5
6
7

CHICHESTER CATHEDRAL
An Historical Survey

Thanks be to you, my Lord Jesus Christ,
for all the benefits and blessings which you
have given to me, for all the pains and insults
which you have borne for me. O Most Merciful
friend, Brother and Redeemer, May I know you
More clearly, love you More dearly,
and follow you More nearly.

St. Richard of Chichester 1198–1253.

To

Dear Alan
to Mark the 25th anniversary of your
Priestly Ordination.
with all My love
Derek
x.

Chichester Cathedral from Westgate Fields by R.H. Nibbs, 1851.

CHICHESTER CATHEDRAL
An Historical Survey

Edited by
MARY HOBBS

Phillimore

1994

Published by
PHILLIMORE & CO. LTD.
Shopwyke Manor Barn, Chichester, Sussex

ISBN 0 85033 924 3

Printed in Great Britain by
CHICHESTER PRESS LTD.
Terminus Road, Chichester, Sussex

CONTENTS

IX **Destruction, Repair and Restoration**
Tim Tatton-Brown 143

X **Deans, Chapters and Bishops from the Boer War to the Cold War: Three Remarkable Men**
The Revd Canon John Halliburton, MA, DPhil,
St Paul's Cathedral; former Principal of Chichester Theological College
The Revd Canon Jeremy Haselock, BPhil, MA,
Vicar of Boxgrove, Chichester; Diocesan Liturgical Advisor 157

XI **The Cathedral Library**
Mary Hobbs, BA, PhD
Cathedral Librarian 171

XII **Archives and Antiquaries**
Alison McCann, BA, DAA
Deputy County Archivist for West Sussex 189

XIII **Church Monuments**
H.A. Tummers
Professor of Art History, University of Nijmegen, Netherlands 203

XIV **The Buildings of the Bishop's Palace and the Close**
Tim Tatton-Brown
with the Right Reverend Eric W. Kemp, DD, DLitt, DTh, Bishop of Chichester
(drawings by John Atherton Bowen) 225

XV **The Musical History of Chichester Cathedral**
The Revd Philip Barrett, MA, BD, FRHistS,
Rector of Compton and Otterbourne, Hants.
with Noel Osborne, MA, FSA, FRSA, former Lay Vicar
and Alan Thurlow, BA, FRCO(CHM), Cathedral Organist 247

XVI **The Cathedral and Modern Art**
David Coke, BA, Curator of Pallant House, Chichester,
with Robert J. Potter, FRIBA, FSA, CGIA, former Surveyor of the Fabric .. 267

XVII **The Immediate Past**
The Very Revd Robert Holtby 283

General Abbreviations 295
Notes 297
Select Bibliography 333
Appendix A. Chichester Cathedral Senior Clergy from 1900 (R.T. Greenacre) 337
Appendix B. The Stained Glass (D. Eagleton) 339
Appendix C. Monuments (H. Tummers) 341
Appendix D. Textiles (A. Blakeney) 345
Appendix E. Plate (R. & M. Moriarty) 347
Appendix F. The Bells 348
Index 349

List of Illustrations

Plans

Colour Plates

Illustration Acknowledgements

(All illustrations are from the Cathedral Library unless otherwise acknowledged.)
Our grateful thanks are due to:

Dr John Birch, 59
The Rt Revd the Bishop of Chichester, 157; Plates XII & XIII
The British Library and H. Tummers, 114, 120
Brian Borton, 45, 92b, 101, 116, 125, 127; Plates III, XI, XV, XVI
Boxgrove Priory PCC and John Moppett, Plate VI
The Syndics, Cambridge University Library, Plate VII
Chichester City Council and Ken Clinch, Plate XIV
Ian Chrismas, 5, 6, 7, 19, 20, 23, 24, 31b, 32, 38, 58, 80, 92a, 93, 94, 95, 96, 100, 110, 113, 115, 119, 131, 136; Plates IV, XII, XIII, XIX
David Coke & Pallant House, 144; Plates XXb, XVII, XXV
John Crook, Plates I, X, XXVI
The Very Revd the Dean, 86
David Dorney 108
Douglas East, Plate X
The Master and Fellows of Emmanuel College, Cambridge, Plates VIII, IX
Leslie Holden, 51, 66
The Huntington Library, San Marino, California, 48, 137
Lambeth Palace, 42
Albert Marshall, 176
Alison McCann & WSRO, 105, 106, 107
Richard Meynell, 128
Julian Munby, 51
Noel Osborne, endpapers, frontispiece, 102, 138, 156
Capt. Blake Parker, RN, 104
Pitkin Pictorials Ltd & Mark Fiennes, Plate II
The Master & Fellows, St John's College, Cambridge, 43
St John's College, Oxford, 90
Society of Antiquaries of London, 11, 26, 31a, 74, 79, 117
Dr. Harry Tummers, 67, 118

Foreword by the Dean of Chichester

For over 900 years the Cathedral Church of the Holy Trinity has stood in a quarter segment of the Roman City of Chichester. A building designed and built, restored and re-arranged over the centuries to conform to new architectural and liturgical fashions, it has stood as a witness to the eternal truths of the spiritual enquiry. It dominates the city and surrounding countryside and attracts visitors and pilgrims from all over the world. The present site was chosen because 'Cicestra' was a centre of commerce and good military communications. Today its geographical position is not ideal as far as the Diocese is concerned, being only seven miles from the western boundary, yet ninety from its easternmost point. Yet distance does not seem to inhibit the affection with which it is held in the hearts of the people of the Diocese. Many devote a great deal of time and energy in support of 'their' Cathedral. Since I became Dean in December 1989, some 340 of the 390 parishes in the Diocese have joined in the Link Scheme and so have a direct personal contact with the Cathedral.

This holy place, where the very atmosphere exudes the prayers of the faithful and the faltering over 900 years, is a 'spirituality zone' for thousands today, including Roman Catholics, who come to say Mass at the Shrine of St Richard, members of the Free Churches who join in ecumenical services led by Churches Together in Chichester, groups and organisations representing many and varied interests.

This present publication is the latest contribution to our understanding of the history and relevance of Chichester Cathedral and I am indebted to those who have contributed so generously by their scholarship and time and, not least, to the editor, Dr. Mary Hobbs, whose honest scholarship and devotion to detail and continuous hard work has now borne fruit. We are also extremely grateful for the generous sponsorship received, without which publication would not have been possible.

In an age of scepticism and doubt the Cathedral is one of the Church's greatest assets. More people than ever come within its walls and it shows so pertinently that there is belief in God, a lively faith in Christ and that prayer and worship are at the heart of the daily experiences within its walls.

As Prof. Adrian Hastings has said (*History of English Christianity*, 1986): 'Simply by being there in very public places cathedrals keep alive the rumour of God, insist that prayer is valid and that worship is at the heart of life. Community courage created our cathedrals as miracles of achievement, with their astonishing tradition of music, choral, instrumental and congregational. Often we are moved by the mere magic of some of the windows, painting and statuary ... The greatest days of the cathedrals lie ahead, as they do for the Church as a whole'.

What a responsibility, what a privilege to lead one of our greatest today!

John Treadgold
The Deanery,
Chichester.
August 1994

Editorial Acknowledgements

My warm thanks are due to what became my unofficial editorial committee, Tim Tatton-Brown, Jeremy Haselock and Andrew Foster (who also acted as historical editor); they helped not only in planning the book but in supervising the chapters. Mrs. Margaret Sparkes generously helped with her experience of the Canterbury volume. Tim and Noel Osborne in addition not only suggested but provided some of our little known illustrations, and many other contributors gave valuable help by reading and commenting on neighbouring chapters. They will join with me in thanking Elaine Bishop for her careful work as research assistant and Ann Hudson for her exemplary index. Our thanks are also due to those whose names appear only in the notes, but who assisted contributors with valuable material: Emlyn Thomas, Richard Meynell, Leslie Holden and Richard Andrewes—while Robert Potter's unique knowledge and archive lie behind more than one chapter. The Cathedral Office undergirded the whole operation, generously contributing their time and talents (in particular Mrs. Jenni Rigby, who undertook with unfailing cheerfulness any and every task as well as typing, and Mrs. Louise Matcham, who also typed, photocopied and generally supported the editor). I owe a particular debt of gratitude to the Communar, Captain Michael Shallow RN, without whose tireless energy and drive the book might never have come to fruition, and to my husband, who put up with my preoccupation and took on the housework. Rachel Moriarty was a stalwart support in many areas, as were our photographers, Ian Chrismas and Brian Borton. I thank Noel Osborne, managing director of Phillimore, most especially, for his constant encouragement, and Nicola Willmot, his assistant, for her patience and hard work in ensuring that we kept on course despite the inevitable hiccups in a major venture with so many component parts.

Mary Hobbs

Sponsors

While commissioned by the Dean and Chapter, any profits from this publication will accrue to the Development Trust, an independent charity, which needs to raise at least £1,000 a day for the continuing restoration of the Cathedral. With this in mind, the following organisations have acted as sponsors and their generous support is gratefully acknowledged:

The Friends of Chichester Cathedral
West Sussex County Council
East Sussex County Council
Chichester City Council
Thomas Eggar Verrall Bowles
Tod Miller Thomas
Chichester Festival Theatre
N P Mander Limited (Pipe Organ Builders)
Willard Electrical Services Limited
Amber Scaffolding Limited
Moore & Tillyer Limited
Geoffrey Osborne Limited
Grant Thornton
Ecclesiastical Insurance Group
The Royal Sussex Regimental Association
The Prebendal School
Barclays Bank plc
British Gas plc (Southern)

List of Subscribers

Colonel M.B. Adams
Major J.F. Ainsworth
Mrs. M.O. Anderson
Richard Andrews
I.V. Askew
The Reverend Canon P.G. Atkinson
John Attwater
Harry and Constance Axton
Terence Banks
Dr. G.L. Barnard
E.A. Bartlett O.B.E.
Eric Bassett
Dr. and Mrs. E.W. Baxter
Andrew H. Benians
Ursula Benker-Schirmer
Corinne G. Bennett
Rev. Cyril Bess
U. M. Bickersteth
Dr. John Birch
R.A. Bishop
David S.W. Blacker D.L.
A.E. Blakeney
B.C. Bloomfield
David, Anne and Jessica Bone
Mrs. Alison Boreham
Penelope Boughton
Mr. W.G. Bowen
Mr. E.W. Boxall
T.K. Boyd
The Revd. I.J. Brackley
Dr. Jean M. Bradley
Revd. Canon Beaumont L. Brandie
The Revd. D.J. Brecknell
Viscount and Viscountess Brentford
John Brider
D.F. Bridger
Bristol University
Commander Henry Brooke M.B.E., DSC
The Venerable the Archdeacon of Chichester and Mrs. Daphne Brotherton
Christopher and Rosemary Bryan
Revd. Canon R. Bullivant
David and Helen Burrell
Anne Butler
Donald Buttress
John Caldicott
Mrs. Hazel B. Campbell White
Canterbury Cathedral Library
Mr. and Mrs. William Capel
The Reverend Graham Carey
Anthony and Wendy Cartmell
Commander and Mrs. Michael Casement
The Reverend Victor Cassam
Sir Robin and Lady Catford
Sheila Chapman
The Dean of Chichester and Mrs. Treadgold
Chichester Cathedral Library
Chichester District Museum
Chichester High School for Girls
Chichester Theological College
D.R. Chrismas
Mr. and Mrs. C.J. Clark
Evelyn Clark
Christopher Clarkson
W. Owen Cole
Mrs. Pamela Combes
The Rev. H.J. Cossar
Mr. M. J. and Mrs. S. Coviello
Mary and Michael Crunden
Lord Cudlipp
Revd. C.G. Francis Dare
Adrian and Valerie Whitsitt Davidson
Max Davies
Lilian Dawson
Mrs. Robin Dean
Mary E. Delves
Kenneth Dickins
Canon Francis H. Doe
Hubert and Sue Doggart
Jane and Peter Dunn
John Dunstan
Durham Dean and Chapter Library
Judith A. Eady
Mr. and Mrs. Douglas Eagleton
Church of St Saviour and St Peter, Eastbourne
Mrs. G.B. Eastwood
Mr. and Mrs. Christopher Edwards
Canon John Edwards
Miss Joan Elder
Frank C. Eldridge
Mr. R.J. Elliott
Mr. and Mrs. R.N. Elphick
Mr. and Mrs. D. Evershed-Martin
Exeter Cathedral Library
The Very Revd R.M.S. Eyre, Dean of Exeter
Audrey Faber
Jane H. Fane de Salis
Ken Farquharson
Denis Fastnedge
Julia H. Ferris
Gordon L. Field
Professor F. Fielden
Nick and Heather Fixsen
Mr. and Mrs. B. Fletcher
Sibylla Jane Flower
June and Cyril Fogg
Anthony Foster
Mrs. Julie François
Miss Daphne Fraser
Anthony Freeman
Jack Freeman
Barbara Frith
D.F. Fromings
Mr. W.F.P. Gammie
Douglas R. Garland
David R.C. Gibbons
Canon Denys Giddey
Eric Gillies
Jack and Margaret Gilmour
Mrs. Kathleen Goddard

Roma Godden
David and Pearl Goodman
Revd. H.I. Gordon-Cumming
Lt. Col. and Mrs. Ian Graham
Ken and Sheila Green
Miss L.J. Greenhill
Canon E. Griffiths
Peter Griffits
Hugo Grimwood
Miss I.D.Groves
Mr. and Mrs. D. Gruffydd Jones
Mrs. J.C. Gurney
David J. Gutteridge
Mr. and Mrs. R.J. Hall
Michael Harlock
Harry Harris O.B.E.
Rosina Harris
E. Hasloch
Professor William Martin Hattersley
John Hawes
Canon Frank Hawkins
Mrs. Geoffrey Hawkins
L.T.S. Hawkins
Celine Healy
The Revd. C.M. Henley
Sir John Herbecq
Hereford Cathedral Library
Angus Hewat
Morris H. Heynes
The Revd. and Mrs. D.A. Hider
Jean and Adrian Higham
Joan P. Hill
The Rt. Revd. John Hind
Dr. Michael Hinton
The Revd. Christopher F. Hopkins
Mrs. G. Patricia Hooley
Robert Geoffrey Howse
Dr. and Mrs. T.P. Hudson
Dr. R.F. Hunnisett
Dr. J. Jago
T.E. James
Cyril and Shirley Jarman
Christopher Jarrett
Jane Jarrett
Mr. J.K. Jasper
Mr. and Mrs. A. Philip Jenkins
J.M. and G.C. Jenkins
Stephen Johns
Vivienne Johnson
Mrs. Mary Joice
David Jones
Richard W. Jones
Donovan Geo Joyce
Michael John Kelly
Beryl King
Mrs. Cynthia King
Joan M. King
Rt. Revd. Edward and Mrs. Knapp-Fisher
Lambeth Palace Library
Dr. D.J.C. Laming
Mrs. Barbara Laming
Lancing College
Mr. P.A. Lawton
Elisabeth Leedham-Green
The Revd. John and Mrs. Clare Lees
Mr. D.E.R. Legg Willis
Roger Levy
Katharine Lippiett
Rear Admiral and Mrs. J.R. Llewellyn
Lilian Lloyd
Garry Long
Geoff Longlands
Peter Longley O.B.E. D.L.
The Reverend K.N.J. Loveless, M.B.E., VRD, F.S.A., F.S.A. Scot, Hon.RNR
The Revd. J.R. Lowerson
Revd. John S. Loxton
John S. McKerchar
Elsie McLeish
June and Donald Mack
John Hugh Mackenzie
Mrs. J.C. Maclean
Bishop Morris Maddocks and Mrs. Anne Maddocks
Georgina Male
Bishop and Mrs. Michael Manktelow
Sally Manley
Revd. Harry Marsh
A.E. Marshall MA CEng FIMechE FIPD
The Rev. Canon B.J. Marshall
The Rt. Revd. Michael Marshall
Keith W. Masters
Dr. and Mrs. Harold W. Matthews
Canon David Maundrell
Mr. W. Mendelsson
Richard Meynell RIBA
Mrs. Jean M. Mitchell
Kathleen E.M. Moody
Mrs. Estelle Morgan (Education Adviser to the Dean and Chapter)
Sherian Morgan
Michael and Rachel Moriarty
The Right Rev. J.H.L. Morrell
Mr. J.L. Morrish
Father Derek Mottershead
K.M. Elisabeth Murray
The Revd. David Nason
The Revd. Canon Arnold Nicholas
Sir Edwin Nixon, C.B.E., D.L.
Norman Oakley
Mr. and Mrs. J. O'Hea
Dympna O'Neill
Marjorie O'Neill
Margaret Orr
Noel Osborne
Mrs. Sybil Papworth
Peter N. Parish
Barbara J. Parker
Blake Parker
Peter F. Parkinson
Mr. P.D. Parsons
Eric Paton
Cllr. Jim Payne
The Dean and Chapter of Peterborough Cathedral
Mrs. Roderick Petley
The Revd. Dr. I.R. Phelps
Jane Pinching
Nicholas M. Plumley
William Porter
Mr. and Mrs. F.E.H. Potter
Jeremy M. Potter
Robert Potter O.B.E.
The Revd. Canon William R. Pratt
Miss B. Quihampton
Dr. and Mrs. Nigel Ramsay
H.D.H. Rance
John Rank, Esq.
John Rankin
Alice Renton
Ringmer Parish Church
Denis Roberts
Miss Audrey M. Robinson
Father Ron Robinson
The Dean and Chapter of Rochester Cathedral
D. Jean C. Rose
Dennis Rushworth
John Sainsbury
St John's College Library, Oxford
Salisbury Cathedral Library

S.A Savill
Tom Saxby
Janet Schofield
Anne Scicluna
Mr. and Mrs. Mark Scrase-Dickins
A.H. Sexton
Wendy Shallow
June and Leslie Shearn
Graham Simcox
The Very Reverend John A. Simpson, Dean of Canterbury
Mrs. Jeremy Smith
Maurice Smith
Mr. and Mrs. Geoffrey B. Soul
Southern Archaeology (Chichester) Ltd.
Mrs. Margaret Sparks
Canon Alan Spray
Jeffrey J. Stanbridge
Alan Stevens BA
Mr. I.G. Stevens
The Revd. Norman Stevens
Derrick and Marjorie Steward
Philip Stroud D.L.
Captain Stephen Stuart
Philip Sturman
Janet Sugden
W.B. Sugden
Sussex Archaeological Society
Mid-Sussex Decorative and Fine Arts Society
Canon John Sweet
Canon Derek Tansill
Mary Tasker
C.V. and L.M.A. Taylor
Jeremy Taylor
Edward Eastaway Thomas
Dr. Emlyn Thomas
Peter A. Thomas
Alan and Tina Thurlow
Mrs. T.M. Thurlow
Major Richard Tolson
Viola I.A. Tomsett
Canon Michael Townroe
Michael Toynbee
The Right Reverend Lindsay Urwin O.G.S.
L.M. Stillingfleet Venner
Dr. John A. Vickers
Nancy Villiers
The Reverend Canon D.M.I. Walters
Dorothy-Joan Walton
Major General Sir Philip Ward
Leslie Weller D.L.
The Dean and Chapter of Wells Cathedral
John R. West
The Dean and Chapter of Westminster
West Sussex County Council Library Service
Bertram White
Leonard G.A. Whyte
Mr. and Mrs. A.J. Wicken
Richard Wilby
Canon Alan Wilkinson
Maev Wilkinson
Councillor John Wilton
The Dean and Chapter of Winchester
The Dean and Canons of Windsor
Barbara W. Wood
Mr. J.R. Worsley
H.R. Wyatt
J.W.P. Yates
Dorothy Young
Dr. Percy M. Young

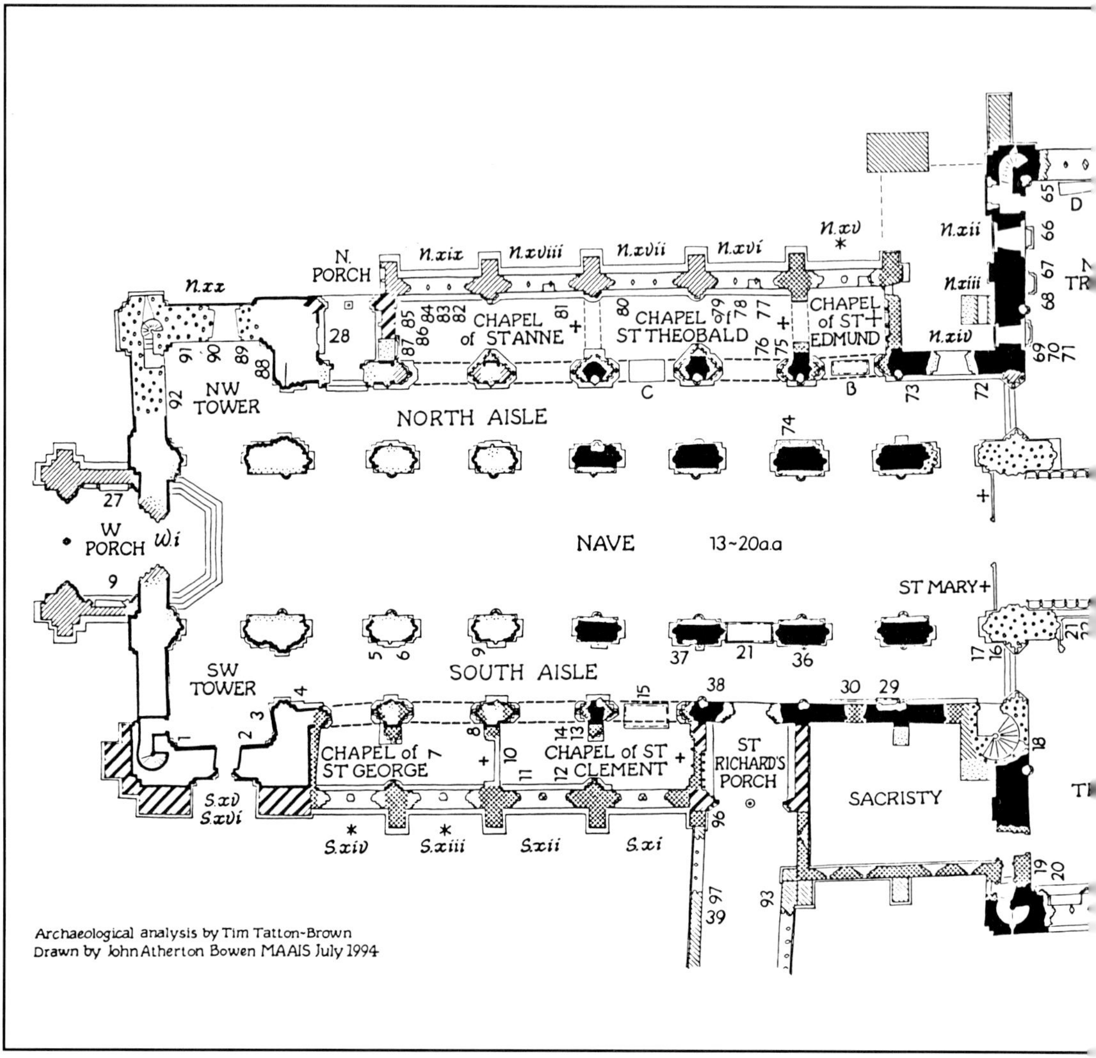

Main phased plan of Chichester Cathedral.

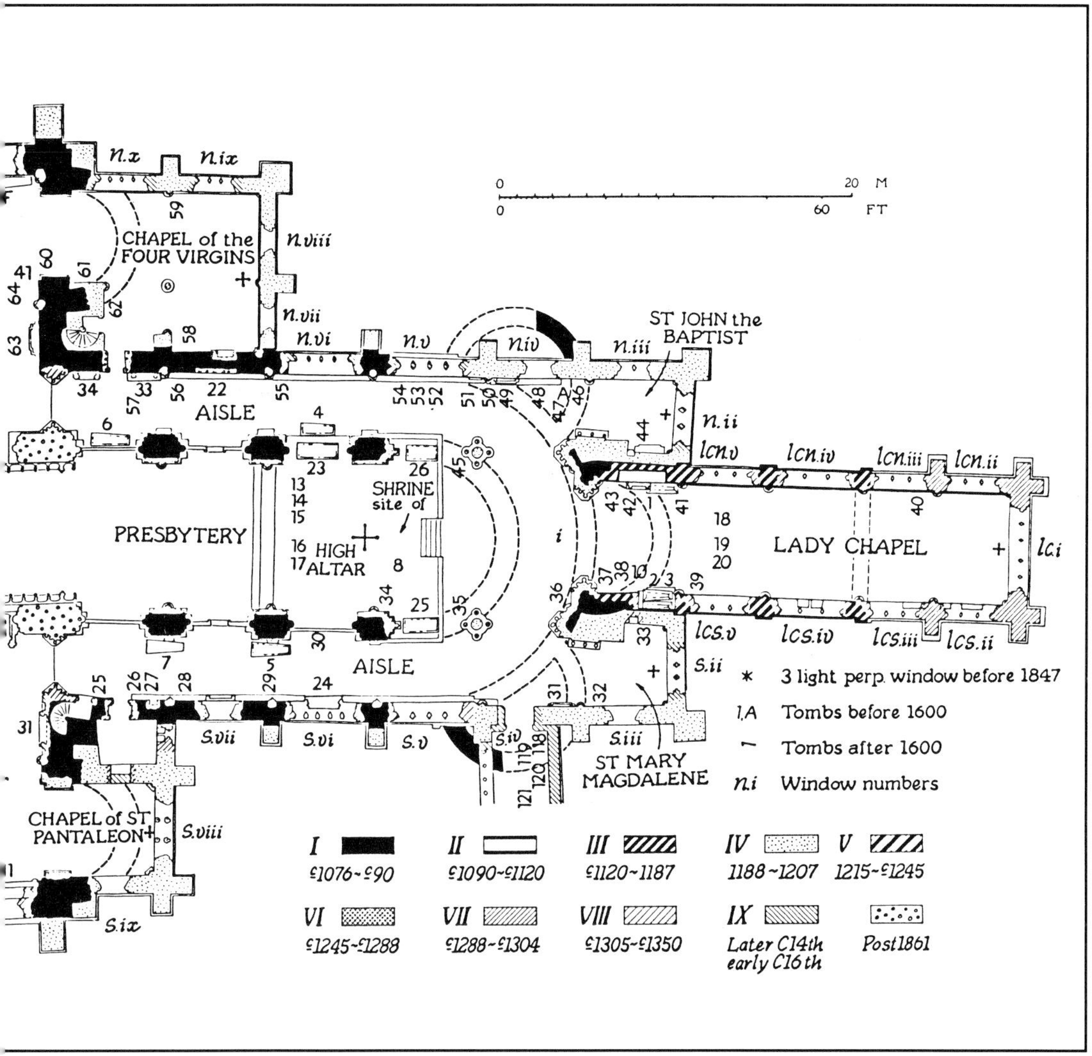

Numerals:

Roman—Appendix (B), windows (north, south and Lady Chapel)

Upright Arabic—Appendix C (Tummers: Chapter XIII) Part I, Monuments to 1600 (augmented from the plan in *VCH* [1935] facing p.112).

Arabic, sideways on—Appendix C Part II, Monuments from 1600 onwards.

I

The Bishopric of Selsey

Susan Kelly

In the south transept of Chichester Cathedral hangs a very large and very splendid panel painting by Lambert Barnard commissioned by his patron, Bishop Robert Sherburne (1508-36) (see Plate II). Sherburne himself appears in the right-hand section, receiving from Henry VIII a formal confirmation of his bishopric. The left-hand part of the panel records a similar confrontation between a king and a bishop, but one that is supposed to have taken place almost seven and a half centuries earlier, and which has traditionally been held to mark the beginning of the bishopric of Sussex. In this case the king, resplendent in ermine and cloth-of-gold and standing with his courtiers (and pet monkey) on the threshold of an impossibly flamboyant Renaissance palace, is Cædwalla of Wessex, a pagan thug who conquered the kingdom of the South Saxons in about 685; while the bishop is the formidable St Wilfrid of Northumbria, by far the least lovable of Anglo-Saxon saints. Wilfrid had a turbulent career, much of it spent in exile as the result of quarrels with various kings and archbishops. In about 680 or 681 he found a temporary refuge in the South Saxon kingdom, still nominally heathen, and there he remained for some five years, evangelising and baptising the people.[1] Barnard's painting shows Cædwalla granting to Wilfrid the land at Selsey which was to be the site of his episcopal see. It is an imaginary episode, in more ways than one.

The South Saxons had already had some contact with Christianity before Wilfrid's arrival. The contemporary king of Sussex, who was named Æthelwealh, had married a Christian wife, and he and his nobles had been baptised at the Mercian court some years previously. A number of priests had followed them back to Sussex to baptise the ordinary people, and there was also a small community of Irish monks living at Bosham.[2] The presence of Irishmen in Sussex in the seventh century is not as surprising as it might seem. At this period many Irish churchmen were inspired by the doctrine of *peregrinatio*, which was the idea that they could gain heavenly merit by leaving their homes and families and voluntarily committing themselves to exile in God's service. They travelled all over western Europe, in the kingdom of the Franks, in Italy and the fringes of pagan Germany, and they also played a major role in the conversion of Scotland and England.[3] The Irish monks at Bosham certainly seem to have preached to the local people; our sources suggest that they made little headway against South Saxon heathenism, but it may be the case that any successes of these earlier missionaries were played down in order to build up Wilfrid's role as the apostle of Sussex.[4] It is likely that Wilfrid's main contribution lay in the area of organisation. He was a consecrated bishop, albeit a bishop in exile, and therefore he had the authority to ordain priests and to set up the structures of a local Church; this would have been an important step towards establishing a permanent Christian presence in the South Saxon kingdom.

One of Wilfrid's most important acts was the foundation of a monastery in the Selsey peninsula, on a former royal estate given to him by King Æthelwealh; the territory is said to have consisted of 87 hides (a hide was the land needed to support one household), and we are told that Wilfrid's first act was to free and then baptise 250 male and female slaves who were associated with the estate.[5] It is rather sad that later tradition at Selsey and Chichester transferred the credit for the land-grant to the barbarous Cædwalla, who murdered Æthelwealh during an incursion into Sussex. This distorted version of events was already current in Selsey in the 10th century, when the community fabricated a foundation charter in the name of Cædwalla,[6] and it is the one that we see in Barnard's painting. Almost certainly Wilfrid's new monastery was built at Church Norton, at the entrance to Pagham Harbour. This may not have been as remote a location as it now seems, for there is reason to think that Pagham Harbour was a trading area of some importance at this period. It would have been at Church Norton that the later Anglo-Saxon cathedral of Selsey was constructed; after the transfer of the see to Chichester it remained the site of the local parish church until 1865. In the background to Barnard's painting can be seen a representation of the later church on the site, with its detached bell-tower that was a well-known sea-mark.[7]

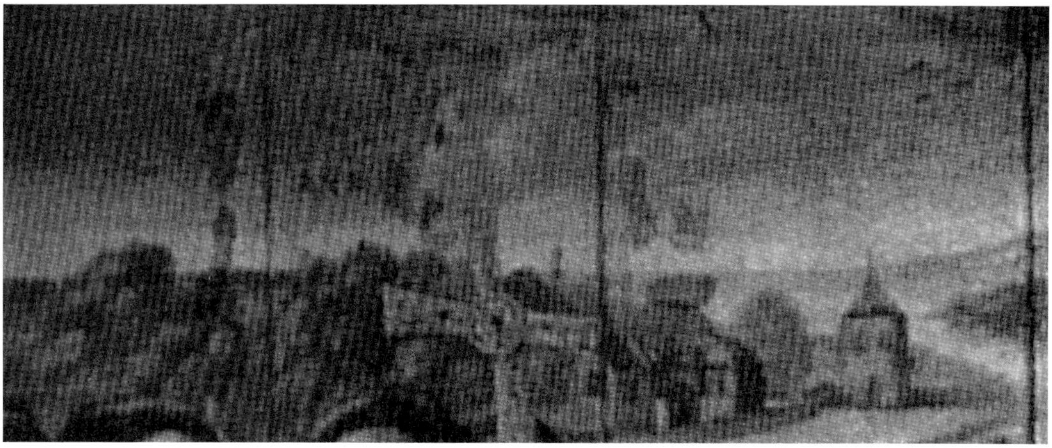

1 *The first Cathedral, at Church Norton (detail from Lambert Barnard's painting).*

It would be a mistake to think of the Selsey community as a monastery in the later sense of the word, with the emphasis on enclosure and the contemplative life. Selsey would certainly have been a centre for prayer and liturgical celebration, but it would also have been a missionary base, from which priests went out to preach and to baptise the local people. In the Celtic parts of Britain and later in England, the monastic ideal of communal life was adapted to cope with the difficulties of establishing a new church among rural populations, in areas where there were few or no cities or small towns which secular priests could use as a base for their pastoral work. Ecclesiastics tended to live together, in small or large communities, often under obedience to an abbot or abbess and following a rule, which might be drawn up by the founder of the house (as Wilfrid drew up a rule for Selsey). A few of these communities would have been concerned exclusively with prayer and worship; many more would also have been involved, to a greater or lesser extent, with pastoral provision to the local people.[8] The Selsey monastery probably began as a mixed community, with some members who lived more strictly monastic lives, devoting themselves primarily to prayer and to the liturgy, and others who were secular priests and ministered to the neighbourhood. Evidence from elsewhere in England shows that, over the course of time, the monastic element tended to wither away, so that by the early 10th century most English monasteries were communities of secular priests or clerks. Many of these clerks may have been married with families, and they often came to have a hereditary interest in the Church's property. There is really no hard evidence about conditions at Selsey in the Anglo-Saxon period, but there is some reason to think that on the eve of the Conquest it was a community of clerks and priests.[9]

Selsey was Wilfrid's base for the few years that he lived in Sussex; he left in about 685 or 686, when circumstances made it possible for him to return to his own see in Northumbria. Just prior to his departure the South Saxon kingdom was conquered most bloodily by Cædwalla of Wessex, an event which ushered in several decades of harsh West Saxon overlordship. In the short run this was a severe setback to the fledgling Church in Sussex. True, Cædwalla seems to have been most impressed by Wilfrid, offering him a quarter of the Isle of Wight after he had conquered it and exterminated most of its inhabitants. But the end result of the West Saxon invasion was that the South Saxons did not have their own bishop for another twenty years. After Wilfrid's departure, the Church in Sussex was treated as part of the vast diocese of the bishop of the West Saxons, whose seat was at Winchester. It was not until about 705, at a time when the West Saxon diocese itself was being reorganised, that it was decided that Sussex should have its own bishop. The man chosen was Eadberht, who had been abbot of the Selsey monastery; he is reckoned as the first bishop of Sussex, since Wilfrid was technically bishop of a Northumbrian diocese.[10]

The episcopal see of the new diocese was established at Selsey, and not at Chichester, which had been the centre of the region in Roman times. The choice is at first surprising. Many of the first generation of Anglo-Saxon sees were set up in former Roman cities. Canterbury, Rochester, Winchester and so on, These were no longer important population centres, but they did have many advantages: they were often centres of political authority, and they lay at focal points in the network of Roman roads (still in use throughout the Anglo-Saxon period); their walls, however tumbledown, had some defensive value; they were sources of building material, and sometimes it might even be the case that a standing Roman building was available for conversion into a cathedral church (as at Canterbury). Moreover, many of the early missionaries to southern England came from Italy, where bishops were always associated with cities and towns; it was assumed that a bishop would naturally have an urban base. Yet Chichester, which had all these advantages, was passed over in favour of Selsey, sited on an apparently remote peninsula well off the main land routes (although it was readily accessible by sea).

The reason for this decision is likely to have been financial. A bishop and his cathedral community needed an endowment to provide an income on which they could live and carry out their functions; they needed money to build and maintain a cathedral church, and to equip it with all those treasures—gold and silver vessels, rich hangings and costly altarcloths—which the Anglo-Saxons thought necessary for God's house. After some decades of harsh West Saxon overlordship, the South Saxon kingdom is likely to have been rather impoverished, and it may have been impossible to endow a see from scratch. One way to get around this difficulty was to take over the endowment of an existing wealthy monastery and set up a bishop there. This seems to have happened in Northumbria in 678, when a new see was established in Wilfrid's monastery at Hexham; another of his foundations, at

Ripon, was also the seat of a bishop for a short period. Wilfrid regarded his monasteries as his personal property, and the loss of them was one of the triggers for his first period of exile; he must have been heartbroken in his extreme old age when his monastery at Selsey was also taken over. Others regarded this procedure with approval: half a century later, when it was clear that yet more Northumbrian dioceses were required, the Venerable Bede advised the then archbishop of York to site the episcopal seats in existing monasteries, and to placate the abbot and monks of the communities involved by allowing them to elect the bishop from among their own number.[11] It seems likely that this is what had already happened in Sussex, with the result that the see was established at Selsey and the abbot of the monastery was chosen as the first bishop; the second bishop, Eolla, also seems to have been a former abbot of Selsey.[12]

The new diocese had a tentative beginning. After the death of Eolla in the 720s there was a lengthy vacancy, ended by an appointment in 733.[13] Thereafter, information fails, and the South Saxon Church enters a period of quite dizzying obscurity which lasts until the 11th century. For the most part our sources are reduced to a bald list of bishops' names (which may be incomplete) and a small collection of land-charters, which pose their own considerable problems. There is a grand total of 21 documents in the so-called Selsey archive, which can be supplemented by a very few charters in other archives which deal with land in Sussex.[14] For a period of three and a half centuries this is far from adequate, and the heart sinks further when it is realised that at least four of the Selsey charters are complete fabrications and that others seem to have been tampered with and partly rewritten. Almost all of these documents survive only as copies in cartularies of the 13th and 14th centuries, with the consequent corruptions; many have lost their dates and witness-lists. There is one exception, a charter dated 780 which survives in its original form, on a separate sheet of parchment; it records a grant of land by a South Saxon nobleman named Oslac to a church dedicated to St Paul, which was probably located in the Witterings.[15] As a written instrument, this charter is far from impressive. The scribe has made use of a spoiled leaf from a psalter, simply turning it over and writing on the other side; he has tried to use a script known as half-uncial, with which he is manifestly unfamiliar, so that the final product has a memorably crude appearance; to make things worse, the orthography and grammar of the Latin text are quite appalling, and the scribe was so incompetent that he seems to have omitted a vital portion of his draft. It is almost certain that this document was produced in the Selsey scriptorium, and so it throws a rather lurid light on standards in the cathedral community in the eighth century. (Wilfrid would have been mortified; he was an immensely learned man.)

From the surviving charters it is possible to make out a rather oblique picture of the history of the diocese in the eighth century. Most of the Sussex documents from this period, like the Oslac charter, are not concerned with Selsey affairs at all: they relate to the foundation and endowment of local churches and monasteries, in the Witterings, at Henfield, Ferring, Stanmer, Bexhill and Peppering near Amberley.[16] The majority of these were established by South Saxon noblemen and women, and were originally largely independent of the bishops of Selsey; they were aristocratic minsters, controlled by the founders and their families. One of the most important themes of English church history in the late eighth and ninth centuries is the gradual expansion of episcopal control over many of these independent churches.[17] In the Selsey diocese the crucial decades for this development appear to have been the 770s and 780s. The houses whose charters were preserved in the archive seem generally to have fallen under the bishop's lordship by the end of the eighth century. The main reason for this was probably the invasion of the kingdom by Offa of Mercia in about 771; for the next half century Sussex was a province of the Mercian empire. The conquest is likely to have weakened the local aristocracy, and to have prompted some independent churches to seek the bishop's protection. An aspect that may have been important was Offa's well-known habit of taking over wealthy monasteries in his sub-kingdoms. They could be treated as family property, and they also ensured that large numbers of ecclesiastics were interceding with God for his sins. One of the houses which he is known to have acquired was a major monastery at Beddingham near Lewes; from this he detached a daughter-house at Denton near Newhaven which he gave to an abbot who passed it on to the bishop of Selsey. This gift caused great difficulties for the bishopric. In the early ninth century two later kings of Mercia, Offa's successors and the heirs of the Beddingham monastery, put pressure on the bishop to return Denton, threatening terrible reprisals if he did not; twice the bishop was forced to defend his ownership of the minster before a church synod, which on each occasion upheld his case. Denton later formed part of the episcopal manor of Bishopstone.[18]

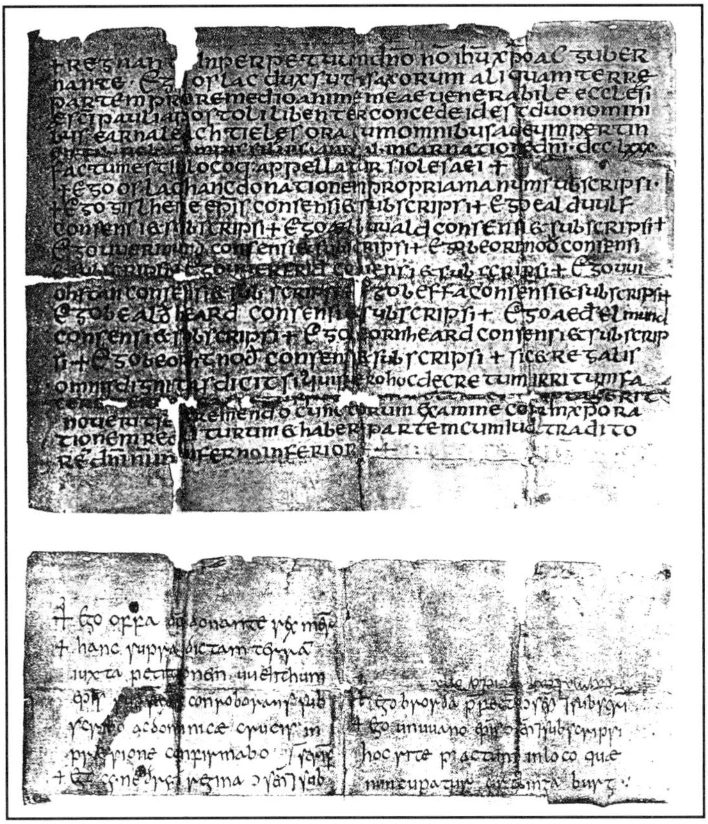

2 *The Oslac charter.*

A contributing factor in the decline of the local monasteries is likely to have been the onset of coastal raids by Viking pirates. They were already a major problem in Kent by 792, and the first attacks on the coasts of Wessex began at about the same time. Thereafter the frequency of such incursions and the numbers of those involved steadily increased. By 836 King Ecgberht of Wessex, who had recently managed to break the Mercian domination of southern England and build up his own empire south of the Thames, was fighting with the crews of 35 Viking long-ships in Devon. In 851 for the first time some of the raiders over-wintered on the island of Thanet in Kent, which is a measure of the weakness of the local English authorities. And then, in 865, a huge force known as the Great Danish Army landed in East Anglia and quickly overran many Anglo-Saxon kingdoms. First they conquered East Anglia, before moving on to Northumbria, which was already weakened by civil war. They then turned their attentions to Mercia, which they partitioned, and finally to the West Saxon empire, where they met their match in Alfred the Great (871-99), grandson of King Ecgberht. By the end of the ninth century only the territory south of the Thames, with the rump of Mercia and perhaps Essex, remained under Anglo-Saxon rule; the Danes now controlled the rest of England.[19]

There is no direct information about the effects of Viking raids on Sussex, but they are likely to have been severe. Due to the nature of the local terrain, the population in Anglo-Saxon times lived mostly on the coastal plain and in river valleys, places which were especially vulnerable to attack by pirates.[20] One of the characteristics of Viking raids, which contemporaries noted with horror, was their tendency to home in on churches, which were largely undefended repositories of treasure and precious objects, as well as of potential slaves (the Vikings were great slave-traders) and of senior churchmen who could be held for ransom. In those areas of England which came under Viking rule all but a handful of churches simply disappeared, presumably because they were sacked or because they could not survive in a pagan climate; in the East Anglian sees of Dunwich and Elmham and in the province known as Lindsey (now Lincolnshire) episcopal succession broke down completely and was not re-established until the middle of the 10th century, while the episcopal community of Lindisfarne began a long wandering that took them, via Chester-le-Street, to Durham. Even in those areas which remained under Anglo-Saxon control, many local churches did not survive the ninth century, either because they had been destroyed or because of the economic pressures caused by the repeated devastation of crops, the payment of tribute and hefty taxation to support the Anglo-Saxon defences. In Kent, where many monasteries were in exposed positions on the coast, some communities seem to have abandoned their churches and taken refuge within the walls of Canterbury (although Canterbury itself was not secure; it was sacked in 851).[21]

Selsey was entirely unprotected, and it was probably during this period that Chichester once more came into its own. To fight the Viking threat, Alfred the Great developed a system of fortified places, known as 'burhs', to which the people of the surrounding countryside could flee when the alarm was given. Some of these burhs were new foundations in strategic places, but in many other cases they were former Roman cities which had walls that could be repaired and defended.[22] There were four burhs in Sussex: at Chichester, at Burpham in the Arun valley, at Lewes on the Ouse and at Hastings.[23] Chichester was already an established burh in 894, when there was a major attack on the area by the crews of some forty Viking ships; the people of the burh are said to have repulsed the invaders, killed some hundreds of them and captured some of their ships.[24] It seems likely that the bishop and the Selsey community retreated to Chichester on occasions, and perhaps even for prolonged periods of time until the security of Selsey itself could be guaranteed.

Against this background, there appears to be an ominous gap in the list of bishops from the 860s until the very early 10th century. We have several collections of Anglo-Saxon episcopal lists, some dating from as early as the ninth and 10th centuries. The entry for each diocese is generally a simple list of names, with no details of the dates of the individual pontificates, but it is usually possible to work out an approximate (often very approximate) date for each bishop by analysing charter-attestations and the few obituary notices. The various versions of the Selsey list generally agree up to the time of Guthheard, who lived in the middle of the ninth century. Thereafter some of them continue with the name of Beornheah, who took up office at some point in the first quarter of the 10th century, while some of them resume with Alfred, who was bishop in the 940s and 950s. This means that we do not have the names of any South Saxon bishops from the second half of the ninth century. It is very tempting to suggest that episcopal succession at Selsey was interrupted for some decades, and perhaps to connect this with an unrecorded but devastating Viking raid on Selsey. However, it may simply be the case that the lists are incomplete and that the gap is just a textual deficiency; it could be significant that there is some evidence for a bishop of Selsey named Wighelm *c.*900, who does not appear in any of the surviving versions of the episcopal list.[25]

Whatever the truth of this, it does appear that the Sussex bishopric was in a rather fragile state in the 10th century. On the wider front, this was an expansive period for England. The descendants of Alfred the Great conquered the Danish-held areas and forged a united kingdom, while the English Church geared itself for a prodigious burst of reform and monastic revival. From Selsey the little evidence we have for the central decades of the 10th century points rather to vulnerability and encroachment on the endowment. There is a charter in the archive dated 945 which records a grant by King Eadmund to Bishop Alfred of land at Bracklesham and Thorney. The unique feature of this document is its statement that this land had previously been part of the episcopal endowment of Selsey; now it was being given to the bishop as his personal property, with the right to dispose of it as he pleased.[26] There may have been some valid and reputable reason for this transaction, but it does seem exceedingly suspicious; there is no parallel for it. A second charter, this time dated 957, is evidence for a considerably more serious attack on the endowment.[27] It concerns the restoration to the Selsey community of numerous estates in Sussex which had been wrongly seized by a certain Ælfsige. The list of properties concerned is quite shocking: the whole of the Selsey peninsula, including the site of the cathedral itself, and large areas of land around Aldingbourne and Amberley. These were some of the most important estates belonging to the bishopric, and the core of its endowment at the time of the Domesday survey; their loss would have been catastrophic.

The charter is very difficult to interpret, but it does appear to indicate that the Ælfsige who had taken control of these lands was the contemporary bishop of Winchester; it would seem that an attempt was made in the 950s to dissolve the independent South Saxon see and to include Sussex once more in the Winchester diocese. By 957 policy must have changed and so the endowment was restored to Selsey, but the episode underlines the relative weakness of the South Saxon bishopric. It may have been at around this time, or a little earlier, that the archbishops of Canterbury came into possession of land which had previously belonged to Selsey. By the time of the Norman Conquest Canterbury had very extensive estates in Sussex; indeed the archbishops in 1066 owned slightly more land in the province than did the bishops of Selsey. Among these estates was a very large manor at Pagham, which included some land in the Mundham area also said to have been among the early estates of Selsey. It is not known when the archbishops acquired Pagham, but it is probably significant that in the 950s a charter was forged at Canterbury claiming that Wilfrid had given the estate to Archbishop Theodore in the 680s;[28] there can be no truth in the story, but it may be justification of a more recent acquisition. It is possible that the bishop and community of Selsey agreed to cede the land in return for receiving the protection and patronage of the archbishops.

Elsewhere in England the 10th century was notable for a prodigious movement of reform and monastic revival, organised by three great religious leaders, Dunstan, Æthelwold and Oswald. Between them these men founded many new monasteries across England, and they also took over existing houses and reorganised them on strict Benedictine lines—some of them were cathedral communities, for it was part of the movement's philosophy that monastic virtues could raise the standards of the episcopate and of the English Church as

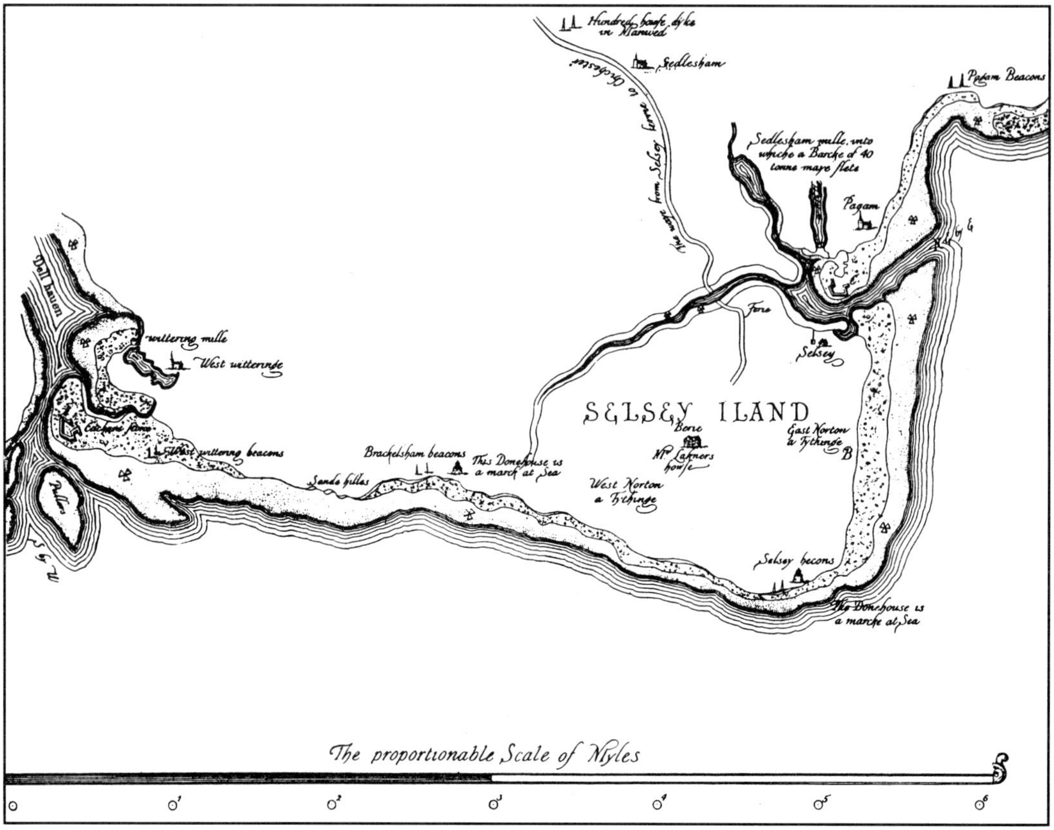

3 *Map of Selsey from a survey made in 1587.*

a whole. Many of the great abbeys of the later Middle Ages took shape in this period: houses such as Glastonbury, Abingdon, Peterborough and Ely, the Old and New Minsters in Winchester. As far as we know (and our evidence is admittedly minimal), not a single reformed monastery was established in the Selsey diocese, and the cathedral community was certainly not reorganised on a monastic basis. King Edgar gave Bishop Æthelwold of Winchester great tracts of land in Sussex, at Harting and Washington, but he did not use this for monastic foundation in the area; instead he exchanged it for other land which he used to endow his monasteries in the East Anglian fens.[29]

But Selsey was not untouched by the monastic reform movement. The only 10th-century bishop about whom we have any information is Æthelgar who was appointed in 980. He was an associate of Bishop Æthelwold, and had been made abbot of the reformed monastery of New Minster, Winchester, in 964.[30] He appears to have retained the abbacy throughout his career at Selsey, only resigning when he was promoted to Canterbury in 988, and there is reason to think that New Minster was always more important to him. There are two surviving charters in his favour, both from the period when he was bishop of Selsey, and one of them granting him land in Sussex, at South Heighton; in both cases he seems to have passed on the land to the New Minster rather than to the Selsey community.[31]

The last decades of the 10th century are likely to have been traumatic for Selsey, as they were for the rest of England. Large-scale Viking raids resumed in 980 and culminated, after widespread devastation, in the conquest of England by Cnut in 1016. Sussex was ravaged on several recorded occasions during this period, and doubtless on many others;[32] it is likely that the bishop and the Selsey community were once more forced to take refuge in Chichester. It is from Cnut's reign that we begin to have fuller information about the individual bishops. Æthelric I (*c.*1032-38) was probably a monk of Christ Church, Canterbury; he was associated with the circle of St Dunstan. The next bishop, Grimketel (1039-47), was a less savoury character; he is supposed to have purchased the bishopric from King Harold Harefoot, and went on to buy the bishopric of Elmham in East Anglia from Edward the Confessor. He also had connections with Christ Church. Little is known of Bishop Heca (1047-57) except that he was a royal priest; he was presumably appointed by King Edward.

The final Anglo-Saxon bishop of Selsey, Æthelric II (1058-70), was certainly a monk of Christ Church, and he also seems to have been a protégé of Archbishop Stigand, a deeply corrupt man who was personally responsible for much of the opprobrium which hung over the English Church in the years immediately before the Conquest.[33] Stigand is known to have exploited financially many of the religious houses which fell into his power, and with his baleful presence in the background and with the continuing legacy of ninth- and 10th-century weakness and of the Grimketel episode, it is not surprising that the Domesday survey reveals Selsey to have been one of the poorest bishoprics in England on the eve of the Norman Conquest. The endowment consisted of only ten manors, with an estimated value of just over £125 a year in 1066.[34] Most of the bishopric's lands lay within twenty miles of the cathedral. In the Manhood peninsula there were manors at Selsey itself, at Sidlesham and East Wittering, while slightly further afield lay extensive estates around Aldingbourne, Amberley, and Ferring on the coast. The other manors were scattered elsewhere in Sussex, at Henfield, Preston (now part of Brighton), Bishopstone (near Newhaven) and Bexhill.[35] In many cases these isolated manors seem to represent the territories of individual minsters which had come under the bishop's control.

The Norman period saw a new beginning for the English Church as a whole and for the Sussex diocese in particular. There was a purge of the English episcopate in 1070. Stigand was deposed, and with him fell four bishops, among them Æthelric of Selsey, probably because of his connections with the archbishop. Æthelric was replaced by a personal chaplain of the new King William, confusingly also called Stigand, who oversaw the transfer of the see from Selsey to Chichester in 1075. This was part of a wider 11th-century movement which saw the removal of a number of sees to more suitable sites; at the same time the sees of Lichfield and Sherborne were transferred to Chester and Salisbury.[36]

By this period Chichester seems to have been a thriving urban centre. Then as now the city was divided into quadrants by the principal roads running north-south and east-west. This feature is one of the few remnants of the Roman street pattern; elsewhere there is little overlap between the Roman and medieval layout, and this is contributory evidence that the city was largely abandoned between the sub-Roman period and the ninth century. Like many Alfredian burhs, Chichester came to have a strong economic role; it was a mint from the early 10th century, and it would have profited from royal legislation which tried to restrict all trading activities to the burhs. Yet Chichester was by no means the largest or most economically important Sussex town in the early 11th century; all the available evidence indicates that it was overshadowed by Lewes.[37] Lewes would in many ways have been a more suitable choice for the new see, in particular because it was more centrally located within the diocese. Once more, it seems likely that the decision about the see was

4 *Early 13th-century Chapter seal.*

largely based on financial factors; most of the bishopric's existing estates were situated in the Chichester area, while it owned relatively little property around Lewes. Moreover, if the bishop and the Selsey community had indeed, as has been suggested above, regularly taken refuge within the walls of Chichester for long periods during the Viking incursions, it may have been the case that a permanent cell had been established there or that a close relationship had been forged with an existing Chichester minster.

By the 11th century there were probably several churches in Chichester, although Domesday Book refers only to one, a dependency of the archbishop's Pagham manor which was presumably All Saints' in the Pallant.[38] The 12th-century historian William of Malmesbury briefly mentions, in connection with Stigand's transfer of the see, the existence in the city of a minster dedicated to St Peter and of a (presumably separate) community of nuns.[39] It is almost certain that St Peter's lay on the site of the present Cathedral, and that it was taken over by Stigand and the episcopal community in 1075; the minster-church was probably used as a pro-cathedral until funds had been raised to start construction of the present building. The later medieval parish of St Peter Subdeanery appears to represent the remnants of the area over which the older minster had jurisdiction; the parochial altar stood at one stage in the nave of the Cathedral, and later in the north transept.[40] St Peter's may have been a very ancient foundation; it may have come into existence at the time of the establishment of the burh, or afterwards when the population increased; it may have been founded as a dependency of the Selsey cathedral, where the community took refuge in those periods when Selsey itself was unsafe.[41] Like so much of the history of the bishopric in the Anglo-Saxon period, almost all is vague and conjectural, and there is little hope that it will ever be possible to come to a more definite conclusion.

A final example of the elusive nature of our evidence is provided by a 13th-century capitular seal from Chichester, which bears the image of a building that is recognisably a Carolingian-style church, resembling those built at Saint-Ricquier in Picardy and at Cologne in the late eighth and ninth centuries; the central tower, with its receding stages of open arcading, is especially characteristic, but also typical are the apse and the small round tower at the west end.[42] It can probably be assumed that the existing seal is a copy of one that had been associated with the bishop and chapter at a much earlier date, perhaps the last of a series of copies. This opens up tempting avenues of speculation. Churches of this type were probably being built in England in the later Anglo-Saxon period. Is this a representation of a particular church? Of a late Anglo-Saxon cathedral at Selsey? Or St Peter's Minster in Chichester? Alas, a deflating but more realistic approach is to look for an iconographical explanation; it is far more likely that the image was borrowed from another source, such as a manuscript illustration of an ideal church, than that it depicts a particular building in Sussex.[43]

II

The Medieval Cathedral

Diana E. Greenway

The medieval Cathedral was, in St Richard's words, 'the mother and mistress' of all the churches of the diocese. Throughout the four centuries between 1100 and 1500, the Cathedral's supremacy was made especially clear every year at Whitsuntide. On Whitmonday there came processions of priests and people from the outlying parishes, bearing their crosses and banners, to proceed through the Cathedral to present their Pentecostal offerings. They came from far and wide, drawn by the power of custom, by the sheer excitement of the occasion, and by the promise of over 400 days' remission of penance for sin. They did not always behave well: there was rivalry between the parishes and from time to time there were disturbances, brawls and even murders among the jostling crowds as they gathered outside the west door, and further disorder, with shouting, chattering and laughing, inside the Cathedral. In 1478 Bishop Storey attempted to control the occasion by forbidding the carrying of long staffs and painted staves and by laying down a precise order in which the parishes were to take their places in the procession: first Arundel; then West Dean; then the inhabitants of Bosham, with its outliers Apuldram, Funtington and Chidham; then Oving; then Sidlesham, with Easton; then Felpham; then Birdham; and finally Selsey.[1]

In origin the requirement on all parishioners to take part in the Whitsun processions to their mother church was introduced into England from Normandy, shortly after 1100.[2] It not only created a powerful tie between the people and their cathedral, but also helped cathedral building programmes, for the Pentecostal offerings, which in Normandy were earmarked for the lighting of the church, tended in England to be used, in part at least, for the fabric. At Chichester as in other dioceses, parishioners were induced to come and make their gifts of alms by remissions from penance: Bishop Ralph Luffa (1091-1123) was the first of many bishops to grant such an indulgence (40 days) for those coming to Chichester at Whitsun.[3]

The pentecostals became a part of the regular income of the Cathedral, which those who could not participate in the processions paid to the rural deans, to be delivered at the Cathedral by the archdeacons. But from time to time parishioners needed to be reminded of their obligation not only to pay but to come. In the 1240s, for instance, the repair and completion of the Cathedral became something of a crusade for St Richard (Bishop Richard de Wych, 1245-53): he identified the duty to come at Whitsuntide with the requirement in the Old Testament to 'appear in the sight of the Lord thy God' at the Solemnity of Weeks,[4] and issued an indulgence of 40 days for those visiting the church at Whitsuntide. He obtained similar indulgences from nine other English diocesan bishops, so that the dean at the time,

5 *St Richard de Wych's seal.*

Geoffrey of Gloucester, was able to make the triumphant calculation that the total remission for visitors at Whitsuntide was 450 days.[5] But by the early 14th century the processions were badly attended 'by the sloth of some, to the grave peril of their souls', and Bishop Robert Rede (1396-1415) issued a further exhortation, with another forty days' indulgence, to parishioners to 'go devoutly and in procession with cross and banner to their kind mother (*alma mater*) the church of Chichester'.[6] This document reveals that at Chichester the Whitsuntide procession was also the occasion when each parish collected the chrism and holy oil, which had been blessed by the bishop on Maundy Thursday, for use in baptism and unction throughout the rest of the year. The Whitsuntide events brought home to the parishioners the motherhood of the Cathedral, binding them to herself in the family of parishes.

But bishops could not expect the impossible. Chichester's location at the far western edge of the diocese rendered it extremely unlikely that people from all the parishes would be able to make the journey to the Cathedral. Similar problems occurred in other medieval dioceses, many of them much larger than Chichester: the solution was to nominate one or more local 'mother' churches to act as surrogate cathedrals. In the case of Chichester, parishioners from East Sussex made their processions to Lewes or Hastings, where their pentecostals were collected by the archdeacon for delivery at the Cathedral; the custom was reinforced by indulgences.[7] Another factor that reduced the number of parishes coming to the Cathedral at Whitsun was the existence of areas that were exempt from the bishop, the ecclesiastical 'peculiars': here the processions were made and pentecostals paid to the major church of the peculiar, such as Pagham (Archbishop of Canterbury's peculiar) and Battle (Battle Abbey peculiar).

Although Whitsun was the highlight of the year for visitors, there was no season when the Cathedral did not receive pilgrims and there were some other very special days when people came in crowds, encouraged by indulgences.[8] One of these was St Faith's Day, 6 October, when during the 12th century there was also a fair at Chichester, and a few days later, on 9 October, was another important feast, the Feast of the Relics. These feasts continued to be observed long after 1204, when the season of the fair was changed. From 1204 the fair began on the Saturday before the patronal festival, Trinity Sunday, and lasted for eight days, thus prolonging for a second week the round of festivities that had commenced at Whitsun.[9]

Another major festival at Chichester commemorated the dedication of the Cathedral on 12 September 1199: festal celebrations and indulgences marked this day every year from 1199 until 1447, when the date of the feast was changed to 3 October. The reason for this change was that the first two weeks of September had become a very busy time, with more assiduous observance of the feasts of the Nativity of the Blessed Virgin (8 September), and the Exaltation of the Holy Cross (14 September) and the introduction of the new reading and responsory, *Peto Domine*, on the first Sunday after 11 September.[10] To the holy days already mentioned we must add, of course, the great feasts of the Christian year and saints' days, and also the many days on which the dead of Chichester were commemorated: of these, St Richard's death, 3 April, and the translation of his body, 16 June, came to be by far the most important.

The Organisation of the Medieval Cathedral

By the middle years of the 12th century there had developed at Chichester an organisational structure that was similar to those in operation at other great English secular cathedrals, such as Salisbury, Lincoln and York.[11] The four chief members of the Chapter were the dean, precentor, chancellor and treasurer. These were the *persone* or dignitaries. First in precedence was the dean, who as chief priest had the care of souls in the Cathedral: he was elected by the canons, and had the power to act in administrative matters only with their consent, determined by majority voting. Second in precedence was the precentor, or cantor. His function was to rule the choir and lead the chant. These two offices came into existence in the early years of the 12th century, before the death of Bishop Ralph Luffa in 1123. Dean and precentor occupied their leading stalls in choir—the dean on the south, the precentor on the north. The other two dignities were established by Bishop Hilary: the treasurership by 1148 and the chancellorship by 1163. The treasurer was responsible for the cathedral treasure, which comprised money and valuables, such as church ornaments, vestments, relics and the archives of the cathedral. The chancellor, although his office was established fourth, took third place in the hierarchy. He was required to oversee the arrangements for reading the lessons in divine service, and for the copying of books and the writing of documents.

6 *Bishop Hilary's seal.*

Beneath the four dignitaries were the canons of the Cathedral, who for most of the medieval period numbered around twenty-six, each of whom occupied a stall in the choir. This cathedral body of thirty was small by comparison with the large chapters of

Salisbury, York, Lincoln and Wells, which all had over fifty canons, but about the same size as Hereford and St Paul's, and a little larger than Exeter. The dignitaries and canons were supported by the produce and profits of the cathedral estates. By the middle of the 12th century, the old system of managing the endowments as a whole so as to produce food and cash for distribution among the members of the Chapter, which had been in operation in 1086 at the time of Domesday Book, had given way to a more individualistic system, in which most of the old common estates were carved up so that each canon had his own piece of property, his *prebenda*, which he managed for himself. A small proportion of the endowment was retained in common, however, so that a canon in residence would receive a distribution of bread and cash from this *communa*, or common fund, as well as what he could make out of his prebend.

Most of the estates of both prebends and *communa* were in the Chichester locality, having their origin in the ancient possessions of the bishopric of Selsey. The *communa* consisted of the income from six parish churches. Similarly, about two-thirds of the prebends were made up of parish churches: in such cases, the prebendary was the rector and received all the rectorial income from tithes, glebe and offerings, apart from the proportion set aside for his vicar (or deputy). The remaining one-third of the prebends consisted of landed estates, usually farms leased out to tenants. The difference between a rectorial and a temporal prebend is neatly illustrated at Hove, where the church constituted one prebend, known as *Hova Ecclesia*, and the landed estates formed another, known as *Hova Villa*. The values of the prebends varied a good deal, depending on the size and profitability of the parishes and estates. In the great valuation of 1291, the four dignitaries were receiving around £50 a year each; half the prebendaries were receiving over £20, of whom the wealthiest had £40; of those below £20, the least wealthy had an income of just £4 13s. 4d.[12]

In addition to the chapter of dignitaries and canons, there were numerous other staff at the medieval cathedral. Before the end of the 12th century, we have our first notice of a group of men who were to become essential to the performance of daily worship in the Cathedral—the vicars. As it became increasingly usual for canons to spend long periods away from the Cathedral, engaged in business on their prebends or elsewhere, so the custom developed whereby the canons appointed clergy to take their places in choir. These clergy were the vicars choral, who from 1232 or earlier received cash and bread from the common fund, as well as a salary, called 'stall wages', and dinner from their respective prebendaries.[13] By this time there were also 10 choir boys, who were supported from the profits of a piece of land set aside by the Dean and Chapter for the purpose. They were taught grammar by the master of the scholars, who was appointed by the Cathedral chancellor.[14] To the vicars and choristers we must add the chantry priests and chaplains, who served the altars of the chantries and side chapels. There were at least fifteen chantries by 1291, and several more were added in the 14th and 15th centuries, but as some of the vicars choral acted also as chantry priests there were not necessarily so many extra clergy. Nevertheless, when we add the doorkeeper and his staff, the sacristans and bell-ringers, and an unknown number of servants,[15] we have a large, complex organisation, that might be difficult to control.

The life of the Cathedral staff was regulated by rules and customs, both written and unwritten. From time to time, an unwritten custom, or more often a collection of unwritten customs, was committed to writing in the form of a 'statute', agreed in Chapter by bishop, dean and canons. One of the first of these, drawn up in 1197 under Bishop Seffrid II, is witnessed by the full Chapter of that period: dean, precentor, chancellor, treasurer, the archdeacons of Chichester and Lewes, and 23 canons. The topics covered by this statute give a good idea of the daily concerns of the canons: the collection of the common fund; the distribution to the canons of their daily bread and weekly 12d. and to the vicars of their weekly 3d.; proper choir dress; the double censing of each clerk 'on the upper step' (i.e. the highest rank of choir stalls); and the bearing of the cross before the gospel book when the gospel was read from the pulpit.[16] The majority of such statutes were made, at Chichester as at most other English cathedrals, in the 13th century. The Chichester statutes of 1232, 1247 and 1251, taken together, provide a fairly comprehensive set of rules, covering most areas of life in the Close: the repair of the fabric of the Cathedral, the duties of the dignitaries and archdeacons, the distribution of cash and bread to canons and vicars, residence requirements and the conditions for leave of absence, behaviour at divine service and penalties for disobedience, the choir boys, the fraternities, the services for deceased canons and the anniversaries of the dead, the chaplains at the altars of St Mary and St Augustine, and the canons' houses within and without the city.[17]

Bishop and Cathedral

At most cathedrals, although the bishop had a general right to oversee the affairs of the chapter, it was accepted that the dean and canons could legislate for themselves on the conduct of services, residence and similar matters. At Chichester, however, there was a quite exceptional dispute in 1314, when a statute made by the Dean and Chapter was annulled by Bishop John Langton because it had been made without his permission. The statute concerned several topics, including the keeping of the feasts of St Wilfrid and St Denis, the prohibition of dogs in the Cathedral, and the dress to be worn by vicars, but it was probably the clauses regulating the payments to vicars and forbidding them to hold more than one stall or to act also as chantry priests that caused the Bishop to take his unprecedented action. He had himself been a noted pluralist before becoming bishop (he had held canonries at several cathedrals, including Chichester) and he gave a sympathetic ear to the complaints of the vicars against the new statute made by the Dean and Chapter.[18] None of the clauses of the annulled statute was re-enacted, and an interval of nearly a century elapsed before Chichester was given another statute: this time, in 1401, it was the Bishop who legislated, with the consent of the canons, for a fifth part of the prebends to be set aside for the next five years for use on the fabric of the Cathedral.[19]

7 *Bishop Langton's seal.*

8 *View of the nave showing the medieval floor and the new 13th-century vertical Purbeck marble shafting lightening the heavy Norman architecture (see Chapter III).*

There was another way in which the bishop might intervene in the affairs of the cathedral chapter: this was through the process of 'visitation'. Increasingly from the second half of the 13th century, English bishops sought to exercise some measure of disciplinary control over clergy in the religious institutions of their dioceses by visiting them to investigate how well they were performing their duties. Not all abbeys and priories received the bishop with enthusiasm, and a bishop who visited his own cathedral chapter was almost certain to meet with opposition. A dispute about visitation at Chichester, and the respective rights of bishop and dean, was referred in 1340 to the archbishop of Canterbury, whose award gave the bishop of Chichester more power in relation to his Chapter than any other English bishop, by virtually suspending the dean's authority during a visitation; it also supplied a list of questions to be asked by the bishop on his visitation.[20]

Naturally there was continued friction at Chichester over this issue. One of the few Chichester episcopal registers to survive from the Middle Ages is that of Bishop Robert Rede (1396-1415), who was a Dominican friar and something of a disciplinarian. He visited the Cathedral three times, on each occasion both pointing out plentiful faults that needed correction and meeting with protest from the Chapter. On his first visitation, in 1397, there was an altercation before the Dean, Treasurer and Archdeacon of Lewes would take their oath of canonical obedience to the Bishop. After the second visitation, in 1403, the Dean riposted by appealing to the Pope against the Bishop's 'molestations.' At the third visitation, in 1409, the Dean and Chapter went further, turning the tables by presenting the Bishop with a list of faults in his own administration that needed amendment.[21] We do not know if relations between bishop and chapter improved in the 15th century: later visitation records report episcopal criticisms of the laxity of the Cathedral clergy but do not reveal how the Chapter reacted.

The Members of the Cathedral Staff

On the whole the dignitaries and canons were men of education, many of whom had university degrees: by the 15th century a fair number of them possessed doctorates in theology or in canon or civil law. From before 1244 the prebend of Wightring (Wittering) was reserved for someone capable of lecturing in theology in the Close, and although from time to time there were complaints that the holder of this prebend was not fulfilling his duties as lecturer, there can be no doubt that in general the prebendaries of Wightring were well-qualified theologians.[22] That the canons had the opportunity to study while at Chichester is attested by the statute of 1226 that allows them to borrow as many books as they wish from the library, so long as they do not take them outside the city.[23]

Theoretically, all the canons were appointed by the bishop, with the exception of the dean, who was elected by the canons. In practice, there might be external pressures on the bishop, chiefly from the king or the pope, who might seek appointments for their own candidates—royal administrators or judges, or papal diplomats or tax-collectors. In times of vacancies in the bishopric, the king had a positive duty to take over the bishop's right to appoint, and if a member of the chapter died while visiting the Roman Curia, the pope might step in and make the next appointment. A dispute that is full of interest and irony started during a vacancy in the bishopric in 1390, when king and pope appointed rival candidates to the deanery, despite the long-established custom that the dean's office was elective. There followed nine years of strife, during which the original nominees were replaced by two others, also candidates of king and pope. Finally, both resigned, and the

King's nominee, John Maydenhith, was reinstated by the Pope.[24] Maydenhith was not a career civil servant, like the usual run of royal nominees, but an ecclesiastical administrator, a Bachelor of Civil Law and Warden of De Vaux College, Salisbury, who had acted as the Bishop of Salisbury's vicar-general in 1391 and had administered the vacant see of Salisbury in 1395.[25] His training and experience made him the sort of man a bishop would have been happy to see as dean of his cathedral. Yet it was Dean Maydenhith who ran into conflict with Bishop Robert Rede over the visitations of 1397 and 1403, as described above.

Maydenhith's successor, John Haseley, was more typical of the medieval deans: he was an Oxford theologian of some distinction and had already been a canon of Chichester for 14 years when he was elected by his fellow-canons. There survives a very full record of this election, which took place on 18 July 1407. After Mass at the high altar of the quire of the Cathedral, the electors proceeded to the Chapter House, where they first sang the hymn *Veni Creator Spiritus* and reviewed the attendance: there were present in person the Chancellor, the Treasurer and nine canons, some of whom were also the appointed proxies for the Precentor, the Archdeacon of Chichester and six more canons; evidence was given that another six canons had been summoned but had failed to appear, and they were therefore declared to be in contempt; and it was shown that it had not been possible to summon three more canons, as they were known to be abroad. One of the canons present was John Haseley, who was elected unanimously, and was led immediately to the high altar as the canons sang the *Te Deum* and the bells chimed. Before the altar Haseley was asked if he consented to his election, and after some deliberation he accepted, 'being unwilling to resist the divine will'. A document recording the election was then drawn up by a notary public, and sealed with the Chapter seal, for delivery to the Bishop at his manor of Amberley, along with a detailed proof of the Chapter's right to elect its own dean and of the correctness of its procedure in this election. The Bishop issued his confirmation on 26 July, and gave orders for Haseley to be installed and to be put in possession of the deanery.[26]

9 *Detail from John Speed's map of 1610 showing the Vicars' Close and Hall.*

The attendance-list at the election of John Haseley in 1407 shows that only 11 members of the chapter were present in person, while 17 were absent. This is in contrast to the attendance at the issue of a statute in 1197 (mentioned above), when all 29 members were present. The fact was that neither the individual prebends nor the common fund at Chichester were large enough to support a fully residential chapter. The problem was perhaps more acute at Chichester than at most other medieval English secular cathedrals, but it was common. A small prebend might not even cover a canon's travelling expenses to the cathedral, as Peter of Blois complained to the Dean of Salisbury in the 1190s. By the middle of the 13th century most cathedrals had modified their residence requirements so that only a proportion of the canons was asked to reside at any one time, thus enabling the others to earn their livings elsewhere—perhaps in other churches, or in the service of lay or ecclesiastical rulers. This also reduced the pressure on the scarce resources of the common fund from which those present at the daily services received their distribution of bread and cash. Chichester adopted the system of 'greater residence', found at St Paul's, Lincoln, York and Hereford, whereby a new residentiary performed a probationary period of very strict continuous residence: at Chichester this was a year. Thereafter, a residentiary canon of Chichester might choose to perform either 'full' or 'half' residence: full residence would allow him full commons and three weeks' absence each quarter, while half residence would allow half commons and six months' absence each year.[27] Houses were reserved for the four dignitaries; otherwise the bishop conferred houses only on resident canons. By the later 14th century, however, the chapter was actually discouraging residence by compelling a canon who wished to reside to pay an entry fine of the substantial sum of 50 marks (£33 6s. 8d.)—25 marks to the chapter and 25 marks to the fabric.[28] Small wonder, therefore, that in the 15th century the number of resident canons at any one time was low: when Bishop Storey carried out visitations in 1478 and 1482 there were only five resident canons, including dean and precentor, on each occasion.[29] The records of Chapter meetings entered in the earliest official act book of the Dean and Chapter, the White Act Book, running from 1472 to 1544, show a similar pattern of residence in the last decades of the 15th century.[30]

The duties of absent canons were carried out by the members of the secondary group of clergy in the Cathedral, the vicars choral. As the number of resident canons dwindled in the 14th and 15th centuries, so the vicars became proportionately more important in the life of the Cathedral. It was no longer a practicable proposition for the few resident canons to entertain the many vicars in their own houses, so a separate residence was built for the vicars by 1403. Soon after, to the south of the Vicars' Hall, two rows of houses were built, facing across an enclosed courtyard, the Vicars' Close.[31] The vicars led a common life, after the style of a medieval college, and were ruled by a Principal. They were incorporated by letters patent in 1465.

The Liturgy

The chief objective of the Cathedral's organisation and the primary duty of its staff lay in divine worship. The outline of the daily services in the medieval secular cathedrals was very similar to that in the monasteries and monastic cathedrals: the seven liturgical 'hours', otherwise called the 'Office'—Matins and Lauds (counted together as one), Prime, Terce, Sext, None, Vespers, and Compline; the celebration of Masses, chiefly the early morning 'Morrow Mass', the Lady Mass and High Mass; and the commemoration of the dead, with prayers, psalms and chantry Masses. The whole Psalter was also recited daily, each canon being allotted one or more psalms. On Sundays, feast days, saints' days, and special anniversaries, there were additional Masses, prayers, and hymns, with processions and sermons. The pattern of worship, although much the same at all cathedrals, varied in detail in the early Middle Ages according to local customs, before more uniform observances were introduced during the course of the 13th, 14th and 15th centuries through the gradual widespread adoption of the customs of Salisbury, known as the Use of Sarum. At Chichester the services followed the Use of Chichester until the 15th century. The Chichester Use had been prescribed for all the churches in the diocese by St Richard in *c.*1250, for both Mass and Office.[32] In 1423, however, the local Use was abandoned, when Archbishop Chichele brought to Chichester service books containing the Use of Sarum, to which the liturgy thereafter conformed.[33]

Throughout the Middle Ages, for much of every day, between sunrise and sunset, worship was offered in the Cathedral, and the visitor would have been aware, perhaps from more than one part of the church at the same time, of the sounds of bells ringing and of voices murmuring, reciting, chanting, or singing, of the flickering light of candles and of the scent of incense. The possibility of having different services going on simultaneously arose from the fact that from the earliest days the Cathedral of Chichester, like other great medieval churches, was not so much a single large area for worship as a series of areas, by virtue of the existence of side chapels and subsidiary altars. The Office was said in the quire and the most solemn Masses at the high altar, but other Masses, prayers and private devotions took place in chapels at various points in the Cathedral.

The first evidence of the dedications of these side altars comes from the early 13th century, but doubtless altars of the principal saints, St John the Baptist and the Virgin Mary, had existed much earlier than our first notice of them, and this may be true also of the altar dedicated to St Cross and St Augustine: it is even possible that these were the dedications of the three flanking chapels at the east end of the first Anglo-Norman church.[34] By the middle years of the 13th century there were also altars dedicated to the following: St Anne; St Catherine, St Agatha, St Margaret and St Winifred; St Mary Magdalene; St Pantaleon; and St Edmund of Abingdon and St Thomas Becket.[35] In the nave the altar of St Peter served as a parish church.[36] At the east end the Lady Chapel was greatly enlarged by Bishop Gilbert of St Leofard, between 1288 and 1305.[37] Other altars within the Cathedral are mentioned in the 15th century, notably St Clement, St George, and St Mary at the choir door.[38] Outside the church, the chapel of St Faith is first mentioned in 1291.[39] But more important than any of these, from 1276, was the altar at the shrine of St Richard.

Shrines and Saints

Relics of the patronal saints were often displayed at medieval altars, but no relic-list survives from Chichester to allow us to know if this was the case with any of the altars that existed before the canonisation of Bishop Richard in 1262. The Cathedral certainly possessed a collection of relics, which were displayed in solemn services held on 9 October, the Feast of the Relics: there is a reference to this practice as early as the 1170s.[40] Doubtless the collection received additions in the course of time. The rarity in England of the dedication to St Pantaleon suggests strongly that a relic of St Pantaleon had been brought to Chichester, perhaps from Cologne, where the saint's head was translated in 1208.[41] The dedication of an altar to two archbishops of Canterbury, St Thomas Becket and St Edmund of Abingdon, is to be associated with Bishop Richard de Wych, who chose to be buried close to it. As he was himself a collector of relics, he may well have arranged for relics of these two saints to be laid in the altar.[42] But before his death there was at Chichester no shrine to attract pilgrims and no cult of a local saint—the body of St Wilfrid, the founder of the see at Selsey, was preserved at Ripon, and claimed also at Canterbury and Worcester. It might be said that Chichester stood in need of its own saint to act as a focus for popular devotion.

There was, however, a strong tradition of commemoration of the dead, particularly the dead of the Cathedral community. The evidence for the endowment of anniversaries and chantries for the remembrance of deceased canons of Chichester is extremely rich, suggesting that from the middle of the 12th century onwards this formed an important part of the religious observance of members of the Chapter. Bishops, dignitaries and canons gave sums of money and pieces of property to pay for the anniversaries of their deaths to be kept each year, with prayers, memorial Masses, bells and candles, and payments to all the participating clergy and to the poor; the names of those remembered were entered in what was known as the 'martilogy' [*sic*] of the church.[43] Chantries, which entailed more substantial endowments in order to secure regular Masses (two or more every week of the year), were established at several of the side altars of the Cathedral before St Richard's death, and more were established afterwards.[44] These chantries were served by priests who were often also vicars choral.[45]

10 *Thirteenth-century wallpainting of St Richard in Black Bourton church, Oxfordshire, depicted not long after his canonisation.*

It is against this background that we should see the career and cult of St Richard. Richard 'de Wych' was so named from the town of Droitwich (Worcs.), where he was born in *c*.1197. After a distinguished career at Oxford, he became chancellor to the Archbishop of Canterbury, Edmund of Abingdon, in 1237, and was present at Edmund's death in France in 1240. Richard stayed on in France, to study theology with the Dominican friars at Orléans, where he was ordained priest. He was back in England in 1244. In the spring of that year, after the death of Bishop Ralph Neville, the canons of Chichester were pressurised by Henry III into electing as bishop a royal administrator, Robert Passelewe, the Archdeacon of Lewes. But Boniface of Savoy, the newly elected Archbishop of Canterbury, supported by other English bishops, quashed this election, after examining Passelewe and finding him wanting in theology: the Archbishop-elect nominated instead Richard de Wych.

The King was furious, and refused to allow Richard his episcopal lands (and therefore his income), even after he had received confirmation and consecration at the hands of the Pope at Lyon. A royal mandate in April 1245, addressed to the custodian of the bishopric, ordered that Master Richard de Wych 'who conducts himself as bishop of Chichester' was not to be allowed into the city-gates. It was not until July 1246 that peace was made between King and Bishop, and the episcopal revenues were released: this was also the year in which Richard's late master, Edmund of Abingdon, was canonised by the Pope. Richard's

11 *The shrine area with its richer carving and medieval floor, drawn by (Sir) George Scharf in 1852 (Society of Antiquaries of London).*

courage and tenacity during the conflict with the King, and his close association with a saint of the Church, were later to be seen as pointers to his own sanctity.

As Bishop of Chichester, he was outstanding for the attention he paid to pastoral care, issuing diocesan statutes and directives covering all aspects of the Christian life, such as the training and discipline of the clergy, the payment of tithes by the laity, the duty to take part in Whitsun processions, and the regulation of the conduct of divine worship. All this added to his holy reputation, as did his enthusiasm for preaching crusades. It was on a preaching tour of Kent that he fell ill and died at Dover, on 3 April 1253, shortly after consecrating a chapel in honour of St Edmund.[46] As we have seen, his will provided for his burial before St Edmund's altar in Chichester Cathedral. It also made numerous bequests: his theological and legal library was divided among more than a dozen houses of Franciscan and Dominican friars; gifts of cash, jewellery, plate and other items were made to servants, friends, and religious (including five recluses); money was also given for the fabric of the cathedral, for the crusade, and for the poor.[47]

The canons of Chichester lost no time after Bishop Richard's death in assembling the necessary documents to pursue the process of canonisation. Evidence was collected of the soundness of his parentage, the holiness of his life, and his working of miracles both before and after his death. His grave in the north aisle was regarded as a holy place, and only eighteen months after his burial a chaplain was appointed to look after it. Formal canonisation by Pope Urban IV followed in 1262, and was accompanied by permission to translate the saint's body to a more prominent place in the Cathedral. The translation was accomplished on 16 June 1276, an occasion of great splendour, attended by King Edward I, when St Richard was reburied in a silver-gilt shrine, encrusted with jewels, behind the high altar, the usual position for the shrines of patronal saints. There was an altar at the shrine, and in the course of time a watch-loft was built close by. It seems that at the time of the translation the saint's head was removed, for veneration separately, and was placed in a silver reliquary in St Mary Magdalene's chapel. The original grave, in St Edmund's chapel, also continued to be a place of pilgrimage and devotion: possibly it was here that the saint's mitre and chalice were displayed. Thus there were three sites within the Cathedral where Masses could be said in the name of St Richard.

Pilgrims were attracted by the remissions granted on the two great annual feast days, 3 April and 16 June, marking respectively the death and translation of the saint, but they were also drawn by the desire to come close to the holy body and by the hope of healing or other miracles. St Richard was held to have performed miracles during his lifetime, most of them reminiscent of the miracles of Christ, such as healing the sick, multiplying a small quantity of food to feed a crowd of poor people, and bringing about a miraculous draught of fishes. After his death, further miracles of healing occurred at his tomb and elsewhere.[48]

The cult flourished, right down to the 16th century, and the Cathedral was commonly known as 'the church of St Richard', even though its true dedication remained the Holy Trinity. St Richard was widely revered, especially in the south of England, and there were small cult centres at Droitwich, the saint's place of birth, and Dover, the place of his death. At Chichester devotees made gifts of various sorts—cash, land, and jewels for the shrine. The most spectacular was the bequest of Bishop Robert Rede: it included items of gold, silver and precious stones. But giving was not confined to the wealthy, and there was a stream of small gifts made by all kinds of people, even those in quite humble circumstances. The record of the large quantity of plate and jewellery taken away when the shrine was dismantled in 1538 reveals something of the scale of the donations that had accumulated over the centuries.[49]

Cathedral and City

This is perhaps all the more remarkable as in national terms Chichester and its surrounding area were neither notably populous nor prosperous. The port of Chichester suffered fluctuating fortunes, and its cloth trade never thrived sufficiently to bring it high rank among the English provincial towns. Estimates of the medieval population suggest that for much of the period between 1100 and 1500 the city had fewer than 2,000 inhabitants.[50] Even when supplemented by visitors to the markets and fairs, the law courts and the Cathedral, the number of people in Chichester at any one time was, by modern standards, extremely low.

Yet the Cathedral's parish of St Peter the Great, served by the subdean at the nave altar, was simply one of eight parishes within the city. All the other parish churches lay in the two quarters on the more prosperous eastern side of the city.[51] With the exception of the most ancient parish church, All Saints in the Pallant, which formed an exempt jurisdiction of the archbishop of Canterbury, the ecclesiastical jurisdiction of the city belonged to the dean, who had the right to institute the incumbents of the parish churches and to carry out disciplinary visitations. It was not unusual for vicars choral of the Cathedral to be appointed to city churches. The indissoluble ties which bound the clergy and people of the city parishes to the Cathedral were manifest in episcopal visitations, when the rectors, vicars, chaplains, and representatives of the parishioners of the city churches were summoned by the dean to appear before the bishop at the subdean's altar, St Peter's in the nave.[52]

Among those appearing before the bishop on such occasions were the warden and chaplain of the Hospital of St Mary. From the early 13th century at least, the hospital was under the direction of the dean and chapter, who appointed its wardens and had a large say in its affairs.[53] Of the 13 inmates, male and female, some were sick and infirm and others in sound health. The latter were required to clean the Chapter House and the enclosure before the altar of the Blessed Virgin in the Cathedral.[54] From the hospital revenues came five pounds of wax each year to keep a candle burning before the same altar on St James's day, and money to pay the clerk who served the altar.[55]

Through its control over the town parishes and the hospital, the Cathedral exercised considerable influence in the daily life of Chichester. It was also the town's major employer, providing both permanent and casual employment for numerous servants and estate labourers, carters and grooms, purveyors of food and drink, suppliers of cloth, artisans in construction and repair—masons, carpenters, workers in glass and metal, and many other craftsmen and traders. The provision of wax candles alone must have involved a veritable army of workers![56]

As property owners, too, dean and chapter were enmeshed in secular affairs, for they were caught up in the land market, where their activities affected their neighbours and vice versa. The mayor and leading citizens were often called upon to act as witnesses to documents recording gifts, sales and leases of Cathedral property, and were drawn into some transactions that might be thought to be purely internal to the Cathedral, such as Dean Roger de Freton's gifts to improve the property of the deanery in 1374.[57] In the field of secular jurisdiction, there was some confusion in the area that was not included in the archbishop's Liberty of the Pallant, for there were competing claims for the courts of the dean, the bishop and the mayor. Settlements of these three-sided disputes were made in 1358 and 1359.[58]

On the whole, relations between the Cathedral and the town in which it lay were harmonious. From the first half of the 13th century, some mayors and wealthy citizens tended to endow their anniversaries in the Cathedral after the style of the canons. The Gild Merchant, which existed from the 12th century or earlier, was re-established in 1446 in union with the Gild of St George: the mayor of Chichester was always to be its Master and it was to maintain a chaplain in St George's chapel. A happy sign of the close ties between the Cathedral and the people of Chichester was Bishop Sherburne's bequest to the Gild in 1534: he gave 20s. annually to be spent on wine on St George's day (23 April), for consumption by the brothers and sisters of the Gild, and by the general public, after 'customary honest merriment' round the City Cross.[59] The medieval Cathedral, 'the mother and mistress' of all the churches of the diocese, the power-house of divine worship, the repository of St Richard's miraculous relics, and the focus of pilgrimage, was also part of the fabric of daily life in Chichester, the well-known neighbour and friend of the townspeople. As with other secular cathedrals, this familiarity doubtless contributed to its survival as a building and as an institution during the perilous time in which the English monasteries were swept away.

III

The Medieval Fabric

Tim Tatton-Brown

The Anglo-Saxon Cathedral

The Anglo-Saxon cathedral of the South Saxons on the Isle of Selsey was almost certainly at Church Norton,[1] as was well-known in the medieval and early Tudor periods. Bishop William Reede, for example, in his will, dated 1 August 1382, says 'My body [is] to be buried in front of the high altar in the chancel of [the church of] the Holy Trinity at Selsey formerly the cathedral church of my diocese'.[2] When the church, which had become Selsey's parish church after the Norman Conquest, was demolished (except for its chancel) in 1865, the nave arcades were taken to be re-used in a new parish church at the south end of the island.

It seems very likely that the Anglo-Saxon cathedral was demolished soon after it ceased to hold the bishop's seat, and was replaced with a new nave and chancel, with the nave acquiring aisles by the end of the 12th century and the chancel being rebuilt in the 13th century. Any remains of the Anglo-Saxon cathedral must now be sought below ground, beneath the chancel ('St Wilfrid's Chapel') and the now-demolished nave. To the south of the parish church site was once a tall, early Norman defensive tower set in a ringwork (an early Norman castle) which later became the church belfry.[3] It is this tower (with a spire) which is depicted in Lambert Barnard's painting in the Cathedral south transept of St Wilfrid receiving the first charter. From the time of William Camden until recent times, however, a myth has grown up that the Anglo-Saxon cathedral was on the south side of Selsey and that it had been washed away by the sea.[4]

Building the New Norman Cathedral

The Cathedral Church of the South Saxon see was moved in 1075 from Selsey to the existing minster church of St Peter in the old Roman walled city of Chichester. For a long time it has been accepted that a new Norman cathedral was not started until at least sixteen years later when Ralph Luffa became Bishop.[5] This is most unlikely, as Dr Richard Gem has shown.[6] The surviving early masonry and early Romanesque architectural details strongly suggest that Bishop Stigand started to construct the present Cathedral soon after the move from Selsey. Robert Willis, who first worked out the architectural history of Chichester Cathedral in 1853, himself stated in a footnote 'perhaps the foundations of the church were prepared by Stigand'.[7] I would go much further and suggest that most of the first church (as far as the fourth bay in the nave—see below) was finished by the time of Bishop Ralph. Although a former chaplain and close friend of William II, Ralph Luffa was in dispute with

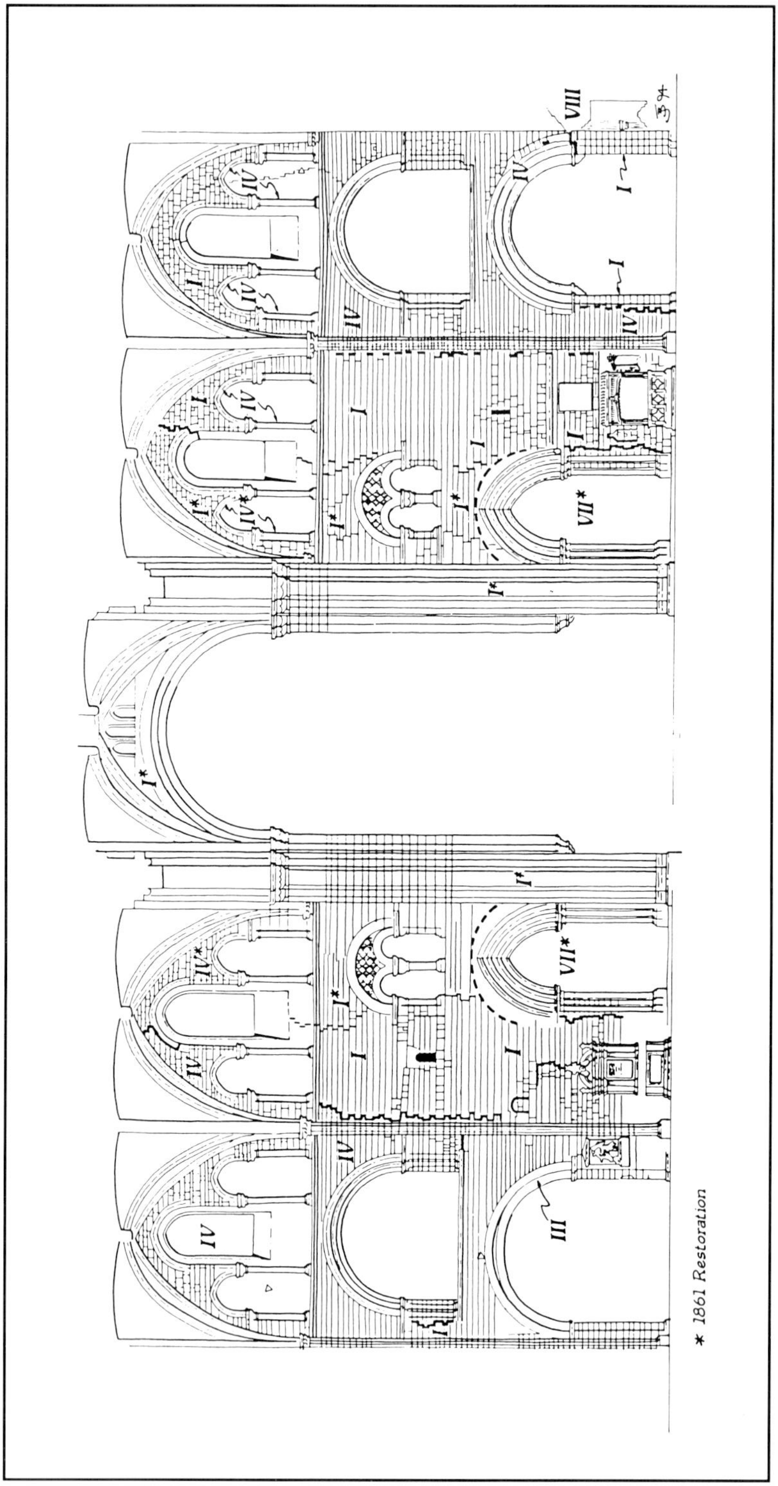

Plan 1 *Elevation of east side of the crossing before the fall of the spire (partly after R. Willis), showing I—original late 11th-century masonry; III—mid-12th-century masonry; IV—Post-1187-fire rebuilding, including vaults; VII—later 13th-century arches into quire aisles; VIII—tomb of Bishop Langton and rebuilt south wall—early 14th century.*

him on behalf of Archbishop Anselm in the later 1090s, and the Cathedral was not formally dedicated until 1108. Ralph's main contribution to the work, which is recorded by William of Malmesbury, was the restoration of the church after a serious fire on 5 May 1114.[8] It is also probable that, by this time, he had completed the western four bays of the nave and the two western towers.

The early cathedral at Chichester consisted of a presbytery of three straight bays ending in an ambulatory that was flanked externally by three small apsidal chapels.[9] The quire was situated under the crossing, and there were north and south transepts which were two bays wide. East of the transepts were small apsidal chapels on two levels, and it is very likely that the outer parts of the transepts originally had galleries in them (perhaps groin-vaulted), but these were removed after the fire of 1187, when the masonry around the western entrance into the upper chapels was completely replaced.[10]

The first Norman Cathedral was probably planned in the mid-1070s with an eight-bay nave with flanking western towers, but the evidence from the fabric shows clearly that only the eastern four bays were built in the first phase.[11] The break can be clearly seen in the outer wall-face at clerestory level, where there is a distinct difference between the wide-jointed early masonry to the east and the better-coursed masonry to the west[12] The stone used throughout, however, is Quarr stone from near Binstead on the Isle of Wight. Inside the nave, the break can also be seen at triforium level in the tympana of the triforium arcading, where there is a change from plain lozenge-shaped masonry to horizontally-coursed masonry.

12 *Earlier view of the south triforium, showing clearly the carved capitals and the point at which the Norman masonry changes to that of the 13th-century retroquire.*

Various other traces of the original Norman Cathedral can also be seen in the masonry, including now-removed blind arcading on the inside faces of the presbytery aisle walls,[13] and roll-mouldings over most of the arches.[14] The external top of the aisle walls, with a crudely decorated corbel-table, can also be seen in the roof spaces above the 13th-century outer nave chapels.[15] The bases for the original great west doorway were also exposed when the floor in the porch was lowered in the early 1970s, but they were boxed in during the porch

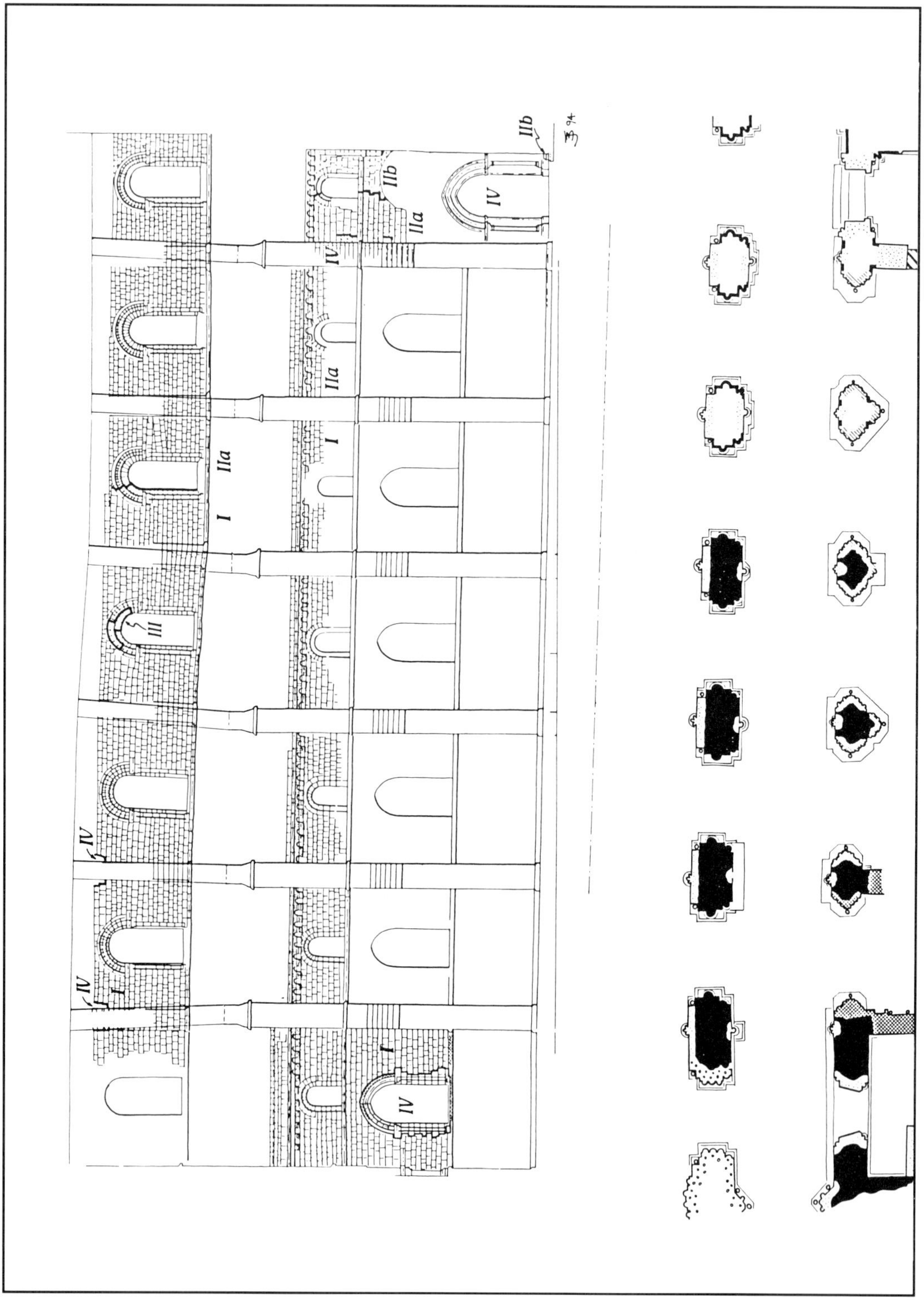
IIb
IIb
IIa
IV
IV
IIa
I
IIa
I
III
IV
IV
I
I
IV

restoration of 1989.[16] The finest early Norman carved work is, however, in the capitals of the triforia in the presbytery. These are rare survivals, though much battered by the 12th-century fires and the 1861 fall of the spire. There is also an early 12th-century south doorway to the south-west tower covered with chevron decoration.

The original Cathedral must have had only a flat ceiling in the presbytery[17] and nave, presumably with groin-vaults in the aisles and apsidal capitals. The whole building was probably complete before the death of Bishop Luffa in 1123, though minor repairs were being made to the fabric a little later in the 12th century, using Caen stone for the first time. This was due largely to uneven settlement of the new Cathedral on its foundations. A triforium arch on the north side of the nave had to be rebuilt, as did the head of the clerestory window above, which had cracked badly. The top of the clerestory wall in the nave now sinks down to the west (settlement seems to have started to occur during the building work) and this caused many problems in the late 12th century (when the high vaults were inserted) and during the 13th century. Willis also noted (before the fall of the spire) that 'the central crossing arches had been rebuilt with their own stones previously to the carrying up of the tower itself in the 13th century, and probably a considerable proportion of the piers also'. This may have been in the early or late 12th century.[18]

The 'Chichester Reliefs', probably part of a stone screen in the quire, presumably date from the decades after *c.*1120, and may therefore be the work of the time of Bishop Seffrid I (Pelochin) or just possibly of Bishop Hilary.[19] It was probably Bishop Hilary who built the surviving three western bays of the Lady Chapel as an enlargement of the earlier apsidal chapel. The two westernmost of these bays still have their later 12th-century quadripartite vaults, probably the earliest in the Cathedral. Below them are some interesting late Norman capitals.

A Century of Rebuilding

The Romanesque Cathedral was finally consecrated on 3 October 1184 under Bishop Seffrid II,[20] but only three years later (20 October 1187) an even more serious fire totally gutted the Cathedral and burnt much of the city, including the Bishop's Palace and the canons' houses.[21] The evidence for this fire can still be seen in many places in the Cathedral; interestingly, instead of carrying out a total rebuilding, only the most severely calcined areas were refaced, as Robert Willis was able to show so clearly.[22] This was probably due to a lack of resources, though at the eastern end of the presbytery much extra money was spent in demolishing the old semicircular ambulatory and apsidal chapels and replacing them with a square east end with new square chapels flanking the Lady Chapel.

In the totally new work, the use of vertical Purbeck marble shafting (with string-courses, capitals and bases in Purbeck and Sussex marble) and the particularly fine large compound piers with very large Corinthian capitals (all in Purbeck marble)[23] are very much a reflection of what was happening at this time in the rebuilding, on a much larger scale, of the cathedrals of Canterbury and Lincoln. There was also the introduction, in stages, of quadripartite rib-vaulting throughout the Cathedral both in the high vaults and in the aisles.

Plan 2 *(facing page) North elevation of the nave, showing phases of Romanesque masonry (note irregular coursing): I—original c1080s masonry; IIa & b—two sub-phases of c.1100 masonry, including N.W. tower; III—mid-12th-century repairs; IV—window(s), flying buttresses and N.W. doorway added after 1187 fire. The plan below is of the north aisle. The key is as for the main phased plan on p.xx.*

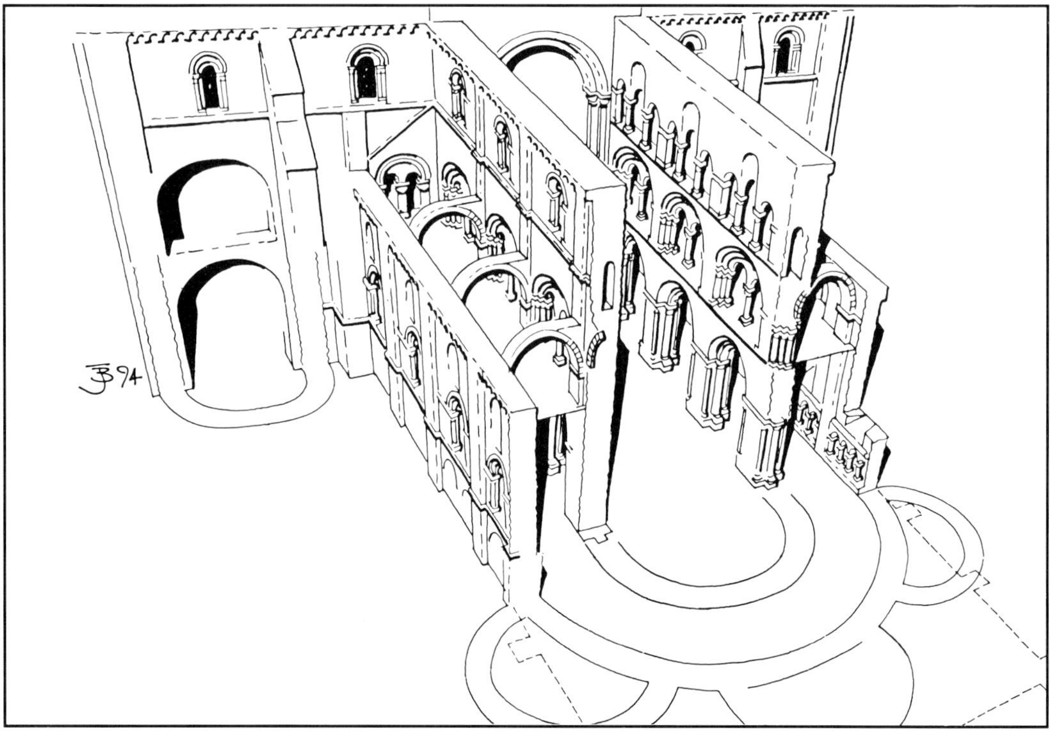

Plan 3a *Reconstructed view of original eastern arm of Chichester Cathedral.*

Here is the beginning of Gothic at Chichester, and, again as at Canterbury, the work seems to have been done rapidly (*c.* 1188-99), allowing the church to be reconsecrated on 12 September 1199. This does not mean, however, that all the work was completed at this time, because two royal licences for Bishop Simon of Wells to bring Purbeck marble 'from the coast of Dorset to Chichester to repair his church' exist for 1205-6.[24]

It seems most unlikely that the whole of the Cathedral had been vaulted in by 1199, but much work remains to be done on elucidating the late 12th- and earlier 13th-century sequences. Exactly when the enlarged transept chapels or the 'sacristry' (now called the Canons' Vestry, and perhaps the original Chapter House), with its quinquepartite vaults, were built has yet to be ascertained. This could only be achieved by a detailed analysis of all the masonry (including the rib-vaults),[25] assisted by dendrochronology and a full study of the mouldings. Apart from the high roofs and doors,[26] medieval timbers for study occur in several other places; for example, the original late 12th-century door into the Canons' Vestry (with original ironwork) survives, and there are early 13th-century centring boards in the triforium above the passage connecting the north and south galleries (*triforia*) at the east end of the presbytery.

Between 1207 and 1215 the see was vacant and the whole of England was under an interdict. It is, therefore, very likely that all work on the Cathedral stopped. It is during this period that another disaster happened to the building; two towers, we are told, were brought down by a great storm in 1210 which also wrecked the towers of Bury St Edmunds and Evesham.[27] One of these towers must have been the south-west tower, but whether the other one was the north-west tower or the crossing tower is unknown. It was probably the former, which collapsed in the early 17th century (see below). The repairs to the south-west tower, using Caen stone to fill in a large crack, can be clearly seen in its west side. This tower was also strongly buttressed on the south and south-west, and an upper stage, with pairs of tall lancet windows, was added.

Plan 3b *Reconstruction of eastern arm as rebuilt in the early 13th century (including mid-12th-century Lady Chapel vault in foreground).*

In 1215 Richard Poore, Dean of Salisbury, was consecrated Bishop of Chichester. Two years later he returned to Salisbury as Bishop and was closely involved in the start of the work on that magnificent new cathedral. At Chichester, he is likely to have restarted the building work and, from the 1220s, work on the Cathedral must have once again been in full swing. The towers were repaired and in 1224 lead 'for the roof of the church' was helped on its way by the king, and during the episcopacy of Ralph Neville much other work is documented or inferred. As Royal Chancellor from 1226 to 1240, Neville was able to get Henry III's help (the King came of age in January 1227), and in 1232 one hundred trees were granted by the King for the fabric. Two years later, he granted a further fifty trees. At this time also, one-twentieth of the common fund was devoted to much needed work on the fabric, and indulgences were granted for contributions to repairs and for carting the royal timber to Chichester.[28] All of this suggests that major roofs were being built, but, as Julian Munby has pointed out,[29] the existing high roofs of the Cathedral (over the nave and presbytery) must date from the later 13th century. If there were new roofs being built in the 1230s, why were they replaced only about half a century or so later? The answer must be that settlement was still taking place, making the wall tops unstable. We also know that early 13th-century roofs usually had no longitudinal ties (purlins), and therefore were commonly subject to racking or leaning.

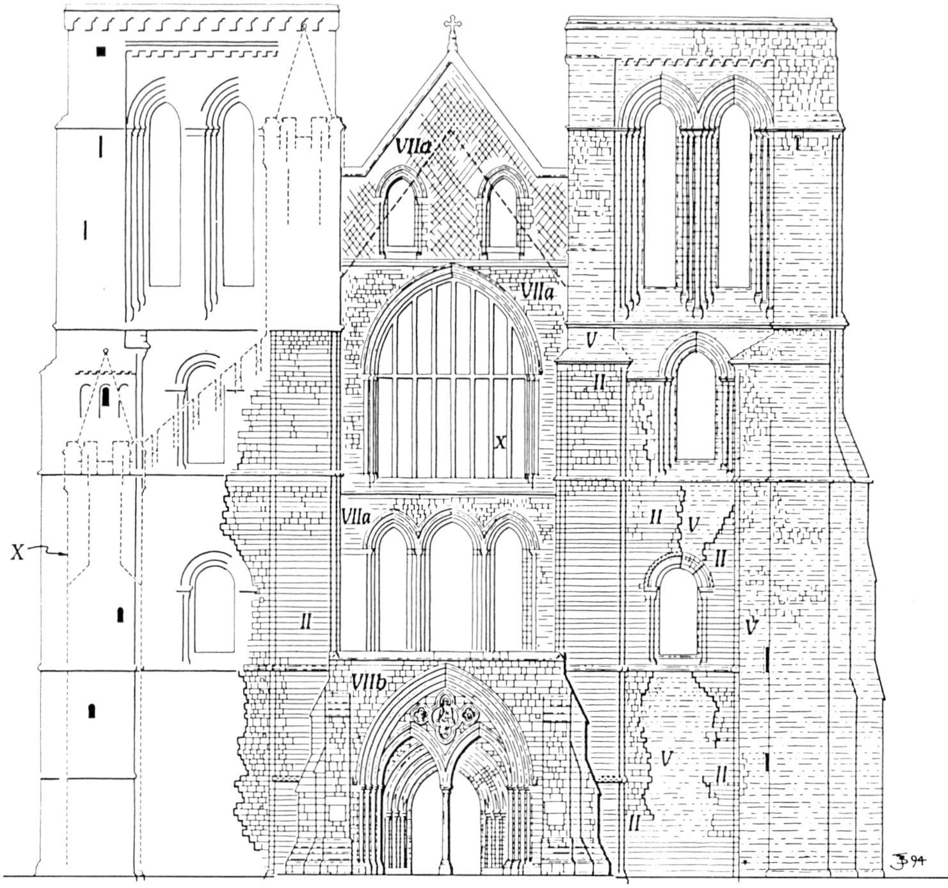

Plan 4 *Archaeological analysis of the West Front: II—c.1100 Quarr stone masonry; V—rebuilding of S.W. tower after 1210 collapse; VII—rebuilt upper gable and added porch of the late 13th century; X—wooden mullions of great west window from mid-19th-century restoration; also outline of north turret before rebuilding of N.W. tower in c.1900.*

In 1240 an important agreement was made by the Dean and Chapter with John the Glazier.[30] In this John agreed that, in return for a daily allowance of food and a yearly fee of 13s. 4d., he and his heirs were to keep the windows of the Cathedral in good repair. This surely indicates that the roofs, vaults and windows in the church were all complete by this time. The contract goes on:

> They shall preserve the ancient glass windows [*vitreolas*], and what has to be washed and cleaned they shall wash and clean, and what has to be repaired they shall repair, at the cost of the church, and what has to be added they shall add, likewise at the cost of the church; and there shall be allowed for them for each foot of addition one penny. And as often as they shall repair the glass windows, in whole, or in part, they shall be bound, if ordered by the keeper of the works, to make one roundel [*roellam*] with an image in each. And if they make a new glass

window entirely at their own cost, which is without pictorial decoration [*pictura*] and is 53 feet in total area [*magnitudinis circumquaque*] they shall receive for it and for their expenses, 12s.[31]

Dr Salzman commented that 53 square feet 'corresponds to the contemporary clerestory windows' (he presumably meant the presbytery). Those windows, however, appear to be considerably less than 53 square feet in area, and it seems more likely that the windows referred to are the wide lancets in the outer walls of the aisles. Most of these window-openings, which were enlarged in the late 12th or early 13th century, have now disappeared. However, one of them can be seen at the extreme east end of the nave north aisle, while another can be found in the south presbytery aisle. They are nearly 50 square feet in area. The north and south windows in all the added eastern chapels are also about 50 square feet in area.

13 *Late 12th-century door into the Canons' Vestry.*

Two other things almost certainly constructed by *c.*1240 were the north and south porches, which predate the construction of the nave aisle chapels.[32] The latter, which is now known as 'St Richard's Porch', and originally had a gabled top, is more likely to have been built by Ralph Neville and therefore before St Richard Wych's time (*c.*1245-53). After the death of Bishop Neville, his executors in 1247 refer to money left to the fabric being put towards the rapid completion of the stone belfry (called *Berfridi* or *turris lapidee*) begun by Neville. 'It had stood for a long time unfinished, and was almost despaired of.'[33] This presumably refers to the central crossing tower, which, although totally rebuilt after 1861 by Scott, is mid-13th-century in style. It is just possible, however, that the stone tower of 1247 refers to a detached stone belfry, like that being built contemporaneously at Salisbury Cathedral, but, if this is the case, it is odd that it had to be replaced only a century and a half later and no trace of an earlier (13th-century) structure remains in the free-standing bell tower of the Cathedral.

The next phase of the construction at the Cathedral must date from the second half of the 13th century. Bishop Richard de Wych was canonised in 1262, and on 16 June 1276 his remains were translated from the nave, where he had been buried in accordance with his will against a column 'near the altar of the blessed Confessor Edmund' (Edmund of Abingdon, Archbishop of Canterbury and friend of St Richard, who had been canonised in 1246).[34] This is amplified by Ralph Bocking, St Richard's contemporary and first biographer, who says that he was buried 'in a humble place before the altar of St Edmund, which he himself had erected in the north part of the church'.[35] After only 23 years his body was moved into the new shrine immediately behind the high altar. As a result of this, much money must have come in, though we are told that Bishop Stephen of Berghsted (1262-87), who had been

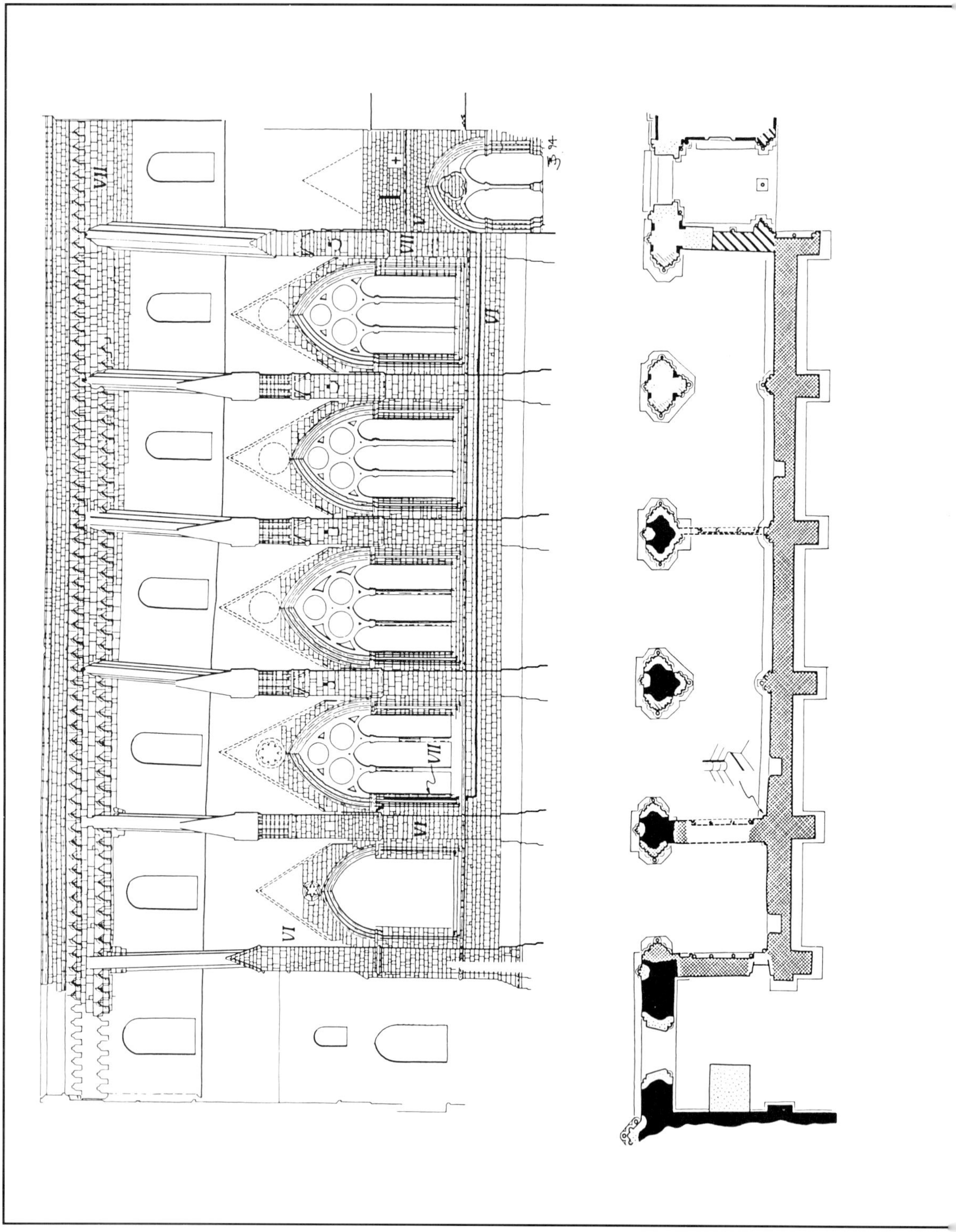

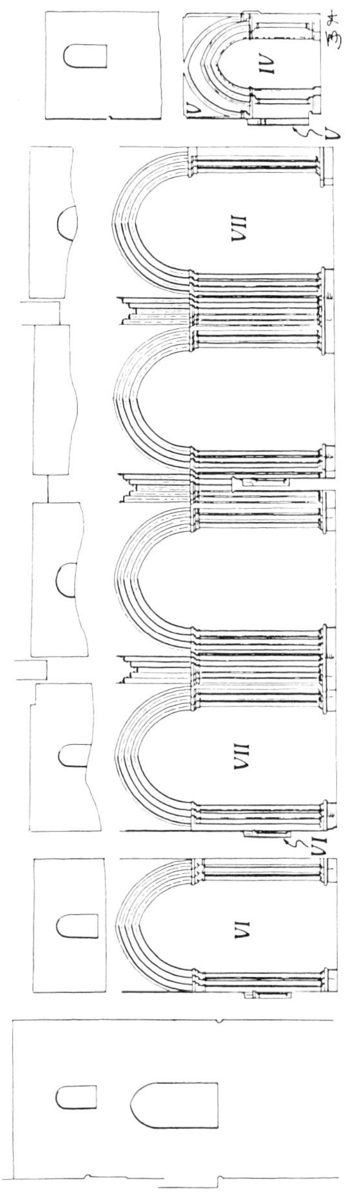

Plan 5 *North elevation of the nave clerestory and outer chapels as rebuilt in the mid- (VI) and late (VII) 13th century. The key to the phased plan is as for the main phased plan. Below that is the north elevation of the arcade cut through the original nave north wall in the mid- (VI) and late (VII) 13th century. The west doorway (IV) was rebuilt in the late 12th century, and the porch was added in the early 13th century.*

St Richard's chaplain, spent more than £1,000 on the translation expenses.[36]

It is very likely, therefore, that St Richard himself started the process of breaching the north and south aisle walls of the nave so that he could add a series of chapels there. He no doubt commenced this on the north-east with a single-bay chapel to St Edmund, and work on this chapel must have started soon after Edmund's canonisation. This small chapel was probably complete by the time of St Richard's death, but the evidence of the fabric on the north side of the chapel shows that the plinth courses for the outer walls of two further chapels to the west were also constructed at this time.[37] The rest of these chapels were not constructed until some decades later, as suggested by the architectural detailing which is stylistically afterwards.[38] These two later chapels were probably those dedicated to St Theobald and St Anne. We know that Dean Walter of Gloucester (1254-75) built a chapel of St Anne, and endowed it for his own chantry. If this identification of the chapel is correct, it suggests that these chapels were being completed in the 1270s, around the time of St Richard's translation. This would make sense of both the documentary and the architectural evidence.

On the south side of the nave, the two two-bay chapels were apparently dedicated to St George and St Clement, but there is no 13th-century documentary evidence to help us here.[39] Stylistically, however, they are of a mid-13th-century date with much of the architectural detailing being similar to that used in the chapel of St Edmund. It seems likely, therefore, that these chapels were also constructed during St Richard's episcopate, and that he intended to build a continuous row of chapels on both sides of the nave in the French manner.

14 *The shrine area, showing the platform restored c.1905 and the contrast between the medieval flooring and the black and white chequered restoration. See also figs. 79a and b.*

Plan 6 *(facing page) Archaeological analysis of the west doorway area.*

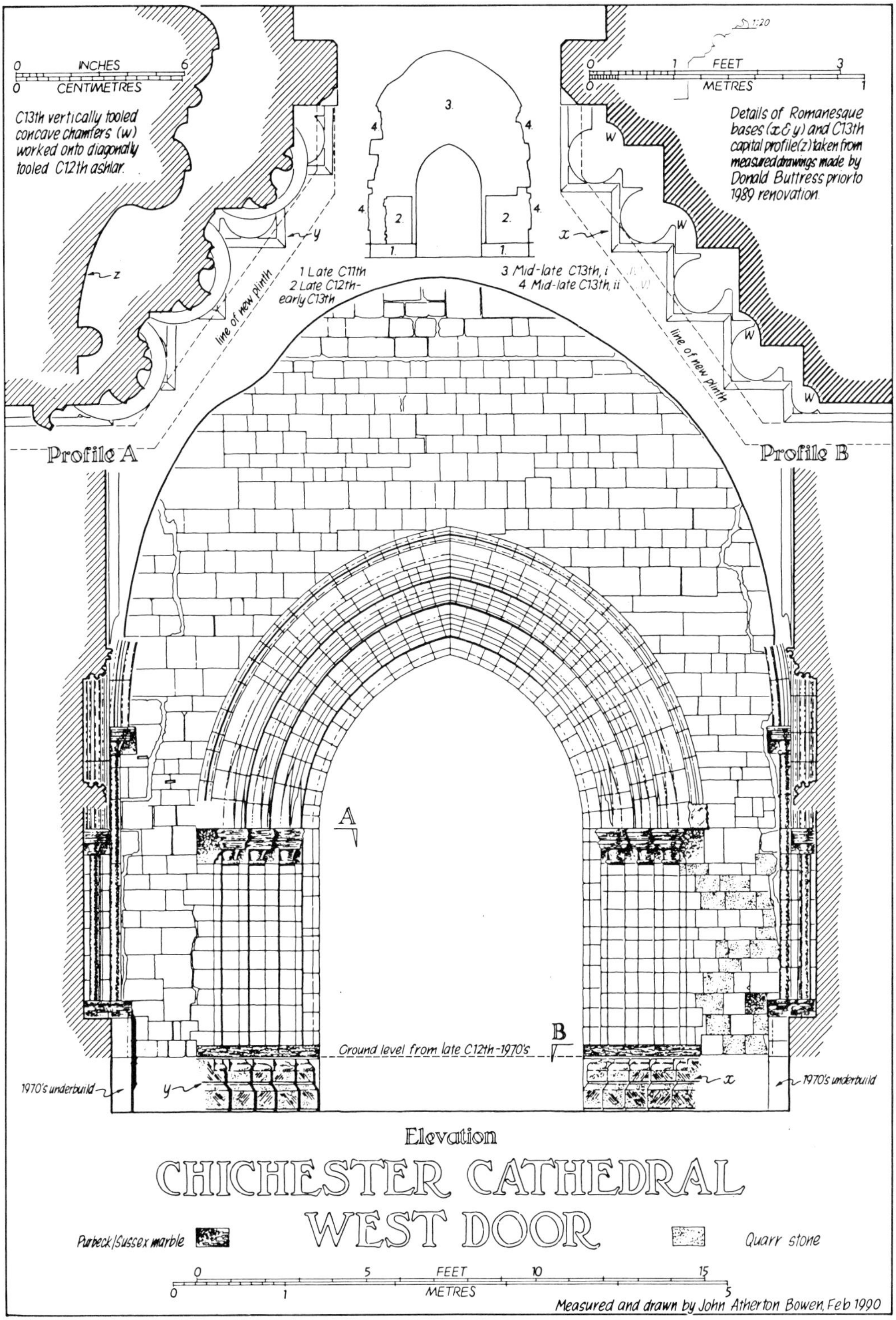
0 INCHES 6
0 CENTIMETRES
C13th vertically tooled concave chamfers (w) worked onto diagonally tooled C12th ashlar.
1 Late C11th
2 Late C12th-early C13th
3 Mid-late C13th, i
4 Mid-late C13th, ii
0 1 FEET 3
0 METRES 1
Details of Romanesque bases (x & y) and C13th capital profile (z) taken from measured drawings made by Donald Buttress prior to 1989 renovation.
line of new plinth
Profile A
Profile B
Ground level from late C12th-1970's
1970's underbuild
Elevation
CHICHESTER CATHEDRAL
WEST DOOR
Purbeck/Sussex marble
Quarr stone
0 5 FEET 10 15
0 1 METRES 5
Measured and drawn by John Atherton Bowen, Feb 1990

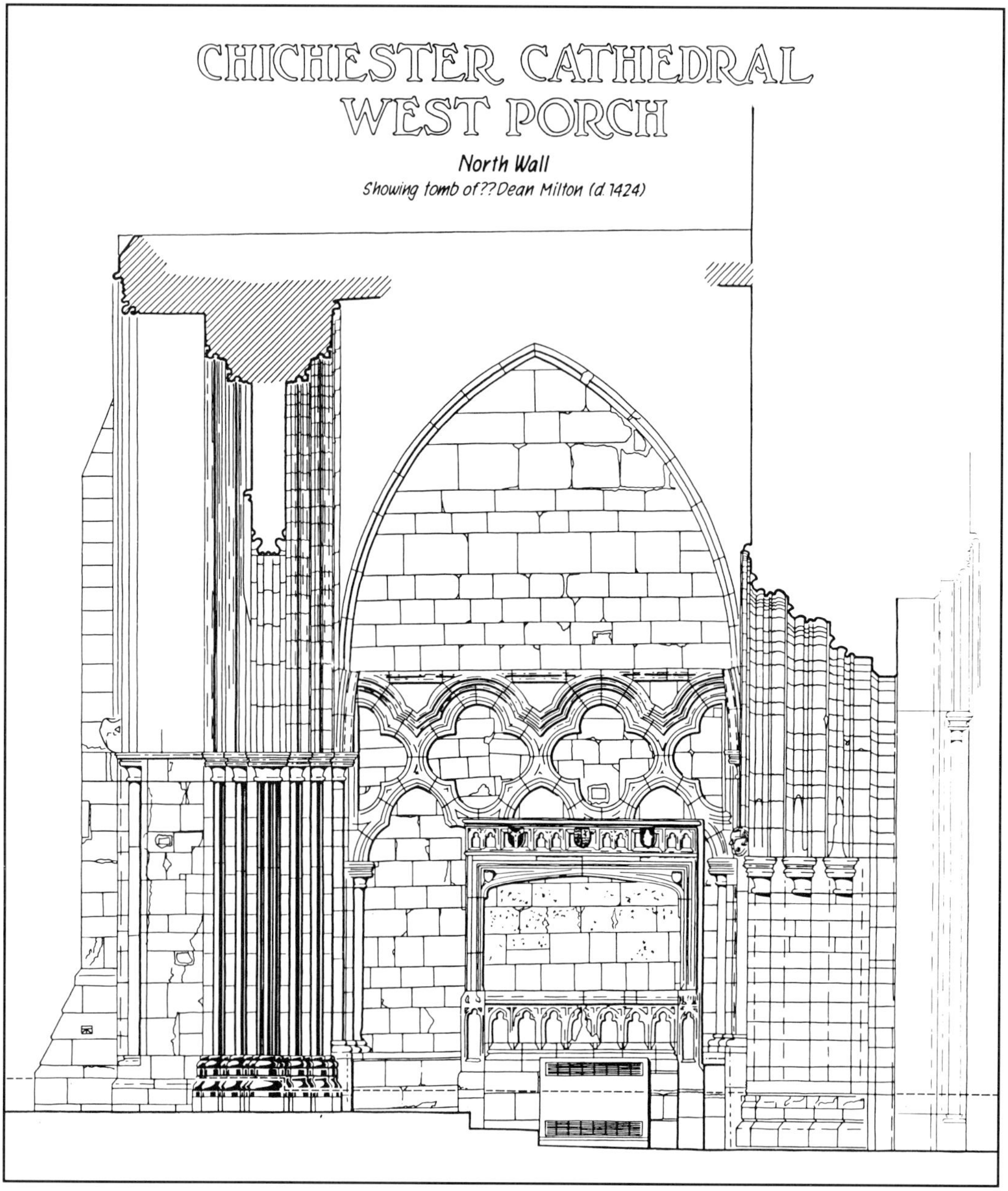

Plan 7 *Archaeological analysis of the north side of the west porch.*

The basic phasing of all these chapels was first worked out by Robert Willis in 1853, but he and later writers thought that they dated from earlier in the 13th century.[40] The situation has been confused by R.C. Carpenter who, in 1847, inserted new bogus plate-tracery into all the mid-13th-century windows.[41] Before this, as earlier engravings show, there was Perpendicular tracery (of a later date) in the windows of both the chapels of

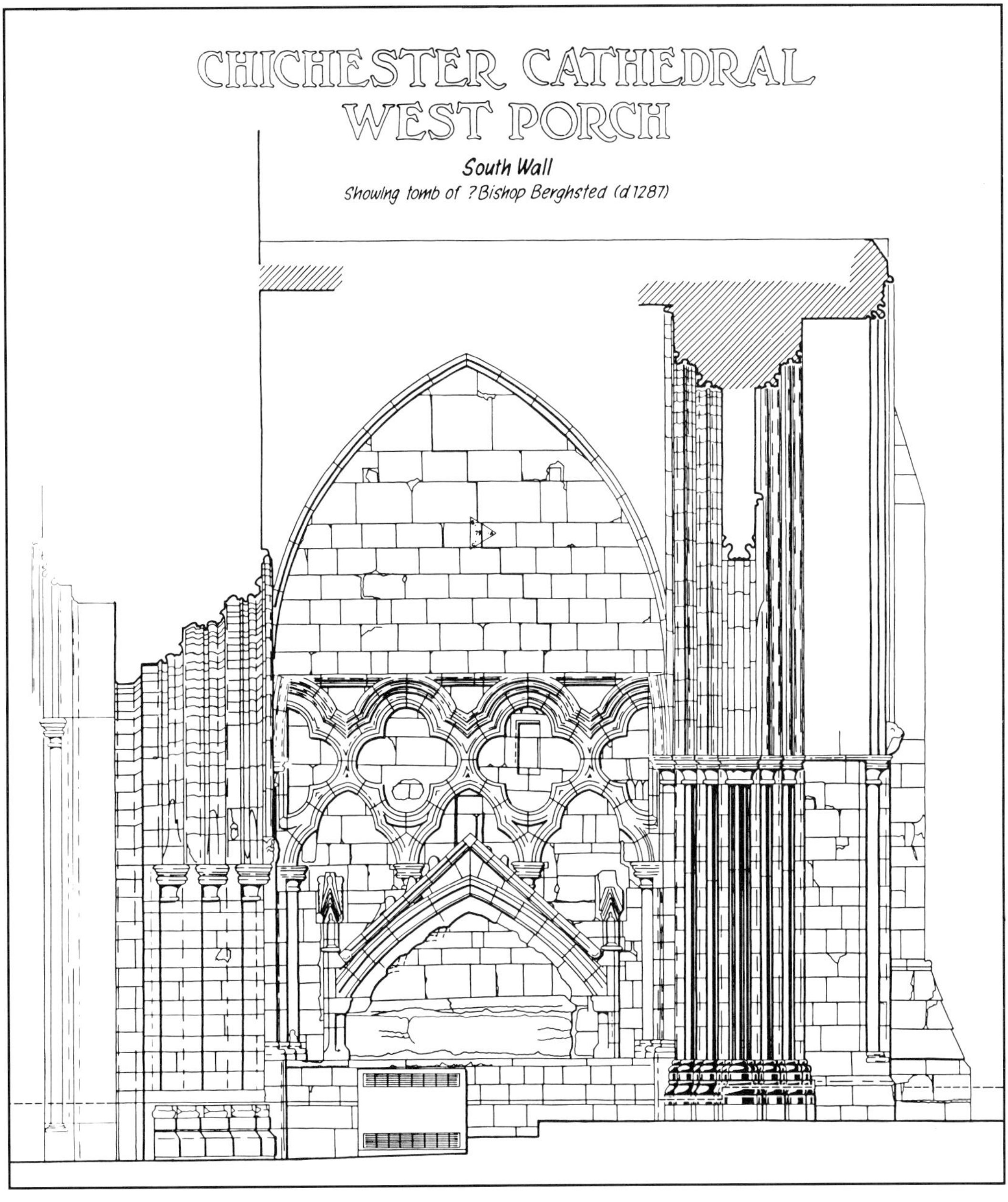

Plan 8 *Archaeological analysis of the south side of the west front.*

St Edmund and St George. Only in the chapel of St Clement did the original 13th-century windows survive until 1847. These consisted of pairs of lancets with apparently large quatrefoils above. All the chapel windows had gables above them, for transverse roofs, but the gable-tops were removed in the 15th century when a continuous parapet was provided. Traces of small round windows in these gables, containing cinquefoils or hexafoils, still survive,[42] as do the small gutters that ran along the outer edge of the gables before turning at right-angles to run along the sides of the buttresses. All the windows in the later north chapels were three-light affairs with triple open circles above. When Carpenter renewed all the tracery in Bath stone in 1847, he added cinquefoil and quatrefoil cusping to these open circles.

R.C. Carpenter also rebuilt the great west window at the same time, adding 'decorated' tracery of his own invention.[43] Below this window is a row of late 13th-century lancets, and below this again is the west doorway, with outside it the western porch which was an even later 13th-century addition.

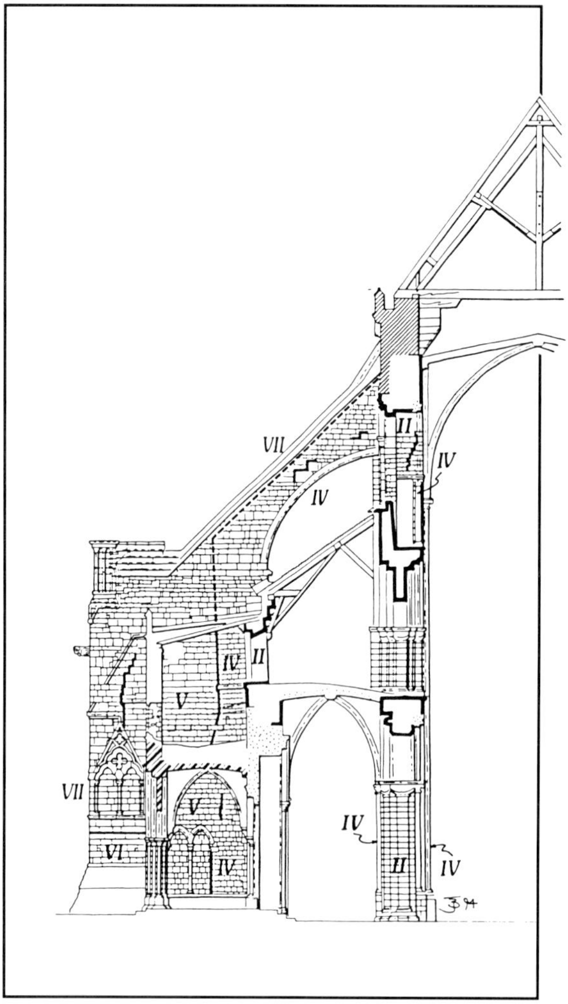

Plan 9 *Phased section through the north porch and north side of the nave, showing: II—late 11th-century north aisle and clerestory masonry; IV—vaults (with added flying buttresses) as rebuilt after 1187 fire; V—early 13th-century north chapels; VII—late 13th-century north chapels with enlarged flying buttress and pinnacle, and heightened clerestory and new nave roof.*

A careful study of the masonry around the west doorway was carried out in 1989 when it was being restored.[44] Apart from the early Norman bases at the bottom, then uncovered,[45] there are three main phases of masonry around the west doorway. The main jambs to the doorway date from just after the fire of 1187, and these were partly recut and given concave chamfers in the late 13th century, when the doorway was remodelled as part of an extensive refacing of the west front. At this time, not only were new Purbeck marble shafts and capitals, and a two-centred arch, put in, but also the three lancets above, and the great west window above that. This complete refacing of the nave west wall, which also involved the raising of the extreme west end of the nave vault, was probably a prelude to the raising of all the high roofs in the Cathedral (see below). The final stage in this work, which was clearly an after-thought, as the masonry shows, was the addition of a west porch with fine internal blind-arcading. The buttressing, and apparently unfinished top to the porch, suggests that an upper chamber may have been intended. All this work in the late 13th century may relate to increased revenue after the translation of St Richard in 1276.

The nave and its aisles still contain some areas of medieval flooring (probably put in after the late 12th-century rebuilding work). This consists of small squares of Purbeck and Sussex marble, with panels set diagonally to give a lozenge effect. There were similar areas of paving in the eastern arm, but these have all been removed by late 19th- and 20th-century repaving schemes.

After the Translation

Throughout the late 11th- and 12th-century building and rebuilding campaigns, there had been many problems caused by the differential settlement of the masonry, as we have seen. By the late 13th century, however, buttressing systems and also timber roof construction had reached a new technological peak, and the decision was taken to rebuild all the high roofs of the Cathedral. Before the new roof-trusses were put in place, however, it was decided to raise all the clerestory walls by about six feet (two metres), as the old Romanesque wall top was very irregular both horizontally and vertically. To achieve a straight and level new upper wall to the nave, much corbelling-out was needed (and stepping in, on the south side). This added weight to the upper wall was also used to give more stability to the vaults themselves. The Romanesque nave wall tops had always been the most unstable, so the flying buttresses here were also thickened up and given a fine new capping[46] along which ran a steep gutter to take the rain water from the parapet gutters of the new high roofs. The flying buttress gutters ended in pipes which ran straight through the outer aisle buttresses[47] to a series of large gargoyles.[48]

15 *Gargoyle.*

When this work had been completed, and a new west gable to the nave had been built (it contains much re-used 12th-century material), the new roof trusses were put in, starting at the west end, and moving eastwards.[49] These magnificent trusses, which still survive in good condition, have been carefully studied, and samples have been taken from them for dendrochronology. The results from these suggest that the re-roofing took place between the 1280s and *c.*1315.[50] This is mostly during the time of Bishop Gilbert of St Leofard, who also rebuilt the Lady Chapel *a fundamentis*, and in his will left 1,250 marks (£416 13s. 4d.) to the fabric. Earlier, he had also directed sums to the fabric fund in his statutes of 1289.[51]

One of the timbers, in the truss behind the heightened east gable (the latter containing a fine rose window), had all its sapwood present. This allowed its felling date to be calculated precisely to 1303. It seems probable, therefore, that this gable was the culmination of all the work after Bishop Gilbert had completely rebuilt the Lady Chapel, and reroofed and heightened first the nave and then the presbytery. His work in the Lady Chapel was first to add two completely new bays to the east, which made this comparatively small Cathedral over 400 feet long. He then put in new Decorated windows, and vaulted the eastern three bays with fine tierceron vaults.[52]

Bishop Gilbert's successor was John Langton, and he is recorded as having spent £341 on 'a certain wall and window built from the ground to the top in the chapter house on

16 *Medieval roof timbers above the north quire aisle.*

17 *Bishop Langton's fine south transept window.*

the south side'. He also left in his will £100 to the fabric.[53] There can be little doubt that this refers to the splendid large seven-light window, with a spherical triangle and curvilinear reticulated tracery above, of the south transept. While this window was being built, new buttresses were added on the south-east side of the transept, and a new gable was built above.[54] Incorporated into the south-east corner of the transept was the Bishop's own tomb, and it seems likely that the transept itself was used as the Chapter House for meetings of the Greater Chapter. Its ceremonial use was accentuated in the early 16th century, when Bishop Sherburne's fine painted panels were added to both the east and west walls.[55] After the rebuilding of the spire, these panels and the wooden benches below were unfortunately not returned to their original positions in the transept.

Bishop Langton was also responsible for giving the quire, under the crossing, its magnificent set of wooden stalls.[56] These were luckily taken down before the collapse of the spire, and in their present form, though re-using much of the 14th-century work, they date from Scott's restoration of 1867. Another architectural feature that was taken down before the fall of the spire is the so-called 'sacellum' at the north end of the south transept. This

Plan 10 *South elevation of south transept tower and spire in the mid-19th century (partly after J. Butler), showing: I—original late 11th-century masonry; IV—added late 12th-century S.E. buttresses; VI—mid-13th-century tower masonry; VIII—rebuilt south transept (including great south window) of early 14th century; also original roofline.*

structure, which abuts the south side of the choir stalls, was not rebuilt until 1904-9, and it has been plausibly suggested that it was the original screen on the west side of the quire until replaced by Bishop Arundel's screen in the late 15th century.[57] Next to the 'sacellum' on its east side is a fine wooden armoire, which apparently has a donation box at its base.[58]

18 *J. Buckler's drawing of the south transept in 1812 showing the sacellum at the north end, with Bishop Stratford's tomb, at that time believed to be St Richard's.*

The Black Death must have caused a pause in any work, but in the later 14th century the final stages of the rebuilding of the Cathedral were carried out. There are no direct documentary references to this work, which is in an early Perpendicular style, but Bishop William Reede was able to get a papal indulgence in 1371 for those who came to the Cathedral and gave alms to it, as it was 'in need of costly repair'.[59]

It is clear that by this time the outer wall of the north transept had become very unstable and was leaning out at an alarming angle. Massive new buttresses were built, including a large new flying buttress on the west, and a completely new five-light north window was put into the north wall of the transept with a new gable above it. On the east and west sides of the transept, the upper clerestory wall also had to be rebuilt, and most of this late 14th-century work was done with large blocks of Upper Greensand that almost certainly came by sea from the Ventnor area on the south side of the Isle of Wight. Similar blocks were used for the detached bell tower at a slightly later date.[60]

Along with the reconstruction of the north transept, a new (perhaps two-storied) vestry area was created on its west side (now demolished), which also connected directly by a small doorway (now blocked) with the chapel of St Edmund. New Perpendicular tracery was put into the north window of this chapel, as well as into the north window of the large chapel east of the north transept.[61] This was perhaps done in the early 15th century because the parochial altar of St Peter the Great (also called the subdeanery church) was to be moved from the nave to the north transept.[62]

The culmination of all the building work at the Cathedral was the construction of a magnificent stone spire. This too is in an early Perpendicular style, and was clearly modelled on the huge stone spire of Salisbury Cathedral which was completed in the early 14th century. It has tall lucarnes and inner pinnacles and two bands of decoration on the spire itself, all inspired by the Salisbury spire.[63] This fine structure, which was of course destroyed in 1861, is now a 277-feet-high replica of the original. Scott, however, raised the whole of the tower and spire by about six feet so that he could 'lift it clear' of the roofs that had

19 *Seal of Bishop John Arundel.*

been raised since the building of the original tower in the mid-13th century.[64]

With the completion of the spire and the reconstruction of the north transept, the rebuilding of the Cathedral was complete, and during the 15th and early 16th centuries only minor works were carried out. The most important of these were the late 15th-century pulpitum screen, apparently put in by Bishop John Arundel. His tomb was nearby on the south side of the nave, and he had a chantry at the altar of St Mary (of Stock), which was 'beside the choir door' under the south side of the screen.[65]

Other works of the 15th century, all undocumented, were the making of a continuous parapet over the north and south nave chapels, the insertion of small crenellated screen walls in the lower triforium openings, and the building of the cloister walks.[66] The upper chamber, above the Sacristry on the west side of the south transept, was heightened and given large new windows and a shallow-pitched roof. It then became an upper chapter house, with a glazed-tile floor and seats around the wall for the canons, and a bishop's or dean's high-backed seat on the west. This was heavily restored in 1910, but it still contains much 15th-century work.[67]

A final pre-Reformation beautification of the Cathedral took place under Bishop Robert Sherburne (1508-36), when he employed the painter Lambert Barnard to decorate all the vaults of the Cathedral with 'a rich and delicate pattern of flowers, fruit and acanthus foliage sprouts from a ring surrounding the central boss'.[68] Unfortunately this only survives in the Lady Chapel and in a few fragments in the aisles. Barnard also made the fine painted panelling for the south transept, and produced decorated inscriptions with the names of all the prebends above the choir stalls. This final decoration was a fitting early Renaissance culmination for this small, but exceptionally fine, English cathedral.

IV

Cathedral and Reformation

John Fines

This study, relying as it does so heavily on the Dean and Chapter Act books (from which all references come unless otherwise stated) produces a picture that is largely about office-holders and how they were funded. What they did, and how they thought is hard to seek, but the evidence we have of how the Chapter managed its estates in an age of acute inflation and urban decay is remarkable. Their care in keeping up what they had was finally defeated by a grasping monarchy, but their relationship with the thriving little town in which they played so large a rôle continued to be that of a good landlord and employer. Citizens may have envied the Chapter and regretted rent-day, but without the Cathedral theirs would have been a hard case.

Personnel 1500-1540

During the period 1500-40 there were 140 men who held office in the Chapter of Chichester Cathedral. They were a distinguished group—we find 102 with recorded degrees—23 at simple bachelor or master's level, six more Bachelors in Civil Law, 12 in Canon Law and seven Bachelors in both Laws. Two Bachelors in Medicine, and one Doctor in a diocese where Sherburne, himself a Doctor of Medicine, was Bishop need not surprise us. Of the 44 doctors four were in civil law, eight in canon law, five in both, with 18 in theology and one in theology and canon law. Four of the group were notaries public.

A significant number, 16, had attended foreign universities—four with doctorates in theology (two from Turin, one from Spain), a doctorate in both laws from Padua, a doctorate in canon law from Bologna and one in civil law from Orléans. Four of our number had studied at Louvain.

Their background was diverse, with a significant number (19) from Winchester and New College, five from Magdalen College, Oxford. Of those from Cambridge we might note three from Queens' College.

At least seven of our subjects were using their benefices for supporting their academic careers. One example, Dr. John Crayford, who had begun his career at Queens', Cambridge, gone on to University College, Oxford, then back to Cambridge before being recruited by Wolsey for Cardinal College. He was later Master of Clare and then Master of University College, Oxford. A distinguished scholar whose views were called upon in the 1540s by the government when he was made a royal chaplain, one cannot imagine that he had much time to give to Chichester in return for his prebend of Eartham.

If the Treasurer, John Colet, ever came to Chichester, which is in grave doubt, he would have been the most distinguished scholar of his generation there. Dean John Young was a friend of Erasmus. Edward Higgins, prebendary of Eartham, was something of a polymath, writing on Geography and possessing a volume of musical settings for the Mass. John Doggett, the Treasurer until 1501, wrote on Plato's *Phaedo*, whilst Edward More, Archdeacon of Lewes, was credited with the skills of an agent, for William Horman bequeathed him a *Chronica Antonini* in three volumes on condition he published Horman's revised *Vulgaria*. Alas, no such new edition is recorded as extant! Thomas Pannell was the most prolific publisher, issuing 20 extant translations, with his contemporary, John Bale (the first great English bibliographer) listing 12 more. Many of these were translations of Erasmus. Pannell left 100 books to St John's College, Oxford, whilst John Fox left eight to Corpus Christi College, Oxford.

20 *Bishop Storey's seal.*

Bishop Storey's refoundation of the Prebendal School forced the Chapter to search out academics. John Holt, who was prebendary of Highleigh from 1501, was born in Chichester, son of William Holt alias Smith. At Magdalen he had naturally become Usher and then went on to Lambeth to become Master to Archbishop Morton's boys. There he wrote the famous introduction to Latin grammar, *Lac Puerorum*, which was prefaced and concluded by verses contributed by Thomas More. More wrote to him when he moved to Chichester, saying he was glad he was in a healthier place than his previous situation, and that the Bishop was so fond of him. He reported to Holt on his own studies, notably Greek, on the lectures of Grocin at St Paul's, to which illiterates flocked to seem smart and pseudo-intellectuals kept away from so as not to admit their ignorance. He gave the news of the arrival of Catherine of Aragon with her weird train, but hopes that the marriage will prove a happy omen for England. The next year Holt was made tutor to Prince Henry himself—neither master nor student could read the future.

After Holt there was a great let-down with William Hoone, who had to be suspended for a three-month absence from his duties in school in 1504. Then came Dr. Nicholas Bradbridge, who had been head of Eton and, after his spell at Chichester, went off to Turin to take his doctorate in theology. He was later mentioned as a learned man who might be consulted about the royal divorce. In 1521 John Goldiff, who also had been head of Eton, was appointed, although he had some years away from schoolmastering as subdean of Chichester. William Frende followed, but retired to a fully clerical career as prebendary of Exceit in 1532. John Tychenor, who took over from him, came from being headmaster of Winchester for six years.

Some of the canons were busy officials who shared their expertise widely, *hommes d'affaires* like Dr. Thomas Wodyngton, who was Treasurer in 1519-20. He was JP for Gloucestershire 1496-9, and in 1500 he had acted as vicar-general of the Bishop of Worcester. In the years 1504-6 he had acted as official of Rochester, Exeter, Ely and Chichester dioceses, *sede vacante*. In 1513 he was Dean of the Arches and he was official of the Court of Canterbury 1520-2.

Such busy fellows there were, but I only find three such in the Administrative Chapter. A bigger group were those who were rising fast, the future bishops—six of them. Robert Sherburne went from being prebendary of Henfield to the see of St David's in 1505, whence he was transferred back to Chichester in 1508. He was replaced by Edward Vaughan, who was not only returning to the diocese of his birth, but moved from the position of Archdeacon of Lewes. John Kyte, a popular courtier, had been made prebendary of Wightring by royal grant in 1507. In 1513 he was made Archbishop of Armagh, but misliking Ireland returned to court in 1516. In 1521 he was translated to Carlisle and, to preserve his archiepiscopal status, given the title of Archbishop of Thebes (in return for 1790 ducats for an impoverished Pope). William Atwater, a noted careerist, was Archdeacon of Lewes 1510-12, when he became Bishop of Lincoln. Nicholas West, who was Treasurer at Chichester in 1507, became Bishop of Ely in 1515. He was very rich and had 100 servants and fed 200 poor folk at his door daily. Perhaps he grew to forget his reputation at Cambridge, where he was credited with setting the Provost's Lodge at King's on fire and stealing silver spoons (no worse than Thomas Wenne, prebendary of Mardon in 1531, who had been sent down ten years before as a result of a town and gown riot). Finally James Turberville, who was prebendary of Wightring 1538-53, became Bishop of Exeter in 1555. There were two suffragans in the diocese in office in this period—William Howe, Bishop of Avara in Phoenicia, who acted for the Bishop of Chichester in 1532 and 1536, and John Young, Dean and Bishop of Callipoli.

The canons and officers of the Cathedral mainly came from the south and south west, but two came from Durham diocese and two from St David's, a distant connection already noted. Surprisingly few (five) came by royal grant although many had royal connections. Two had interesting connections with the Lady Margaret, mother of Henry VII: Thomas Burwell, Chancellor, had been her secretary in 1489 and Gabriel Sylvester, prebendary of Colworth, was also dean of her chapel in 1511. Eight were royal chaplains and one had been chaplain and tutor to Prince Arthur (John Reed, prebendary of Hova Villa and later of Bracklesham) and, as already noted, John Holt was tutor to Prince Henry.

Relatively few earned their benefices by heavy diplomatic activity—notably Nicholas West, John Young and Thomas Pannell. Both William Howe and John Kyte served Lord Berners in diplomatic ventures on occasion and Oliver Pole, Archdeacon of Lewes, was chancellor to Charles Brandon. Edward Finch, prebendary of Woodhorn, was physician to Cardinal Wolsey, whilst Thomas Barrett, prebendary of Bury, and Roger Dyngle, prebendary of Wightring, were associates of Thomas Cromwell.

A few were the recipients of episcopal patronage. John Doggett, Treasurer, was a nephew of Cardinal Bourchier, while Thomas Wardall, prebendary of Colworth, was a nephew of Bishop Storey, who left him a concordance, the *Works* of Jerome in three volumes and a commentary on the *Sentences*, book iv. Storey also seems to have patronised the Burrell family, of whom more later. Nicholas West was strongly promoted by Bishop Foxe of Durham, and no doubt Gabriel Sylvester, prebendary of Colworth, also benefited from being Dean of Chapel to Archbishop Warham.

Yet it would be a great mistake to view this body of men as venal, rushing around accumulating offices merely to serve their own ends. When one looks at their careers, it is clear that a substantial group served out their time in the diocese, doing no doubt good service. I count at least seventeen, of whom John Worthiall, Bachelor of Canon Law, may stand as a good example. Originally from Exeter diocese, he began in Chichester diocese in 1518 as rector of East Wittering, becoming priest of Ferring Chantry the following year. He held benefices in Icklesham, West Wittering, North Mundham, Sutton, Warnham, Northiam, Ardingly and Burwash and was by turn prebendary of Firle, Selsey, Colworth, Selsey again, then Gates, which he exchanged for Hova Villa. He was Chancellor from 1525 to 1532, and Archdeacon of Chichester from 1532 to 1555. He had been commissary general to Sherburne, was official principal 1543 to 1551 and was vicar general *sede vacante* 1563.

In a church ruled by clerical celibacy one tends to forget the rôle of family. The Stephen Darrell who was prebendary of Heathfield from 1536-41 may well have been the elder brother of Richard Darrell who took over the position until his deprivation in 1554. A similar situation may be suspected with the prebend of Ferring held by one family, the Blythes, 1501-58. The three Burrells, Gerard, Thomas and Ninian, Archdeacon, Chancellor and prebendary of Hampstead, seem to have been related, two of them, Gerard and Ninian, being remembered in Bishop Storey's will. John Cloos, Dean of Chichester, appears to have had a deep respect for his relative of the same name who had been prebendary of Bracklesham, in that he requested to be buried by him in the entry to the Chapter House, five years later.

Finance 1500-1540

The White Act Book,[1] the first attempt at a concentrated record of Dean and Chapter activities, seems at first a most confusing document. There are, early on, signs of great activity in recording finances, but there seems to be no regular and settled chronological process instituted until the late 1520s, and even then a good deal of carelessness seems to prevail. Yet the superficial confusion covers a more orderly situation than one might expect. Bishop Barlow annotated it carefully (strangely enough restoring the word 'pope', which had been stricken out throughout following the injunction of 1538) and obviously saw it as a useful financial record. The community, of usually four residentiaries, 18 vicars choral, eight choristers and a floating number of chantry priests, needed to manage itself with some care. In 1522 they set up a muniment room over the south door of the Cathedral, facing the dean's residence (Peckham, *Acts* (1) 55) and in 1544 we have the first note of appointment of a registrar, acting in the same capacity to the bishop and the dean and chapter (312). Sherburne noted a set of regulations for the auditor of his Liberties in 1529, but the chapter had had its own auditor as early as 1501 (103 and 399). In 1439 the Chapter made Ellis Bradshaw receiver and surveyor of the lands and tenements of the Cathedral and in 1539 they made Thomas Bishop life-holder of the stewardship of the demesnes of the Dignity, with a fee of 40s. a year (205, 246). In 1542 they noted another life grant, of the stewardship of Coleworth prebend (307).

They were not short of officers to manage their affairs, but what of their income? The clear values of the Cathedral Chapter as recorded in the *Valor Ecclesiasticus*, a survey of the worth of livings conducted by Thomas Cromwell in 1536, were £554 19s. 9d., ranging from the Treasurer's income of £62 6s. 8d. down to Firle prebend worth only 10s. Only the Dean and the Treasurer topped £50, with three prebendaries in the £30s, three in the £20s, 16 in the £10s, the remainder below £10 p.a., with two, Seaford and Firle, below £1 p.a.[2] Of course there was other income from benefices—Worthiall got as much as £120 per annum and Dean Fleshmonger £210.[3] The biggest source of income for most was from residence—but to enter residence there was a fee of £33 13s. 4d. which must have been hard to find. Dividends for residents varied but after 1555 it averaged £40 each.[4] The residentiary had to give an admission banquet to the other residentiaries and all comers. During the first year he had to entertain his vicar, two other vicars choral, the porter, two sacrists and a chorister every day. If he missed one service he had to undertake this entertainment for a second year. In return, the residentiary had a dole of bread and a weekly payment of 12d. on Saturday after Chapter, with payments for services and a share in the income and other doles.[5]

Money came from a diversity of sources, and the Treasurer seems to have accounted simply enough—paying out expenses, putting some in the building fund, some in the Elsted box (386), an unexplained entity that sounds as though it was for a rainy day, and dividing the rest between the residentiaries. In 1505/6, for example, there was money from first fruits, from legacies, from the schoolmaster's indemnity and from the use of the common seal (6s. 8d. a time) which totalled £14 2s. 0d., so that each residentiary got £3 10s. 6d.

There were incidentals like pensions—East Wittering paid 40s. to the Dean and Chapter each year (317) whilst Amport church in Winchester diocese paid £10 (43). Eartham, a poor enough church at the start, had to pay the Dean 20s. a year (45 and 450).

St Richard's pence gave a regular, if declining income; in 1501 it was near enough £5 whilst in 1506 it was down to 33s. (380 and 33).[6]

Bishop Sampson sold wood eagerly from his properties (219, 261, 299) but the Chapter was much more conservative, forbidding its tenants to fell trees without permission, and providing wood to them (mainly from Wilmington) for any necessary major repairs. In 1534 they sold 30 acres of Wilmington Great Wood but there is no further record of such sales (181). They were indeed much more interested in acquiring land. In 1523 they took in the Nonington land of West Wittering to provide for a dole of wine (55) and in 1529 they had recently purchased lands in Hunston and Merston (332/3). In 1520 a clerk, Richard Bramley, gave the Chapter four closes (319 and 379). There were numerous bequests, from the 6s. 8d. from Simon Wood of the Pallant, through £8 from Bishop Storey for lead (most of which was spent on quite other expenses, one should mention) to the £20 legacy from John Doggett for the fabric (£16 14s. 2d. being spent immediately on the fabric), all in 1503 (403, 404, 29). The following year Dean Cloos's estate rendered 110s. (405). In 1505, 40s. came from the legacy of Edward Bartlet and, in 1506, 6s. 8d. came from the legacy of Sir John Kendal (32, 33). 1535 was a famous year—they had a bequest of lands in Rudgwick, West Thorney, Selsey, Hunston, the Pallant, Amberley and elsewhere and a mitre and jewels value £193 13s. 6d. and ornaments value £132 14s. 9d. given to them by Bishop Sherburne (192).

The rental of 1533-4, prepared by William Samford (and transcribed by W.E. Thumwood),[7] provides the most detailed survey of Dean and Chapter properties we have. There were in Chichester some 88 tenements, with 36 separately let gardens. There were an additional 26 tenements with their own gardens attached. Only two houses are noted as ruinous. There are only three barns and two cellars noticed, with one storehouse.

21 *Bishop Sherburne (detail from his tomb).*

Clearly the town was quite thickly occupied and several people, from the Chancellor downwards, were willing to pay substantial sums for outlets to the street.

We learn where people lived, including Hans Jugell of 'Moy', the barber, 'Lambert Barnard the painter' and Richard Cobbler of Bosham who is recorded as 'gittons'—maybe a guitar player! We learn also that the 'fire rack' stood just south of the lane leading off North Street to St Cyriac's. There is little reference to the length of agreements—more and better details are to be found in the Act Books.

The whole rental comes to £40 16s. 3½d. This record, thoroughly detailed as it may seem, is in fact considerably less than a comparable (though much less detailed) rental of the city made on 25 March 1558 and recording 138 rents (whilst Samford has 150) yielding £53 17s. 1½d. (which includes 14 unpaid rents totalling £1 19s. 11d.).[8] It is possible that Samford was rather more generous than his successors, as we shall see, but the discrepancy is large and may perhaps be explained by subtle rent rises that do not seem to figure in other documentation.

Samford also records receipts from properties outside Chichester. These yield £262 14s. 6d. (giving a grand total of £303 11s. 0d.). We might note the three really big estates—East Dean, yielding £20 a year, West Dean £32 6s. 8d. and Wilmington £41 5s. 0d. Wilmington estate spread widely over East Sussex, and included five woodlands and rich properties—one tilehouse made 2,000 tiles a year, for example.

Where did all this money go? We are lucky to have Samford's Communar's Accounts for 1533-38,[9] and a later set for 1544.[10] The Communar seems to have been responsible for repairing Chichester (and Stoughton and Wyke) tenements, for Cathedral repairs, for obits and the expenses of the choristers and for services.

Samford receives in 1533-4 £84 2s. 11d. and spends £76 4s. 4d. By 1544 the job was much larger—the Communar received £422 3s. 2d. and spent £293 15s. 8d. Again we have a huge difference, which is hard to explain in so short a period.

The choristers had to eat, and this cost £17 6s. 8d. a year—a substantial outlay, for their accommodation and clothing is additional to this sum. Albs needed washing by Alice Lee and repairing ('like a net'—darning? more often 'edging') at Whitsuntide, Easter and Christmas. The cost of keeping up the vestments was high: in 1544 they spent 2s. 5d. on ribbons of green, tawny, black and white caddis; 2s. 10d. on new altar cloths and diapers and Thomas the embroiderer was employed for three weeks after Christmas on repairs that totalled 10s. There were also costs on books—the repair of an antiphoner cost 1s., and 12 little processionals were bought for the choir, at 3d. each.

The choir was well cared for—Thomas Moreys (not, be it noted, the foreign barber Hans) got 8d. each for shaving and polling the choristers. In 1544 the choir got 4d. worth of wine for a *Te Deum* for the victory over the Scots (the Chapter's 10 infantrymen had cost them £17 0s. 1d., so no doubt they were glad the war was over). Later that year Blewett left the choir to be taken by the Subdean to the election at Eton. We do not know whether he got a place (he does not figure in Sterry's Eton registers) but this seems a good example of the Chapter's care for the boys. They were less well pleased with the men—Sir Robert Smith is fined ever larger sums for his absence from choir, and Arthur Rode is fined 1d. for ringing early for 6 o'clock Mattins after a previous warning (this last in 1550).

Apart from the choir there were other costly entertainments: 6s. 8d. to the King's minstrels in 1534 and 1537; at Christmas came the Earl of Arundel's players 'as usual' and got 20d.; in 1544 in July another 20d. went to the players of the Prince Edward.

The organs (one in the choir and one in the Lady Chapel) and the bells needed constant and expensive attention. 'Choice skins' had to be bought for repairing the organs in 1534 and also a pillar on the east side of the south aisle of the Lady Chapel had to be hewed down, in order to set the organ there closer to the wall. In 1536 they rehung a bell and replaced a cable of the chime. In 1538 they rehung the whole set of bells and repaired the organs yet again. Perhaps that was something to do with the organist, William Campion, whose playing is described as 'pulsatione'—a perfectly correct medieval Latin term, but in classical Latin meaning 'beating'. 1544 brought more repairs to the organ and a new bell rope as well as further work on the bells themselves.

The services had to be prepared for—there were 50 anniversaries and seven special feasts which cost usually around £20 0s. 0d. in wine alone. It is difficult to come to a figure for wax, but they seemed to have kept about 80lb in hand, which at 6d. a lb was a substantial cost. And then there was the staff to pay and the dividends, which in 1544 came to about £20 a quarter for the Dean, £3 6s. 8d. for the Treasurer and £3 10s. 0d. for the Archdeacon.

There were legal costs, which could be large, especially in visits to London in search of great men. In 1544 they totalled £6 18s. 6d. One trip involved an attempt to get Sir Thomas Wriothesley on their side, and 4d. was given to the porter of his London house, 1s. to another of his servants, and the Cathedral servants ate up a further 1s. hanging about ('expectando et observando') for the chance of a word with the great man. The Chapter tried its best to keep in with the mighty, but, far from London, they were often behind the times. On 16 August 1550, the Chapter sent the Duke of Somerset ten fat sheep, presumably in response to his work for restoring order in the county noted by the King, 26 July.[11] If they could have looked a year ahead to his coming imprisonment in the Tower, they would have saved their flock.

The fabric was, as ever, one of the biggest charges to be met. The operation was huge—in 1534, for example, Samford had to oversee the purchase of 28,600 blue slates—the pilot had to be paid to see the ship into the harbour at Dell Quay, Helyer had to be paid to check that the right number of slates was brought ashore, Sandon and Garden had to be paid to carry them and Capper to store them—the whole operation costing £6 17s. 10d.

The cloisters constantly needed attention, and there was a lot of work for Arthur Rode, clearing snow from the roofs after a heavy fall in 1534, and for 25 days' glazing after high winds which did damage to the 'liberary windows'. The steeple was repointed in 1536 and work was done on Canon Gate and the choristers' chamber. Keys were constantly lost—in 1536 they even opened a tomb in the Lady Chapel to look for the Church door key. The same year they were repointing the arch over St Richard's shrine, unaware of what would overtake their efforts all too soon.

In 1544, Lambert the painter was paid 3s. for renewing the reredos canvas of the crucifixion. The same year John Somer and his mate came over from Portsmouth to examine the condition of the tower and steeple, at a cost of 3s. 4d. There was another great wind that blew out a lot of glass.

Only two pieces of repair work mark great events. In 1544 a mason was paid 15d. for mending a tomb in the Lady Chapel that was broken 'when the commissioners were here from the Council searching for treasure'. The reference is to the destruction of St Richard's shrine, for sure, but I wonder whether the damage was in fact caused by the men hunting for the lost key mentioned above. In June 1550 there is mention of the sale of five altars and two coffers and a long chest.

Perhaps the most revealing feature of these accounts, however, is the very detailed statements of repairs to Dean and Chapter properties, mainly in Chichester. It will be recalled from the rental that only two of these were considered ruinous, so we are not in the middle of some special repair campaign, yet in 1534, 26 properties were repaired, at a cost of £14 3s. 11d. (their rents totalling £10 16s. 3d.) and in the following year they repaired 14 houses.

John Knott's house was re-roofed in 1534 with a loft being added with new dormer windows. An additional loft was put over the passage between this and the next house. 'Loft conversions' were common and suggest a shortage of space in Chichester in this period. The work cost 25s. (more work was done in 1538 at a cost of 29s. 1d. and even more in 1544 costing 6s. 8d.).

A chimney and a brick privy were installed at Thomas Godley's house, again common features of work done at the time. The chimney was furnished with an iron fireback. There were new hinges, locks and keys, as in many other houses.

Sills were commonly replaced and penthouses installed—some in the nature of 'storm porches'. Cellars were cleared out—obviously storage space was short. Several houses had hoists installed to get goods up to the new-built lofts. Others had to have subsidence dealt with. There was a lot of roofing (mainly tiles, rarely thatched) and a good deal of painting and re-daubing of walls.

New shutters for shops were commonly required, and various craftsmen required special circumstances—the mind boggles at the needs of one who was a feather-bed drier! Many tenants were prepared to do their own repairs and claim rent rebates, sometimes being supplied with materials from the Cathedral stores.

The work was not stinted—at John Matthews' house they installed a 'great' window which entailed half a day's work and cost 1s. 5d., including charges for hinges and catches. Ovens were installed in several houses, one had weather-boarding put over a gable end and another had a post and rail fence set up to demarcate the boundary with next door.

Without doubt the Cathedral had a good care of its investment in property, and there are good indications that they took equal care of distant properties, which they would travel to inspect, at the cost of the tenant, of course.

The Cathedral was not always such a good landlord, as may be seen in its own accounts, and its servants were not averse to using rough methods to resolve problems. In 1521 Ellis St John charged the Bishop with denial of the execution of his wife's first husband's will (to the value of £100 and above). A commission of Sir Davie Owen and Sir John Dawtry was set up, but nothing was done, and meanwhile the Bishop had hired a gang to dispossess St John of Drongwyke Farm.[12] One might think little of this case, but in 1529 we hear of a band led by Ellis and James Bradshaw repossessing Chapter property by force in Upper Marden.[13] Clearly some agents of the church were rough diamonds—in 1533 a former keeper of the palace so threatened a citizen of Chichester after a drinking session in the *White Horse* that he picked a flint out of South Street and killed him in self defence, and had to seek sanctuary with the Dominicans.[14] In 1540 John Cressweller and confederates broke the garden wall of Richard Awdeby, and when he repaired it they came and broke it again, but he was foiled in his suit by the Mayor, a friend to Cressweller, and so was forced to go to the Court of Star Chamber in London.[15] When a citizen tried to get a mayor who would favour the people of Chichester, Bishop Sampson got Lord de la Warr, John Caryll and Richard Sackville to stop such revolution.[16]

It is interesting to discover, through his will, how Cressweller saw himself. In 1527 he left £5 to be delivered to the poor at his funeral, and £4 for the poor at his month's mind. He wanted one of the great bells of the Cathedral rung for him between 7.15 and 8 o'clock for 28 days after his death, for which he left money for the ringers as well as the Cathedral. Ellis Bradshaw wanted (in 1544) to be buried in the midst of the south aisle, with his portrait in brass or free stone on the pillar. He wanted 4d. to go to 100 poor people, not beggars (for whom there was food and drink provided). Eight poor householders were to have a black gown each, value 6s., to bear tapers of 1lb each around his hearse. Later 200 poor householders (certainly 1 in 100 of the citizens) would benefit from a legacy of £20.[17]

In a time when many parishes were in dire poverty, with ruinous churches (Peckham, *Acts* (1), p.104) unions of parishes (118, 134, 169, 176, 187, 200, 239, 240, 283) and augmentations of vicarages (e.g. 450), it seems astonishing that leases of rectories, vicarages and their tithes should yield the largest income for the Chapter. Yet 21 leases in the period yielded an income by 1540 of over £200 p.a. Some were extensive—one for life, one at 90 years, one at 80, seven in the 40s, four in the 30s, two at 21 and one at ten.

The leases were good business (a vicar cost £5 6s. 8d. per annum to put in place) and one gets some notion of the value from a note in 1528 of a widow surrendering 'to our great profit' the lease of Burpham rectory. She was granted an annuity of 40s. (not to begin for two years) and she was 'seized' of this by a mere 4d.—the Chapter finally kept

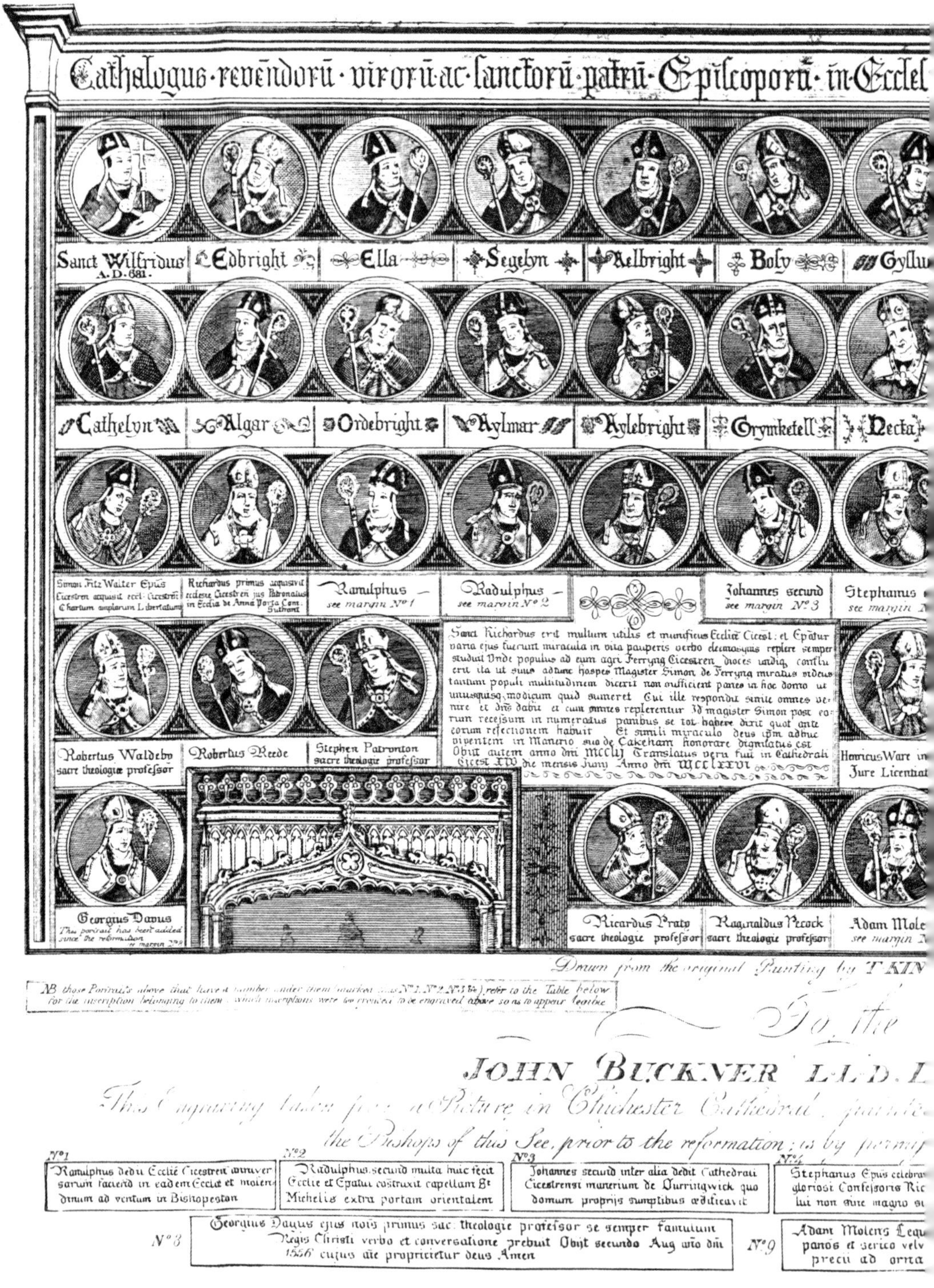

22 *Lambert Barnard's panel of the bishops, drawn in 1812 by Thomas King, the Chichester artist and engraver.*

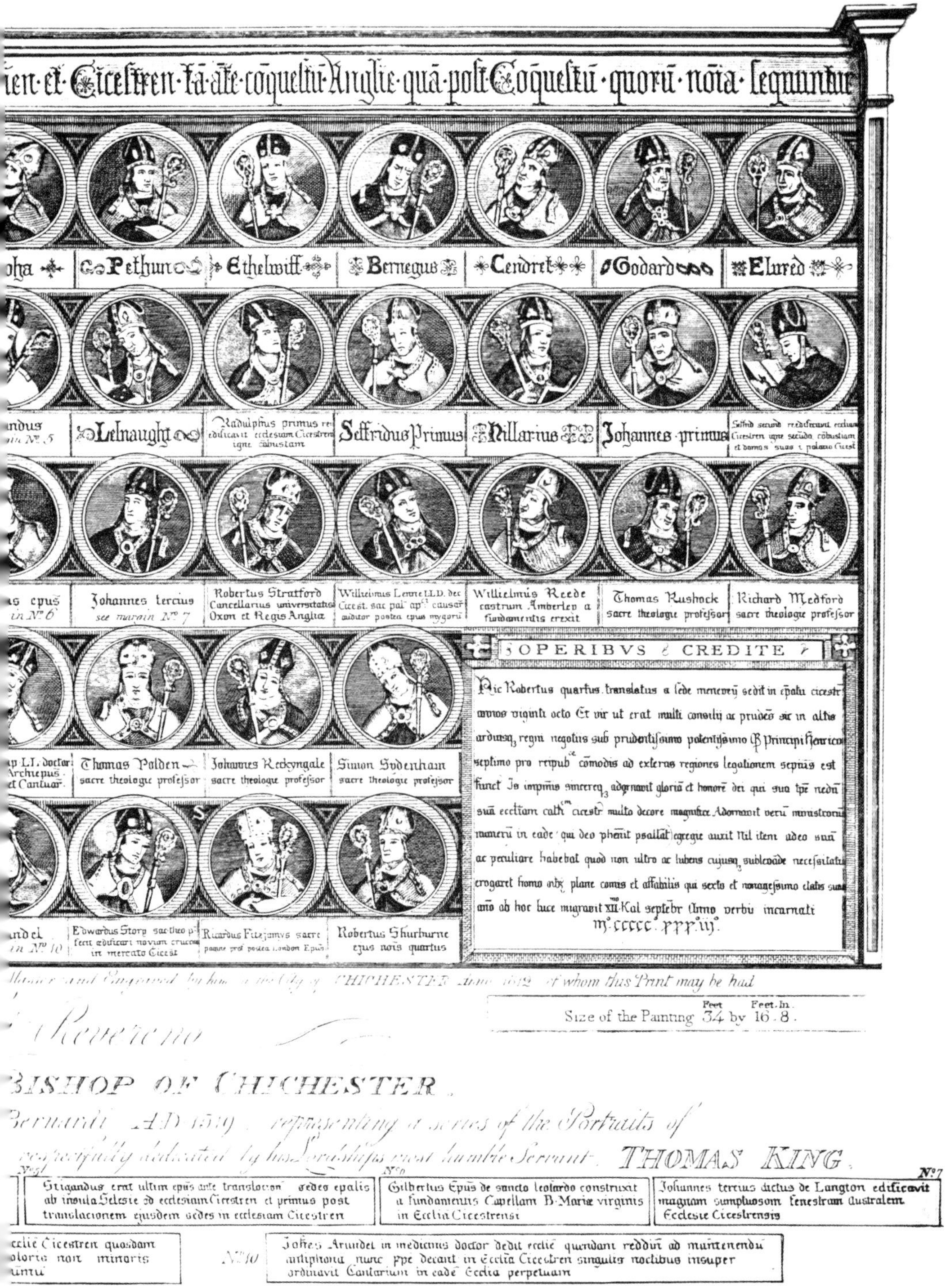
Bernegus
Cendret
Godard
Elured
Seffridus Primus
Hillarius
Johannes primus
Johannes tercius
Robertus Stratford
Willielmus Reede
Thomas Rushock
Richard Medford
sacre theologie professor
OPERIBVS CREDITE
Thomas Polden
Johannes Reckyngale
Simon Sydenham
Edwardus Story
Ricardus Fitzjamys
Robertus Shurburne
ejus nois quartus
Size of the Painting 34 by 16 . 8.
BISHOP OF CHICHESTER
THOMAS KING

its nerve (328)! Some of the leases clearly yielded a vital provision to the Cathedral. In 1531, for instance, the Chapter leased John Knott of Chichester West Dean parsonage with Chilgrove, Binderton, Singleton and Didling. They reserved for themselves the presentation of the vicarage, escheats, wards, marriages and heriots. For this extensive and valuable estate, John Knott had to pay 60 quarters of wheat, and £17 6s. 8d. The wheat was to be delivered weekly to Chichester. In addition there was a purveyance charge—for six years Knott had to deliver 20 quarters of wheat for which he would be paid, good or bad, high prices or low, 5s. a quarter. The Chapter was anxious about its supply—Knott had to leave the tenancy with 10 acres sown with wheat or barley (344).

Grants of next presentation to a living may not have brought in much in the way of specific income, but they proved in Chichester a fast-increasing instrument for gaining influence. On 6 February 1543 eight such grants were confirmed—14 days later a further six (306-7). The White Act Book records 55 such grants, none before 1535, when there were nine, including grants to Cromwell, Audley, John Uvedale (Anne Boleyn's secretary) and Cranmer (190, 191, 204, 205). In 1540 they began the year with grants to Cromwell's protégés Thomas Wriothesley and Richard Moryson, and ended it with grants to the Duke of Norfolk and Thomas Audley once more (251, 265, 271). In 1541 they granted the presentation of both archdeaconries to Catherine Howard, and in 1543 they made two grants to Sir Anthony Browne and one to John Jennings, another gentleman of the King's Chamber (306, 307, 309).

Browne, of Cowdray, was a local as well as a national notability; other such favoured with grants were the Gorings, the Gages and the de la Warrs (206, 236, 253; 202, 302, 308, 314; 99, 100, 101, 102).

There is evidence of consortia bidding for grants of next presentation, some from outside the diocese—one hot little team of Devon men led by Francis Everard did considerable business in Sussex preferments (303). But the outsiders needed local brokers and indeed the Cathedral needed to rely on a team of largely Chichester-based investors and officials. The Knotts and the Creswellers were already building up their position in Chichester, and Ellis Bradshaw figures largely, too. In 1528 he leases Burpham parsonage for the substantial sum of £15, and he takes on the large task of purveying corn to the Chapter and baking their bread (329/330). The next year he was leasing lands in Hunston and in 1530 took on Highleigh lands and Graylingwell—a substantial estate that cost him £8 a year in rent (332, 338, 337). In 1531 he was made porter or verger of the Cathedral, for which he would receive 20s. a year and a gown worth 8s. at Christmas (339). In 1535 he was made receiver and surveyor of the lands, rents and tenements of the Cathedral (206). In 1538 he leased a tenement in North Street, and the following year takes on more Cathedral land (225, 199). In 1540 he joined with the Archdeacon of Chichester in the lease of Wilmington, and with Sir John Gage in a grant of next presentation. In 1547 he was again involved with Gage, and a team of investors from Dorset interested in getting the grant of next presentation of a prebend (248, 262, 302). We last see him in the White Act Book leasing more Cathedral land outside Westgate (379).

One other character who comes from outside the diocese, Anthony Wayte of Clapham in Surrey, is worth following for he begins on the clerical side and ends as an official. We meet him first as MA and Archdeacon of Lewes, but by 1530 he is the Bishop's steward and later warden of the Palace (121, 193). He leases Ticehurst in 1533, Cowdray farm (along with Lettice his wife) in 1540 and a share of Aldingbourne farm in 1542 (197, 270,

304). He stands as a good symbol of the new order. Starting as definitely a cleric, he ends as a lay administrator.

Before we leave the topic of incomes we should consider the more personal finances of the prebends themselves. Sixteen of the 35 prebends were leased during this period, and one can understand, for example, that the prebendary of Ipthorne would have been hard put to it to exploit his own quarries at Slinfold, nor could the prebendary of Waltham be expected to manage his own dovehouse (120 and 159). But even though the leases are quite long (one at 21, seven in the 30s, three in the 40s, two in the 50s, two in the 60s and one at 80 years) some of the prebendaries do want to keep some control—the prebendary of Highleigh requires the use of a room in his mansion, and the Treasurer requires the lessee of the Wyndham lands to keep two geldings for him and to purvey hay and wood to the parsonage at fixed prices (160 and 112). The yields were not substantial—£8 3s. 4d. for the Treasurer's lands, £8 for the prebend of Ipthorne, £8 for Waltham, £14 3s. 4d. for Highleigh and £12 for Henfield (122, 120, 159, 160, 166).

And this does depend on people actually paying what they had promised. When John Chamber, the prebendary of Wisborough, died in 1503 he left a sorry record of debts himself, including three years' arrears of rent of his own house in East Street (405).

Pensions and annuities were a major charge on income. The pension for a retiring prebendary was £15 to be paid out of the prebend itself (e.g. 81, 133, 156, 161). The Treasurer got £22 in 1540, whilst still being prebendary of Bracklesham. Indeed several prebendaries who changed places took pensions with them, willy nilly—thus the retiring prebendary of Highleigh took a pension from the prebend in 1532, although he seems to have flourished as prebendary of Exceit until 1555. Similarly a retiring Master of St Mary's Hospital took an annuity, even though he had a long career ahead that involved a return to the said mastership (261, 165, 62). Something distinctly odd was happening on 15 July 1529, when John Colyns was installed to, retired from and took a pension of £6 from the prebend of Mardon (91).

A chantry priest got considerably less—£4 6s. 0d.; and a parish priest £3 (269 and 248). One may compare this with the £5 a farm worker might have earned in this period.[18] Chantry priests and vicars choral also improved their own financial positions by taking on cures in Chichester and its suburbs.[19] The dean and chapter and the bishop granted a number of annuities out of the Cathedral: 13s. 4d. for 'faithfulness and good counsel'; £3 13s. 4d. to a servant for 36 years' service, in and out of the country; the assurance to one of his favourite musicians' wife that if he predeceased her she should continue to have his £10 16s. 8d. whether she married another musician who might serve in his place or no; and of course the retainer for Lambert Barnard of £3 6s. 8d., with the promise that, whilst he worked for the Cathedral on tasks 'no meaner than he had done before', he should have £14 8s. 0d. and his materials above that (335, 151, 130, 360).

Chantries[20]

The fear of the pains of purgatory, and the sympathy with those enduring them, funded a whole area of Church life that was to disappear at the Reformation. During our period there were 24 chantries operating in the Cathedral (of which 15 were noticed at their Dissolution), and 77 obits (or yearly remembrances) were funded in the rest of the town churches. Twenty-two clergy working in their field were noted at the dissolution, of whom 18 were pensioned (10 of whom were still in receipt of their pensions in 1556). The total annual income for chantries and obits was just over £189, out of which only £1 11s. 3d. was specifically set aside for distribution to the poor, although probably a great deal more than that was given in money, bread and wine doles.[21]

The average income for a Chichester chantry priest was £4 19s. 4d., which looks poor in comparison with the areas studied by Alan Kreider.[22] Only one priest, Robert Hunt, served two chantries, and some chantries were served by prebendaries like Lawrence Woodcock. Chantries sometimes had houses attached;[23] the income needed collection of rent: collectors charged as much as half a mark, which for Arundel's chantry, with only four tenements and four gardens in Chichester, seems rather a lot (3 and 188-9).

The duties were clearly extensive—the endowment was made for a very important purpose, and even old obits, like that for Bishop Seffrid II, were carefully kept going. The more recent and well endowed Mortimer obit required 16 vicars, the King's chaplains, the subdean, eight choristers and a thurifer, the porter, the sexton and four bellringers.[24] Thomas Dean of Lichfield's third chantry priest (Lawrence Woodcock, prebendary of Exceit) had to say three masses a week and each day *placebo* and *dirige* with nine lessons.[25] Let us hope they did remember for whom they were praying—the cheerful way that Ralph Nevill was transmogrified into 'Raph Randal', a term used in every source for this period, does not give us much confidence.

Two of the chantry priests had degrees—one Nicholas Hycket, who also held the post of subdean until his deprivation in 1554, was still drawing his pension from Thomas Dean's number one chantry in 1556, so his education had taught him something (143)!

The chantries appeared to possess little in the way of furniture—at the Dissolution all that could be found was a parcel-gilt chalice weighing 14½ ounces in Nevill's chantry, a chalice and patten double-gilt weighing 18¾ ounces and a silver bell weighing one and a quarter ounces in the Brotherhood of St George (113 and 132).

The average age of the chantry priests at the Dissolution was just under fifty, and the commissioners were generous with pensions, often awarding only a little less than the real income.

Interlude—Autumn 1538

The second half of the year 1538 was a year of crisis in the English church, when Thomas Cromwell, recovered from the outburst of the Pilgrimage of Grace, was driving on with all his major projects for change—the Bible in English, the dissolution of the remaining monasteries and friaries, the taking-down of the images and the major shrines and the attack on his enemies. In all of this Chichester was to feel the effects of change, and indeed attempted to resist them.

Already in the early 1530s there were signs of opposition to the main trend. Christopher Plummer, prebendary of Somerleigh, for instance, opposed the king's divorce and was sent to the Tower on 6 July 1535.[26] (He had been Queen Catherine's chaplain in 1518.) Even though Plummer was released on 8 March 1536, clearly he was still pursued: on 11 June, a petty canon of Windsor reported to Cromwell that he had received from Plummer's servant Bryan a chain and cross of gold, 10 gold rings, a pair of jet beads and eight gaudes of gold. Could it be that Plummer's real crime was concealing donations at a shrine as, maybe, the Dean and Archdeacon of Chichester were to attempt a short while later?[27]

At the Dissolution, about a hundred religious were put out of their houses in Sussex, some of whom found their way to Chichester. By and large the ex-religious were kindly

23 *William Bradbridge with his family (memorial brass, 1592).*

treated. Nicholas Duncke, a canon of Shulbrede, was licensed to wear the habit of his order under the robe of a secular priest.[28]

John Collins, the Bursalis prebendary, was chaplain to Lord Montague, eldest of the Pole brothers, who read him letters from the exiled Cardinal de la Pole and spoke with him indiscreetly about the royal family. Even more deeply involved was George Croft, the Chancellor of Chichester. He was chaplain to Sir Geoffrey Pole and a close associate of Lord de la Warr, and Lord Montague was often with him.

On 9 December 1537 Croft and Collins were executed at Tyburn and their heads set on Tower Bridge—the episode frightened the conservative Chichester community witless.

Clearly some people were profiting from the changes and were as a result eagerly supporting the administration. John Cressweller, William Bradbridge the mayor and Ellis Bradshaw were in the business. On 15 December 1538 William Earnley wrote to John Huberden, one of Cromwell's secretaries, sending in a little book which 'had marvellously aggrieved these papistical fellows in Chichester'. He writes bitterly against de la Warr (who was in the Tower) saying there have been very many suspicious-looking night visitors to his house at Halnaker recently, and that he once entertained Cardinal Pole there, as Canon George Croft, Chancellor of the Cathedral, did at Chichester. He also asked for Cromwell's arms with his 'possey' to set up over his house.[29] In fact the order for the destruction of St Richard's shrine had already been addressed to Sir William Goring and 'Earnley' (when the account was rendered, when they got £40 for doing the job, he is called 'Mr. Will'—he must have been annoyed).[30]

The commission was to take down the shrine, deliver silver, gold, jewels and ornaments to the Tower, also relics, and to raze and deface it to the ground and take away any images that were abusing simple people's goodwill. This to be done so that God should not have His glory stolen from him and simple folk deceived.

On 20 December they took away six coffers, a casket and a little box. In a ship's coffer they put 55 images, silver and gilt. In a long coffin that had contained St Richard's bones they placed 57 images of silver and gilt. A sixth coffer with three locks was delivered to them by the Dean and Archdeacon containing relics and jewels from the shrine. The casket contained 51 jewels set with stones and pearls, and the little box had 31 rings with stones and three other jewels.[31]

The Period 1542-1569

Personnel

There were some 130 members of Chapter in all during this period. Their qualifications were 12 Bachelors of Arts, 28 Masters of Arts, four Bachelors of Canon Law and three Bachelors of Civil Law with six Bachelors of both Laws. Eighteen were Bachelors of Theology, nine Doctors of Theology. Three were Doctors of Canon Law, one Doctor of Civil Law and three Doctors of both Laws. Fifty-three degrees came from Oxford (13 from New College—the Sherburne connection holding up—and six from Oriel). Thirteen came from Cambridge, and seven had obtained degrees abroad.

Thirty-six give no degrees at all (Miles Man did not take the degree upon which he had started, and John Satwell was nominated to Bargham prebend late in 1560 as 'sufficiently instructed in grammar' but was refused (Peckham, *Acts* (2), p.620). Rather more worryingly, 23 who are recorded in Chapter Acts as having degrees cannot be traced in standard reference works on Oxford and Cambridge graduates. Clearly the Chapter was concerned with scholarship, in 1560 charging Francis Cox, prebendary of Wightring, with lack of qualifications, failure to preach at Wittering and failure to lecture in the Cathedral Close (720). The same year they had appointed another scholar to a prebend, so clearly they were hopeful of the experiment (714). We should note also the bequest of Thomas Carpender of Kingsham in February 1566 of £4 a year for exhibitions of Sussex students to Oxford.

The canons come from the same wide geographical spread as the previous group studied, with only four recorded as from this diocese. Five were ex-religious (Brisely, Clerke, Crowham, Johnson and Pannell). A significant number of former chantry priests were appointed to Chapter in this period (Angell, Hall, Hicknett, Lancaster and Lloyd). But we should recall that even such high and mighty members as Archdeacon Worthiall had not despised the office of chantry priest.

Influence played some part in appointments. George Day looked after his family, notably his brother Thomas, who was in fact a good scholar and worthy of his place. A

24 *Bishop Day's canting arms, the daisy ('Day's eye').*

number of members of Chapter held chaplaincies—seven of them royal, Maurice Gyttans was chaplain to Cranmer, William Pye to Wriothesley, Richard Caurden to Sir William Fitzwilliam, John Chauntler to the Earl of Arundel, John Sherry to the Duke of Norfolk and Alban Langdale to Viscount Montague.

Five (Bradbridge, Curteys, Overton, Turberville and White) went on to become bishops, whilst others suffered in the many reverses of the period. Roland Swinburne, Master of Clare Hall, was dismissed by the Visitors in 1549 (to be reinstated in 1554) but did not seem to suffer in his prebend of Eartham, to which he came the previous year (475). In 1553-4, nine members of Chapter went, the majority for marriage, with three being reappointed. Robert Oking might have reason to be cross: as commissary to Bishop Capon of Bangor he had sold indulgences at risk of physical attack by the Registrar. Having moved on with Capon to Salisbury he had been involved in the trial for heresy of John Marbeck. However, despite a good Catholic record he was, in fact, married, so he was deprived. In October 1555 he found refuge at Highleigh prebend. Similarly William Devenish, who had been deprived of his Canterbury prebend for marriage in 1554, moved back to the diocese of his birth to become prebendary of Exceit in July 1556. The great survivor was George Carew, third son of Sir Edmund of Anthony, whose career seemed to crash in 1554 for the same reason as Oking's, but by March 1555 he was prebendary of Bury, and ended, in 1571, as Dean of Exeter. Clearly he was unrepentant, for his son and heir was born in 1555, let us hope discreetly.

In the period 1558-61 there were seven members of Chapter deprived. There was, too, at least one reappointment—Robert Raynold, who had lost prebends in Lincoln and Winchester dioceses, came to Windham in April 1562 and on to Hova Villa in 1563.

There were seven more deprivations to follow (ending with that of Thomas Fryer) by 1571. It was a troublous time, as John Smythe, deprived of the treasurership in 1562, noted in his will, referring to his books 'miserably dispersed and stolen away' in various places.[32]

Chichester diocese was so physically isolated that it learned little of novelties in religion, and that almost entirely in the eastern part.[33] When Latimer was brought to Chichester, under the care of Bishop Sampson in late summer 1539, with just two servants, having resigned his bishopric in protest at the Act of Six Articles, he came to a Catholic community, but one that was threatened with change. Sampson himself was to be imprisoned a year later.[34]

Other Protestants made the adventurous journey to Chichester. In November 1551 Bartholomew Traheron, a layman, was made dean. He had been fostered by a noted Protestant, Richard Tracy, and at Oxford he had associated with John Frith, a pupil of William Tyndale. He travelled extensively, becoming a friend of Bullinger and of Calvin, and married on his return. He became keeper of the Royal Library and was one of those who particularly welcomed Swiss students in Edward's reign. He found it almost impossible to cope with the Chapter at Chichester and resigned in 1553, becoming a prebendary of Windsor. In Mary's reign he withdrew to Frankfurt and moved on to Wesel. He wrote against the Arians, against Mary and on the subject of providence, dying in Wesel in 1558.

Richard Tremayne returned from exile in Strasbourg to be presented by the Queen to the archdeaconry of Chichester in October 1559, but the presentation was apparently ineffective, and he made the remainder of his career at home in the West country. Thomas Spencer had a longer career: he had been in Zürich and then in Geneva as a member of Knox's congregation, and returned to be ordained by Grindal in January 1560, when he became rector of the well-known Protestant centre of Hadleigh, in Suffolk. He was made archdeacon of Chichester in April of the year, where he remained until his death in 1571, strangely little used by Barlow, who complained bitterly at his lack of 'lieutenants'.

Finally we should notice the appointment of the Saxonist and Marian exile Lawrence Nowell to Ferring prebend in August 1563. Like Spencer he does not seem to figure in the business of the diocese, having richer and more important positions elsewhere.

The diocese was, and was to remain, substantially loyal to the Catholic faith. One of the leading nobles of the diocese, Lord Montague, spoke in parliament against the supremacy:

> foreasmuch as the catholics of this realm disturb not, nor hinder the public affairs of the realm, neither spiritual nor temporal: they dispute not, they preach not, they disobey not the queen, they cause no trouble nor tumults among the people ... I do entreat, whether it be just to make this penal statue [*sic*] to force the subjects of this realm to receive and believe the religion of the protestants upon pain of death ... naturally no man can or ought to be constrained to take for certain that that he holdeth to be uncertain: for this repugneth to the natural liberty of man's understanding: for understanding may be persuaded, but not forced.[35]

Some members of Chapter are hard to nail. George Day's brother Thomas was Precentor and may well have assisted in the interrogation of Philpot, yet his book collection contained work by the Protestant Luther, Bugenhagen, Melanchthon, Bullinger, Calvin and Peter Martyr.

William Pye, Dean, and William Tresham, Chancellor, were members of the team set to debate with the Protestant bishops imprisoned at Oxford, and there is no doubt of the loyalties of Bonner's chaplain, John Harpsfield, who held the Bursalis prebend at Chichester. John White, who had been prebendary of Ipthorne and then Seaford until he was made bishop of Lincoln in 1554, was one of the ablest of Queen Mary's bishops and was clearly much feared by the new Elizabethan administration, which made elaborate regulations for his detention.

Alban Langdale, Archdeacon of Chichester, was also a member of the team set to dispute with Cranmer, Ridley and Latimer. He was chaplain to Lord Montague and was set by him to preach in disaffected areas. On his deprivation he was ordered to stay with Lord Montague, but went abroad. He was remembered in the will of Nicholas Hickett, former chantry priest and subdean, who left Dr. Langdale his second best gown.[36]

Two others who also left the country were Edward Goddesalve and Thomas Stapleton. Goddesalve was nominated by Henry VIII as one of the first fellows of Trinity College, Cambridge, and during the Marian visitation of the University he had held the office of peruser of books. He was a friend of Christopherson (who translated one of his works into Latin) and was made prebendary of Ferring in November 1558, shortly afterwards leaving for Antwerp, where he became Professor of Divinity in the monastery of St Michael.

Thomas Stapleton was born in Henfield, and was made prebendary of Woodhorn in February 1559. He retired to Louvain and shortly became Professor of Divinity at Douai. He became a leading controversialist, and the *DNB* lists 27 of his works, collected, as they comment ruefully, in four 'huge' volumes. Stapleton and Goddesalve attended the Council of Trent as representatives of Chichester diocese, and were not deprived until 1563. Indeed Goddesalve was abroad under royal licence!

The Archiepiscopal Visitation of 1569 names four people who were sending money to Stapleton, one being Davie Spenser, possibly the prebendary of Fittleworth, who was also looking after Stapleton's property.

The Visitor was shocked to find old people in Chichester taking Latin primers to Church and keeping Rosary beads at home. The Cathedral was not exempt from this. In

October 1569 William Waye, who had been a Sherburne clerk from 1564 until his resignation in August 1566, was proceeded against by the Dean and Chapter for possession of Romish relics. He had a *Legenda Aurea* in English, a *Pilgrimage of Perfection*, a manuscript great Psalter, Fisher on the Psalms and a super-altar. He had got some of these from the sub-treasurer, whose son had sold the super-altar after his father's death for 1d. Waye claimed his wife wanted it, and that the young man had also offered to sell him a 'faire newe greate portise'. He said he did not approve of purgatory, prayer to saints, the Mass, transubstantiation and the supremacy of the Pope 'or else there should be many heads if every prince were supreme governor in their own realm'. The Chapter deprived him of his lay vicarage but seemed disinclined to go further—after all, over in Battle everything was held in readiness 'to set up the Mass again within 24 hours warning'.[37]

Of course there were lots of people other than members of Chapter needed to run the Cathedral. The staff list in October 1568 gives four lay vicars and a supernumerary (three of the singers being appropriately surnamed Base), eight choristers, their master, an organist, a verger, four bellringers, two sextons, a baker and four vicars choral (707).

There were in addition a number of deputies of whom we hear from time to time—an under-communar in 1565 (671—he got £10) a sub-treasurer and a succentor in 1569 (716). Edward Amyers was Chapter Clerk and Registrar, first to the archdeaconry of Chichester and then to the diocese (503 and 625). There were auditors (486 and 552—cost 53s. 4d.) and stewards, to deanery and prebends (468, 479, 550, 552, 682—William Stapleton and Thomas Bishop seem to have mopped up most of this work). Lord Montague fulfilled the feudal task for Christopherson of 'leader of all my farmers, tenants and others in my liberties to array them in time of war for the defence of the realm' (570—all for 40s.).

Certainly the most bothersome staff were the vicars choral and lay vicars. John Mekyns was pensioned from Stubbes chantry aged 40 and became a vicar choral. He appeared in Chapter in July 1551 for speaking insulting words against the prebendary of Firle and striking him with his fist in the Close. He was ordered not to do this again on pain of dismissal. Four years later he was deprived of Rumboldswyke rectory.[38] In 1561 Richard Paine complained to Chapter at the injustice of having been put out of his teaching post for brawling with Edward Piper.[39]

In 1568 three of the vicars choral were ordered to re-establish their common eating in hall and the following year one of their number was committed to prison (707 and 723). Also in 1569 William Payne was appointed Master of the Choristers at a fee of 58s. 4d., given charge of their chambers and the key to their garden (William Overton also had a key). Payne declared John Morris 'unmeate and unhable' to serve as a chorister any longer (727). All sounds well, yet within two years Payne was charged with threatening the verger that he would 'fill his skinne full of hayleshotte'.[40]

Finance

Money was clearly going to remain one of the biggest focuses of attention for the Chapter, particularly as the rapacious agents of Queen Elizabeth got to work, stripping the Church of its foundation property. There were other problems—such as Christopher Perne who ran off with lead and bells in 1554 (526). By 1562 repairs were urgently needed, particularly to the spire, and there was no cash in hand. They got permission to have a sale. They had certain redundant silver, such as the chrysmatory and the figure of Christ from the cross. Other furnishings were poor—19 copes in all, four of them 'very bad', 14 vestments, a pall, a canopy, four 'corporas' cases (three again 'very bad'), a sepulchre cloth, seven cushions and an old chair of red velvet. Sad though the case was, William Bradbridge took all the silver to London and got £128 19s. 9½d. for it, buying a standing cup for Communion, paying their arrears of subsidy and bringing back the rest to cover repairs.[41]

The sources of money supply were very much as before. One hundred and eleven leases are recorded for the period. There seems to have been a decrease in leasing in the early years (or had they leased all they possessed?) 1551 brings nine leases and there are six in 1555 and six in 1556. In 1562 there are nine, 16 in 1566, 11 in 1569. There is a certain amount of post-dated leasing—in 1569 one lease was struck to begin in 1592 and another in 1589. The length of the leases is at first well controlled, with most being for 21 or 31 years, but in the early days of Elizabeth's reign we get five leases for 99 years (and one for 500 years—almost a grant, to Lord Lumley, son-in-law to the Earl of Arundel [615]). By the late 1560s leases are commonly of 41-year term, with six at 60 years. The income from the leases is not always recorded, so our total is defective—£216 5s. 8d.

Some leases caused problems—in 1564 the Town Clerk of Chichester forged the Chapter seal to authenticate a lease and two years later a lease was held to be void because Austin Bradbridge had sealed it alone at night in his house after the death of the Dean (665 and 690).

Fourteen prebends were leased out in this period (usually at their *Valor Ecclesiasticus* prices). There were some reservations; the prebendary of Woodhorn wanted a chamber and stabling in his mansion when he came to preach and once again the prebendary of Highleigh reserved the chamber over the parlour for times of pestilence in Chichester (53 and 628). Ipthorne was again leased with its quarries 'found or to be found' in Slinfold (689). Most commonly the term of the leases was 41 years, but there were three as high as eighty.

Again there are some indications of a desire to improve and conserve—some tenants being instructed to build barns, for example (590 and 624). Whilst the Bishop continued to sell wood (472, 550, 645), the Chapter was pushed in 1561 to extend a lease to a tenant to fell for his own use between Christmas and Lady Day, so long as he made no waste, nor cut elms for sale and he should preserve the young wood under pain of £60 (628).

During the period there were 18 leases of rectories, mostly for the term of 40 years, the whole (again not always noted in the source) yielding £160 7s. 7d. Three of the leases were to London tradesmen whom one finds regularly coming out into the provinces to invest (564, 647, 673). Two leases were more in the order of grants—some of the Chapter's richest possessions: Willingdon, going to Sir Philip Hoby in 1548 (for 80 years) and Chiddingly for 70 years to Sir Richard Sackville in 1561 (475 and 621).

The Chapter was very aware that it needed the aid of royal counsellors and local gentry. In 1545 the Dean granted Thomas Saunder of Chorleywood 20s. for life 'for his good counsel' (476). The following year John Gunter of Racton received 13s. 4d. from the Chapter 'on account of many benefits received' (468). In 1560 Robert Bowyer, gentleman, of Chichester was also granted an annuity of 13s. 4d. 'for faithful service given and to be given' (606). Eight years later Thomas Bowyer got 40s., a considerable improvement (712). John Caryll of Warnham received an annuity of 20s. (664). The biggest grant of all was to the Queen herself, in December 1564, when the Chapter turned over to Sir Richard Sackville, her sub-treasurer, some of its best properties, including Wilmington, Willingdon, Friston, Sutton, Heathfield, Eastbourne, Westham, Hartfield and Chiddingly (667).

There were 11 grants of next presentation made in this period, many to men of influence like Edward Gage (594), Matthew Parker (617) and Robert, Earl of Leicester (690). Such grants were clearly valuable. In 1556 the grant of a Sherburne clerkship was bought back for £11 (558).

The times were changing fast. The Chapter was much less in control of its income, and the income was depleted whilst prices rose. The problems of a substantially Roman Catholic community had by no means been resolved, and relations with the city which had once been so good were beginning to decline. As the choral institutions declined and civic dwelling encroached upon the Close, as properties began to fall into ruin, a new and somewhat sadder age began.

V

Art in the Cathedral from the Foundation to the Civil War

Trevor Brighton

Chichester Cathedral is a very plain building in terms of decorative stonework and sculptural features. Little remains externally or internally of this aspect of Romanesque art. From the bases that survive, the west door must have been a fine Norman example, but we have no idea whether any sculptured frieze extended above it in the manner of that at Lincoln Cathedral, although there are remains of 12th-century decorated work in the west gable and below the west window inside. The rest of the building was probably not elaborate, judging by the simple billet ornament that decorates the string courses and window heads and by the plain cushion capitals. The blocked doorway of the south-western tower, with its zig-zag, chevron and rope mouldings, is the only survival amounting to a mild decorative flourish.

The corbel table which once extended around the outside of the Cathedral represents the best survival of early-Norman sculpture. Corbel tables were common decorative features around the eaves and at principal roof level and helped to conceal and strengthen the wall-plate where the roof timbers rested. These tables may be plain or sculpted with a variety of motifs such as human, animal or grotesque heads, sometimes interspersed with simple, patterned corbels. At Chichester the corbel tables are sculpted, and much evidence, though largely hidden from view, exists to allow some assessment.

What survives is at the level of the original roof line of the outer aisles, but these tables were concealed in the later 13th century when new stone roof vaults were added along with three new chambers. It is above these vaults that one is able to examine 37 of the hundreds of corbels which once studded the Cathedral's eaves.

The largest number, 17, can be viewed in what is now the Cathedral Library,[1] originally a chapel over the Chapel of the Four Virgins. The stairs to the library pass an original, outer-wall Norman window with billet moulding in pristine order. Above this survives a portion of the outer corbel table of the north choir aisle. Two of the corbels are broken and one is a modern replacement, the head of Archdeacon Mason's labrador dog, Victor. The remainder are contorted human faces and masks, conjoined heads, a horse, a bull and numerous writhing monsters. One corbel has an X-patterned frieze on a rope moulding which is, in turn, supported by three plain miniature corbels.

Another 11 corbels are visible in the chamber over the south porch, now the Choir Library. These are more worn and broken but again the two-headed motif occurs, a head with one eye closed and one open, another head with hands beneath holding what appears

25 *a. The Cathedral Library: part of the row of corbels; b. Corbel of monster with man in his mouth, viewed from beneath; c & d. The modern corbel next to it: Victor the labrador, seen with his master, Archdeacon Lancelot Mason, and his carver, Richard Mitchell.*

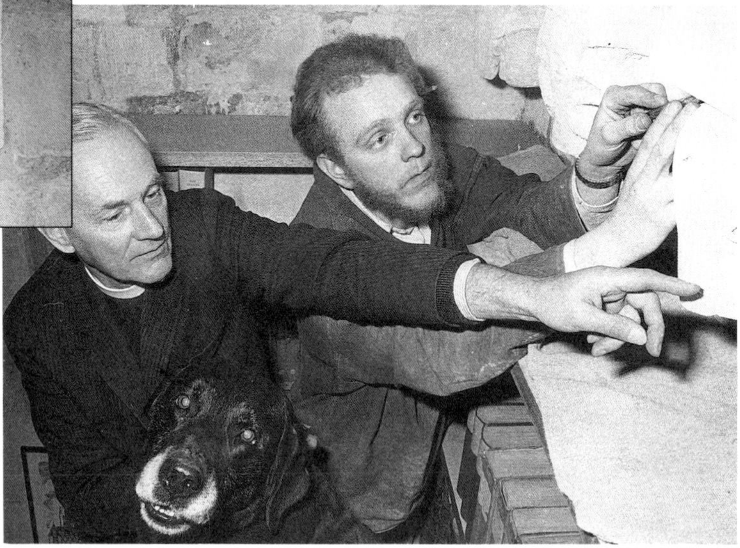

to be a heart, and decorative examples with a crude cross and chequered patterns. The chamber over the north-west porch contains a further nine which again comprise animal and human heads, a griffin (or eagle) and a plain incised saltire motif.

If one ventures along the triforium and enters the unlit recesses of the vaults above the nave aisles, many more corbel heads can be picked out in the thick cobwebs by the beam of a powerful lamp. Again they scowl, snarl and stare from their black recesses. They reveal little or no evidence of Christian iconography.[2] As a group, the corbel sculptures are bold and crude in execution. They show some weathering after a century or more gazing upon the houses and citizens of Norman Chichester.

The work is that of masons rather than sophisticated carvers; such detail as there is has been achieved by simple grooving with a chisel and the forming of eye-sockets with a drill or a punch. Similar work can be found at the top of neighbouring Bosham church tower and at Boxgrove Priory and suggests a late 11th-century, early 12th-century group of masons, possibly settling at Chichester in the time of the first bishop, Stigand.

The otherwise plain appearance of the Cathedral's Norman exterior was repeated inside. The quire triforium has some rare survivals of early Romanesque capitals (*c.*1080). Otherwise the solid mass of the lower arcades with their plain cushion capitals is relieved only by 13th-century stiff-leaf capitals on the Purbeck shafts.

Polychromatic mural paintings once enlivened the architecture and two notable fragments of these survive. The first and earliest is the painting of banded ashlarwork under the soffit of the fifth bay from the west of the south nave arcade and under those of the sixth bay from the west of the north triforium. If such detailing in contrasting light and dark tones was repeated throughout the nave, the effect may have been similar to the interior of Vézelay in Burgundy.

More striking is the surviving early wall-painting in the Treasury.[3] The technique used here appears to be true fresco, where the artist applies dry powder pigments, mixed in pure water, to the freshly applied, wet lime-plaster on the wall. The colours dry and set with the plaster to become a permanent part of the wall. Three areas in the Treasury have fragmentary remains. The earliest, most important and most striking are to be found on the south side of the large Norman arch which formerly gave access from the north transept into an eastern apsidal chapel. Above the impost, in a square frame, are the lower parts of three standing figures, facing east. They wear sandals and their garments are elaborately painted with folds in green, blue, ochre and red. Below the impost is a frontally enthroned bishop, similarly framed, against a delicately draped background in red, ochre and green.

Stylistically, Dr. Gärtner has compared these paintings to the Romanesque examples in St Anselm's Chapel in Canterbury Cathedral and he ascribes a similar date, of about the mid-12th century. Furthermore, the palette of the Chichester artist reveals a comparable use of precious pigments such as ground lapis lazuli and malachite.

Unfortunately the figures did not escape the attention of iconoclasts and their faces, as usual, have been hacked away, most probably at the Reformation or during the Civil War.

The two other remaining areas of painting are on the north wall of the Treasury and in the south-east corner along the window. Both are much later in date than the figures and are so fragmentary that little beyond architectural decoration can be defined. Nevertheless, these fragments, together with the celebrated roundel of the Virgin and Child in the private chapel of the Bishop's Palace,[4] give some indication of the very high quality of painting that once adorned Chichester Cathedral.

26 *The Chichester Reliefs drawn in 1852, before the fall of the spire, by George Scharf.*

The greatest pieces of sculpture surviving in the Cathedral are the two stone panels known as the Chichester Reliefs.[5] They were discovered, one above the other behind boards on the south-east pier of the Norman crossing, above the choir stalls, in 1829 and their removal to their present position saved them from destruction when the tower and spire collapsed in 1861. They can now be viewed at eye level on the south wall of the south quire aisle.

These reliefs, reckoned by many to be the Cathedral's greatest treasure, rank highly among Romanesque artistic achievements in Western Europe. Here we have a sophistication of treatment that renders the grotesques of the corbel tables almost barbaric in comparison. The reliefs depict two scenes from the story of the Raising of Lazarus, as told in John 11: 1-44, and are cut from a number of blocks of stone placed together in six courses. This was not a unique process in early Norman England; other examples of this technique may be found, for example, on early tympana such as that at Barton Seagrave in Northamptonshire, or the *Deluge* on the west front of Lincoln Cathedral and in the relief of the *Crucifixion* at Barking in Essex.

The first of the two Chichester Reliefs has a top border of eight acanthus motifs and portrays Christ arriving at Bethany where Lazarus had been dead for four days. Behind Christ are four disciples and before him, suppliant at the town gate, are Martha and Mary, sisters of the dead man. In the second relief Christ, accompanied by his disciples, two sextons and onlookers, raises the dead Lazarus. Martha and Mary look on, stricken with grief and awe.

Originally these sculptures were almost certainly painted, though no colour now remains and the gems or glass which once filled their drilled eye sockets have long gone. Nevertheless, allowing for this and damage sustained over centuries, the figures are sharply and deeply cut, to give movement, drama and, above all, pathos.

When they were rescued in 1829, 13 fragments of other panels were preserved and are now deposited in the Library. Although fragments of architecture, wings, drapery and grotesque creatures are identifiable on these blocks of stone, three of which are carved on both sides, there is insufficient material to deduce the subject of a further panel.

The original purpose, arrangement and date of these sculptures still provokes debate. The cult of Lazarus was prominent in the early 12th century, especially in Burgundy at Vézelay, Avallon and Autun. The relics and tomb of St Lazare were, according to legend, at Autun whose church, now a cathedral, was built in 1130 and dedicated to the saint. In England, however, associations with St Lazarus are so rare that some scholars considered the Chichester Reliefs may have had continental origins. They have been attributed to the Ottonian schools in Germany or to a 'Channel school' of artists which merged French and English styles.

Debate about the dates of the Reliefs began following the display of a cast of one of them in the Great Exhibition of 1851. Since then, writers have assigned them to dates ranging from the late Anglo-Saxon period to the last decade of the 12th century, a span of almost 150 years.[6] Most scholars would now agree with Professor George Zarnecki's dating to the second quarter of the 12th century. Zarnecki also postulates that the place where the Reliefs were discovered in 1829 was their original location and that they were part of a chancel screen extending from the south-east to the north-east crossing pier. He calculates that the screen would have consisted of eight panels arranged in four pairs of sculpted scenes, two on each pier and two either side of the gateway in the centre of the screen. Scholars would also agree in general with Zarnecki that the sculptures are English, though not with his precise assertion that they are carved in Purbeck stone. The material used was Caen stone, which has suffered some discoloration from what would appear to be the effects of fire, so that it must predate at least the second of the two conflagrations the Cathedral suffered in its infancy, in 1114 and 1187. The second fire damaged the east end and burned the wooden roof. When new roofing with stone quadripartite vaulting was gradually extended throughout the Cathedral, the masons were set to work to carve the bosses.[7]

There are pre-fire bosses only in the two western bays of the Lady Chapel. The earliest post-fire bosses may be those in the quire aisles and the nave. They are rigid, geometric forms with leaves on stiff stems radiating from the central pierced hole. All are foliate types, with one amusing exception in the third bay of the south quire aisle.

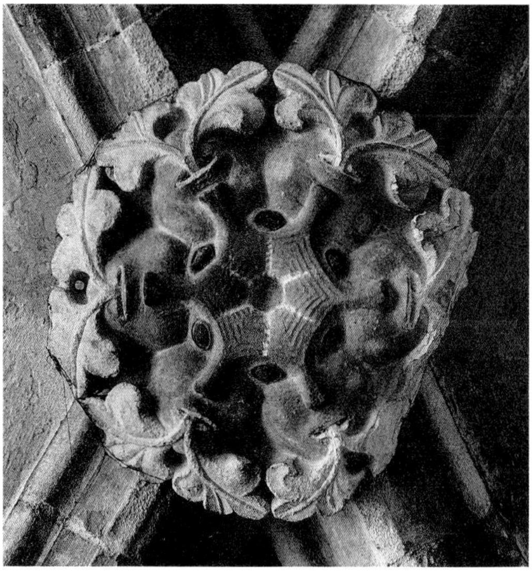

27 *The* trompe l'oeil *boss in the south quire aisle.*

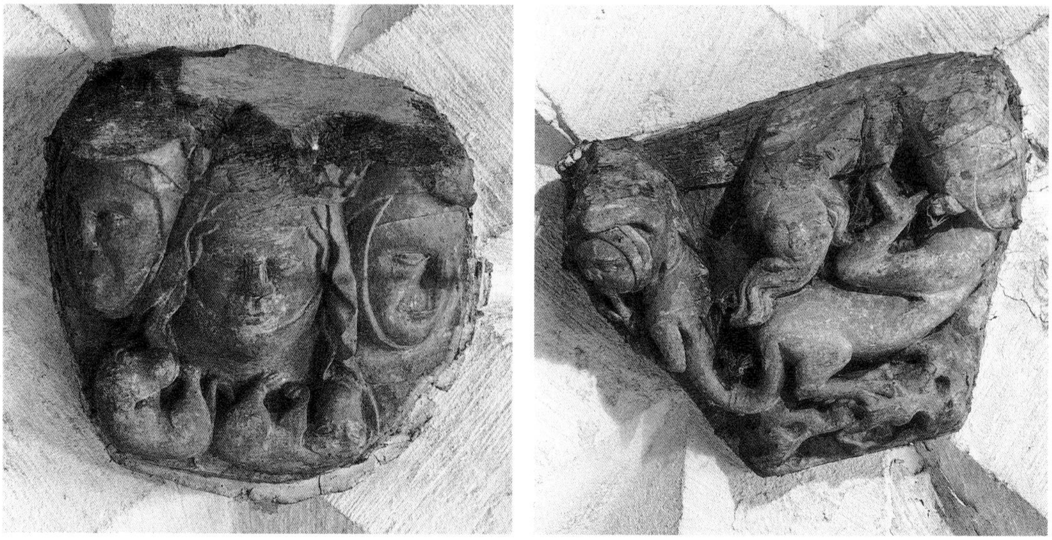

28 The two 'bosses' in the Canons' Vestry, photographed before being painted to simulate stonework.

Here the boss is domed, not pierced, and radiates six human noses linked to one another centrally by an arching brow. Beneath each nose is a mouth which merges into the outer frond of leaves, serving as a beard. These six faces, each with two eyes but only six in total, are a perfect example of *trompe l'oeil*. The effect is repeated in Boxgrove Priory, where the boss (possibly as late as mid-13th-century) is eight-faced.

From these low-relief, formal patterns one turns to the later bosses of the retroquire. Here the leaves radiate from the central piercing of the boss with greater depth and delicacy of carving. This style in turn gives way to the freer forms in the central ridges of the quire, south transept and nave. The sculptor here allows the foliage to swirl and interlace, always in a clockwise direction. This more rhythmic treatment belongs, with the spandrel sculptures of the retroquire, to about 1240.

The Cathedral's bosses are not figurative in form, with three exceptions of a still later date. In a Cathedral lacking medieval heraldic decoration, one must remark on the fine armorial boss from the early 15th century in the second bay of the choir, east of the crossing. An elegant spread-winged angel, reminiscent of those carved on the Derbyshire alabaster tombs of the period, holds across its breast one of the coats of arms attributed to St Richard: (gules) a cross between four covered cups (argent).

Finally, two in the Canons' Vestry, later insertions in that location, belong to the late 14th century. They have been revealed recently, however (by Ralph Tireman, the CWO site supervisor), to be painted wood, not stone. Tim Tatton-Brown plausibly suggests they may be the misericord carvings from the two returned stalls removed during the quire restoration after the fall of the spire. The first is a curious composition of three female heads; the central one wears an ornamental head-band, a wimple and a veil which drapes, either side of her head, into the jaws of two beasts curled upside-down on her chest. The other heads wear Phrygian-peaked hats. The second 'boss' is also tripartite in form; here three human heads are part of a chimaera, on its shoulders, its rump and the end of its tail.

I *View of the Cathedral from the south east.*

SANCTVS WILFRIDVS

OPERIBVS CREDITE

II *The historical paintings by Lambert Barnard, now in the south transept: King Cædwalla of Wessex grants land at Selsey to St Wilfrid for his monastery, the traditional site of the new see, and (below) King Henry VIII gives Bishop Sherburne a formal confirmation of his bishopric.*

III *Remains of 12th-century frescoes on the west arch of the Treasury.*

IV *13th-century roundel in the Bishop's Chapel.*

The fire of 1187 also led to the rebuilding of the eastern arm of the Cathedral in a contemporary modern, that is, transitional Early English, style using Purbeck shafting from the ground level. The retroquire is finely proportioned, with the richest carving in the Cathedral; the huge composite Purbeck pillars with their graceful stiff-leaved capitals are in harmony with the foliate bosses. The decorative theme is continued in the spandrels of the triforia which contain fragments of gothic sculpture. At the same time these sculptures are an enigma.

There are seven sculptures, six of which are set in trefoil, quatrefoil and septfoil recesses in the triforium spandrels—two at the east and two in the adjoining north and south bays. The seventh is central at the east and appropriately so; it portrays Christ enthroned in majesty, seated on a corbel carved with two figures, between the two round-headed triforium arches.

Within the arches either side of Christ are rich, asymmetrical carvings. On the north side, under the soffits of the triforium, are processions of grotesque birds and other creatures, including an ape-like figure which appears to be urinating on the high altar! On the south side, the trefoiled spandrel is flanked by cloud-like foliage among which an open-winged monster clasps a book. From within the trefoil, a censing angel leans out and is balanced on the south side of Christ by another angel in a trefoil whose arms are broken.

On the southern triforium, from the east, is a crowned king enthroned within a septfoil, his hands broken off. To the west, in a trefoil, is a seated bare-headed man who stretches out his left hand to unfurl a scroll.

On the northern triforium, reading from the east, are three very mutilated figures in beautifully draped costume framed in a septfoil. The adjacent sexfoil contains a spread-winged angel holding a chalice.

The six sculptures, excluding Christ on his corbel, have been inserted into the stonework of their surrounds. This can readily be seen from ground level, where the stonework appears uneven around the figures. What cannot easily be detected from ground level is the amount of restoration that the sculptures have received and it is this that leads to misinterpretation of their meaning.

All commentators agree that, though the figures do not fit well into their foiled frames, they are basically very fine examples of 13th-century work. George Gordon thought he detected the work of at least two sculptors,[8] spanning the period between 1220 and 1280. Ian Nairn, who liked the French style of the drapes and felt that the sculptures complemented the rhythm of the retroquire, argued more acceptably for their insertion some time after 1240.[9]

How much of the sculpture is original, however? It is necessary to view them from triforium level: they are easily reached from the triforium with a long-handled implement and one can readily see how their heads and hands could have been smashed off by iconoclasts. In the case of Christ in Majesty, it would appear that the whole figure was knocked off its corbel, for the present one is not 13th-century work; nor are the rest of the heads nor the angels' wings. All these replacements must have been added either about 1818, when the Cathedral's painted vaults were scraped bare and there was much 'tidying', or when the galleries were removed in 1829, possibly inflicting further damage to the figures. The result was that a king's crowned head was fitted to a seated figure with bare feet and what now appears like a prophet with a scroll might well have been an apostle with a halo. Only one of the seven sculptures has not been restored—the one with the remains

29 *Thirteenth-century sculptures above the retroquire.*

of three figures on the north side—and it is not difficult to see why it was not touched. Quite simply the restorers could not understand what it represented. Gordon had no doubts; he considered the group represented the Marriage of the Lamb to His Bride or the Coronation of the Blessed Virgin Mary. He also offered a convoluted conjecture about the symbolism of the sculptures:

> The revelation to the Old Testament saints of the Gospel of the future, depicted by the King, who may be David or Solomon, an ancestor of Our Lord, and the Prophets, Isaiah, Jeremiah, who prophesied of the coming of the Saviour of Israel. The ministration of the Sacraments in the Choir, and at the Altar in the church, and the services sung there, [symbolise] plainly salvation in process of application to the redeemed.

The enigma of the sculptures must remain! They are too fragmentary to allow a feasible interpretation of their original iconography.

30 *The unrestored sculpture.*

Linked stylistically with the retroquire are the three porches at the west, south and north of the Cathedral. The earliest, most elegant and most interesting, sculpturally, is the south porch into the Cathedral from the cloisters. On its exterior face above the slender Purbeck trumeau is a large, recessed and elongated quatrefoil with a corbel of carved leaves at its base, almost identical to that in the centre of the retroquire which now supports Christ in Majesty and to others in the Bishop's private chapel. What figure originally occupied this recess is not known; its present occupant, St Richard, was carved by H. Hems in 1894. The tripartite capitals beneath this tympanum have crisp, stiff-leaved acanthus and, above the innermost, wide-mouthed grotesque masks as it were spew out the springer of the quadripartite vault within. The central boss is unremarkable but little sculptural details capture the eye at the base of the vault: a bearded and mustachioed head opposite a clean shaven one to the north, balanced by two half-human, half-animal creatures to the south. At first glance the elegant, Early-English blind arcading on the west wall of the porch appears to have finely detailed leaved capitals; closer inspection reveals that the second from the south is decorated with four geese.

The woodwork of the stalls (see fig.32a) had been dated to *c*.1330[10] until Charles Tracy, in a careful comparison of their architecture and carving with similar work at Exeter, Westminster and Winchester, attributed them to the episcopate of John Langton, between 1305 and 1320.[11] The original plan and structure of the stalls are incomplete and much restored. The return stalls were removed after the fall of the spire, the sub-stalls have been replaced by 19th-century work and of the original back stalls only 38 remain of what Tracy reckoned were originally forty-two. Each surviving back stall has a carved misericord beneath its seat and, together, these form rare survivals of Gothic wood carving in the Cathedral.

The misericords may not be among the most celebrated examples in England but they are notable for their robust if occasionally crude execution. Individually they lack fluidity and uniformity of style; for instance, the balancing motifs on either side of the backed seat—human, animals and monstrous heads, writhing creatures or simple leaf stops—effect little continuity of line between the bracket and the corbel beneath. One notable exception on the north side of the quire allows the ends of the bracket to scroll gracefully down and terminate in the heads of two roaring lions with a central lion's mask as the corbel. Otherwise the corbels portray human faces and forms with grotesque contortions or hybridisation with some animal or monster, as in the 'bosses' of the Canons' Vestry. Two brackets, one with a harpist and a flautist and the other with a fiddler and a dancing woman, are rare examples of human normality. Heads are arranged in twos and threes, as

31 *(left) St Richard's porch (drawing by George Scharf), showing the 13th-century bracket of leaves, the Romanesque blind arcading and the string course spouting from the mouth of an upturned grotesque (below left).*

32 *(below) Example of the dog's-head ending to the pinnacles of the choirstalls.*

33 *(facing page) Misericord carvings.*

on the roof-bosses and earlier corbel tables, and eight of the misericords are simple leaf studies, comparable with the more fluid of the foliate roof bosses. Otherwise there is a predominance of fantastic chimaerae, harpies and mythical monsters such as were illuminated in contemporary bestiaries. Beneath the seats of the stalls this menagerie represents an underworld of demonic creatures, squirming and clinging, often bat-like, to their ledges.

The stalls remain as part of a richly decorated eastern arm of the Cathedral which included a sumptuous Lady Chapel, erected about 1300 by Bishop Gilbert of St Leofard, and a retroquire embellished with the shrine of St Richard. The former, containing shrines and altars together with its founder's tomb, was desecrated about 1548 and again during the Civil War and remained ruinous until 1750. St Richard's shrine, which stood before the entrance to the Lady Chapel, was despoiled in 1538. Little now survives except pieces of the wrought-iron grill which may have formed part of the costly clausures made for the saint's relics in 1276. Two of the fragments, which had been later used for gates in the Arundel Screen, are now incorporated centrally in the Victorian gates of the Lady Chapel. They are composed of reticulated and collared quatrefoils.

The larger and more interesting survival of the Cathedral's 13th-century wrought-ironwork is now in the Victoria and Albert Museum.[12] It is a grill composed of eight, different-sized panels attached to a plain iron frame topped with a

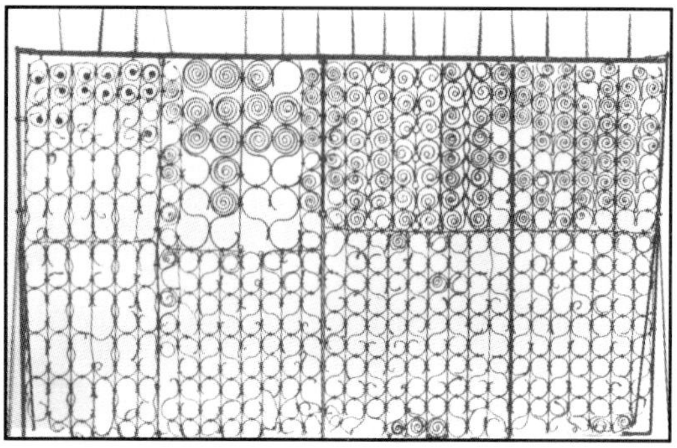

34 *Thirteenth-century ironwork grill, possibly from the shrine, now in the Victoria and Albert Museum.*

spiked rail. The panels are traceries of collared and addorsed Cs and Ss, together with Ys. These decorative elements are in turn clasped together and to vertical rails within the frame. The terminals of the Cs and Ss are curled and spiralled, tipped with a loop or stamped with a fleur-de-lys on either side.

This important surviving example of English wrought-ironwork must have been part of a scheme that was very delicate, varied and colourful (traces of red paint and gilding were still visible when the Museum acquired the grill). A similar example was recorded in Boxgrove Priory but has now vanished.[13]

The Cathedral would have been adorned with medieval stained glass, if not in the Norman window apertures then certainly in the Lady Chapel and in the 13th-century windows and the new, enlarged transept windows. Of this nothing remains, with the exception of one shield of arms in the south choir aisle above Bishop Sherburne's tomb. The coat has been attributed to Edward More, who was Archdeacon of Lewes and Warden of Winchester during Sherburne's episcopate.[14]

Indeed it is to Robert Sherburne we must look for the major artistic refurbishment of the Cathedral at what might be termed the close of the Middle Ages: the work began in the reign of Henry VIII and continued during the Reformation.

Sherburne (fig.21) was a prelate-diplomat, a scholar and man of taste, one of the contemporary bishops who followed Wolsey's lead as a patron of the arts. Like Wolsey, he embellished his palaces, in Amberley and Chichester, but unlike the Cardinal he spent much time and money beautifying the Cathedral where his monument was to be placed.

For this work Sherburne employed Lambert Barnard, who also worked in his palaces, at Boxgrove Priory and perhaps at Winchester. Whether Barnard was Flemish or French, an Englishman or a native of Chichester is not known. Certainly the style of his work is continental, but his use of distemper on wood and plaster rather than oil paint is an English technique and suggests that he may have been trained by the court painters of Henry VIII. Wherever he was born or trained, he gave the Cathedral a Netherlandish flavour in the painting he executed on its walls, columns, vaults and quire.[15]

George Vertue (1684-1756), the father of English art history, says that Barnard was painting in the Cathedral as early as 1519, but Edward Croft-Murray has suggested a date about 1535-6, towards the end of Sherburne's episcopate, which is confirmed by the Communar's Accounts (see Chapter IV). The bishop's biographical Latin epitaph, now in the south transept and painted by Barnard soon after his patron's death, records that 'he adorned his cathedral church at Chichester with much beauty'. Indeed the Accounts reveal that much of Barnard's work in the Cathedral after 1536 was paid for from Sherburne's bequest.

Barnard's most extensive work in the Cathedral was the painting of the plastered vaults. This was done in a Netherlandish fashion of accentuating each central boss within a medallion of distempered foliage, flowers and vine-scrolls. From this emanated four extended flourishes to fill the sections of each quadripartite bay. Among these branches were hung armorial shields and some branches bore mottoes or texts at their extremities.

35 *Lambert Barnard's painted vaulting: a bay of the Lady Chapel drawn by Thomas King.*

Only one such decorated roof bay, much faded and retouched, survives, in the Lady Chapel. It bears the Tudor badges of the red and white rose together with the pomegranate of Aragon. In one compartment appears the Wykehamist motto 'Manners makyth man'—Sherburne had been at Winchester and New College. The ghost of other painted bays can be detected on a wet day in the south nave aisle. However, some idea of the total effect may be gained from two drawings in the British Library—a view of the nave by S.H. Grimm in 1781 and a sketch from the south across both transepts by J. Buckler in 1862-63.[16] There is also an early 19th-century watercolour by Thomas King in the Cathedral Library depicting the vault of the quire looking west (Plate XVII). However, the best idea of Barnard's effect of a floral arbour can be gained by visiting neighbouring Boxgrove Priory, where he worked for Thomas, Lord de la Warr, c.1525-30.

The Cathedral's painted vaults were destroyed when the building was 'tidied up' in the early 19th century. James Dallaway, writing in 1817, declared that 'Sherburn's painted ceiling was destroyed, as it merited to be'.[17] *The Gentleman's Magazine* in 1829 reported that 'a Goth prevailed on the Chapter to whitewash the building'. Unluckily in most places the action seems to have been more drastic and the paintings appear to have been scraped off first.

Barnard's largest surviving works in the Cathedral were executed in distemper on oak boards in the south transept. They consisted of two 'history' paintings accompanied by

36 *S.H. Grimm's drawing of the nave with painted vaulting, 1781.*

portraits of the kings of England from William the Conqueror and the bishops of Selsey and Chichester from St Wilfrid (see Plate II and fig. 22). Most of this work survives, though it was vandalised in the 17th century, overpainted in the 18th and damaged and reorganised in the nineteenth.

The two large 'history' paintings concern the Cathedral and the see of Chichester; the first shows King Cædwalla of the West Saxons and Bishop Wilfrid of Selsey; the second depicts Henry VIII and Bishop Sherburne of Chichester. The theme is the establishment and continuation by royal authority of the see of Selsey which was replaced by that of Chichester. Interestingly, there is no acknowledgement of papal involvement in either.

These are propaganda pieces such as Henry VIII himself commissioned from Holbein and others to illustrate the claims and strengths of the Tudor monarchy. The first is curious in that Barnard sets the scene against a seascape including the last cathedral of Selsey, shown as part gothic, part renaissance in its architectural detail. St Wilfrid and his clerical officials are dressed in Tudor ecclesiastical vestments, the bishop wearing the red and ermine robe of a spiritual lord, his mitre and processional cross held by attendants. Cædwalla wears a Tudor crown, a collar of red roses and carries a Tudor sceptre. Behind him stands a royal official in lawyer's cap and robe whilst the courtiers wear fanciful renaissance garb and headgear. The episcopal and royal parties stand either side an elaborate renaissance column surmounted by St George slaying the dragon; at its base is the King's monkey engaged in cracking walnuts. Further bizarre decoration surrounds the plaque indicating 'Sanctus Wilfridus'. The Bishop addresses the King by way of a scroll bearing the words 'Da servis dei locū habitation' p[ro]pter Deum' ('Grant God's servants a dwelling place according to His will'). The King points to an open book bearing his reply, 'Fiat sicut petitur' ('Let the petition be granted'). Framed below the picture is an account in Latin of Wilfrid's life and work.

The companion picture balances it in almost every way; the two are like type and anti-type from the Old and New Testaments. This time the scene is set indoors against elaborate renaissance stalls. Sherburne and his party are attired like Wilfrid's and attendants hold his mitre and crozier. The Bishop is identified by his quartered arms on a gilded renaissance plinth and by his motto, 'Operibus Credite', on a framed plaque beneath his initials. The royal party stands beneath a tasselled canopy beside a luxuriant silver pedestal bearing the Plantagenet shield. Henry VIII wears a crown over a cap of maintenance, a collar and pendant of the Garter about his neck and a sword of justice at his hip. He is accompanied by his father, Henry VII, who was Sherburne's first patron, also crowned and wearing the Garter collar. A secretary carries the Great Seal and stands with the courtiers, again extravagantly dressed. Sherburne petitions the King in Latin, on a scroll which recalls the subject of the companion picture. Translated, it reads: 'Most sacred King on God's account confirm your church at Chichester, now the cathedral, as did Cædwalla, King of the South Saxons, with the Church at Selsey, once the cathedral'.

Henry VIII indicates his reply in an open book, 'For the love of Jesus Christ I grant your petition'. The panel giving Sherburne's biography in Latin appears beside his 'portrait' in Barnard's catalogue of the bishops of Selsey and Chichester, now in the north transept. Finally the two pictures described are drawn together by an overall Latin inscription acknowledging the King's early omnipotence and justice, 'All the kings of the earth shall acknowledge that you are the great king above all kings. Straight is the road which leads to life'.

These rare local and religious 'propaganda paintings' are accompanied by Barnard's medallion 'portraits' of the English kings from William the Conqueror. Each bears his name and the duration of his reign. These were painted, no doubt, to strengthen the idea of the continuity of the see and its royal protection. The painted kings, collared, crowned and sceptred, are typical of those which head so many contemporary genealogies. They are arranged in horizontal sequence like the 'ring pedigrees' that date from the 13th to the 17th centuries.[18] The bishops, similarly arranged and named, each in cope and mitre with crozier, owe even less to portraiture. Only George Day, Sherburne's successor, was added to this *cathalogus* and the whole sequence was originally displayed on the east wall of the south transept. John Buckler's drawing of 1812 shows it *in situ*.

These paintings by Barnard were abused by the parliamentary soldiers of Colonel Waller in 1642 and were considerably restored and overpainted by one Tremaine about 1747.[19] The fall of the Cathedral's spire in 1861 destroyed several of the kings' portraits including that of William the Conqueror.

Barnard carried out other decorative work in the Cathedral of which little remains. This was largely lettering, as in the painted frieze which was placed above the choir stalls, denoting the seats of the dignitaries. The only original fragment hangs now on the Treasury wall, with three labels denoting two residentiary canons and an archdeacon. The lettering is in gold gothic script on black; the serifs on the letters are flourished and interlaced in imitation of penmanship and the titles over each stall are separated by plain, vertical renaissance balusters. Today the choir stalls are topped with a faithful copy of Barnard's work in the style of this fragment.

Barnard continued working in the Cathedral after Sherburne's death and into the reign of Elizabeth. He died about 1567. Thus he experienced the changing demands of his patrons as the Reformation and new legislation put pressure on them to promote Protestantism, then revive Roman Catholicism and finally support the Elizabethan Settlement.

37 *Fragment of Barnard's original frieze above the choirstalls.*

The Chapter Accounts give some small insights into these developments. In 1543, for instance, Barnard was paid 'for removing the cloth of the Crucifixion in the middle of the high altar'. In 1561 he was paid for a replacement of the Ten Commandments painted on 6¼ ells of canvas. Both these changes presumably have their origins in the Injunctions issued by Thomas Cromwell in 1536 and again in 1538, which required, among other things, that images and shrines should be taken down and that the clergy should preach and teach from the new English Bible with particular emphasis on the Ten Commandments. This Henrician legislation was further endorsed in the reign of Edward VI by an Injunction concerning the Altar (1550) and the Act against Superstitions, Books and Images (1550). The last may have promoted the Dean and Chapter of Chichester to remove the rood screen in the Cathedral but in Mary's reign we find Barnard being paid for repainting the carved figures on the re-erected rood (1556). In 1558 further payments were made for his making and mending of the wings of two angels.

The Chapter Accounts also tell us that Barnard painted a clock in 1550 and some fragments of his black-letter texts from the English Bible survive on two of the nave piers. This non-figurative wall-painting, together with his Ten Commandments behind the altar, demonstrates the new ecclesiastical decoration that was to become the vogue in the Protestant Church.

Perhaps in this early period, the Reformers did not wreak the havoc and iconoclasm that has often been attributed to them. In the diocese of Chichester, at any rate, a report compiled in 1568 revealed that change was very slow and reluctant.[20] Many parishes concealed their old chalices, awaiting the return of the Mass, rather than profane them in administering Communion. Images were likewise hidden and many rood lofts were left standing ready for the replacement of the Crucifixion together with 'other popish ornaments ready to set up Mass again within twenty-four hours warning'. In Chichester Cathedral we are told that a painting of the Passion of Christ had been whitewashed over in the early 1580s, but 'some well-wishers of that way' rubbed at the whitewash so that 'it is almost as bright as ever it was'.[21]

The major desecration of the Cathedral was carried out at a stroke when the City of Chichester surrendered to the parliamentary commander, Colonel Waller, in 1642. Bruno Ryves, later Dean of Chichester, described what happened to Barnard's paintings on 30 December when the soldiers burst into the Cathedral:

> in the South cross Ile on the one side, the History of the Churches Foundation was very artificially pourtrayed, with the Pictures of the Kings of *England*; on the other side over against them are the Pictures of the Bishops as well of *Sealsey* as *Chichester*, began by *Robert Sherborn*, the 37 Bishop of that See, ... These Monuments they deface and mangle with their hands and swords, as high as they could reach: and to shew their love, and Zeal to the *Protestant Religion* established in the Church of *England*, one of those Miscreants picked out the eyes of King *Edward the sixth's* Picture, saying, *That all this mischief came from him, when he established the Book of Common-Prayer*.[22]

VI

THE DEAN AND CHAPTER 1570-1660

Andrew Foster

What were cathedrals for in the 16th and 17th centuries? What did they, or rather their deans and chapters, do? How was that work perceived by their contemporaries and how should we judge success or failure? Such blunt questions smack of current debates concerning the Church in the 20th century, but they also have great relevance when applied to the past. The existence of cathedrals as mother churches of their dioceses (and often, like Winchester, the homes of monastic foundations) had been taken for granted before the Reformation, but given Puritan doubts about the structure of the Elizabethan Church, it is remarkable that the cathedrals survived relatively unscathed until the 1640s. In Puritan literature of the day, cathedrals were either seen as dens of thieves—over-staffed with idle clergy who consumed valuable resources—or they were centres of crypto-Catholic worship, where music and superstitious rituals overshadowed vital preaching.[1] Given that cathedrals certainly were great centres of privilege, it is indeed remarkable that they not only survived until the 1640s, but gained re-instatement with the rest of the Church of England, in 1660. This testifies to the strength of vested interests, both clerical and lay, but it also suggests that we would do well to investigate closely the many valuable functions performed by cathedrals during this period.

Dividing the 'early modern' section of this book at 1570 has enabled John Fines to draw attention to often neglected continuities between the pre- and post-Reformation Church. He has offered clues as to how cathedrals survived the first phases of the Reformation and has set the scene for the consolidation to come. 1570 happened to witness a flurry of activity, as an energetic dean, Richard Curteys, was promoted to bishop of Chichester diocese and factions were organised to constrain his influence on the Cathedral. The new Dean Rushe was soon pressurised into agreeing to regulations which severely restricted influence in the Chapter to a small oligarchy of residentiary canons, truly the 'Masters of the Church' as they were known.[2] The Chapter which ruled after 1570 and was returned to power on the Restoration was a tightly-knit body which to protect itself developed clearer rules of procedure than ever before. It is useful to take the story through to 1660, because the Restoration—as the label suggests—virtually marked the re-establishment of the Church of England. This was certainly so at Chichester, for although 22 members of the Chapter lived to see the Restoration, eight had never been formally installed before 1660, two had converted to Catholicism while in exile on the continent, one was instantly promoted to another cathedral, one had resigned his post long before, and four promptly died in all the excitements of 1660. That year was clearly an *annus mirabilis* in the Cathedral's history.[3]

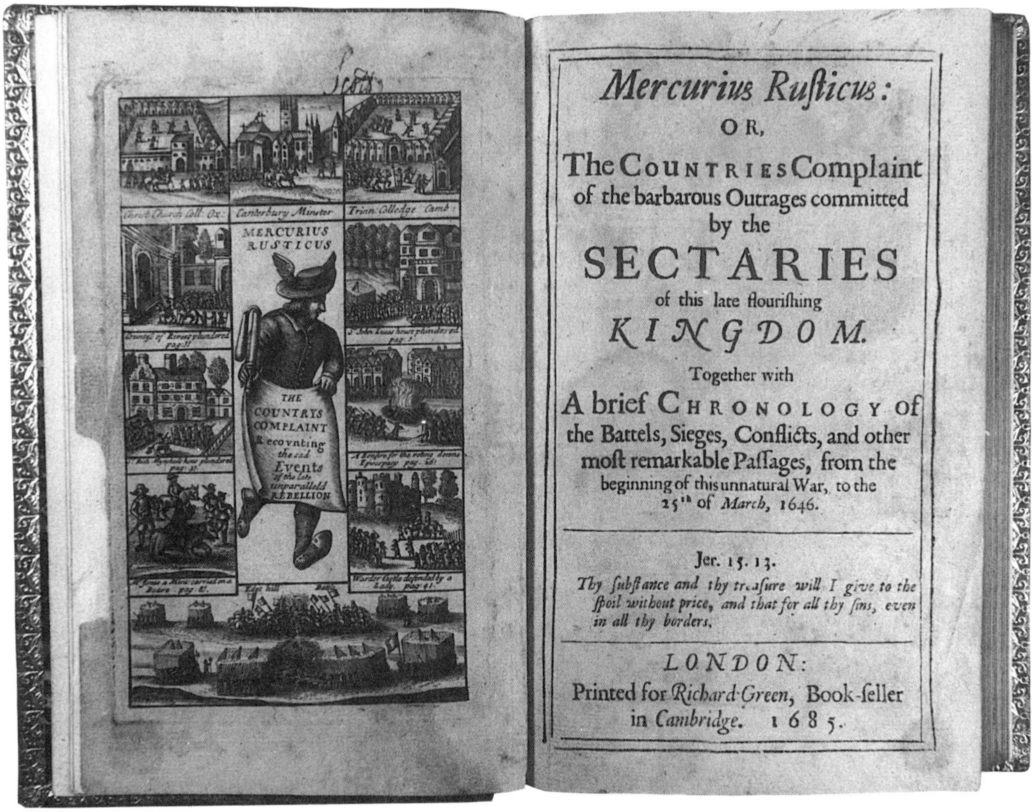

38a *Title page of Dean Bruno Ryves' description of the 'Barbarous outrages' committed by the Parliamentarian troops.*

The Cathedral Chapter had survived the vicissitudes of the Reformation relatively unscathed. It had its four main dignitaries in the persons of the dean, treasurer, precentor and chancellor, 27 prebends—not counting Oving which had been attached to the precentorship, and Henfield which had been annexed to the see of Chichester before the Reformation (belatedly confirmed by a test appointment in 1627)—and the four Wiccamical prebends of Bishop Sherburne's foundation.[4] This figure includes the Highleigh prebend, even though that was held by masters of the school who were not necessarily in clerical orders and who were not entitled to become residentiary canons.[5] The two archdeacons of Chichester and Lewes have only been taken into account when they were also members of the Chapter, something not achieved by five of the 19 archdeacons who held office during this period, even if they may have been familiar visitors to the Palace and Close.[6] The position of the Chapter as a whole was simplified in 1618 when the four Wiccamical posts were recognised as full prebends.[7] A complete Dean and Chapter was thus a comparatively large establishment for the day, theoretically comprising 35 individuals, not counting the two archdeacons or the vicars choral. At its best, this meant that the Cathedral offered relatively wealthy prebends to attract the service of about 30 scholars and preachers in the diocese at large; at worst, these became sinecures for already wealthy, non-resident pluralists.

As Alison McCann reveals below, the historian of this period can turn to a fair selection of source materials: a full run of Chapter minutes up to 1641, a superb set of

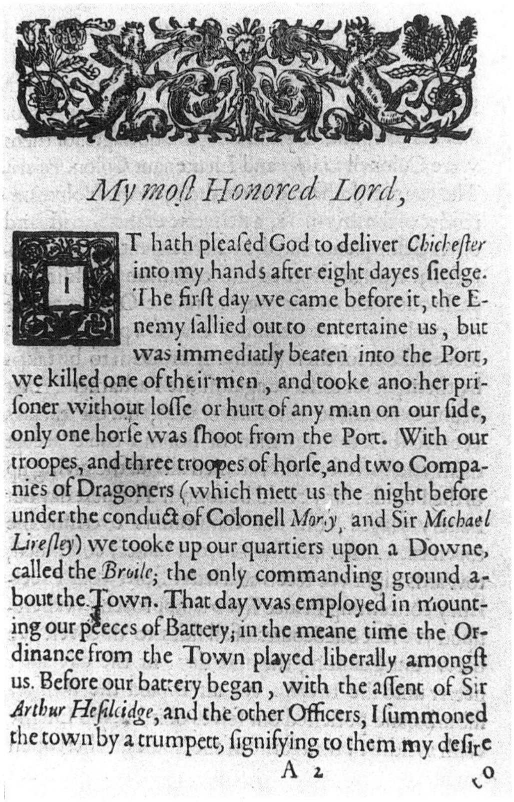

My most Honored Lord,

IT hath pleased God to deliver *Chichester* into my hands after eight dayes siedge. The first day we came before it, the Enemy sallied out to entertaine us, but was immediatly beaten into the Port, we killed one of their men, and tooke another prisoner without losse or hurt of any man on our side, only one horse was shoot from the Port. With our troopes, and three troopes of horse, and two Companies of Dragoners (which mett us the night before under the conduct of Colonell *Mor.y*, and Sir *Michael Livesley*) we tooke up our quarters upon a Downe, called the *Broile*; the only commanding ground about the Town. That day was employed in mounting our peeces of Battery; in the meane time the Ordinance from the Town played liberally amongst us. Before our battery began, with the assent of Sir *Arthur Hesilrige*, and the other Officers, I summoned the town by a trumpett, signifying to them my desire

A 2 to

38b *Sir William Waller's letter to Cromwell announcing his capture of Chichester.*

Communars' Accounts to the same date, and a good supply of lease books and miscellaneous papers.[8] There are always tantalising gaps, of course, notably when it comes to the survival of visitation material. And full though some of the records might appear to be, they reveal much more about routine administration than they do about personalities and conflicts behind policies pursued within the Close. All cathedrals yield little for the period 1646-60, when deans and chapters had been voted out of existence and their revenues were employed to support a wide range of preaching initiatives. Nevertheless, it does not seem unduly rash to claim that Chichester possesses a set of capitular records for this period amongst the best in the country.[9]

The Cathedral itself was one of the smallest, described by Camden in the 1580s as 'not very large, but extreamely neat'.[10] Camden was impressed by the paintings of monarchs and bishops commissioned by Bishop Sherburne which today adorn both transepts. The Reformation was slow to take effect in this diocese. Even in the Cathedral, it was as late as 1586 that it was reported that a recently whitewashed painting of Christ's passion had been restored: 'since that time some well-wishers of that way (as there are too many) have taken some pains that it is almost as bright as ever it was'. Moreover, there were 'monstrous and idolatrous monuments in the High Cross' and 'the common people are used to reverence unto them'.[11] Old habits died hard. Many people could still remember the changes of the 1540s and '50s and may have secretly hoped for a return to the old faith. Will bequests still mentioned gifts to the mother church of St Richard.[12] The very location of Chichester in the Catholic stronghold of west Sussex, adjacent to the Hampshire border and yet more influential Catholic gentry, made it hard to throw off old allegiances. Key families like the Brownes, the Shelleys and the Gages provided the recusant leadership of this region. It was in this context that Richard Curteys strove to carry out Protestant evangelism, not always eagerly assisted by his colleagues in the Close.[13]

In the 17th century, visitors picked out problems of neglect rather than undue reverence. One Lieutenant Hammond, who toured many cathedrals in the 1630s, noted that Chichester Cathedral was 'not very large, but reasonable fair; her Organs small, and voices but indifferent'. He also noticed that 'the monuments in her are not many nor rich, but ancient and plain'.[14] In 1635, while carrying out Archbishop Laud's metropolitical visitation, Sir Nathaniel Brent reported that the Cathedral was 'somewhat out of repair, especially one tower'.[15] This was the north-west tower and in 1636 a large part of it came crashing down.

(This can clearly be seen in fig.68.) A contemporary estimate put the cost of repairs at close to £3,500, a very large sum for the times, so it is perhaps not surprising that nothing substantial was undertaken until as late as 1901.[16] The Communars' Accounts reveal an average expenditure of about £30 per annum on routine maintenance of the Cathedral throughout this period. £79 was spent in 1592 and £87 in 1635, but these high points do not alter the impression that little out of the ordinary was done.[17] Indeed, it may yet turn out that less was spent on maintaining Chichester Cathedral than on most other cathedrals in this period.

This image of long-term neglect should be borne in mind when reading descriptions of the notorious sacking of the Cathedral in December 1642 provided for us by Bruno Ryves in *Mercurius Rusticus*. Ryves claimed that:

> ... their first business [the rebels] was to plunder the Cathedral Church; the Marshal therefore and some other Officers having entred the Church went unto the Vestery, there they seize upon the Vestments and ornaments of the Church, together with the Consecrated Plate, serving for the Altar, and administration of the Lords Supper; they left not so much as a Cushion for the Pulpit, nor a Chalice for the Blessed Sacrament: the Commanders having in person executed the *covetous part* of Sacrilege, they leave the *destructive* and *spoyling part* to be finished by the Common Soldiers: ... They break the Rail about the Communion-Table, which was done with that fury, that the Table itself escaped not their madness, but tasted of the same fare with the Rail, and was broken in pieces by them.[18]

Books, vestments, pictures and monuments were apparently destroyed or defaced by an almost mutinous rabble of soldiers, all while their commanders looked on with unconcern. It is a black picture, but it comes from a very prejudiced source and recent research on the Civil War suggests that the harm

39a *The Chapter House, with the secret door behind which Sir Arthur Haselrigg's men found the Cathedral silver.*

carried out in cathedrals was significantly less than has often been supposed.[19] It has always been too easy to blame Cromwell's soldiers for damage caused to churches in the 17th century, but, while cathedrals were clearly neglected between 1646 and 1660, the major structural problems at Chichester stemmed at least from the 1630s.

The gift of the deanery was in the hands of the Crown, but virtually all of the prebends were at the disposal of the Bishop of Chichester. Highleigh and Bargham were in the hands of the Dean and Chapter, and appointments to all four Wiccamical prebends were technically restricted to members of New College, Oxford.[20] In theory, this gave the Bishop considerable power in the Close but, in practice, a Dean and Chapter once formed constituted an hotly defended island of privilege. It is possible to argue that they became steadily more insular in outlook as the period progressed. Bishop Curteys may have had grand plans to use Chapter clergy—and revenues—in his campaign to spread the Protestant word more effectively in his diocese, but they were baulked in 1573 when he was forced to sign new regulations concerning the operation of the Chapter, which gave greater power and wealth to the residentiary canons than ever before. Set dates in October, January, May and August were established for the sealing of leases, none was to be admitted to residence without a clear majority and the consent of the Dean; in the absence of the Dean, the senior residentiary canon—revealingly styled the President—would take charge of affairs.[21] In 1575 these orders were clarified and extended, confirming the power of the residentiary canons and limiting their number to four; they were aptly described as the Masters of the Church for they took precedence even over the dignitaries of the Cathedral.[22] They were entitled to a share in all surplus funds, which generally amounted to a total of £120 per annum in the late 16th century and rose to an average of £155 per annum in the early 17th

39b *The door opened.*

40 *Bishop Thomas Bickley, from his memorial.*

century. Only when Cathedral maintenance costs rose sharply in the 1630s did the surplus dwindle to around £60 per annum.[23]

Bishop Curteys made strenuous efforts to impose his will on the Dean and Chapter, but his zealous temperament had already alienated conservatives during his time as dean. Nearly half the total of all resignations of prebendaries over this period occurred in the 1570s, which may be one intriguing testimony to his efforts! Yet even though he was able to make more appointments than any other bishop of this period, Curteys still found it difficult to make real inroads into the administration of the Cathedral itself. He was not helped by the fact that his successor as dean, Anthony Rushe, held lucrative church preferments at Windsor and Canterbury, which distracted his attention from Chichester. Curteys should have been aided by the nomination of the new Archdeacon of Lewes, Thomas Drante, for residence in March 1570, on account of his splendid record for preaching and scholarship. Yet when Drante came formally to be admitted, it was strictly on condition that he was 'not to meddle in Chapter business'.[24] Just days before the formal election of Curteys as Bishop, the rival conservative factions had mobilised to seize control of key Cathedral positions, the coup being ratified on 15 April when they admitted Henry Worley, William Clarke, Thomas Willoughby and Francis Cox to residence in one group 'to deal with the more weighty business of the Church'. This represented game, set and match to the Chapter and ensured that the unpopular Curteys failed in his efforts to control Cathedral policy.[25]

Bishop Bickley, a distinguished warden of Merton College, Oxford and another fervent Protestant, succeeded Curteys at Chichester in 1586. He too, questioned the tight-knit nature of the Dean and Chapter, but was fobbed off with assurances that it was better to have such rules than be dictated to on the whim of a particular dean. He was informed

V *Lambert Barnard's Lady Chapel ceiling, carefully restored, with a scroll bearing the Wykehamist motto, 'Maners Makyth Man', described in early Cathedral guides as recurring in many other places on the vaulting. The 19th-century 'pious pelican' lectern can be seen in the circle left for it on the contemporary tiled floor.*

VI *Part of Barnard's similar work on the vaulting of Boxgrove Priory (also restored).*

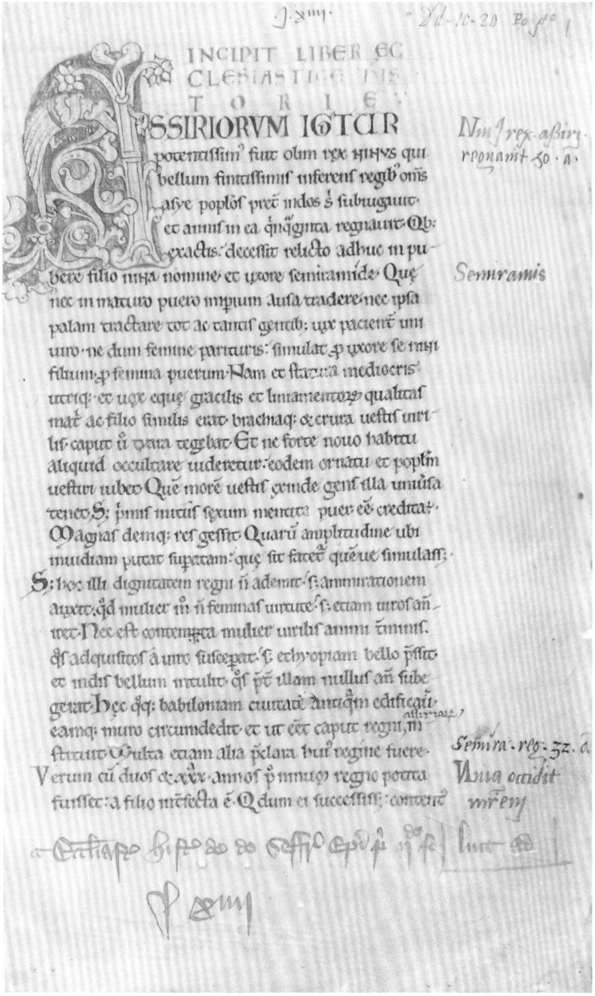

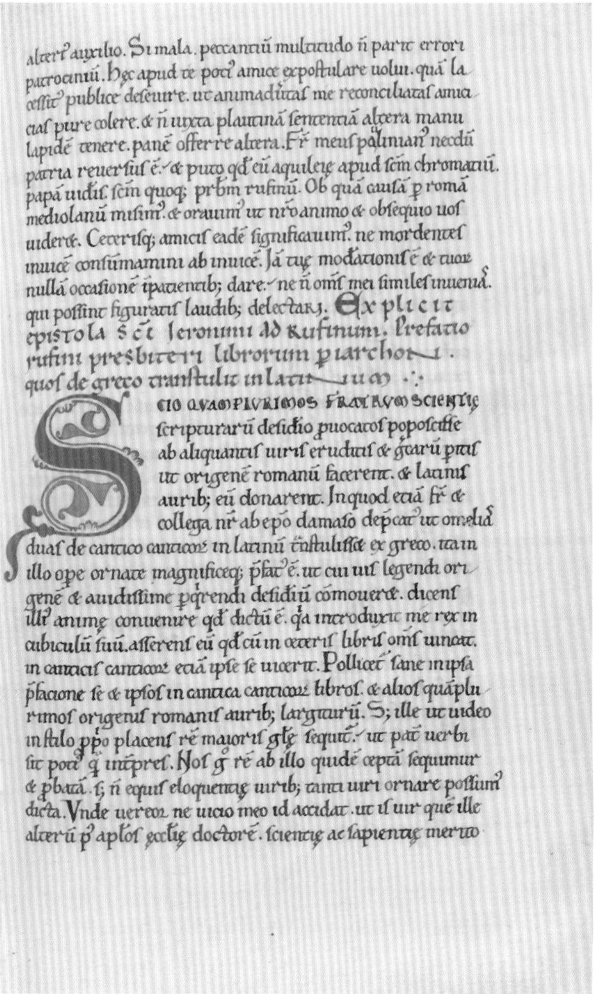

VII *(above left) The first page of a 12th-century copy of Hugo Floriacensis (Cambridge University Library MS Dd.10.20), showing (top) a 14th-century shelf mark (I.xiiii) and at the bottom, an inscription naming Bishop Seffrid as donor, found on several former Chichester MSS; also an illuminated initial influenced by Celtic design.*

VIII *(above centre) Page from St Jerome,* Contra Rufinum *(Emmanuel College Library, Cambridge, MS 25, fol.36) showing the red and green arabesque-type initials found on others of the 12th-century Chichester MSS.*

IX *(above right) Page from a 13th-century Boethius* de Trinitate, *(Emmanuel Coll. Library MS 28, fol.4), in a hand similar to that of Plate X, with characteristic red and blue initials.*

X *(right) MS of St Augustine in the Cathedral Library, possibly listed in the* Old Catalogue *(perhaps, therefore, an original Chichester volume). The page, in process of restoration by Douglas East, shows how the poor quality of the skin has obliged the scribe to write round holes.*

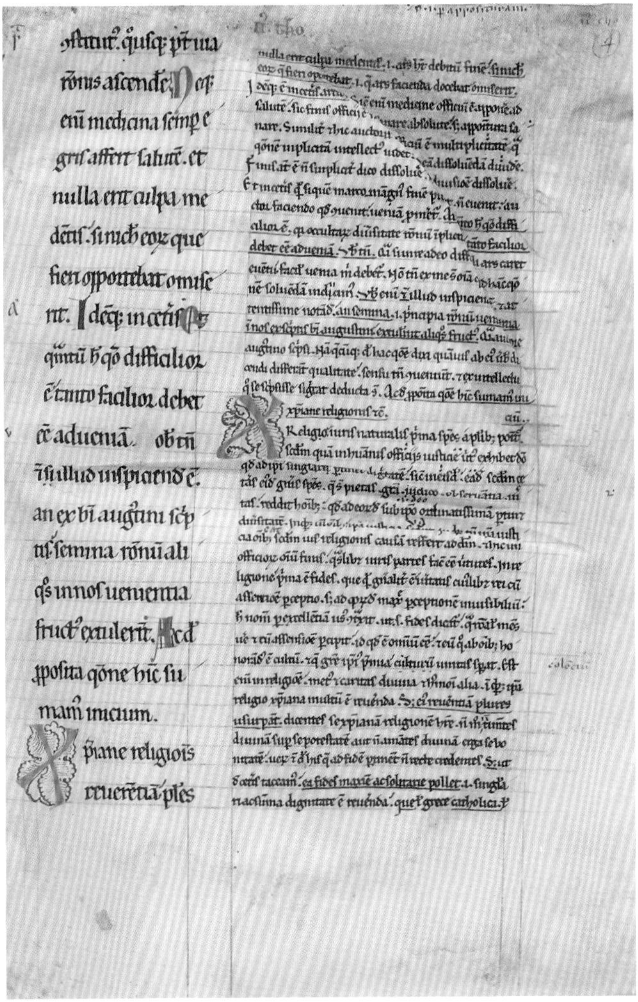

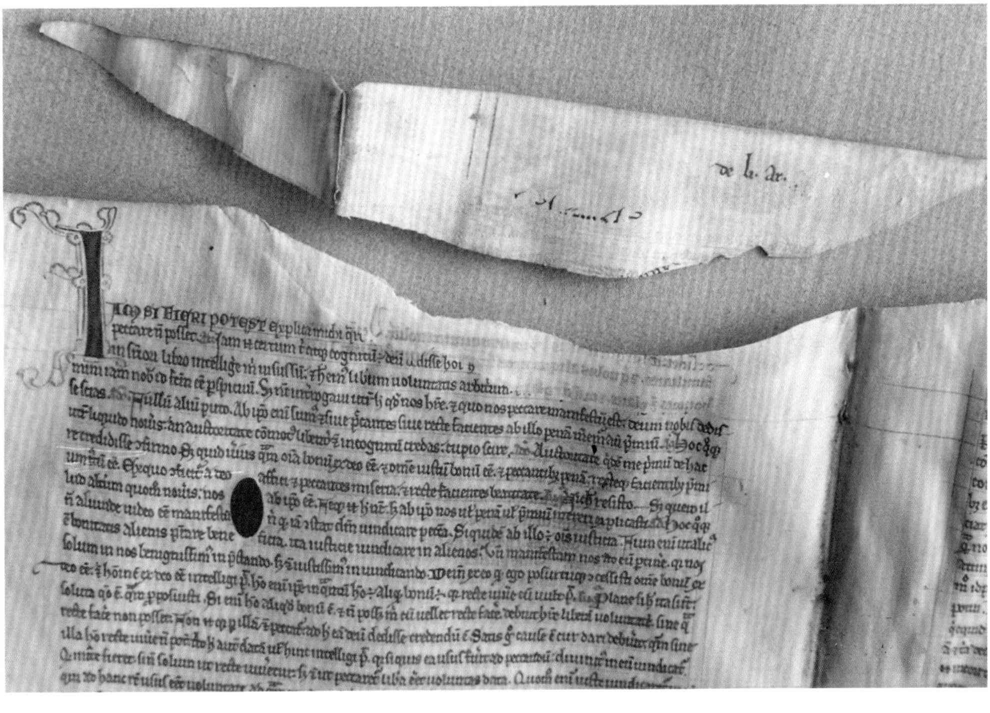

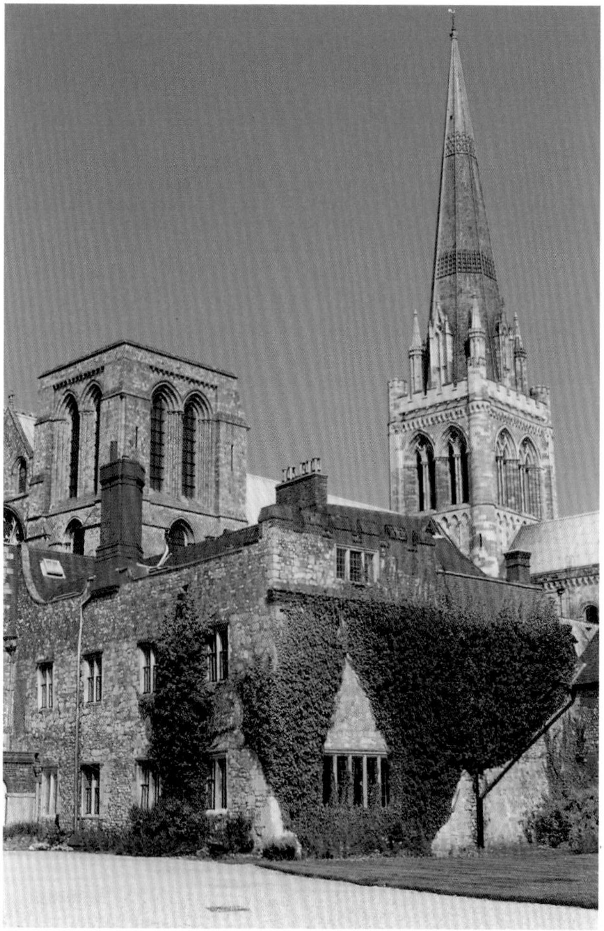

XI *The Palace: the south-east wing, with the Cathedral beyond.*

XII *(below left) Thomas Bickley, Bishop 1585-96 (portrait acquired for the Bishop from his descendants by Geoffrey Parks and restored by Joy Woolley).*

XIII *(below right) Lancelot Andrewes, Bishop 1605-9 (portrait in the Palace).*

that Dean Rushe was in the habit of attempting to carry out business 'when most of the Residentiaries were from home and drawing one or two into his Faction, to grant and confirm with the Chapter Seal what he would'. There were unseemly stories of chest locks being picked as rival groups sought to gain access to Cathedral documents![26] Later bishops also attempted to investigate Cathedral affairs, but with equal lack of success. Initially the rivalries between Palace and Close seem to have concerned a lack of synchronisation between the efforts of Protestant reforming bishops and a more conservative Dean and Chapter; there was later a degree of harmony so long as Cathedral interests were respected. Over the latter part of the period the Chapter had to deal with a marked tightening of discipline, as Arminian bishops with High Church leanings exerted their influence. Whichever the case, it looks as if bishops and the Cathedral Chapter were frequently at loggerheads with each other. Of the nine bishops who served the diocese between 1570 and 1660, only Richard Curteys, Samuel Harsnett and possibly George Carleton and Richard Montagu seem to have had much impact on life in the Cathedral Close.[27] At least Henry King actually lived in the Palace close by—most of his predecessors seem to have preferred the better air at Amberley or Aldingbourne.[28]

41 *Bishop George Carleton.*

Samuel Harsnett, who was Bishop of Chichester between 1609 and 1619, was something of a bully, an individual fond of hectoring his flock, somewhat similar in temperament, if not theological inclinations, to Curteys.[29] As a member of the Arminian faction within the Church of England he had strong views on the nature of worship. Thus he set himself to attempt to reform the admittedly low standards which prevailed within the Cathedral, where some of the vicars choral had a reputation for bowling and brawling rather than for singing. In a series of orders in 1611, 1614 and 1616—all made following visitations—Harsnett tried to compel the canons of Bishop Sherburne's foundation to keep residence, tried to ensure more seemly conduct of worship, introduced penalties for those departing the Cathedral during times of service, established tests for the choristers and laid down rules concerning the work of the choirmaster and, perhaps most significant of all—given the apparently deplorable standards of the times—

attempted to curb the drinking excesses of members of the Cathedral Close, chiefly the vicars choral.[30] Several of these people actually owned or ran alehouses, and as even his most gifted organist and choirmaster, Thomas Weelkes, was found guilty of various offences while drunk, it is hardly surprising that an exasperated tone entered into Harsnett's later visitation articles, when he pointedly enquired whether anything had been reformed in the last six years![31]

Surviving records of later visitations reveal that constant pressure was required to maintain standards in the Cathedral. Few of the statutes were not broken in Bishop Carleton's days, when even the requirement on the canons residentiary to preach regularly was not always kept. John Cradock confessed in 1622 that 'most of the dignitaries and best prebends seldom or never preach in their own persons',[32] which perhaps explains the rancour of Bishop Montagu in 1632 when he complained of William Hicks for sending substitutes 'whom he can get, sometimes good sometimes bad, any riff-raff, whom he can light upon, shifters, unconformicants, curates, young boys, puritans, as the whole city hath often spoken against it'.[33] Laud's busy Vicar-General, Sir Nathaniel Brent, also tried to give orders for reform arising out of the metropolitical visitation in 1635, noting 'divers things for reverence in the church which before were not observed'. This included compelling members of the congregation to remove their hats in time of divine service, something that even some aldermen had to be spoken to about. Brent was concerned that greater respect should be shown during times of service; he spotted the lack of copes, but accepted that 'the choir is well furnished, though their allowance be small'.[34]

The picture which has emerged thus far is of a cathedral 'corporation' quietly running its own business, occasionally troubled by the antics of a rather zealous bishop. It is not a bad image to keep in mind, for the Chapter controlled extensive estates, including about a third to half of Chichester, and managed a business with a turnover of approximately £500 per annum.[35] Its chief officer, namely the Dean, took a salary of roughly £60 per annum, a figure actually exceeded by the Treasurer. The wealthiest prebends, like Woodhorn and Wightring, yielded their incumbents approximately £20 per annum.[36] And these are nominal figures, for it is impossible to calculate what these clergymen really earned from their estates and dues, not forgetting that those who also served as canons residentiary received a share of the considerable common profits made each year. It is hardly surprising that Cathedral posts were seen as highly desirable billets by clergymen of this period, and also apt targets for reform in the 1640s.

★ ★ ★ ★ ★

What kind of men came to serve the Chapter between 1570 and 1660? Should we see them as careerists and high-fliers on their way to high office in the Church? Were they local clergymen made good? Were they a more distinguished bunch of clergymen than their parish counterparts? How many of them actually contributed much to the life of this Cathedral? 202 individuals served as members of the Chapter between 1570 and 1660. (The 26 who served as dignitaries of the Cathedral, together with another 28 canons residentiary receive closer attention later.[37])

In characterising the group as a whole, we are dealing with highly educated people. 161 or approximately 80 per cent of the group held degrees, usually several, leaving only 41 unaccounted for, all but one of whom were 16th-century appointments. This supports the findings of scholars concerning the raising of educational standards of clergy during this period and suggests that Chichester Cathedral was in the vanguard of such developments.[38] Cathedrals had always been havens of scholars, however, and even before the Reformation it would probably be safe to assume that they contained a high proportion of graduates.[39] Oxford scholars predominated with 91 of the graduates so far known, while Cambridge accounts for 65 graduates. Given this diocese's long-standing links with New College, Oxford, it is hardly surprising to find scholars from that college topping the list with 20 of our Chichester personnel, but Christ Church came a close second with 15, with Merton and Magdalen next with nine apiece. Scholars from 21 Oxford colleges were represented on Chichester Chapter within the period. Cambridge colleges were less well represented in our list—12 in all—and significant numbers of graduates came from only three colleges, St John's with 15, Trinity and Pembroke 10 apiece. Technically, the four Wiccamical prebends founded by Bishop Sherburne (*c.*1524), had to take scholars either from his old Winchester College, or New College, Oxford. The figures above suggest that Curteys made good use of his old connections at St John's College, Cambridge when making appointments, while the same could be said of Bickley with Merton, Andrewes and Harsnett with Pembroke, and Duppa and King with Christ Church, Oxford.[40]

42 *Archbishop William Juxon, formerly High Steward to the Dean and Chapter.*

The image of a well-educated Chapter should not be exaggerated, however, for, although Chichester included in its midst the usual sprinkling of Oxbridge Fellows, the odd Master of a college, and some famous writers, philosophers and mathematicians, it is almost as if the more famous they were, the less likely they were to spend time at Chichester! It is also the case that some of the best examples of scholars appointed to Chichester, like the Oxford Professor of Philosophy, Edward Fulham, the theologian John Gregory, and the mathematician, William Oughtred, all come from the 1640s, when they had scant opportunity to visit Chichester because of the Civil War. There were, of course, notable exceptions. In the late 16th century, the medical Doctor Martin Culpepper was Warden of New College, Oxford while also Dean of Chichester. Jerome Beale, the

Wightring prebendary between 1609 and 1620, achieved fame in the 1630s as Master of Pembroke College, Cambridge. Christopher Potter served as Chichester's precentor after 1631, when he was also Provost of Queen's College, Oxford. Yet these examples still beg the question as to how much time famous clergymen of the period might devote to Chichester. We are perhaps on safer ground when we turn to a few of the illustrious civil lawyers who held office here, for proximity to London seems to have helped Chichester to attract the services of 17 such people. William Clarke was one time Regius Professor of Law at Cambridge; Edmund Weston, John Beacon, Henry Worley and John Drury all held office as Chancellor of Chichester diocese, often combined with influential posts in London.[41]

Undoubtedly Chichester's most famous son in this period was William Juxon.[42] Both his father and a brother served as Cathedral registrar, while William himself was educated locally at the Cathedral School before also taking up civil law. He went on to a career in the Church which took him eventually to Canterbury after the Restoration. He was the loyal chaplain who attended Charles I to the scaffold in 1649. Such was the Chapter's pride in his achievements and awareness of his political clout, that they happily made Juxon—when he was merely President of St John's College, Oxford and Dean of Worcester—Principal Steward of their properties on the death of the Earl of Pembroke in 1630.[43] It was a shrewd decision, since Juxon stood at the right hand of Archbishop Laud and came to hold the influential job of Lord Treasurer of England in 1636. Juxon might have thought of Chichester more than many, but one could hardly expect this busy man to exercise much influence in the Close as prebendary of Mardon between 1622 and 1633.

43 *Richard Neile, Archbishop of York; Cathedral Treasurer, 1598-1610.*

Dean William Thorne was probably the only really distinguished scholar who devoted much attention to Chichester Chapter affairs. A Fellow of New College, Oxford and Regius Professor of Hebrew at Oxford between 1598 and 1604, Thorne devoted himself quite assiduously to his work as Dean of Chichester between 1601 and his death in 1630. He is possibly the dean who made most impact on the Cathedral during this period, although uncharitable voices might note that, while he attended more meetings than many, as with many an academic, little actually came of such deliberations. He may have thrown himself into his work at Chichester precisely because an otherwise illustrious career had already been blighted! Yet he did have influential backers like the Bishop of London who still urged his promotion in 1606.[44] Other notable scholars included Thomas Lockey, prebendary of Thorney between 1639-42, who went on to become Librarian of the Bodleian in Oxford after 1660.[45] Thomas Drante, the archdeacon already spoken of, was a fine poet and translator who had worked closely with Edmund Grindal—hence perhaps his strong reputation for preaching. Dean Richard Steward was also a fine theologian who dared to defend episcopacy at the Uxbridge Conference in 1645. Yet it remains broadly true to say that, although Chichester Chapter embraced educated clergymen, it held few of real distinction, and therefore—perhaps not surprisingly—few who went on to enjoy illustrious careers within the Church of England. This picture contrasts sharply with that drawn by Professor Fines for the earlier 16th century, when Chichester was part of a European theological establishment.

In common with all cathedrals, a small band of theologians undeniably used a Chichester living as a perquisite, just passing through on their way to better things. This was most obviously the case with Richard Neile, who has the dubious distinction of serving as treasurer of the Cathedral between 1598 and 1610, despite the fact that he hardly ever set foot in the place. For at least 67 people, a Chichester living proved to be a temporary platform to higher things, and one which may have rarely troubled them to visit the city. It is as significant, however, that, for at least 80 of the 202 Chapter members, a Chichester prebend represented the peak of their career. Far from Chichester Cathedral being used as a temporary training ground to groom selected clergy for better things, it may have actually provided genuine and much coveted honours for able clergymen in the region.

This picture of Chichester as a rather sleepy backwater is confirmed when one looks closely at those who gained high office in the Church. While the diocese may have been seen as ideal for the induction of newly consecrated bishops in this period, relatively few members of the Chapter were elevated to episcopal office.[46] Only eight gained episcopal appointments, a much smaller proportion than during the early 16th century. Of the Elizabethan appointments, Richard Curteys gained Chichester, William Bradbridge became Bishop of Exeter in 1571, and the hard-working William Overton gained Lichfield and Coventry in 1580. All these three had impeccable Calvinist credentials, but the three who came next before 1640 were all of the minority Arminian wing of the Church. These were Richard Neile, the most complete careerist the Church of England has produced, who ran through six dioceses in his life;[47] William Juxon who gained London in 1633; and Francis Dee who was promoted to Peterborough in 1634. Two appointments made after the Restoration complete the group of eight: in 1663 Joseph Henshaw went to Peterborough and William Paule moved to Oxford.[48]

At least 132 people, or approximately 65 per cent of the group, died in post here, which also serves to underline the insularity of Chichester. It represents something of a double-edged comment on their character and ability, for it either suggests the ultimate in commitment to this region or an inability to gain promotion![49] It would be interesting to discover in which period Chichester was most heavily involved in the life of the Church as a whole and when members of its Chapter were most mobile. In many ways, of course, this analysis is as deceptive as it is cold-blooded; it assumes that all members of the Chapter played a full and equal part in the life of the Cathedral during this period. The existence of such a group as the Masters of the Church clearly shows this was not the case; it was this oligarchy which really controlled Chichester Cathedral between 1570 and the 1640s.

★ ★ ★ ★ ★

A total of 26 clerics served as dignitaries of the Cathedral during this period; 28 other individuals were canons residentiary. In fact, when scrutinising the careers of these people, we can probably reduce still further the number who really counted. Of the eight deans who served between 1570 and 1660, only three may have actually exercised much clout: Richard Curteys, who promptly became Bishop, Martin Culpepper MD, who served between 1577 and 1601, and the scholarly William Thorne, who served for 29 years before his death in 1630. Some might claim that Francis Dee was influential during his short period of office between 1630 and 1634, if only because he engineered the removal of some notorious vicars choral, but certainly, of the other four, there is scant evidence that they ever became heavily involved in Chichester affairs and, of course, a large question-mark hangs over Culpepper too, who served as Warden of New College, Oxford for most of his time as Dean.[50] It has been wryly remarked that, while deans have large responsibilities—and may possess some influence—they are seldom blessed with real power and authority in the complicated politics of the Close![51]

It is the same story when one turns to other office-holders. Of eight precentors during this period, three gave long service over 15 years: Thomas Willoughby, Henry Ball, and Thomas Murriell, but only Ball served as an important residentiary canon, thanks to the influence of his friend Bishop Bickley.[52] And Willoughby should in theory at least have been more concerned with his post as Dean of Rochester, while Murriell became Archdeacon of Norfolk during his time as precentor. If we are to believe the extravagant praise on his Cathedral monument, the passing of Ball was genuinely lamented, for he was 'to the poor a father; solace to the sick, and to these walls, alas, deservedly a pride'.[53] There is little evidence of much involvement in Chichester affairs of the other five precentors.

The tale gets worse when one looks at the treasurers, the most highly paid officers of the Chapter at £62 6s. 8d. Four people held this office—all providing suspiciously lengthy service, of course (with the communars obviously doing the real work of keeping finances in order). William Overton was probably the most conscientious, before he gained promotion in 1580. Stephen Chatfield was really more fully engaged as Master of Kingston-on-Thames Grammar School, where he was also the vicar. Richard Neile was busy pursuing a lucrative career in the Church which took him steadily from Dean of Westminster to Archbishop of York. It looks as if he only visited Chichester on one occasion, and that was when his half-brother and successor as treasurer, Robert Newell, first petitioned for a residentiary position in 1611.[54] There is no evidence that Newell ever took much part in Chapter affairs either, but he held on to the lucrative treasurership until his death in 1642!

It was the same with the chancellors. Of six people, three became residentiary canons and gave lengthy service in the post: William Bradbridge, Henry Blaxton and the ubiquitous Roger Andrewes, brother of the more famous Lancelot (see Plate XIII). Roger Andrewes is often cited as a classic example of nepotism and pluralism during this period, and indeed he held a range of offices at Chichester, including the chancellorship, the Wightring prebend, and an all-important canon residentiary position. He became Archdeacon of Chichester in 1608 and held a number of cathedral sinecures elsewhere, for example at Ely and Winchester. Yet it has to be said that he seems to have served Chichester most conscientiously until his death in 1635. His brother Lancelot Andrewes may have been a famous court theologian and scholar, but Roger probably contributed more to the smooth administration of the Cathedral than Lancelot achieved for the diocese during his short spell as its bishop between 1605 and 1609.[55]

What cannot be denied after this analysis, however, is that, in the running of Chichester Cathedral between 1570 and 1660, remarkably few individuals really played a prominent part, bearing in mind that activities were severely curtailed after 1641 and ceased entirely in 1646. We are possibly talking of less than 20 people.[56] All of them were highly educated, with three or four degrees apiece, all of them served for significant periods of time, often in a variety of capacities, all bar one died in post. Of those who played a critical part as residentiary canons in the late 16th century, we should single out Francis Cox, DD of New College, Oxford, who served the Cathedral for 42 years, acting as the Wightring prebendary, becoming a residentiary canon in 1570, also Warden of St Mary's Hospital after 1602 until his death in 1613, at which point he was justly buried in the Cathedral. Another key figure during the late 16th century was Richard Kitson BD, a canon residentiary for 31 years before his death in 1602—he also lies buried in the Cathedral. Daniel Gardiner BD, of Clare College, Cambridge was another, buried in the Cathedral in 1592 after 17 years' service. Henry Worley LLD served for 14 years before his death in 1586. These are the less famous, unsung heroes of the Chapter, the clergymen on the ground, who maintained Cathedral services during the late 16th and early 17th centuries.[57]

The golden days of lengthy service were definitely between 1570 and the 1620s; it is difficult to judge the next generation, of course, because of the Civil War after 1642. Lengthy service could also reduce significantly the real influence of a bishop, particularly if the important canon-residentiary posts were already taken. Hence, it took many years before the appointments of the 1570s ceased to hold considerable sway in the affairs of the Chapter, and some later canons like Roger Andrewes, Richard Buckenham and Owen Stockton served for 25, 14 and 18 years respectively. 123 of the canons (60 per cent) held office for over 10 years, while a significant 65 (32 per cent) gave over 20 years' service.[58] Between 1570 and the 1640s a bishop could probably count on being able to make approximately 19 appointments a decade, but these were to the General Chapter, and even this figure is boosted by the 43 appointments made by Curteys in the 1570s. The 1630s witnessed another flurry of activity with 24 appointments, as Montagu and Duppa gained positions for friends like Richard Steward, Lawrence Pay, Robert Bostock, John Scull and John Gregory, but none of these canons ever gained a really firm foothold in the Chapter.[59] At the very time that we know Archbishop Laud was orchestrating changes in cathedrals across the land, the records at Chichester start to falter and provide little more than rudimentary information.

Two other groups perhaps deserve special mention, namely the Highleigh and the Wightring prebendaries. The prebendary of Highleigh was automatically the Master of the Grammar School, nominated by the Dean and Chapter, and not eligible to serve as a residentiary canon. Also, before 1662, he was not necessarily in holy orders.[60] Ten people served the Chapter in this guise between 1570 and 1660, one George Elgar LlB, being reappointed to serve for a second distinct period of office after a Chapter row in 1632. When one considers that just two of these individuals—Elgar and John Woodhouse—held the Mastership from 1602 to 1647, it becomes clear that there was a high turnover of personnel before 1600. Several of the more obscure individuals out of the 202 come from this group. Even though we might expect them to be highly educated and therefore to appear in *alumni* registers,[61] it is very difficult to pick up people who held this post at the very outset of their careers. Hugh Barker, the civil lawyer, was probably the most famous man to emerge from a short spell of teaching at the school in the 1590s. He gained his DCL from New College, Oxford in 1605 and went on to become Chancellor of the diocese of Oxford and also to serve in London on the Court of High Commission and that of Delegates.[62] Clearly the school prospered in this period, for in 1619 rising pupil enrolments enabled the Chapter to make the position of usher more profitable and secure.[63]

The Wightring prebend had to be given to a theologian qualified to give Cathedral lectures in theology.[64] Seven people served between 1570 and 1660 and, while we know more about this group than that above, it is difficult to say how well they performed. There were problems at the very outset of the period when Francis Cox was charged with not preaching, on which he relinquished the post to Anthony Corano.[65] The latter was probably the famous Anthony Corro, a Protestant refugee from Spain who later caused trouble with his novel views on predestination; as he only served for two years until 1572, it is difficult to detect what influence he had on Chichester.[66] We know equally little of how well Blaxton and Andrewes performed; further problems materialised after 1620 when Jerome Beale resigned in order to devote himself to the Mastership of Pembroke College, Cambridge. One William Hicks was installed in the post, but it looks as if he soon fell out with the Chapter, for he was twice refused his application to become a canon residentiary and only succeeded in becoming one thanks to a royal mandate in May 1632.[67] Hicks had also made the mistake of alienating Bishop Montagu, who had reported him to Laud for failing to perform his lecturing duties personally, sending substitutes 'whom he can get, sometimes good, sometimes bad, any riff-raff whom he can light upon'![68] When Hicks died in 1637, Montagu must have sighed with relief for he wrote swiftly to Laud recommending Aquila Cruso for the post as 'a man of unequalled learning', fit 'to revive' the practice of the Cathedral lectures.[69] Montagu's disagreements with Hicks were probably of a personal nature, for the latter clearly held 'high church' views like his own and felt strongly enough about Chichester to leave £5 towards the high altar in his will.[70] It is intriguing to note, given the Catholic traditions of the area, just how many of the holders of the Wightring prebend held Arminian or high church views.

It is difficult to discern much about relations between the Cathedral Close and the City of Chichester during this period, for the Corporation minutes have not survived to complement the excellent Chapter records.[71] In the hostile climate of the 1630s, when the city fathers were apparently at loggerheads over rights of precedence during services in the Cathedral, attention was also drawn to charter changes which had been effected in 1622.[72] These gave the City the right to levy taxes within the Cathedral Close, a matter which was referred to the Privy Council in 1636.[73] The dispute included questions concerning the extent of clerical power in the City, and the right of clergymen to act as local justices of the peace. Brent picked up hints of the quarrel at his visitation in 1635, for 'the Mayor and his brethren came not to visit me, because I lodged in the close, there being some difference between them and the dean and prebendaries'.[74] Brent made it clear where his sympathies lay when he noted of the Corporation that 'they are puritanically addicted'; hence his admonition to one of the aldermen over wearing a hat during services. Brent also sided with the Dean and Chapter when he forced William Speed of St Pancras, friend and correspondent of the philanthropist Samuel Hartlib, to confess 'his error in being too popular in the pulpit' and to agree to remove a gallery which had been erected to cater for a larger congregation. Speed had clearly drawn many who should have been attending Cathedral services![75] We cannot tell whether Cathedral clergymen and officials ever served on Chichester City Council, as happened in other cathedral cities.

It is a cruel irony that, when Chichester Cathedral seemed to be assembling the best qualified and most illustrious band of prebendaries for some time in the late 1630s and early 1640s, the whole Church of England should be held to account for past failings. Defeat of the Royalists in the Civil War led inexorably to the abolition of episcopacy and, with that system, so too deans and chapters in 1646.[76] It must have seemed as if the Puritan Curteys was to have the last laugh after all. Between 1646 and 1649 the property of Chichester Cathedral was shared amongst 16 towns and villages, the lion's share going to provide for 'three learned divines' in Chichester, each of whom was to receive £150 per annum. The total sum disbursed in this manner eventually came to £897 3s. 4d., at which stage it was realised that there was not enough money to go round.[77] This figure included, however, money taken from many of the prebends. Perhaps because of the continued presence of Bishop Henry King in southern England, nominations continued to be made for Chapter posts well into the 1650s, but there was never the slightest chance that the Chapter could be re-formed until the miracle of the Restoration in 1660. In his magisterial *Sufferings of the Clergy* published in 1714, John Walker recorded the woes of 38 members of the Chichester Cathedral Chapter, but it is fair to say that very few of them, including Bruno Ryves, ever became ensconced in the city before the war broke out in 1642.[78] The siege and his eventual escape to the relative security of Surrey via Petworth certainly remained in Henry King's mind, for, when giving a commemorative sermon on the execution of the King in 1665, he recalled the unusual event of a Parliamentary woman captain parading her troops each morning 'with drums beating and colours flying' through the streets of Chichester. No wonder the period seemed to represent for many a world turned upside down![79]

* * * * *

It is difficult to formulate a final judgement on the rôle of Chichester Cathedral between 1570 and 1660. For many people, the Cathedral must have seemed an expensive anachronism, particularly in the 1640s and '50s, but this was also the perspective of Puritans in the 1570s and '80s. For others, the Cathedral offered a real link to a Catholic past and retained its pull as a pilgrimage centre long after the shrines had gone. Clearly, the Cathedral as a tourist centre is not just a feature of the 20th century, for many descriptions of this period come from such travellers, and many of the orders suggested by bishops and deans alike concerned disturbances made during services by those who were obviously not there to pray or worship. Such visitors could also, alas, prove to be vandals, prompting frequent orders to the vergers and sextons not to allow visitors indiscriminately to climb the steeple to admire the view; their numbers were causing damage to the bells, while some were even stealing the lead![80]

The Cathedral played a vital part in community life, as host to church courts, a place where worship was conducted with the full panoply of choir music and ceremony in a grand architectural setting, as an educational centre for the region, and not least, as a source of employment to many in the city. It was truly a large corporation with extensive business interests. The careers of the vicars choral, choirmasters and organists, stewards, chapter clerks, auditors, porters, vergers and sextons provide an host of names almost as extensive as the 202 clergymen who formed the Chapter over this period. Both groups played their part in maintaining the Cathedral, but between 1570 and 1660 it is difficult to claim that they played a large rôle in ensuring the success of the Protestant Reformation. The Cathedral was never known as a citadel of good preaching, nor did it really maintain high standards of worship. Vicars choral were all too frequently cited for drunken brawling in the cloisters; even the quality of the bread baked for those in residence and the poor was often considered sub-standard. The Dean and Chapter may have proved good stewards of their estates, they certainly protected their income and positions, but only major further research can hope to reveal how well the Chapter as a whole served both the Cathedral and their local parish congregations.[81]

VII

The Restoration to 1790

Robert Holtby

From the Restoration to the Glorious Revolution, 1660-1689

There is a legend that William Oughtred, the distinguished mathematician, died from excess of joy at the vote of the Convention to recall Charles II.[1] In fact Oughtred became prebendary of Heathfield in 1660, and died on 30 June that year, aged eighty-six. But the legend conveys the mood of the day at the re-establishment of the Church of England, and Oughtred's appointment indicates the speed at which it was accomplished.[2]

Bishop Henry King (Plate XIV) was restored to his see by 20 June 1660, and the first Chapter meeting was held on 11 July, when Bruno Ryves, nominated in 1646, was elected Dean by Joseph Henshaw and William Paule (the latter by proxy). Paule was shortly to become Dean of Lichfield and then Bishop of Oxford—symptomatic, in that early stage, of the rapid promotion of Chichester divines. Ryves had been one of Charles I's chaplains. He was also a pluralist, a characteristic of senior clerics which the Restoration Church did nothing to reform. But his installation on 12 July 1660 was followed immediately by his appointment to the deanery of Windsor.

Joseph Henshaw followed him. Born in 1603, he was already (from 1628) prebendary of Bishopshurst. His appointment as precentor dated formally from 1658, but, when installed as dean in July 1660, he continued to hold his existing offices. He was also a residentiary (from 1638), and, as such, with the deanery, benefited from two-fifths of the Common Fund until he resigned his residentiaryship in 1663. Eleven years older than Ryves, he also had an impeccable Royalist background, having been chaplain to the Earl of Bristol and the Duke of Buckingham, and, in addition to his prebendal stall at Chichester, had held the livings (until the sequestration) of Stedham with Heyshott and East Lavant. His family name was well known in Sussex. In 1663 he became Bishop of Peterborough, and was succeeded by Joseph Gulston, who also held the precentorship, as did his decanal successors until 1688, Charles II having tried in 1684 to make permanent the joint appointment. The argument was that the Deanery had been 'totally ruined' during the Rebellion and that revenues were insufficient to fund a replacement. The 'chantership' included the benefit of 'a large and good house', with the accession of about £90 a year. (The sub-chanter, it was pointed out, normally performed the office of chanter.) The King, having 'advised with' the Archbishop, therefore proposed that the two offices should 'for ever hereafter be united'.[3] But the offer came to nothing.

The custom (since 1574) was re-established by which the Dean and residentiaries conducted the normal business of the Chapter, each residentiary officially qualifying by virtue of a prebend already held. The formal requirements demanding the presence of the whole Chapter were rare, episcopal elections being one such occasion. The full number of residentiaries (four) was not always achieved. For instance, when Nicholas Garbrand resigned in January 1661, he was not replaced. In 1663 Lambrook Thomas (Chancellor) made the residentiaries up to four, but he continued to hold that office when Dean (1671-2) after which deans did not occupy the two together. Four remained the norm, and their importance politically became glaringly apparent in the next century. There were two houses in the Close to accommodate them.

Chapter meetings were held four times a year, on 20 January, 2 May, 1 August and 10 October, and days following if required. The names of two Residentiaries in the early years are particularly interesting: Oliver Whitby (1660-79) and Henry Edes, who held office from 1662 for 41 years, and who played a prominent rôle in the visits of the Duke of Monmouth in the later years of Charles II's reign.

Thomas Ballowe joined the Chapter in 1660. He was a former Whyte Professor of Philosophy at Cambridge, who held the livings of Sutton with Seaford and South Stoke with his residentiaryship until his death in 1669. Two Residentiaries appointed before the Civil War did not continue in office—Thomas Hook, who resigned in 1660, and Stephen Goffe, who was deprived in 1661, having joined the (Roman Catholic) Oratorians in Paris.

What the Restoration had achieved was the re-establishment of the Church and its Liturgy, with all its accompanying defects—notably pluralism. Whitby, for instance, was rector of Ford, vicar of Climping and Selsey, and, in 1672, Archdeacon of Chichester. The ecclesiastical regime was to last until the 19th century, despite social change. The retaking of Church estates, and of property within the City, was rapidly achieved, and the records reveal early attention to rents and renewals.[4] Apart from those in Chichester, the Chapter

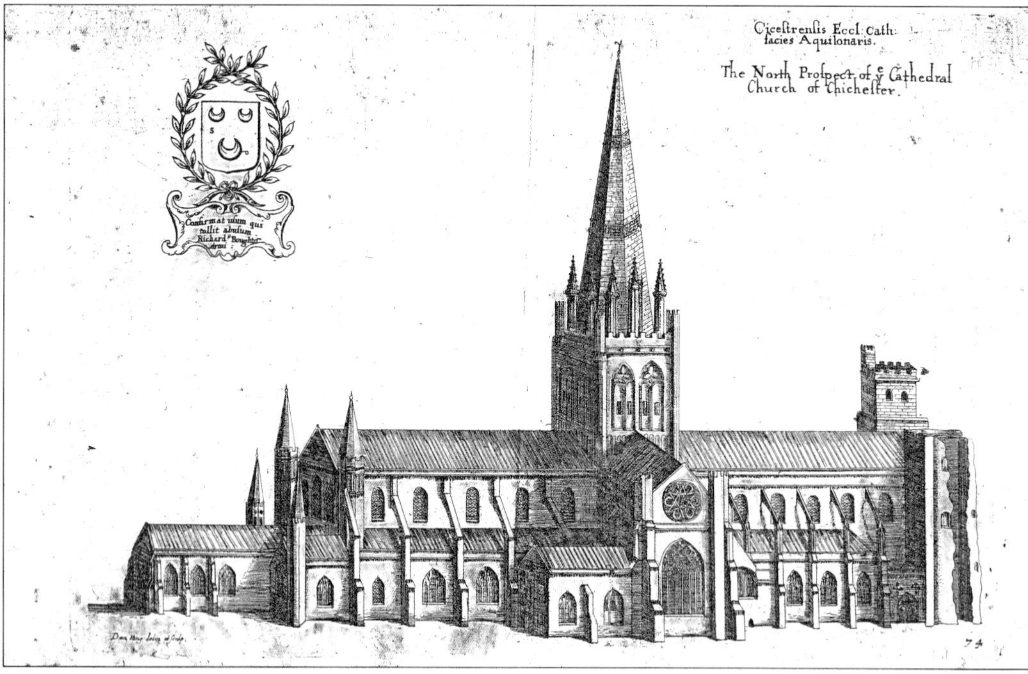

44 *Daniel King's engraving of the exterior of the Cathedral, c. 1660, showing the unrepaired south-west tower and east end.*

owned in Sussex upward of 68 properties, of which at least fifty were in the western division of the County. The return of the ecclesiastical landlord evoked the temper of pre-Commonwealth days—the inevitable resentment of the power of the closed corporation within the City, of which temper there had been telling evidence before the arrival of Waller's troops.

Immediately after the re-establishment of the Chapter, instructions were issued formally for the regulation of the duties of Cathedral servants. Thus, on 17 October 1660, payment to the Dean's verger was authorised—13s. 4d. at the four principal feasts, 'also 6 loaves of Bread weekly at the common bynn for keeping the clock and chimes', and fees for funerals 'and other extraordinary occasions', as well as for cleaning pews, seats and forms. The aforesaid verger was to 'wait before ye Dean with his virge at all times to Prayers and Sermon in ye Church'—or before the President of the Chapter in the Dean's absence. The 'common virger' was to attend the preacher to the pulpit. Provision was to be made for 'reasonable' sums of money for seats in the quire.[5]

Thus the old order was restored. It seems that Chichester did not experience the difficulty of some other cathedrals in re-establishing the choral foundation, partly perhaps because of the existence of the Cathedral school, which had continued during the Interregnum. By 1666 it was laid down that the choristers should have one-fifth of 'such monies as shall be given for funerals'.[6] By then the choir was clearly well-established, and playing its accustomed part in the daily worship. It is not known whether Thomas Lewes, organist and Sherburne clerk, resumed his offices at the Restoration. After September 1661, John Floud, Sherburne clerk, became Master of the Choristers, but the post of organist was not always combined with that office and, although in 1668 Bartholomew Webb was appointed organist, Master of the Choristers and Sherburne clerk, that arrangement did not last.[7]

The Fabric

Waller's troops had done major damage to the Cathedral. It is therefore astonishing to find in the Sussex volume of a highly reputable series, *The Buildings of England*, the statement that the Cathedral had 'never been sacked'.[8] On the contrary, the depredations, together with the already ruined state of the north-west tower, give to the whole period an aura of neglect—reflected also in the condition of the Close. A board still in the South Transept indicates the beginning of efforts at repair envisaged by Bishop King: 'A Memorial of the Names of such Honourable Worthy and Pious Persons who have Freely and bountifully Contributed to ye Repairing and Beautifying of ye Cathedral Church of ye Holy Trinity in Chichester with ye severall summes of money by them given 1664' (fig.45). These accounts, the notice records, were examined and approved by Bishop Brideoake (1677) and Bishop Lake (1686). Between 1677 and 1680 a general repair was set on foot, to which, earlier, the Bishop (Brideoake) had contributed £100. The Chapter sold some plate which raised £128.[9] Bequests were made in 1678 towards the rebuilding of the ruined tower—£50 by John Sefton, clerk (a project realised 220 years later). Sefton also left £50 for repairs to the Vicars' Hall ('if it maybe had to make a Library'). The testator's other directions show clearly that there was doubt about the feasibility of the tower project.[10]

The most memorable aspect of the fated enterprise was the visit of Sir Christopher Wren in 1684, recorded in Henry Edes's memorandum,[11] 14 August of that year:

> An account of Sir Christopher Wren's opinion concerning the rebuilding of one of the Great Towers at the West end of the Cathedral Church of Chichester (one third part of which from top to bottom fell down, about 50 years since) which he gave after he had for about two hours

45 *South-transept list of contributors to the Restoration Fund after the Civil War.*

viewed it both without and within and above and below, and had also observed the great want of repairs, especially in the inside of the other Great West Tower and having well surveyed the whole West end of the said Church: Which was in substance as followeth, viz; That there could be no sure building to the remaining part of the Tower. That if this could and it were so built there could be little uniformity to that of the other, they never having been alike, nor were they both built together, with the Church. And when both were standing at the west end could never look very handsome. And therefore considering the vast charge

> of rebuilding the fallen Tower and repairing the other he thought the best way was to pull down both together, with the west arch of the nave of the Church between both; and to lengthen the two northern aisles to answer exactly to two southern and then to close all with a well designed and fair built west end and Porch which would make the west end of the Church much more handsome than ever it did, and would be done with half the charge.[12]

Fortunately, the lack of finance alone ensured that the scheme was never realised. Some urgent repairs, however, were undertaken, such as Wren's taking down and rebuilding the upper part of the spire of the cathedral.[13] The principal features of the building at this time were the wrecked condition of the north porch, the ruinous state of the gables of the transept, and the total absence of the high-pitched roofs of the upper room over the subdeanery church, the Lady Chapel and the south arm of the transept. Relatively minor expenditure on the fabric contrasted strongly with these defects.

Clergy and Government

From the Restoration to 1689 two deans were prominent, one locally, the other nationally. Both served for very short periods. Joseph Henshaw established the pattern of capitular government,[14] and was the principal agent in the restoration of old order. From 1669 to 1671 Nathaniel (later Lord) Crewe was dean (and precentor), having been in orders for five years: Charles II was said to have expressed his gladness at a gentleman undertaking the service of the Church. Like other senior churchmen, he was a pluralist, and his offices included the rectorship of Lincoln College, Oxford, the statutes allowing its head to hold that office *cum quocumque beneficio ecclesiastico*. His biographer records that at Chichester an appropriation held by lease for the Dean and Chapter fell in, and for its renewal a fine of £1,000 was set. Crewe carried a resolution in Chapter that half the sum should be applied to the augmentation of the vicarage and half divided among Chapter members, who otherwise would have shared the whole sum.[15] Appointed Bishop of Oxford in 1671, he was translated to Durham in 1674. Sycophantic to James II, he withdrew his loyalty when the King fell on evil days.

46 *Nathaniel, Lord Crewe, Dean 1669-71 (anonymous portrait in the Deanery).*

Stuart affairs impinged on Chichester when Guy Carleton was bishop (a kinsman of George Carleton, bishop 1619-28). Imprisoned at Lambeth during the Civil War, he escaped overseas. The year after his appointment to Chichester, 1679, he had a mortifying experience when the Duke of Monmouth arrived in the City to an enthusiastic, even rapturous, reception, an event which throws light on the character of Henry Edes, one of the more colourful personalities of that period.

Carleton described the humiliating events in a letter to Archbishop Sancroft. Writing on 17 February 1679, he recounted the events of the seventh of that month. The Duke had a 'noisy' reception from fifty or sixty of 'the lower sort', and at the Cathedral the 'great men' welcomed him

> with belles and bonfires made by wood from the houses to flare before his lodgings, personal visits made to him, complemented at the lighting from his horse, with all that was in their houses professed to his service. Dr. Edes (the Precentor)[16] that night officiated as his Chaplane, supped with him, and herded himself there with such companie as no man that had a loyal harte towards the King, or bene really a cordiale sonn of the Church of England would have bene amongst.[17]

Next day Monmouth was ushered into the dean's seat in the Cathedral, 'with a voluntarie upon the organ', Edes having conducted the Duke into the quire from the cloister. A part of Psalm 1 was sung before the sermon, 'He shall be like the tree that growes, fast by the river syde'. The words of the anthem were taken from the account of the slaughter of King Saul and the people upon the mountains of Gilboa—but not a word about the warning that the King's enemies shall perish or that on his head shall a crown long flourish. Amidst these 'bell and bonfire solemnities', and after it was dark, a 'clubb companie of these zealous brethren' demanded wood from the Bishop for bonfires—as, they said, other clergymen had done of their own accord. When the request was refused, the Bishop was called 'an old popish rogue', and they fired three shots into his house, throwing stones also. Neither the Mayor, however, nor the gentlemen of the City had gone out to meet the Duke, and only three of the country gentlemen joined him for the hunt which followed his visit to the City. On the other hand, the Mayor and Aldermen called on him and gave him wine. Carleton reported that he had been much criticised for not 'doing homage'.[18]

Monmouth had already been disgraced and stripped of his offices, so Edes and his colleagues exposed themselves to the charge of disloyalty to the Crown, and Edes himself was later imprisoned on suspicion of Jacobitism, but the 1679 episode was of little significance. It merely provided an opportunity for the mob to riot, and for ecclesiastics to make a show of independence.

The Duke came again to Chichester in February 1681, to stay with Lord Grey at Uppark, and yet again in February 1683. On two Sundays when he was in Chichester he attended the morning service in the Cathedral, and on one occasion the Bishop's chaplain preached on the text, 1 Samuel, 15.23, 'For rebellion is as the sin of witchcraft', and 'made as full a parallel of rebellion and witchcraft that the Duke did not stay', though some of his party did, 'and cursed the preacher'.[19]

Edes continued to act in an eccentric fashion, disrupting the Cathedral services. On 29 May 1683, 'all things were done in so ridiculous a manner that the whole congregation was amazed, and the order of service was so strangely perverted, the second lesson being read before the first, that confusion lasted throughout the time'.[20] The date was significant—the annual commemoration of the return of Charles II to England and deliverance from the Great Rebellion—for which day there was an order of prayer and thanksgiving provided in *The Book of Common Prayer*. It is difficult to penetrate the mind of Edes, who, so the Bishop declared, wished to demonstrate his loyalty to Church and King.

In the background was the Exclusion controversy, the attempt to hinder the accession of the Duke of York and the possibility of Monmouth's succession. A trivial local event may well have reflected national affairs. On 10 July 1679, there was a royal recommendation for the appointment of Thomas Woodward, rumoured to have supported Parliament during the Commonwealth, as a residentiary at the next vacancy, but the recommendation was subsequently cancelled. The Dean and residentiaries, however, in December 1681, petitioned against the cancellation on the grounds that Woodward had already secured a vested interest. In January 1682, Woodward was duly elected, but there were two absentees, and Woodward and Edes voted by proxy. It would not be amiss to suspect that discretion was indicated in all the circumstances.

A more serious issue was that prompted by the abdication of James II in 1688. John Lake, bishop from 1685 to 1689, was among those who scrupled to take the oaths of allegiance and supremacy to William and Mary on the grounds of breaking previous oaths to James II and his successors. Lake died before formal deprivation. Two of the Cathedral clergy, as non-jurors, were deprived. Robert Jenkin, Precentor from May 1688, was Lake's chaplain, and held the vicarage of Waterbeach with his Chichester preferments. He witnessed Lake's dying confession of faith in the Church of England. But his years in the wilderness were not unpleasant—residing at Burghley as Chaplain to the Earl of Exeter, then attending Lord Weymouth at Longleat. In due course he was able to take the oaths to Queen Anne, and in 1711 became Master of St John's College, Cambridge, where he had been allowed to retain his fellowship, and also Lady Margaret Professor of Divinity. It is said that it was with reluctance that he had to dismiss Fellows who refused the abjuration oath![21]

William Snatt had a more rigorous adherence to the demands of conscience. He was prebendary of Sutton from 1675, and was a notable pluralist—rector of Benton and Cliffe St Thomas, and vicar of Seaford, Cuckfield and Bishopstone. He was deprived in 1690, and in 1696 attended Sir William Parkyns and Sir John Friend on the scaffold, both of whom were guilty of High Treason for plotting to assassinate William III. Snatt joined in pronouncing absolution and consequently, with others, was imprisoned, though released shortly afterwards.[22] Another victim was the Chapter Clerk, Nicholas Covert, who was imprisoned for an offence against the Statute of *Scandalum Magnatum* and had to forfeit his office; but by 1691 he was restored.[23]

The residentiaries at this time of national crisis, and Francis Hawkins, a considerable pluralist, appointed dean in May 1688, seem to have sailed with the tide, and accommodated themselves to change. Hawkins, nominated by James II, had no difficulty in taking the oaths to William III.

Policy and Persons

Throughout the period a very instructive source of information on Chapter affairs is to be found in successive episcopal visitations and the injunctions which followed the replies to the questions. Certain issues persisted, and the repetition of enquiry about them suggests at best a feeble response in practice to episcopal admonition.

On a personal level there was evidence of occasional strain. Thus Bishop Peter Gunning in 1674 delicately pointed out that he was not seeking to infringe Chapter rights:

> Whereas I appoint a servant of mine to carry a virge before me into the Cathedral Church (wch I doe for Decency and Order Sake) I doe by these presents declare that I doe not designe thereby, or to take upon me anything of Jurisdiction or Authority wch was not in me before, nor to diminish in ye least way any of the Jurisdiction wch ye Dean and Chapter of this Church hath had at any time heretofore.[24]

However, the issue did not end there. In 1714 Bishop Manningham renounced his right to have a verger; in 1727 Bishop Waddington agreed to have a verger at his own expense. Such were the delicacies in the relationship between the Bishop and 'his' Chapter.

Waddington (1723-31) was a Whig, and was at loggerheads with the Tory Canon, Thomas Gooch. The story is told of how Waddington, preceded by the aforesaid verger, proceeded to the Cathedral and gave the blessing at the end of the service. He attended again for Evensong, but met a rebuff. Gooch, who had read the prayers at both services, determined at Evensong to obstruct the episcopal blessing, concluding the service himself 'with the Grace of our Lord Jesus Xit [*sic*]'.[25] Gooch was yet to be converted to the Whig camp, and so to become a considerable beneficiary of the patronage of the Duke of Newcastle, the 'Ecclesiastical Minister'.

One of the persistent issues in episcopal enquiries was that of the proper registration of leases. Bishop King shortly after the Restoration gave instructions on this requirement.[26] It was to be a constant matter of concern: a considerable number of rentals survive (there were, for instance, 270 entries in a rental for 1712),[27] but the registration seems to have been slack.

Very little is said in the records about the fabric of the Cathedral or its furnishings. Bishop King in 1662 ordered that the galleries and seats 'in the Sermon place' should be taken down and replaced by moveable seats.[28] There were enquiries about the state of the Close houses and the condition of the Close itself: garbage in Canon Lane was all too evident to the inhabitant of the Palace. Chapter administration was a continuing matter of concern, as was the behaviour of the officers. Personalities emerge over disciplinary issues, like the vicar John Allen's 'very great misdemenour', or Organist Kelway's drunkenness (Allen had enjoyed a convivial evening with Kelway). Edward Barnard in 1695 was rebuked for slackness at Morning Prayers in the Subdeanery Church,[29] and again in 1742, Edward Barnard, Clerk of the subdeanery parish, was rebuked for being negligent in his duties.[30]

Bishop Waddington's Statutes, following his Primary Visitation in 1727, illustrate the range of matters into which enquiry was made. There was a question about the Cathedral grammar school, and the admonition that account should be taken of the headmaster's age. The ordinances and statutes of Bishops Brideoake and Lake were to be observed. Conformity was required to instructions on the copies of leases belonging to dignitaries and prebendaries and to any other matters 'concerning the preserving to them and their successors their undoubted right to the estates so leased out by them'.[31] Copies of such ordinances were to be distributed. As the 'inquisitors' had had no satisfactory returns to their articles of enquiry for lack of knowledge of the statutes ancient and modern, it was directed that all must know the statutes to which they swore obedience.Vicars choral, lay clerks and choristers were never in future to be allowed 'to officiate in Divine Service in the said Cathedral Church without their surplices and other canonical habits, upon any pretence whatsoever'.[32]

Francis Hare, Waddington's successor, in 1733 laid down rules on residence and Chapter administration. The senior canon was to start residence on 1 October. Sometimes no one had resided in the first days of that month before the Chapter meeting on the 10th. Residence was to be settled at the August meeting. Nothing was to pass the Chapter unless agreed by a majority, and proper registration of decisions was to be made. No prebendary or vicar was to let his house except to another prebendary, vicar or singing man, or some other officer of the Church (under pain of deprivation). If houses stood empty, they could be let to persons 'not belonging to the Church,'[33] but only with Chapter consent, and such permission was required also in the assignment of house leases. Doors recently made into the churchyard from the street and into the Cloisters were to be 'stopped up', unless Chapter approval had been given. The rest of the instructions concerned the proper registration of leases, the auditing of accounts and the clarifying of the duties of officers.

The first half of the 18th century is remarkable in the history of Chichester Cathedral for two reasons: the appointment of some Chapter members who held, or were yet further to hold, major office elsewhere; and, secondly, after much internal struggle,[34] the emergence of a capitular body strongly in support of the Whig party in Sussex, and, indeed, an influential aid for the Duke of Newcastle and his family in their domination of County politics.

Free from such political manoeuvring, an engaging and eirenic personality was William Clarke, a remarkable contrast to contentious divines characteristic of the period. A former chaplain to the Duke of Newcastle, he was appointed by Archbishop Wake to the benefice of Buxted in 1724. Prebendary of Hova Villa in 1727, he became a residentiary in 1738, and Chancellor in 1770, a year before his death. Though a considerable pluralist—he added the Chapter living of Amport in Hampshire to his benefices—he eschewed ambition for high office, content to pursue his antiquarian studies and managing 'the jarring passions' of the Chapter. It was said of him that 'the peace of the Church at Chichester died with Mr. Clarke'.[35]

Edmund Gibson, 'Dr. Codex', the eminent authority on Church law, who was to be successively Bishop of Lincoln and London, was Precentor of Chichester (with the prebend of Oving) from 1703 to 1717, for the last year holding the offices *in commendam*, as he was appointed to Lincoln in 1716. Until that year he was also a residentiary. Known as an ardent Whig, the ecclesiastical adviser of Walpole, he was temperamentally the antagonist of Thomas Sherlock. Their personal animosity remained, even when Sherlock changed his political allegiance. Still Rector of Stisted in Essex, where residence was not expected, rector of Lambeth and archdeacon of Surrey, Gibson nevertheless undertook the duties of residence at Chichester conscientiously, 'living there every year from Midsummer to Michaelmas', as he wrote to Arthur Charlett, Master of University College, Oxford.[36]

Thomas Sherlock was Tory in politics and conservative in theology—a strong opponent of Bishop Hoadly in the Bangorian controversy (Hoadly's contention was that the Gospels showed no warrant for any visible Church authority). Gibson's dislike of Sherlock was political, and he was said to have been most indignant at Sherlock's promotion to the deanery of Chichester.[37] However, in 1728 Sherlock was advanced to the bishopric of Bangor, from which office, helped by the patronage of Queen Caroline, he rapidly ascended the ladder of preferment, modifying his Toryism, eventually accommodating himself to the policy of the Duke of Newcastle, and working with him in ecclesiastical affairs, though never losing his characteristic streak of independence. He became, after Bangor, Bishop of Salisbury, and then of London, refusing both archbishoprics.

When he came to Chichester he was still Master of St Catherine's Hall in Cambridge, and Master of the Temple, an office he held until 1753. He is notable as Dean for the erection of the Deanery in 1725 and for his reforms at St Mary's Hospital. In the Chapter he colluded with his brother-in-law, Thomas Gooch, forming a Tory clique. But his conversion to the Newcastle interest was a potent factor in the development of the political rôle of the Chapter.

'As the body moved, so did the shadow.'[38] It was said of Thomas Gooch—he who had discomforted Bishop Waddington—that his sole merit was to be the brother-in-law of Sherlock. He was prebendary of Somerleigh from 1719 to 1738 and a residentiary. At

Cambridge he was Master of Caius College, and Vice-Chancellor in 1717, a Tory opponent of the Master of Corpus Christi, Matthias Mawson, who was to become Bishop of Chichester in 1740. The records at Caius, taken with those at Chichester, show that Gooch, at least in the early years, performed his quarterly residence, and played his part in the social life of Chichester:

> Although he was still Vice-Chancellor when collated to his prebend at Chichester until late 1720, he aimed and succeeded at full residence—at preaching in January and residing from Lady Day to Midsummer—from 1720 to 1722. In 1723 he missed his sermon and started residence late, and from then on the sermon was usually given by proxy. Still the residence persisted; and, although his brother-in-law, Thomas Sherlock, left Chichester in 1727, he acquired other links by marrying the daughter of a local magnate (Sir John Miller of West Lavant) in the same year. In 1728-9 his residence was curtailed, and he was clearly much involved in affairs in Cambridge. In February 1730 he was installed at Canterbury, and over the next two years he evidently tried conscientiously to keep his residence in both cathedrals.[39]

Perhaps in the light of this a somewhat more favourable view of Gooch might be taken, though his career is an instance of contemporary extensive pluralism. His conversion to the Newcastle camp was not without reward—the bishoprics of Bristol, Norwich and Ely.

The Chapter had its internal differences,[40] but was itself moving towards undisguised support for the Newcastle interest. And the chief actor in the ecclesiastical-political drama was the notorious Thomas Ball.

Significance of Thomas Ball

The career of Thomas Ball reveals the interlocking of political and ecclesiastical affairs in Sussex in the middle decades of the 18th century. Ball migrated from Brasenose College, Oxford, to Caius College, Cambridge, and was ordained in 1723, being that year admitted to the vicarage of Boxgrove. He was presented by Lord Derby, who had an estate at Halnaker, and he held that living for 30 years. He was prebendary of Hampstead from 1727 to 1730, and prebendary of Eartham from 1730. He succeeded Thomas Hayley as a residentiary when Hayley became dean (1735), declined the office of dean in 1741, and accepted it in 1754. He continued as dean to hold the archdeaconry of Chichester, to which he was appointed in 1736.

The proximity of Boxgrove to Goodwood was an important factor in Ball's political machinations, for the Duke of Richmond was the ally of the Duke of Newcastle, and the key political figure in the west of the county. Newcastle's dominant influence in Sussex politics had to be sustained by the constant activity of agents, of whom Ball was

47 *Dean Thomas Ball (portrait in the Deanery).*

one of the most watchful. And a major objective was to secure the support of a Whig Chapter: 'Ball was a miniature of Newcastle. He loved in his heart a Whig Chapter as the Duke loved a Cabinet of friends. His joys were politics, intrigue and insinuation'.[41]

The importance of residentiaries was particularly evident in Ball's time, when they, with the Dean, were the effective governing body of the Cathedral, with the influence that entailed. To secure a Whig Chapter required a deft hand at the local level of manoeuvres in Chichester, and close liaison with the Whig chiefs in the county. Among the factors contributing to Ball's achievement was the conversion of Gooch to the Whig cause, the resignation of the deanery by Sherlock in 1728 (and his conversion to the Whig interest, albeit continuing to oppose any scheme of Gibson), and the providential death of Canon William Sherwin, who had been the ally of Gooch in the latter's unregenerate days.

The key rôle of Ball was indicated in a letter from Newcastle to Richmond in 1740: 'I reckon he [Ball] is the best agent we have in our parts, and will do whatever you would have Him'.[42] In connection with the by-election of 1741, Richmond thought that the Bishop should be 'wrote to ... to order his people to be a little more vigilant'.[43] Such was the ducal hauteur towards the senior clergy. It was between the General Election of 1734 and that by-election that the Whig cause triumphed. Naturally, therefore, when the Dean, James Hargraves, died in 1741, the two Dukes thought of Ball as a strong candidate for the succession. But their intention was frustrated by the desire of Ball to retain the archdeaconry as well, with its political influence wider than that of the deanery. He was also begging for a 'snugg' addition, the benefice of Selsey, and hinted also at the chancellorship of the Cathedral (which had two benefices annexed).

Beneath his sycophantic demeanour Ball had a genuine belief in Whig principles: 'An amiable divine, who had received from nature very sprightly talents, with benevolence and conviviality of temper'.[44] His untiring devotion to the Whig cause as embodied in the Duke of Newcastle was expressed, for instance, on the appointment of Hargraves as Dean in 1739, when he promised to concur with the new Dean on all occasions, 'especially where the common interest (that I mean of your Grace and our country) is concerned'.[45] 'Civil and Religious Liberty, and their best support, the Protestant Succession'[46] was the watchword, and Ball combined a detailed awareness of the nuance of party difference in Sussex with respectful tributes to Newcastle, referring to the Whig interest in the County as that of which 'I take your Grace and your family to be the main supports'.[47]

Ball, having failed to secure the deanery of Worcester, was appointed Dean of Chichester in 1754, when William Ashburnham became Bishop. The correspondence with Newcastle continued almost to Ball's death in 1770, the Duke reflecting on 'the Cause in which you and I have been so long engaged'.[48] Ball's memorial in the Cathedral (by Flaxman) suggests a cleric of enormous energy, with an unequalled capacity for electoral business, and for the political use of ecclesiastical influence, but, alas, with a degree of servility which often obscured his undoubted gifts.

Cathedral, City and Close

The Close occupied nearly a quarter of the city within the walls, and so large an enclave was bound to arouse resentment, particularly when the Chapter took deliberate measures to insulate the Vicars' buildings in South Street from the life of the city:

> The leading merchants found this situation of a city within a city intolerable. Thus, alleged a petition of the cathedral clergy after the Restoration, 'under the pretence and under colour of

> the large and comprehensive expressions in their Jacobean charters, the mayor and aldermen have thereon inferred and concluded the Close as part of the city to be within their liberty and have by degrees attempted to bring the precinct of the said Close ... under their government and jurisdiction.[49]

Discontent at capitular privilege was a gnawing irritation in the civic-ecclesiastical relationship. It is perhaps significant, therefore, that there is little recorded in the official contemporary civic records. For instance, between 1737 and 1783 there occurs but one reference to the Cathedral (21 February 1770): 'At the Assembly, it was Ordered that six new Common Prayer Books be bought for the use of the Corporation in the Cathedral'.[50] Doubtless the relationship was eased politically by the rôle of the Duke of Richmond as

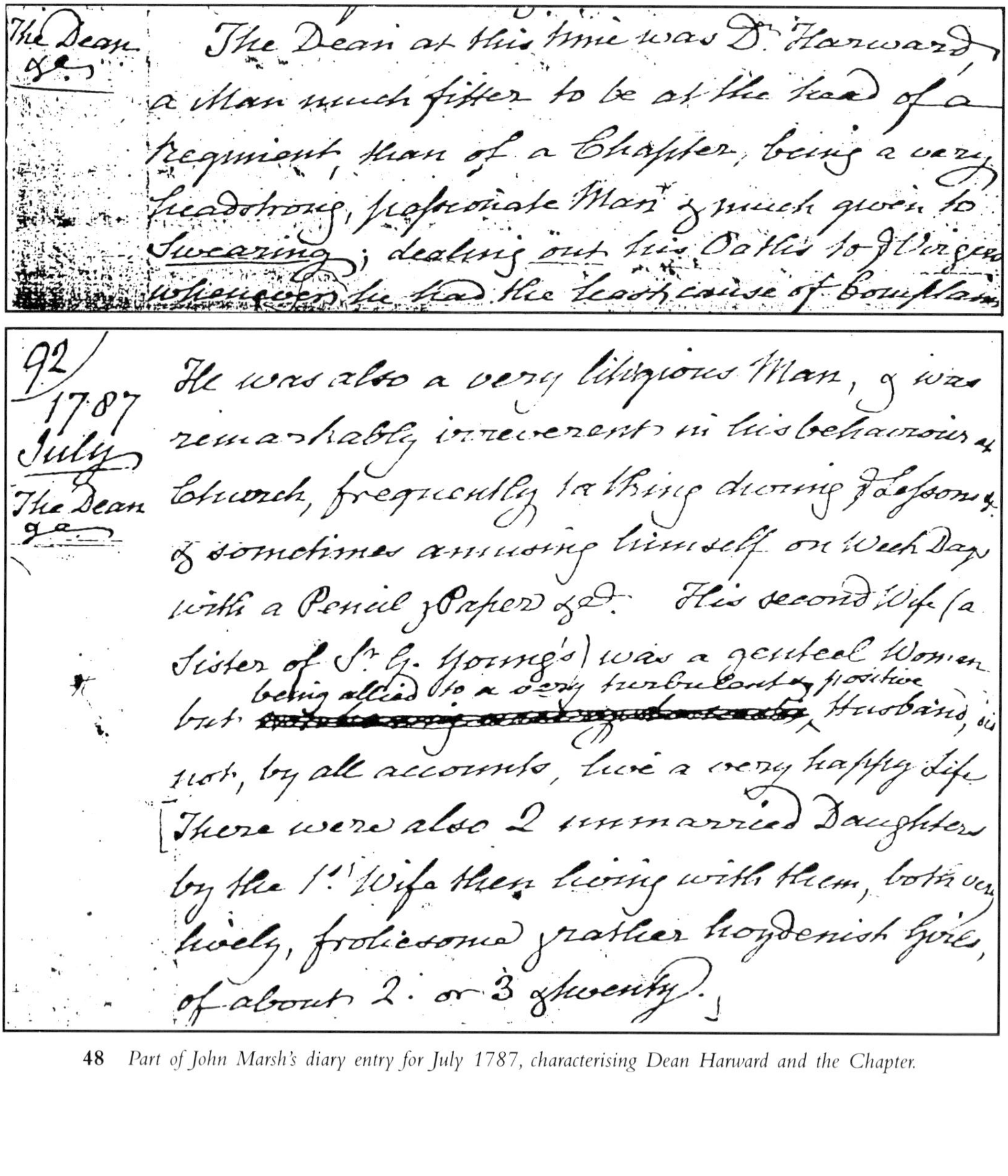
The Dean &c.

The Dean at this time was Dr Harward, a Man much fitter to be at the head of a Regiment than of a Chapter, being a very headstrong, passionate Man & much given to Swearing; dealing out his Oaths to Vergers whenever he had the least cause of Complai

92
1787
July
The Dean &c.

He was also a very litigious Man, & was remarkably irreverent in his behaviour at Church, frequently talking during the Lessons & sometimes amusing himself on Week Days with a Pencil & Paper &c. His second Wife (a Sister of Sr G. Young's) was a genteel Woman but being allied to a very turbulent & positive Husband, did not, by all accounts, live a very happy Life. [There were also 2 unmarried Daughters by the 1st Wife then living with them, both very lively, frolicsome & rather hoydenish Girls, of about 2 or 3 & twenty.]

48 *Part of John Marsh's diary entry for July 1787, characterising Dean Harward and the Chapter.*

successively mayor, alderman and (in the 1750s) high steward. It was a time of close amity between his Grace and the Whig Chapter.

In 1740 there were 785 houses in Chichester, and the Chapter derived income from 92 of them.[51] Alexander Hay's *History* and the *Memoirs* of James Spershott provide some idea of the state of the city. Hay said that at the beginning of the 18th century

> the condition and appearance of the dwelling houses in Chichester was not meliorated in any degree, except a few belonging to the dignitaries of the Church, or the most opulent of the gentlemen of the corporation, and a very few independent gentlemen who resided here. Many of those in the lanes and almost every one in St Pancras were thatched.[52]

In 1753 by an Act of Parliament the eight parishes of the City were united with the Close for the maintenance of the poor, with 30 elected guardians. Spershott, a Baptist pastor born in 1710, confirmed the mean appearance of the City when he was young. Houses in the Pallants were for the better sort, but the main streets were the scene of much riotous behaviour, doubtless fuelled by the 45 public houses:

> and on Shrove Tuesday the most unmanly and cruel exercise of 'cock scailing' was in vogue everywhere, even in the High Church lighten [i.e. Cathedral litten or burial place], and in many other places in city and county.[53]

The figures already quoted are reflected in what appears to be an elementary census based on Hay, a transcript of which survives. It gives 3,712 as the City's population in 1740 (in 783 houses), followed by a decline; 3,970 in 859 houses in 1769; and 4,203 in 844 houses in 1774. The 'great men' of the Close were perceived as property owners, and among the tenants and tradesmen was the 'Church baker', the annual account in respect of whom in 1727 included 21 white loaves and 10 cobs for the Dean, 14 loaves and seven cobs for the 'vickers', and seven cobs for the four lay clerks.[54]

Two Chichester institutions, the Cathedral grammar school (the Prebendal School) and St Mary's Hospital, had a continuing existence during the Interregnum. The school was maintained by George Collins, an Oxford graduate who himself had been a pupil at the school. In 1660 Collins moved to Lewes Grammar School, and was succeeded by Thomas Barter, who held office until 1665, the year when the Great Plague affected Chichester. The author of the School's history wrote of the succeeding century:

> Whereas there had been no fewer than twenty-five masters between 1497 and the end of the seventeenth century, the eighteenth century was remarkable in that the school was ruled by only six men, each of whom enjoyed a long term of office. This century also witnessed the foundation in 1702 of the Bluecoat School under the will of Oliver Whitby, son of the Archdeacon of Chichester, and a former pupil of the Prebendal School.[55]

Among the long-serving masters of the school were Thomas Baker (1701-30) and William Wade (1730-68). James Hurdis (1763-1801), the poet and Professor of Poetry at Oxford, attended the Cathedral school. The better known poet, William Collins, almost certainly attended Whitby's Bluecoat School, one of several rival establishments appearing in the 18th century. In 1818 the Cathedral school had 40 pupils, day and boarding.[56]

St Mary's Hospital, under the care of a Custos or Master, himself a residentiary, passed into the hands of the mayor, Corporation and citizens of Chichester (appointed Wardens) in 1656 but in 1660 the previous regime was restored, and Dean Ryves installed as Custos. In 1683 the mercurial Henry Edes, then Custos, sued the widow of Oliver Whitby, his predecessor, on the grounds that Whitby had withheld income from fines (for rent renewals)

49 *James Hurdis's chamber organ (now in the retroquire).*

from the Hospital. A suit in Chancery before Archbishop Sancroft followed, and, among other decisions on finance, the Archbishop found that £171 14s. 8d. should be repaid to Edes by Mrs. Whitby. Edes showed an active care for the Hospital: he repaired the building and erected the huge brick chimney stacks which served the eight apartments. Edes's term of office was therefore of benefit to the pensioners, but it was Dean Sherlock who initiated reforms which were to shape the conduct of affairs until recent times. The Hospital finances were placed on a sound basis, and salaries were allowed to increase over the years. The fabric was to be regularly inspected and proper records kept. (The inspection of the property was the duty of the Cathedral Communar.) The provision of a chaplain or reader in Sherlock's statutes was to ensure that 'house prayers' were said every day, save Sundays and holidays. The office of chaplain later in the century was held by Alexander Hay. Sherlock's reforms, effective as they were, stood in remarkable contrast to the record of the Chapter in other areas of responsibility—a ray of light in a dim period. There was also another scheme of Sherlock's—the conversion of St Mary's Chapel into a church for Chichester inhabitants at large.[57] This was abandoned, as was Sherlock's plan for the combination of five smaller parishes, a proposal supported by Bishop Bowers. But the City authorities opposed the scheme—perhaps another indication of an uneasy relationship between Cathedral and City.

If the condition of the city was squalid, the Close was hardly a notable contrast. The Deanery had been ruined by Waller's troops, and it was said in 1742 that the Chancellor's house 'is and has been for many years quite dilapidated' (the house between the Bishop's Chapel and the west porch of the Cathedral, the area subsequently known as the Chancellor's Garden).[58] During the Interregnum a Parliamentary Member, John Downes, acquired most of the Close, and was reputed to be responsible for demolishing the Chancellor's house.

As to the Vicars' Hall

In 1661 the vicars choral leased the undercroft to the occupiers of the White Horse Inn opposite ... 'for the receipt of wines and other sweet and unnoisome merchandize'. The lessee was prohibited from using the premises as a dwelling and had to pay one pint of sack or twelve pence to the vicars each Lady Day for their feast called the King's Feast.[59]

In October 1686, a vicar choral, Roger Collins, answered an article of Bishop Lake to the effect that 'the Cellar under thye Vicars Hall [was] a great nuizance for that Mr. Booker the Tenant keeps therein swine'.[60]

The vicars lived in their own dwellings, and the four houses in Vicars' Close 'took their present shape in 1743 and were generally occupied by the Vicars, who owned them and those opposite, now shops in South Street; also the house in the Close known as Blackman House, Vicars' Hall and its undercroft, and two houses in the churchyard. A Vicar had to swear to see that the doors of Vicars' Close were shut by 9 p.m., to keep the keys himself, and to prevent sedition and brawls'.[61] The perils attendant on too easy access to South Street and the city were exemplified in an order of 1 August 1713, when the Chapter laid down that a clause should be inserted in leases, forbidding doors and windows opening onto the street.[62]

THIS MONVMENT WAS ERECTED BY A VOLVNTARY SVBSCRIPTION,
IN HONOR OF WILLIAM COLLINS,
WHO WAS BORN IN THIS CITY. MDCCXXI.
AND DIED IN A HOVSE ADIOINING TO THE CLOISTERS
OF THIS CHVRCH. MDCCLIX.
WHO HOLD MISFORTVNE SACRED, GENIVS DEAR,
REGARD THIS TOMB! WHERE COLLINS, HAPLESS NAME!
SOLICITS KINDNESS, WITH A DOVBLE CLAIM:
THO NATVRE GAVE HIM, AND THO' SCIENCE TAVGHT,
THE FIRE OF FANCY, AND THE REACH OF THOVGHT,
SEVERELY DOOM'D TO PENVRY'S EXTREME,
HE PASS'D IN MADD'NING PAIN LIFE'S FEVERISH DREAM;
WHILE RAYS OF GENIVS ONLY SERV'D TO SHEW
THE THICK'NING HORROR, AND EXALT HIS WOE.
YE WALLS THAT ECHOED TO HIS FRANTIC MOAN,
GVARD THE DVE RECORD OF THIS GRATEFVL STONE!
STRANGERS TO HIM, ENAMOVR'D OF HIS LAYS,
THIS FOND MEMORIAL OF HIS TALENTS RAISE;
FOR THIS THE ASHES OF A BARD REQVIRE,
WHO TOVCH'D THE TENDEREST NOTES OF PITY'S LYRE;
WHO IOIN'D PVRE FAITH TO STRONG POETIC POWERS,
WHO IN REVIVING REASON'S LVCID HOVRS,
SOVGHT ON ONE BOOK HIS TROVBLED MIND TO REST,
AND RIGHTLY DEEM'D THE BOOK OF GOD THE BEST.

50 *William Collins the poet, from Flaxman's memorial (1795).*

The Cathedral gardens were a problem, particularly Paradise, sometimes called the Paradise Garden. Thomas Woodward, the residentiary whose appointment had been made in spite of the withdrawal of royal nomination, was given a lease of Paradise on 2 May 1687, to be used only 'as a garden, orchard and green plot'.[63] He was required to prevent all nuisance there, and to allow burials as the Dean and Chapter authorised. In 1695 Woodward was still the tenant, but was instructed that the garden was not to be 'dug up for turnips or such uses whereby the bones of any person there buried may be disturbed'.[64] The 'Choristers Garden' next to the Chantry, with two wooden houses, stables and coach house, was also let. The rent of 26s. 6d., charged in 1715 was still unchanged in 1828, reflecting a custom applicable also to Chapter estates, that rents generally remained unchanged, but that fines for renewals were imposed at higher levels.

But the general state of the Close remained untidy, and episcopal admonition did little to change it. When Bishop John Williams conducted his visitation in July 1700, there was a response about the churchyard which 'lays very disorderly, particularly about the west end where the great porch is full of nastiness. Some of the graves are so ordered as to give offence, and tombs are settled there without leave'.[65] Earlier, the vicars (in 1675) had commented that their common hall was 'out of repair, and the ancient customs there used wholly neglected'.[66] The overall impression is one of disorder such as is unimaginable to the visitor who passes down Canon Lane today.

51 *Henry Edes's initials on the great chimneypiece of St Mary's Hospital, signifying his restoration of the building while Custos.*

52 *The Vicars' Hall undercroft before alterations.*

Towards the End of an Era

What impression of the Church in this period is left as the evidence is surveyed? 'Complacency, it is true, is the quality which fits neatly into the stereotype picture of the 18th-century Church of England, the image which the corrective work of Norman Sykes and his heirs took such a long time to dispel'.[67] Certainly that Church was not guilty of the wholesale neglect with which it is often charged. Nevertheless, Chichester Cathedral in the period from the Restoration to the 19th century sadly displays the unattractive character of a closed community, fulfilling minimum statutory obligations, and singularly conservative, failing to show any endeavour beyond the demands of basic duty. The Restoration restored, but did not renew, and the succeeding century was marked by Erastian subservience to the Whig establishment, particularly exemplified by the career of Thomas Ball as residentiary, archdeacon and then dean. Such a judgement does not deny genuine Christian faith to the Whig parsons. Nor were they evil men. But there is no evidence of evangelistic zeal: that had to come from the Methodists.[68] A 'Whig Chapter' was identified with the interest of the Church, and to Chichester City that Chapter was perceived primarily as a landlord. Chancellor Clarke stands out because of his personal disposition—scholarly and peaceable, but even he was a pluralist, who owed his preferments to Newcastle. It was a dry period in Anglican history, and Chichester exemplified both its sober temper and its contentment with the *status quo*.

In July 1798, Bishop John Buckner conducted his Primary Visitation.[69] The 36 questions, and the answers by the Chapter, reflect the same issues of administration and discipline which characterised previous episcopal enquiries and injunctions. In reply to a question about St Mary's Hospital it was stated that, as neither the Dean nor the Custos was present, no reply could be given! The dean was Combe Miller, a baronet, one of the Lavant family, who had been a prebendary and Treasurer, and was in office as Dean from 1790 to 1824. From 1772 he held two parishes in Norfolk. The answers assert that statutory duties were performed, including preaching and residence. Singers and organist were commended for discipline except that some did not receive Communion (a familiar complaint). Vergers, sextons and bell-ringers attended on Sundays to stop people 'walking about and making a noise in the Cathedral' (also familiar). Repairs on the fabric were not yet complete, though it was claimed that the state of the building was much better than it had been for a long time. £2,100 in bank stock and £200 in South Sea Old Annuities,[70] together with admission fees (*sic*), profits from the sale of wood, and funeral fees, all contributed to Cathedral repairs. £3,900 had been spent since 1769. The Library was in good order. Externally, the ground was 'tolerably free from filth', though some gravestones were 'unimpaired', and Paradise was not as good as it ought to be. The houses were in good order, including those of the Sherburne prebendaries, let to respectable tenants. There was no immorality nor crime among the community. 'Tolerable singing' was the verdict on the choir, and it was not clear who catechised the choristers. There was very little about the estates. The Bishop's injunctions required, *inter alia*, continuing effort in the repair of the Cathedral, the wearing of proper habit in the services, more efficiency in the assignment of leases, and, generally, a stricter adherence to Cathedral statutes. The Visitation pointed to the defects of the time, at any point of which similar observations could have been made. There was little promise of reform.

The optimism of the Chapter on the subject of the fabric was not shared by 'An Architect' who, in the *Gentleman's Magazine* (Part 1) in 1803, recorded the depressing state of the Cathedral and Close at the turn of the century. He described the upper parts of the gateways as being converted into habitations 'for the lower order of people'. The north side of the Close was 'defiled by hovels filled with the lowest and most profligate part of the community':

> while on the southern side stand the Bishop's Palace, Deanry [*sic*], and other buildings occupied by the clergy. How these opposite degrees of people can accord in situations so neighbourly seated I cannot possibly devise.[71]

The writer continued with comments on the Cathedral itself: 'in the interior few innovations have been effected'. The west window had its mullions and other works 'knocked out':

> and your common masoned muntings [mullions] and transoms stuck up in their room without any tracery sweeps or turns, of the second or third degrees: which work may before long be construed by some shallow dablers in architectural matters into the classical and chaste productions of our old workmen. On the north and south sides of the church are buttresses, with rare and uncommon octangular columned terminations; but they have likewise, to save trifling expense in reparation, been deprived of their principal embellishments, and are now capped with vulgar house coping—it may be well to speak of the west porch as an excellent performance; and the statue over the double entrance is remarkably so.[72]

53 *Engraving from Dallaway (1815).*

But the north porch was in a wrecked condition, both gables of the transept were in ruins, and the high-pitched roofs of the old Library, the Lady Chapel and the south arm of the transept 'were absent altogether'. The Lady Chapel 'had been turned into a reading room, a depot for books, stationers' almanacks, and other furniture—with a chimney piece at the east end, the east window being mortared up'.[73]

The author referred to 'pew lumber' in the nave, and described an area to the north (presumably the outer aisle) as a 'vault', probably indicating a walled-in area, which enclosed the figure of a Cynic philosopher, denoting the triumph of Greece and Rome over 'Apostolic example'.[74]

This was a gloomy account, though consonant with evidence on the condition of the Cathedral in the previous century. It was relieved, however, by a reflection on the morning service:

> The office of the Litany was more devoutly and solemnly delivered and the Responses from the Choir more harmoniously and sweetly chanted, than I had ever before heard: and so devoutly was the whole of the service gone through, that I heard one of the attending Dignitaries observe, after consulting his watch 'that the morning's duty was longer at this time, by half an hour' than was the usual custom.[75]

A sad observation on the fabric was thus followed by a witness to the continued enactment of the *opus Dei*, even in the bleak ambience of the Georgian Church. It is a Church of England vignette, even to the dignitary's comment (as is ever the wont of canons) to note any departure from 'the usual custom'.

VIII

Change and Continuity, 1790-1902

Nigel Yates

The history of Chichester Cathedral between the late 18th and early 20th centuries explodes two popular myths about the overall development of the Church of England in this period. The first myth is that until the middle of the 19th century the church was both decadent and somnolent. The second is that the church was transformed from that date by a revolution, both pastoral and theological, that shook it to its very foundations.

Is Chichester untypical? Or is it more the case that the worst excesses of pre-1840 corruption, and the more dramatic manifestations of the post-1840 revolution (or revival as some would term it), were restricted to relatively small, but extremely well-publicised, pockets of the Church of England, widely dispersed through the length and breadth of the provinces of Canterbury and York? Recent research suggests that the picture of gradual, and almost imperceptible, change that characterises the history of Chichester Cathedral in the 19th century was actually very widespread within the Church of England.[1] It is not a case of saying that change did not occur, and with hindsight quite radical change if comparing the church of say 1900 with the church of 1800, but of saying that this change was less noticeable to those actually experiencing it, and that change has to be seen in perspective, and with a careful understanding of its impact at the time.

The Cathedral and Reform

Despite the qualifications with which I have introduced this chapter, it was undoubtedly the case that, by the first quarter of the 19th century, the Church of England in general, and its cathedrals in particular, were under enormous pressure from the reform lobby, which, though mostly outside the Anglican establishment, among dissenters and anti-clericalists, nevertheless had considerable strength in Parliament. Cathedrals were seen by many as useless and outdated institutions. Durham tried to deflect public criticism by giving up property worth £80,000 to fund a new university in 1832,[2] but no other cathedral was in a position to make so generous a gesture. It was therefore no surprise that, when an Ecclesiastical Commission was set up to reform the administration of the Church of England, the reform of the cathedrals was at the very top of this agenda. There is, however, reason to believe that criticism of the cathedrals was much exaggerated. At Chichester, despite the criticism levelled by later deans at their predecessors, the Cathedral had been generally well maintained and its services decently conducted during the first three decades of the 19th century. The main criticism that could be levelled at the Dean and Chapter was that they were an inward-looking body, with little influence in the diocese, or even in the city of Chichester itself, outside the narrow confines of the Cathedral precincts. All three deans between 1790 and 1830 held other preferment. Combe Miller (1790-1814) had been advanced from within the Chapter, having been collated to a prebend in 1769 and the treasurership in 1785; he was also rector of two Norfolk parishes, Snetterton and Winfarthing. Christopher Bethell (1814-24), who held the Yorkshire rectory of Kirby Wiske from 1808 until 1830, was a leading member of a group of distinguished high churchmen known as the Hackney Phalanx,[3] and became Bishop of Gloucester in 1824, being translated first to Exeter and then to Bangor in 1830. As Bishop of Bangor until his death in 1859, he was the only Welsh bishop before the last quarter of the 19th century to show any sympathy towards the Oxford Movement. [4] Samuel Slade (1824-9), also vicar of Staverton (Northants) and rector of Hartfield, might have advanced beyond the deanery of Chichester had he not died at a relatively early age.

A major overhaul of the fabric of the Cathedral was carried out in 1812-17 under the supervision of James Elmes,[5] the architect of St John's church in Chichester (a building, now vested in the Churches Conservation Trust, which fortunately retains its early 19th-century fittings virtually unaltered). The work included repairs to the spire and the covering of the vaults in a yellow wash which, unfortunately, obliterated much earlier decoration now known only, apart from the restored bay in the Lady Chapel and traces visible in damp weather, from the sketches made before the wash was applied (as can be seen in fig.36).[6] The 18th-century pattern of daily choral services was maintained, the Chapter resolving in 1822 that 'the Morning Service shall begin at 10 o'clock, thro'out the year and the Evening Service at 4 o'clock, except during November, December and January, when it shall begin at 3 o'clock.'[7] On Sundays, Morning Prayer began at 10.30 a.m. and a sermon was preached. An elderly alderman of the city, describing the services in the Cathedral in his youth in the 1820s and 1830s, recalled:

> During the morning service there used to be an adjournment to the 'Kings and Queens' portion of the building for the sermon, and many people took the opportunity to leave. .... the preacher wore a black gown, yet the choir was surpliced. There were Corporation pews in the Chancel, very near to the Lord's Table. The singing at that time was very good but not as excellent as it is now.[8]

Holy Communion was celebrated on the first Sunday of each month, after Morning Prayer, and also at the great festivals of Christmas, Easter and Whitsun. There is some evidence of a slight overall decline in the number of communicants in the last decade of the 18th and first decade of the 19th centuries. The surviving Sacrament accounts for the period 1789-1807 indicate the highest level of communicants' offerings, at £21 16s. in 1789/90, tapering to the lowest level, at £11 17s., in 1799/1800. Thereafter there was a gradual recovery, the size of the offerings fluctuating between a low of £14 7s. and a high of £16 2s. 3d. in the years between 1802 and 1807.[9]

Only the quire of the Cathedral was fitted up for services, though the north transept was occupied by the congregation of St Peter the Great, or the subdeanery church, where a service was held on Sundays at 2.30 p.m. In order to accommodate the required number of worshippers, there were galleries in the north and south quire aisles and, until 1829, across the screen behind the altar (see Plate XVIII). Such arrangements were not uncommon. New galleries in the quire aisles were erected at Winchester Cathedral in 1818, and there were double galleries in the transepts of Norwich Cathedral until 1837, when they were demolished.[10] Stalls and pews were 'appropriated to the families of the bishop, dean and other members of the cathedral, and one to the mayor and corporation, and some few are let'. Pressure on the available seating meant that from time to time the Chapter was obliged to restrict access to it. In 1792:

> The Dean and Chapter wishing to accommodate as many families as possible with seats in the Galleries, it is ordered that no more than two of each family be permitted to sit there; that the doors of the galleries be kept lock'd; and that each lady who accepts a seat therein do engage to pay the sextons two shillings annually at Christmas.[11]

In 1802:

> The seat in the Sermon place ... appropriated to the accommodation of the female part of the residentiaries' families having been for some time past used to their great inconvenience (inadvertently it is presumed) by other ladies, the chapter find themselves under the necessity of intimating that it is their intention in future to keep that seat for the accommodation of their own families in the first place, and in the next, so far as it may be convenient, for that of the families of their predecessors. And the vergers were directed to communicate this to all persons not coming under the above description.[12]

The Cathedral choir consisted of seven lay clerks and ten choristers. The Lady Chapel was occupied by the Cathedral Library which comprised some 2,500 volumes. There were no almshouses specifically attached to the Cathedral but there were 'certain poor persons, to the number of about fifty, who receive a weekly dole of bread, but there is no requirement to attend the services'.[13]

Visitations of the Cathedral were carried out by Bishop Carr in 1825 and Bishop Maltby in 1832.[14] About half the Chapter were present on each occasion. The outcome was generally favourable. In 1825 it was reported that 'the churchyard and cloisters are so much frequented with idle children and others, that they are seldom so clean as they would otherwise be'. Carr himself commented that 'the service of the church is scandalously interrupted by the indecent and improper behaviour of idle and disorderly persons who are walking about the aisles and nave of the church and making a noise and disturbance', and directed the sextons and bell-ringers to be more diligent. He also instructed the choristers, 'who frequently conduct themselves in a very improper and disorderly manner', to improve their behaviour. He reserved his strongest condemnation for the neglect of the Sacrament.

> Whereas it appears that the lay clerks and other inferior officers of the church do seldom or ever come to Holy Communion; we do hereby admonish them for their gross neglect, and do recommend the Dean ... to repeat such admonitions as may prove effective in case of future omissions of this duty.

Both neglect of the Sacrament and the state of the cloisters were continued causes for concern in 1832. The cloisters were described as 'often upon the Sunday a scene of confusion and gross indecency'. Maltby also noted that the house of the treasurer was 'in a bad state of repair'.

The Dean and Chapter Act of 1840 made major changes at all English and Welsh cathedrals including Chichester. The principal effect was on residence. Before 1840 the arrangements for residence varied from one cathedral to another according to custom and statute; each prebend had its own endowment but the income of those prebendaries who were also residentiaries was increased by a share in the common fund, normally calculated on the number of days they were resident. The 1840 Act reduced the number of residentiaries in most cathedrals to four and, on the expiry of the existing life-interests, transferred the endowments of all the prebends to the Ecclesiastical Commission. Future prebendaries who were not residentiaries had the same status as the honorary canons that were established at those cathedrals that did not have prebends of pre-Reformation foundation. Chapters retained their corporate patronage but the patronage attached to individual dignitaries and prebendaries was transferred to the appropriate diocesan bishop and sinecure rectories abolished.[15]

Following on from the 1840 Act the Ecclesiastical Commission endeavoured to negotiate with individual chapters better arrangements for securing capitular incomes that did not fluctuate from year to year. The income at Chichester averaged £4,639 per annum between 1845 and 1852 but this figure disguised fluctuations from a low of £2,414 in 1848 to a high of £7,793 in 1846. In 1859 the Chapter considered an initial proposal to transfer their estates to the Ecclesiastical Commission in return for an annual income of £4,500, plus an additional £200 to be paid to the chapter clerk to compensate him for the loss of profits on the renewal of chapter leases. After prolonged negotiation a re-endowment scheme was approved in 1864-5 which secured the Cathedral an annual income of £5,000, of which £1,000 was to be paid to the dean, £500 each to the four residentiary canons and £2,000 to a new fabric fund. The Chapter also agreed to transfer the corporate property of the vicars choral to the Ecclesiastical Commission.

The income of the dean and residentiaries under the scheme represented a considerable increase on earlier arrangements, the annual income of the deanery in the early 19th century being only £300. The re-endowment scheme, however, fell victim to the agricultural depression of the late 19th century. The fabric fund could not be maintained as had originally been envisaged, and by 1899 the annual incomes of the dean and residentiary canons had been reduced to £560 and £280 respectively.[16] The Chapter might have been better advised to settle for the fixed annual payment offered by the Ecclesiastical Commission in 1859, rather than the re-endowment scheme actually agreed; cathedrals that adopted the former course of action seem to have fared somewhat better.[17]

One of the lasting financial reforms agreed by the Chapter was to abolish all payments in kind and to substitute cash payments instead. In 1860 the Chapter resolved that, instead of the corn rents and bread distributed among the vicars choral, the officers of the Cathedral, and the recipients of the weekly dole, money payments should be made equal to the value of the payments in kind over the previous seven years. It was agreed that the two sextons and the dean's verger should each be paid an annual salary of £30 and cease receiving the pew rents and fees for admission to the Cathedral or for guided tours that had previously been a major part of their incomes.[18]

The impact of the statutory provisions of the 1840 Act on the cathedral establishments were, like the financial reforms that followed from them, by no means immediate. Like most of the other cathedral and collegiate foundations, the Chichester Chapter had opposed the Act,[19] much to the embarrassment of the bishop, William Otter, who was one of the most enthusiastic episcopal supporters of ecclesiastical reform. Otter's brief episcopate was notable for the establishment of a Diocesan Association, 'to promote the building, restoration, or enlargement of churches and schools, the augmentation of poor livings, and the increase and maintenance of curates' in 1838, and of a theological college in 1839, for the revival of ruri-decanal chapters and for encouraging schemes for the better training of school teachers. It was in recognition of the last of these that Bishop Otter College was founded in his memory and the buildings paid for by public subscription in 1849-50. Otter's successor, Philip Shuttleworth, whose episcopate was even briefer, was another reformer, whose most significant action was the replacement of his two elderly archdeacons.[20] The new post-holders, Julius Hare and Henry Manning, were young and vigorous. Hare (1795-1855), rector of Herstmonceux and Archdeacon of Lewes, was a leading advocate of church restoration and the replacement of closed pews by open benches. Manning (1808-92), rector of Graffham and Lavington and Archdeacon of Chichester, was an Evangelical who was deeply influenced by the Oxford Movement; he might have become one of the first Tractarian bishops had he not instead seceded to the Roman Catholic Church in 1851 and succeeded Nicholas Wiseman as the second Cardinal Archbishop of Westminster.

54 *Bishop William Otter: his memorial bust by John Towne.*

The beginnings of reform in the diocese may have engendered some nervousness on the part of the Dean and Chapter. Bishop Otter had declined to collate to prebends as they fell vacant so that by 1840 no fewer than a quarter of the prebends (8 out of 32) were available to be filled under the terms of the 1840 Act. The remaining prebends only fell vacant gradually; a further nine between 1840 and 1850, ten between 1850 and 1860, two in 1863, two in 1870, and the last one in 1876. The diocesan reform programme was slowed down, however, after the death of Bishop Shuttleworth. His successors, Ashurst Turner Gilbert and Richard Durnford were traditional high churchmen, very much more in the mould of the Dean and most other members of the Chichester Chapter. Six of the prebends, because of the special nature of their establishment, were exempted from the disendowment provisions of the 1840 Act. These were the four Wiccamical prebends of Bargham, Bursalis, Exceit and Wyndham, together with the prebends of Highleigh and Wightring.

The prebendary of Highleigh was Master of the Prebendal or Cathedral grammar school, his salary being provided by the prebendal endowment. This school had had 40 boarders and eight day pupils in 1818, but the total number of pupils had declined to 18 by 1854 and was still that figure in 1866. A new scheme for the operation of the school was not implemented until 1880. The prebendary of Wightring was obliged by statute to deliver divinity lectures in the Cathedral.[21]

Little immediate change was made to the structure of the Chapter by the residence requirements of the 1840 Act. Initially the residentiary canons were chosen exclusively from the ranks of the existing prebendaries; the first residentiaries were Charles Webber senior, Charles Edward Hutchinson, Charles Webber junior and Sir George Shiffner, all serving prebendaries. Barré Phipps, appointed to succeed Webber senior in 1848, had been a prebendary since 1804, and Charles Pilkington junior, appointed to succeed Webber junior in 1850, had been a prebendary since 1834. Shiffner and Phipps remained residentiaries until 1863, Hutchinson and Pilkington until 1870. It was not until 1870 that Arthur Ashwell became the first residentiary canon who had not previously been a prebendary.

All the first residentiary canons after 1840 held other, usually parochial, preferment. Even in the last quarter of the 19th century the lack of accommodation attached to the Cathedral for the use of residentiary canons meant that normally only two out of four were resident in Chichester, the other two normally holding a parochial living in the diocese; R.E. Sanderson succeeded T.F. Crosse as both a residentiary canon and as vicar of Holy Trinity, Hastings.[22] Another part of the Cathedral establishment little affected by the 1840 Act was the Corporation of Vicars Choral, which was not formally dissolved until 1935.[23]

The Personnel of the Chapter

The slow impact of the 1840 Act on the Cathedral is shown in the differences between the composition of the Chapter in 1825 and 1875. One might have expected a Chapter in 1825 full of excessive pluralists, and one in 1875 clearly shaped by the changes in the Church of England in the intervening period, yet neither was wholly the case. In 1825 only four prebendaries held more than two benefices in addition to their prebend. Thomas Heberden, prebendary of Bracklesham, held two livings in Devon and prebends at both Exeter and Wells Cathedrals; George Frederick Nott, prebendary of Colworth, held two livings in Kent and one in Devon and was also a prebendary of Winchester Cathedral; James Dallaway, prebendary of Ferring, held one rectory each in Glamorgan, Surrey and Sussex; James Webber, prebendary of Somerley, held one living each in Lancashire and Yorkshire and a prebend at York Minster. The two most distinguished prebendaries in 1825 were George Pelham (Middleton), who was Bishop of Lincoln, and David Williams (Bursalis), then headmaster of Winchester College and a future warden of New College, Oxford. In both 1825 and 1875 the majority of those people holding office in the Cathedral, as the accompanying table shows, were local men, and it is difficult to draw a distinction in practice between prebendaries in 1825 who might reside for a small part of the year and those in 1875 who might attend some of the Cathedral services, sitting in their stalls, and take their turn to preach.

Preferment of Chichester Dignitaries, Prebendaries and Vicars-Choral, 1825 and 1875

	1825	1875
Other preferment in more than one diocese	11	1
Other preferment outside Chichester diocese	6	4
Other preferment within Chichester diocese	17	29
No other preferment	3	7
TOTAL	37	41

One of the factors determining the slow change in the overall composition of the Chapter was the great length of many prebendal tenures. In 1825 exactly half the prebendaries had held prebends in the Cathedral for more than twenty years; six had done so for more than thirty years, three for more than forty and one for more than fifty. The statistics were not vastly different in 1875; then 11 prebendaries had been in office more than twenty years, nine more than thirty and one more than forty. Thomas Heberden was prebendary of Bracklesham from 1784 until 1843, Sir John Ashburnham was chancellor and prebendary of Gates from 1796 until 1854, Barré Phipps was prebendary of Mardon from 1804 until 1863, and Richard Bingham was prebendary of Bargham from 1807 until 1858.

A similar longevity of tenure applied to the office of vicar choral. In both 1825 and 1875 one of four vicars choral had held office for more than forty years. In 1825 all the vicars choral held at least two parochial livings in or near Chichester, and one was also vicar of Bapchild, a Kent living in the patronage of the Dean and Chapter. In 1875 two of the vicars choral held local rectories, one held the curacy of East and Mid Lavant and only one held no other preferment.[24]

The exact size of the General Chapter was not fixed, since the dignitaries and, after 1840, the residentiary canons might or might not hold a prebend. The exception was the precentor who was automatically prebendary of Oving. In 1825 the then precentor also held another prebend and only the Archdeacon of Lewes was without one. In 1875 both Archdeacons held prebends but the Chancellor, Treasurer and two of the four residentiary canons did not. Henry Wagner, vicar of Brighton, was Treasurer of the Cathedral from 1834 until 1870 but never held a prebend. The use of parochial livings within the city of Chichester, or its immediate environs, to boost the income of both Chapter members and the vicars choral was general throughout the 19th century. Whilst this created an additional bond between the Cathedral and the local community, it had the disadvantage of dissipating the energies of, and from time to time creating a conflict of interests for, the relevant post holders. The Chapter also used its own corporate patronage of livings to advance those connected with the Cathedral or their relatives. This patronage was not extensive. It comprised six livings in the city of Chichester, 14 others in Sussex, Bapchild in Kent, and Amport and Appleshaw in Hampshire. All the presentations to the vicarage of Amport between 1808 and 1870 were to serving prebendaries: Charles Webber senior in 1808, Charles Webber junior in 1828, Sir George Shiffner in 1848, Charles Hutchinson in 1864 and Charles Wollaston in 1870.

Some prebendaries carried particular weight within the Chapter over and above that of their fellows. The most prominent of these were Charles Webber senior, Sir George Shiffner and Charles Swainson. Webber was prebendary of Bishopshurst 1803-48 and Archdeacon of Chichester 1808-40. His influence secured the collation of his brother, James Webber, a future dean of Ripon, to the prebend of Somerley in 1813, and his son and namesake to that of Highleigh, and the mastership of the Prebendal School, in 1824. Another son, George Henry Webber, succeeded his uncle as prebendary of Somerley in 1827, and secured, through that same uncle's influence, a prebend in the collegiate church of Ripon two years later. Sir George Shiffner, prebendary of Eartham 1829-63 and one of the residentiary canons from 1848, was until that year rector of St Peter and St Mary, Lewes, and also of Hamsey, where he was the local squire and patron of the living. When he resigned Hamsey, he presented his own son to succeed him in that living, and the son duly succeeded to the baronetcy when Shiffner died in 1863. Charles Swainson, prebendary of Firle 1856-87 and a residentiary canon between 1863 and 1882, came to Chichester as Principal of the Theological College in 1854. He was a distinguished theologian who held, successively, two of the divinity chairs at Cambridge, being appointed to the Norrisian professorship in 1863 and the Lady Margaret professorship in 1879.

55 *Dean George Chandler.*

The rôle of dean was a difficult one, at Chichester as it was elsewhere, as it involved the exercise of responsibility without power. The dean could not control his chapter; he could only seek to influence it and he might frequently be frustrated in these efforts. Between 1830 and 1902 the dean who clearly had the greatest rapport with his chapter was George Chandler. Although a high churchman of the pre-Tractarian school, he was a close friend of Archdeacon Manning and active in both the Ecclesiological Society and the Society for Promoting Christian Knowledge. Until 1847 he was also rector of All Souls', Langham Place, St Marylebone, residing at Chichester only for the 90 days required by statute.[25] The belief that deaneries ought to be full-time appointments, with their holders lacking any other preferment, may well have made a significant contribution to the strained relations between deans and their chapters which was such a marked feature of cathedral life in the late 19th century.[26] All four deans at Chichester between 1859 and 1902 had difficult relations with the Chapter. Those with a parochial background like Walter Hook, Francis Pigou and Richard Randall felt frustrated by the lack of things to do. Hook had been, as vicar of Leeds from 1837, one of the most effective parish priests in England. He saw his period at Chichester as one of quiet retirement in which he could devote his time to completing the *Lives of the Archbishops of Canterbury* which he had been commissioned to write in September 1859.[27] Pigou had been vicar of Doncaster 1869-75 and Halifax 1875-88 and accepted the deanery, worth considerably less than his former living, as he had 'not enjoyed good health for the past few years'.[28] He soon regretted the move:

> The City affords quiet for the students of the Theological College, but lacks opportunity for their training in parochial work. The fact of there being nine Parish Churches is not favourable to the spiritual life of the people, but the parishioners are so Conservative that they will not hear of the removal of any of the Churches, and of the union of Benefices.[29]

He accepted the offer of the deanery of Bristol, where he could have the opportunity to make his cathedral relevant to the special needs of a large city, with a mixture of enthusiasm and relief. Randall had deliberately sought, through the discreet lobbying of friends, the deanery of Chichester, as an opportunity to raise the spiritual life of the Cathedral, but he was disappointed in his lack of success and tendered his resignation towards the end of 1901. Randall was no stranger to Sussex. He had succeeded Manning at Graffham and Lavington, on the latter's secession to Rome in 1851, and was the subject of attacks by his own curate and some of his parishioners for his ritual innovations and his doctrinal teaching.[30] He moved to Bristol in 1868 to become the first vicar of All Saints', Clifton, a parish which had been deliberately created to secure Tractarian teaching in that part of the city. Randall was one of the few early ritualists to receive major preferment, owing his appointment to the High Church sympathies of the prime minister, the Marquess of Salisbury.[31]

By far the most controversial of Chichester's deans was John Burgon. Unlike his immediate predecessor and successors, Burgon had no real parochial experience. He had been a fellow of Oriel College, Oxford, since 1846; vicar of the University Church of St Mary since 1863; and Gresham Lecturer in Divinity since 1868. He was conservative to the point of being reactionary and 'devoted his life to maintaining the Church of England exactly where it stood about 1850'.[32] He opposed most university reform, particularly any aimed at opening up the university to women. He defended the use of the Athanasian creed at a time when many were wishing to abolish this. Above all he deplored the revised version of the Bible and did everything in his power to prevent it from replacing the Authorised Version as the one read at church services. He was by nature a quarrelsome person and wholly unsuited to become a dean, a position which required the exercise of tact and understanding. One of the residentiary canons told his biographer that 'the history of Dean Burgon's relations with his chapter was this. He declared war on his Residentiary Canons by sending them one of those scoldings with which we are all familiar'.[33] A reviewer of the published biography, commenting on Burgon's relations with his chapter, wrote in the *Quarterly Review* that 'he turned that peaceful circle into a ring of unceasing and acrimonious controversy, his idea having been that the relation of a Dean to his Canons was pretty nearly equivalent to that of a Rector to his Curates'.[34] When one of those 'curates' was a

56 *Dean Richard Randall.*

57 *Dean John Burgon.*

58 *Canon Charles Swainson (see also fig. 66).*

distinguished Cambridge professor and a future Master of Christ's College there was bound to be trouble, and it was indeed with Charles Swainson that Burgon had his most violent disputes. Burgon was irritated that Swainson's combined income as a residentiary canon and university professor outstripped his own as dean. Burgon was also the inferior scholar and the fact that Swainson took a very different position on many contemporary theological issues, notably on the Athanasian creed, did not help. Burgon described Swainson as 'insufferable'. Swainson seemed to take every opportunity available to humiliate Burgon in public. In 1878 Swainson had persuaded the Chapter, in the Dean's absence and without his knowledge, to re-organise the seating in the eastern part of the nave as it obscured the general view of the pulpit. These seats had, however, been used by the lady members of the Dean's family and Burgon alleged that they had been 'molested' by their removal, and that it was his duty to protect them and 'maintain them in the quiet enjoyment of their seats'.[35] The only member of the Chapter that Burgon found congenial was T.F. Crosse, who became one of the residentiary canons in 1882.[36] Nevertheless, despite the endless quarrels with the Chapter, Burgon made some positive contributions to Church life in Chichester, starting a Bible class and giving evening lectures at Bishop Otter College.

The Building and its Services

The maintenance of the fabric and the daily round of choral services had always been a priority for all cathedral chapters, and Chichester was no exception. To a large extent these activities went together. During the 19th century there was in the Church of England as a whole a significant shift in the relationship between the two. Whereas formerly the requirements of divine worship had determined the design and liturgical arrangement of the building, one of the results of the ecclesiological movement of the 1830s and 1840s was to place the emphasis more firmly on the design and symbolism of the building, and then to adapt services so that they were more consistent with this new architectural vision.[38] Chichester was one of the first cathedrals to embark on a programme of both building restoration and liturgical innovation. In 1829-30 the gallery across the top of the altar screen was removed and a new bishop's throne erected.[39] The core of the seating in the quire was the medieval stalls but on to these had been grafted more recent box pews (as in Plate XVII). The arrangement of the quire was not dissimilar to the one that survives in York Minster, where the quire was completely refitted after a fire in 1829. Within three years of his appointment to the deanery in 1830, George Chandler had persuaded the Chapter to remove the yellow wash from the walls and vaults of the Cathedral and to embark on a scheme for filling the windows with stained glass.[40] The new glass included work by the leading artists of the period including O'Connor, Wailes and Willement. Contemporaries were very appreciative of these additions to the Cathedral, mostly the result of specific memorials and subscriptions,[41] but later generations were more critical: 'to the example thus set by the Dean the Cathedral is indebted for the richness of its stained glass, now of unusual quantity, but generally of indifferent quality'.[42] In 1839 the Cathedral was lit by gas and Chandler introduced, for the first time in more than a century, a weekly celebration of the Holy Communion.[43] Chichester was not the only cathedral to move to a weekly celebration; Canterbury also did so at about the same time, but even in the 1850s a significant number of cathedrals still only had a monthly celebration.[44]

In 1847 Chandler embarked on the most significant stage of his restoration programme. In a statement to the whole diocese he explained that one of his main motives was to reverse 'that insensibility and deadness to the proprieties of Sacred Architecture which characterised the generations recently passed away'.[45] The distinguished architect and ecclesiologist, R.C. Carpenter, was appointed to superintend the work, the cost of which was estimated at £22,000. This was to include not only the restoration of the Cathedral but also the building of a new church for the parishioners of St Peter the Great, whose accommodation in the north transept of the Cathedral was described as 'unsightly and sordid'. It was also inconvenient, since its proximity to the quire of the Cathedral meant that services could only be held at times which did not conflict with those in the Cathedral quire. A meeting was held on 14 January 1847, attended by Bishop Gilbert and Archdeacon Manning, to interest the diocese in the project, since the Cathedral had no fabric fund to meet the costs, and a committee was set up to assist the Dean and Chapter to raise the necessary money. A site for the new subdeanery church was acquired just to the north-west of the Cathedral on the other side of West Street, and a design for the new building by Carpenter approved in the autumn of 1847. By December 1848 the appeal had raised £8,785 in promised subscriptions, but thereafter money was very slow in coming in and the work could only proceed in stages. By 1852 the new church of St Peter the Great had been completed and the pews and galleries in the north transept removed.[46]

Work began on adapting the nave of the Cathedral for public worship in 1853 when Chandler was given permission 'at his request to erect at his own expense a stone pulpit in the nave of the cathedral'.[47] Chandler, by now in poor health, handed over the chairmanship of the restoration committee in 1857 to one of the residentiary canons, Sir George Shiffner, and in 1859, the year of the Dean's death, work on the nave was completed.[48] By 1855 the whole restoration programme had cost £9,010—£5,650 on St Peter's church and £3,360 on the Cathedral—but there was still a long way to go. Nearly half the money had been contributed by members of the Chapter, Chandler himself putting up at least £3,000 towards the restoration and adding to this a bequest of £2,000 in his will, to benefit either the Cathedral, the Theological College or a new church in Chichester. The executors decided that the whole sum should be devoted to the restoration of the quire of the Cathedral, which had not been touched since the improvements of 1829-30, and which was considered inadequate for the size of the congregation. In 1849 it had been noted that 'the attendance on weekdays is much more numerous than formerly; and at each service on Sunday, the quire is invariably filled'.[49]

The new dean, Walter Hook, was somewhat sceptical of both the reasoning behind and the actual plans for the restoration of the quire:

> I confess I do not take much interest in the present movement to alter the Cathedral, and I think if it would have been delayed a year or two, the thing would have been done better; but the step was taken before my appointment and I can only go on with it. You should make a demand before you think of a supply; as far as I can see, the present choir is sufficiently large for the congregation, and the present movement will give offence to certain respectable persons who have long slumbered in their pews, and do not like the idea of being ousted from their aristocratic position. Why enlarge the choir before the enlargement is demanded? Why not look first to the spiritual fabric and see whether that can be enlarged? If it cannot, we may as well remain as we are.[50]

Hook endeavoured to enlarge the 'spiritual fabric' by introducing a sermon at Evening Prayer on Sunday afternoons. Whereas at Morning Prayer the Dean took his turn with the prebendaries, Hook instituted an arrangement whereby the Dean himself normally preached in the afternoons. The proposal for the restoration of the quire involved the removal of the 15th-century screen erected by Bishop Arundel across the western arch of the crossing supporting an 18th-century organ case, the destruction of the returned stalls against the eastern side of the screen, and the sweeping away of 'the pews and galleries by which the quire was encumbered and disfigured'. The component parts of the Arundel screen were still lying around the Cathedral 40 years later.[51] In order that the quire could be completely refitted, the Cathedral restoration committee, now under Hook's chairmanship, resolved 'to fit up the Nave temporarily for Service'. The full cost of the restoration was estimated at £6,000. By removing the screen and throwing the nave and choir together it was calculated that the Cathedral could be made to accommodate 3,000 people if necessary. All the seating was to be free and the 'sextons will be prohibited from taking fees'.[52]

The nave was opened for worship on Advent Sunday 1859. Early in 1860 all the quire fittings and the Arundel screen were removed, and the costs of this part of the restoration programme had already reached £2,916. By the end of the year an appeal for the restoration of the quire had attracted gifts, including Dean Chandler's bequest, totalling nearly £5,022. Then a disaster occurred. The screen's removal put such pressure on the foundations that by the summer of 1860 remedial works had to be undertaken to shore up the piers of the crossing. In January 1861 the Chapter approved further emergency repairs: 'it was determined that the bulging of the piers should be checked by the application of a jacketing of solid timber, powerfully looped together with iron bolts and balks of timber'. On Sunday 17 February the afternoon service had to be 'interrupted by the urgent necessity for shoring up a part of the facing of the south-west pier which had exhibited new symptoms of giving way'. Further efforts to shore up the crossing piers were completely unsuccessful and on Thursday 21 February the spire 'was seen to incline slightly to the south-west, and then to descend perpendicularly into the church, as one telescope tube slides into another, the mass of the tower crumbling beneath it'.[53]

Hook's initial attitude was one of deep despondency. The plans for his quasi-academic semi-retirement had been shattered. Neither he nor any of his residentiary canons was in the prime of life. As someone who had been able to work up little enthusiasm for the modest restoration scheme then in progress he was now faced with an obligation to rebuild a partially ruined cathedral. A public meeting was held five days after the collapse of the spire on 26 February 1861. Hook rehearsed the measures that had been taken by the Chapter to save the spire, pointing out that neither the Cathedral architect, William Slater,[54] nor Ewan Christian, whom they had consulted for a second opinion, thought that collapse

59 *Dean Walter Farquhar Hook.*

60 *The Restoration Appeal—song written and composed by the wife of Canon Barré Phipps: 'No horrid crash betray'd its fall, The beautiful the grand! But gently like a ship at sea, Sank down no more to stand!'*

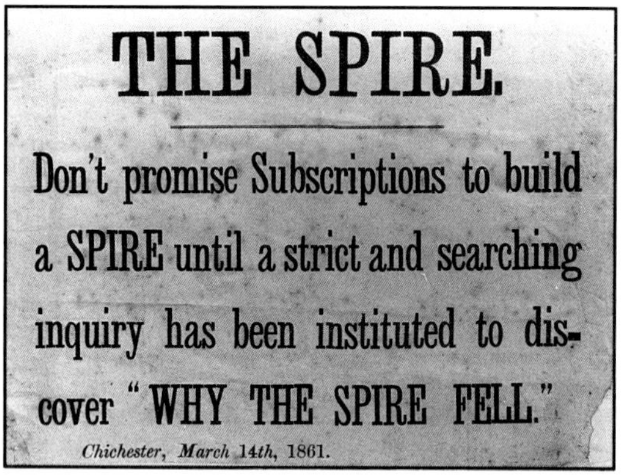
THE SPIRE.

Don't promise Subscriptions to build a SPIRE until a strict and searching inquiry has been instituted to discover "WHY THE SPIRE FELL."

Chichester, March 14th, 1861.

61 *Warning poster in Chichester.*

was imminent. The meeting, chaired by the Mayor of Chichester, resolved that, despite the likely astronomical cost, the spire, being the city's 'most noble ornament', had to be rebuilt. A special committee was appointed to raise the necessary funds and to oversee the work, and almost £28,000 had been raised in a very short period, half that sum being raised at the initial meeting alone.[55] Hook himself contributed £1,000, his income from the deanery for a whole year.[56] The eventual cost of the replacement of the spire was £70,000.[57]

For some months after the collapse of the spire the Cathedral could not be used for public worship. All the services were held in St Andrew's church until 17 August 1861 when the Cathedral nave was reopened, the Dean and Chapter donating £10 to the parish clerk of St Andrew's for the privilege.[58] The rebuilding committee felt that the restoration of the spire required a more competent architect than Slater and called in Sir George Gilbert Scott; Slater, however, was permitted to complete the restoration of the quire as originally planned. The first stone of the new spire was laid on 2 May 1865.[59] Work on the restoration of the quire began again in 1866 when the architect was instructed to proceed with the foundations of the stalls and the laying of concrete under the pavement. In January 1867 Slater was asked to submit a design for the new Bishop's Throne. Many of the fittings in the restored quire were personal gifts. These included the 'beautiful gas standards', the altar table, the eagle lectern and the altar frontal, kneeling stools and cushions worked by a team of ladies under the supervision of the Dean's wife.[60] The restored quire was formally opened on 17 November 1867. There was an octave of special services with distinguished guest preachers, a repetition of the celebrations Hook had held in Leeds for the reopening of the parish church in 1841. The accompanying jollifications of a more secular character included balloons, fireworks and a public dinner.[61]

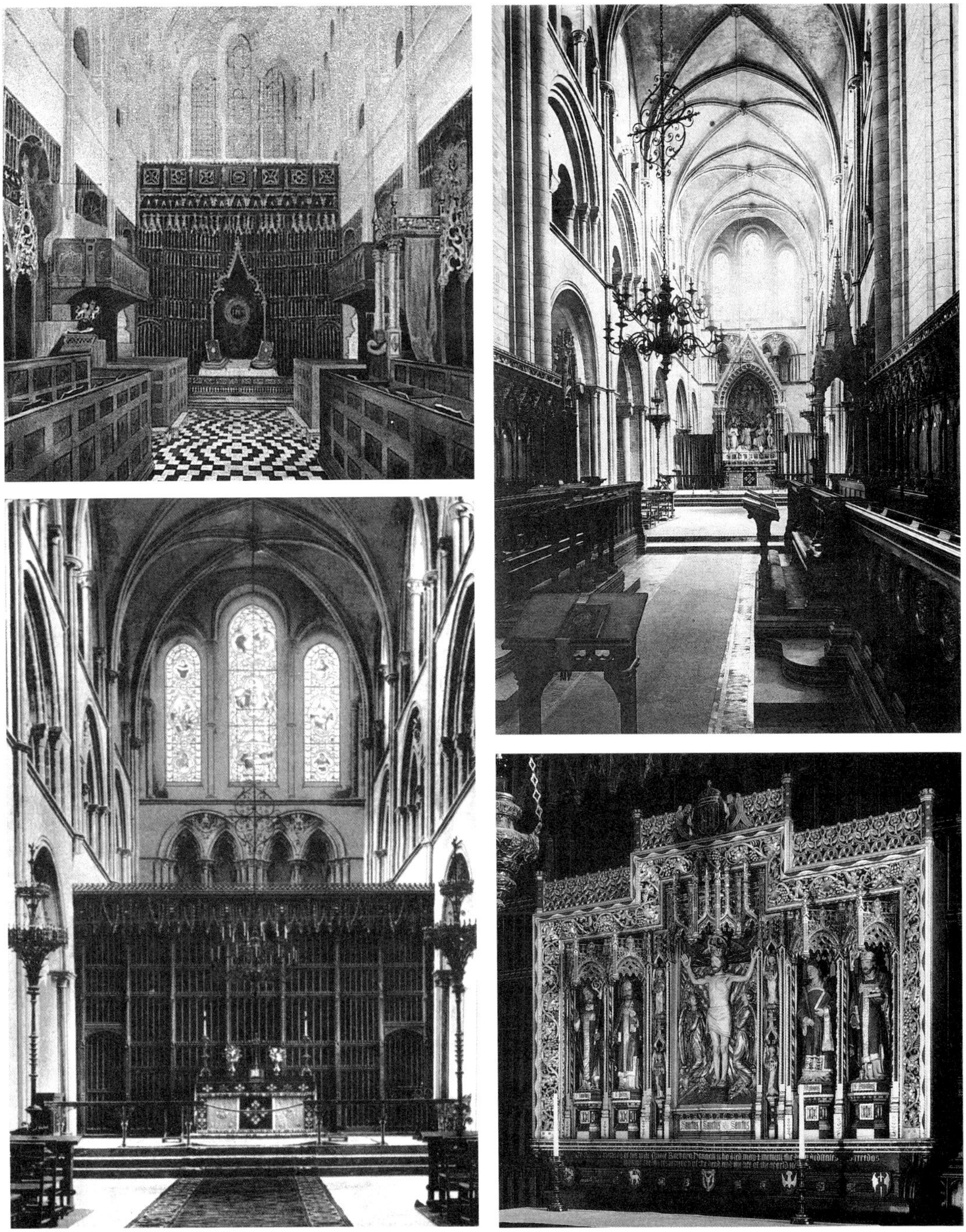

62 *The reredos (clockwise from top left): a. Before the 1829 restoration (drawing by Thomas King); b. Slater and Carpenter (1871); c. Interim after its removal; d. Somers Clarke (1910).*

The quire was finally completed with Slater and Carpenter's new reredos, to which Charles Swainson contributed £500. The new reredos was generally disliked. Within forty years it had been moved to St Saviour's in Brighton and replaced by a new high altar and reredos designed by Somers Clarke.[62] The rest of the new quire was generally appreciated by contemporaries when compared with the previous arrangements:

> There were ranges of high pews, besides galleries, under the arches. All this has been swept away; and the stall work which now exists is for the most part that of Bishop Sherborne, cleaned and repaired. The bishop's throne with its canopy, and the canopies above the return stalls at the west end, are altogether new, and perhaps hardly improvements on the old design. The front seats and desks are modern... It should be added that the reconstruction was greatly aided by the zeal of the Dean of Chichester, Dr Hook, who saw it brought to a happy conclusion.[63]

Several local churches benefited from the restoration, the former altar and its frontal being offered to Aldingbourne and its candlesticks to Funtington.[64]

Although the completion of the quire marked the end of the major work of restoration begun by Dean Chandler, a significant number of smaller-scale improvements were carried out in the last three decades of the 19th century. In 1871-2 the Lady Chapel was restored. The Duke of Richmond's family mausoleum and the Cathedral Library were dismantled and the library moved to the north transept chapel which had once formed part of the old subdeanery church.[65] In 1876-8 a new pulpit, designed by Sir George Gilbert Scott in Caen stone and Purbeck marble, was approved as a memorial to Dean Hook, and the former pulpit, given by Dean Chandler, offered to Pevensey parish church.[66] Rather more controversial was the proposal for the erection of a new screen across the west end of the choir as a memorial to Archdeacon Walker:

> The late Archdeacon of Chichester was an exceedingly popular man amongst all classes, and it will surprise many to read that very little money has been subscribed towards the memorial. Disagreement is apparently the cause of this apathy. The High Church party object to the screen because it will tend to hide the internal beauty of the Cathedral, and on the other hand, the Low Church party are entirely opposed to its erection at all, on the ground that it savours too much of Ritualistic-like adornment.[67]

After a good deal of discussion, the screen, designed by Bodley and Garner, was eventually installed in 1890.[68] On the initiative of Dean Pigou the cloisters were restored and re-opened for public use, also in 1890.[69] In 1891 the Lady Chapel was fitted out for weekday celebrations of Holy Communion and under Dean Randall several other side chapels were brought into use and fitted up with altars; the chapel of St Mary Magdalene was consecrated by Bishop Durnford in 1897. In 1894 Dean Randall offered £1,000 to restore the sanctuary pavement in the choir and to provide a sedilia, piscina and credence table to be designed by J.L. Pearson.[70]

Up until 1860 liturgical developments at Chichester were in line with, even to some extent in advance of, developments at most other cathedrals and large parish churches. After 1860 Chichester failed to keep in line with some innovations in cathedrals elsewhere, most notably in the provision of a Sunday evening service. The Chapter resolved to introduce one in Advent 1881 but it was abandoned within a few months; the idea was mooted again in 1890 but rejected. According to Dean Pigou 'we could not have a Sunday evening Nave Service, for if it had not depleted some of the city churches, it might well have seriously affected them, and have caused no little ill-will'. An even stronger motive was opposition

63 *The controversial Bodley and Garner screen in memory of Archdeacon Walker (1889-90), and the Hook memorial pulpit.*

THE CHICHESTER EXTINGUISHER.
BISHOP OF CHICHESTER. "GO! GO! YOU INSOLENT, REBELLIOUS BOY. WHAT WITH YOUR NONSENSE AND INCENSE AND CANDLES YOU'LL BE SETTING THE CHURCH ON FIRE."
MASTER P-CH-S. "JUST WHAT I'D LIKE TO DO. THERE!"
PUNCH, OR THE LONDON CHARIVARI.—OCTOBER 24, 1868.

64 *Cartoon on the celebrated confrontation between John Purchas, vicar of St James's, Brighton, and Bishop Durnford (judgement was passed against Purchas in 1871).*

from the vicars choral, most of whom held parochial preferment, and who could only combine this with their Cathedral duties if the latter were not too arduous. Pigou felt so frustrated at having so little to do on Sundays that he spent them, when not preaching at the Cathedral, in 'helping my brothers throughout the Diocese, for which they were more grateful than Chichester people were pleased'.[71] Another factor in delaying liturgical change at Chichester was the conservatism of Deans Hook and Burgon. At Leeds Hook had initially adopted and indeed put into practice the liturgical ideas of the Oxford Movement; early Communion services to permit communicants to receive fasting, the eastward position at the Holy Communion and preaching in the surplice. But he had reacted badly to the rows over ritualism in the 1840s and 1850s, and to his own personal experiences with the clergy of St Saviour's, Leeds, many of whom seceded to Rome between 1847 and 1851.[72] His attitude to ritual innovations as dean of Chichester is summed up in his comments on the prosecution of the ritualist Brighton incumbent, John Purchas.

> The chief blame in this case rests with Mr Purchas. He obtains notoriety by defying his superiors, and damages the Church by refusing to defend his case when he is prosecuted ... I signed a protest against the judgement, because for two and twenty years, at Leeds, I had consecrated in the eastward position. But I show that while claiming liberty for others, if liberty is granted by the Church, I consider the position of the celebrant a thing indifferent, as we do not use it in this cathedral.[73]

Burgon's anti-ritualistic stance was part of his all-embracing and deliberate conservative position. According to his biographer, 'Burgon adhered throughout his life to the views that the church movement, as originated by the primitive Tractarians, had nothing in common with that effervescence of Ritual, which indeed succeeded it historically, but which he held to be merely its running to seed and degeneration'.[74] Thus it was not until Pigou became dean that the eastward position was taken at celebrations of the Holy Communion in Chichester Cathedral, by which time the innovation had ceased to have much theological significance. Pigou himself commented that 'there are not a few of us, dubbed "High Church Evangelicals", who can consistently adopt the Eastward Position as the right interpretation of the rubric and as more convenient, without for one moment associating it with a sacerdotal act'.[75]

Under Hook and Burgon changes in the Cathedral services were few and far between and, it would seem, mostly adopted under pressure from the residentiary canons, especially

Swainson. Preaching on the State Days—the anniversaries of the execution of Charles I, the restoration of Charles II and the discovery of the Gunpowder Plot—was discontinued in 1860, and with the restoration of the quire in 1867 the practice was adopted of reading the lessons from the newly-donated eagle lectern, an innovation which occasioned a letter of mild reproof from Bishop Gilbert:[76]

Xmas Eve 1867

My Dear Dean

There can be no necessity for your reading at the Eagle when you take either the first or the second Lesson, or, as you have occasionally both, in the Cathedral Service. I believe mine is the worst place of all for hearing, before the Holy Communion, but I always hear you fully and clearly when you take any part of the prayers. Your stall, it appears to me, is the best, and I know it to be a sufficient position for you until you go within the Communion Rails. Nor can I forbear adding I think our chief Cathedral Dignitary ought not to be walked up and down as you humbly have condescended. Please excuse the boldness of

Yrs faithfully and affectionately

A T Cicestr:

The Chapter resolved to adopt the revised lectionary from 1 January 1872,[77] and between 1873 and 1877 the Cathedral moved gradually to the adoption of a weekly early celebration of the Holy Communion on Sundays at 8 a.m.[78] The numbers of communicants were never very large. Between 1870 and 1880 they averaged about ninety at Easter, seventy at Whitsun, sixty at Christmas, and somewhat fewer on an ordinary Sunday.[79] *Hymns Ancient and Modern* was used from the beginning of Advent 1877, somewhat later than in many other cathedrals, and the full sequence of coloured altar frontals introduced early in 1878,[80] but these were minor tinkerings with an attitude to worship at Chichester which was beginning to look distinctly old-fashioned by the last quarter of the 19th century. In the words of Dean Pigou, 'Morning Service in the Cathedral, lasting from 10.30 to 1, is the most sleep-inducing I have ever had to attend'.[81] During Pigou's tenure of the deanery, collections were introduced at all the Sunday services, a regular weekday celebration of the Holy Communion was begun on Thursdays, additional early celebrations at 7 a.m. took place at Easter, Whitsun and Christmas, choral celebrations were introduced on the first Sunday of each month after Morning Prayer, the vergers made to wear cassocks when on duty, and the organist instructed to play 'some soft and suitable music' during the administration of Holy Communion.[82]

As might have been expected from his ritualist background, Dean Randall saw it as his mission to make the Cathedral services both more colourful in terms of ceremonial and more parochial, with a greater measure of congregational participation. Both moves were unpopular, one being seen as ritualistic, the other as an attack on the Cathedral music. The liturgical outlook of the Cathedral changed more in the period of Randall's brief tenure of the deanery than it had at any time during the previous two centuries. Randall's first act was to make the late Communion service choral every Sunday, the parts to be sung being the introit, *Kyries*, responses before and after the Gospel, Nicene Creed, offertory sentence, *Sursum Corda*, Preface, *Sanctus*, *Gloria* and, on the greater festivals, a seven-fold *Amen*. In 1894 an additional early celebration on most Sundays was introduced; from 1895 Holy Communion was celebrated daily in Advent, Lent, the octaves of Christmas, Easter and the

Ascension, and between Whitsun and Trinity Sunday; a daily celebration throughout the year began in 1896.[83] In 1898 the Chapter resolved that the 8 a.m. celebration on Sundays, Wednesdays, Fridays and Holy Days should take place in either the choir or the Lady Chapel, and the 7 a.m. celebration on Sundays, and the 8 a.m. celebration on Mondays, Tuesdays, Thursdays and Saturdays in St Clement's Chapel.

The resistance to change on the part of some members of the Chapter is, however, revealed by the fact that Randall did not introduce the use of Eucharistic vestments at Chichester, though he had worn them at Bristol for more than twenty years, and even coloured stoles were not worn in the Cathedral until 1900; the altar candles were lighted at all Communion services, but they were not lit at Evensong until 1901, and only then between Michaelmas and Easter.[84] In 1897 there was considerable opposition to Randall's attempts to change the main morning service in the Cathedral. He persuaded the Chapter to agree firstly that the singing of the Litany and the hymns should be made more congregational and that to achieve this the organist should play louder, and later that the *Agnus Dei* and a hymn should be sung at the Communion.[85] Shorter settings were adopted for the anthems and canticles. The Dean was attacked in the local press and, after a campaign clearly orchestrated by the organist and choir, a petition was signed by over 400 residents of Chichester complaining that the standard of music in the Cathedral was being reduced to the level of a mere parish church.[86] Local objections to the relatively modest ritual innovations in the Cathedral came to a head on 6 October 1900 when Divine Service was interrupted by the Evangelical rector of St Pancras', Chichester, who was subsequently disciplined by Bishop Wilberforce.[87]

The Cathedral and Theological Education

In their search for a future rôle for cathedrals in the 1830s, some churchmen, anxious to respond positively to those clamouring for reform, suggested that they could provide post-graduate theological training for those wishing to become ordained clergymen of the Church of England. Colleges for the training of non-graduate clergy had been provided at St Bees and Lampeter in 1816 and 1822 respectively. Only two cathedrals, Chichester and Wells, had decided to co-operate with their respective bishops, William Otter and G.H. Law, in the establishment of a theological college by 1840, though colleges were later founded at Lichfield (1857), Salisbury (1861), Exeter (1861), Gloucester (1868), Lincoln (1874), and Ely (1876). The college at Chichester, founded in 1839, had the full support of the Dean and Chapter from the start and a particularly close relationship between the Cathedral and the college—much more so, for example, than at Wells—was maintained throughout the 19th century.

In its return to the first Cathedrals Commission the Chapter reported that 'a theological college has been established with very considerable success. One of the two residentiary houses is given up for this purpose free of rent, the dean and chapter paying the rates and taxes'. In fact the early years of the Theological College were somewhat shaky. Otter and Chandler had secured as first principal Charles Marriott, fellow and tutor of Oriel College, Oxford, and an avowed, though not extreme, Tractarian. The establishment was small and there was, unlike the college founded by Bishop Wilberforce at Cuddesdon in 1854, no common life. The curriculum was restricted. There was no practical training. The students 'read in the Bible daily from twelve to one.' Apart from this there was the study of doctrine and Church history, with the emphasis being on the early Fathers or Anglican divines of

65 *View of the Palace gateway about 1907, showing (on the left) 4 Canon Lane, one of the two residentiary houses accommodating Theological College students in the 1870s.*

the late 16th, 17th and early 18th centuries: 'the students are expected to abstain from public amusements, and from sporting' and to inform the Principal 'when they wish to be absent from our meals, and never to miss a lecture without leave'.[90]

Marriott was in poor health and, as a result, forced to return to Oxford, and hand over the principalship to Henry Browne. In 1845-6 the college was suspended for five months and revived under Philip Freeman, who was succeeded as principal by Charles Swainson in 1854. Under Freeman the college attracted between six and ten students a year, and occasionally admitted non-graduates. The college went through another difficult period in the late 1850s. Its future looked so insecure that Dean Chandler, in a codicil to his will, revoked the bequest of his library to the college. When Chandler died in 1859 his executors were able to decide whether his legacy of £2,000 should go to the Cathedral, the Theological College or a new church in Chichester. Swainson applied to the executors for £300 to improve the college's accommodation and his own salary, which fell well short of those received by the principals of the other cathedral theological colleges at Wells and Lichfield. His application was rejected when it was decided that the whole £2,000 should be offered to the Cathedral for the restoration of the quire. Swainson thought that some of the prebendaries had lobbied the executors against the college. Meanwhile student numbers failed to rise. Because of the college's limited accommodation, the students were obliged not only to meet the cost of the fees but also to pay the rent of lodgings licensed by the college. The policy of trying to maintain the college as one designed largely for post-graduate training was finally abandoned by Arthur Ashwell, who succeeded Swainson as principal in 1870.

The close relationship between the Theological College and the Cathedral was strengthened when Charles Swainson was collated to the prebend of Firle in 1854. The difficulties over the principal's salary were also partially resolved by the appointment of the principal to one of the residentiary canonries. This arrangement began with Swainson in 1863, and continued under Ashwell and his immediate successors. In 1875 Dean Hook's son-in-law and future biographer, W.R.W. Stephens, then lecturer at the Theological College, was collated to the prebend of Wightring, the holder of which was obliged to deliver divinity lectures in the Cathedral. When the restoration of the Lady Chapel was completed in 1872, the Dean and Chapter agreed that it might be used as the chapel of the Theological College.[92] In addition the students of the college attended one of the Cathedral services each day wearing their gowns and hoods.[93]

The Cathedral and the Wider Community

One of the greatest changes in the rôle of cathedrals in the 19th century was their relationship to the local community and the diocese of which they were the mother church. At the beginning of the century, and in most cases until well into its second half, this rôle was virtually non-existent. Cathedral chapters were nervous that if they developed a closer link with the diocese they would lose that independence which they had jealously preserved over the centuries against the attempted encroachments of successive bishops. Until 1845, when they were swept away in the reforms emanating from the Ecclesiastical Commission, deans had their own peculiars within which they exercised all those powers normally reserved to bishops and their archdeacons. Within the municipal communities of which they were geographically a part, deans and chapters were an exempt corporation, the precincts of the cathedral being, in effect, a city within a city. This was another area in which cathedral chapters had been particularly jealous of their rights and privileges. Another area of potential difficulty for the Cathedral lay in its relationship with the city's parish churches. The Cathedral was expected to maintain services for its own Chapter and for those who lived within the precincts which was, in effect, the Cathedral parish, but it was not expected to poach worshippers from other parish churches in the city.

The religious condition of Chichester in the mid-19th century is not very accurately revealed in the returns made in response to the religious census of 30 March 1851.[94] The parish of St Peter the Great also included the new district church of St Paul but it is unlikely that the parochial census return of 360 adult worshippers includes those at St Paul's as well as those worshipping at the subdeanery church in the Cathedral. Neither the Cathedral nor the extra-parochial district of St James returned the forms. The minister of the Unitarian Chapel returned the form but declined to answer any of the questions. Many returns omitted vital information, especially in relation to sittings and to Sunday scholars and, for the Church of England, the adult congregations of three of its places of worship. Altogether the returns show total adult congregations of some 2,722 in the 12 Anglican places of worship, 467 in the two independent chapels, 490 in the two Calvinist chapels and only 300 in four other meeting houses: Unitarian General Baptists, Society of Friends, Wesleyan Methodists and Bible Christians. When one takes into account the missing or defective returns, which may well have underestimated Anglican congregations by over a thousand worshippers, it becomes clear that the Church of England had retained a dominant position over all the other religious groupings in Chichester. In a somewhat overchurched community of only 8,647 people, it had succeeded in attracting over 80 per cent of the adult attendances in the city.

SAFETY OF THE CATHEDRAL

FROM FIRE!!

It is now a matter of public notoriety that the Dean and Chapter of Chichester have received the highest legal opinion that it is beyond their power to lease to the Chichester Water Company the Campanile for the purposes of a Water Tower. But, in the face of this adverse opinion, we understand the Directors of the Company have not yet relinquished their endeavour to push forward their measure, but are now busy in scheming to carry out in some way or other, their proposal, which has caused such anxiety and alarm.

Notwithstanding the impartial verdict of public opinion, in spite of the illegality of their endeavour, against the well-grounded fears and anxieties of all true Churchmen and admirers of the beautiful in art and lovers of antiquity, setting aside a petition against the scheme, signed by the Mayor and Corporation of the City, and by over 200 individuals, representing, not a narrow section, as is stated, but a large and influential body of the inhabitants, among whom are seen the signatures of many of the Clergy, the Dissenting Ministers, legal and professional residents, and citizens, representing every shade of opinion in the City, the Company still show the want of common sense by persisting to push their proposal to an ultimate issue.

The question has been so well ventilated, and its demerits exposed, that I must apologise for introducing it again to the public; but there appears to me to be a point in the argument that has not received the careful attention which I think its importance deserves, and that is the *presumed advantages* of the Campanile Tank in case of a fire in the Cathedral.

Canon Swainson, in his efforts to place before the public in a plausible manner his plan, of which he openly avows that he is "prepared to take upon himself the responsibility of proposing," has chosen to base his strongest argument on the possibility of a fire occurring in the Cathedral. He has, so far, succeeded in awakening the anxieties of a few of our timid neighbours, by arguments for the furtherance of his aim. But, I ask, has he fairly placed the question before us? He says, "The advantages of the Campanile for a Tank over the Company's Tower are enormous in case of fire." In a letter to the *West Sussex Gazette*, he also states, "*The Company's Reservoir, when completed will only furnish pressure of a head of water three quarter's of a mile distant at an elevation of fifty-four feet. My plan* (*i.e.* the conversion of the Campanile) *gives security to the Cathedral beyond measure, infinitely superior to that we anticipated three months ago.*" He here forgets to remember that the Company are bound by their Act to erect a Water Tower which will give an additional pressure of fifty feet, making the *pressure at the Cross* 104 *feet*, which, accordingly to their own Engineer, when examined before the Committee of the House of Lords *on oath*, will be amply sufficient for all requirements in case of fire and which shows clearly and conclusively that if the Company carry out their works in their *legitimate* way, our Cathedral will be quite as safe as Canon Swainson would lead us to believe the appropriation of the Campanile will render it.

The following is extracted from the Evidence of Mr. William Shelford, Engineer of the Company, when examined on the 24th of March last, before the Committee of the House of Lords:

Have you measured the roof of Chichester Cathedral?—No, except in my eye.

It is mere guess work?—I give you a good idea.

What is it?—Between seventy and eighty feet.

And the (*Company's water*) tower?—That will throw water over it.

What is the height?—104 feet above the cross.

The height of the tower of the cathedral—could you touch it?—We have a special arrangement for that. If a conflagration occurred at the cathedral, the general water supply would be shut off out by a stop-valve, and the pump would force water through the pipes to a height which would be only limited by the capability of the pipes to stand the pressure.

Suppose a fire happened in the night, when the works are not working?—The fires are kept banked up.

You are to keep the fires banked up in case of a conflagration in the roof and tower of Chichester Cathedral. Is that so?—If we are obliged to do it we should keep the fires banked up, but not for that purpose.

Without having them banked up, and having the engines ready for forcing the water up, **you could not touch the roof and Tower of Chichest-r Cathedral?—The main body of the building WE COULD,** but not the stone Spire.

And send word to your engine-house for the purpose of having the fire stirred up—the engines put to work, and so to obtain water—that is what you suggest as necessary?—Putting out a fire at the top of Chichester Cross is a thing that would not be likely to occur.

I am speaking of the Cathedral?—I am speaking of the tower of Chichester Cathedral—I mean the Spire. There is no necessity to provide engine power to put out a fire on the top of Chichester Spire.

At the top of the Tower I am speaking of?—That is very much lower.

It is a great deal higher than the top of the Cross?—Yes.

Could you touch that without having your fires banked up, and everything ready to force the water in the manner you describe?—The top of the spire we could not touch, the top of the tower is eighty feet above the ground.

Have you measured it?—No; there is no roof.

From your eye you gave an opinion—what should you say with an ordinary supply of water and the fires not banked. **Could you with the ordinary pressure put out a fire?—WE COULD PUT OUT ANY FIRE THAT IS LIKELY TO OCCUR.**

But is the tower which you propose of fifty feet amply high enough for supplying the whole of the City of Chichester with water, and all the purposes for which the water is required?—Yes, amply high.

Now with your present tower, your fifty feet tower, you can throw water over the roof of Chichester Cathedral, you said so I think?—**Yes, over the nave—all that part which is liable to fire.**

With your present head of water are you able to extinguish any fire that is likely to take place in Chichester?—Yes; we can supply any quantity that is required in case of a fire.

This evidence establishes beyond controversion that the endeavour to convert the Campanile into a Water Tower is for no other purpose than to serve the Company, and I defy Canon Swainson or any of the Directors to gainsay the fact. It is a proposal that is alike indecent and unwarrantable, and cannot be defended with any sense of logic, reason, truth or justice.

In the face of these facts is it possible for us to be mis-led as to the safety of the Cathedral?

In conclusion, the only possible advantage that will be effected by the Company's plan will be the gain of a few months in making the Cathedral safe; but 900 years having passed without such an catastrophe occuring, are we prepared to give our adhesion and sanction this haste, at the expense of destroying the charm that pervades our "unique Campanile" with the recollections of its antiquity, and giving it over to the relentless and desecrating hand of the utilitarian.

Chichester, October 17th, 1873. **CLERICUS.**

MOORE, PRINTER, EAST GATE, CHICHESTER.

66 *Another warning poster, this time involving Canon Swainson!*

The Cathedral was drawn into much closer contact with both the City and the Diocese because of its need to attract financial support for its restoration programme after 1847, and even more so after the collapse of the spire in 1861. In 1852-4 the Cathedral and City authorities co-operated in the demolition of the shops and houses on the south side of West Street, with the result that, for the first time, the Cathedral was fully visible from one of the main streets of the city.[96] In 1872 the Chapter resolved that, as the recipients died off, the Cathedral bread money should no longer be paid to individuals but instead offered to the Chichester Nurses Association.[97] In 1865 special collections were started in the Cathedral for various educational and missionary societies, for the national Additional Curates Society and for the Diocesan Association founded by Bishop Otter, and in 1866 an annual service was established in aid of funds for the Chichester Infirmary. [98] An even more significant move was the use of the Cathedral for major Diocesan services, such as the festival of parochial choirs in Chichester and its environs, first held in 1868.[99]

The changes that took place at Chichester in the 19th century were replicated, to a greater or lesser extent, in every one of the ancient cathedrals in England and Wales. There is no doubt that these changes were considerable but they should not be exaggerated. The element of continuity was very great as well, so that change was slow and sometimes painful. It is clear that at Chichester the initial impetus for change came in the desire of Dean Chandler to do something about the fabric. The restoration of the Cathedral, complicated by the fall of the spire, was to dominate completely the business of the Chapter for a 20-year period between 1847 and 1867. The early positive response in Chichester to the idea that cathedrals might promote theological education was also well ahead of contemporary attitudes elsewhere. There were other respects in which the Cathedral was very slow to respond to the pressure for change and anxious to maintain long-established traditions. This was particularly so in respect of the Cathedral services, but it can also be seen in the very slow recognition that the Cathedral had a more positive rôle to play as a spiritual centre for both City and Diocese. The key to all this was the length of time it took for the composition of the Chapter to change, with prebendaries brought up in the tradition of the pre-reform Church of England still present within the chapter until almost the end of the 19th century. The history of Chichester Cathedral in the 19th century provides evidence of both change and continuity. In chronicling the former we should not disregard the latter, nor should we undervalue the strengths of the pre-reform Church of England and that group of conservative high churchmen like Chandler, Hook and Burgon, who continued to represent many of the values of an older tradition whilst at the same time endeavouring to meet the challenges of new generations with different needs.

IX

Destruction, Repair and Restoration

Tim Tatton-Brown

As so often, the first major acts of destruction occurred in the Cathedral in 1538. The shrine of St Richard, which was at that time the third most popular in England (after St Thomas of Canterbury and Walsingham), was demolished on Friday 20 November and all the silver, gold and jewels were ordered by Henry VIII to be taken to the Tower of London. His instructions to his commissioners, through Thomas Cromwell, went on:

> And also that ye shall see bothe the place where the same shryne standyth to be raysed and defaced even to the very ground, and all such other images of the church as any notable superstition hath been used to be taken and conveyed away.[1]

This was no doubt efficiently carried out, and at the same time the Commissioners seem to have ordered the 'breaking up' of a tomb in the Lady Chapel (probably Bishop Gilbert's tomb in the niche on the south side) which they evidently thought was also being 'abused' as a shrine. In 1544 Wolsey, the mason, was given the job of 'amending of the Tumbe in our Lady Chapel', cost 15d.[2] In 1550 the stone altars were also ordered to be 'plucked down', and replaced by a communion table, but Bishop Day objected to this and was subsequently deprived of his see in 1551, and replaced by Bishop

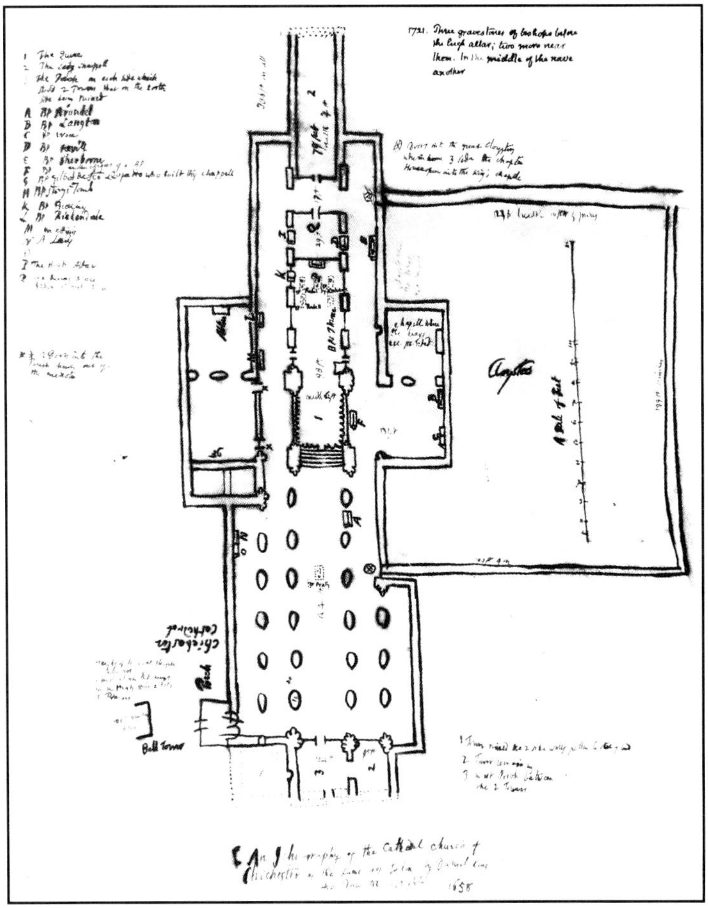

67 *Daniel King's plan of the Cathedral 1658 (now lost): copy by Browne Willis in the 18th century.*

68 *Detail from Wenceslaus Hollar's engraving of the Cathedral showing the crenellations to tidy up the north-west tower.*

Scory.[3] Bishop Day returned, however, under Queen Mary and preached at Edward VI's funeral, and Mary's coronation, and in 1556, as Dr. Brighton has shown, Lambert Barnard was painting the carved figures on the re-erected Rood. Finally under Queen Elizabeth (in 1561) he painted the Ten Commandments on 6¼ ells of cloth behind the altar; this, as Edward Croft-Murray says, 'is one of the earliest recorded instances of an embellishment which was to become so characteristic of the Anglican East End'.[4]

With the destruction of the stone altars in the outer nave chapels it is likely that the reredoses behind them were also destroyed, and, at the same time, the screen walls between the chapels were removed to turn the space into outer aisles. During this period of change, the fabric was 'made good' after the removal of the stone altars, images, and St Richard's shrine, and the body of the Cathedral became, from the time of Elizabeth, more of a preaching house. After the final destruction of the great Rood above the Arundel Screen, the organs were apparently removed from the Lady Chapel to the top of the screen, and in 1588 repairs were done on them.[5] In 1563, repairs to the spire had been the cause of the sale of Cathedral plate.

By the early 17th century the cathedral fabric was in poor condition, and a major calamity, the collapse of the north-west tower, happened in or shortly before 1636. Dr L.F. Salzman discovered and published a most interesting 'estimate of the new building of the Tower that is now fallen downe at the West end of the Cathedrall Church of Chichester 1636'.[6] It gives full costings for the '12,000 foote of Portland Stone Ashler' to be used, as well as interesting details about how the work was to be done. It is followed by detailed estimates for the repair of the subdeanery (i.e. north transept) roof 'most of it very rotten and much decaied and like to throwe downe the walls ...'. There was also a proposal to rebuild one quarter of the vault here because it was 'very dangerous to those that sitt under it and readie to fall upon them'. There are then other estimates for mending almost all the other roofs in the Cathedral, and for moving the bells into the newly rebuilt north-west tower, with a total estimate of £3,404 and 3 shillings for all the work.

None of this work seems to have been carried out, and only six years later, on 30 December 1642, Sir William Waller entered the Cathedral with his rabble of soldiers.[7] It was probably at this time that the tracery in the great west window was destroyed (and that in the great south window was damaged). The great west window was packed up after 1660 with plain wooden mullions until 1847, while 'wooden props served instead of mullions for many years to hold up the tracery above' in the great south window.[8] The steep-pitched medieval roofs over the two transepts, the first-floor chapel east of the north transept (now the Cathedral Library), and the Lady Chapel, were also probably destroyed at this time. They were all later replaced with low-pitched roofs, presumably in the late 17th century. New steep-pitched roofs were again restored to the transepts in the mid-19th century. The surviving triforium roofs were probably also made in the late 17th century.[9]

After the Restoration, Bishop Henry King set in motion a campaign to 'repair and beautify' the Cathedral, as the list in the south transept of donors to the fund (fig.45), and the amount raised (£1,780), shows, with even the altar plate being sold to increase the funds. By 1675, however, there was still much to do as Bishop Ralph Brideoake's Visitation makes clear,[10] and it is at this time that we have our first large-scale depiction of the Cathedral, a 'North Prospect' done in *c.*1660 by Daniel King (fig.44), who also seems to have made a plan of the interior of the Cathedral at the same time (now lost; it had been copied by Browne Willis in the early 18th century).[11] A little later (*c.*1684) Sir Christopher Wren suggested that the south-west tower should also be demolished, and that the west end be entirely rebuilt at 'half the charge' of rebuilding the north-west tower.[12] Luckily this advice was not acted upon, and instead only the dangerous upper parts of the tower were removed (and made good against the Cathedral nave). A little later a low façade was made on the west with a north-west turret and an upward-sloping crenellated wall.[13] In 1707 the crossing tower into the north transept was found to be dangerous and was repaired.

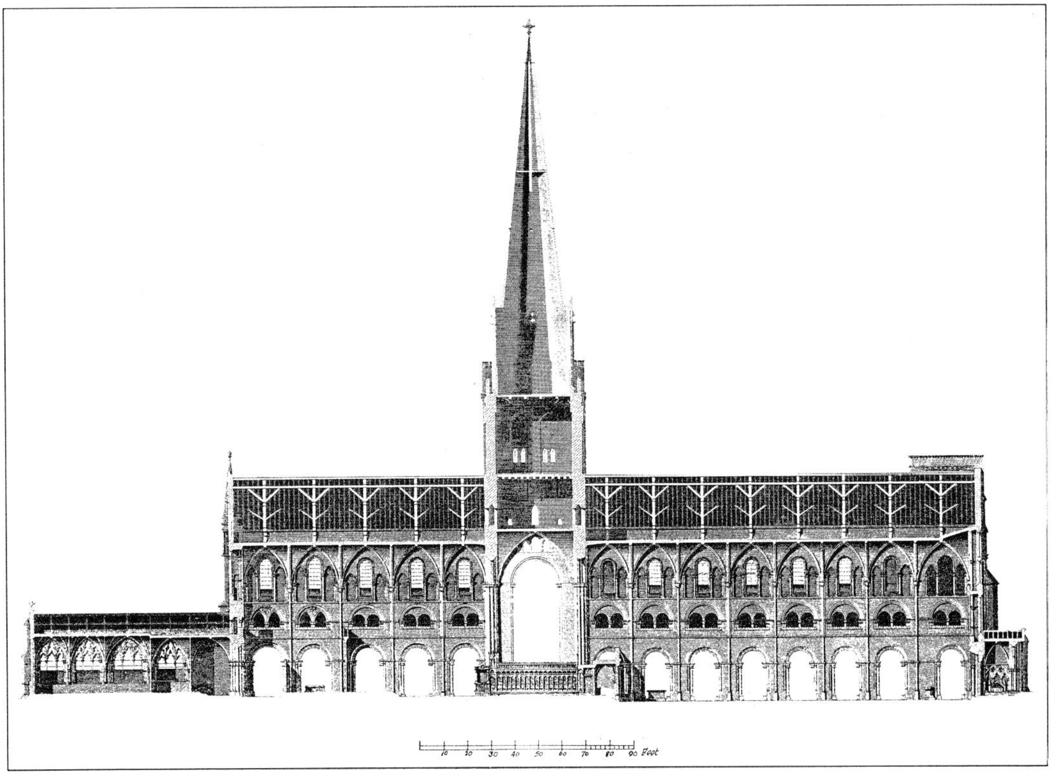

69 *Le Keux's section through the Cathedral, c.1815, showing the ruined north-west tower and east end.*

During the 18th century various works are recorded, starting with repairs to the upper part of the spire after a lightning strike in 1721. At the end of the previous century, the top of the spire had also been strengthened by Sir Christopher Wren who, according to James Elmes,[14]

> took down and rebuilt the upper part of the spire of the cathedral and fixed therein a pendulum stage to counteract the effects of the south and south-westerly gales which act with some considerable power against it, and had forced it from its perpendicularity.

This 'pendulum' stage is depicted in Elmes' book as well as in Le Keux's fine longitudinal section of the cathedral of *c.*1815; it seems likely that Wren got some of his ideas for installing this after studying the timber-scaffold inside the spire of Salisbury Cathedral.[15] The Chichester pendulum was 'taken down and reinstated' by James Elmes when he carried out repairs in 1813-14.[16]

As usual in the 18th century, tidiness and neatness was what was required, and new paving was introduced into the 'great chapter house' (presumably the south transept) in 1729 and into the quire in 1731.[17] The latter was completely refloored with black-and-white marble, and the many floor slabs, with indents for brasses, were moved into the nave and aisles. The quire and presbytery were refurbished at this time with new pews, and galleries were also put under the arches of the presbytery. It should not be forgotten that, apart from the subdeanery area (which was still a parish church), the quire and presbytery area was the only part of the Cathedral used for worship between the Restoration and the mid-19th century.

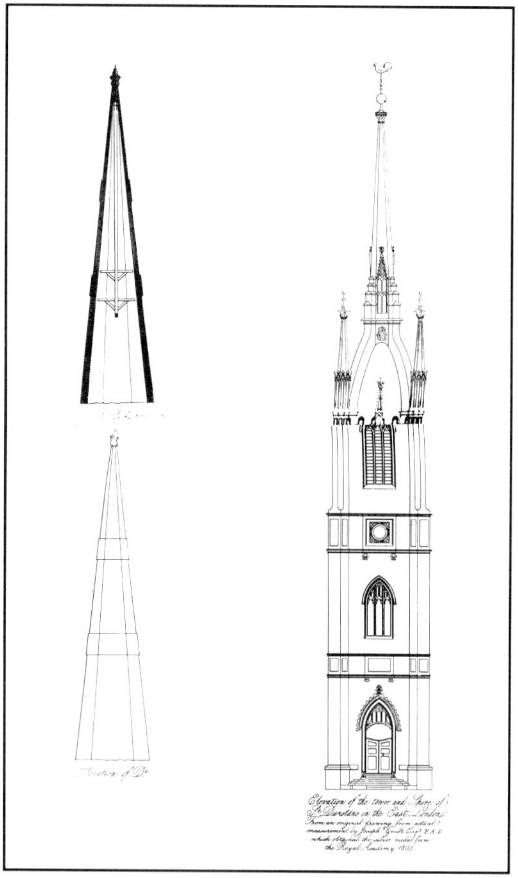

70 *Sir Christopher Wren's pendulum structure, restored in the 19th century by the Cathedral architect James Elmes.*

In 1750 the Lady Chapel, which was said to be partly ruinous, was granted to the Duke of Richmond as a family mausoleum, and a vault was 'diged and made'. The floor above this was then raised over the vault and the east window and the lower parts of the other windows were plastered up.[18] Finally a fireplace and chimney were built in front of the east window of the Lady Chapel. The three eastern bays then became the Cathedral Library, with an ante-room in the bay beyond at the top of a flight of steps. Steps also went down into the Duke's vault.[19] The Lady Chapel remained in this state until 1871. This was done in Bishop Mawson's time and it is possible that he employed the architect, James Essex, to do other works in the Cathedral, but no details seem to exist.[20] Little else appears to have been done in the Cathedral for over half a century, and Grimm's fine drawings of the late 18th century give a good

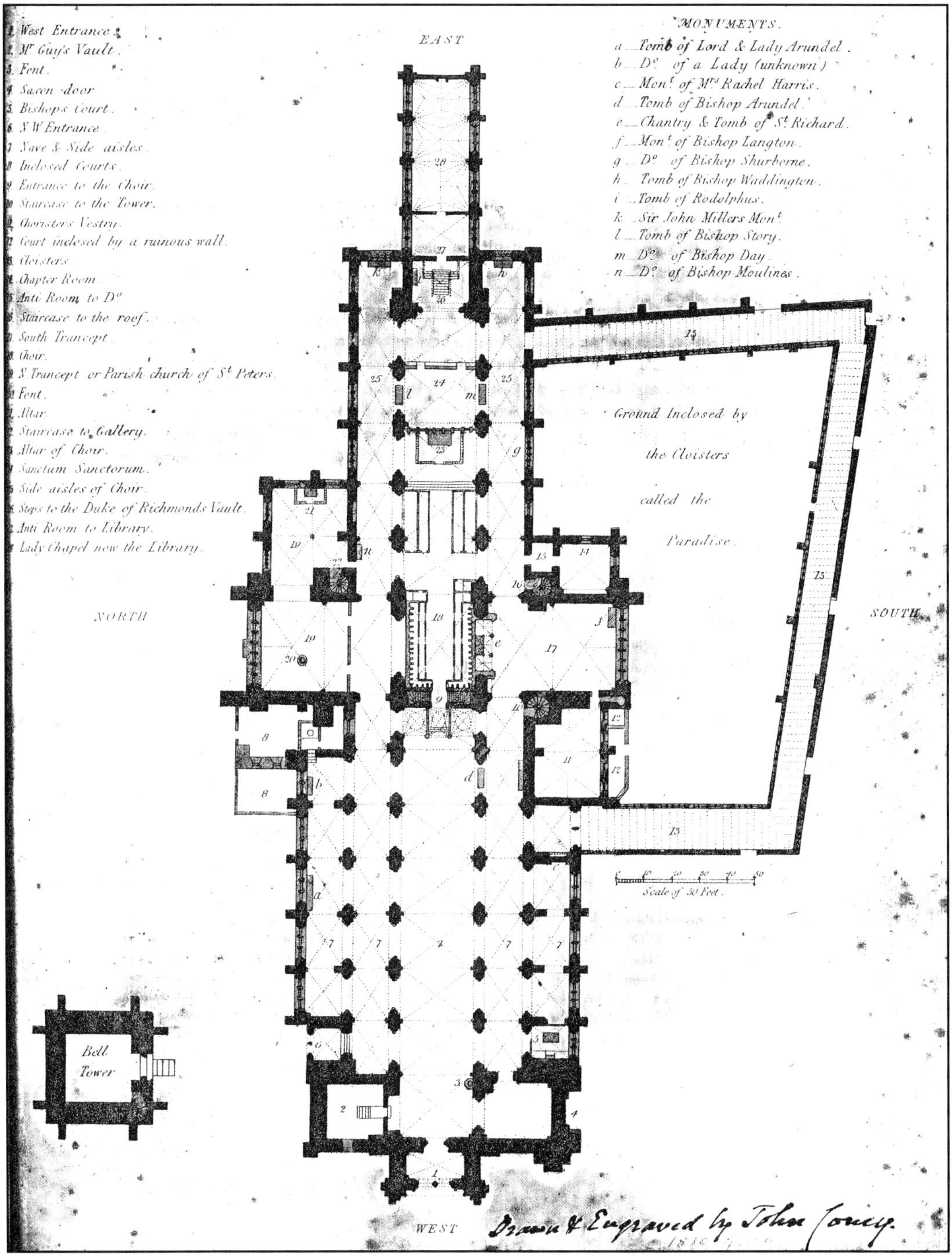

71 *John Coney's plan of the Cathedral (1826).*

idea of the state of the buildings, inside and out, before its many 19th-century alterations.[21] In 1800 a large burial vault was built in the shell of the north-west tower for Mr. Guy and his family. He was an eminent local surgeon.

72 *S.H. Grimm, the south-east exterior, 1781.*

The 19th Century

By the beginning of the 19th century, the Cathedral was in a very poor state of repair, and the first restorations were from 1812-17, when, as we have seen, James Elmes, a London architect, was brought in to make repairs. By 1817 almost all of Lambert Barnard's fine vault paintings were covered with a 'dirty yellow wash' and later destroyed when this was removed in the 1830s.[22] Most of Elmes' other repairs seem to have been largely cosmetic. Then in 1829 'major repairs and improvements' were carried out in the quire and presbytery. Between May and November, this area of the Cathedral was closed for extensive work to be carried out and it was at this time that the famous 'Chichester Reliefs' were found 'just above the choir stalls' on the eastern crossing piers, and removed to their present position in the south quire aisle.[23] At the same time the galleries (and their brick supports) and some tombs around the high altar were removed, including the gallery/bridge over the 15th-century reredos screen behind the high altar. The early Romanesque arches were then 'made good' with many new masonry voussoirs. Portions of the very fine late 13th-century ironwork screen which had perhaps originally surrounded the shrine of St Richard were also removed at this time.[24] These screen fragments were sold to a 'marine store dealer', and eventually bought by the Victoria and Albert Museum in 1896.[25]

The year following the major works in the quire saw the arrival as dean of the 'new broom', George Chandler. After having Elmes' wash removed and new stained glass put in, he also apparently removed the late medieval embattled parapet walls in the triforium galleries, throughout the nave and presbytery. In 1841, after Joseph Butler had been appointed architect and surveyor, the subdeanery church in the north transept was opened up to the rest of the Cathedral and, less than a dozen years later, as we have seen, it was removed to the fine new church of St Peter the Great, now redundant. The architect, R.C. Carpenter, restored the tracery of the great west window and the nave side chapel windows in 1847.[26] (His bogus plate tracery in the south nave chapels, and in the chapel of St Edmund, was the least successful part of his work.) With the opening of the new church in 1852, the pews and galleries were removed from the north transept and the two transepts were given new roofs at their original medieval pitch. For the first time in at least 400 years the north transept was therefore reintegrated into the Cathedral, and shortly

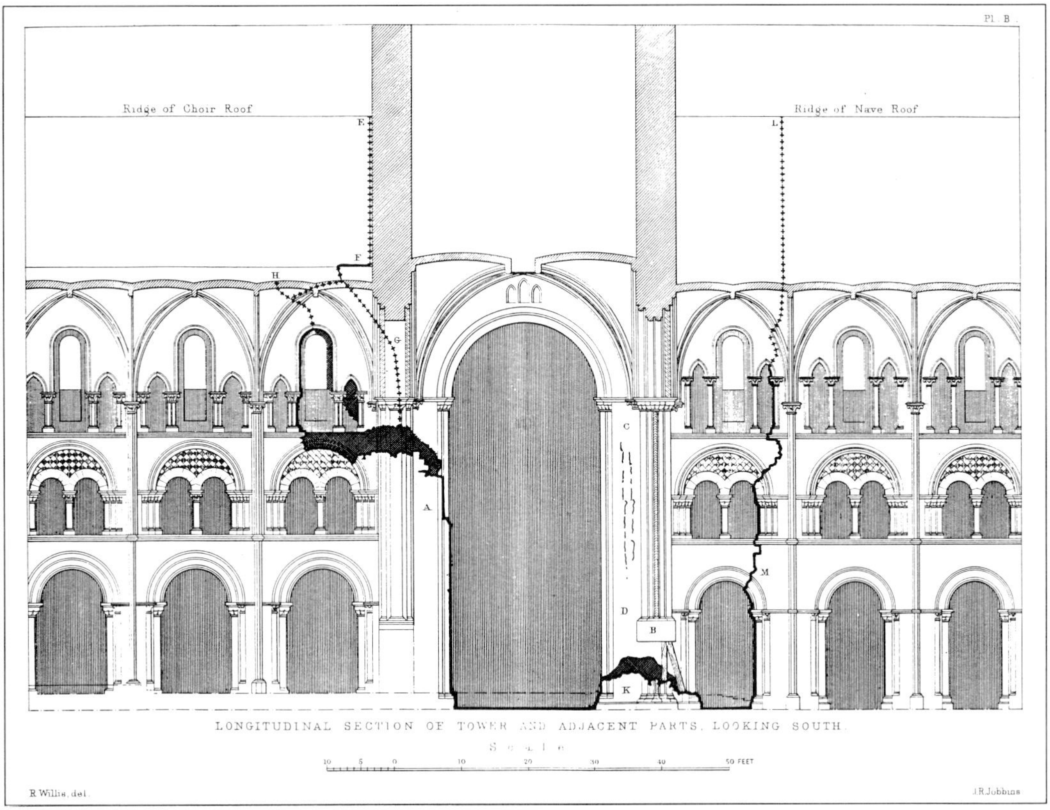

73 *Professor Robert Willis's section of the tower and adjacent parts (Plate B).*

afterwards (1853) the nave was fitted out with Chandler's pulpit and pews, for use once again for services.[27]

In July 1853 the Archaeological Institute of Great Britain and Ireland visited the city for a week, and on Wednesday 13th, Professor Robert Willis delivered his celebrated lecture on the architectural history of the Cathedral, followed in the afternoon by his guided tour.[28]

In 1859, work was started on yet another major restoration in the quire, this time under the architect William Slater. The Arundel Screen and the great organ above were taken down early in 1860 (the individual blocks of the screen were carefully numbered for re-erection in a different location and stored in the north aisle of the nave[29]), and the 14th-century return stalls behind the screen were removed. (The huge cracks revealed in the crossing piers were fully described by Slater.)[30]

Work was undertaken to repair these defects during the summer and autumn of 1860, but by November fresh settlement had begun in the new work. In desperation much shoring was put in, but still the cracking continued, as Nigel Yates vividly describes above. The timber jackets with iron hoops were of no avail and soon it became apparent that the total collapse of the tower and spire was imminent. Seventy men worked from 3.30 a.m. on Thursday 21 February 1861 but the inevitable happened and at just before half past one the spire fell.

74 *Drawing of Chichester Cathedral by George Scharf from room 28 of the* Dolphin Hotel.

Robert Willis had returned to Chichester soon after the disaster and his account is a masterly record of the events, as well as a careful analysis of the reasons for the collapse. It was published soon afterwards (as an introductory essay to his *Architectural History*) and is accompanied by a very useful set of drawings, which can be supplemented by quite a large number of early photographs taken immediately after the fall. The heart of Willis' report is in his analysis, which is worth quoting in full:

> [of] the history of the failure of the south-west pier, which was weakest. It began slightly to bend to the south in the middle of February last: this was shown by the closing up of the old fissures, which had divided it from the south transept ... The eastern respond of this pier, belonging to the south tower arch, began to split from top to bottom (CD, plate B), and a fissure extending into the nave arch became manifest. On the Sunday preceding the fall, the bulging of the facing of the pier was observed to increase so alarmingly, that men, as already stated, were set to work to apply shores, during the service in the nave. This bulging increased on the succeeding days, rapidly, and the arches of the triforium assumed gradually the peculiar elliptical form, which is produced by the unequal settlement of the piers of a semicircular arch. On Wednesday, the facing of the pier, about seven feet from the ground, bulged out about three inches on the south side, and strained and bent the timber struts, which connected it with the north-west pier. The pier then settled down about three-quarters of an inch, crushing in the centre, in such a manner, that, on its north face, at about four feet from the ground, the front of the stones stood at their original height and perfect, while the back part of the same stones was crushed and pressed downwards three-quarters of an inch. On Thursday morning, the

75 *The Cathedral after the collapse of the spire on 21 February 1861.*

upper part of the pier was found cracked, and audibly cracking in many directions, flaked stones fell from it, whole stones burst out and fell. Finally, at half-past one, the whole gave way as above related.[32]

In the recriminations after the fall of the spire, the architect Slater became the scape-goat and was replaced by Gilbert Scott as architect for the rebuilding. Both Willis and Scott himself knew that it was not Slater's fault, and Scott generously said he would work alongside Slater, rather than replace him, even though the official restoration committee would not recognise Slater in this rôle.[33] As the mass of rubble was cleared away, Scott left his son, Gilbert 'to "spot" and identify every moulded and carved stone found among the debris, and to label and register them so that we might have every detail of the old work to refer to and, if sufficiently preserved, to re-use'.[34] Then, after creating massive new 'cement concrete' foundations with great blocks of Purbeck stone laid on top, new piers were built, followed by a replica of the old tower and spire (using the measured drawings

76 *Sir George Gilbert Scott (top hat on right) viewing the damage; the other top-hatted figure is the Clerk of the Works, John Marshall; the boy in the middle, his son, was father of Albert Marshall, who supplied this illustration.*

of a former resident architect, Joseph Butler). However, Scott raised the height of the whole structure by about six feet (the total height of the spire is now about 277 feet), because:

> The four arms of the cross had been (probably in the 14th century) raised some five or six feet in height, and thus had buried a part of what had originally been the clear height of the tower, and with it an ornamental arcading running around it. I lifted out the tower from this encroachment by adding five or six feet to its height ... I also omitted the partial walling up of the belfry windows.[35]

77 *The rebuilding of the spire glimpsed from South Street in 1866.*

The work was completed in just over five years and on 28 June 1866 Gilbert Scott the younger refixed the old weathercock to the top of the spire. Work on restoring the interior continued after the Cathedral opened for worship again in 1867. In that same year the library-enclosing wall (in the Lady Chapel) was removed and in 1871 the Duke of Richmond allowed the top of the family burial vault to be removed and the floor lowered again;[36] the library had been removed. The Lady Chapel was then rededicated in 1872 in memory of Bishop Ashurst Turner Gilbert, and it became as well the chapel of the Theological College.

In 1870 the reredos screen behind the high altar was removed and replaced in 1871 by the massive and elaborate new reredos (designed by Slater and Carpenter). This was never completely finished, and it too was swept away only a few decades later (see figs.62a-d). Besides the reredos, a new oak high altar was constructed as well as a new presbytery pavement made up of coloured marbles soon worn (and restored in 1894 and 1994). The early 14th-century choir stalls were reconstructed and put back under the crossing with new dean's and precentor's stalls, and Slater's episcopal throne. Until 1889 when an openwork screen was added, the choir stalls were open to the nave. Just west of the Dean's stall, the new pulpit designed by Scott was installed in memory of Dean Hook.[37] Perhaps the saddest (and most unnecessary) demolition of the 1870s was of the platform behind the high altar and reredos on which St Richard's shrine had probably stood. This was totally removed, and

78 *The completed spire awaiting unveiling.*

the two north and south flanking table tombs (probably of the 16th-century Bishops Day and Barlow) were lowered to the surrounding floor level. Only just over thirty years later (in *c.*1905) a new platform was built, with West Hoathly sandstone blocks around it, and the table tombs were once again raised up.[38]

In 1875 the new surveyor, G.M. Hills, made a report on the state of the fabric, and then went on to carry out various repairs, culminating in the restoration of the cloisters (in 1890). In succeeding years after a 'Cathedral Restoration Committee' had been set up in 1894 to raise £12,000 (to include the rebuilding of the north-west tower), much new stained glass was put in, which was described only a few years later in the Bell's *Cathedral Guide* as mostly 'of the worst possible kind'.[39] In 1889-90 the new 'Rood-screen' designed by G.F. Bodley and T. Garner had been erected at the entrance to the choir in memory of Archdeacon Walker, and these two architects went on to restore the chapels of St Mary Magdalene (1894) and St Clement (1898). Externally the east end of the Cathedral was restored in the 1890s by G.P.G. Hills (son of G.M. Hills), including the now rather strange-looking tall pinnacles on the clasping buttresses outside the chapels of St Mary Magdalene and St John the Baptist. The Lady Chapel roof was also rebuilt with once more its steeper medieval pitch.

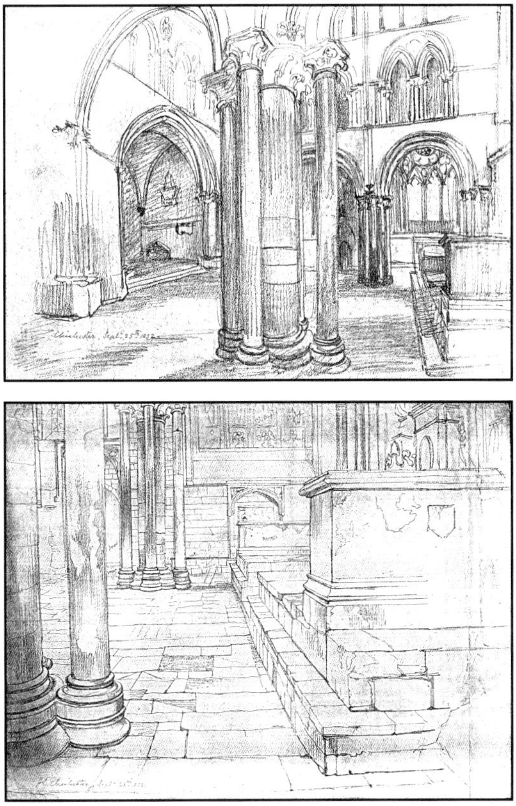

79 *Two views of the shrine area by George Scharf in 1852 before the reordering of the retroquire; the second shows dramatically the original height of the platform.*

In the early 1890s Sir Arthur Blomfield was brought in, to advise on the restoration of the south-west tower. The large windows of the top storey, which had been walled up, were re-opened and glazed and the inserted floor at this level was removed, leaving the whole tower open to the roof. The arch from the nave into the shell of the north-west tower had been reopened in 1873, and 20 years later discussions got under way on how to rebuild it, with various ideas being put forward.[40] In 1899-1901 the north-west tower was finally rebuilt to the designs of J.L.Pearson (his son actually supervised the work after his father's death). The new work, in Chilmark stone, is sympathetically done and matches the surviving Norman work (in Quarr stone), though Pearson had hoped to build upper stages onto both towers and to add spires (fig.80).

During the earlier decades of the present century, the work of restoration has continued, with many inaccessible and disused areas of the Cathedral gradually being opened up. Most of the nave chapels were restored and refurnished, starting with G.F. Bodley and T. Garner's restoration of the chapel of St Clement in memory of Bishop Durnford. In 1921 the chapel of St George was restored, followed by that of Saints Thomas and Edmund in

80 *J.L. Pearson's designs for the restoration of the north-west tower.*

1923, and St John the Baptist (north-west of the Lady Chapel) in 1924. This work culminated in the creation of a new altar (dedicated to St Michael), and a 'children's corner', later the Naval Chapel, under the north-west tower in 1931.[41] Other external repair work was also carried out including major repairs in 1931 under P.M. Johnston, still using Chilmark stone, and the restoration of the south transept gable in 1932.[42]

Just after the war, some repair work was carried out using Clipsham stone (from Rutland). This was in 1946 when the flying buttresses on the north side of the presbytery and the nave north chapel windows were repaired after air-raid damage in 1943-4. Not long after this the lead coverings of the high roofs were replaced in copper, which has given the Cathedral roofs, for nearly half a century now, their 'famous' turquoise-green colour.

X

Deans, Chapters and Bishops from the Boer War to the Cold War: Three Remarkable Men

John Halliburton and Jeremy Haselock

John Julius Hannah came to Chichester to be installed as dean in 1902. He had been for 14 years vicar of St Peter's, Brighton, was a prebendary of the Cathedral and prominent in diocesan affairs. A sadness overshadowed his coming to Chichester since, only a year before, his eldest son had been killed in action in the South African campaign. And there was more grief to come. Annie, his wife, whom he married in 1873, began to fail and five years later died, leaving him for the next 22 years a widower, father of three and master of the destiny of a great cathedral church.[1]

At the age of 63, this represented something of both an awakening and a challenge to John Julius Hannah. For years, he had lived under the shadow of his father, the Archdeacon of Lewes and vicar of Brighton. The latter, John Hannah, had remarkably brilliant beginnings, a double first at Oxford, and a fellowship at Lincoln College. Then at the age of 29 he was elected Rector of the Edinburgh Academy, choosing only seven years later to become Warden of Trinity College, Glenalmond. His son, Julius, was 10 at the time; becoming a boy at the school was his first taste of experiencing his father's authority both at home and at work. This was to last for another 30 years. Apart from his years at Balliol, brief training at Cuddesdon and curacies at Brill and in Paddington, John Julius Hannah was to be his father's employee until 1888. Even then, he simply stepped into the parish which his father vacated. For in 1870, John Hannah had made the decision to abandon teaching and to take a parish. He accepted the vicarage of Brighton from the

The Dean of St Paul's (Dr Gregory) walking with his nephew the Dean of Chichester (Dr Hannah) from the Deanery, to dedicate the reredos in the Cathedral; the last official act he performed. September 16th 1910.

81 *Dean John Julius Hannah and his uncle, Dean Gregory of St Paul's.*

Bishop of Chichester and his son immediately became his curate. They lived together *en famille* at St Nicholas' vicarage until in 1873 John Hannah moved to St Peter's, leaving his son as vicar of St Nicholas, with a benefice to himself and at last free to marry. In 1887, at the age of 70, John Hannah retired from St Peter's in favour of his son. In the space of 15 years the new vicar not only commanded a respect and popularity similar to his father but, like him, became rural dean and a prebendary of Chichester. The only way in which his career veered away from the paternal footsteps was that he was not considered for the archdeaconry of Lewes. Instead, the new King called him through his ministers to the deanery of Chichester.[2]

John Julius Hannah was to be Dean of Chichester for 27 years. During his time there, the world around him would change, probably more dramatically than throughout the whole of his father's career. Born into the ruling classes, by no means wholly dependent on the income from his benefice,[3] he lived, like most Brighton clergymen, in a style appropriate to his calling. At the same time, he was fully aware of the strong undercurrents of protest against the immense social divisions of the country. Education came high on the list of reforms that were being called for. A vital education bill concerning secondary education was going through Parliament in the year of Hannah's appointment to Chichester and by the end of his time at Brighton he had become Chairman of the Brighton and Portsmouth School Board, a significant appointment for a clergyman and an indication of this being one of his special interests.[4]

At the same time, Hannah must have been aware of the beginnings of the break up of the old social order. Chichester before the Great War was a Georgian city with some fine Victorian additions to house the wealthy. The working classes who were not in service were by and large comfortably tucked away in cottages mostly to the west and to the east or deep in the surrounding countryside, to service an economy which was wholly rural and basically untouched by the developments that had been going on in the great cities. The franchise was not yet universal. There were no passports. There was little social benefit for certain classes of worker who were insured against sickness and unemployment, and the needy over 70 could draw a very small pension. Children stayed at school till the age of thirteen.[5]

But when Hannah retired at the age of 85, he looked out onto a very different England and in some ways a very different Chichester. There was to begin with not a family in the land which had not been affected by the grim conflict of the First World War. To be Dean of Chichester during that time meant a sensitivity to a whole variety of attitudes to the war, an acceptance of and provision for the military presence in Chichester (special services for the military were held in the Cathedral at 9.30 on Sundays before the 11.00 Mattins),[6] and a suitable remembrance of the fallen. Among Hannah's many recorded works at the Cathedral is his restoration of the chapel of St George and the setting up of the memorial to the dead of the Royal Sussex Regiment.[7] In addition, and in common with other churches, Hannah called for the silencing of the peal of bells in the Bell Tower and also for the cessation of the chimes in the Cathedral clock.[8] At the end of the war, in 1918, the Dean and Chapter ordered a 'simple service' at 6.00 p.m. on Sundays to be arranged, 'intended principally for airmen, soldiers and women workers now in Chichester'.[9]

From the outset, Hannah clearly believed that the music of the Cathedral stood in need of improvement, both as to the regular services and with regard to additional musical occasions. Early in his time at Chichester (in 1904) he promoted the formation of the

Oratorio Society, which by 1906 was contributing to 'three Oratorio services' in the Cathedral and by 1907 was also assisting at Lent services.[10] F.J.W. Crowe was on the organ stool when Hannah became dean and the Oratorio Society may well have been formed to make good deficiencies in what Crowe had to offer. This is made all the more probable by the fact that in 1923 the Chapter minutes record a unanimous vote of thanks to the 'new' organist, Dr. Read, for the way in which he had so drastically improved musical standards.[11] Sadly, Read died four years later. But undoubtedly the Chapter now had a clear idea of the talent they were looking for and were not prepared to tolerate anything else.

82 *St George's Chapel, restored as the chapel of the Royal Sussex Regiment.*

Hannah resigned in 1929 and died two years later. His obituary in *The Times* is dedicated mostly to his career as a parish priest in Brighton. Of his time as dean, it mentions principally his being a valuable ally to the bishops under whom he served (Ernest Roland Wilberforce, Charles John Ridgeway and William Burrows), to his making the Cathedral the centre of the diocese, and to his work for the restoration of the fabric. In his time, it is reported, he oversaw many works of restoration and repair, including the chapel of St Edmund and St Thomas, the chapel of St Catherine, the chapel of St George and the re-erection of the Arundel Screen in the Bell Tower. For all this work he raised the sum of £150,000 and at the same time abolished all charges for visitors.

At the age of 85, however, when he gave up office, he must have wondered at the state of the country and the state of Europe. The year marked the beginning of the great Depression, plunging two and a half million British into unemployment in a world almost totally devoid of social security. 1929 was the year of the collapse of Hindenburg and the German economy and the vacuum of power which led to the rise of Hitler. 1929 also saw Ramsay Macdonald as the first prime minister of a government in which the Labour party held a majority of seats; 1929 was also the year of John Julius Hannah's retirement. He was

83 *(above) Dean Hannah surveys the stones of the Arundel Screen lying in the Bell Tower; (below) The Screen re-erected there.*

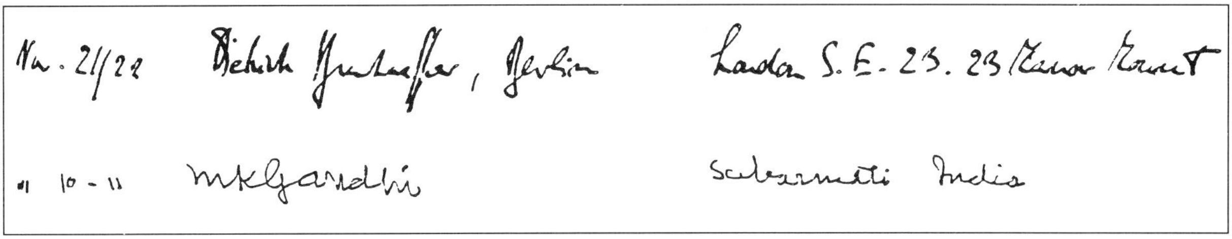

84 *Dietrich Bonhoeffer's signature in the Palace Visitors' book, after his first meeting with George Bell 1934; Mahatma Gandhi's signature on his visit in 1931.*

old and tired, and needed to yield to a younger man. So did the Bishop of Chichester, William Burrows. In their places, to the Palace came the former dean of Canterbury, George Kennedy Allen Bell; and to the deanery, Arthur Stuart Duncan-Jones.

Bell first of all (of whom much has already been written).[12] After reading Lit. Hum. at Christ Church, training at Wells for ordination, serving a curacy at Leeds parish church and returning to Christ Church as junior lecturer, he was then appointed domestic chaplain to Randall Davidson, Archbishop of Canterbury from 1914-24, key years in which he was to be involved in much and to contribute much. Bell was undoubtedly a visionary, a visionary moreover with incredible drive and determination. For him, the divisions in Christendom were not insuperable. No more were the divisions in Europe. Those with heart and mind greater than the narrow minded so-called integrities of nation or denomination needed to gather, share and plan. Such ideals marked the beginning of Bell's relationship with the German Confessing Church which, he felt, unlike the national Church, had the right spirit (through men like Niemöller and Bonhoeffer) for promoting European reconciliation and opposing crude Aryan domination. The peace of mankind was possible.

Bell's career, as is well known, was fraught with opposition. He stood for justice, righteousness and in a sense for a tough opposition to all that threatened peace and human dignity. But there was at the same time a major disinclination in his declared policy to sacrifice the enemy and his blind supporters in the interests of those who were on the side of right and deserved to win. What he knew of the plot to assassinate Hitler we shall never know. But we do know that he stood firmly against the planned bombing of German cities involving colossal loss of innocent lives in the hope that the Nazi régime would thus be brought to its knees. That to him was not part of the furniture of the just war ('debito modo').[13] It is said that his opposition to this grim throw of the British War Cabinet classed him as a turbulent priest and cost him the archbishopric of Canterbury.

Ronald Jasper in his biography of Bell records that at the outbreak of the Second World War, the Dean of Chichester, Arthur Stuart Duncan-Jones, voiced the feelings of most Englishmen at that time in tones of quite justifiable patriotic pride in all that the nation stood for, coupled with the desire that the enemies of the King might rightly be confounded. At the end of morning service, however, George Bell appeared and calmly reminded the congregation that the ordinary people of Germany were much as they were, reluctant to engage in any conflict, and longing for peace. Mutual hatred would get no one anywhere. We were all part of one human family. We needed nationally and ecclesiastically to respect one another's differences and to work together.[14]

It is significant that Bell and Duncan-Jones should have stood together in the Cathedral at Chichester on that first Sunday of the War. Both were keen students of European society,

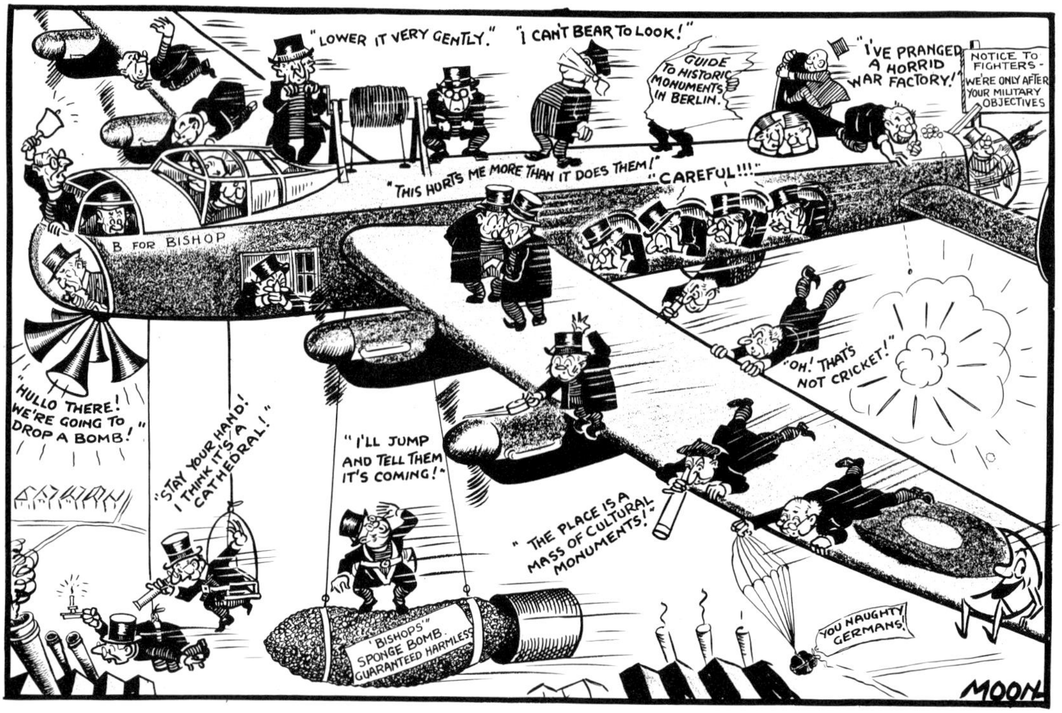

85 *Cartoon occasioned by Bell's condemnation of the indiscriminate bombing of civilians in German cities.*

both were well travelled, each much concerned about the way things had developed in Germany and indeed in Russia during the past two decades. Duncan-Jones himself had actually met Hitler in 1933, on which occasion the new Chancellor had reassured him that he would in no way interfere with the churches. But Duncan-Jones was soon to be disillusioned and during the 1930s wrote powerfully about the Nazi threat, notably in his book *The Struggle for Religious Freedom in Germany*.[15]

Bishop and Dean therefore stood together in their growing awareness and horror of events in Germany, their concern for the German clergy and people and their conviction that the Allies had to stand firm against Fascism and indeed against other forms of totalitarianism. The Russian threat to small European countries was a continuing concern. The whole idea of the protection of the small state against the imperialism of either Germany or Russia, which was certainly a part of British foreign policy at the outbreak of the Second World War, was here fully supported by Chichester's leading churchmen. Duncan-Jones and George Bell between them sustained an interest in oppressed minority voices in big countries and in majority voices in equally oppressed small countries, which has continued to bear fruit ever since.

At home in Chichester the Dean looked to his own household, domestic and capitular. His large family fitted the 18th-century deanery (with not much space to spare) and his Administrative Chapter (at that time four in number—Bishop Southwell of Lewes, Archdeacon Hoskyns of Chichester, Canon Mortlock and Canon Campbell) served him in the guidance of Cathedral affairs. Duncan-Jones became dean a year after the proposed Prayer Book of 1928 had been rejected by a majority vote in the House of Commons. It was a difficult time for him and those like him who considered themselves the heirs of the Oxford Movement in the Church of England.

As early as 1911 the liturgical scholar Walter Frere CR, later Bishop of Truro, had pointed to the urgent need for a radical rearrangement of the Eucharistic Prayer in the Communion Service: 'It will probably be recognised that the present state of our liturgy at this point is gravely at variance, both with the oldest and most universal liturgical tradition, and also with the practical needs of today'.[16]

Since then a great deal of liturgical scholarship, time and effort had been invested in the reforms proposed for the Book of Common Prayer. When Duncan-Jones was vicar of St Mary's, Primrose Hill, London, he supplemented a meagre stipend by working part-time for *The Guardian* and *The Times* newspapers and through these connections he obtained an advance copy of the 1927 proposals. At once he enthusiastically welcomed the revised Eucharistic Prayer[17] and thereafter maintained a consistent support for the whole new Eucharistic rite, later delivering a paper on the subject to the Alcuin Club in December 1934.[18] As with so many parish priests of his persuasion, loyal to the Church of England and its historic formularies but Catholic in their interpretation of its rites and ceremonies, Duncan-Jones had been assiduous in teaching the congregations committed to his charge at Blofield, Louth and Primrose Hill that the Church of England was an integral part of the one holy catholic and apostolic church. At St Paul's, Knightsbridge, to which living he was preferred in 1927, he went to considerable lengths in the Parish Paper to explain that the really quite moderate additions and supplements to the Prayer Book liturgy from sources ancient and medieval were an enrichment rather than an alteration of what loyal Anglicans believed. His clearly expressed views also lay behind the editorial stance taken by *The Times* in favour of the Revised Prayer Book.[19] All this to no avail. Members of Parliament, Christian and non-Christian, Anglican and non-Anglican, considered the Church of England's request for an improved and enriched Prayer Book and politely said 'No'.

This left the Catholic wing of the Church of England in some difficulties. It was in these years, the 1920s and '30s, that classical Anglo-Catholicism began its era of 'civil disobedience'. While taking care in public services to observe what was legal, many adopted what was tantamount to the Roman Missal in English, from which they said the Canon of the Mass silently, breaking out only to say the Prayer Book 'Prayer of Consecration', and then lapsing back into silence for the rest of the canon until the doxology. Ceremonial was similarly adopted from the Roman usage. Some religious orders abandoned the Prayer Book altogether, and there were some parishes also, notably along the South Coast, where the book was little in evidence.

To this anarchic situation George Bell addressed himself in the articles of inquiry in his Primary Visitation of the diocese of Chichester in 1936.[20] As he expected, the returns to his articles gave evidence of 'an extraordinary liturgical chaos'[21] prevailing in the diocese. So disquieted was he by the number of unauthorised alterations made to the liturgy and the remarkable variety of Eucharistic rites admitted to by his clergy that he analysed them and categorised them by degrees of enormity in his Charge. 'I cannot believe', he declared, 'that clergy of any school of thought in the Church of England can be content to acquiesce in the continuation of such confusion, when they realise the extent to which it has reached'.[22] While undoubtedly sympathetic to liturgical reform himself, he was opposed to individuals taking matters into their own hands. With the many Anglo-Catholics in his diocese clearly in mind he took a firm stand on the question of authority, contrasting a

Catholic ideal of the worshipping Church, glorifying God with one mind and one mouth, with a Congregationalist view of the local assembly ordering its own worship according to its own tastes and preferences.

> The adoption outside the Roman Catholic Church of practices used by authority within the Roman Catholic Church does not of itself make 'Catholic' worship. It lacks the primary Catholic requisite of due authorization. A certain uniformity in rite (i.e., things said) and ceremony (i.e. things done) is necessary to the Catholic idea, because this uniformity at one and the same time effects, preserves and symbolizes the unity of the Body.[23]

Bell proposed to achieve this desirable uniformity in rites and ceremonies within his diocese by insisting on strict adherence to the forms of service prescribed and authorised by law. In the admittedly embarrassing circumstances following the rejection by a secular Parliament of the Church's own efforts to reform its liturgy Bell, in common with his brother bishops, was prepared to interpret the phrase 'authorised by law' to include the additions to and deviations from the 1662 Book of Common Prayer set out in the Proposed Book of 1928. Though it lacked both statutory and formal canonical authority, the 1928 Book, with its Alternative Order of Holy Communion, was regarded by the Upper Houses of the two Convocations as having very high authority of an informal kind. The Archbishop of Canterbury, Cosmo Gordon Lang, declared in 1929 that in the 1928 Book they now possessed 'a norm or standard by which to determine what usages may or may not be regarded as in accordance with the principles of the Church of England'. Thus it was that the clergy of the diocese of Chichester were directed by their bishop that if they had to break the law of the land in their manner of celebrating the Holy Communion they should see to it that they only broke the law in a way authorised by their bishop. As Duncan-Jones later observed, 'the bishops could not, in the circumstances, do more. They could not, consistently with the responsibilities of their office, do less'.[24]

Duncan-Jones came as Dean of Chichester into this confused and controversial scene with particular gifts. He had all the sense and instinct for catholic liturgy and devotion but none of the turbulence and angular awkwardness of some Anglo-Catholic clergy. His predecessor as incumbent of St Mary's, Primrose Hill, had been Percy Dearmer, a skilled populariser of the liturgical scholarship of others and the author of an enormously influential book, *The Parson's Handbook*.[25] In the book he set about expounding his ideas on the adaptation of medieval English

86 *Cartoon of Dean Arthur Duncan-Jones.*

ceremonial—the 'English Use'—to the rites of the Book of Common Prayer. Succeeding Dearmer, Duncan-Jones entered into a rich inheritance which above all things stressed the continuity of the worship of the Church of England with that of the Pre-Reformation Church. Duncan-Jones was an active member of the Alcuin Club (which was founded with the object of promoting the study of the history and use of the Book of Common Prayer), serving on its executive, its publications committee and eventually becoming its chairman. Through the Alcuin Club, its members and its publications, and through his incumbency at Primrose Hill Duncan-Jones acquired both scholarly and practical expertise in the field of medieval liturgy and ceremonial which was to come to fruition in the ordering of the worship at Chichester and in the publication of the *Chichester Customary*.

In 1921 Duncan-Jones and two other members of the Alcuin Club edited what was to become the best seller of all their tracts, *A Directory of Ceremonial*.[26] This little book was in many ways a first airing of the principles Duncan-Jones was to put into practice in Chichester. The ceremonial is a little more 'advanced' than that deemed suitable for the Cathedral but the method of presentation, not so much a series of directions but more a description of the service as actually carried out, is very similar to that adopted in the *Customary*. The *Chichester Customary* was not actually published until 1948 but the ceremonies it prescribes go back to the earliest years of Duncan-Jones' time as dean and were worked out over the course of a complete liturgical cycle in order to cope with all the eventualities of cathedral life.

Given both Duncan-Jones' advocacy of the 1928 Prayer Book and the liturgical policy of George Bell spelled out in *Common Order in Christ's Church*, it is not surprising that the rites of the Cathedral church were those of 1662 with the additions and deviations permitted by the Bishops' resolutions of 1929. 'They are, in fact', wrote Duncan-Jones in the preface to the *Customary*, 'the most practical guide to worship in the Church of England at the present day, and at the same time are the instrument possessing the greatest moral and spiritual authority in that sphere.'[27] Some twenty years after it had all taken place, Duncan-Jones still thought it important to devote several pages of his preface to the *Customary* to an account of the Prayer Book controversy of 1927-9. In today's climate of rapid liturgical change it seems surprising that this apologia was considered necessary.

The *Customary* gives evidence of three of the many gifts Duncan-Jones brought to his tenure of the deanery: an aesthetic sensitivity, which showed itself not only in liturgical good taste but also in the furnishings and fabrics with which he clothed the worship; careful scholarship which showed itself in the notes he appended to the book; and practical good sense in tailoring the ceremonial to the dictates of the Cathedral itself. The aesthete in him would see the necessity for some continuity in style between what was essentially English before the Reformation and what could be achieved without slavish imitation of Rome in the contemporary Church. The scholar in him would save him from declaring to be Catholic that which was in fact Roman Catholic. Genuflecting at the consecration, for example, he judged to have been a custom devised in the 12th century and not before and therefore not integral to the modern liturgy. Incense, from the evidence, was designed to be used in procession but not to be waved at objects or people. The practical liturgist in him would understand the great building in which the worship was to take place, with all its various, clearly defined areas, and determine to use it to the full. He understood how the building had been used before the Reformation and devised contemporary forms of worship which reflected those early uses. Great festal processions, for example, using the

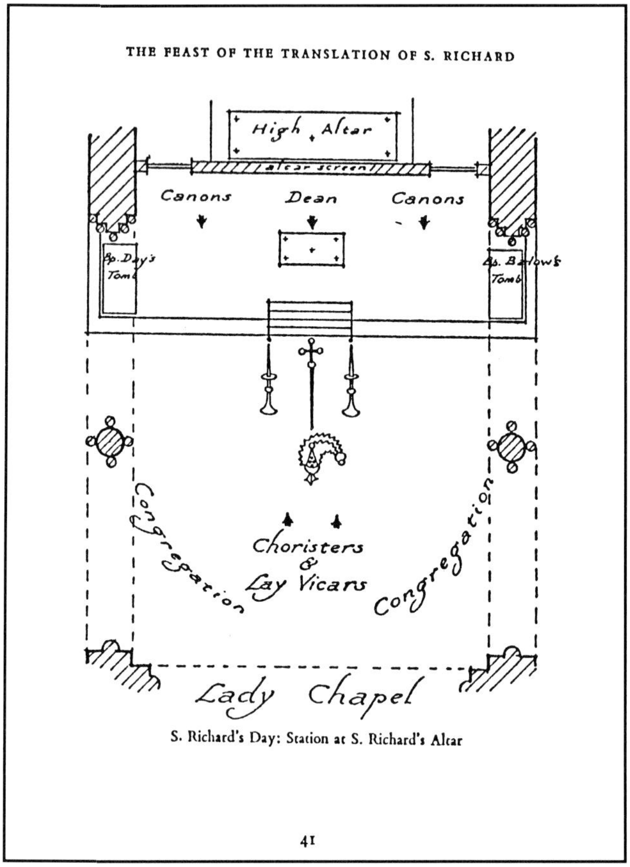

87 *A page from* The Chichester Customary.

whole building and with stations at suitable places according to the seasons of the liturgical year, became a regular feature of the worship. The Litany was sung in procession through the nave on ordinary Sundays, and at Epiphany a dramatic procession with a tableau of the Three Kings was devised to appeal particularly to children.

Precise details for the liturgical observance of the principal feasts and seasons of the Christian year are given in the *Customary*, with notably rich provision for Holy Week. Carefully-drawn diagrams are provided, after the model of those in late, printed versions of the *Sarum Cæremoniale*, to show exactly where the sacred ministers and servers are to stand at critical moments in the services. On Maundy Thursday, in accordance with medieval custom, the altars are to be stripped and washed with wine and water. For Good Friday Duncan-Jones at last clarified what could be a really constructive way for the ordinary Anglican to spend the three hours from noon till 3.00 p.m. Neither the Three Hours, preaching of the Passion nor the Roman Catholic Good Friday Liturgy really, in his opinion, met the Anglican need. Why not offer what the Prayer Book supplied—Mattins, Litany and Ante-Communion, with a good preacher and the Passion solemnly sung? To complete the remainder of the time he devised a very simple procession to the Cross—no creeping nor genuflecting, but a simple walking up to the Cross set up in the sanctuary while the choir sang the centuries-old chants of the Reproaches, opportunity for each individual to kneel and pray and then to return quietly to their seat for a hymn and then Evensong.

The remainder of the book is given to precise instructions for the regulation of Mattins and Evensong, the use of altar and other candles, the days on which the Cathedral flag may be flown, the sequence of liturgical colours to be used and collects to be used at the various processional stations prescribed for the year. There is also a section on forms and Offices to be used in the installation of new prebendaries, the admission of choristers, on hearing of the death of a dignitary or bishop and in receiving pilgrims at the shrine of St Richard. All of these provide evidence of Duncan-Jones' eye for detail and fondness for precise planning. If some of this seems today a trifle precious it was certainly not seen as such when the book was published. Long before its appearance as volume XXXVI in the Alcuin Club

Collections, the Use it describes was having an influence on cathedral and parish church worship throughout England. Randoll Blacking, a distinguished ecclesiastical architect and close friend of the Dean, summed up his achievements in the *Customary* in this way:

> This is surely the model of a modern Cathedral Use, in which every aspect of the worship of the place is carefully set forth, and in which the dignified and logical ceremonial with which the English Rite may be accompanied is described without the slightest taint of ritualism or antiquarianism.[28]

Throughout the *Customary* Duncan-Jones shows a remarkable capacity to offer the Catholic tradition in worship to the whole Church and not just to those who prefer the High Church way. It is probably for this that he will be most remembered. Chichester Cathedral today is a home for Anglicans of most persuasions. It is very rare to hear a voice raised in protest because the ceremonies are 'too Catholic'. Incense is still used, the servers still wear albs, Good Friday continues much as it was, the clergy are vested in alb, stole and chasuble. There are candles at the shrine of St Richard, enormous processions at Epiphany, but nothing jars. You never have the sense of 'High Church' being forced upon you. Most of this sensible catholic reserve in the conduct of the Cathedral's worship is due to the wisdom and initiative of Duncan-Jones.

In his day Duncan-Jones was respected for his enthusiastic reception of liturgical reform. Bishop and Dean, in a liturgical partnership represented by their two publications, *Common Order in Christ's Church* and *The Chichester Customary*, were working at the forefront of modern applied liturgy. Bell's liturgical interests are not sufficiently well-known; amongst his many other achievements he should be remembered for hosting ecumenical liturgical conferences in 1933 and 1936 at the Palace in Chichester where A.G. Hebert and scholars representing the Liturgical Movement in mainland Europe forged the framework of what was to become the Parish Communion movement in England. Hebert's book, *Liturgy and Society*,[29] published in 1935, and the collection of essays *The Parish Communion*[30] he edited in 1937, were a powerful spur to this attempt to put Eucharistic worship once more at the heart of parish life, and his influence can be detected in Bell's Visitation Charge of 1937. Bell in time appointed a Diocesan Liturgical Missioner, Henry de Candole, later Bishop of Knaresborough, who was to play a key rôle in the Parish and People Movement. Through de Candole's work and Bishop Bell's encouragement the diocese of Chichester was to become a stronghold of the Parish Communion movement.[31] At the Cathedral Duncan-Jones showed how liturgy could be presented—not just the impressive ceremonies of the main festivals and big diocesan occasions, but also the simple daily celebration of the Eucharist and the right ordering of the Prayer Book Offices. Both the traditional style and the forward-looking attitude of the Cathedral could be emulated in the parish churches of the diocese by those clergy who, having visited the Cathedral, would return home inspired. Such should surely be the rôle of the Cathedral today where the exciting new liturgical material produced in recent years ought to be as prominent as was contemporary liturgical revision in Duncan-Jones' day.

In 1945 Duncan-Jones acquired an ally in matters liturgical on the Chapter in the person of W.K. Lowther Clarke. In 1932, Lowther Clarke had very successfully edited an important collection of essays on the history of worship in the wake of the 1928 debacle over the proposed reforms to the Prayer Book. The book was called *Liturgy and Worship*, it was published by SPCK, in which society Lowther Clarke played a leading rôle, and is still even today immensely valuable as a treasury of the researches of some very prominent

88 *George Bell receiving the Freedom of the City, 10 June 1954, with the Mayor of Chichester, Mrs. Alice Eastland, and the Town Clerk, Eric Banks.*

scholars (Oesterley, Brightman, Ratcliff, A.J. Maclean, Srawley, Wickham Legg, Kenneth Mackenzie and Eric Milner White, to name but a few). Duncan-Jones also contributed. Coming to Chichester therefore, and appointed Bursalis prebendary (one of the Wiccamical prebends) it was only natural that a man of Lowther Clarke's scholarly reputation should be given responsibility for the Library.

The Cathedral Library at Chichester is of modest size but of rare interest and is very warming to the heart of scholar and bibliophile alike. But in 1947, the Library and its contents were to form the subject of considerable controversy.[32] The late Eric Banks, formerly Town Clerk of Chichester, told the present Librarian that in November 1947 George Bell, Bishop of Chichester, was dining at the Athenaeum when a fellow member came over with a Sotheby's catalogue in his hand. 'Ah, Bishop', he said, 'I see you are selling your books!' For there in the catalogue was a list of books from the Cathedral at Chichester about to go under the auctioneer's hammer. Bell is reported to have returned immediately to Chichester and confronted the Dean. Duncan-Jones was apparently impenitent, affirming that the books were the property of the Dean and Chapter and nothing to do with the Bishop. Bell thereupon took legal advice and, though the sale of 120 books went ahead, he was able to arrange for the withdrawal of 10 volumes.

The usual arguments were adduced in favour of the sale. 'Nobody reads these books in the Library.' 'We can't look after them properly, better that someone else conserve them.' The real issue was financial. The Chapter needed funds; Lowther Clarke, knowledgeable through long experience at SPCK, knew the value of a rare book. He was also Communar and responsible for the day-to-day running of the administration and financing of the Cathedral. But it was of course Bell who raised the real moral issue. The Chapter, he argued, did not own the books in the Library, but were merely trustees. He therefore personally took immediate action to limit the damage of the sale by withdrawing what he could; and then he ordered a visitation of the whole Cathedral.

Bell's Visitation Charge,[33] delivered at the annual meeting of the General Chapter on 4 November 1948, is a masterly account of the purposes and aims of any cathedral church and contains many a wise recommendation for the Cathedral at Chichester in particular. Bell begins by quoting the Church Assembly Commission on Cathedral and Collegiate Churches which reported in 1927. The Commission outlined four principle aims and purposes for cathedrals:

> The first and supreme aim of a cathedral is, by its own beauty and by the religious services held within it, to give continuous witness to the things unseen and eternal, and to offer continuous and reverent worship to Almighty God. To this supreme object, all others must be subsidiary.
>
> A cathedral, as the place of the bishop's seat, is the mother church of the diocese. To it, as the centre of their diocesan life, the clergy and people will be encouraged to come; within it, they will be made welcome; from it will go out into the diocese many activities helpful to the religious life of the people.
>
> The spirit and work of the cathedral are maintained by the corporate religious life of the dean and canons and of the other officers and servants of the cathedral.
>
> The cathedral is a home and school of religious art—architecture, craftsmanship and music—and of religious learning.

Bell then turns to those who are responsible for fulfilling these aims at Chichester—the Dean and Chapter first of all, the General Chapter who share responsibility, the

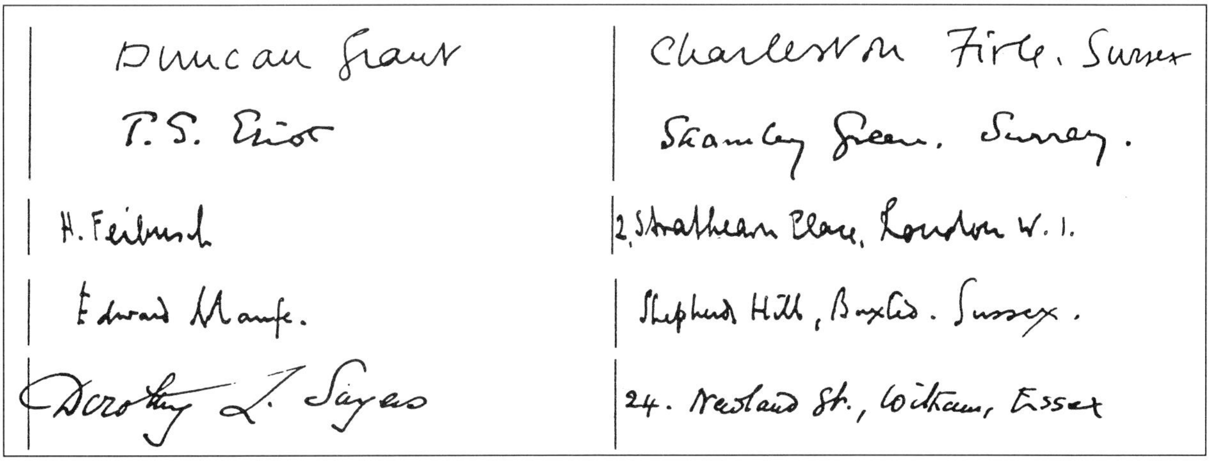

Duncan Grant	Charleston Firle. Sussex
T. S. Eliot	Shamley Green. Surrey.
H. Feibusch	2, Strathearn Place, London W. 1.
Edward Maufe.	Shepherds Hill, Buxted. Sussex.
Dorothy L. Sayers	24. Newland St., Witham, Essex

89 *Conference on the Church and the Artist, 15-18 September 1944, one of several such convened by Bell.*

dignitaries. He then reviews the provision for daily worship and comes next to the Library. His discussion of the Library is all part of his exegesis of the declared aim of a cathedral as being a 'home and school ... of religious learning'. Already, in his discussion of the rôle of the Chancellor, he has underlined the importance of one member of the Chapter being responsible for 'extending sacred learning' and for religious education in general. He quotes Dean Colet of St Paul's who was of the opinion that: '[The Chancellor] is the teacher in erudition and doctrine and is bound to lecture publicly in divinity unto the knowledge of God and instruction in life and morals'. The Chancellor at the time of this Visitation was in fact John Moorman, Principal of the Theological College and later Bishop of Ripon. Lowther Clarke was a man of similar learning but much occupied with being Communar, i.e Cathedral Administrator, as well as Bursalis prebendary. In Bell's view, Lowther Clarke was to Chichester what the Chancellor of the Exchequer was to the country—and therein lay a fatal flaw. Bell makes himself absolutely clear:

> There is one point about the Librarian which requires attention. By Statute XII the Librarian is charged to make a report 'from time to time to the Dean and Communar concerning the repairs that are needed in the Library'. He is also authorised to purchase new books as funds permit, after consultation with the Communar. The present Librarian is the Communar. This is clearly not in accord with the intention of the Statutes and I direct therefore that the Librarian and the Communar shall be always be different persons.

Never again, therefore, would a Communar, unable to balance his books, turn to the Library to solve his financial nightmares. Bell is quite open about what has happened. One hundred and twenty rare books were sold in 1947 without the General Chapter being fully aware of the action taken on their behalf by the Administrative Chapter. All of these books, he continues, were of a kind in which the General Chapter would have a definite interest. Now they are lost, irrevocably.

He does, however, go on to recommend a future policy for the Library. Post-17th-century books of little significance or value, he says first of all, should be disposed of. The remainder should be housed in what he calls the upper library (i.e. the present Library) with the lower library fitted out as a Treasury (as it is today) to display the rare treasures of plate and ornament in possession of the Dean and Chapter. With these treasures should be kept the precious books, charters and documents of special interest, thus leaving the upper library free as a reading room for students. The lower room would be in the charge of the Treasurer!

The Visitation Charge of 1948 is something of a landmark in the Cathedral's history. So much seems to have stemmed from this vision of the rôle and work of a cathedral. In the years that followed, the Cathedral was to thrive as a home for religious art, its worship was as ever of the highest standard of simple catholic dignity, there was learning on the Chapter, a growing Theological College and a well-cared for Library and Treasury. Duncan-Jones, like John Julius Hannah, died without seeing the full consequence of a lifetime's labour. But others, like us, have entered into those labours and even now reap the reward of so much personal love and dedication to a unique cathedral.

XI

The Cathedral Library

Mary Hobbs

> This is the custom ancient and approved, and in the year from the Incarnation of the Lord 1226 renewed in the presence of [here follows the name of the dean and the residentiary canons], namely that when any canon wishes to take books from the Church, he may be allowed to take as many as he wishes, except an excessive quantity, and to keep them as long as he is in the city; but when he shall leave the city, he shall restore the books to the Church; but if he shall wish to keep any with him, let this be done by the Dean's leave. So however that in the place of the books he should leave to the Church a sufficient and equivalent bond.[1]

This unusually generous arrangement is the first written reference to the Cathedral's books. The 'ancient custom' goes back at least to 1197, when Bishop Seffrid II, who rebuilt the upper eastern part of the Cathedral after the disastrous fire of 1187, presided at a chapter meeting to regularise Cathedral matters.[2] One Seffrid (they thought in the 14th century he was the first one) was clearly interested in the library: he is named as donor on the title-page of nine of the extant 12th-century Chichester manuscripts, listed by Neil Ker in libraries at Oxford, Cambridge, London, Lincoln, Glasgow and Paris. None has survived continuously at Chichester.[3] Seffrid's benefaction was an early one by most English cathedrals' standards. The books seem to fall into two, possibly three, distinct styles of copying. One would like to know their origin: it seems unlikely that a small foundation like Chichester copied its own manuscripts as the Salisbury canons did, though, like theirs, these are working manuscripts, often on poor skins, with holes round which the scribe's pen had to skirt. The two 12th-century groups have smallish painted capitals in red, green and occasionally blue. Beginnings and important sections are decorated more elaborately, sometimes with a large initial but chiefly with smaller square ones, either of Celtic design, with writhing foliage, serpents and other creatures and small grotesques, or with larger, flowing arabesque shapes (Plates VII and VIII). Where the first page is still present, at top or bottom a 14th-century hand has written the author and a brief title, sometimes also the donor, followed by the pressmark, beginning with capital C, F, H, I and L (which may represent shelf names) followed by small roman numerals. Similar marks in the same 14th-century handwriting appear on the early 13th-century manuscripts which form another distinguishable group of Chichester books. These are for the most part copied in a small neat hand, with finely drawn initial letters, blue on red or vice-versa, with delicate background designs, usually abstract but one, an initial in a Boethius *De Trinitate*, now at Emmanuel College, Cambridge, depicting intertwined strawberry leaves (see Plate IX).

Actual library rooms are not recorded in English cathedrals before the late 14th or early 15th centuries, and then only if some cleric bequeathing his books to the cathedral

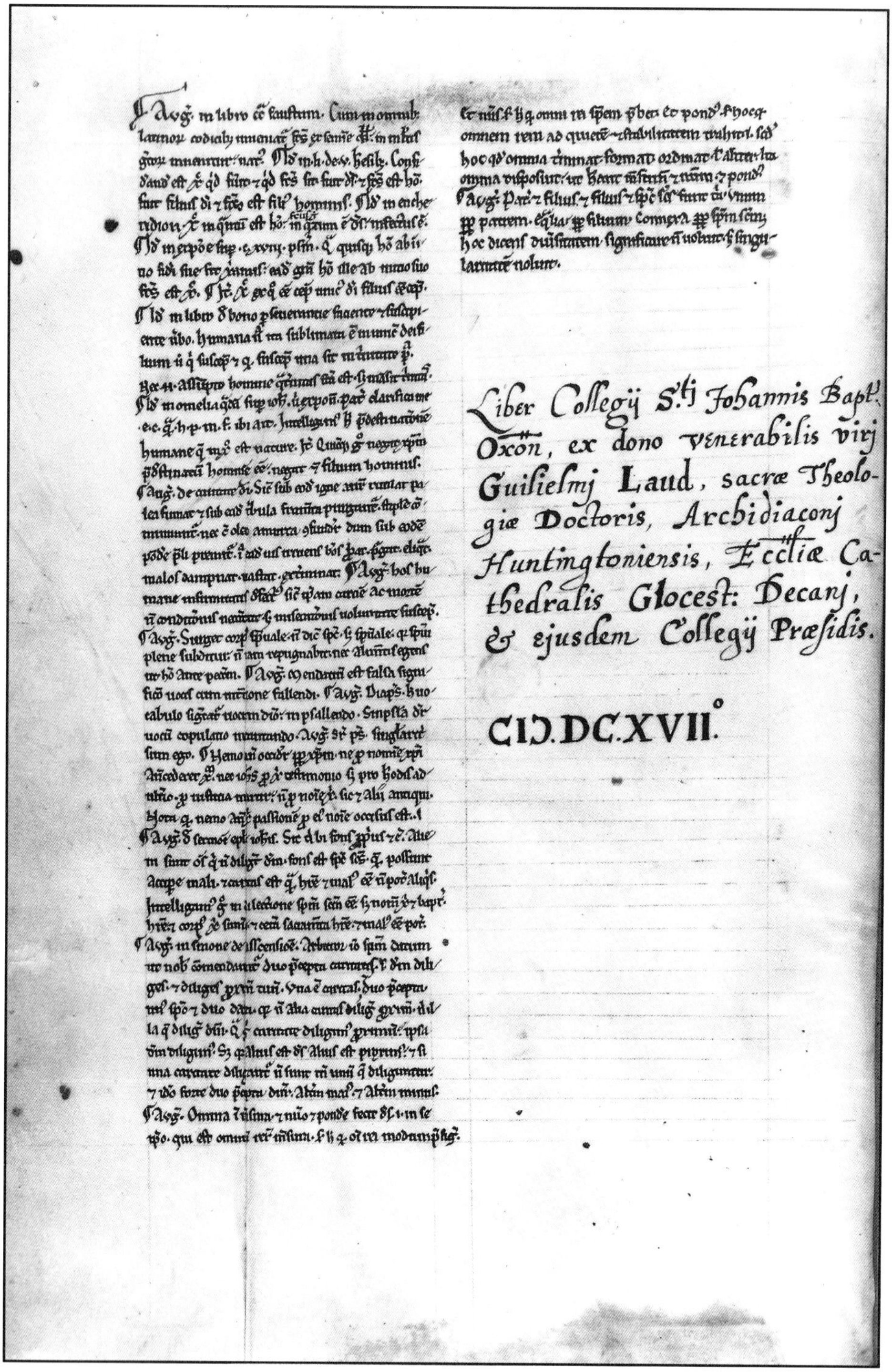

90 *Twelfth-century MS of Peter Lombard, just possibly that referred to in 1475 (note 7): vol.4 of the* Sentences *concerned the Sacrament. William Laud acquired a number of Chichester MSS, some, like this, given to St John's College, Oxford, in 1617, when he was President.*

(as Dean Roger de Freton left his law books in 1381 to Chichester) was rich or generous enough to endow a room as well—he was not! Otherwise, it was usual for books to be kept in locked boxes or cupboards, often in a cloister or tribune (a wider triforium, like Chichester's). By 1534/5, when William Samford the Communar records payment to 'Artur Rode' for the repair of 'the liberary windows',[4] there must have been an actual part of the Cathedral building set apart for books for study, as opposed to service books and grammar books for the choir school (the rebinding of which occurs from time to time in the Chapter Acts). Moreover, the plumber is paid 18d. for casting 'archbuttmentes on ye sowth syd of y[e] church for lyberary'. This confutes Mackenzie Walcott's assumption in 1877,[5] apparently followed thereafter without question, that the present site over the Treasury was the original one. The most likely chamber is that of the post-Reformation consistory court (now called the Muniment Room), with timbered roof and a round east window, perhaps that 'O window' repaired by John Glasiar in 1473/4 for 12d.[6] Charters and other muniments were at that time guarded in the Treasury ('aeriarius') across the south transept.

So little evidence remains of Chichester's early library, unlike more fortunate cathedrals such as Salisbury and Exeter, which not only retain substantial groups of their early manuscripts, but medieval catalogues which show the extent of what once was present. There is nothing to identify the 14th-century librarian (the Chancellor or his deputy) who must have catalogued the books at the time the pressmarks were written on them. As there is no mention of a Vicars' Library, it seems likely both that the vicars were allowed to use the canons' books and that the assistant or working librarian was from the first drawn from their ranks. Glimpses of the Cathedral's books occur in the Chapter Acts: John Kybow, a residentiary canon, took over the loan of a complete set of Decretals (which Richard Hapsynall [Aspinall], then a vicar choral, had from Robert Gest, another residentiary, possibly at the time of his death in 1475) together with the sixth book of the Decretals, a commentary on it by John Andrew, and a book on the Sacraments by the Master of the Sentences, Peter Lombard.[7]

Books left to the early library by will are described only in general terms. The first identifiable bequests are both post-Reformation: in 1554 Archdeacon John Worthiall gave 'Dionisius Cartusianus uppon y[e] evangelists, Paules Epistolles and the Canonycall Epistolles [i.e. those of the other apostles included in the New Testament], Erasmus workes upon Paules Epystalls [a nice example of the way spelling varied before printing gradually standardised it!] and also y[e] Hole Course of Sylar (except upon the New Testament) and one Vocabylar namyd Catholicon'. The vicar of Findon, John Marynge, in 1549 left 'My concordance and my calopeyn or cronacle' to be 'chayned in the quyre, at M. Worthialles discretyn'[8]—Worthiall, a former Chancellor, was presumably still responsible then for the Cathedral books.

Reformation and Civil War

After St Richard's shrine was despoiled in 1538, the use of the library room seems to have been in abeyance, at which time many of the books and manuscripts were no doubt dispersed. (A manuscript from the Dominican friary at Chichester, William of Heytesbury's *Sophismata* [now at St John's College, Oxford], was already in the hands of Francis Whyte of Southwick, near Portsmouth, in 1555.) When William Way, a vicar choral, was deprived in 1569, in Elizabeth's reign, for Romish opinions and having pledged for money Romish books: 'A great [Golden] Legend in English and The Pilgrimage of Perfection; A great Psalter; Fyssher upon the Seven Psalms' and 'a super-altar',[9] it may be that the books had

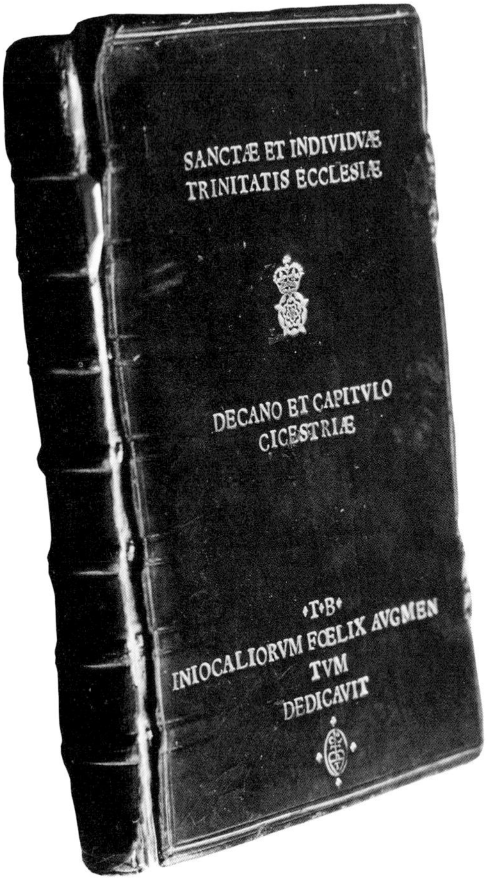

91 *Bishop Bickley's gift of the controversy between Bishop Jewel of Salisbury and the Jesuit Thomas Harding.*

come from the old Cathedral Library. After that, except for the Dean and Chapter Statutes of 1616, which show the sub-treasurer holding the library key (so some attempt had probably been made to refurbish a room), the records remain silent about the library until the time of the Civil War. Yet from 1639-42, Thomas Lockey, who at the Restoration became librarian of the Bodleian at Oxford, was prebendary of Thorney and might have been expected to interest himself in it.[10]

After the siege of Chichester in 1642, the books of Dean, Chapter, Bishop and 'other delinquents' were dumped in the ruined, roofless deanery.[11] The County Committee for Sussex wrote in 1651 to the Committee for Compounding at London for permission to sell them in London, 'as they have received much damage, and will do still more by lying where they are' (a sentiment reiterated by the dean and librarian after the Second World War!). When Bishop Nicolson wrote in 1696 that 'they never recovered more than 3 books belonging to the Chapter', his statement is possibly supported by the fact that only one book can now be identified with certainty from the earlier Cathedral Library, William Whittaker's edition of the controversy between Bishop John Jewel of Salisbury and the Jesuit Thomas Harding. This bears on its front cover the date 1585, the Tudor rose, and in large gilt Latin capitals the pleasant legend: 'T.B. gave [this] happy increase of their *Jewels* to the Dean and Chapter of the Cathedral Church of the Holy and Undivided Trinity at Chichester'. The volume, bound in dark calf, was printed at Geneva in the year Thomas Bickley, formerly Warden of Merton College, Oxford and a Queen's Chaplain, was consecrated Bishop of Chichester: there seems little doubt he was 'T.B.'.[12]

The King Library

Henry King, Civil War bishop and the friend and executor of the poet John Donne, complained in his will, drawn up during the Interregnum, of a large library 'taken from me at Chichester, contrary to the condic[i]on and contract of the General and Council of war'. Nevertheless, when at the Restoration he returned to Chichester, he must have had in his possession most of the 974 old books left after he died in 1669 to his son John (including the Jewel book, which may have been bought back for him from the sale in London). John's own will two years later left to the Cathedral: 'all my Latine books w[i]the some others I shall choose out ... to the use of Schollers in this Diocese of Chichester hopeing this example will move others to do the same'.[13] It is interesting that, just as Bishop Seffrid's books virtually founded the first Cathedral Library, so we owe its refounding at the Restoration to the books of another bishop. Though it was the Chapter's library, his successors, in particular John Williams and Matthias Mawson, also interested themselves in it and gave important benefactions. John King's will also voices a problem which remained for the next 50 years: 'so [tha]t [th]e Deane and Chapter will assigne a place to dispose [the books] in as their disicrec[i]on shall approve'.

The contents of the bequest (which I have described in detail elsewhere)[14] are preserved in a catalogue marked only 'Old Catalogue of books before 1735'. A scribbled entry gives Cathedral dignitaries for the year 1684, possibly the date of the original list, and there are a few 18th-century additions. The books listed date from the earliest days of printing to the end of the Civil Wars, with only two slightly later Commonwealth exceptions. Some 300 are extant, at Chichester or elsewhere. Several show marks of ownership by the Bishop and his family: John King, Bishop of London, Henry's father, and his four brothers, besides John Donne (six signed copies but another 14 identifiable as his). There is a list of six manuscripts at the end, just possibly, like the Jewel book, rescued from the pre-Civil War Cathedral library. Only one of these, a St Augustine written in England in the late 12th or early 13th century, is still at Chichester today: it closely resembles the 13th-century Boethius at Emmanuel College and the Bodleian Library commentary on Job, both originally at Chichester. It is tempting to conclude that this may have been one of ours, too, but it lacks the first page on which the medieval callmark would have appeared. None of the many incunabula listed (printed before 1501) is still present: most were already lost or sold for newer editions by the late 18th century.

As one would expect, the majority of the books are theological works: Bibles, prayer books, even, perhaps surprisingly in a Calvinistic family, four Missals (one formerly owned by Thomas Cornwallis), and Classical literature. European and English history, in Latin even where originally written in the vernacular, come second (Henry King's sermons show that his own favourite was his heavily annotated Seneca, now in Reading University Library). Next are rhetoric, poetry (again chiefly in Latin even where the writer, like John Owen or Alexander Gill, was English, though there is a magnificent Italian Petrarch), science and medicine, falconry and magic. John Donne's graphite marks occur against passages in books of his which he quotes in his sermons; Henry King's hand and characteristic markings are found in *his* books.

There are many curiosities, such as a 1534 collection of school books printed at Antwerp for Wolsey's Ipswich grammar school: it contains a manuscript class-list with the name 'Kynge'. Elias Reusner's genealogical account of European royal families has all the coats of arms painted in its wide margins by the owner, probably William King, Henry's younger brother and fellow of All Souls', Oxford. Copious manuscript notes against the Spanish chapter suggest that it may have been decorated in 1623, the year of Prince Charles's projected Spanish match. The puzzle of Sir Henry Spelman's *Glossaria* with Henry King's proud inscription on the flyleaf, 'ex dono auctore', and a date two years *after* its publication in 1626, was solved when Sir William Trumbull's papers (now in the British Library) were auctioned at Sotheby's in 1989: a catalogue illustration of a 1628 letter signed by both men shows that, in that year, they had become members of the Guiana Company of Merchant Adventurers. Many of the books have titles inked on their foredges, not only because on a leather book there was nowhere else to write, but also in accordance with

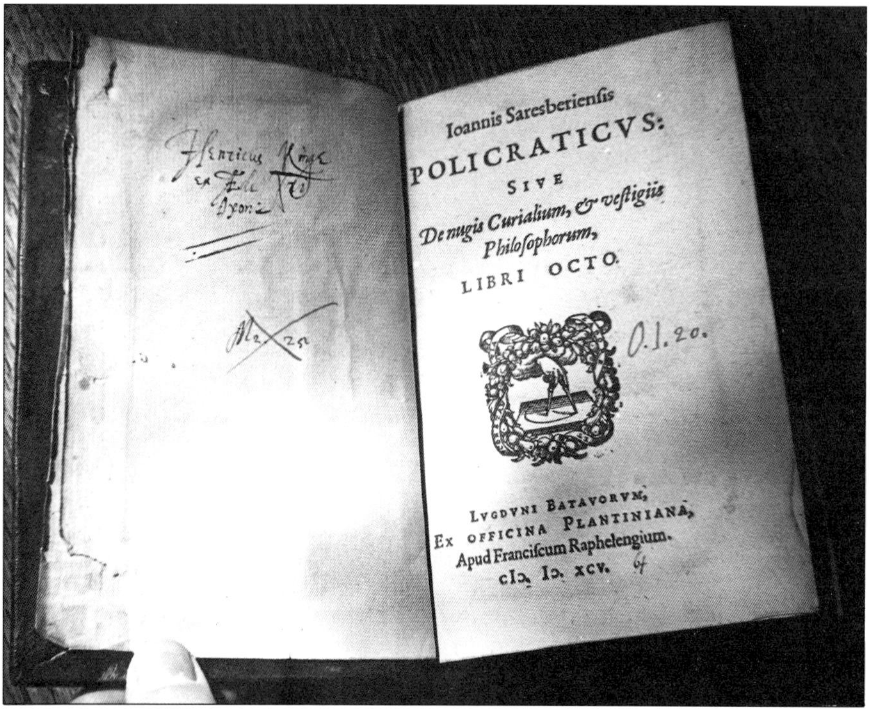

92 *(above) Signature of Henry King while at Christ Church, Oxford, from one of his books; (below) The Dean cutting the cake at King's 400th-anniversary celebrations in 1992, watched by the Librarian and others.*

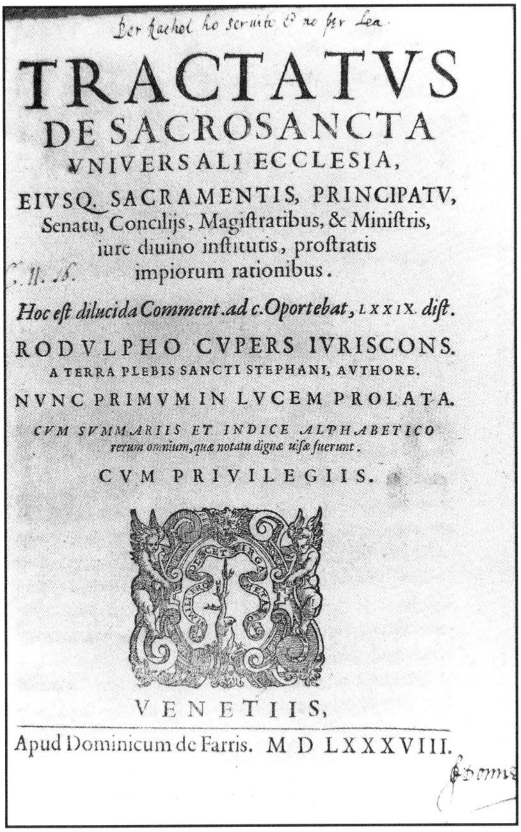
TRACTATVS
DE SACROSANCTA
VNIVERSALI ECCLESIA,
EIVSQ. SACRAMENTIS, PRINCIPATV,
Senatu, Concilijs, Magistratibus, & Ministris,
iure diuino institutis, prostratis
impiorum rationibus.
Hoc est dilucida Comment. ad c. Oportebat, LXXIX. dist.
RODVLPHO CVPERS IVRISCONS.
A TERRA PLEBIS SANCTI STEPHANI, AVTHORE.
NVNC PRIMVM IN LVCEM PROLATA.
CVM SVMMARIIS ET INDICE ALPHABETICO
rerum omnium, quæ notatu dignæ uisæ fuerunt.
CVM PRIVILEGIIS.
VENETIIS,
Apud Dominicum de Farris. M D LXXXVIII.

93 *John Donne's signature and motto (from Petrarch) in one of the books from his library.*

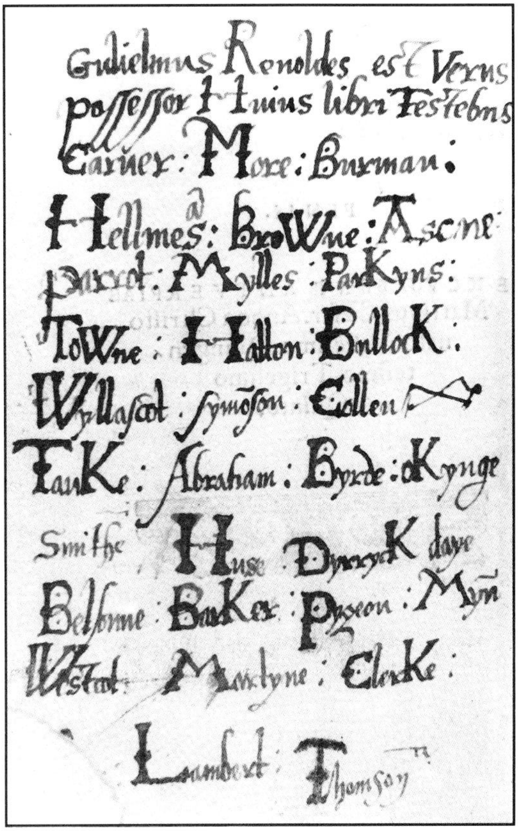

94 *Sixteenth-century class list (including the name Kynge) written into a school book printed for Cardinal Wolsey's grammar school at Ipswich.*

contemporary fashion for housing books foredge forward, to pretend one had an antique chained library.

The books' bindings have suffered from neglect and damp, but there are still some fine specimens. A very early gilt-stamp (1561) on a seven-volume Augustine printed in Paris in 1555; decorative blind-stamped calf and pigskin; green morocco; heavy red-dyed calf with gilt armorial centre devices still make a show, along with the cheaper serviceable vellum bindings favoured by 17th-century scholars, with traces of their original red or green cloth ties. From the catalogue's press marks, it is possible to recreate the original position of the books, from case A (Bibles) to N (Law), and to guess from known volumes the size of the shelves which contained them. In volumes still containing their original flyleaves, these press marks have been crossed through and replaced by later 18th-century marks.

In 1679, Canon John Sefton left the Dean and Chapter 100 books by his will—providing they repaired the Vicars' Hall to house them, and provided 'all parties concerned shall be agreed to make a Publicke Library of it'. There seems no trace of these volumes in the donors' books,[15] nor evidence for the use of the Vicars' Hall, so the conditions may not have been fulfilled in time. Inscriptions dated between the King bequest, 1671, and the 1735 early catalogue show that many other gifts to the Library were not included there, confirming that, until then, the King bequest must have been kept separately: our copy of one of Cranmer's books, Hermann von Wied's *Simplex ac Pia Deliberatio*, was given by Bishop Williams in 1705, and in 1707 Nicholas Covert, the Chapter Clerk, inscribed in Latin a folio Peter Canisius of 1585 in his own untidy hand for the Dean and Chapter, in order to advertise his relationship to 'the never-to-be-conquered Lord John, Duke of Marlborough': second cousin once removed!

The Golden Age—The 18th Century

From the last years of the 17th century, not only the clergy, but townsfolk and other friends of the Cathedral constantly gave books to restore the library. Chichester Cathedral has four remarkably informative 18th-century catalogues and borrowers' lists (though Paul Kaufman did not use them in his study of such books),[16] from 1735, 1753, 1757 and 1761. The latter shows how the shelves and room must have been arranged in the Lady Chapel to which, according to Walcott, Bishop Mawson removed the library in 1750.[17] A second 1735 catalogue, of the whole library, bears a note of the books 'missing of this catalogue when the Library was moved' (had it perhaps been previously housed for a time in the present room, producing the tradition that this was 'the old library'?) Another hand has added 'N.B. The Library was moved to its present position in the time of W. Clarke': the latest addition to this catalogue is dated 1751. The Communars' Accounts, of which Dr. Emlyn Thomas has very kindly made me an analysis, have a separate library section in 1725 and again from 1740—possibly the year the new library room in the Lady Chapel was first projected—to 1771. In 1748, 12 mahogany chairs (still used in the Cathedral) were bought for it; it was 'repaired' in 1750, when two [terrestrial] globes (lent to Bishop Otter College in 1891, present whereabouts unknown) were bought. In 1751/2, 'a grate, brass fender, etc.' for the library cost £1 13s. 0d.

Beriah Botfield later describes this room as having large windows, royal portraits and a fireplace.[18] This stood below the blocked-up east window of the chapel; since the Lady Chapel, according to Charles Crocker's 1849 guide, 'was more completely desecrated by Sir William Waller's soldiers, in 1642, than any other part of the Church',[19] this is not as extraordinary as it might seem. A 'new chimney board' was bought in 1760 and painted with the library coat of arms (recently found preserved in the offices of Rapers the solicitors, the former registry),[20] while in 1795, five bavins or bundles of twigs were bought for 1s. 0½d., 'to light fires in the library at Chapter time'.

The 1761 catalogue gives the new layout of the shelves, which Botfield describes as three bookcases a side. Where before, the whole alphabet was used, we now find the cases labelled only from R to Z, each divided into sections labelled from 1 to 3, with seven shelves each, A to G. Shelves H and I ran above four desks. There were in addition corner shelves labelled 4 to 8, on which large illustrated works like Sir William Chambers' architectural works and the *Table des Cartes des Pays et des Frontières de France* (Brussels, 1712) were laid open. Two of the catalogues have borrowers' sections, covering somewhat spasmodically the periods from 1745 to about 1786.[21] As today, there was a workaday librarian as well as a canon librarian and, as in the Middle Ages, the deputy was usually a vicar choral.

For much of this crucial period of relocation and development, at least from 1731 until his death in 1771, William Clarke the witty antiquarian[22] was the Canon Librarian; his neat hand occasionally makes devastating comments in margin or on flyleaf about the contents of Popish and other books. In 1761, John Smyth signs himself as the 'librarian' or deputy

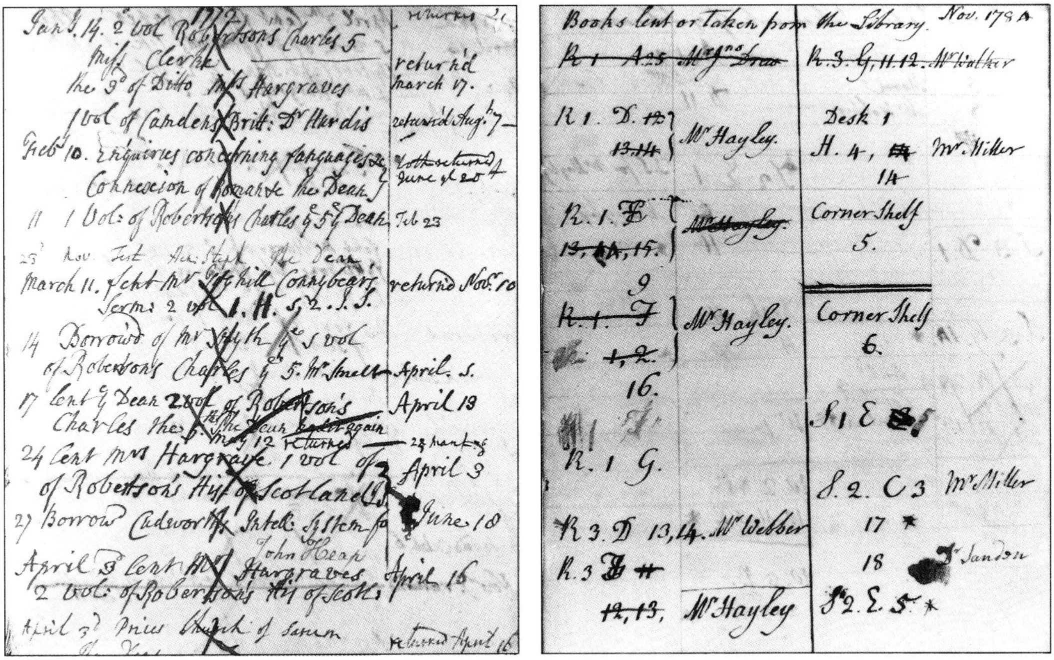

95 *Pages from the 1772-89 Borrowers' Book and the 1761 Catalogue.*

but, from at least 1775, the deputy librarian was Richard Shenton, vicar choral and soloist, and vicar in turn of various parishes in and around Chichester, together with St Andrew, Oxmarket. He was also a music teacher and a correspondent of the scholar Thomas Wharton; William Hayley wrote an admiring epitaph for him.[23] He seems to have been an active and painstaking librarian, even though his revealing scribble in the 1772-89 borrowers' book shows that in 1784 the librarian's salary was only £2 a year, at which figure it remained throughout the 19th century.

Dr. Thomas deduces that, on average, the Dean and Chapter bought six volumes a year until the 1770s, some by subscription. Duplicate volumes were sold by William Clarke to help finance acquisitions: and early editions (were the King Library incunabula among them?) were replaced by those more up-to-date—a first setback to tracing the fate of Henry King's books today. Dr. Thomas is nevertheless right to call this the Library's golden age, in particular the year 1769. Incoming prebendaries gave or paid for books on installation, London booksellers, printers, civic dignitaries, doctors, country gentlemen, military and naval men, widows of clergy and female members of the congregation, not all related to the dean or chapter (20 ladies in all), contributed and frequently borrowed books: John King's pious wish that others might follow his example was fulfilled, and this had become, as John Sefton had desired, a public library.

The subjects included biography and memoirs (as in other cathedrals, the *Biographia Britannica*, Robertson's *Charles V* and Lyttelton's *Henry II* were chief favourites among borrowers), travel books, topography, natural history, architecture and numismatics. Henry Peckham the wine merchant gave Cudworth's *Intellectual Systems* and Ussher's *Annals* in 1713, the year he built Pallant House; Benjamin Martin, the distinguished scientific lecturer who lived in Chichester during the 1730s, presented Speed's *History of Great Britain*, and

Alexander Hay, author of *The History of Chichester*, gave two books, while the teacher at the Presbyterian Meeting House, Mr Heap, an indefatigable reader, gave *The Travels of the Jesuits*! Kaufman[24] expresses surprise at finding dissenting ministers borrowing frequently from cathedral libraries: they were, of course, debarred at this time from universities and their libraries, and many cathedrals had useful parallel collections open as a public lending service to any worthy borrower.

William Hayley the poet, friend of William Blake, gave Gibson's *Camden*, Perrault's *Les Hommes Illustrés* and his own poems. Among the 30 per cent lay borrowers, he was one of those who used the Library most frequently, a fact he acknowledged in the manuscript dedication of his poems in 1779: 'To the Librarian of Chichester Cathedral as a small memorial of Gratitude for the Use of many valuable books'. Since these included a wide range of Church Fathers, most of them in early 16th- or 17th-century editions, he ought indeed to have been grateful—they would not have been allowed to leave the shelves today! He is carefully distinguished in the useful 1759 donors' books (where nobility, bishops, Cathedral canons, other clergy and the laity 'not members of the church', are firmly segregated): 'Mr William Hayley, grandson of the late Dean Hayley'.

This last catalogue contains a neat copy of the working accessions book of 1753. It implies that the Duke of Newcastle's gifts were higher esteemed than those of the Duke of Richmond: he gave the complete set—23 folio volumes—of the *Corpus Byzantinæ Historiæ*, together with two enormous folios, a Baskett Vinegar Bible and a matching Prayer Book, red calf gilt with some of the original blue silk ties and gilt tassels still present. A letter from Dean Ball and the Administrative Chapter calls these 'lasting Monumentals of your Grace's invariable zeal and attachment to the Protestant Cause in general and of your steady adherence to the primitive and very considerable branch of it, the Church of England in particular'.[25] Nevertheless, Richmond's volumes of Chambers' *Civil* and *Chinese Architecture* are splendid, too, and all are still with us. Since no incunabula from the King Library survived to this date, great importance was also attached to a gift from Mr. Brereton, rector of Westbourne, of Higden's *Polycronycon* (the 1525 reprint), printed by Wynkyn de Worde, along with Fabyan's *Chronicles* and those of Grafton and Holinshed; a Virgil printed at Venice in 1499 was later acquired. Bishop Mawson took an active interest in the library and gave some 48 volumes before he was translated in 1754. His books all contain a splendid Latin eulogy in William Clarke's most elegant calligraphy: 'To whom we owe not only such a great wealth of useful, elegant and sumptuous Books; But also in great measure the Library itself', with the date, 1753.[26] He is closely followed by 32 volumes from Canon William Clarke, while Richard Shenton himself gave nine volumes.

The 19th Century

Our authority for the contents of the early 19th-century library is once more Beriah Botfield, who praised Chichester highly in his *Notes*. He gives long lists of the books and benefactors, and commends the fine engraved book plate which 'all chartered or collegiate bodies would do well to imitate'. The century fluctuated between periods of eager activity and dismal neglect, sometimes remarkably close to one another.[27] The hazard has always been that a change of dean or of librarian can lead to the books being no longer seen as important. The room was used for various diocesan meetings. *DNB* records that Henry Manning's last meeting as archdeacon of Chichester before becoming a Roman Catholic, a 'No Popery' gathering of his clergy in 1850, was held there! After all the excitement of the second half

96 *The 18th-century engraved bookplate.*

97 *S.H. Grimm's 1781 drawing of the Cathedral seen from the south west, showing the blocked-up east end of the Lady Chapel in use as the Library.*

of the 18th century, however, there is silence about the Library in the Chapter Acts until 1859, when Canon Charles Pilkington was made canon librarian and that splendid poet-verger, Charles Crocker (Plate XVI), author of *The Vale of Obscurity, Kingly Vale etc.* was appointed deputy librarian. (This was perhaps the beginning of the custom which still obtained earlier in this century, that the vergers showed the library to visitors.) Crocker died in August 1861 (had the fall of the spire hastened his end?). His son was appointed in this father's place, but there is a sharpish directive on 27 December 1867 that the sextons (the vergers) are not to show the library any longer and that the key must be surrendered to the Chapter Clerk. In 1868, H.H. Moore, later head verger and the sculptor Eric Gill's father-in-law, was appointed; in 1869, a vicar choral, Mr. John Parker, Master of the Prebendal School, became deputy librarian—the salary remaining at £2 a year.

It is intriguing that in August 1877 Dallaway's *West Sussex* was to be bound 'and then to be kept locked up'. Only six years earlier, the Chapter Acts record a time of great activity. The first printed catalogue of the library had been undertaken by Mr. Edwin Wilmshurst at his own expense in 1871. He had rearranged and numbered the books, showing there were at that date 1,465 volumes (there are some 6,000 today). He printed 100 copies of his book, possibly to the embarrassment of the Dean and Chapter who had to get rid of them: they eventually decided to send them to local dignitaries, the British Museum, Lambeth, the universities of Oxford and Cambridge and other cathedrals (there was still a small stock left when I became librarian in 1978). Yet in 1884, Chancellor Parish, then Canon Librarian, put to the Chapter his proposal for publishing yet another catalogue at his own expense, to be distributed to every beneficed clergyman in the diocese. For centuries, it seems, librarians have struggled to rationalise this library.

The Early 20th Century

1878 marked the appearance of James Fraser, made deputy librarian in order to draw up library rules and aid in checking and recataloguing. The Dean and Chapter lamented to the Commissioners in 1881 that their library was 'in a state of utter decadence for want of funds'. They wanted to offer someone undertaking the care of the books the modest stipend of £25, but the Commissioners were not prepared to assist. Nevertheless, Fraser accepted appointment as Canon Librarian in 1901. A distinguished antiquary, he became an outstanding librarian, restoring the books and raising the profile of the Library by exhibitions and regular articles of Library news in the *Diocesan Gazette*. His scrapbooks contain a wealth of historical interest.

There is a steady trickle of thanks in the Chapter Acts from now on for gifts of individual volumes or unspecified piles of books. A later Librarian accurately if unkindly commented that these latter were mostly bequests 'by the widows of clergymen of the rest of their deceased husbands' books after booksellers had already taken the more valuable items'.[28] Others were of great value, however, given by Fraser himself, by Archdeacon Mount and by Canon Cooper, who in May 1901 was thanked for his gift of 'manuscripts': presumably our few really important ones other than the 12th-century Augustine in the King catalogue. They include a beautifully illuminated late 13th-century Benedictine missal.

The attitude towards old books which caused our post-Second World War troubles is nevertheless already in evidence. The *Diocesan Gazette* of February 1916 records a munificent gift of nearly 180 volumes from the late vicar of Chertsey—'Handy editions of the Fathers in octavo and duodecimo size are far more useful to students than the ponderous folios and quartos which usually remain on their shelves, except for periodic dustings'. Losses could also occur; witness an agonised letter in the *Gazette* of 1917: 'Aldingbourne, Jan. 16th: Dear Sir—Last year I borrowed the Stowe Missal from the Cathedral Library, and being desirous to make known that ancient Irish Liturgy, lent it to a friend. I cannot remember to whom I lent it. Would you make this known in the Gazette, as it may meet his eye and bring repentance to him?' It evidently did not: I wonder where it is now.

In 1916, there is also the first written confirmation that the Library is now on the north side of the building, in the present Treasury. (It had moved there at least by October 1895, when Archdeacon Mount was given permission to place an iron gate at its entrance, perhaps the one still in position.) The Chapter Acts record that 'the large room above the Library has been furnished with a substantial table and chairs' as a reading room for clergy: 'laymen and ladies would also be welcome'. Downstairs, in place of two former bookcases (possibly the plate-glass ones insured in 1894) which have been moved to the new room, they have been given by Dean Hannah 'a most handsome mahogany bookcase' once purchased by his father John, who first edited Bishop Henry King's poems (1843). In 1918, we read that the Dean 'has fitted up, at no slight cost [they were fixtures and had to be rebuilt], the book cases lately removed from Brighton Vicarage ... we now have ample space for the present'. For the first time, the Librarian tells *Gazette* readers, he has now 'a small sum to spend annually, through the generosity of the Dean and Chapter' with which he has purchased 'a few books of local value'. (Local history, especially ecclesiastical, is still one of the few areas where the Library buys books.)

Prosperity had further been ensured by the appointment from deputy to Canon Librarian in 1918 of Cecil Deedes, one of its greatest benefactors. He was a dedicated book

98 *Librarians: a. Canon James Fraser; b. Canon Cecil Deedes.*

collector. I suspect he had worked out the connection between the 1735 Old Catalogue and John King's bequest, for he seems to have bought for the library some of the very editions from that catalogue lost to it in former years. He died in 1921, and little more is recorded about the books until after the Second World War, when more spectacular losses occurred.

Canon Halliburton has shown the part these losses played in the relationship between Chapter and Bishop. Of great interest for the Library are some forgotten facts in Bishop George Bell's correspondence file on the affair.[29] A letter from Norman Sykes, then Dixie Professor of Ecclesiastical History at Cambridge, reveals something forgotten until now alike at Chichester and Emmanuel College: 'During the war the college housed a good many books and manuscripts of your dean and chapter; and our librarian, H.S. Bennet[t] ... spent a good deal of time in unpacking the contents of the packing cases from Chichester, disposing the books and MSS; and in repacking them when the war had ended'—for which he had received 'not even a formal acknowledgement of their safe receipt ... not to mention the courtesy of a letter of thanks.'

The scandalous sale of books described in Chapter X went ahead on Monday, 24 November 1947. Ten books the Cathedral was allowed to withdraw included Fabyan's *Chronicle*, Higden's *Polycronycon*, and the King Library copy of Solinus's *Polyhistor*, with a map carrying the first printed reference to America. A Mr. Clarke was allowed to buy in one of our six texts carrying John Donne's signature and three books containing the signature of Bishop Henry King, besides two of those classified by Sotheby's 'very rare': St John Fisher on the seven penitential Psalms, printed by Wynkyn de Worde in 1508, and Sir Thomas More defending Henry VIII against Luther in 1525. 'Mr Clarke' was Canon

99 *The Library while in the present Treasury, with the bookcases from Brighton Vicarage.*

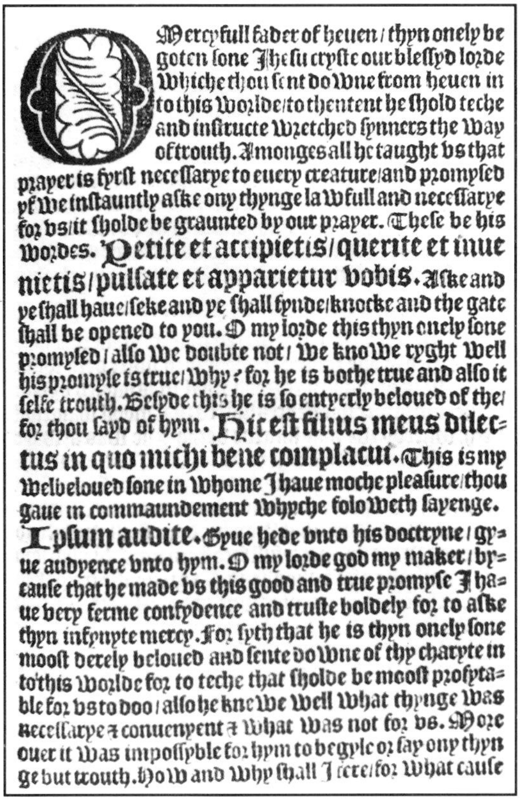

Mercyfull fader of heuen / thyn onely be
goten sone Jhesu cryste our blessyd lorde
whiche thou sent downe from heuen in
to this worlde / to thentent he sholde teche
and instructe wretched synners the way
of trouth. Amonges all he taught vs that
prayer is fyrst necessarye to euery creature / and promysed
yf we instauntly aske ony thynge lawfull and necessarye
for vs / it sholde be graunted by our prayer. These be his
wordes. Petite et accipietis / querite et inue
nietis / pulsate et aperietur vobis. Aske and
ye shall haue / seke and ye shall fynde / knocke and the gate
shall be opened to you. O my lorde this thyn onely sone
promysed / also we doubte not / we knowe ryght well
his promyse is true / why? for he is bothe true and also it
selfe trouth. Besyde this he is so entyerly beloued of the /
for thou sayd of hym. Hic est filius meus dilec=
tus in quo michi bene complacui. This is my
welbeloued sone in whome I haue moche pleasure / thou
gaue in commaundement whyche foloweth sayenge.
Ipsum audite. Gyue hede vnto his doctryne / gy=
ue audyence vnto hym. O my lorde god my maker / by=
cause that he made vs this good and true promyse I ha=
ue very ferme confydence and truste boldely for to aske
thyn infynyte mercy. For syth that he is thyn onely sone
moost derely beloued and sente downe of thy charyte in
to this worlde for to teche that sholde be moost profyta=
ble for vs to doo / also he knewe well what thynge was
necessarye & conuenyent / what was not for vs. More
ouer it was impossyble for hym to begyle or say ony thyn
ge but trouth. How and why shall I fere / for what cause

100 *Page from the rare treatise on the seven penitential Psalms by Bishop John Fisher (1508), withdrawn from Sotheby's sale.*

101 *Wynkyn de Worde's colophon at the end of the book, inherited from his predecessor and master, William Caxton.*

Lowther Clarke, the Cathedral's Communar and Librarian. He had already sold a 1579 Saxton's Atlas and the incunable *Hortus Sanitatis* (Mainz, 1491) for £250 after commission, '£100 to be given to the Restoration Fund and £150 invested in P.O. Savings Bank for the Library', without telling the Chapter until after the event, and the consultations with Sotheby's were not made public. Lowther Clarke's subsequent correspondence with the Bishop exudes defeatism and truculence. 'We ... should not be justified in spending [money] on what is used by no one.' As for readers, 'we have nothing to be studied, our original MSS etc. having been dispersed at the Civil War time'.

Letters from the only two people who apparently used the library regularly, Hilda Johnstone and Walter Peckham, 'one an ex-Professor of History and the other an antiquarian, one my Archivist and the other theirs', as Bell described them, are our source of information about the library room at the time. Peckham says that, 'Unfortunately, since Canon Bicknell's rearrangement [of which we now know nothing] it has often become practically impossible to lay hands on a book, even when one has verified from the catalogue that it is somewhere in the library ... I might have to take down perhaps a couple of hundred folios and look at the title pages of each. I have not done it.' Hilda Johnstone 'had to crawl behind or push aside the servers' hanging rack to get at [Rymer's *Foedera*] in the present room, which was also used as the servers' vestry'. (The rest of the books were

102 *Francis Steer, drawn by Nigel Purchase, 1965.*

in the lower library, today's Treasury.) Moreover, 'after the bell by which it used to be possible to summon a verger was removed and not replaced, and while the staff of vergers was at a minimum, readers without keys found it difficult to spare the time needed, before they could begin to work, to effect an entrance'. ('Find the verger' is still sometimes a game to be played!)

On 27 November, Peckham wrote to the Bishop, 'I have always liked to picture a Cathedral library, not so much as a place round which visitors are herded by a verger, but rather as a help to learning'. He calls the books to be sold 'exclusively show-case specimens', instancing the Fisher, 'of which a reprint would serve my purpose just as well' (shades of 1916). He goes on to justify the Dean and Chapter's action: 'From my point of view the loss of Dickinson's printed text of the Sarum Missal would be more serious than that of half a dozen incunabula'. Sotheby's had suggested to the Bishop that scholars' and antiquarians' work was 'far more conveniently carried out in larger and more specialized libraries than by being forced to visit a comparatively small library, quite out of their ordinary beaten path'.

As an antiquarian, Peckham was more concerned over the Chapter's treatment of their manuscripts, which could 'contain information which exists nowhere else'. His own abstract of part of Bishop Sherburne's Register had been put away by the then Librarian uncatalogued 'in a locked case with the (supposed) *obscaena* and the (presumed) *incunabula*'. In 1950, indeed, it was Peckham who obtained the removal of the Cathedral's archives to the Record Office, where they remain.[30]

Protest at the Chapter's irresponsible action escalated. Professor Owst at Cambridge, who had written to *The Times* after the earlier sale of the Saxton atlas, told Bell

> they should have promptly requested Bodley's Librarian, or the University Librarian here, or a sister Cathedral to house the volumes temporarily, until such time as the Cathedral Library could be put in repair ... There must be many close links with such institutions at the two ancient Universities in the long history of Chichester, which an enthusiastic Chapter might

> well have exploited, not to mention the many interested in our ancient Libraries and Cathedrals in the United States!'

He foresees that 'the Cathedral chapter will bitterly regret its folly' and concludes with the crucial question, 'I suppose that some one at Chichester has at least a record of the purchasers of last Tuesday's victims?' They had indeed: Lowther Clarke sent Bell a list of buyers, but Sotheby's had told him that '90% of all their sales are to booksellers, buying on commission for public or private collectors', so that it proved of little value in tracing the books' subsequent ownership. The dealers refused at the time (and later were unable) to throw light on the books' subsequent homes.[31]

The Visitation Charge was delivered, but there are sad postscripts to the affair. Lowther Clarke and Bishop Bell both sanctioned the sale at Sotheby's in 1949 of further manuscripts and books, some of them from the library of Bishop Henry King (his copy of one of his favourite Fathers, St Ambrose, heavily annotated but in poor condition, sold for just £4.) Francis Steer records in his *Chichester Paper* on the Library,[32] that other 'books' (unlisted) were later sold to 'the newer Universities'. I have traced only a relatively small number of volumes, in the libraries of the universities of London (which has kept together a 'Chichester Collection'), Bristol and Reading. The rest may have been lost in what today, with our higher regard for the value of old books, seems more criminal fashion: 2,000 unnamed books were sold for pulp during the chancellorship of Canon Cheslyn Jones.

103 *The Library today.*

104 *Chichester Decorative and Fine Arts Society cleaning the books in 1982.*

Dr. Francis Steer succeeded Lowther Clarke and guarded the Library faithfully and well for about 20 years until his death in 1978, though he had an understandable mistrust of deans and chapters—especially after the '60s, when the books were pitched from the triforium to be placed in sacks on the stone floor of the present Treasury while the room was reroofed and refloored. It was given back to him without shelving: we owe the present shelves to the generosity of the Pilgrim Trust in 1969. In his day, few were admitted without difficulty to the sacred precincts. The painstaking, neatly written card index compiled by Steer is a joy to look at, if infuriating to use, since he catalogued the books by editor, without cross-reference to the often much better-known authors!

The Library today is visited not only by a small band of scholars, albeit from all over the world, but by many interested groups such as librarians, members of societies such as NADFAS, the National Trust, the English-Speaking Union and the newly formed Chichester Centre for Ecclesiastical Studies. As in other cathedrals, the Library and its treasures are increasingly recognised as part of the Cathedral's wider outreach and mission. We seem to be once more in a golden period. As in the 18th and 19th centuries, benefactors contribute gifts, in money as well as in kind (space and weight restrict us to accepting only those books in keeping with the existing library). Verena Smith FSA before her death in 1993 gave us many useful ecclesiastical art and history books, with rare books from her own and L.F. Salzman's fine collections. They include one of our greatest treasures, an illustrated 1503 French Book of Hours printed on vellum by Thielmann Kerver. By her generous will and two smaller previous legacies, we can at last create a proper endowment fund to care for the books.

XII

Archives and Antiquaries

Alison McCann

The earliest reference to any sort of record keeping at the Cathedral is in the statutes of 1232, when it was noted that it was the duty of the chancellor to provide a notary for the secretarial work of the Chapter, and to repair the books of the church.[1] It was emphasised again in the Constitutions of 1247, that the chancellor should keep the Chapter seal, and was responsible for compiling letters and charters.[2] Not long after this, the compilation of the earliest cartulary (Liber Y) began,[3] a positive step in the preservation of the contents of the Cathedral muniments as well as episcopal ones, though it may have resulted in the disposal of some of the original charters.

At this period, the documents were stored in a chest in the treasury,[4] a facility also used by the local population. Adam de Wandrasy, in granting an annual rent to the Dean and Chapter in c.1250-1255 to pay for the observance of his anniversary, referred to the deeds of the properties concerned which were deposited for safe keeping in the 'muniment room of the Church at Chichester'.[5] The chancellor had by 1299, however, not yet employed a notary, nor repaired the books.[6]

The earliest surviving reference to someone acting as a possible chapter clerk is 1333,[7] though the title is not used until 1382.[8] The late 14th century was also the next period of record collection under Bishop William Reede, who instigated the methodical compilation of books of evidence 'from various old copies and documents which could be found'.[9]

The motivation for record keeping was of course the need to preserve the proofs of Cathedral possessions and privileges, as well as to have a record of Chapter decisions and finances. The first Chapter Act Book was begun in 1472 and the earliest entries are in what is probably the hand of John Vincent, Notary Public, who also kept the Bishop's Register.[10] A memorandum, recorded in the Act Book in 1479/80,[11] to look for evidences of the foundations of the Cathedral chantries, implies that the records were not immediately to hand. There had been complaints at the Bishop's Visitation in 1478 that Dean Waynflete kept many muniments and writings of the church in his own hands, and had abstracted several documents concerning Chapter rights.[12]

There is reference to a communar's account roll as early as 1496,[13] though the earliest surviving account book dates only from 1555.[14] The first lease book (lease book *Hobby*), recording the leasing out of the Dean and Chapter's numerous properties in and around Chichester, started in 1548;[15] previously, details of leases had been entered in the Act Books. At the 1573 Visitation it was ordered that the Act Books and Registers of Leases should be kept in the custody of the chapter clerk, unless they were needed by the dean or residentiary.

Even the dean and residentiary were not to keep them for more than a few days without special permission.[16]

It would seem that some of the early archives of the Cathedral had already been lost by 1616. Article 18 of Bishop Harsnett's Visitation asked 'by whose default principally are your evidences wanting and lost'.[17] It is usual to blame the Parliamentarians' sacking of the Cathedral in 1642 for the loss of the early archives, and there may well be some truth in this, although the sacking was not sufficiently disruptive to interfere with the sitting of the Consistory Court.[18] Certainly both the Lease Book and the Act Book for the period before the start of the Civil War have gone. Bishop William Nicolson, later Bishop of Carlisle, writing in 1696, believed that

> Most of the Ancient Records of this Church were squandered or lost, upon the City's being taken and plundered by Sir William Waller in our late Civil Wars, and after the Restoration they never recovered more than 3 books belonging to the Chapter, and a Register or 2 of the Bishops. These do not reach above 230 years backwards; so that the prime antiquities of this see before are either wholly lost, or in such private hands as have hitherto very injuriously detained them from their right owners.[19]

However, he was at the very least overstating the case. If such 'prime antiquities' did survive at the start of the Civil War, it is astonishing that John Swayne, NP, Chapter Clerk, and a keen antiquarian, should not have made notes from them, as he did from the earliest cartulary (Liber Y) and the surviving Act Books.[20]

We know of the existence of the 'Leiger Book', which had certainly vanished by the late 17th century, through the compilation of an index, which survives.[21] However, there are other possible explanations of its disappearance. The Church's rights were often called into question in a litigious age, and the archives were frequently in demand for use in legal proceedings, which generally meant that they were taken to London. A number of references survive to documents being requested in this way. In 1609 the Bishop asked the Dean to look out any evidence about the Manor of Bishopstone for a court case, which he thought might be 'in your house of evidences'.[22]

The question about the loss of muniments in the 1616 visitation may well have been prompted by an incident dating from Dean William Thorne's time.[23] Some Chapter deeds had been entrusted to William Harrison 'of Westminster, gent.', presumably a lawyer. Harrison died in 1613, and his widow subsequently remarried. Her second husband pawned the documents for £10 to one Thomas Bradford, who demanded money from the Dean and Chapter for their return. The Dean and Chapter brought a case in Chancery to recover the deeds, but they did not know exactly how many 'deeds, charters, patents and evidences' were concerned, or of what date, or whether they were sealed or unsealed! The result of the case is not known.

The Decrees following the visitation instructed the Chapter Clerk to make a schedule of 'all the church books, counterparts, writings and evidences in his custody' and not to loan them out even to the Dean and Chapter without their being signed for.[24]

In 1636 the then dean ordered John Swayne, the deputy chapter clerk, to produce 'the Leiger Book and the old white Book of evidences' to be taken to London for the use of Mr. Pay, residentiary 'in defending the rights and privileges of the church'.[25] One assumes that the Leiger Book came back safely. After the Restoration, it was thought by the anonymous annotater of Dean Hayley's book to have been in the hands of Sir Richard Farrington,[26] of the Puritan faction, but his descendants could find no trace of it. By *c.*1665-71, it was lost.

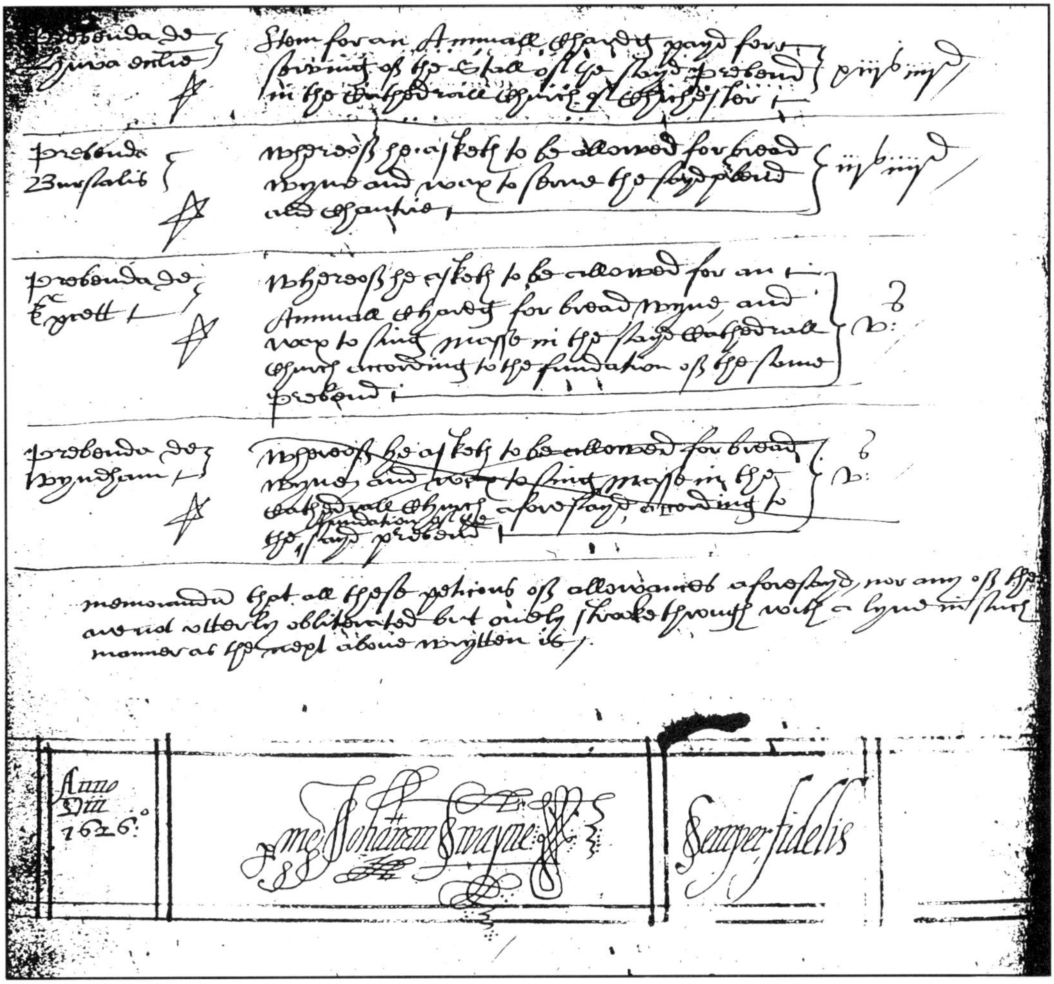

105 *John Swayne's signature, 1626.*

Certainly the abolition of the Cathedral establishment during the Interregnum caused an interruption in the regular series of records, which all start again in 1660. There was, however, continuity in personnel, Richard Bragge being procurator of the Dean's Court from at least 1619 and continuing to write the Dean's Court diary until local probate jurisdiction ceased in 1652. At the Restoration, he became Chapter Clerk, until just before his death in 1672.[27]

The post-Restoration visitations always questioned the care of the records. 'Have you the deeds, writings, and grants in safe custody, and by whom are they kept?[28] Have you terriers and surveys of all lands and revenues ...?' These questions, and variations on them, were asked throughout the 1670s. A certain amount of dispersal of the records is suggested by the Bishop's injunctions of 1675 that the muniments, which were in 'various places, nests and vaults' should be promptly found and kept in a place of safety.[29] This was despite the recorded answer of the Dean and Chapter that their 'books and evidences were faithfully kept and none detained'.[30]

There are other indications that this may not have been entirely true. In 1683 George May, one of the residentiaries, wrote to the Treasurer, Henry Maurice, to complain that 'Dr. Edes hath for many years had the sole possession of all the books of our church till of late (not a year since) I extorted as many of them as he thought good to own out of his hands ... I am apt to believe there are books belonging either to the church or [St Mary's] Hospital which he reserves for his own use'.[31] Henry Edes, residentiary canon 1662-1703, was leader of one faction in a chapter which was bitterly divided. May believed that Edes had got the church's books and records into his own hands 'to make [himself] ... necessary to the church or for other private ends', and had 'concealed them from the knowledge of the Dean and Chapter'. At the end of 1684 May was still not confident that he had got all the documents back from Edes.

Records could in fact easily become dispersed for very practical reasons. In 1686 the Vicars Choral reported at the Bishop's Visitation that their muniments were kept in a public chest.[32] However, one of their number, Roger Collins, gave a dissenting reply: 'We have no court rolls or evidences kept in a public chest or other place'. The court rolls were in the hands of Mr. Raynes, the steward of their manors, and one of the vicars choral, Mr. Haslock, had an 'old book wherein are some memoranda concerning lands and possessions'.[33] It was quite understandable that the steward should need the earlier court rolls when running the manorial courts, but this could lead to problems. In 1733 the Vicars Choral were injoined not to renew any leases of their land to Mr. Medly until he had handed back the court rolls in his custody, to be kept in the public chest.[34] In 1742, the Vicars could report that they had got the court rolls back from the steward.[35]

As time went on, the stewards and chapter clerks were usually local solicitors. It was obviously more convenient to have the relevant documents to hand. This presented no problem if their successor in office was another partner of the firm. However, if the office moved to a different firm, earlier records could easily be forgotten and were left behind.

Glimpses of the extent of the Cathedral archives in the 18th century are given by lists of the archives compiled by prebendary, later Dean, Thomas Hayley in 1722[36] and Canon William Clarke, residentiary, in *c.*1739.[37] When Thomas Hayley made his list in 1722, the 'books, evidences and papers' were kept either in the 'Long Chest with three locks' or the 'Deal Press', both of which were in the Chapter House. The Deal Press was obviously a large one, since it contained over 40 volumes. One volume which was missing from the press was the Dean's Statute Book,[38] but a careful note was made that it was 'now in Dean Sherlock's hands in London, for which he has given his note of hand to be accountable for it'.

Hayley's list of the archives is less detailed than that of Canon Clarke, but substantially the same. The capitular archives which Clarke listed were stored on three shelves in the Chapter House, and in the chapter-house chest. At that date, the Dean and Chapter held their Act Books, Communar's Accounts, rentals and registers of leases. They also had the registers of Bishop Sherburne's donations. None of the records about capitular or prebendal land were in the Chapter House. These were presumably in the hands of the Chapter steward. Also missing from the lists are most of the early original charters of the Cathedral, although the earliest surviving charter, that of Oslac in AD 780, was there. A few volumes now considered to be capitular were listed with the Bishop's records.

Clarke listed a number of documents which cannot with any certainty be identified with documents in the present capitular archives. Some of their descriptions are very tantalising. What was a 'very ancient Terrar, much defac'd'? Was there really an incorporation of the Vicars Choral in 1334? Some 28 items are either inaccurately described, or have not survived. We know that at least one item disappeared quite soon after the list was compiled. This was King James' charter of exemption to the church of Chichester, granted in 1686. By February 1750, a search had been instituted in the Rolls Chapel in London for a copy, so presumably the charter had vanished from the Chapter House.[39] As a document of some importance to the Cathedral, it evidently had not shared the fate of those 'Numbers of Articles cross'd' which, according to Clarke's note at the end of the list, had been 'thrown out since, as of no use'. Among the papers which were destroyed was a list of 'Goods left by Bishop Bowers to the Palace', 1724, which might have proved interesting.

Clarke's list is valuable, showing as it does that all the major series of records which now survive were in the archives by then. None of the title deeds were listed, being presumably in the office of the Chapter Clerk. The vagaries of these officers would of course affect the care afforded the documents. In 1685 Nicholas Covert, the Chapter Clerk, was in prison and consequently was unable to fulfil his duties.[40] All the 'Chapter Books and Muniments' had been in his care, and they were to be surrendered to the Communar. John Wakeford was appointed in his place, though Covert was later reinstated.[41] John Wakeford's nephew and probable partner, Wakeford Bridger, became Chapter Clerk on his uncle's death in 1731, and was also appointed steward of the manors, and solicitor.[42] However, in 1738, the Dean and Chapter were complaining that Bridger had 'absented himself for some time from his duty'. He was to be warned to appear, otherwise the Dean and Chapter would elect a new chapter clerk.[43]

Evidence concerning the state and care of the archives in the 19th century is sparse. In 1800 a select committee was appointed to 'enquire into the state of the Public Records of the Kingdom'. In their report, William Fowler, then registrar and Clerk to the Dean and Chapter, stated that the Chapter records were 'lodged in the Chapter Room within the Cathedral Church aforesaid which is as secure and commodious for the keeping thereof as any building can be'.[44] Most of the documents were arranged in compartments in presses, and all of them were under lock and key. He made no comment on what they actually comprised.

In 1825 and 1832 it was reported at visitation that all the 'evidences' were well kept.[45] 1833 saw the beginning of the long tenure of the chapter clerkship by partners in the firm of solicitors which became Raper and Co. This gave the documents relating to real estate a more settled home. In 1854 Rev. Thomas Brown asked to see Bishop Sherburne's statutes (Cap I/14) and was only allowed to do so at the Clerk's office. The Chapter were not, however, always so careful of their archives—in 1872 Rev. F.H. Arnold was allowed to borrow the earliest communar's account roll (Cap I/23/3) for six months.[47] However, when Lane Poole inspected the Cathedral archives on behalf of the Historical Manuscripts Commission in 1901, the then Chapter Clerk, Sir Robert Raper, 'was so little acquainted with the collections under his care' that he thought all the contents of the Cathedral muniments room belonged to the bishop. The older volumes were kept at that time in a press in the Cathedral muniments room with 'other miscellaneous books of no special interest'. The more modern act books were in a strongroom in the Bishop's Registry in Rapers' office, in West Street. Twenty-five original charters, including the 'Oslac' charter of AD 780, had been discovered a few years before in a drawer in the Canons' Vestry, and put into the Cathedral Library.[48]

One of Lane Poole's comments concerned the two major works on the Cathedral which had been published at the end of the 19th century, *Early Statutes of Chichester Cathedral* by Mackenzie E. Walcott, the precentor (1877), and *The History and Constitution of a Cathedral of the old foundation* by Canon Swainson (1880). Both relied very heavily on the archives. Lane Poole had to record that 'for reasons which it is unnecessary to mention, neither of these volumes is to be found in the Cathedral Library'.[49] The next great work on the Cathedral was Bennett, Codrington and Deedes' *Statutes and Constitutions of the Cathedral Church of Chichester*, which appeared in 1904. Shortly after this, Canons Bennett and Deedes gave an account of the 'papers, plans and books etc. in the Dean and Chapter cupboard' in the muniments room over the Canons' Vestry in the south transept.[50] Their list is tremendously detailed and, assuming that they listed individual documents as they found them, it would seem to imply that the documents were very mixed up in date and subject, and between the Dean and Chapter, St. Mary's Hospital and the Vicars Choral.

There were estate papers there, too, leases and manorial account books: Bennett and Deedes' descriptions are very detailed and thorough. The most interesting is what they described as a copy of Bishop William Reede's Register, made in 1646 by Stephen Humphry. This volume was listed in earlier lists, but Bennett and Deedes' description enables it to be firmly identified with Cap I/12/1 in the West Sussex Record Office, which is a copy of Bishop Reede's cartulary (Ep V1/1/4).

Not all the documents listed were in good condition. Among the items was a 'bundle of about 195 documents on paper and parchment of which many are almost wholly illegible having been gnawed by rodents and rotted away or previously injured by damp'. These were described as being mostly bonds or mandates, and may now be among those in Cap I/9 and Cap I/10, some of which were certainly in a poor state.

At the beginning of the Second World War, in 1940 Miss K.M.E. Murray, then assistant bursar of Girton College, was asked by Bishop Bell to supervise the removal of all the Cathedral Archives from the triforium down to the nave. The Cathedral was felt to be at risk from air raids or invasion, and the documents were packed in boxes and dispatched to Cambridge.[51]

This did not of course include the estate records, which were still in the basement of the Diocesan Registry. Other ecclesiastical material was still in the strongrooms of Rapers. There they were at risk during the waste paper drives for the war effort. Fortunately Leslie Holden, who had started work for the firm in 1942, took an interest in the material, which had been put aside for possible disposal. He spent many evenings in the cellar, sorting through the piles of paper, abstracting the interesting material. Eventually Professor Hilda Johnstone, an eminent historian and archivist to the Bishop, and W.D. Peckham, who became Dean and Chapter archivist in 1943,[52] became involved. Documents were picked out, identified, and sent to the appropriate place of deposit.[53]

In 1946, the Pilgrim Trust carried out a survey of the Chapter archives, as part of its survey of the principal collections of archives of the Church of England.[54] Chichester was a very tiny collection, comprising only 120 linear feet, compared with York with 4,000, or Lincoln with 1,114 feet. The Trust drew attention to the danger the capitular archives were in, from fire or damp, in the basement of the Diocesan Registry. In 1948 it was reported at the Bishop's Visitation that the archives of the Dean and Chapter were in the Chapter Clerk's office, except for a few which had been for many years in a store-room in the triforium and were allowed to stay when it was used for the Bishop's muniments. W.D. Peckham, Honorary Archivist to the Dean and Chapter, 'makes constant use of them and requests concerning them are referred to him'.[55]

This state of affairs was shortly to change. In 1946 West Sussex County Record Office had been established in the basement of County Hall, Chichester. In February 1948 the question was first raised of the establishment of a Diocesan Record Office under the wing of the County Record Office. In June of that year part of the east wing basement of County Hall became available, and as from 1 April 1949 the Diocesan Record Office came into being. The report on its accommodation described the Diocesan Record Office as being 'accessible with some difficulty from the present Record Office'. People moving from one office to the other had in fact to negotiate a long tunnel, in which no one could stand upright.

The Dean and Chapter asked their archivist, W.D. Peckham, to report on the question of whether their archives should be transferred to the new Diocesan Record Office. On his recommendation, in December 1950 the Administrative Chapter agreed to deposit all the Chapter archives up to 1850. Before they were deposited, Peckham made a complete list of them. The Act Books and a few other volumes were in the strongroom at the Diocesan Registry; the estate records were in a damp basement; about 12 feet of records were in the Cathedral Muniment Room.

In June 1951 the formal agreement was signed between the Dean and Chapter and West Sussex County Council. The first documents to arrive at the Record Office were the manorial records, which were in immediate danger from damp and mildew. In March 1952, the Chapter asked the County Archivist, B. Campbell Cooke, to arrange for the transfer of the whole of the pre-1850 capitular archive to the Diocesan Record Office. They also asked him to advise them as to 'whether you think any of them could be properly destroyed', to which he replied that there was little, if anything, which was worthless.

Documents which had become detached from the main body of the archive were gradually being returned. In May 1952 Canon Lowther Clarke, the Cathedral Librarian and Communar, sent over 21 of the 25 ancient deeds, the remaining ones being on display in the Cathedral. In September of that year he sent over an 18th-century statute book. In April 1953 Campbell Cooke was trying to trace the whereabouts of a Chapter charter which had last been seen in the Cathedral Library some years before. Lowther Clarke admitted that his predecessor, Rev. R.S.T. Haslehurst, who had left Chichester in 1945, had several years later returned a charter, which for some reason he had taken with him. Some of the early Chapter leasebooks were not with the archives handed over in 1952. These were found with the Church Commissioners, as too was the Parliamentary Survey. The Church Commissioners agreed to transfer all their Chichester documents to the Diocesan Record Office in 1956.[56]

With the transfer of the archives, W.D. Peckham transferred too, becoming a daily visitor to the Diocesan Record Office. A gift from the Pilgrim Trust in 1955 enabled some repair work to be done on the archives and, with support from the Marc Fitch Fund, a catalogue was prepared and published in 1967.[57] It was prepared and produced quickly, to provide a working list of the archive for the benefit of scholars wishing to use it. Since its publication, many sections of the catalogue have been expanded. More modern material has been added to the archive by the Dean and Chapter over the years, and the lists of such items have been added to the catalogue.

The Diocesan Record Office now shares the accommodation of the modern West Sussex County Record Office, purpose-built in 1989. The environmentally controlled strongrooms and the professional administration of the archive should ensure that the Dean and Chapter archive survives for at least another 700 years of recorded history.

In terms of the amount of documents which actually survives, the Chapter archives are very disappointing. There is very little from before 1500, which is tragic for a Cathedral of the Old Foundation. Less than 120 original medieval charters survive, although there is of course much relevant material in the cartularies which now form part of the episcopal archives. Other early material survives in later copies and collections, in which the archives are quite rich. Of the major archive series, only the Chapter Act Books start before 1500. These record the decisions made by the Dean and Chapter, and the business transacted at Chapter meetings. From the mid-16th century on, there are communars' accounts and lease books. The accounts are quite detailed initially, but from the late 16th century they are only a formal presentation of accounts, containing less information. The lease books, which also survive from the mid-16th century on, record all leases of land granted by the Dean and Chapter and the prebendaries. The information in these is supplemented by a good series of rentals. In all these sources there is the inevitable gap during the Civil War and Commonwealth. A complete copy of the Parliamentary Survey of Chapter, prebendal and Vicars Choral estates, in 1649-50 gives detailed information on church property at the time. Manor court books survive from the late 17th century, and title deeds mainly from the 18th century on, for many of the prebendal estates. Records of visitations, injunctions and decrees survive from the 16th century.

One major deficiency of the archive has been the lack of personal papers of the deans and residentiaries. The only exception to this is Dean Hussey, who bequeathed his personal papers to the Dean and Chapter, in whose archives they are now deposited.[58] Dean Hussey's papers are especially important in documenting his pioneering patronage of the arts. It is to be hoped that his example will be followed by his successors, so that the Dean and Chapter archives may continue to grow, in both formal and informal series of records, and reflect the life of the Cathedral in the centuries to come.

The Antiquaries

Chichester Cathedral has been fortunate in numbering among those closely associated with it several talented antiquaries. First in this honourable succession came William Reede, Bishop of Chichester from 1368-85.[59] He was a Fellow of Merton College, Oxford, 'the most excellent mathematician of the age', and 'most learned in theology and in all the liberal sciences'. Chichester Cathedral already had one cartulary, compiled in the mid-13th century, but Bishop Reede's contribution in Chichester was the systematic compilation of cartularies, gathering together all the charters and writings concerning the church. The Cædwalla charter of AD 683 certainly made an impression on him. He anathematised anyone who presumed to alter his collection in the very words quoted from the charter.[60]

The compilation of the cartularies was done in a methodical way, by scribes from the Bishop's own household. The object was to provide the Bishop and his successors with a working set of episcopal documents, the charters and evidences, rentals and custumals, constitutions and statutes. The scribes' only deficiency was in Anglo-Saxon, so a number of charters in that language were omitted, their titles only being listed. Bishop Reede even thought to mention the cartularies in his will.[61] Reede was of course collecting documentary evidence for himself and his successors. His cartularies do, however, preserve almost the only early documentary evidence about the Cathedral. Less than fifty original charters survive in the Chapter archives dating from before his compilations.

The next person of antiquarian interests associated with the Cathedral of whom we have information is John Swayne NP (*c.*1590-1654), deputy Chapter Clerk from 1613.[62] The Cathedral archives seem to have been his particular concern, for he made copious abstracts from them. They seem to have been in his care, for in 1636 the Dean ordered him to produce 'the Leiger book and the old white book of evidence' which were needed for a court case in London.[63] It is to him that we owe the earliest description of Liber Y, the first Cathedral cartulary, compiled in the mid-13th century. Swayne describes it as 'a very auncient leiger booke, in a somewhat great quarto; bound up in boordes, covered over with leather of a whiteish russett colour, with a brasse pinne set in the midst of the cover of one side of the booke'.[64] His description of the earliest Chapter Act Book (Cap I/3/0) from which he also made abstracts, is similarly detailed, and includes observations on the various systems of foliation, and the differing hands involved in the compilation.[65] He was himself a careful copyist, taking care to reproduce exactly the abbreviations and the spellings of proper names. According to Richard Bragge, Swayne also compiled in 1628 a 'thin book' concerning the election and installation of Bishops, which may possibly be identified with Cap I/6/6.[66]

Perhaps the most valuable contribution which Swayne made by his compilations from the archives, was the preservation of at least some of the contents of Liber Æ, known as the 'Leiger Book', which was subsequently lost. Thanks to Swayne, we know what the Leiger Book looked like: 'a leiger booke, with parchment leaves, in a very great folio, bound in bords, and covered over with leather of a Murrey colour; and with two claspes'.[67] He adds that most of the entries were in the hand of John Stilman NP, who was Bishop Sherburne's registrar from at least 1523.

More work on the Leiger Book was done by William Paul, residentiary from 1636-62, who compiled an index of the contents up to page 137. The index was copied into Statute Book B, with a note that it had been done by Dr. Paul, late Bishop of Oxford, who had seen the Leiger Book and transcribed the index thus far, 'which book is since lost'.[68] If the copying into Statute Book B was done by Richard Bragge, whose writing it would seem to be, the index was copied between 1665 when Dr. Paul died, and 1671 when Bragge retired, so the Leiger Book was lost by then. Dr. Paul also annotated an 'old vellum rental', which he dated (inaccurately) to 1335. Our only knowledge of the original comes from Canon William Clarke's note at the beginning of the copy of the rental in Cap I/23/1, observing that it must have been legible in Dr. Paul's day. It vanished after Clarke's day.

Canon William Clarke (1696-1771) is one of the most attractive characters associated with the Cathedral archives.[69] William Hayley commented on his 'engaging mildness of face and manner ... it was his custom to devote a shilling in every guinea that he received, to the services of the poor'. Clarke described himself, with due modesty, as 'a meek, quiet thing, not vain enough to desire to be thought a scholar'. He also had a sense of humour. When the inscription 'Haec est Domus ultima' was placed on the Duke of Richmond's family vault in the Cathedral Lady Chapel, Clarke was prompted into verse:

> Did he, who thus inscrib'd the wall,
> Not read, or not believe St Paul,
> Who says there is, where'er it stands,
> Another house not made with hands,
> Or may we gather from these words,
> That house is not a house of Lords?

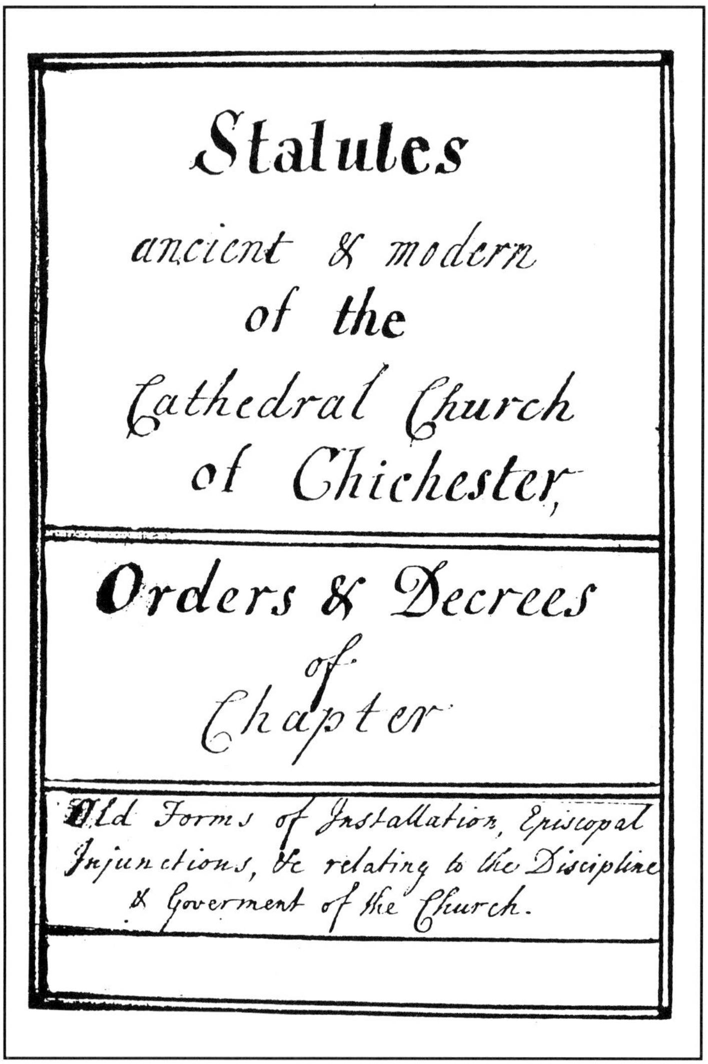

Statutes
ancient & modern
of the
Cathedral Church
of Chichester,

Orders & Decrees
of
Chapter

Old Forms of Installation, Episcopal Injunctions, &c relating to the Discipline & Goverment of the Church.

106 *William Clarke's transcript of the Cathedral Statutes.*

Clarke's attitude to ecclesiastical preferment was expressed in 1737: 'I was for a few days in great fear of an Archdeaconry; but was happily delivered from that dignity'.

He worked extensively on the Cathedral archives as he did on the Library catalogues. He compiled a list of both the capitular and episcopal archives.[70] He made an ordered compilation of Cathedral statutes, forms and customs, episcopal injunctions and chapter decrees. He indexed the copy of the early statutes of the Cathedral which the Chapter had made from the original in University College, Oxford, in 1725.[72] His erudition is neatly demonstrated by his annotation on the back of what was thought to be the earliest original charter, made in either 725 or 775 (Cap I/17/1): 'a part of a Saxon grant forged to support the estates of the church against Norman c[laims] but probably an honest fraud'.[73] Modern scholarship concludes from internal evidence that the existing document was written *c.*1000, and it is quite probable that it was written, or the substance copied from an original, to maintain existing church rights, rather than falsely to claim new ones.

In *c.*1750 Bishop Mawson asked Clarke to compile an account of 'the Antiquities of Chichester Cathedral'. This was never published as a separate work. It was used, though much criticised, by Alexander Hay in his *History of Chichester* published in 1804.[74] The Bishop's request seems to have been prompted by some remarks on the Cathedral by another antiquary, Charles Lyttleton, Dean of Exeter. Clarke's manuscript begins with the slightly waspish remark, 'I was surprised that the Dean of Exeter, in such a transient view of this church, should distinguish the several dates of the building so exactly.'

James Bennett Freeland (1782-1852) was a partner in the firm of Raper and Freeland, which has over the centuries provided a number of clerks and registrars for both the Dean and Chapter and the bishop. He was admitted clerk, steward and solicitor to the Chapter in 1833.[75] His was the pioneering work on the clergy. His papers contain abstracts of institutions from the episcopal registers and subscription books, and of installations of Cathedral clergy. His son, F.E. Freeland, transcribed and abstracted documents for him in the British Museum.[76] Freeland does not seem to have published any work on the Cathedral, though it seems he was at one time contemplating writing a life of St Wilfrid.[77]

C.A. Swainson and M.E.C. Walcott are the two 19th-century antiquaries who compiled major works on the Cathedral, neither of which were in the Cathedral Library in 1901. The reasons which R. Lane Poole found it 'unnecessary to mention' were that both Swainson and Walcott had in fact had differences with their deans.

C.A. Swainson became principal of the Theological College in 1854, and a prebendary in 1856. He wrote many theological works, but his first local work, in 1866, was in fact concerned neither with theology nor history. It was a spirited pamphlet about Chichester's urgent need for a drainage system.[78] This was a controversial subject, over which opinion in the city was very much divided. Swainson also held controversial views on the relationship between the Dean and the Chapter which brought him into conflict with the newly appointed Dean Burgon.[79]

It is possible that Swainson acquired his views in the course of his research for his work on the *History and Constitution of the Cathedral*. He had published an article on the history of St Mary's Hospital in *Sussex Archaeological Collections* in 1872, but the *History and Constitution*, published in 1880, was his major work. It was intended to be published in two volumes, and the first volume covers only up to 1503, ending curiously in the middle of a word. It was intended to continue the history up to the time of the abolition of the Dean's Peculiar jurisdiction. A note by Dr. A. Jessopp,[80] in the copy of the volume given to him by Swainson,[81] explains the non-appearance of the second volume. 'When Professor Swainson gave me this volume he assured me that, so far as he knew, only a single copy had been sold. "I meant" he said, "to go on with it; but I really could not afford to do so without some encouragement."' It must have been very disheartening to have done so much work and provoked so little response.

Mackenzie E.C. Walcott (1822-80) came into conflict with the whole Chapter over his interpretation of the rôle of the precentor, to which office he was appointed in 1863. Dean Hook certainly had no great opinion of his historical accuracy. When M.A. Lower wrote to him in 1865, enquiring about Walcott's suitability as editor of *Sussex Archaeological Collections*, the Dean was rather scathing: 'Mr. Mackenzie Walcott is a grandiloquent as well as an inaccurate writer ... I do not think that the Sussex Archaeological Journal will gain much if he shall be appointed editor ... He has much miscellaneous archaeological information, but is very inaccurate.'[82] W.D. Peckham, a later Cathedral antiquary, in his own copy of Walcott's *Statutes* does note many inaccuracies and misreadings.

Bennett, Codrington and Deedes, who together compiled the *Statutes and Constitutions of the Cathedral Church of Chichester*, published in 1904, were each in their own right distinguished men. R.H. Codrington (1830-1922), as F.G. Bennett told W.D. Peckham, did most of the copying work for the book. In earlier years he had been a missionary, and had created a *lingua franca* for Melanesia. When he came back in 1887 he became vicar of Wadhurst, and in 1888 prebendary of Sidlesham. He lectured at the Theological College and, according to an anonymous recollection of him, 'Dr. Codrington was a saint; he would have been distressed to hear himself so called'.[83] He was remembered in old age as 'a very old rotund man, black skull cap firmly on head, pottering about his banana tree' which he grew in the garden of No.2 St. Richard's Walk, Chichester. He had an influence on the career of Eric Gill, whom he invited to tea many times while Gill was in Chichester. According to Gill

> He was great on heraldry and medieval architectural archaeology ... He gently ridiculed the enthusiasm of the 'restorers' and ... laughed at the idea that modern Gothic should look like old ... In his quiet way ... he was a keen critic and he smiled to scorn the foibles and foolishness of our little ecclesiastical society and its snobberies and pretences.'[84]

It was through Codrington that Gill was found a place in the office of the architect to the Ecclesiastical Commissioners, W.D. Caroë.

Codrington found time to write two articles in *Sussex Archaeological Collections*, one in 1892 on the Selwyn family, one in 1905 on coats of arms in the Cathedral.[85] A letter from him to Cavis Brown, the rector of Selsey, who was collecting material on the history of that place, gives an idea of Codrington's high standard of historical accuracy. In discussing the dating of the early stone sculpture panels in the Cathedral he wrote,

> What they call a 'tradition' of those stones being brought from Selsey is but a conjecture. They were not known to exist 80 years ago and there can be no tradition about what is not known to exist. Of all things in the world a man who wants to write a good book should beware of the local antiquary.[86]

F.G. Bennett (1844-1937) was head of the Prebendal School from 1879-1911, when he became prebendary of Gates until his retirement in 1923. His particular interest was in the fabric of the Cathedral. An obituary in the *Chichester Observer* described him as having been almost an unofficial honorary clerk of works, the confidant and friend of successive Cathedral architects, with a profound knowledge of the history and architecture of the Cathedral and its precincts, which he was happy to share.[87] In 1913-19 with Cecil Deedes he compiled the tremendously detailed list of 'papers, plans and books etc. in the Dean and Chapter cupboard',[88] the fruit of many hours' work.

Deedes (*c.*1843-1921) became a prebendary of Chichester Cathedral in 1902. The *Statutes and Constitutions* with Bennett and Codrington was his first published work based on the archives. He then undertook editions of the earliest surviving episcopal registers, those of Richard Praty, and Robert Rede,[89] published in 1908 and 1910. In 1909 he published the order of the *Consecration of St. Bartholomew's Hospital*, the manuscript of which was in John Swayne's book. In 1911 Deedes was busy checking the original sources in the Cathedral archives used by E. Heron-Allen for his major book on Selsey, and reading the proofs. He offered to transcribe Cædwalla's charter to Wilfrid, but admitted that he would have to get expert help with the Anglo-Saxon boundaries.[90] He wrote to Heron-Allen in 1911, 'We ought to have a critical edition of all these pre-Norman charters and perhaps the next generation may see their way to doing this. If I were a good deal younger than I am I might attempt it, but "the night cometh" etc. and there are other more important things.'[91]

When Canon Deedes retired in 1920, a presentation was made to him. The newspaper report spoke of his 'affectionate nature and kindly disposition'. Tribute was paid to his hard work on the Cathedral Library.[92] He was to remain Librarian and intended to visit Chichester four times a year to oversee the Library but he died the next year. A great collector of books himself, when he left Chichester, he sold his own library. The *Chichester Observer* reported that it comprised 89,000 (*sic*!) volumes, which fetched prices ranging from 2s. to £20.[93]

107 *Walter Divie Peckham in Balkan dress.*

Cecil Deedes' other great contribution to the Cathedral archives was introducing to them in 1920 the man who was to do more research on the Cathedral and its history than anyone before or since. He placed Liber P, one of the cartularies, in the hands of Walter Divie Peckham, who had then just retired, at the age of 37, from the Diplomatic Service.[94] He was to devote his long retirement to research on the archives. During this period of nearly sixty years, he gained an immense knowledge of the history of the Dean and Chapter and the Cathedral. It was so profound, that it almost seemed that he had personally known all the people associated with the Cathedral over the centuries. He was fascinated by oral tradition, and the sense of playing a part in it. He would recite with pride small anecdotes about the prebendaries of the late 18th century, emphasising that these were unpublished, and had been recounted to him by their 19th-century successors. Some of his knowledge was incorporated in his numerous published articles and editions of documents. Peckham himself described these as 'some solid, not to say stodgy, papers on archaeological subjects'.[95]

His published works included four volumes for the *Sussex Record Society*—of medieval custumals of episcopal manors; of the earliest cartulary, Liber Y; and of Chapter Acts from 1472-1642. He contributed articles to 19 volumes of *Sussex Archaeological Collections*, and notes to nearly every volume of *Sussex Notes and Queries* for 50 years. Peckham said, modestly, in his memoirs, 'A succession of papers ... and other published work ... are, I claim good evidence that I have not been a useless idler since I last earned a salary'.

But only a proportion of his extensive research was published. Among his unpublished papers in the County Record Office are editions of Chapter Acts from 1660-1778; transcripts of accounts and obits 1513-71; lists of institutions to Sussex livings 1279-1857; a *fasti* of the Cathedral establishment; and transcripts of registers of 19 parishes.[96]

Peckham continued working on aspects of Cathedral history until shortly before his death in 1979, although his contact with others in the same field had been hampered for many years by his increasing deafness. While he was still in Chichester, and able to do so, he was a daily visitor to the Diocesan Record Office. In summer, he made a memorable figure, dressed only in shorts and sandals, with his hearing-aid battery taped to his bare chest. When his infirmities increased, he worked at home, and eventually in his nursing-home room, from photocopies of documents. He wrote in 1978, 'time hangs very heavy on my hands unless I have something to occupy my mind'.[97]

It is ironic that at the end of over half a century immersed in ecclesiastical documents, Peckham's funeral service was at his express request not a conventional Christian one. Afterwards his ashes were scattered by his family on the garden of Nutley Old Vicarage, where he was born, to the accompaniment of the Catullus lament which finishes 'Frater ave atque vale'. W.D. Peckham was always pleased to share his knowledge, particularly with the professional archivists who had taken over the care of the Chapter archives, so that they felt themselves to be the latest representatives in a succession of those who had cared for the Cathedral Archives.

XIII

Church Monuments

H.A. Tummers

In remembrance of Canon Geoffrey Parks, M.C.

In Pevsner's *Buildings of England* series, the furnishings in Chichester Cathedral are called meagre and the monuments few and small.[1] This judgement is too harsh and incorrect. Other cathedrals may boast of greater collections of church monuments but Chichester has a collection that can stand the test of criticism, with some remarkable objects not seen elsewhere. The scope of the memorials is very broad: there are very early and very late ones. The quality is sometimes very high—John Flaxman called the effigial tomb to Joan de Vere the finest medieval monument in England, while his own finest memorial, to Agnes Cromwell, is also found here. And further it is the great variety in sorts of monuments, of the 18th and especially the 19th century, that attracts attention.[2]

What follows will not be a chronological or enumerative description of all the Cathedral monuments by their present position, but a study of their characteristics from three viewpoints: firstly, their original sites and the oft-recurring practice of moving them about; secondly, the persons commemorated, their profession or state in life; and thirdly, the type of monument chosen in specific periods and the sculptors employed. This may result in repeated mention of some of the monuments, chiefly the most remarkable ones, yet I think that this method of procedure should bring about a renewed attention to their characteristics.

Monuments *in situ*

The best documented medieval monument in Chichester Cathedral is the niche tomb to Bishop Robert Sherburne (d.1536).[3] Ordered during the bishop's lifetime, it was set up in the south wall of the south choir aisle, where it has remained, well cared for, till this day.[4] The type of niche and effigy is a style that lasted for more than two centuries, yet some details make it a clearly early 16th-century monument (fig.109). The effigy shows nothing of the broad manner of Bishop William of Wykeham's effigy in Winchester Cathedral (1404) with praying hands protruding and the upright, sitting attendant figures. With Sherburne everything is kept low. The praying hands are in line with the body, the attendant puppet-like angels are lying on their backs and the vestments have softly rippling drapery. The effigy is an elongated figure, in which there is more stress on the sumptuous effects of small details than on extrovert accents reaching out into the space around.

Bishop Sherburne himself stands on the borderline between the Middle Ages and modern times and so does his tomb. Strongly in sympathy with the old tradition, he

108 *Agnes Cromwell's memorial by Flaxman (1800).*

nevertheless delivered a sermon promoting the King's supremacy over the Church, but only as a last act. After it he resigned; he died six months later. His sumptuous, somewhat nostalgic tomb may be old-fashioned in conception, but it is still an imposing memorial.

We are unusually well informed about how the Bishop's memorials were to be organised and his tomb taken care of. A curtain was drawn over it to keep it clean, only to be opened on certain days. Yearly three shillings and fourpence were spent on washing and repairing the tomb. For every day that, after a mass to the Holy Virgin, eight choristers made a procession to the tomb and said a 'De profundis' there, 24 shillings had to be divided among them annually ('My Lord Robert's dyvydent money'). And on Bishop Sherburne's anniversary there was a procession to his tomb by the Dean and Chapter and eight choristers.[5]

As the tomb is still in its original place, such provisions, similar to well-known examples elsewhere, help us to understand how parts of the liturgy took place in the medieval Cathedral. The monument is thus not only an important art-historical memorial in itself but also historically, for the part it played in the liturgy.

Other medieval tombs have kept their original positions inside the Cathedral, though for the most part it is no longer clear whom they commemorated. On 3 June and 16 July 1829, four coffins were found between the piers of the north and south arches of the quire. The opening of them revealed remarkable grave objects that even nowadays attract attention. Less attention has been paid to the decoration of the lids of two of the coffins, which show incised croziers, and to the exact place where the monuments were found, between the piers six inches below the pavement. After the discovery they were moved to the eastern side-chapels, to return, in 1925, to the places where they were found. Careful analysis of the meagre contemporary accounts of the finds shows that the two eastern tombs can tentatively be attributed to Seffrid II (d.1204) and Simon of Wells (d.1207) and the two western ones to Ranulph Wareham (d.1222) and Ralph Neville (d.1244).[6] The present position of the coffins, in the north and south aisles of the quire, must be very near their original position. The suggestion that they came from other parts of the building is not based on any serious proof and would be against all logic. The contents had not been disturbed and the coffins were unknown in the 17th and 18th centuries. Moreover, other cathedrals show that a place under the arcade near the high altar is the traditional site reserved for early bishops and founders. It is their position near the high altar that makes them part and parcel of the liturgy that was celebrated there daily.

The niche tomb in the south wall of the first bay of the Lady Chapel and the one in the south transept have not been moved either: they were cut into the wall. The former can be attributed to Bishop Gilbert of St Leofard (d.1304), because it was he who built that part of the Lady Chapel. The two coped coffins now housed in the niche do not, on the face of it, belong there. Whether the niche formerly possessed an effigy is hard to say. If so, it has completely disappeared. The two now in the south transept can never, because of their measurements, have been there, as has sometimes been suggested. Another recent suggestion, that one of the coffin slabs from the quire aisles may have belonged to Bishop Gilbert, is not very convincing either.[7] The assumption is based on two possible indents for brass letters, ER. The strong tapering of slab and coffin is not only stylistically out-of-date for the beginning of the 14th century, but it too could not have conveniently fitted the niche in the Lady Chapel.

Both the early 14th-century niche tomb in the Lady Chapel and Bishop Langton's tomb in the south wall of the south transept were set up away from the quire, at places where the dignitaries commemorated had contributed to the embellishment of the fabric. This practice signals a phase in the disposition of medieval ecclesiastical monuments of which Bishop Berghsted's tomb (*c.*1300) in the west porch, if it is his, is an early example. Another example is Bishop Arundel's tomb under the third arch of the southern nave arcade; its original position was under the second arch, nearer the so-called Arundel screen.[8] About 1829, at a time of much internal refurnishing, it was moved to the south-west tower, followed in 1860 by the screen. After the rebuilding of the

109 *Bishop Sherburne's tomb (see detail, fig.21).*

tower and spire following their collapse, the tomb was brought back to its original position somewhere between 1865 and 1874; the Arundel screen was not re-erected until 1961. In 1966, when a new pulpit was put in, the tomb had to move one bay further west.

At present there are voices in favour of moving the tomb once more, with an eye to the possible erection of a nave altar.[9] Historical reasons would plead against such a decision, unless, of course, it could be moved one bay eastwards towards its original site. Screen and tomb should not be further separated. The Arundel tomb chest, with its indent of a bishop's figure in brass on the top slab, is a typically 15th-century monument and deserves to be treated carefully.

The first two post-Reformation bishops' tombs in Chichester Cathedral have also apparently never been moved, though the contents were disturbed.[10] They are the chest tombs under the first arches behind the high altar. The names of the bishops that were buried in them were forgotten by the middle of the 17th century. The brass set into an older indent in the top slab of the tomb to the south was made by Thomas King somewhere between 1832 and 1842, repeating the account of Bishop Day under Barnard's portraits of the bishops, but the small side brass on its south side with his canting arms (see fig.24) is much older, and was there long before the 1780s. The other tomb chest is now commonly supposed to be that of Bishop Barlow. The two tombs show something of the spirit of the beginning of the Reformation period: sober chests with a minimum of decorative motifs, solely for identification and without an effigy. The site chosen is remarkable, as it was near the place where, up till a few years before, in 1538, the shrine of St Richard had stood. Bishop Day was a moderate man, sympathetic to reform; Barlow appears to have more or less consistently stood on the side of the Reformation. Both, still feeling for a continuing tradition, however, must have had uneasy thoughts on the destruction of St Richard's shrine. At least they started to use the space behind the high altar, the place of the venerated saint of Chichester, for interments: 'the burial place', as it was to be called for a long time. The effigial wall memorial to the clearly new-style Anglican bishop Thomas Bickley (d.1596), now hanging in the Lady Chapel, also hung originally near this burial place, on the north side.

The change in liturgical practices due to the Reformation led to a change in the choice of places for monuments. Moreover, more and more lay people wanted monuments erected for themselves and their families, for which a suitable place had to be found. The direct connection that existed in the old religion between liturgical practices and monuments disappeared. Gradually one sees the space outside the quire become a lay area to walk around in, to ponder in front of memorials or admire them. All this led to a far greater freedom in the selection of an appropriate site. And the appropriateness could quickly be obscured by the erection of a new memorial that might well cause another one to move on a little. Yet in spite of all this there are instances where it is absolutely clear that a specific site was chosen for specific reasons and adhered to in subsequent times. A few examples may suffice to give a general idea of this in the period from the 16th to the 20th centuries.

What is now again the chapel of St John the Baptist, at the east end of the north quire aisle, lost that name in the course of the 17th century. From the end of that century it was known as 'Miller's vault': the Miller family had appropriated it as their family burial chapel. The impressive monument, erected shortly after 1701, which is now against the south wall of the chapel, probably stood originally against the east wall, at the site of the altar.[11] According to the inscription, it was set up, in the first place, to Margaret Miller, then to her son and daughter, her husband, the latter's second wife and her children, and to her husband's parents. In 1924, the connection between chapel space and Miller's vault was still remembered: the chapel was renovated with money from Sir Hubert Miller, a late descendant of the family, in memory of Sir Hubert's son, who was killed in World War I.

The cenotaph to Bishop Durnford (d.1896) was put up under the influence of the Gothic Revival. The erection was part of a greater project of restoring St Clement's Chapel to its original use as a chapel. The whole design was approved in 1897. A large monument consisting of a big chest with an open canopy structure housing the effigy was to occupy the north arch of the chapel. A grille and an iron entrance gate were added in 1898. The installation of the monument and the chapel was a great affair, with a special service and an unveiling by the Duke of Richmond on 23 May 1898.

It is the most ambitious monument in neo-Gothic style in the Cathedral, in a grander style and more successful in execution than the neo-Gothic niche tomb in the south transept to John Smith (d.1848), a banker and politician, a tomb expressly meant to be a companion piece to the nearby tomb of Bishop Langton.[12] Contemporary comments on Durnford's tomb rather quickly changed from 'magnificent' and 'admirable' to 'sham' and 'stone dead', but it certainly tells us something of the ideas about the functioning of the Cathedral and the style of restoration chosen for it at the end of the 19th century. It will perhaps be better valued by future generations.[13]

In 1922/3 the chapel of St Edmund and St Thomas was restored

110 *Memorial to Margaret Miller and family.*

to the memory of Lt Noel Roland Abbey of the Grenadier Guards, who was killed near Dieppe in 1918. It was done very much in the ecclesiastical manner of the 1920s. In 1979 it was refurbished, as a memorial to the former Librarian and County Archivist, the antiquarian Francis Steer (d.1978).[14]

The Moving of Monuments

In 1731 the floor of the choir was repaved with black and white marble tiles; as a result, the Purbeck marble slabs with indents of brasses for bishops and others were removed to the nave. Commenting on this, Godfrey wrote in 1935: 'Thus an unfortunate practice began, or was continued, of moving the monuments of the church, which has been the cause of irreparable confusion in their identification and generally in the history of the church'.[15] Some examples will show more clearly distortions in historical evidence and the difficulties of tracing the original state of affairs.

111 *Indent formerly believed that of Bishop William Reede, but possibly from the original resting place of St Richard.*

A recent debate concerns a remarkable marble slab with the brass indents of a bishop's figure and a number of stars and crescent moons.[16] On the basis of the crescent moons and stars the slab was until now thought to commemorate Bishop William Reede (d.1385), who had been an amateur astrologist. John Bertram suggests that it belonged to Bishop Richard de Wych, placed there on the occasion of his centenary in 1352. The slab lies by the column in the nave where the saint was first buried and the style suggested by the indent is too early for 1385 but would just fit 1352.

This latter is a strong argument. Much more is known about brasses and their indents nowadays and the slab certainly fits the 1340s and 1350s best. Moreover, there is no Chichester bishop of the period who is not commemorated by another monument. The later argument is far less strong. A 19th-century inventory of slabs with indents of brasses[17] enumerates eight slabs with brasses for bishops, one of them for the tomb chest of Bishop Arundel. Browne-Willis's notes of the late 17th and early 18th centuries[18] (see fig.67) tell us of three to five brass indents in the quire and three more in the Lady Chapel.

112 *Chest tomb of Bishop Robert Stratford (formerly believed that of St Richard) after the fall of the spire and before the rebuilding of the superstructure in 1904. (Note the new position of Barnard's historical pictures and the 19th-century organ case.)*

Thus, in the 17th century there seems to have been none in the nave, except the one for Bishop Arundel. If the quire pavement in 1731 had been treated with more respect for the old slabs, this puzzle would not have occurred; the floor would not necessarily have been the worse for it, and fewer feet would have worn out the memorial inscriptions.

Removing monuments is of course better than destroying them. The wilful destruction of St Richard's shrine in 1538 illustrates this. Within a century the knowledge of the exact site of the shrine was lost. The tomb chest on the south side of the retroquire (the 'burial place') was then thought to be St Richard's tomb. When at the beginning of the 19th century it was recognised that this tomb chest was of a later date and was probably that of Bishop Day,[19] the free-standing tomb chest with effigy under the so-called Sacellum in the south transept was attributed to St Richard. Even when this tomb was opened in 1845, the contents were interpreted in this way: remnants of hazel twigs were found 'such as pilgrims were accustomed to cut by the way, and which were afterwards hung by the shrine as a token of the zeal by the faithful'. Only gradually between 1847 and 1861, by the researches of W.H. Blaauw, did it become clear that, as in other cathedrals, the great shrine to the Chichester saint had been situated in the retroquire.

A more modern appropriation of a tomb on doubtful grounds concerns the tomb chest with effigy now standing below the arch to the north of the high altar. Mackenzie Walcott, Gordon M. Hills ('the learned architect'), Matthew Bloxam (an expert from London) and Canon F.G. Bennett together came to the conclusion, in the 1880s, that the great Bishop Storey must certainly have had a great tomb and, none being known, they decided between them that it must have been the niche tomb with effigy in the north wall one bay further west. With money from H.L. and E. Storey of Lancaster, family descendants, the tomb was moved to its present place in 1908 and attributed to Bishop Storey.[20] This attribution, however, is wrong; the present tomb comes from another place where without doubt it commemorated Bishop Rickingale. Not only does the style of both chest and effigy point to this, it is also proved by 18th-century drawings and the wills of the two bishops. The will of Bishop Storey only speaks of a monument on the north side of the altar, whereas Rickingale's will explicitly mentions an effigy (fig.120). An old plan of the

113 *Weepers from the tomb of Joan de Vere.*

Cathedral[21] also shows only a tomb chest without an effigy to the north of the high altar. One must conclude that the place of Bishop Storey's grave was deduced rightly, but that the present monument is a 19th-century assumption.

If the three striking effigial monuments to the Arundel family, the heart burial to Maud, the chest with effigy to Joan de Vere and the double tomb to Richard Fitzalan, the second Earl. and his wife, had not been moved to Chichester from the dissolved priory at Lewes, they would almost certainly have been lost sight of. That they come from Lewes is all but certain, not only because of the presence of the Arundel arms, but also because of the fact that the tombs, not originally present in Chichester Cathedral, can all three of them together be connected with figures mentioned in the Lewes cartulary.

The effigy of Joan de Vere (d.1293) is important, in art-historical terms, because it is the first of a series of female effigies that can be connected with the work of a court school around 1300.[22] The attribution of the double tomb has recently been called into doubt: in my earlier paper.[23] I had not the benefit of two pieces of rather conflicting evidence describing the shipping of two marble tombs for the second Earl of Arundel (d.1376) and Eleanor his wife (d.1372) from Poole harbour to London in January 1375 and of the Earl's desire, as stated in his will of December 1375, that his tomb in the Chapter House of Lewes should not be higher than his wife's.[24] This creates a puzzle. The two facts mentioned are not quite in agreement with each other, while the wording in the Lewes cartulary would suggest that the two are lying closely next to each other. If the word 'marble' is taken at its face value, the present chest in Chichester cannot be the original one. But the phrase 'a tomb ... no higher than' does not exclude the two effigies for husband and wife being made at the Earl's death. Further, the stylistic evidence points to the 1370s and no other couple of the Arundel family is mentioned in the same cartulary for the second half of the century. Without further evidence to the contrary the present attribution may, I think, still stand.

Though, as said before, post-Reformation tombs are less intricately bound up with liturgical practices, moving them about can still result in loss of historical evidence.

The three baroque monuments to the bishops Henry King, Guy Carleton and Robert Grove, now set up against the west wall of the north transept, may serve as an example. From the 17th century until 1829 the monuments were in the area east of the high altar. That of King appears to have stood against the east wall and that of Grove against a pillar, both on the south side; Carleton's was apparently against the east wall on the north side. In 1829 the three tombs were moved, within the same area, to the back of the wooden reredos of the high altar. This

114 *The effigies of Richard Fitzalan, 2nd Earl of Arundel, and Eleanor his wife, drawn side by side by S.H. Grimm (BL Add. MS 29925, fol.26). This shows why E.A. Richardson thought the monuments were originally joined together, as he proceeded to make them.*

115 *Bishop Grove's memorial.*

was thought, probably correctly, a more conspicuous and elevated position. They are thus seen in a drawing of 1836.[25]

However, somewhere in the 1870s, after the erection of the new alabaster reredos by Carpenter and Slater, the monuments had to be moved further away. King's monument went at once to its present position in the north transept, whereas the two other tombs were first put in the cloisters, before reaching their present situation around 1889/90.[26]

The choice of 'the burial place' was deliberate, not infringed by the first move of the bishops' funerary monuments. It expressed the historical continuity between the old and the new order. Nowadays, only the tomb chests to the bishops Day and Barlow testify to such a continuity.

Another result of the latest removal was that the original floor slab marking Bishop King's grave was more or less lost sight of. In her edition of the sermons of Henry King, Dr. Hobbs refers to the fact that King's will was not followed in the erection of the monument.[27] He had asked for a plain stone with the words 'Redditurae animae depositum'. These words are indeed found on a big black slab now lying in the chapel of St John the Baptist, proving it to be Bishop King's. The combination of a slab and a monument is not exceptional; there are several examples to be found in the Cathedral. In King's case the erection of the baroque monument came later. It was ordered by his daughter-in-law, no doubt as more fitting to a bishop. Her husband, King's eldest son, is also commemorated in the monument. It was then recut by his great-niece in the 18th century. The present position of the large monument opposite the library may be regarded as having a symbolic meaning, but this was not the aim of the removers in the 19th century. The baroque monuments had by then lost their aesthetic appeal for the reformers of the church space.

Several times the church was cleared of monuments that were thought to be too cumbersome. The cloisters, carefully restored in the later 19th century, were evidently looked upon as most fitting for the superfluous monuments. The wall monument to Percival Smalpage (d.1595) is an early example. The rectangular frame showing the bust of a man in toga originally hung against the south wall of the south transept, but already before 1865 it was to be found in the west alley of the cloisters. A comparable wall monument, to John Cawley (d.1621) and his son the regicide, William Cawley (d.1666), recently moved from the redundant parish church of St Andrew's, has been better preserved and gained a more conspicuous position inside the church building.[28]

In contrast to Smalpage's memorial, that to William Chillingworth (d. 1643/4) will have hung in the cloisters from the start. He was buried there and the memorial was put up by his friend, Oliver Whitby, whose son founded the Oliver Whitby School in Chichester.

116 *Bishop Henry King's memorial, at the time of the 400th-anniversary celebrations.*

The Persons Commemorated

The oldest monument in the Cathedral is the sarcophagus for Bishop Ralph Luffa (d.1123), a great promoter of the new Cathedral. Its raised top is decorated with a crozier and a mitre and, most exceptionally for the time, bears an inscription with the Bishop's name. The latest episcopal memorial is the one to Bishop George Bell, a rectangular tablet with a brass roundel showing his head in profile. This plaque, which has been modelled with feeling, has been affixed to his real memorial, the Arundel screen re-erected in 1961. These two monuments span the whole period of the Cathedral and, as one would expect, both were put up for the clergy.

All medieval bishops who are known to be buried in the Cathedral can be connected with monuments, though it is not always clear which bishop belongs to which monument. For the post-medieval bishops not all the facts relating to their deaths and burials are clear, but from 1840 till the present there is an uninterrupted sequence of bishops' tombs.[30] Episcopal memorials are only occasionally simple affairs, like the one to John Buckner (d.1824), a tablet with a minimum of decoration in the form of a draped urn and a mitre between palm leaves, or to Philip Shuttleworth (d.1842), a floor tablet of brass with a mitre. Mostly they are ostentatious pieces of work: the two to William Otter (d.1840) and to Ernest Wilberforce (d.1907) may serve as examples.

117 *The 'Burial Place', drawn by George Scharf (1852), showing the bishops' memorials in their earlier positions.*

The monument to Otter consists of a large rectangular slab with an extensive inscription topped by a smaller stone with two armorial shields and a bust in a niche. Bishop Otter was a great educationalist and ecclesiastical reformer and his monument (fig.54) in the Cathedral (there are others elsewhere[31]) was put up by his wife and children in 1861.The bust especially, already made in 1844, has a strong and expressive head and a finely draped toga.

The monument to Wilberforce consists of an alabaster relief of the bishop kneeling before a prayer desk fitted into a Tudor arch. The composition as a whole, however, is disappointing; the arrangement within the relief of the kneeling bishop and his books, crozier, desk and armorial shield does not make a happy design.

The memorials to deans of the Cathedral are equally conspicuous.There is the memorial tablet to Thomas Hayley (d.1739), showing a fine balance of baroque and classical elements in the side decoration, an inscription plate with two cherubs' heads below and an urn on top.[32] Two monuments in the Cathedral that show a 19th-century style of their own, something rather exceptional, are those to Deans Walter Hook (d.1875) and John Burgon (d.1888).The former is a tomb chest made up of six different sorts of coloured marble for both the chest itself and the top slab. This cenotaph is at once simple in design, rich in texture and wholly typical of the period in which it was made.

The black marble slab to Burgon has a fine brass figure of the Dean in ecclesiastical vestments with an extensive border inscription also in brass.[33] It is especially the head that strikes us: an unrelenting 19th-century theologian.The inscription on the banderole across his chest reads: '*Credo* [I believe] quod redemptor meus vivit' (for the biblical 'scio'—I know). One wonders if Burgon, who so sternly adhered to the traditional text of the Bible, would have approved of such a change of words, or was the new emphasis intentional?

The memorials to dignitaries and prebendaries are on the whole less remarkable. The brass inscription plate to Henry Ball (d.1603) commemorates the archdeacon who was a particular friend of Bishop Bickley. The only memorable aspect of the memorial is its rhyming epitaph with the refrain 'Balle jaces' ('Ball, you lie there'). The memorial to Chancellor Henry Blaxton (d.1606) is unusual for the different stones used and the grotesque Renaissance decoration of the borders. It was restored, when 'almost obliterated', in 1770 by the pharmacist Edward Blaxton, a descendant and once Mayor of Chichester, and again in the late 1970s—the colours are still strikingly fresh.[34]

The memorials to Charles Pilkington (d.1828) and Thomas Baker (d.1831) are somewhat more elaborate. Both consist of a rectangular block of white marble on brackets on which a piece of cloth is gracefully draped. The first tablet shows a table set for the sacrament with a chalice, a paten with pieces of bread, and an open book; the second an open book with a dove appearing from clouds above.

The few memorials to other priests are also simple affairs, like those to vicars of St Peter's parish church when it was in the present north transept and Treasury, and the one to Evan Griffith (d.1954) in the cloisters.

The absence of monuments to lay persons of rank for the medieval period is rather exceptional for a great church like Chichester Cathedral, but finds an explanation in the

118 *Dean John Burgon's brass by C.E. Kempe, whose own memorial is on the wall above.*

neighbourhood of Arundel Castle and Lewes Priory, favoured as burial places by the earls of Surrey and Arundel. For the 16th and 17th centuries ecclesiastical monuments still outnumber memorials for laymen, and in the 20th century again the ecclesiastical memorials are in the majority, if only just. For the 18th and 19th centuries, however, the lay memorials reach double the numbers of those for clergymen. For Chichester, this was the age of the laity.

It is quite usual to find that a monument for a layman was used for more than one person. The names of several members of a family or related family have often been added to an existing memorial. An early lay monument is the exceptional brass plate to William Bradbridge (d.1546) and his family (see fig.23).[35] In a Renaissance-style room with columns and a receding tile floor, we see William and his wife Alice in contemporary dress kneeling before a prayer desk facing each other, with six sons behind him and eight daughters behind her. From the inscription we learn that William was mayor of Chichester three times and that the brass was erected in 1592 by Alice their daughter, who had married Francis Barnham, alderman of London. The brass is unusual in that it shows an important layman and his family in homely surroundings at an early date.

The rich wall monument to 'Rachel the wife of George Harris Citizen and Alderman of the City' (d.1734), an early example within the Cathedral of a memorial set up for a woman, was clearly intended to be used later for other members of the family, though eventually only her husband George Harris (d.1741) was added. The coat of arms on the tomb shows the arms of Harris impaling those of his wife, yet the dates and wording show it to be the monument to Rachel in the first instance, not the other way round, though historians invariably refer to such tombs as set up to the man and his dependents.

Another monument to a woman is the classical wall tablet showing a female figure kneeling at a desk, visited by an angel, set up for Eliza Huskisson (d.1856). Her husband William Huskisson (d.1830—the first to be run over by a train) had received his public monument in the form of a freestanding statue on a pedestal, clad in a toga, with a fulsome civic tribute beneath. The wife's name could hardly be added to that; she got one for herself, put up by the sculptor John Gibson, who was a personal friend.

In the south alley of the cloisters there is a group of three wall memorials, the middle one being a classical tablet between shafts and a cornice and the two side ones being baroque cartouches. The middle of these commemorates Thomas Briggs (d.1713) Chancellor, the right one his daughter Elizabeth (d.1759) and the left one her husband John Shore (d.1721). The three tablets are meant to form one group, in which the cartouches to husband and to wife are of equal size. Another group of three is very different, the big rectangular tablets, resting on two consoles each and topped by a triangular gable, to the whole Johnson family in the south cloister. The second and third one are just continuations of the left-hand one, which starts with the name of Mary Johnson (d.1784), while the right-hand tablet ends with the name of Eleanor Weller-Poley (d.1945).

A good example of the place that memorials to women take is the one to Frances Waddington (d.1728). It is a classical wall monument of variegated marble, still with a touch of the baroque in the top decoration. It was set up by her husband, Bishop Edward Waddington, and in an extensive inscription the virtues of the lady, sister under the skin to Jane Austen's Lady Catherine de Bourgh, are extolled: 'While she treated her Inferiours with Candour and Humility, She knew well how to maintain her Character, and Preserve the Esteem and Respect of Persons of the First Quality'. Almost as an afterthought, her husband (d.1731) got his inscription, in Latin, on a tablet at the base. Other interesting examples commemorating women are those to Dorothy Lane (d.1807, wife of William Lane), a very simple round tablet and to Mary Lennox (d.1843, daughter of Lord George Lennox), a slab with a brass cross standing on a brass inscription tablet.

Many professions are represented on the memorials to men: mayors, aldermen, a town clerk, recorders of the city, lawyers, doctors of medicine, a scholar, a poet (the early Romantic, William Collins), a glassmaker, a pharmacist, a bellringer, sacristans and members of parliament, among them Charles Cullen (d.1830), who 'was a candidate at the late General Election to represent this City in Parliament on the constitutional principle of unbought suffrage' and among whose virtues were 'energy in the cause of freedom and the most inflexible integrity'. As for musicians, one should gaze with reverence at the tablet with a modest inscription to the great Elizabethan composer Thomas Weelkes (d.1623), erected as a tercentenary memorial in the south transept. The modern composer Gustav Holst (d.1934), friend of Bishop Bell, is commemorated by a floor tile nearby.

119 *Capt. Thomas Allen RN, memorial by Charles Harris.*

A large group of lay monuments commemorates military and naval servicemen. From an aesthetic point of view, it is especially the four wall monuments with a seascape that catch the eye. These seascapes stand in a tradition that goes back to the 17th century. In 1957, the naval memorials were collected from elsewhere in the Cathedral into the north-west tower, which was then called the Sailors' Chapel.[36] This, however, is misleading, as the simpler naval monuments have remained in other places, and there appear to be far more military monuments. The Royal Sussex Regiment have had as their own St George's Chapel since 1921 (fig.82).[37] The only memorials there, however, are a number of unremarkable 20th-century brass inscription plates in the floor. The monuments to the Dukes of Richmond and their family are similarly not out of the ordinary. Most are found in or near the Lady Chapel, which served as the Richmond vault until the 1870s.[38] The largest wall monument, of black and white marble, is to Charles, 5th Duke of Richmond, with an extensive inscription but for the rest a small, rather sloppy head in profile above and his coat of arms beneath.

The Nicolls family, of whom one rose to the rank of General, three to Lieutenant-General and one more to Major-General, have similarly undistinguished black-and-white

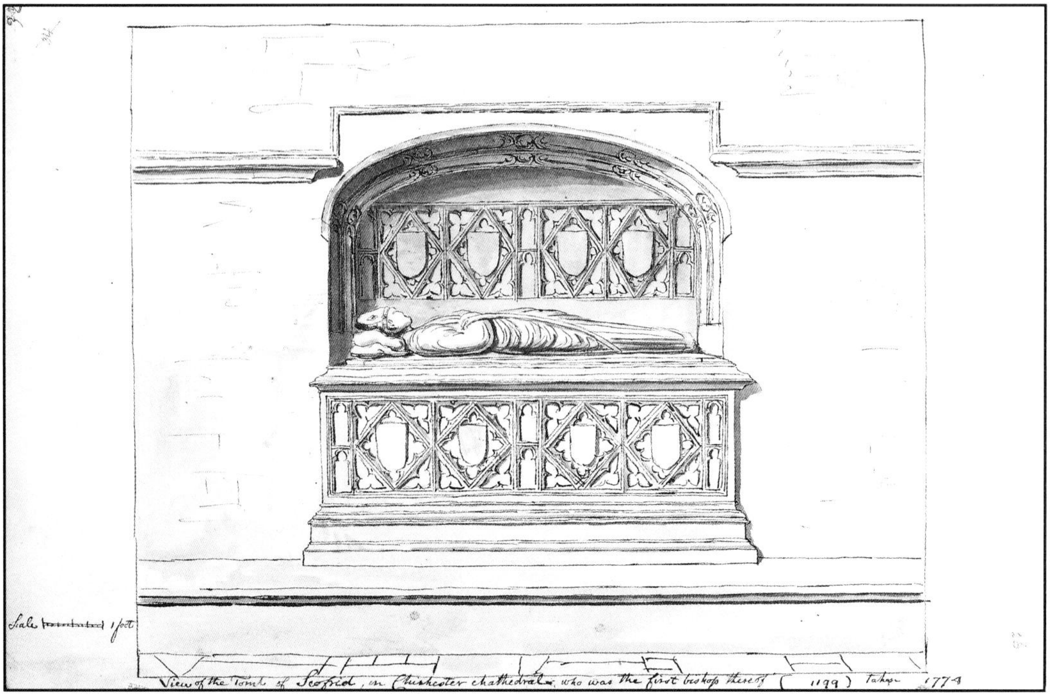

120 *Effigy of Bishop Rickingale, formerly believed to be that of Bishop Seffrid II, and now in place in the sanctuary as that of Bishop Storey, drawn by J. Carter, 1774 (BL Add. MS 29925 fol.26).*

inscription tablets, totalling eight, which now hang as an homogeneous group in the east alley of the cloisters, where they can hardly be seen, as the place is used for storage. Originally, they hung in St Clement's Chapel, but when this was restored in 1896, the Nicolls tablets were removed, with the consent of the family, to the south-west tower. In the 1970s they had to move again to their present position. At least the tablets have been kept together as a group and as such testify to a family that may not have had great aesthetic aims, but whose members served their country well.[39]

Church Monuments and Sculptors

Church monuments can be viewed as artistic objects in themselves. Certain periods of time favoured particular types of monument, sometimes resulting in an all-pervasive form for that period or for a certain group of people, sometimes in an amazing variety within a limited sphere. Later, the influence of sculptors, famous or less so, who designed and executed the monuments, begins to be felt. Fashion or specific request on financial or aesthetic grounds will have played their part. Chichester Cathedral is no exception. It can boast all the different types of known monuments. For the medieval period, there are some remarkable coped and flat tomb slabs to early bishops, some almost perfect niche tombs with recumbent effigies, freestanding tomb chests with or without effigies, and impressive floor slabs with indents of brasses (the brasses themselves having mostly been lost before the Civil War).[40] With the Tudor period, another sort of monument comes into vogue, the altar tomb in a niche, of which there are five in Chichester. Though still in their original position, built into the wall as they are, they have suffered so much in course of time that any attribution is no longer possible. They are all made of Petworth marble and consist of a base with quatrefoils, a niche built into the wall with shafts at the sides, and a depressed arch at the top with a panelled frieze. On the back wall of some of them we see the indents of brasses, mostly kneeling figures of a man and a woman with banderoles. Dallaway's suggestion that they were put up for members of great families who were benefactors of the church may

121 *Wall-niche altar tomb in the south transept.*

well be true.[41] These niches served a double purpose, being both a memorial and a side altar, where the many Masses so typical for the late medieval period were held. To judge from the style, they all date from the end of the 15th and the beginning of the 16th century.

Of the makers of medieval tombs we do not know very much. Surprisingly, neither do we know the sculptors of the three baroque episcopal tombs of the 17th century. A very similar tomb to the one for Bishop King is found in Boxgrove Priory, commemorating Sir William Morley (d.1701) and erected in 1718. Though they are on a smaller scale than the really great baroque tombs elsewhere in the country, the one to Bishop Grove is a most successful design, although now situated rather unhappily, with the bust on top interfering with the window behind. The monument may originally have had a truncated pyramidal background slab. The composition would then be well balanced, with finely sculpted putti holding a cloth with inscription, and topped with a bust of more than ordinary quality. Bishop Carleton's monument has a less balanced design but shows two engagingly cheerful cherubs lifting his mitre.

The 18th century is characterised by a few striking standing wall monuments and great wall tablets by anonymous masters. An early signed monument is the fine wall tablet to George Farhill (d.1790) on the north wall of what is now again the chapel of St Mary Magdalene. (The monument, originally on the east wall, bears witness to the fact that the chapel served for a time as the family vault for the Farhill family, just as the chapel on the north side served as the Miller family chapel.) It has the form of a sarcophagus on which a mourning female figure is leaning over a large urn under a well-draped curtain. A prominent inscription mentions that it was made by Charles Harris of the Strand, London, the sculptor of a similar but less successful wall tablet to a member of the related Peckham family (Sarah, d.1784). The same sculptor also made at least two of the exceptional naval monuments in the north-west tower, to Capt. Thomas Allen, RN (d.1781) (fig.119) and Lt. George Alms, RN (d.1782). Though the one to Capt. James Alms RN (d. 1791) has also been attributed to him by Katherine Esdaile, what remains of the inscription ('E .. L .. UR .. NDO') must refer to another sculptor. Harris's monuments, including the Chichester ones, have great charm and are in the best 18th-century tradition.[42] The fourth naval monument, picturing the battle of Copenhagen, is by the sculptor J. Kendrick.

The earliest signed monument in the Cathedral is the rather simple wall tablet, a pyramid shape on a base with, in front of it, an urn on a small cartouche, to Richard Smith (d.1767) by William Tyler. He was a prolific sculptor, a pupil of Roubilliac, and though he could make well-modelled busts, he also produced many mediocre works, of which the Chichester monument is one.

The best-known name here is that of John Flaxman, who signed eight of the monuments, of which much has been written elsewhere, at times rather confusingly.[43] His earliest monument in the Cathedral is the one to Dean Thomas Ball (d.1770), which was made in 1785/6 and not in 1817 as is sometimes said. William Hayley, the poetaster of Eartham, was very active as the self-styled 'patron of genius'. He counted among his friends William Blake and George Romney and, through them, John Flaxman. Hayley's grandfather was Dean Thomas Hayley, whose fine wall memorial has already been described. William Hayley was responsible for the erection of the monument to his parents-in-law (the Ball memorial mentioned above) as well as for the one to the Chichester poet William Collins (d.1759), installed in 1795 (see fig.45). Their and other memorial inscriptions in the Cathedral were also written by him. The harsh criticism voiced, for instance, in the *Buildings of England*

THEY SHALL IN NO WISE LOSE THEIR REWARD. MATT. CHAP. X. VER. 42.

122 *Flaxman's memorial to Dean Ball.*

about the Collins memorial does not take into account that it was designed to hang on a pier in the north aisle, where the converging outer lines would be seen as a contrasting play to the clear vertical lines of the pier. About 1930, all monuments hanging on piers were removed from fear that they were harming the fabric of the church. Collins's monument then went to the north-west tower and, when this became the naval chapel, it again moved to its present position in the baptistry, the south-west tower.

In Flaxman's monument to Agnes Cromwell (d.1797), erected in 1800 (fig.108), his outlines are at their purest, and the expression of Christian immortality in a neo-classical form is at its best. Other good examples of Flaxman's works are the monument to Jane Smith (d.1780) showing the spirit of marriage reclining on an extinguished torch, and the one to Sarah Udny (d.1811), which combines a touch of neo-Gothic with Neoclassicism and rejoices in Hayley's splendid inscription beginning: 'Udny! How few thy excellence transcend,/In three most honor'd names, Wife! Mother! Friend!'. Then we come to the products of Flaxman's atelier, similar designs to be found all over the country in all kinds of variation. Here we have those to Francis Dear (d.1802) and Henry Frankland (d.1814). The monument to Matthew Quantock (d.1812) is again remarkable in as far as the design of a father and mother kneeling in grief against a Gothic arch is a close study of medieval sculpture. Hayley's inscription in verse below is less attractive:

> Dear to the friendless whom he oft reliev'd
> Dear to the social whom his loss has griev'd ...
> Found fit for heaven in our Redeemer's eyes
> Benignant angels bore him to the skies.

Flaxman's pupil John Hinchliff signed the inconspicuous tablet to John Quantock (d.1820). The Flaxman design of two intertwined reclining figures in a pediment shown on the Collins memorial was copied by Edward Richardson in the tablet to Alicia Murray (d.1853). His other monument, to John Smith (d.1842) in the south transept, was also a copy, of Bishop Langton's niche tomb nearby.[44]

123 *The north aisle, showing the memorials to William Collins (see fig.50) and Matthew Quantock in their earlier positions, and the Arundel tombs. In Thomas King's drawing (1814), the latter are end-on to the right; in the photograph (facing page), they have reached their present position together.*

The standing wall monument to Joseph Baker (d.1789) with the elaborately draped standing female figure in rococo style leaning on a pedestal seems to be the work of the Irish sculptor John Hickey, appointed sculptor to the Prince of Wales in 1786, although the inscription calls him 'F. Hickley'.[45]

From the first half of the 19th century there are a number of mediocre monuments by sculptors of whom better might have been expected: Henry Westmacott (Ernest Udny, d.1808), John Bacon the Younger (Edward Madden, d.1819), William Pitts (John Farhill, d.1830), M.W. Johnson (George Teesdale, d.1840) and Robert Brown (Richard Buckner, d.1837).[46] Much better works of art are found by John Towne (a famous anatomical modeller: this shows in his bust of Bishop Otter), by J.E. Carew (well known for his statues at Petworth and one of the reliefs on Nelson's column in Trafalgar Square, London—his are the statue to Huskisson and the impressive monument to Edmund Woods, d.1833), and John Gibson, R.A. (who worked almost exclusively in Rome; when in England he made the famous 'Tinted Venus' and the Chichester monument to Eliza Huskisson).[47]

After the medieval period it is the 19th-century monuments which show the greatest variety. Besides George Gilbert Scott's rich marble tomb chest to Dean Hook and Charles Kempe's fine brass to Dean Burgon, there are others of exceptional form and quality. George Bodley and Thomas Garner designed Bishop Durnford's monument and L.J. Chavalliaud made the effigy. William Tower is responsible for the well-carved wood tablet to Charles Eamer Kempe, the stained-glass artist, and John Tweed, a pupil of Rodin, for the notable monument to Bishop Wilberforce.[48]

Even in the 19th and 20th centuries, many memorials are not signed, not to be wondered at for very simple affairs, but rather strange for more remarkable memorials, such

as the retable-like monument to Bishop Ridgeway (d.1929), the last neo-Gothic memorial in the Cathedral.

Sometimes monuments are signed by a firm's names, which raise more curiosity than the actual memorials. Little is known of 'A & N. Aux C.S.L. London' (Lt. Col. Sir Edward Wheeler, d.1903), 'Culn Cawthorpe & Sons, London' (Col. Hector Gem, d.1918 and Lt. Edward Tyacke, d.1918), 'Clark & Son, Reading' (John Mackie, d.1831) and 'T. Gaffin. sc. 63 Regent St. London'.[49] The latter firm not only produced the large, rather ordinary tablet to the 5th Duke of Richmond, but also, very probably, the eight tablets to the members of the Nicolls family, one of which was signed. This firm is notorious for thousands of such tablets all over the country, neatly described as 'postage stamps ... stuck on the walls of aisle and chancel ... looking like the mourning cards of our grandparents'.[50] Happily the group in Chichester Cathedral is not so large, but it sets one thinking if two important families connected with the Cathedral drew on this wholesale firm. Another little known name, that of 'G. Karn/Chichester' is found on the far more pleasing memorial to Charles Cullen the reformer (d.1830) with a relief showing a book on which is written 'Reform of Bankrupt Court' and a scroll on a desk with 'Petition against Negro Slavery'.

Twentieth-century artists at Chichester include well-known names. Eric Gill made the inscription tablet to his father-in-law, H.H. Moore (d.1911), the head verger. (Gill's lettering stands out from the two neighbouring inscription tablets.) Mary Gillick was commissioned, on the recommendation of Kenneth Clark, to make the tablet to Bishop Bell, and Alec Peever carved the black marble roundel to Dean Hussey.[51]

The number of memorials put up after the Second World War is very small indeed. And the few there are show, perhaps as a sign of the times, a modest or even simple form,

124 *(left) Plaque by Mary Gillick to Bishop Bell, for the re-erected Arundel screen, 1961.*

125 *Roundel for Dean Hussey by Alec Peever in St Mary Magdalene's Chapel.*

the latest being that in the south quire aisle by Douglas Garland, clerk of the works, to Archdeacon Lancelot Mason (d.1990). Bishop Bell and Dean Hussey, as has been said, have tablets of some distinction. Very simple are the stone floor tablets to Archdeacon C.P.S. Clarke (d.1947) and Dean Arthur Duncan-Jones (d.1955). We really see an 'extreme of simplicity ... so unobtrusive that (the memorials have) to be discovered'.[52] The traditions of commemorating contributions to the fabric and memorials to the dead have now rolled into one. Thus Muriel Cox (d.1970) has an inscription tablet saying that Cecil Collins' altar frontal of the Icon of Divine Light was given in her memory and the statue of St Richard on his porch in the cloisters was restored in memory of Canon Vernon Lippiett (d.1980). The latest memorials are in the same vein: small roundels of black marble affixed to the jambs of the window traceries in the cloisters commemorating people whose relatives or friends paid for the restoration of that particular tracery. In shape offshoots of Dean Hussey's roundel, they are not to be distinguished from others commemorating the name of an institution or a firm that paid for a similar restoration.

See Appendix C: the position of the listed monuments is indicated on the Cathedral plan, p.xx.

XIV

The Buildings of the Bishop's Palace and the Close

Tim Tatton-Brown

Early in the 12th century, perhaps in the later part of the episcopate of Ralph de Luffa, a Close was being created around the new Romanesque Cathedral. A cathedral establishment had been set up with a dean and the other customary dignitaries, as well as between twenty and thirty canons. Besides the bishop's own house, new residences were required for the dignitaries and for some of the canons, though from an early date many of them were non-resident. A large area around the Cathedral in the south-western quarter of the Roman walled city was acquired, and the building then started. In 1147 Bishop Hilary was able to get from Pope Eugenius III a confirmation of a grant of the whole of the south-western quarter of the city,[1] and a second confirmation of this came in 1163 from Pope Alexander III.[2]

The Bishop kept for himself much of the western half of this area, while around the Cathedral in the north-east part of the precinct a cemetery area was reserved with a wall on the north and east sides (the Close wall). This left only the south-east area for the houses, though by the late Middle Ages the chancellor was found a plot immediately opposite the west front, and the sub-dean (not a prebendary) and school master had houses north of this, fronting onto West Street. Other plots fronting onto the western part of West Street and the southern part of South Street were early leased out by the Dean and Chapter for houses and shops.[3]

The south-eastern area, which ran down to the city walls, was probably crossed by two east-west lanes. On the south was the principal lane (Canon Lane), while a small lane probably ran west from South Street along the north side of the later Vicars' Hall and St Faith's chapel to the Bishop's Palace. In its central section it was later covered by the south cloister walk, and to the north of this the land was always the consecrated ground of the churchyard, called Paradise.[4] There was always a north-south lane (later called St Richard's Lane or Walk), leading from the churchyard down towards the Deanery; the latter was built on the largest plot east of the bishop's house and gardens, and south of Canon Lane. Two further plots were created on the south side of Canon Lane, one of which was for the precentor. By the mid-12th century, posterns were beginning to be made through the city wall to give direct access to the Chapter's meadows beside the river Lavant beyond. This large extra-mural area was later called Deanery farm. On the north side of Canon Lane, smaller plots were created, with the houses built at the north end of the plots, the most westerly of which was the Treasurer's House.

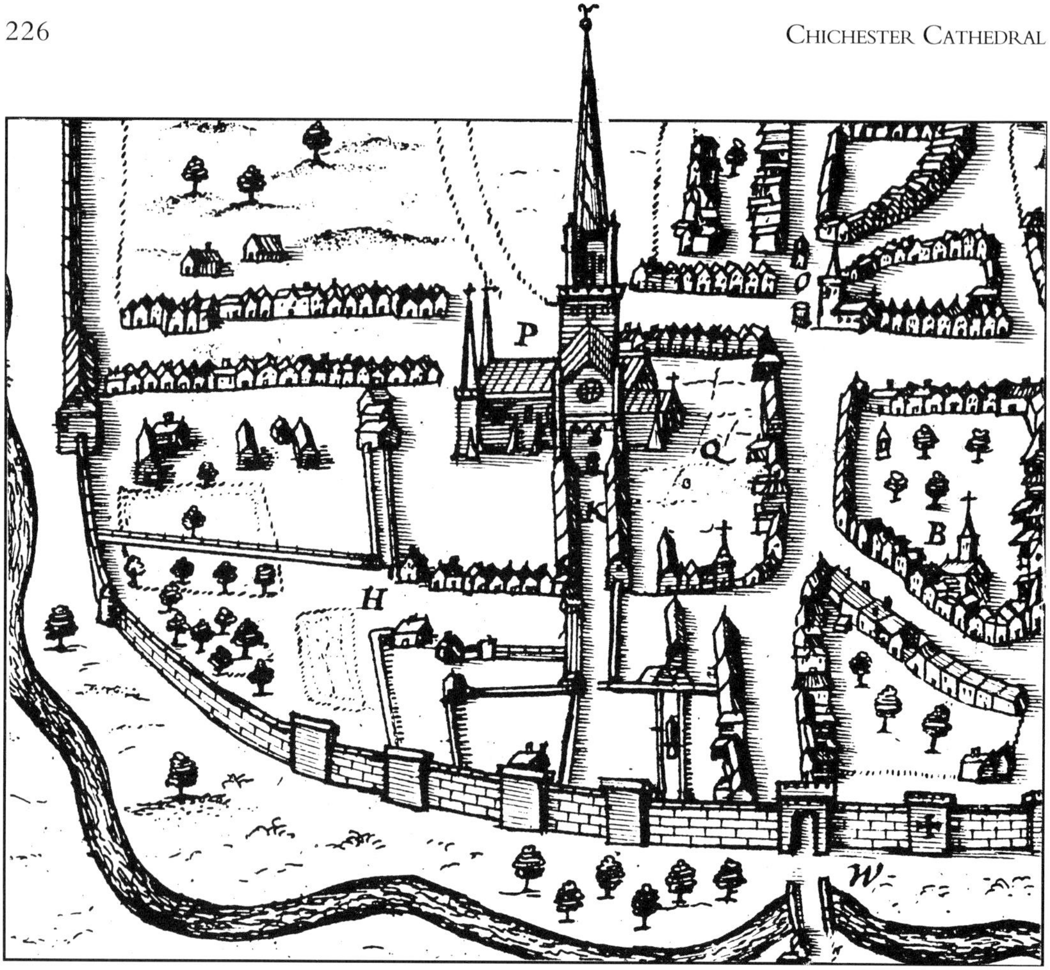

126 *Detail of the Close in 1610, from John Speed's map.*

The building of stone houses on these plots was probably started by the mid-12th century at the latest and, though interrupted by the great fire of 1187, which Hoveden tells us burnt the houses of the bishop and canons,[5] the main phase of the building must have been completed by the mid-13th century. In the early 1260s a final confirmation of the grant of the Close was made by Pope Urban IV:[6] this charter also forbade rape, theft, arson, bloodshedding, imprisonment, killing or any violence within the Close! From the early 13th century shops were being made, outside the Close wall, on the north and east sides of the churchyard that fronted onto the streets of Chichester.[7]

In the 15th century there were major additions to the Close with the building of a separate Vicars' Close, a cloister and a new bell tower. Other houses were enlarged or reassigned (like that for the two royal chantry priests in 1413), and the number of other resident prebendaries probably decreased. More shops and houses were made along and inside the churchyard (or Close) wall. After the Reformation, other changes took place with the reduction of vicars choral to four, who were allowed, as indeed were all the canons, to be married. The residentiary canons were fixed at four in 1574.[8]

Plan 11 *(facing page) Plan of Chichester Cathedral Close.*

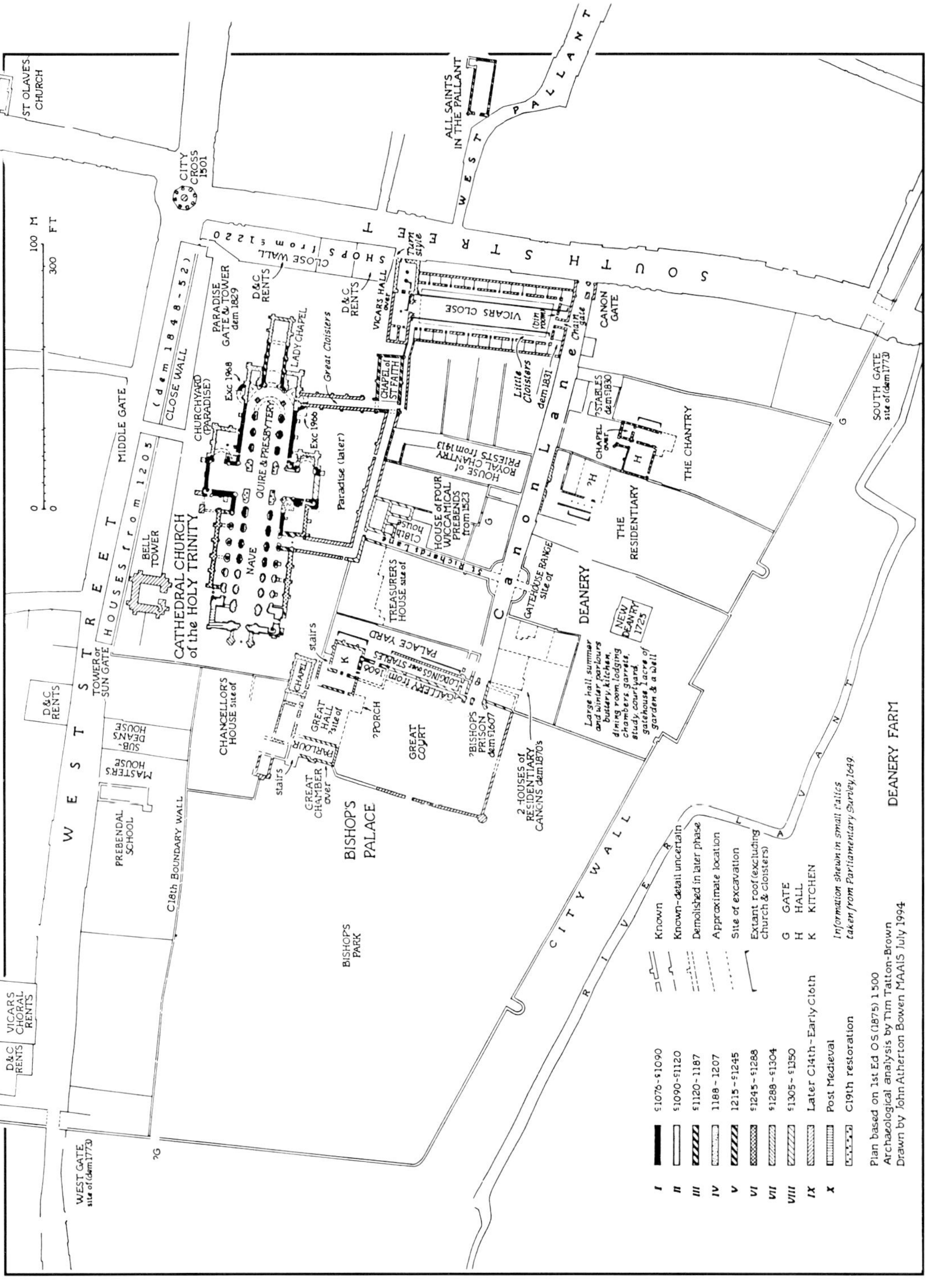
ST OLAVES CHURCH
CITY CROSS 1501
ALL SAINTS IN THE PALLANT
WEST PALLANT
SOUTH STREET
WEST STREET
MIDDLE GATE
CLOSE WALL (dem 1848-52)
HOUSES from 1205
BELL TOWER
CATHEDRAL CHURCH of the HOLY TRINITY
CHURCHYARD (PARADISE)
PARADISE GATE & TOWER dem 1829
D&C RENTS
SHOPS from c1220
CLOSE WALL
Turn style
VICARS HALL over
VICARS CLOSE
LADY CHAPEL
Great Cloisters
Exc 1968
Exc 1966
QUIRE & PRESBYTERY
NAVE
Paradise (later)
CHAPEL of ST FAITH
Little Cloisters
CANON GATE
Chain gate
Canon Lane
STABLES dem 1830
HOUSE of ROYAL CHANTRY PRIESTS from 1413
HOUSE OF FOUR WICCAMICAL PREBENDS from 1523
C18th house
St Richard's Lane
CHAPEL over
THE CHANTRY
THE RESIDENTIARY
TREASURERS HOUSE site of
GATEHOUSE RANGE site of
DEANERY
NEW DEANERY 1725
Large hall, summer and winter parlours, buttery, kitchen, dining room, lodging chambers, garrets, study, courtyard, gatehouse, 1 acre of garden & a well
PALACE YARD
STABLES
LODGINGS over
GALLERY from 1606
TOWER or SUN GATE
D&C RENTS
CHANCELLOR'S HOUSE site of
SUB-DEAN'S HOUSE
MASTER'S HOUSE
CHAPEL
GREAT HALL site of
?PORCH
GREAT COURT
?BISHOPS PRISON dem c1607
PARLOUR
stairs
GREAT CHAMBER over
BISHOP'S PALACE
2 HOUSES of RESIDENTIARY CANONS dem 1870's
PREBENDAL SCHOOL
C18th BOUNDARY WALL
BISHOPS PARK
CITY WALL
RIVER LAVANT
SOUTH GATE site of (dem 1773)
DEANERY FARM
VICARS CHORAL RENTS
D&C RENTS
WEST GATE site of (dem 1773)
0 100 M
0 300 FT
I c1076-c1090
II c1090-c1120
III c1120-1187
IV 1188-1207
V 1215-c1245
VI c1245-c1288
VII c1288-c1304
VIII c1305-c1350
IX Later C14th-Early C16th
X Post Medieval
C19th restoration
Known
Known-detail uncertain
Demolished in later phase
Approximate location
Site of excavation
Extant roof (excluding church & cloisters)
G GATE
H HALL
K KITCHEN
Information shewn in small italics taken from Parliamentary Survey 1649
Plan based on 1st Ed OS (1875) 1:500
Archaeological analysis by Tim Tatton-Brown
Drawn by John Atherton Bowen MAAIS July 1994

The greatest changes to the houses came during the 'Great Rebellion' of the 1640s. First, much destruction was caused during the siege of 1642. Many of the houses were in ruins when a survey took place in 1649,[9] and though some major rebuilding took place after this, at the Treasurer's house in *c.*1686, and at the Bishop's Palace and at the Deanery in the early 18th century, the Close must have remained rather uncared for and semi-ruined during the next half century or so.

Finally, further demolitions took place in the 1830s, notably the Treasurer's house, and the eastern range of vicars' houses were turned round to become shops in South Street. A little later (between 1845 and 1852) the churchyard was opened up on the north by the demolition of all the houses and shops around and east of the bell tower,[10] and the removal of all the gates here and in Canon Lane. The Paradise Gate, surmounted by a small tower, on the north-east near the Cross, had already been demolished in 1829.[11] In the later 20th century, the biggest changes have been the expansion of the Prebendal School[12] and the removal of gravestones and lowering of the ground level around the Cathedral.

The Bishop's Palace

As we have seen, by far the biggest area of the Close on the west was earmarked from the beginning for the bishop,[13] and it is, in fact, at the Bishop's Palace that the earliest building remains survive. On the outside of the south wall of the great kitchen can be seen two round-headed (blocked) windows at a lower level. Immediately to the left of them is an inserted late 12th-century doorway (also now blocked), and it is clear that we are looking at the inside face of the wall of an early to mid-12th-century building. Also just visible in this wallface are scars for the north end of two bays of semicircular vaults (presumably groined vaults) with, above, a pronounced set-back in the wallface, no doubt at the level of the original first floor. Part of the east wall of this building may also survive, where the first-floor joist-level-slot and the top of the doorway, with a semicircular head (and a possible tympanum), are filled with 17th-century brickwork. This fragment is almost certainly the only surviving part above ground of the Bishop's Palace that was burnt in the fire of 1187 and was rebuilt by Bishop Seffrid II. We are told specifically, '*Seffridus reaedifacavit Cicestriam et domus suas in palatio*',[14] and there can be little doubt that the chapel range, which is at the heart of the present Palace, was new-built by Seffrid at the end of the 12th century.

This range, which is just over 110 feet long by 25 feet wide (external measurements), seems to have started out as two separate buildings with a north-south passageway between them. Of the western building, which has been called a hall (internal dimensions 48 by 19 feet), little original evidence is visible except the shell of the walls.[15] In the later Middle Ages, this building was floored over, and given a new roof.[16] The building to the east is the justly famous Bishop's Chapel, still in use after 800 years. It must have been built, with its two bays of sexpartite vaulting, in about 1200 (i.e. under Bishop Seffrid II, who was also building the Cathedral presbytery at this time), but many of the decorative details suggest a remodelling after *c.*1220, perhaps under Bishop Ralph Neville. The elaborate lancets, though mostly blocked or replaced by early 14th-century traceried windows, can still be seen in several places. The round-headed doorway on the south-west is a strange mixture of the latest Romanesque and Early English. On the south wall of the chapel is the wonderful painting of the Virgin and Child in a roundel (Plate IV), which must be similar to other painted early 13th-century roundels on the walls of the Lady Chapel (though only

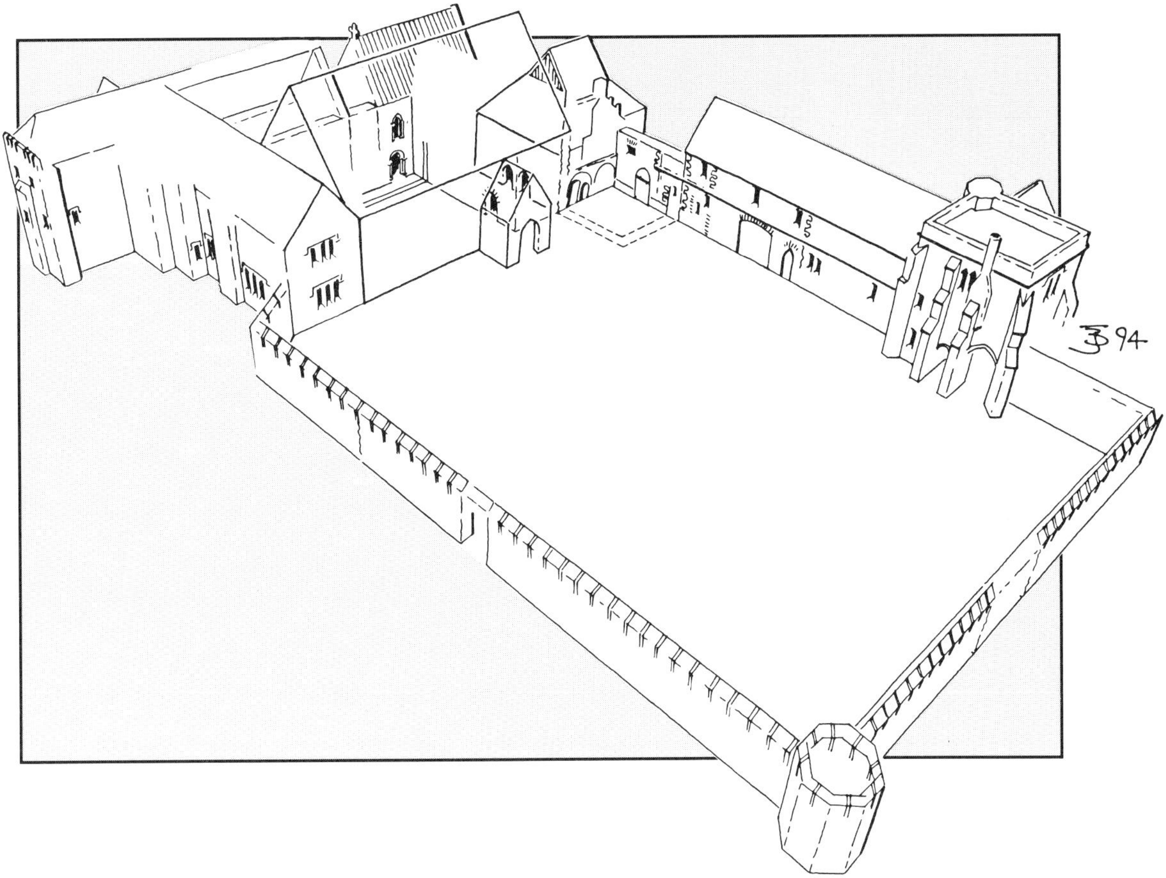

Plan 12 *Cut-away from the south west of the Bishop's Palace, showing medieval and Tudor features. The probable form of the great hall and its porch is outlined.*

very faint traces of them survive in the Cathedral).[17] The Bishop's Chapel roundel was only rediscovered in 1829; it had presumably been covered over at the Reformation.

In the years following 1642, the most important building at the core of the medieval Palace, the great hall, had disappeared. The ground plan of the Palace, as remodelled after 1660, is a half-H, and it is almost certain, from a recent reappraisal of the surviving documentary and fabric evidence, that the great hall stood across the now-open space between the south-east and south-west wings, with the screens-passage and buttery and pantry on the east side (where the south-east wing is situated) and immediately beyond this the still-surviving great kitchen. This great hall was almost certainly built in the late 13th century, and would have followed a pattern being set by bishops at their palaces all over England.[18] During the Civil War years, almost all these great halls were stripped of their lead roofs and left as ruins, like the Bishop's Palace at Lincoln, where a large hall and detached kitchen had been added to a smaller and longer 12th-century hall (on a basement and with an attached chapel) in the early 13th century.

In the lower part of the west wall of the south-east wing, a 13th-century doorway can still be seen, cut into by the ground-floor late 17th-century windows. This doorway is nearly opposite the pair of doors in the west wall of the great kitchen, and it seems likely that in the intervening area there was a central east-west passage from the kitchen to the great hall, flanked north and south by the pantry and buttery.[19] The great hall itself presumably then ran west as far as the south-west wing, whose external east wall was completely rebuilt after the Civil War, making the hall about 67 feet long internally. Its width must have been at least 34 feet, the internal width of the great kitchen.

North of the great hall was presumably a passageway leading east to the doorway into the churchyard. The last part of this, a covered passage, still survives. It must have been built in the early 14th century, when the windows on the south side of the chapel were blocked. The south wall of this passage still contains an early 14th-century square-headed window, now also blocked.[20]

South-west of this passage is the kitchen with its remarkable hammer-beam roof,[21] built, there seems little doubt now, for the Bishop's new great hall at the end of the 13th century. On the south, it was built against the 12th-century block mentioned above, while to the west it had doorways[22] to the great hall, buttery and pantry. The north and east walls of the great kitchen were external walls with pairs of shallow buttresses in them, though a brick staircase turret was built onto the north-west side of the kitchen in the 16th century. South-east of the kitchen was a long range that leads down to the fine early 14th-century gatehouse. This range must have contained lodgings as well as service buildings like a granary and stables.[23] Along its west wall there is some evidence to suggest that a timber-framed long gallery was built at first-floor level in 1606-7,[24] but probably did not survive the Commonwealth period. East of the lodgings and stable range was an open yard which still survives, with the bishop's boundary wall with early 16th-century brick crenellations[25] to the north and east of it.

The gatehouse, built at the end of Canon Lane in *c.*1327, must originally have had ribbed vaults over the two passageways (a foot-passage on the north).[26] There was a porter's room on the north side, with a staircase up to the large chamber at first-floor level with an original fireplace and chimney in its west wall. Adjoining the gatehouse on either the south or north-east was the bishop's prison, which was demolished in 1608-9.[27] The gatehouse was built in the episcopate of John Langton to complete the work of his predecessor, Gilbert of St Leofard: he built almost certainly the great hall and kitchen.

Nearly a century later, Bishops Stephen Patrington and Henry Ware were leaving money in their wills for the retiling of the chapel, great cloister and hall roofs, as well as for completing the parlour.[28] At this time the great or principal chamber was above the parlour at the west end of the great hall, in what is now the south-west wing. This range was, however, completely rebuilt by Bishop Sherburne, about a century later, and his magnificent ceiling still survives in the parlour (later a great dining room).[29] Though heavily restored, the fireplace and late Perpendicular windows in this range probably also date from Sherburne's time.

Sherburne also added a new north-west wing in brick which is still the core of the private rooms of the Palace. Internally this wing has been completely rebuilt, but externally a few of its small original windows are still visible in a garde-robe tower on the west, and a stair turret on the south-west. Part of a larger original window (now blocked) can also be seen in the south wall. The west gable of this wing is a crow-stepped brick gable and Sherburne also added a crow-stepped gable to the east wall of the chapel, and put brick crenellations on the Palace boundary wall of the churchyard.[30] He also had built a series of brick walls with crenellated tops around the great court to the south, and in the south-west

127 *Sherburne's north-west wing of the Palace today.*

corner there is a small octagonal turret. Sherburne was also rebuilding his seaside palace at Cakeham, near West Wittering, at about the same time, where he added a unique brick pentagonal tower. The high point for the Bishop's Palace came on Good Friday 1535 when Bishop Sherburne gave a great fish dinner for Henry VIII's commissioners and all their retainers. A contemporary account tells us that 'about 700 persons dined in his palace; some in the hall, which is not small; some in the parlour, and the great chamber above, where he [i.e. the bishop] dined for warmth, with other of the commissioners.'[31] Sherburne was about eighty years old at the time, and died the following year.

A small number of other additions were made to the Palace before its destruction in the Civil War. These include a gallery down the east side of the great court, in front of the lodging and stable range. Documentary evidence tells us that this was done in Bishop Lancelot Andrewes' time, in 1606-7.[32]

Unfortunately no parliamentary survey of the Palace survives, but there can be little doubt that much was destroyed during the 1642 siege and in the years after it had been sold to Colonel John Downes for £1,209 6s.[33] After the Restoration, Bishop Henry King effected repairs, and it is likely that he rebuilt the south-east wing with its casement windows.[34] Large quantities of re-used masonry can be found here, which may well have come from the destroyed great hall. There was also a brick south-facing gable, though the top of this was removed in the early 19th century.

The final phase of rebuilding was carried out under Bishop Edward Waddington, who rebuilt the whole of the central block between the two wings, soon after his arrival at Chichester.[35] He also added the fine staircase in the west range and the covered passageway, originally open on the south, along the outside of the south front. Inside the Palace, much new panelling was put in, and a fine new dropped ceiling was inserted into the great chamber (then the drawing room) in the south-west range. At the beginning of the 19th century, under Bishop John Buckner, other alterations were effected, the most important of which was the making of a finely decorated lobby in the western two bays of the covered passageway.[36]

The Right Rev. E.W. Kemp, Bishop of Chichester, adds:
During the Middle Ages, the Palace at Chichester would have been the seat of such of the diocesan administration as did not move around with the bishop. Other episcopal residences were Amberley castle, Drungewick (in the parish of Wisborough Green), Aldingbourne, Cakeham in West Wittering, and a house off Chancery Lane in London. Certain of the bishops were closely connected with the government and would have spent much time in London. While in Sussex they would have moved from house to house, taking much of the administration with them.

Through the ages, the Palace has from time to time found itself caught up in outside affairs—Henry VIII's visit, for instance, and the Royalist prisoners housed after the siege of Chichester in Bishop Sherburne's great painted room, where their names can be seen scratched on the embrasures of a window. A 19th-century picture in the Palace hallway shows the great Kitchen still very much in use at that time, with hosts of servants: by the time the Bells arrived in 1929, living styles had become less lavish and the staff considerably reduced. The greatest changes, however, came with the Second World War, when Bishop Bell moved to Brighton to be at the geographical centre of his diocese and handed over the Palace to the Education authorities (free of charge apart from repairs) to house a succession of refugee schools from the London area. When the Bells returned, the Bishop offered the whole of the south-east wing to the Theological College, which reopened with at first only 15 students, using the Old Kitchen for lectures and the Chapel for worship. Now the Prebendal School has the use of that wing, and comfortable, less formal and more easily kept family rooms have been designed for the Bishop on the ground floor of the remainder. He and his immediate clergy staff still use the Chapel daily.

The Palace building has undergone so many changes that its precise history is difficult to determine. In the 16th century, some of the building works at the north-western corner may have been the result of bishops being allowed to marry. In the 18th century, when Bishop Waddington gave the Palace its present appearance by joining the east and west wings to his new Georgian façade, he may also have been responsible for the attic floor which extends over the former hall, chapel and east wing. The range of buildings which ends with the gatehouse entrance to the Palace grounds, at one time the stables and coach house, has now been made into three cottages and two garages.

The Palace remains the home of the bishop and his family and is also the place of work of his chaplain and secretaries. The legal work of the diocese is also centred in Chichester, but the diocesan office itself is in Hove. The diocese has therefore two focal points. One is in Chichester, where the Cathedral is situated and the bishop lives, nine miles from the western border, the other in Hove, part of the main centre of population and more central to the diocese as a whole. If the present county divisions persist, one is in West Sussex, the other in East Sussex. The diocese itself still consists, however, of the whole of Sussex, the ancient kingdom of the South Saxons.

Canons' Houses

As we have seen, apart from the Chancellor's House opposite the west porch, all the canons' houses were in the block of land south of the Cathedral. So much destruction took place in the mid-17th and early 19th centuries, that little of the fabric of the medieval houses survives. However, documentary evidence and some material remains allow us to understand something of their form.

After the Bishop's Palace, the Deanery occupied the largest adjoining site and by the later Middle Ages it had expanded through the Roman city wall, with a large new building, perhaps the hall range, astride the wall. At about the same time, the river Lavant seems to have been moved southwards and this dogleg in the watercourse can still be seen today. During the siege of December 1642, the Deanery was a weak point in the city's defences, so that much was destroyed here.[37] The Parliamentary Survey of 1649 does, however, give us something of the medieval topography of the site, mentioning a large hall, with summer and winter parlours, a buttery, kitchen and dining room as well as lodging chambers, garrets, a study, the courtyard and one acre of garden (and a well). All the main buildings were of stone with tiled roofs, and on the north side was a stone gatehouse, which was converted into a coach house in 1674.[38] By 1649 the house was in very poor condition and for a time, after the Restoration, the Dean had to live at the Chantry and then at a house in the Pallant, before moving back into the Deanery.

In the later 16th century, a plot of land for a house for a residentiary canon was probably cut out of the north-west corner of the Deanery site (perhaps associated with the fixing of the number of residentiaries at four).[39] By the early 19th century, there were two houses here, but they were demolished and replaced by the present Archdeacon's house, no.4 Canon Lane, in the 1870s. The front doorway of the house is, in part, a reused one of the mid-12th century,[40] but whether it once formed part of the 12th-century Deanery or of a canon's house is unknown.

The present Deanery was built in 1725 for Dean Thomas Sherlock, and he no doubt landscaped the site and removed the old gatehouse on the north, creating instead brick gate piers with iron gates and a circular turning area outside them. The house is a rather plain brick box-like structure with pediments on all four wall-tops. It is three and a half storeys high and is plainly visible from beyond the city walls, as Samuel and Nathaniel Buck's engraving of Chichester from the south in 1738 was the first to show. Under Dean Hook, the house was extended eastwards, but this Victorian wing was demolished in the 1960s and replaced by a single-

128 *The Deanery.*

129 *The Treasury: view from the Palace stableyard, 1821, before the rebuilding by Canon Wagner.*

storey extension. To the north of this wing were the service-yard and servants' quarters, well screened-off from the front drive. The shell of the old Deanery buildings on the city wall was filled in and turned into an enlarged bastion.

Of the other medieval houses in the Close, not a great deal remains. A fragment of the front wall (with some blocked windows) of the Chancellor's House can be seen nearly opposite the 'Galilee' or west porch of the Cathedral. It was ruined in the siege of 1642 and never rebuilt.[41] The southern part of the site was taken into the Bishop's Palace after the debris of the Chancellor's House was cleared away in the later 18th century. The rest of the site was sold in 1803. It now forms part of the enlarged Prebendal School.

The Treasurer's House occupied the whole of the north end of the plot immediately west of St Richard's Walk. Unfortunately it was demolished in 1834, and replaced in 1835 by a small-scale replica of the new vicarage at Brighton, where the Treasurer was vicar. All that now remains of the original house are parts of the east wall adjoining St Richard's Walk (where one open, and two blocked, windows can be seen), and a section of the north wall, which is also the south-west corner of the cloister. It is clear from a study of the fabric in this area that the north-east corner of the house had to be demolished to make way for the cloister south walk. The outer wall of this part of the cloister contains a reset window and doorway into the treasury. When the house was being rebuilt in 1686, Chapter were told of its

> long time being ruinated and dilapidated and such dilapidations happened chiefly in the years 1644, 1645, and 1646 or thereabouts and that amongst other things the great hall belonging to the said house was made wholly useless so that it was indeed a burthen only and a charge to keep up same ... and that the said hall was so ruinated by Collonell [*sic*] Downes and by him converted to a stable and the wall and roof likely to fall. And further alleged that the ... Treasurer ... hath at his own great charge caused to be well repaired the said house and edifice saveing the said Hall which for reasons aforesaid he desires that he be permitted to take down.[42]

The rebuilt Treasury is depicted in a drawing (dated 1821) of the Cathedral from the south-west,[43] which shows various casement windows, no doubt from the 1686 restoration.

The best-preserved of the medieval canons' houses is the building called 'The Chantry', on the south side of Canon Lane, the residence of the Precentor (or chanter), now divided into flats. The core of the present building is a late 13th-century stone hall, with a vaulted porch to the north, and a principal chamber over an undercroft on the east. Over the porch and extending eastwards over another small undercroft, later given a brick vault, is another chamber that was probably the chapel. It has a pair of lancets in both its east and west walls, with a round window above in the gable. Internally the lancets have a rere arch, suggesting a date in the later 13th century. Unfortunately most of the rest of the building was heavily rebuilt in the post-medieval period, and in the early 19th century a whole series of architectural features added that had apparently been brought from Halnaker. The roof over the principal chamber is, however, still a 15th-century crown-post one, and next to it on the west an original late 13th-century chimney flue can be seen built into the east side of the east gable wall of the hall, no doubt for a fireplace in the principal chamber.[44]

South of this chamber was another wing which was demolished in *c.*1830, perhaps the kitchen or service wing. At the same time a large block of buildings around a courtyard in the north-east corner of the site was also demolished. These were almost certainly the stables and associated buildings.[45] The Chantry had been sold by Dean Hayley in 1736, but in 1860 it was bought back again by Chapter. In 1897 it was given a new east wing by Archdeacon Walker, and new garages have been built to the north.

Next to the Chantry on the west is a house known today as 'The Residentiary'. It lies along the northern side of the plot and was probably built in the later Middle Ages for one of the residentiary canons. It too has been much rebuilt in more recent centuries, but the main east-west range on the north side must be medieval, while another two-storied range, running south from its west end, has three bays of a 15th-century crown-post roof over it. On the north-west corner of the site is a gatehouse with a service courtyard to the south.[46]

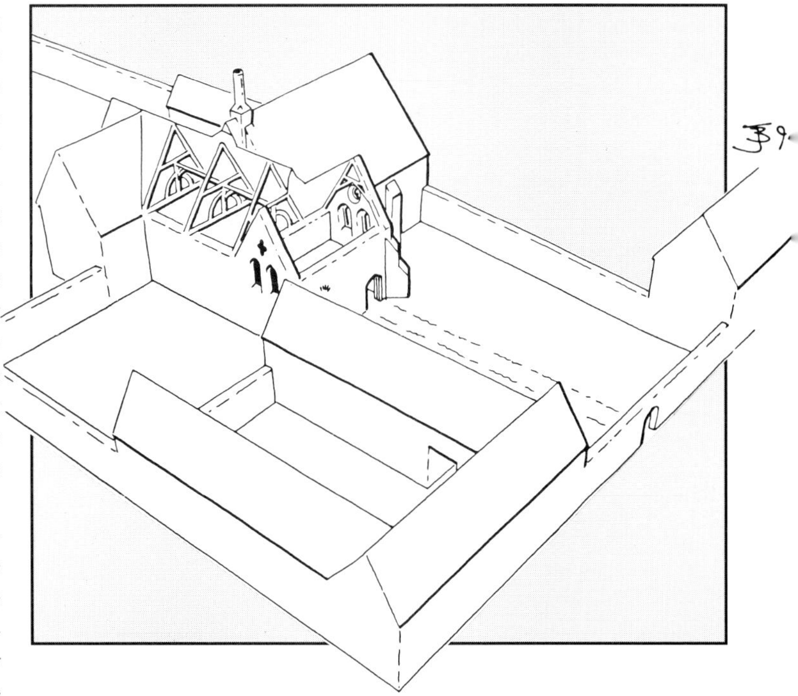

Plan 13 *Cut-away of the Chantry from the north east to show probably medieval features.*

The two other medieval canons' houses deserving mention are the buildings later known as the houses of the Wiccamical Prebendaries, and of the Royal Chantry priests, which are entered from the south walk of the Cloister. The former house was built in the early

14th century, as can be seen from the doorway and two square-headed windows (now blocked) on the north side.[47] Under this main range on the north is a fine rib-vaulted cellar, while another contemporary cellar runs off to the south-east. In 1523, Bishop Sherburne had this building divided into four residences for the occupiers of his new 'Wiccamical' prebends (the details of this are fully documented in the Bishop's register).[48] Once again the house has been very thoroughly rebuilt in the post-medieval period and another 18th-century house has been built onto the south-west side, with an entry directly from St Richard's Walk.

The building now known as the Royal Chantry was originally an east-west hall-like building on an undercroft first constructed in the 13th century. In its north wall, still visible, are the three small (three-feet-high) rectangular windows (now blocked) that originally lit its undercroft, as well as one tall lancet for the room on the main floor. Though all now blocked, they still contain some of their original ironwork. High up in the west wall of this building is a blocked round window containing a cinquefoil, which must have lit the hall roof. Unfortunately a second storey was added to the Royal Chantry in the early 19th century, which has mutilated the earlier gable and destroyed the roof. The south-east wing also appears to be a later addition, possibly medieval, but now containing only 18th-century and later features.

130 *The doorway of the Royal Chantry, which today leads to the Cathedral Offices.*

In 1413, the Chichester prebend of Wilmington, which had hitherto been held by the Abbot of Grenstein, a foreigner, was confiscated by King Henry V, along with other 'alien' holdings. Its revenues were then used to found a new chantry in the Cathedral's Lady Chapel for the King's parents and Nicholas Mortimer, a kinsman who was buried here. The two royal chaplains, who then had to say daily masses, were given this building as a residence, hence its later name. In the late 15th century a fine new doorway was inserted into the north wall of the building,[49] while above it a high-relief panel of Henry VII's arms was fixed, supported by a dragon and greyhound, above a now-defaced figure of Our Lady. On either side are defaced kneeling figures, probably members of the Mortimer family.

The Vicars' Close and Cloisters

By the 14th century, the Close at Chichester contained fine houses for the bishops and the four dignitaries, as well as perhaps for the two or three residentiary canons. At this time there were also between twenty-eight and thirty-two vicars choral,[50] who occupied the splendid new stalls in the Cathedral quire and sang the daily services. These young men, however, had no proper residence in the Close, so at the very end of the century the Bishop decided to create a new Vicars' Close on the east side of the Cathedral Close, following the pattern already set at other secular cathedrals such as Lincoln and Wells.[51] In 1394 a late 12th-century stone 'gilden halle' in South Street was conveyed to King Richard II and then passed on to the Bishop as the first stage in this process. By the spring of 1397 plans were sufficiently far advanced for a fine new Vicars' Hall to be started. On 6 March 1397, four new foundation stones were formally laid by the Dean and canons around the old Guildhall undercroft and work on this large new structure was put in hand.[52]

The old late 12th-century rib-vaulted undercroft was retained (fig.52), and a pair of barrel vaults were added on the west (below the kitchen, which had a large fireplace in its west wall). In the centre was an unvaulted undercroft with 'sampson posts' to hold up the floor, and above this a fine open hall was created, with a separate chamber or parlour to the east (beyond a timber partition). This parlour was situated at a slightly higher level on top of the old vaulted undercroft. The original three-bay crown-post roof (with wind braces) still survives in the central part (the hall), and there are several original two-light trefoiled ogee-headed windows with external square hood-moulds. On the south side of the hall is a fine moulded doorway, with opposite it a large wash-basin set in an ogee-headed niche (fig.131). On the south-east side of the hall is a small projection which acted as both a pulpit (for meal-time readings), and the place where the statutes, written in a book, were kept in a box that was chained to the wall.[53]

Beyond the principal doorway on the south side of the hall was a small landing with steps leading down from it to the east and west to connect with the little cloister around the Vicars' Close to the south. Only in the early 18th century, when the hall itself was first leased out, was a new entrance created on the north, connecting with the passageway on the north side of the Vicars' Hall that led to a small postern gate in South Street. This tiny gateway (earlier called the Turnstyle) still survives, but the chamber above it, which was joined to the Vicars' Parlour, has disappeared.[54]

The Vicars' Hall was finished and ready for use in 1403, and at about the same time the two ranges of houses to the south were being constructed with return ranges and a gateway at the southern end.[55] Recent careful study of these houses, particularly of their crown-post roofs, has shown that, as originally built, there were 28 pairs of chambers, which corresponds closely with the known number of vicars choral at this time.[56] The outer walls of the ranges are of masonry, while the internal partitions are timber-framed. Though many alterations were made to the houses from the 15th century onwards, it is still possible to reconstruct the positions of all the original partitions, and to see several of the original doors and traceried windows in the front walls. Each house had a front door leading into a ground-floor chamber, with a staircase opposite the door that led up to a first-floor sleeping chamber. In the back wall there must have been other windows and fireplaces, as well as probably a garde-robe.

Outside there was a small yard. At least one original chimney stack base survives in the rear wall,[57] and there are traces of others. There is little doubt that there was once a covered walk all the way round the internal courtyard. This seems to have been destroyed in 1736 when James Essex, the architect, was employed to take it down. He is quoted as calling it 'a very old cloister mostly built with wood, but of what age I cannot tell'.[58] This cloister is shown on the 1749 map of Chichester (fig.132), and in the Parliamentary Survey of 1649 it is called the 'Little Cloisters'. There was a 'Pump Yard' in the centre of the court.

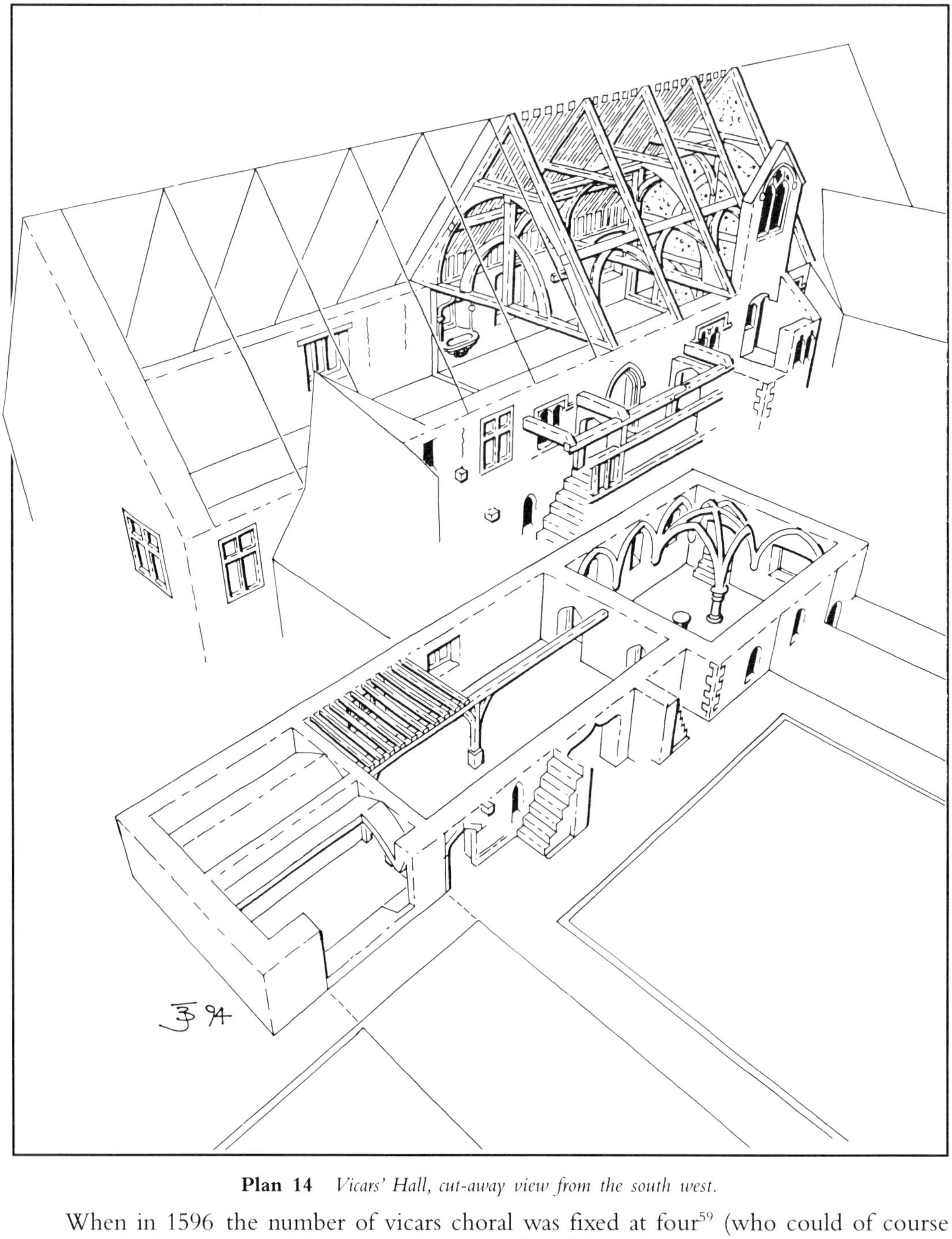

Plan 14 *Vicars' Hall, cut-away view from the south west.*

When in 1596 the number of vicars choral was fixed at four[59] (who could of course be married), the 12 original houses on the west side of the Close were rearranged into only four large vicars' houses which had larger gardens at the back. Many extensions were also added to the rear of these houses over the centuries, though the houses on the east side of the Close (which were leased out) were hampered by the proximity of South Street. Eventually in 1825, these houses were given up, and new fronts with shops in them were built, so that they could be 'turned round.' The eastern half of the old courtyard was then turned into back yards for the new shops, with a nine-foot-high wall to screen off the surviving vicars' houses.

At the southern end of Vicars' Close, four slightly larger houses flanked a gateway called the Chaingate. Above this gate were 'chambers used for the Register office', according to the 1649 survey, while alongside the gate was the 'Common Bread Binge', later called the Bin Room.[60] Sadly all of this was demolished in 1831, along with the chambers to the west. Immediately adjoining the south-east side of the Vicars' Close is the Canon Gate, at the end of Canon Lane. It has a double gateway (for vehicles and pedestrians), and above it a chamber where the bishop's court of Pie Powder for Sloe Fair was held.[61] The gateway was very heavily restored in 1894 by Ewan Christian, but it still displays some fine early 16th-century carvings, including demi-angels holding shields on either side of the main arch (*in situ*) and in niches above the main outer arches. These niches once contained statues, but since their destruction, in presumably the mid-16th or 17th century, shields have been set there.[62]

Vicar's House, Chichester Cathedral c1450
A provisional reconstruction
John Atherton Bowen March 1991

Plan 15 *Reconstruction of one of the late medieval vicars' houses.*

When many of the vicars' closes were built at English secular cathedrals, special provision was made for the vicars to get from their close to the cathedral choir via covered passageways. Some of these, like the passage from the Bedern in York, or from the Vicars' Close at Wells, had elaborate bridges over the road.[63] At Chichester no bridge was required, but a long covered passageway was built from the Vicars' Close after the Vicars' Hall was completed, in the years after 1400.[64] A little later still, this passage became the eastern alley of a three-sided cloister that was built around the south side of the Cathedral.

Plan 16 *(overleaf) Plan and elevations of the cloister walks and St Faith's chapel.*

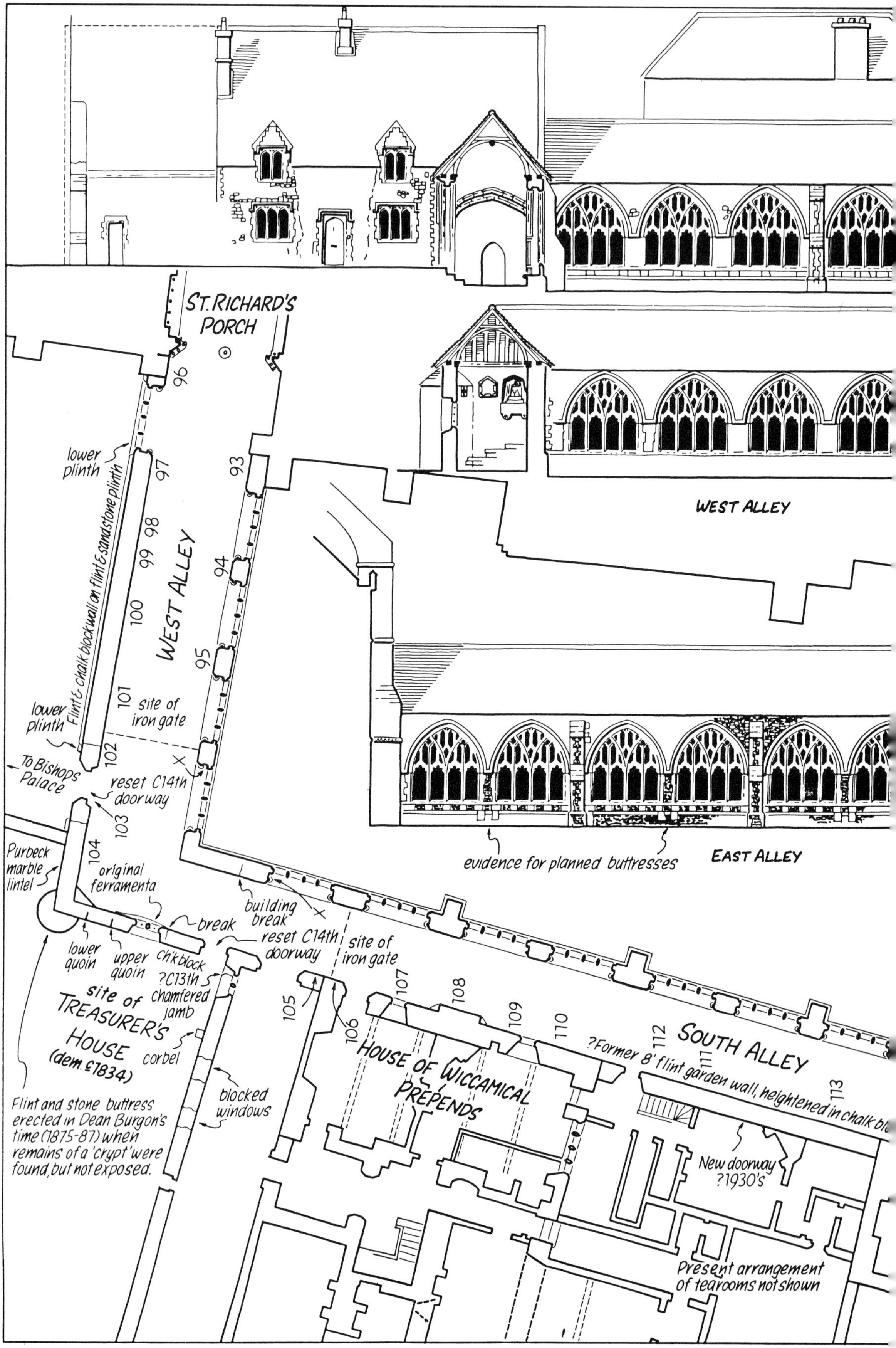

ST. RICHARD'S PORCH
96
lower plinth
97
98
99
100
101
102
Flint & chalk block wall on flint & sandstone plinth
WEST ALLEY
93
94
95
site of iron gate
lower plinth
To Bishops Palace
reset C14th doorway
103
104
Purbeck marble lintel
original ferramenta
break
building break
reset C14th doorway
site of iron gate
lower quoin
upper quoin
ch'k block ?C13th chamfered jamb
site of TREASURER'S HOUSE (dem. c1834)
corbel
blocked windows
Flint and stone buttress erected in Dean Burgon's time (1875-87) when remains of a 'crypt' were found, but not exposed.
105
106
107
108
109
110
111
112
113
HOUSE OF WICCAMICAL PREPENDS
SOUTH ALLEY
?Former 8' flint garden wall, heightened in chalk bl
New doorway ?1930's
Present arrangement of tearooms not shown
WEST ALLEY
evidence for planned buttresses
EAST ALLEY

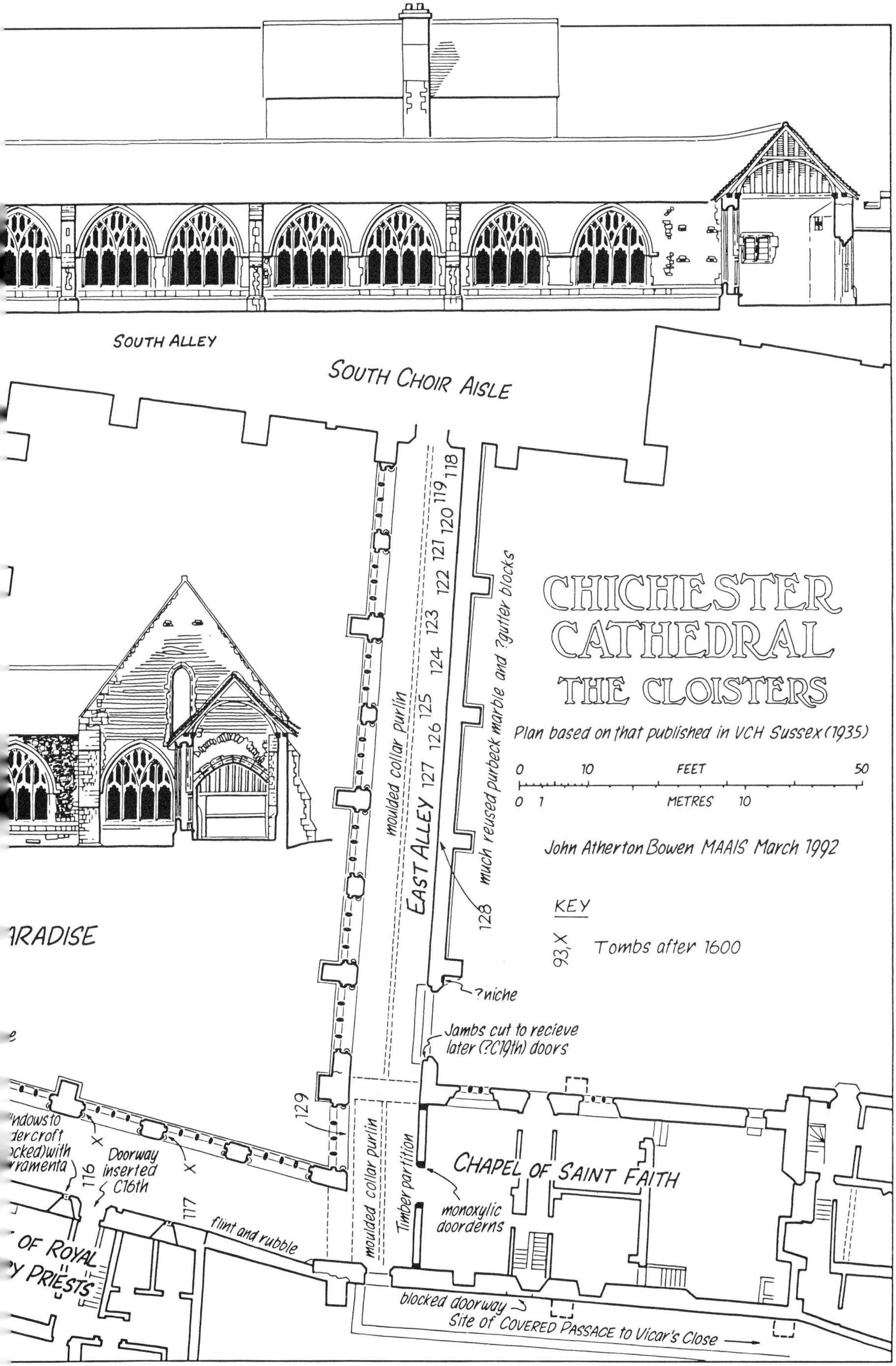

SOUTH ALLEY
SOUTH CHOIR AISLE
118
119
120
121
122
123
124
125
126
127
128
moulded collar purlin
EAST ALLEY
much reused purbeck marble and ?gutter blocks
CHICHESTER CATHEDRAL
THE CLOISTERS
Plan based on that published in VCH Sussex (1935)
0
10
FEET
50
0
1
METRES
10
John Atherton Bowen MAAIS March 1992
KEY
93, X
Tombs after 1600
?niche
Jambs cut to recieve later (?C19th) doors
129
116
117
Doorway inserted C16th
moulded collar purlin
Timber partition
monoxylic doorderns
CHAPEL OF SAINT FAITH
flint and rubble
blocked doorway
Site of COVERED PASSAGE to Vicar's Close

131 *Vicars' Hall today, with wash basin, and detail of pulpitum (left).*

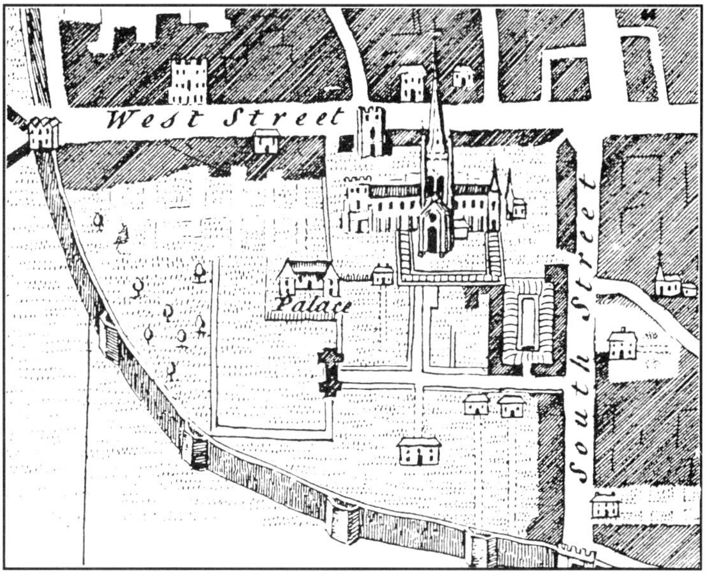

132 *Emanuel Bowen's 1749 map, showing the 'little cloister' in Vicars' Close.*

To build this covered passage, a way had to be made through the west end of St Faith's Chapel. One of the canons, John Paxton, had been summoned before the Bishop in 1402 for making a common path from his lodging through the chapel of St Faith 'against the ordinance of the founder of the said chapel and the great loss and alienation of the goods and things of the [cathedral] church deposited in the chapel for safe custody'. Paxton's defence was that a residentiary canon living in his lodgings always had the right to go through the chapel into the Cathedral. (He was also accused of taking timber stored in the chapel for works on the high altar of the Cathedral: he promised to restore these to John Mason, master of the works.) Five years later in 1407, however, Dean Maidenhith left half the residue of his estate '*ad fabricam domorum per communicate vicariorum infra clausum construendam*.'[65] This suggests that the situation had been regularised and that the construction of the cloister was underway.

The Cloisters at Chichester are unusual in several ways.[66] First their position around the south transept is unique, and then the fact that all of the three alleys are different suggest that their form was evolving as they were being built. Perhaps they should not be thought of as cloisters at all, but merely as three covered walks. The east alley was built first, as we have seen, and this was planned to be heavily buttressed on both sides, possibly suggesting that a stone vault was to be built. However, only every second buttress on the west side was built above plinth level, and anyway the buttresses are not opposite each other. The south alley had buttresses on its north side for roughly every other bay, but the plinth shows no evidence for more buttresses having been planned. The west alley had no buttresses at all. The large Perpendicular traceried windows are, however, the same throughout, with benches on their insides. Another difference is in the fine timber roofs: where the east alley has a nearly semi-circular barrel-vault with a moulded central purlin, the south and west alleys have moulded wall-plates, but no central purlin, and the vaults are more four-centred in cross-section. There is also a very ingenious framing for the roof in the south-west corner, where it turns around an obtuse angle.[67]

When the east alley was cut through the west end of St Faith's, large holes were cut in the earlier walls and wide four-centred arches (with relieving arches above) were put in. The west gable of the chapel with its single lancet was left standing, and a new timber partition and doorway were added. The chapel itself, which may also have acted as the vicars' chapel,[68] was a fine early 13th-century, originally free-standing, building which was converted to a private house after the Reformation. The eastern end was left as an open shell, though beyond it further east another small house was inserted into the space next

133 *Canon Gate in the early 19th century, with the original entrance to Vicars' Close and the Bin Room.*

to the Vicars' Hall in the 18th century. Along the south side of St Faith's a covered passage, called the 'Dark Cloister', was also created in the 15th century. This was unroofed by the early 19th century, but corbels and other traces of the former roof can still be seen. The passageway joined the 'little cloister' in the Vicars' Close with the west alley of the 'great cloister' and, where it goes through the chapel wall in the south-east corner of the Cloister, a re-used 13th-century doorway (presumably from the chapel) can still be seen.

The south alley of the Cloister, as we have seen, runs along, and incorporates, the north walls of the houses for the Royal Chantry priests and the Wiccamical prebends, and then cuts through the north-east corner of the Treasurer's House, before turning north to form a short west alley which runs up to St Richard's porch on the south side of the Cathedral nave. This alley is unusual in having one window, at the north end, on the outside. There may originally have been a second window in the outside wall at the south end, but the opening for this was soon filled up, and a smaller, probably re-used, doorway (perhaps from the Treasurer's House) was inserted instead. Whether there was ever a covered walk from here to the Bishop's Palace is, as yet, unknown. There are, however, some remains of a porch, or possibly the covered walk, outside the door into the Bishop's Palace, at the south-west corner of the churchyard.

During the 18th and 19th centuries the Cloister walks and 'Paradise' were much used for burial; large vaults were dug beneath them and monuments were added to the walls. The original paving was, therefore, much disturbed, and several medieval brass indents from the Cathedral were deposited here. In May 1786, doors were ordered to be put up 'at the east and west entrance (to the cloisters) and at the end of the Dark Cloister, leading to the Vicars' Close, and that the said doors be shut every evening and opened every morning by the sextons'.[69] Over a century earlier than this, in the Parliamentary Survey of 1649, the 'rooms and chambers called the Cloisters School' are mentioned, and it seems possible that the Cloister alleys, with their benches under the windows, were used for a time as a school, just as they were at Winchester College. Perhaps this was before the Prebendal School was properly established by Bishop Storey in 1497.

The Bell Tower

Finally, the bell tower, called Raymond's or Ryman's Tower at an early date, ought to be mentioned. This was built in the years around 1400 in the early Perpendicular style.[70] It is just over 107 feet high and is made from large ashlar blocks of Upper Greensand, that were probably brought from Ventnor on the south side of the Isle of Wight. There are also some original quoins and jambs of the harder Bembridge limestone, though the harder yellow-brown quoins are of West Hoathly stone which were put in during the 1902-8 restoration.[71] In 1965, the octagonal top stage, the lantern, was rebuilt completely with Purbeck stone from Worth Matravers. Sadly the very fine merlons, pierced with trefoiled arches, were replaced at this time with plain ones.

When the Bell Tower was put up, it was probably already surrounded on the north and east by houses and shops.[72] Hence these two sides of the tower are completely plain in its first stage. On the west, there is a doorway which leads down into a basement (now a Cathedral shop), while a larger doorway on the south with steps leading up to it opens into a large ground-floor chamber. This is lit by two-light windows on the south and west. In the south-west corner is a spiral stair leading to the upper floors, though the door into the first-floor level is blocked, and the floor itself has been removed. The second floor, the ringing chamber, is well-lit with two-light windows

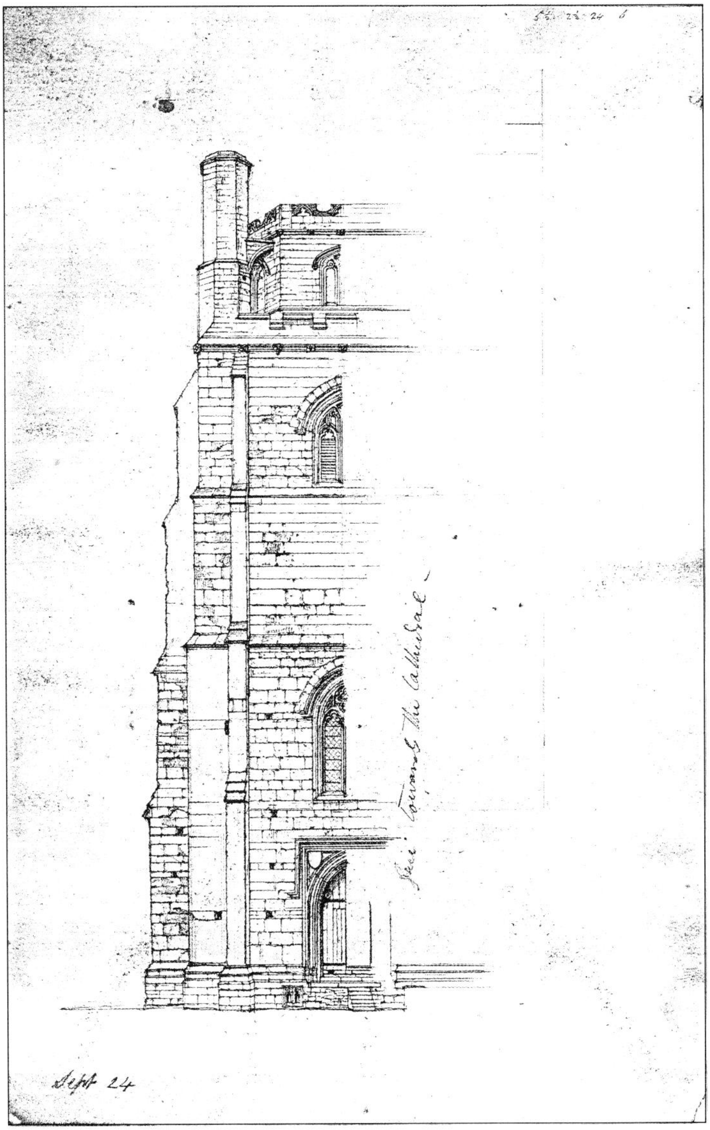

134 *Bell Tower.*

in each face, and above it are two large oak beams, supported by wall-posts and braces. These, in turn, support the bell-frame, which in its present form dates from 1731. The bell-chamber itself is octagonal and supported on squinch arches (Plate XIX). It contains a fine ring of eight bells of the late 16th, 17th and 18th centuries, as well as quarter chimes and an hour bell for the clock, added in 1877 as a memorial to Dean Hook.[73] It seems just possible that the Bell Tower was once capped with a timber spire, but, if this was so, it had gone by the 16th century.

With the removal of the surrounding houses in the mid-19th century, and the land-scaping of the surrounding area in the 1970s, the Bell Tower now stands in splendid isolation; a unique survival in a cathedral close of what was once a fairly common feature.

XV

The Musical History of Chichester Cathedral

Philip Barrett

The Middle Ages

As a secular or 'old foundation' cathedral, Chichester's music in the Middle Ages was performed by the vicars choral and choristers. The earliest evidence of vicars choral comes from the late 12th century.[1] By 1397 there were 31 vicars, of whom 28 were named at Bishop Robert Rede's visitation.[2] At first, each of them lived in the household of the canon who was his master and we know that in 1232 he shared with him in the daily distribution of bread. A college for the vicars was begun in 1397 and was ready by 1403. Later they

135 *Vicars' Close in 1783, before the east side was turned round for shops.*

had separate houses in Vicars' Close, and their college was incorporated in 1467.[3] There were 10 choristers in 1232 and 12 by 1481.[4] The Constitutions of 1247 emphasised that the precentor or 'chanter' was to direct the choir:

> he has the power of raising and lowering the pitch; he ought to note the readers and singers for night and day on the board; to introduce the inferior clerks into the choir; at the celebration of orders [i.e. ordinations] to recite the names of the clerks who are admitted.[5]

Our knowledge of the music sung in the Cathedral is fragmentary. A 13th-century Psalter in the British Library[6] contains some later Chichester antiphons at the beginning and end of the book. The volume of Cathedral Statutes in the library of University College, Oxford[7] also contains some music which Walcott described as 'a Tropar of the Use of Chichester'.[8] Was there a separate Use of Chichester distinguishable from the uses of other old-foundation cathedrals such as Salisbury, Hereford and Lincoln? There is little actual evidence for this, though, as Dr. Greenway has shown, during the episcopate of St Richard, the Use of Chichester Cathedral was prescribed throughout the diocese.[9] The Use of Sarum was certainly introduced into the Cathedral between 1414 and 1443, and in 1423 Archbishop Chichele gave the Cathedral some books of this liturgy. In his will of 1424, Dean Milton left a Sarum Missal to the Cathedral.[10]

The antiphon *Honor virtus* was sung at the enthronement of bishops as the new bishop was led to the west door of the Cathedral, and the responsory *Triuna Trinitatis* was sung as he was led to the high altar. At the enthronement of Bishop Robert Rede in 1397 the choir sang the antiphon *Summae Trinitati* in procession, and three psalms, *Deus misereatur, Ad te levavi* and *Ecce quam bonum* were customarily sung at the installation of a dean.[11] According to the Constitutions of 1247, when a canon died the other canons, for seven days, visited his tomb 'chanting fifteen psalms in going, but in returning five psalms'. The Mass for the Departed was then begun.[12] In 1504 the Dean and Chapter agreed to say prayers for Henry VII at each High Mass at the high altar, with additional psalms and prayers at every capitular mass at any altar. They further undertook that, when he died, they would have a special Requiem Mass

> with special collects, naming your majesty and with other prayers, suffrages, lights, knell and other ceremonies necessary and convenient, with chants, as solemnly as any exequies have ever been celebrated in our Church.[13]

As at many other cathedrals, there were disciplinary and other problems with the choir. At Bishop Rede's visitation in 1402, 'it was complained that the books of the choir were deficient in notes and binding, through defect of the Chancellor'. Another problem was that 'the vicars are accustomed to take away books from the choir to their own chambers contrary to the customs of the church'. In 1409 it was said that 'the vicars often leave the choir without reasonable cause, before the completion of the Divine Office'. In 1441, Bishop Praty found that

> The vicars choral attend matins abominably so that frequently there are scarcely two on one side of the choir and the service cannot be duly rendered. The worst is that the stronger and the younger among them lie in their beds in the morning notwithstanding their oath.[14]

Bishop Storey discovered in 1478 that many vicars were still absenting themselves from the services, leaving only two or three in the quire. Talking during services was a problem, as it had been in 1409, and even the succentor and rulers of the choir were often late: 'some come in after the middle of the first psalm, some at the end of it'.[15] In 1481 Bishop Storey required the most junior of the vicars to sing an antiphon of the Blessed Virgin Mary with the customary collect and suffrages before her image next to the quire door at the usual times daily throughout the year.[16] Bishop Arundel had required an antiphon to be sung here when he founded an altar of the Virgin (St Mary at Stock) in this position some years earlier. Sometimes outsiders took part in the musical worship of the Cathedral. The merchants' guild, which was refounded in 1446 as a Fraternity of St George, sang an antiphon on St George's Day each year, and a mass of St George was celebrated daily.[17]

Our fullest information about the medieval musical life of the Cathedral comes just before the Reformation. In 1529 Bishop Sherburne added four lay clerks to the choir.[18] They were required to be singers of polyphonic music, with voices that blended well and together had a range of fifteen or sixteen notes. They sang at High Mass and the Lady Mass in the Lady Chapel each day, meeting the choristers and their master at Sherburne's tomb daily to sing the psalm *De profundis* on their way to the Lady Mass, and at Matins on the principal feast-days. The vicars and choristers were also instructed by Sherburne to sing an antiphon of St Katherine on the vigil of her feast-day (25 November). Each singer was to be provided with his part, written and noted, and given a candle to hold. The next morning, six vicars with the choir-master and choristers attended the Mass of St Katherine. Afterwards the boys were given refreshments.[19] In 1534 Sherburne gave new statutes to the Vicars Choral.[20] Before the election of Bishop Richard Sampson in 1536 a Mass of the Holy Ghost was sung. After the *congé d'élire* had been read, the election proceeded with the customary music: the hymn *Veni Creator* was sung and after the actual election the Dean and Chapter 'adjourned to publish the election and for the singing of the Te Deum'.[21] In 1544 William Samford was given a payment for the antiphon *Nunc Christe* and William Campyon was paid to play the organs in the quire and Lady Chapel.[22] The Peterhouse partbooks of 1545 include polyphonic antiphons by the Chichester composer John Mason.[23] Detailed instructions concerning the distribution of lights at Lauds, the singing of the *Venite*, and the distribution of the 'venite-loaf' have survived from about this time.[24]

From the Reformation to the Restoration

The musical life of the Cathedral between the Reformation and the Restoration has received considerable study from several scholars, who have been chiefly attracted by the figure of Thomas Weelkes.[25] During the hundred years or so preceding the Civil War, the standard number of singers was probably four vicars choral, eight lay clerks and eight choristers.[26] Both the vicars choral and the clerks were frequently in trouble with the Dean and Chapter over their behaviour. Fights, drunkenness and neglect of duty were quite common.[27] Christopher Payne was appointed choirmaster in 1581 with a fee of 50s. 4d. and 3s. 4d. from the City of Chichester. He was allowed the chambers belonging to the choirmaster and the choristers' garden for a rent of 4s. 8d. A few months earlier he had been given an annual allowance of 6s. 8d. 'for paper and ink for altering the choir books'. When John Cowper was admitted as a lay vicar in 1587 he was obliged to 'pryck his own part', as were John Foster in 1589 and Jacob Hilarie in 1590. Clement Woodcocke, a vicar choral who was organist off and on from 1570, seems to have resumed the post of choirmaster in 1589, when he was given 'six books of paper, partly pricked and partly unpricked', for the vicars, 'according to every man's parte'.[28] William Lawes, the succentor, was given authority in 1596/7 to 'appoynte what songs shulde be songe daylye and that all the syngers shulde stande upp the tyme that they dyd synge that they might be the better herde'.[29] Peter le Huray has shown that at least 67 choristers were in the Cathedral choir at different times between 1545 and 1603, with a further 64 between 1604 and 1644. The average time spent in the choir was six years in the 16th century and four in the early 17th century, though the expected time was seven years. The Dean and Chapter educated the choristers, giving them food and shelter and £2 3s. 4d., provided their parents handed over a bond of £10, to be forfeited if a boy was removed from the choir without permission. Many of the choristers came from the families of graduates, though there was a gradual trend towards a wider social background in the 17th century, as the proportion of boys with a cathedral family background declined.[30]

The Cathedral services were often in disarray, interrupted by 'unreverend gesture or unseemly talking' among the vicars choral and lay vicars, who were also wont to bring a 'dogge or bytche' with them to the services. The Dean and Chapter tried hard to prevent them wandering out of the stalls during the services and to ensure that the choristers were given a sufficient musical training of three hours a day.[31]

Thomas Weelkes, the most famous musician at Chichester at this time, was probably admitted as a Sherburne clerk in 1601, though the earliest evidence of his holding such a post is in 1605. He had become organist and *informator choristarum* by October 1602. Before coming to Chichester he was well-known as a madrigal composer while he was organist of Winchester College.[32] He was evidently appreciated by his fellow-musicians at Chichester. When Archbishop George Abbot conducted a metropolitical visitation of the diocese in 1615, he asked other members of the Cathedral choir whether they had 'a skillful organist'. Two of the Sherburne clerks, Valentine Austen and Anthony Buttery, said that there was a fair pair of organs and 'a sufficient and skillful organist'. Two of the singing-men, Thomas Clifford and Thomas Young, replied that 'our organist is very skilful and exquisite in his p[ro]fesssion', while Godfrey Blaxton, one of the vicars choral, said that 'the organist [is] as able a man as most quyers in England hath'. Another vicar choral, John Lilliatt, described Weelkes as 'most exquisite in his profession and place; causinge the instrum[en]t to seeme much the better, by his arteficiall finger'.[33]

As the years passed, so Weelkes' manner of life caused concern at Chichester. He was absent from Lancelot Andrewes' visitation in 1609 and accused of drunkenness in 1613.[34] In 1616, he was presented at Bishop Harsnett's visitation as 'a common drunkard and a notorious swearer and blasphemer'. In January 1617 Weelkes was sentenced to be deprived of his offices as a Sherburne clerk and choirmaster.[35] In 1619 he was again described at Bishop George Carleton's visitation as 'a common drunkard':

> Thomas Weelkes ... very often comes so disguised eyther from the Taverne or ale howse into the quire as is muche to be lamented, for in these humours he will bothe curse and Sweare most dreadfully and so prophane the service of God (and especially on the Saboth dayes) as is most fearfull to heare, and to the great amasement of all the people p'sent'.[36]

Towards the end of his life, Weelkes seems to have spent more and more time in London. His wife died in 1622 and he followed her to the grave in December 1623.[37]

Weelkes was unfortunate in his noble patrons, who were either recusants or otherwise fell from official favour, and this really ruined his career. His unruly later life may have been the result of his disappointments rather than the cause of them.[38] In Weelkes' collection of *Ayeres or Phantasticke Spirites for three voices*, published in 1608, he described himself as a Gentleman of the Chapel Royal. Although there is no direct evidence for this, it may be that Weelkes' connections with the Chapel Royal accounted for his various absences from

Chichester.[39] Weelkes' full anthems were probably written for the Chapel Royal choir, whereas his simpler verse anthems may have been more suitable for Chichester.[40]

Bishop Samuel Harsnett was keen to improve the musical standards at the Cathedral. In his visitation in 1611 he ordered 'that the master of the choristers bestowe three hours at ye least in every day in teaching the choristers'.[41] There were more detailed instructions following his visitation in 1616. The Master of the Choristers was told to teach the choristers 'each morning from eight to ten and so conduct them to Church to and fro: likewise from three to fower each afternoon and so again bring them to church, ranking them orderly two by two thus shall he guide them more especially on Sundays and holy days'.[42] The Dean and Chapter amplified this order with an act on 6 May 1616, in which they decreed:

> ... that John Juxon, John Lytle, Thomas Trigges and Richard Mose, choristers, shall henceforth every day goe to the songe school to Mr Weekes organiste and instructor of the choristers at nyne of the clocke in the forenoone by him to be instructed and made more perfitt in singing untill tenn and then to goe with the rest of the choristers orderly to church, and lykewyse in the afternoon to be there present to the entent aforssayde from three to fower and then to goe to church as aforessayde ... that Nicholas Windres, Thomas Weekes, Robert Randoll and Thomas Butcher, junior choristers, shall from henceforth every daye repayre and goe to the sayde songe schole at eyghte of the clock in the forenoon to be there instructed and to practisse theire singing untill ten and then to goe to church as above-sayde, and soe lykewysse in the afternoone at twoe of the clocke there to remayne to the same entent untill fower, and then allsoe to go to church according to the same order above sett downe.[43]

Each boy was to have his own prayer book and 'his surplice white and cleane'.[44] According to an old laudable custom, the choristers were

> to serve in the quire by weeks, two each weeke specially, the one a senior and the other a junior, and that they sort their books every week once only with another, lest by negligence hereafter they be lost, as heretofore they have been.[45]

There is also a rather enigmatic instruction to the organist, who was told to

> ... remaine in the quire untill ye last psalm be sung and then go to ye organs, and then having done his duty to return into ye quire again to beare his part ... this is thought a meete manner in all double quires, much more is it necessary in all half quires as ours is.[46]

From this we may deduce that the psalms were sung unaccompanied and that the organist played a middle voluntary. The subchanter was also required to make an immediate survey of

> ye Church songbooks, what they are, how conditioned, preserved and pricked, that he bring in a catalogue thereof within one week next. And for that we are informed our best services are conveyed away, that he enquire them out, if he can, and that henceforth he permit no book or service to be had out of ye quire without express leave of the Dean *in scriptis*.[47]

Such a list, written by John Lilliat, survives from the year 1621.[48] From this we learn that the Cathedral choir had a library of over an hundred books and thirty-two 'scrolls' of music. There were at least six service settings by composers who included Byrd, Sheppard, Farrant, Nicholas Strogers and William Cox.[49] There is some evidence from this list to show that Weelkes' music was in the repertoire at Chichester. One anthem, entitled *A poor desire I have to amend mine ill* is probably the first chorus of Weelkes' anthem *If King Manasses*. A set of books 'of Mr Weelkes his pricking' was probably a set of part-books which he himself had written out. A ten-book set labelled 'of Gunpowder Treason' may well have included Weelkes' long verse anthem *O Lord, how joyful is the King*, apparently written for the annual commemoration on 5 November.[50]

Disciplinary problems in the choir were not confined to Weelkes. Absenteeism and neglect of duty were common. In particular, two vicars choral, John Meade and Godfrey Blaxton, were often in trouble with the Chapter.[51] Sometimes they were absent for two or three months at a time.[52] One of the canons residentiary recalled in 1623:

> One Saturdaye night the seconde of November 1622 for want of a vicar Mr Deane was compelled to reade divine service, and that for wante of a competente number of vicars and singingmen, prayers in the Cathedrall church ar often reade as in a parochiall church.[53]

Apparently the vicars choral were so slack and irregular at this time that one idled away his time as a fortune-teller, while another openly referred to his housekeeper as 'his whore'. The buildings, community life and finances of the vicars choral were in a disgraceful state.[54]

Little is known about the Cathedral's music during the reign of Charles I, but it evidently came to an end with the riot on 28 December 1642 when the Parliamentary soldiers not only destroyed the organ but also forced open

> all the locks, either of doors or desks wherein the singing-men laid up their Common-Prayer Books, and their singing Books, their Gowns and Surplesses: they rent the Books in pieces and scatter the torn leaves all over the Church, even to the covering of the Pavement.[55]

From the Restoration to 1800

Indeed, it was not until over a year after the restoration of Charles II in May 1660 that the Cathedral choir was fully reconstituted. On 14 September 1661 the Dean and Chapter admitted two new Sherburne clerks in place of two who had died some years previously, three other lay clerks and eight choristers. John Floud became Master of the Choristers in place of the long-serving John Fidge.[56] Both some of the vicars choral and the lay clerks continued to cause disciplinary problems in the 1660s.[57] By the time Bishop Gunning was enthroned on 24 March 1669/70, there were two vicars choral, four Sherburne clerks and four other lay vicars.[58] Gunning's visitation articles in 1673 enquired

> whether the choristers be well learnt and instructed in the art of singing, rightly and duly catechized in the principles of religion and by whom?

A few years later, in reply to the visitation articles of Bishop Ralph Brideoake, the vicars choral said:

> the choristers at some times do not demeane themselves so decently and orderly in the quire as they ought to do, neither do their duty in singing and reading as they should.[59]

A Chapter Act of 2 May 1678 throws some light on the musical and liturgical life of the Cathedral at this time. The choice of anthems was the responsibility of the sub-chanter or succentor, and the singing-men were instructed to 'chant the second anthem after the *Te Deum* on Litany days'. We may infer from this that on Wednesdays and Fridays the *Jubilate* was sung to a chant rather than to a full setting of the canticles. Mattins began at 9.00 a.m. on Sundays and 'preaching Holy Days', at 9.45 a.m. on Litany days and on all other days at 10.00 a.m. From Michaelmas to All Saints' Day, Evensong was at 3.30 p.m. and at 3.15 p.m. from All Saints' Day to Candlemas. From Candlemas until 1 March, the service began at 3.30 p.m. 'except Candle nights, and then and on all other evenings prayer shall begin at four o'clock'. The bell was rung 15 minutes before each service, with a warning bell 15 minutes before that.[60] In 1680 it was decided that each vicar choral should take a turn in being succentor and choosing the music in consultation with the organist.[61] This plan swiftly broke down and in 1684 John Harrow was appointed succentor and ordered to rehearse the choir every Monday morning in the music to be sung during the week.[62] In 1679 Bishop Guy Carleton asked whether the vicars 'and other lay singing-men' met twice a week to spend at least an hour with the Master of the Choristers

> to practice [sic] and improve their skill in musick thereby the better to enable themselves more solemnly to perform the service of God in their places in the Cathedral.[63]

Bishop Lake discovered in 1686 that the choristers were rehearsed for only two hours a day instead of four and that some of the lay vicars were infrequent communicants.[64]

The Dean and Chapter told Bishop Robert Grove in 1695 that the daily services were not performed 'so reverently by some as may be wished', and that some of the lay vicars were 'very negligent' both in their attendance and in receiving Communion. There were fewer choristers than the statutory number 'and we apprehend that they are not so carefully taught in the art of singing and principles of religion as is required'.[65] The vicars choral complained that three of the lay vicars and some of the choristers were negligent in their attendance at services 'and they sometimes behave themselves indecently and irreverently in the time of it'.[66] Grove was clearly keen to enforce improvements and ordered the Master of the Choristers to bring them every Saturday after Mattins 'to the schoolmaster of the free school to be by him examined and instructed in the church catechism'. On Sundays both the lay vicars and choristers were ordered that, after Mattins, they

> when they goe out of the choir do go into their seat in the body of the Church and joyne in singing the psalm before sermon and continue there all the sermon time and till after the blessing pronounced and the Bishop, Dean and Residentiaries or such of them as are then at church be gone by their seat.[67]

Four years later, Charles Leaver was in trouble with the Chapter not only for his frequent absences and persuading others to go with him, but also

> for being guilty of a most horrid and abominable Impiety in putting up at Evening prayers A mock Thanksgiving (written with his owne hand) to the great Dishonour of god and Scandal of the Congregation.[68]

Bishop Williams' visitation in 1700 contained several searching questions about the choir and the Cathedral services. The Dean and Chapter told him that the Litany was always read by two lay clerks and that the prayers on solemn occasions were read by the Dean and residentiaries 'in their turns'. The vicars choral and lay vicars attended services 'pretty well but they are apt to enter the choir disorderly in a crowd'. Holy Communion was celebrated on great festivals and on the first Sunday of each month, but most of the lay clerks were accustomed to 'scandalously neglect it'. There were only six choristers.[69]

Disciplinary problems came to a head in 1701 when three vicars choral—Roger Collins, Thomas Kelway, Charles Leaver—and a lay vicar (Charles Collins) were hauled before the Chapter over their persistent quarrelling.[70] In 1708 it was ordered that verse anthems (*anathemata carmine composita*) should be sung on Sunday, Tuesday and Thursday mornings. This order was confirmed in the following year and any singer who refused to take part was to have his bread stopped or pay a fine of 6d. The new chanting of the psalms was to be performed daily.[71] In 1710, Samuel Pearson, the organist, shocked the Dean and

136 *Page from the contemporary MS of Kelway's services in the Cathedral Library.*

Chapter by saying that William III was 'a pickpocket'. He had seen him at the Chapel Royal 'and he had noe more Religion or Devotion in him than a dog'.[72] In the same year Bishop Manningham allowed the choir to have cakes and ale on 'waiting days' when they escorted him to the Cathedral, and he also ordered that at clergy visitations a psalm should be sung before the sermon 'as is usual before the sermon on Sundays'.[73] Another unseemly row on Advent Sunday 1714 involved a lay vicar, Robert Clarke, who refused to sing the anthem and quarrelled with Thomas Evans, the succentor, while in 1716 Charles Leaver's misbehaviour included having 'an intimate acquaintance' with a Mrs. Maggot who lived in the Close, and walking around the Cathedral in his surplice during services without taking his place in the quire. He was eventually deprived.[74] The younger Thomas Kelway, who was organist from 1720 to 1744, was also a difficult character and in frequent trouble with the Dean and Chapter.[75] Bishop Waddington tried in 1727 to enforce the wearing of surplices by members of the choir at services,[76] and Bishop Hare told the Dean and Chapter in 1733 'to inspect into and correct and reforme the morals of the organist, lay clerks and other ministers of the Church'.[77] James Allen, a vicar choral, was a persistent drunkard and even disturbed services in 1746 by his inebriated behaviour.[78]

A detailed catalogue of the music books belonging to the Cathedral in 1767 has survived.[79] This is divided into three sections and lists music kept in the organ loft and the quire, some 'anthems in score' and a quantity of music bought the previous day from Thomas Capel, the organist from 1744 to 1776. Capel had been ill and unable to do his work since 1765.[80] This catalogue includes services by Croft, Gibbons, Aldrich, King, Farrant and Boyce, and anthems by Rogers, Croft and Greene. The anthems in score were composed by such composers as Croft, Stroud, Greene, Clarke, Kent, Boyce, Goldwin, Tucker, Nares, Turner and Bishop. The music bought from Capel consisted of 14 individual service settings, all the services and anthems written by Thomas Kelway, several anthems by Kent and individual anthems by Byrd, Clarke, Turner, Richardson, Purcell and Aldrich, and some psalms set by Tallis. Because some of the entries in this list are very vague—such as 'ten books of services and anthems by different hands'—it is impossible to determine the full range of the repertoire in the 1760s, though it was clearly quite extensive. Christopher Dearnley has pointed out that most of the music is from the 18th century, with only four Tudor composers in the list.[81]

The information in this list may be supplemented in two ways. First, from the Communar's Accounts in the 18th century we know of several purchases of music. For example, Boyce's anthems and the three volumes of his *Cathedral Music* were bought in 1753, 1769 and 1773, and further anthems by Nares and Hayes in 1795.[82] Secondly, there are various manuscript books which survive from the 17th and 18th centuries. The County Record Office has a volume of sacred and secular music which belonged to John Walter in the late 17th century. Other volumes contain 29 anthems by Greene, transcribed by Kelway, and three evening services and three anthems by Kelway.[83] The Cathedral Library possesses a single counter-tenor part book of unknown date, but probably of the mid-18th century.[84] This contains many of the typical 18th-century composers we have already mentioned, but also includes five anthems by Blow and seven by Wise. The most popular anthem composer was William Turner, who died in 1740, but there is nothing by Boyce. At the other end of the book there are 18 different service settings, including five by William Child. The setting of *Purcell in B flat* is marked 'corrected from Dr Boyce's *Cathedral Music*'. The services contain some little known settings of the *Cantate Domino*, *Deus misereatur* and *Benedicite* by Child.

John Marsh and his Diary

Our knowledge of the music of the Cathedral in the late 18th and early 19th centuries is vividly illuminated from the diary of John Marsh. He was an amateur composer and performer who lived in Chichester from 1787 and was a leading figure in the musical life of the City, especially in the management of concerts at the Assembly Rooms, until his death in 1828. Marsh's first visit to the Cathedral was in 1770, when he was eighteen:

> Being St Luke's day we had the complete service with a voluntary before the first lesson and another after church, the organ being played by Rev. Tireman a Prebendary, as we thought in a very good church style. In the afternoon I had a full leisure to go to the Cathedral again and sat in the organ loft. Having been practising chants much lately, I felt a desire (especially as there were not above 3 or 4 people in the church besides those concerned in the service) to try and play the chant myself, which indeed Mr Hall offered me to do, but thinking I might make some mistake, I did not venture it. Just however at the concluding Gloria Patri I could no longer refrain, but as I stood beside Mr Hall, put my hands round him down upon the keys of the Great Organ and thus made my first attempt in this way.[85]

Richard Hall was the troublesome deputy organist between 1765 and 1771, but by the time Marsh came to live in Chichester the organist was William Walond. During his first year, Marsh was careful not to press his compositions on him too eagerly, and records that only his anthem *O give thanks* and 'a little Hymn of mine done at y^e charity sermon' had been performed in the Cathedral.[86] On Easter Day 1788 Walond rather grudgingly allowed

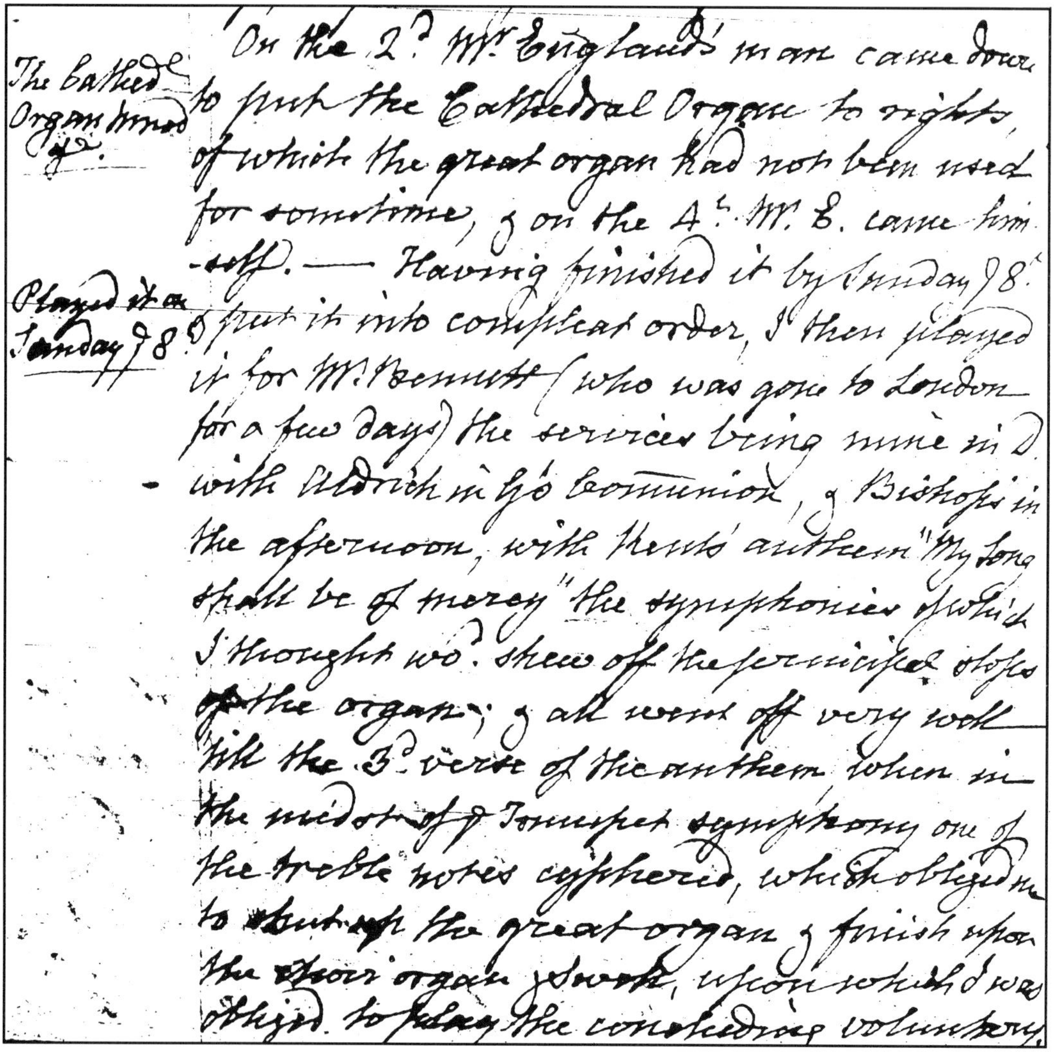
The Cathed.l Organ tuned &c.

Played it on Sunday ye 8.

On the 2.d Mr England's man came down to put the Cathedral Organ to rights, of which the great organ had not been used for sometime, & on the 4.th Mr E. came him-self. — Having finished it by Sunday ye 8.th & put it into compleat order, I then played it for Mr Bennett (who was gone to London for a few days) the services being mine in D with Aldrich in G to Communion, & Bishop's in the afternoon, with Kent's anthem "My Song shall be of mercy" the symphonies of which I thought wo.d shew off the principal stops of the organ; & all went off very well till the 3.d verse of the anthem when in the midst of ye Trumpet symphony one of the treble notes cyphered, which obliged me to shut up the great organ & finish upon the choir organ & Swell, upon which I was obliged to play the concluding voluntary.

137 *Entry for April 1810 from John Marsh's diary.*

Marsh's settings of the Sanctus and Kyries to be sung. One of the lay vicars, Thomas Barber, asked Marsh if they could perform his complete Communion Service in G

> as they wanted another *easy*, *practical* Communion Service, fit for their small choir, for want of which they had lately done nothing but those of *Aldrich in G* and *Rogers in D*.

Marsh had practised it with the choir, but Walond wanted to accompany the service. They had an unseemly argument in the organ loft.[87]

From time to time Marsh deputised both for Walond and his short-lived successor James Target, who was organist from 1801 to 1803. On Easter Day 1802 he

> played *King's in C* for the morning and evening service and my new double chant in C for ye Athanasian Creed; and in ye afternoon accompd. ye anthem of Boyce's 'If we believe that Jesus

> died' which I introduced with a spirited and appropriate Prelude or Voluntary on the Trumpet and Swell, having for ye 1st voluntary played 'I know that my Redeemer liveth', and concluded with the Hallelujah in ye Messiah.[88]

Marsh had a good relationship with the next organist, Thomas Bennett, often deputising for and playing with him. Marsh wrote a Sanctus in E flat to match a setting of the *Kyrie eleison* which Bennett had brought from Salisbury. This was sung the next Sunday

> and went very well, on which morning I sat in ye organ loft and played a new chant of mine in G and my trumpet piece for 2 performers with Mr Bennett.[89]

Bennett and Marsh persuaded the Dean and Chapter to have the organ repaired in 1805-6 by G.P. England and 'were much pleased with its improved state'.[90] In June 1806 Marsh deputised for Bennett twice a day for 10 days,[91] while in Easter week 1807 be 'played the organ on Easter Day, *King in F, Smith in D*, my Sanctus for 3 trebles and Stanley's trumpet voluntary'. In April 1810 he was again deputising for Bennett and played his own service in D

> with *Aldrich in G's* communion, and Bishop's in the afternoon, with Kent's anthem *My song shall be of mercy*,

during which the organ cyphered.[92]

The Nineteenth Century

Several of the vicars choral and lay vicars were prominent in the musical life of the City at this time, taking part in concerts at the Assembly Rooms, St John's Chapel and elsewhere. Two of the best known were Moses Toghill, a vicar choral from 1768 to 1790, when he became a prebendary and was later a canon residentiary from 1798 to 1825:[93] and Robert Atkins, a lay vicar from 1827 to 1861.[94] Sylas Neville's diary gives details of a concert in January 1803:

> In the evening we were at a concert, which ... was one of the best both for music and company ... Mr Toghill, one of the Vicars of the Cathedral, has a most powerful and at the same time melodious Bass voice.[95]

Thomas Bennett and his son, Henry Roberts Bennett, served nearly sixty years between them as organist at the Cathedral, from 1803 to 1860. During this time there was a slow improvement in the standard of the choir, despite many difficulties. The six choristers were augmented to eight in 1849, to 10 in 1865 and to 12 in the following year. Some attended the Prebendal School, but most of them were educated at a special choristers' school established in 1850 in St Faith's,[96] though three years later there were 'complaints' from the boys' parents.[97] This was certainly an improvement on earlier arrangements. When Maria Hackett visited the Cathedral in 1818 she said that

> there is no choir in England, with the single exception of Carlisle, which promises so few advantages to the young persons educating under the auspices of the Chapter. The choristers have occasional lessons in singing from the organist.[98]

At this time they were allowed 'an half quartern loaf of bread each week', and so it may have been hunger which led to complaints of 'irregularities and acts of disobedience' in the following year when new rules for the choristers were drawn up by the Dean and Chapter. They were required to attend Mattins and Evensong daily, 'to be attentive to their duty and to conduct themselves decently and quietly during the time of divine service'. They must obey their master, 'behave in an orderly and respectful manner', and were not allowed to sing in any concerts or private parties without the master's permission, and certainly not at any public house, club or 'convivial evening'. Nevertheless, their conduct was still liable to criticism. A boy called Alfred Angel was expelled in 1828,[99] and Bishop Carr's injunctions of 1825 remarked that the choristers 'frequently conduct themselves in a very improper and disorderly manner'.[100] In 1857 they had the sole right to play in Canon Lane, any other children being prevented from doing so by the police.[101] Until shortly before 1865 they roamed the streets at Christmas, singing carols and asking for money.[102]

When Bishop Carr complained in 1825 that the four lay vicars seldom came to Holy Communion, they used the opportunity of his visitation to point out that they believed that their annual salaries of £24 13s. 4d. were the lowest in the country.[103] They were raised to £30 in 1826,[104] and varied in 1831 between £50 and £20. On weekdays there was only one man to a part. In 1849 there were seven lay vicars, including two tailors, one schoolmaster and the town crier.[105] Henry Bennett, the organist, told the Cathedral Commission in 1854 that the six lay vicars had 'to strain their voices to produce the effect of chorus'.[106] Their annual stipends were raised to £55 in that year 'in consequence of the continued high price of provisions'.[107]

In 1823 Thomas Bennett published the collected works of the anthems then sung in the Cathedral. This gives us some idea of the repertoire, though it does not include details of the service settings. Some 155 anthems were in use. Many composers, such as Battishill, Byrd, Haydn, Travers and Tye, were represented by a single anthem. The most popular composer was Maurice Greene, with 15 anthems, but the Cathedral had owned his printed *Forty Anthems* since 1743 and Kelway had transcribed 29 of them.[108] Kent with 14 anthems and Hayes with 10, followed by Croft with nine, came next. Altogether some fifty composers are represented, only five of them being from before the Restoration. The resources available to the Cathedral choir were rather greater than Bennett's collection indicates. Several dozen bound volumes of 18th-century and early 19th-century music have survived, but not all the contents were apparently in current use in 1823. For example, the Cathedral's copy of Crotch's anthems contains 10 pieces, but only five of them are listed by Bennett.[109]

Philip Armes, who was organist at Chichester from 1861 to 1863 before going to Durham,[110] was followed in quick succession by six other organists in the next 24 years before the arrival of F.J. Read in 1887. During the years following the fall of the spire in 1861 the Cathedral choir was in a poor condition, though efforts were made to improve it. A form for the formal admission of choristers was drawn up in 1866, and the rule that they must not sing elsewhere was stressed in 1871, 1876 and 1890.[111] Maria Hackett reported that there was an agreeable custom whereby each of the canons arranged an outing for the boys during his annual residence.[112]

In 1875 the Dean and Chapter took urgent action to prevent the lay vicars from singing glees and part-songs once a fortnight at Shoreham Gardens.[113] In 1876, in reply to an House of Commons enquiry, it was stated that the six lay vicars, who were nearly all in their thirties, were paid £60 p.a. plus gratuities, sang twice a day except Mondays and attended regularly.[114] About two years later they told the Dean and Chapter that they did not like to hear Dean Burgon's frequent complaints about them:

> as we have been trained from boyhood under eminent organists and are not entirely ignorant of the art of singing, it is unfair to stigmatize our efforts as 'a disgusting noise', and etc.[115]

In 1880, the lay vicars told the Cathedrals Commission that they attended two rehearsals each week,[116] but that their stipends were quite inadequate:

> we believe ours to be the lowest paid choir in the kingdom and beg respectfully to mention that the character and excellence of the music performed will bear comparison with many cathedral choirs of which the members receive double the amount of our remuneration ... it has been a great struggle for years past for several of us to support our families on so small and totally inadequate a stipend.[117]

F.J. Read combined his work as organist at Chichester between 1887 and 1902 with teaching at the Royal College of Music. He brought with him as his assistant Hugh Allen, later to be a distinguished Oxford organist.[118] These two young men began to transform the Cathedral's music. J.H. Mee, who was appointed precentor in 1889, admired their enthusiasm and said that the lay vicars were reverent with good voices, but that none of the choristers was so gifted. He suggested that some of them should be boarders, so that the choice could be widened beyond those who lived locally. The earliest surviving music list, for the week beginning 30 December 1888, shows that the canticles at Mattins on Wednesdays and Fridays were sung to chants, while the remainder of the week included music by Mendelssohn, Croft, Nares, Goss, Sullivan, Barnby, Hopkins, Boyce and others—a fairly typical scheme of the period.

Dean Randall disliked music, except at the Eucharist, and would even leave his stall when the anthem at Sunday Evensong began. In 1897 an attempt was made to shorten and simplify the musical content of the services. The Mayor and Corporation and about 400 citizens sent a petition to the Dean and Chapter complaining about the changes. The *Chichester Observer* claimed that the Cathedral was

> necessarily regarded as being the home and nursery of high class ecclesiastical music ... 99 out of every 100 who attend the services at the cathedral avowedly go there to reverently listen to and enjoy beautiful music so sweetly rendered by the highly-trained and accomplished choir.[119]

The Early Twentieth Century

Efforts to improve the musical life of the Cathedral in the early years of the present century included an order to sing anthems instead of a hymn at the Wednesday services, and the canticles were to be sung to short settings instead of chants. A Cathedral Oratorio Society was formed, the cathedral choirs of Salisbury and Winchester attended the re-opening of the Cathedral organ (from this grew the annual Southern Cathedrals Festival) and a carol service was introduced at Christmas.[120] The Dean and Chapter kept open the appointment of lay vicars who volunteered for active service in the First World War.[121] In 1918 a Rogation Day of Continuous Prayer for the Empire was held, while, at the St George's Day Service in 1919, all the notables of the county and diocese attended to honour the fallen of Sussex, 'the service concluding with a great burst of triumph in the singing of the Hallelujah chorus by the augmented choir'.[122] When F.J. Read returned to succeed F.J.W. Crowe as organist, the Dean and Chapter praised 'his unremitting care and wonderful success in the training of the boys and men'. When he died in 1925 they referred to 'the magic of his presence' and said that the music 'was maintained by him at the highest level which could possibly be expected'.[123] Dr. Marmaduke Conway, who was organist between 1925 and 1931, was praised for his care for fine psalm-singing and 'reverent and beautiful sung eucharists'. He was keen to encourage the Cathedral choir to sing unaccompanied.

138 *Gustav Holst in the Palace courtyard with his 'heavenly host' for Whit Monday: his daughter Imogen kneels before him holding the music.*

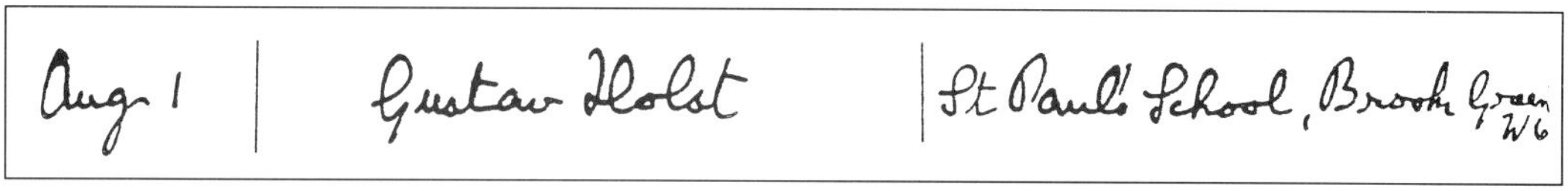

139 *Holst's signature in Bishop Bell's Visitors' Book in 1928, on his first visit to Chichester.*

The advent of George Bell as Bishop and Arthur Duncan-Jones as Dean in 1929 began a distinguished chapter in the life of the Cathedral. The Chapter Acts are full of liturgical and musical changes introduced by the new Dean, who appointed Harvey Grace as his organist in 1931.[124] Grace was also editor of the *Musical Times* and an experienced broadcaster and examiner.[125] Bell's meeting in 1928 and subsequent friendship with Gustav Holst led to the composer transferring his 'heavenly host' in 1930 from Canterbury to sing at Whitsuntide in the Cathedral and the Palace gardens at Chichester. Although Holst died in 1934 (his ashes are interred in the north transept), the singing and dancing continued each year and was resumed after the Second World War.[126] Plainsong began to be used more frequently at the Cathedral services.[127]

Harvey Grace resigned in 1937 and after a long interregnum Horace Hawkins, the organist of Hurstpierpoint College, was appointed to succeed him when it became apparent that Geoffrey Shaw was unavailable.[128] Aged 58 when he came to Chichester, Hawkins stayed for 20 years.[129] Soon some of the lay clerks began to be called up to the forces,[130] and a lady, Mrs. Eve Salwey (later Powell) was appointed to fill one of their places.[131] Mrs. Anne Sheail (now Maddocks) helped Hawkins with the choir-training as assistant organist and later acted as choir librarian.[132] Chamber music recitals helped to brighten the dark days of the war and attracted crowded audiences.[133] The poverty of the Cathedral immediately after the war caused difficulties for the music, though gifts from the *Hymns Ancient and Modern* Trust obtained by Canon Lowther Clarke, and the willingness of the students of the Theological College to sing during the choir holidays kept the services

140 *Horace Hawkins and the choir at practice in the old Song School (now the Canons' Vestry).*

going.[134] One of the most characteristic services was the lovely Epiphany Procession, where the voices of the choristers and the congregation were accompanied by the recorders of the Dolmetsch family.[135] The haunting beauty and devotion of this service had a memorable effect on the writer as a small child.

Soon after the arrival of Walter Hussey as dean in 1955, Archdeacon Lancelot Mason discussed with Dr Boris Ord at King's College, Cambridge, the possibility of ex-choral scholars coming to Chichester as lay vicars and teachers in the Prebendal School.[136] It took some time for this approach to bear fruit. In 1958 Hawkins, who was nearly 79, was asked to retire and John Birch began his notable reign on 17 October when he took the oath as organist and choirmaster.[137]

In Quires and Places ... 1958-1980

Noel Osborne

The recruitment around 1960 of former choral scholars to the cathedral choir brought about a significant change. Beyond four or five collegiate choirs in Oxford and Cambridge, and the London choirs of St Paul's Cathedral and Westminster Abbey, there were few, if any, provincial cathedrals in the top choral flight. It was Dean Hussey's ambition, and one shared by Archdeacon Lancelot Mason, that Chichester should join the élite of the unique British choral tradition. In John Birch—half a century younger than his predecessor Horace Hawkins—the Dean and Chapter appointed an organist of rising international reputation and a Master of the Choristers who soon gathered about him a choir well suited to the new

141 *An early Epiphany Procession.*

challenges of live broadcasts and recordings, of festivals and new commissions, of public concerts and promotional tours. In this he was supported by, among others, Richard Seal (now Dr., and organist and Master of the Choristers at Salisbury Cathedral since 1969) who through the 1960s combined the rôles of assistant organist of the Cathedral and director of music at the Prebendal School.

This close link between Cathedral and choir school was echoed in the appointments of new lay vicars. By 1963 half the lay vicars were former Oxbridge choral scholars, who also taught at the Prebendal School. That these appointments were influenced more by music than by academe is perhaps borne out by subsequent careers, as the choir provided one third of the first-generation King's Singers and several others who became full-time professional musicians.

The Cathedral choir's chief responsibility was, as ever, to sing the daily services; in the early 1960s this meant eight services a week for 48 weeks of the year. The quality of such choirs is measured, not from spectacular showpieces, but through the day-to-day performance of the liturgy. Chichester has long been renowned for the beauty and sensibility of its psalm singing, even against the background accompaniment, during '60s winters, of the noisy refuelling of the coke stoves. It was not by accident that three-quarters of choir practice time could be taken up with one Psalm.

142 *John Birch after receiving a Lambeth Doctorate of Music from Archbishop Runcie in 1990.*

The choir's experiences of reaching beyond the Cathedral had been limited. The BBC broadcast live on Wednesday afternoons the service of choral Evensong. Chichester took its turn on the rota, for a while at that time produced by the Rev. Colin James (now Bishop of Winchester). In 1962 the choir paid its first visit to Chartres, a visit inspired by the new 'twinning' arrangements between the two cities. Also in that year the Chichester Festival Theatre played its first season. John Birch was appointed its Musical Adviser, and at an early stage introduced Christmas concerts in an unheated theatre: the Cathedral choir took part, the audience took blankets and hip flasks.

In 1960 John Birch—together with Alwyn Surplice (Winchester) and Christopher Dearnley (Salisbury)—had re-established the Southern Cathedrals Festival, an annual long-weekend of services and concerts for the three choirs, visiting each cathedral in turn every three years. This is not the place for a chronicle of this major choral festival, but the 1965 Festival in Chichester witnessed the première of Leonard Bernstein's *Chichester Psalms*, conducted by John Birch in the presence of the composer, one of the most successful commissions the SCF is ever likely to make. The circumstances of this commission have been described by Walter Hussey, Humphrey Burton and others, but those who were there will not forget the excitement and the drama of the performance itself.

It was a measure of the esteem in which the choir came to be held that it was invited by EMI to contribute the 20th-century disk in the five-volume *Treasury of English Church Music*, issued in 1966. Other recordings and broadcasts followed, as public interest in sacred choral music increased and Chichester Cathedral choir became better known.[138]

The decade of the 1970s inevitably focuses on the celebrations in 1975 of the Cathedral's ninth centenary. Much has been written elsewhere of 'Chichester 900', the three-week festival under the charismatic direction of Richard Gregson-Williams whose success gave birth to the Cathedral-based Chichester Festivities each July. The opportunity was grasped in this and subsequent festivals to demonstrate the excellence of the Cathedral's music, both in the performances of established works, and in the vision of new commissions, which have so evidently stood the text of time. The list is, to say the least, impressive; and is constantly growing, including from the 1970s: William Walton, *Magnificat* and *Nunc Dimittis* (1975); William Albright, *Chichester Mass* (1975); Lennox Berkeley, *The Lord is my Shepherd* (1975); Kenneth Leighton, *An Evening Hymn* (1979).

The year after the ninth-century celebrations, the choir went back to France, and sang in Chartres (where Bishop Eric presided in the Cathedral at an Anglican celebration of the

Eucharist), in the Château de Brissac-Quincé (already informally twinned with Goodwood House) and in Paris. Three years later, in 1979, another tour celebrated the Year of the Norman Abbey, a chance to sing in some of Normandy's finest Romanesque churches.

In the meantime, Dean Walter Hussey had retired (December 1977) and in 1980 John Birch did likewise, after 22 years at Chichester. One does not say 'in' Chichester, for it is well known that, as a recitalist, examiner and an ambassador for the Cathedral and its choir, he travelled—and still travels—the world. Indeed, 'God is everywhere, John Birch is everywhere but here!' was the plaintive cry that sometimes escaped Dean Hussey's lips. He, though, more than anyone, knew what had been achieved during those two decades. John Birch was succeeded by Alan Thurlow, one of whose immediate tasks was to set in motion the appeal for the restoration of the main organ, which had been silent for too long.

The Organ

Alan Thurlow

Chichester Cathedral organ can claim a special position in the history of English organ building. That there was an instrument in the Cathedral before the Commonwealth is recorded in the Chapter archives although we have no details of the specification or of where the organ was placed. In common with that of other foundations this instrument was destroyed by Cromwell's troops, Bruno Ryves's account relating 'they break down the organs, and dashing the pipes with their pole-axes, scoffing said "Harke, how the organs goe"'.

In the years after the Restoration cathedrals had to work hard to re-establish their musical traditions. Two famous organ-builders, 'Father' Smith and Renatus Harris, vied with each other to build the new organs which were needed. After the organ for Gloucester Cathedral in 1663-5, Chichester, in 1678, gave Harris his second opportunity to build a new cathedral organ, a one-manual instrument of eight stops situated on the Arundel Screen. He went on to build seven more cathedral organs, culminating in the four-manual instrument for Salisbury in 1710.

Thereafter, the story at Chichester followed the normal pattern; organs were rebuilt at periodic intervals and were enlarged on each occasion to take account of increasing musical requirements and the opportunities afforded by the developing skills and technology of the craftsmen. In 1725 Byfield added the second (choir) manual, a division of four stops placed in a case behind the player's back on the east side of the screen; the two flute stops in the choir organ today date from that period. In 1778 a five-stop Swell organ was added by Thomas Knight and at the same time a second, new, Open Diapason was added to the Great Organ, the pipes forming a new front for the instrument on the west side and facing down the nave.

It was, however, the 19th century which provided the distinctive part of the history of the instrument. In the early years of the century the previous pattern was maintained. G.P. England worked on the organ in 1806 and added the first pedal-board ('pull-downs' to work the manuals rather than a pedal organ with pipes of its own). Pedal pipes were added by Pilcher in 1829 and Gray & Davison carried out further work in 1844.

In 1849 the great English builder William Hill became involved with the Chichester organ and ten years later, following the fashion of the time, was responsible for moving it from the screen to its present position in the north transept. This allowed for the removal of the screen in 1860 and the subsequent unification of the nave and quire. In 1861 the

143 *The restored organ, 1986.*

collapse of the tower and spire had important consequences for the organ as well as for the building, for this was the period when the historic organs which had evolved during the previous two centuries, and which provided important evidence of the work of the earlier builders, were being removed in favour of the larger and more powerful romantic organs pioneered from the time of the Great Exhibition by the legendary 'Father' Willis.

Fortunately, in Chichester this was not to be. All the funds that could be raised were needed for the restoration of the building and the internal furnishings which had been destroyed or damaged by the falling masonry. The organ casework had been destroyed but the pipework had been saved so, in order to provide music for the services once the building was re-opened, the organ was first rebuilt with no case and with all the workings visible. Later, in 1888, Arthur Hill built the distinguished front case which we know today and which was eventually completed in matching style at the sides and back in the restoration of 1986.

In 1904 the organ was again rebuilt, this time by Hele of Plymouth, and the playing action was changed from mechanical to pneumatic. In terms of the pipework, however, Hele's alterations were conservative and it is due to his foresight that the character of the organ appears not to have been altered in any adverse way at this period of its history. Hele's pneumatic action lasted until 1972 (no mean feat for an instrument in constant daily use), by which time many of the soundboards, which dated from earlier periods, were in very poor condition. In the autumn of that year the organ was deemed unplayable and as the money for a full and proper restoration could not be raised (this was a time when much money was needed for structural work on the building) it was abandoned in favour of an Allen electronic organ which remained in use for all services for the next fourteen years.

In 1982 an organ committee was established under the chairmanship of Sir John Barnes. By 1986, when the pipe organ came back into use, £300,000 had been raised to pay for the work. The fine craftsmanship of N.P. Mander Ltd. was completed in time for the Royal Maundy service in that year although the actual service of dedication, at which the preacher was the Right Honourable Edward Heath, did not take place until June.

The organ was enlarged to four manuals (in keeping with Hill's suggestion of 1873) but the additions were carefully styled in the manner of Hill. A new mechanical action was built, the casework was completed, and the original painted decoration of 1678 on the distinguished Harris pipes of the front case was restored by Anna Plowden. A new nave section was added, playable from the great or solo keys of the main organ or from its own console at floor level on the north side of the building; this provides valuable support for congregational singing in the building on Sundays and on large occasions.

Through good fortune the Chichester organ survived not only removal during the Victorian era but also the electrification and enlargement which characterised English organ-building in the middle years of the 20th century. Today its clarity and gentle, unforced tone provide a rare insight into the beauty and delicacy of the work of early English organ-builders.

XIV *Henry King, Bishop 1642-69 (portrait in Chichester Council Chamber).*

XV *18th-century overmantel to the fireplace in the Lady Chapel Library (now in the library of Rapers, Solicitors).*

XVI *Charles Crocker, 19th-century verger, poet and sub-Librarian.*

XVII *The quire in the early 19th century, looking west (water colour by Thomas King), with box pews, returned stalls and the painted ceiling beyond.*

XVIII *The quire in the early 19th century, looking east (water colour by Thomas King), showing the galleries above the quire, members of Chapter and ladies of the Close, the dress of the choristers and vicars, a charity school to the east, and the pre-1829 reredos.*

XIX *The ringing chamber of the Bell Tower in the late 19th century, showing the squinch arches which convert it into an octagonal room, and the paintwork of the 19th-century restoration.*

XX *The two versions of Sutherland's 'Noli me tangere' (that on the right chosen for the Cathedral by Chapter, the other retained by Dean Hussey) and the restored Mary Magdalene Chapel.*

XXI *The* Baptism of Christ *by Hans Feibusch in its original position, masking the blocked-up south-west (Bishop's) door into the Cathedral.*

XVI

The Cathedral and Modern Art

David Coke and Robert Potter

> Through works of art man probably reaches the highest achievement of which he is capable, and so such works are surely the most appropriate offerings to God.
>
> Walter Hussey in *Time*, 21 July 1947, p.31

The creation of a body of successful works of art in a major cathedral church is only possible with a very unusual set of circumstances and combination of personalities.

In Chichester, this has happened twice since the building of the Cathedral. Once, as already described, in the early 16th century; the second time over three hundred years later.

The right circumstances were provided by the existence of a dynamic school of young and inspired artists in this country, a general need for renewal and hope for the future, and a strong Church. The combination of personalities in Chichester included the bishop, Dr. George Bell; his chosen dean, Walter Hussey and an artist, the German, Hans Feibusch (b.1898).

144 *Walter Hussey. Drawing by Hans Feibusch.*

For the purposes of this chapter, a work of art is considered to involve the creation of something new, unexpected or challenging, something to make the viewer think, something that can become a focus for our imagination. A work of art should set up a dialogue with the viewer that is more than just a one-way aesthetic appreciation. A work of art is the realisation of the artist's personal conception of a particular theme. Furnishings, embroideries, calligraphy, inscriptions, or other items of craftwork or design will not be considered, although the metalwork (1953-75) of Desmond Clen-Murphy to be seen in Stephen Buzas' Treasury (1979) and in the cross over the altar in St George's Chapel at the west end of the south aisle is worthy of notice.

Artistic activity in the Cathedral for the first half of the century appears to have been almost entirely non-existent. Our time span is entirely post-war (*c.*1950-85) and begins at a period of great change in British art; to most people, 'modern art' was alien, mysterious, or a subject for ridicule. Emotional or romantic art was unfashionable; the arts had become secularised, abstracted and introverted, involved in an endless search for novelty and the church authorities had been frightened off.

To Bishop Bell though, modern art was a vital part of life and so a vital element of modern religion. In the visual arts he was strongly influenced by Hans Feibusch, whose revolutionary book, *Mural Painting*, was published in 1946.[1] This book, ostensibly a practical guide to its subject, is more importantly a rallying-call to the church authorities, urging them to make good use of the emerging school of young and powerful British artists.

> The artists are more than ready; modern painting possesses the requirements to a degree not reached for more than one hundred years. It is for the leaders of the Church to take the initiative, to commission the best artists, the real representatives of our time, to give them intelligent guidance in a sphere new to them, and to have sufficient confidence in their artistic and human quality to give them free play.[2]

The friendship between Bell and Feibusch led to a series of commissions for churches within the see of Chichester. But two of the most important of Feibusch's works for Bell are in Chichester: The *Baptism of Christ* in the Cathedral baptistry (painted in 1951 when the artist was already 53) and the *Ascension* in the Bishop's private chapel (1953). Bishop Bell had received a gift of £200 that he wanted to devote to a mural painting in the Cathedral.[3] The baptistry was, at the time, free of ornament and had a rather unsightly filled-in doorway that had lost its purpose due to the build-up of soil outside in the churchyard. This, then, was to be the site of the new mural. But the Chapter were not happy and at their meeting of 15 June 1951 it was

> resolved that the Dean should write to the Bishop explaining that if the mural had been offered by anyone else but his lordship, the Chapter would have felt bound to decline it, as they were not convinced that it was a great work of art.[4]

In an article written only three years after the completion of the *Baptism* mural, Hans Feibusch wrote of it that

> the setting, a three-foot-deep niche underneath a window, demanded a relief-like, strongly modelled panel, with large forms, easily readable and strong in colour in the dim light. The simple and rather austere character of the Cathedral asked for a similar style in drawing and the avoidance of naturalistic colour; but, while using simple forms, I tried to resist the temptation to archaise them. The colour is based on the grey-green of the Cathedral stone, which helps to relate my painting to the surroundings; contours and deep shadows are black or mahogany, and there are some patches of yellow and orange, and in the background, of bright blue.[5]

Earlier in the same article he explains that,

> A work of art in a church is there to help the worshipper, to lead his thoughts from the tumultuous outer world towards an inner spiritual one, and to serve as a point of departure for his meditations.[6]

Representations of the Baptism of Christ in the history of art are surprisingly uncommon, but one that would certainly have been known to Feibusch is the Piero della Francesca in the National Gallery, London, painted in the 1450s. The composition of the Chichester mural is almost identical to Piero's except in the position of Christ's arms. Also, Piero introduces many ancillary figures in a perspectival landscape, whereas Feibusch respects the flatness of the wall surface, presenting a hieratic image, transcending the humanity of the figures, isolating them in a symbolic abstraction that some viewers find disturbing.[7]

In the early 1970s, when the churchyard was levelled, the old doorway was re-opened for the benefit of wheelchairs. The work was thus displaced, much to the artist's displeasure and in its present position, on the west wall, appears to float. The mural is signed '51/77' denoting the original date, as well as the date when it was touched up and repaired by Feibusch himself after the move.

Bishop Bell was well acquainted with another churchman who not only shared his belief that churches should give a lead in the 'revival of that association of religion and art which has meant so much to the whole religious and spiritual life of the country',[8] but who also had the courage and vision to act upon that belief. That man was Walter Hussey, vicar of St Matthew's church, Northampton, since 1938. So when the post of dean of Chichester Cathedral fell vacant on the death of Dean Duncan-Jones on 19 January 1955, Bell's suggestion that Hussey should be appointed was accepted, so ensuring that Chichester would play a leading rôle in the 20th-century renaissance of church art.

Walter Hussey also knew and admired Hans Feibusch; he agreed strongly with Feibusch when he wrote

> I should like to shake up both architects and painters to overcome the anaemia and whimsicality that have become a characteristic of mural painting, or, at any rate, to keep them in their place in ladies' drawing-rooms and nurseries; but to let churches be decorated by such men as Georges Rouault or Graham Sutherland, in whom there is fire ... There is another danger against which I would like to warn church authorities, architects, painters and sculptors: that of talking baby language ... The men who come home from the war, and all the rest of us, have seen too much horror and evil; ... The voice of the Church should be heard loud over the thunderstorm; and the artist should be her mouthpiece, as of old ...[9]

Whilst at St Matthew's, and under the difficult conditions of war-time and its aftermath, Hussey had commissioned two of the outstanding works of 20th-century religious art: Henry Moore's life-sized *Madonna and Child* of 1944, and Graham Sutherland's dramatic and tortured *Crucifixion* of 1947. He had also persuaded Benjamin Britten to compose a setting of Christopher Smart's poem *Rejoice in the Lamb* and sponsored performances by some of the greatest singers, musicians and literary figures of the time.

Arriving in Chichester in 1955, Hussey was well aware that his reputation as a patron of avant-garde, controversial and deeply suspect artists had preceded him. He therefore lay low for a while, allowing the Cathedral and City of Chichester to get to know him, gaining their confidence and support so that they would become willing partners in his future projects for introducing the 20th century into the Cathedral. Apart from some minor works in partnership with the Naval Association, in the Sailors' Chapel,[10] for which John Skelton provided a simple wooden cross, the first intimations of Dean Hussey's eagerness to replace some of the 'tatty and makeshift' elements of the Cathedral fittings with something new come in a letter from the Dean to the Cathedral architect Robert Potter of 16 January 1957[11] in which Hussey invited him 'to come and advise on the redecoration of St Mary Magdalene's chapel in the Cathedral. The Friends have allotted some money for this purpose.'

The Chapel had been restored and furnished with a reredos and panelling to the designs of G.F. Bodley in 1909; it was towards the end of this distinguished architect's life and it is more likely that the refurnishing of this little chapel was the work of his partner Hare. The walls were decorated by Miss Lowndes with frescoes illustrating the life of St

145 *Cross by John Skelton for St Michael's (the Sailors') Chapel.*

Mary Magdalene and St Richard of Chichester. The frescoes were peeling and a panelled dado painted by Miss Lowndes had perished as a result of damp and fungal attack.[12]

In his report to the Dean and Chapter of 21 June 1957, Robert Potter said he did not regard this late work of Bodley's of sufficient merit to be worthy of preservation and he recommended the entire removal of these furnishings. He proposed a freestanding altar in stone set upon a footpace: behind the altar he suggested figures of Our Lord and Mary Magdalene to be executed by a contemporary sculptor, possibly Barbara Hepworth.

The Cathedrals Advisory Commission agreed that both frescoes and reredos should go. In his subsequent report to the Dean and Chapter dated 21 April 1958 Potter wrote:

> My first thoughts were of sculpted figures of Our Lord appearing to Mary Magdalen on Easter morning, but with further thought, I feel that after the removal of the present panelling and pictures the Chapel will require colour and this should be provided by a painting.

This letter also confirms that Graham Sutherland had been appointed to undertake the commission, but it was the autumn of the following year before Sutherland had applied himself to thinking seriously about the project.[13] He was already very busy that year on the Coventry tapestry design and preparation for a major American exhibition of his work, as well as a portrait of Walter Hussey, a private commission from the Dean.

Hussey had wanted a Sutherland work for the Cathedral, and the Mary Magdalene altarpiece provided just the right vehicle. The subject, a *Noli Me Tangere*, was unusual, challenging and full of potential, and the chapel itself a small but very important site. Sir Basil Spence described the view down the south aisle with the Mary Magdalene chapel at the end as 'one of the most beautiful in Europe',[14] and the painting had to work from a hundred yards away as well as from a few feet.

From the start, Sutherland was uneasy and insecure about the commission. In a letter to Hussey of 22 October 1960, he confesses,

> I won't pretend that I don't start such projects like a fish out of water—since we, the artists of today are (alas!) not acclimatised at the start. Be that as it may, I'm always intrigued to try something for you, and so strong is my feeling for your example that I must confess I do push myself to the limit. Everything you ask poses a problem and I suppose I like problems![15]

Sutherland brought to the Cathedral a number of sketches and trial versions for the picture to show to members of the Administrative Chapter. He provided on 21 October 1960 two final versions for consideration: one was accepted for the Cathedral and the other is now, with the rest of Dean Hussey's bequest, at Pallant House (Plate XX).

Even more than the *Baptism of Christ*, the *Noli Me Tangere* is a real rarity in the history of art. Only two other predecessors spring to mind, those by Fra Angelico (*c.*1440, Convent of San Marco, Florence) and by Rembrandt (1638, Royal Collection, Buckingham Palace), despite the fact that this moment, recorded in the Gospel of St John, chapter XX: 11-18,[16] is one of the most significant of early Christian history, the first realisation by a mortal that Christ had risen from the dead. Sutherland's composition owes nothing to Fra Angelico, and to Rembrandt only the inclusion of Christ's hat, and the steps as a central motif.

Sutherland's painting is full of tensions, both artistic and emotional. The distress, shock and confusion and ultimate amazement of Mary Magdalene are highlighted by the strong horizontals and verticals, by the startling colour combinations, and by the relationship of the two zig-zag figures that dominate this small but immensely powerful work, all illuminated by a strong light from the left, casting strong shadows. The symbolism of the painting is highly complex and largely personal to the artist (the setting is said to derive from his garden in the south of France). Sutherland is fighting against the illustrative and narrative tradition of church art, avoiding any obvious or accepted version of the Bible.

To complete the refurbishment of the chapel, the Cathedral Friends, through Hussey, commissioned a pair of candlesticks (1960), and a Communion rail (1962) from that 'tough and unsentimental' artist,[17] the versatile Geoffrey Clarke (b.1924)—also involved at Coventry—and a new altar designed by Robert Potter. Clarke's metalwork is all in cast aluminium and absolutely plain, depending solely upon its shape and texture. 'I feel,' said Clarke, 'this is what will look best in the chapel.'[18] The artist also gave a bookrest for the altar of this chapel.

The altar was made to the architect's design in Purbeck stone, quarried and fashioned by W.J. Haysom of Worth Matravers. It was installed by Norman and Burt on 30 May 1960. The work to the chapel was paid for by the Friends of the Cathedral, and the chapel was re-dedicated on 5 April 1961,[19] before the arrival of the Communion rails in July of the following year.

The chapel was the subject of a major notice in *The Guardian* newspaper on Friday, 7 April 1961 by one of the most eminent critics of the day, Eric Newton:

146 *St Mary Magdalene's Chapel: a. before the 1909 restoration*

> The altar itself, a flat slab of grey-white stone, giving an effect of enormous weight and resting on a stone block, devoid of ornament, with nothing to arrest the eye but its inherent beauty of proportion, is entirely successful seen from any distance. The two candlesticks rise from heavy bases on either side in gentle but robust curves that frame the rectangular monolith between them and give it unexpected vitality. Sutherland's altarpiece—necessarily modest in size or the chapel itself would have been dwarfed—is bright and jewel-like in colour, and therefore equally telling at almost any distance ...

> That Graham Sutherland is almost the only living artist capable of expressing the full intensity of a Christian theme is now proved ... this small-scale interpretation of a miracle ... involves more than effective symbolism. It required the visualisation of a human situation with supernatural implications. To paint the Son of God momentarily mistaken for a gardener is surely more difficult than to visualise Christ crucified or Christ enthroned.

Not all the citizens of Chichester agreed that it was the jewel in their crown, but it took Mabel Winifred Norris, a 46-year-old spinster of no fixed address, but smartly dressed and spoken,[20] to translate this feeling into action when she defaced the picture with a biro, causing £50 worth of damage. 'This picture fills me with loathing', she said, 'this is a Cathedral that belongs to the people ...'

While work was progressing on the chapel, Hussey was not content to wait before commissioning other works. Reynolds Stone produced an engraved design for the cover of the *Chichester Cathedral Journal* in 1958 (still in use), and was involved in the design and layout of the journal itself into the following year.[21] John Baker made a small octagonal stained-glass window, *Christ Rescuing St Peter from the Sea*, for the Sailors' Chapel in 1960. The Dean had also been in correspondence with John Piper since 1952 about the design of vestments. On his retirement from Northampton, Hussey was presented with a cope by Piper. The design and making of this were not actually complete until early in 1958.[22] It was made in silk appliqué by Scott Gray and with an enamelled morse by John and Daphne

b. with Miss Lowndes' panels on the life of St Richard.

Lord. Hussey recalls that he wore it on festival days, when it tended to emphasise the drabness of the other vestments,[23] so it was suggested (whether by the clergy themselves or by Hussey is not clear) that a new project for the Friends' consideration could be the provision of a new set of copes. 'They all wanted copes that would register', Hussey later recalled, 'and I remember when I told Kenneth Clark about them he said that Ceri Richards was our best designer. Kenneth Clark was a marvellous adviser and wonderful publicity agent.'[24]

Richards (1903-71) agreed to work on the project, and was visited by Hussey and Robert Potter in February 1960.[25] After discussions in detail, the artist agreed to submit some sketches. The emphasis was upon powerful coloured patterns for the hoods against plain orphreys (two red, two blue and two light yellow). After accustoming themselves to Ceri Richards' *avant garde* approach, the Chapter accepted with enthusiasm the designs for six copes. They were made by the Embroidery Department of Bromley College of Art and paid for by the Friends and by a bequest from Miss Younghusband (see Plate XXV).

All the copes were complete by August 1962, when Richards writes to Hussey: 'I was pleased to hear from you and to know the news about the arrival of the copes, and your agreeable reactions. I am so very pleased that you like them so much.'[26]

The great effectiveness of these designs is that they work so well at a distance, unlike the traditional cope, covered with embroidery and metallic thread, that really needs to be seen at close range in order to appreciate the design and workmanship. Richards's original designs are now amongst Walter Hussey's collection at Pallant House (133-142).[27]

In parallel with these activities the Dean and Chapter decided to re-erect, as a memorial to Bishop Bell, the Arundel Screen, the stones at this time were cemented into the base of the bell tower. Robert Potter, employing Benfield and Loxley of Oxford, now implemented plans by W.H. Randall Blacking which had retained the visual link between the nave and quire by creating arched openings in the solid rear walls. The completed project

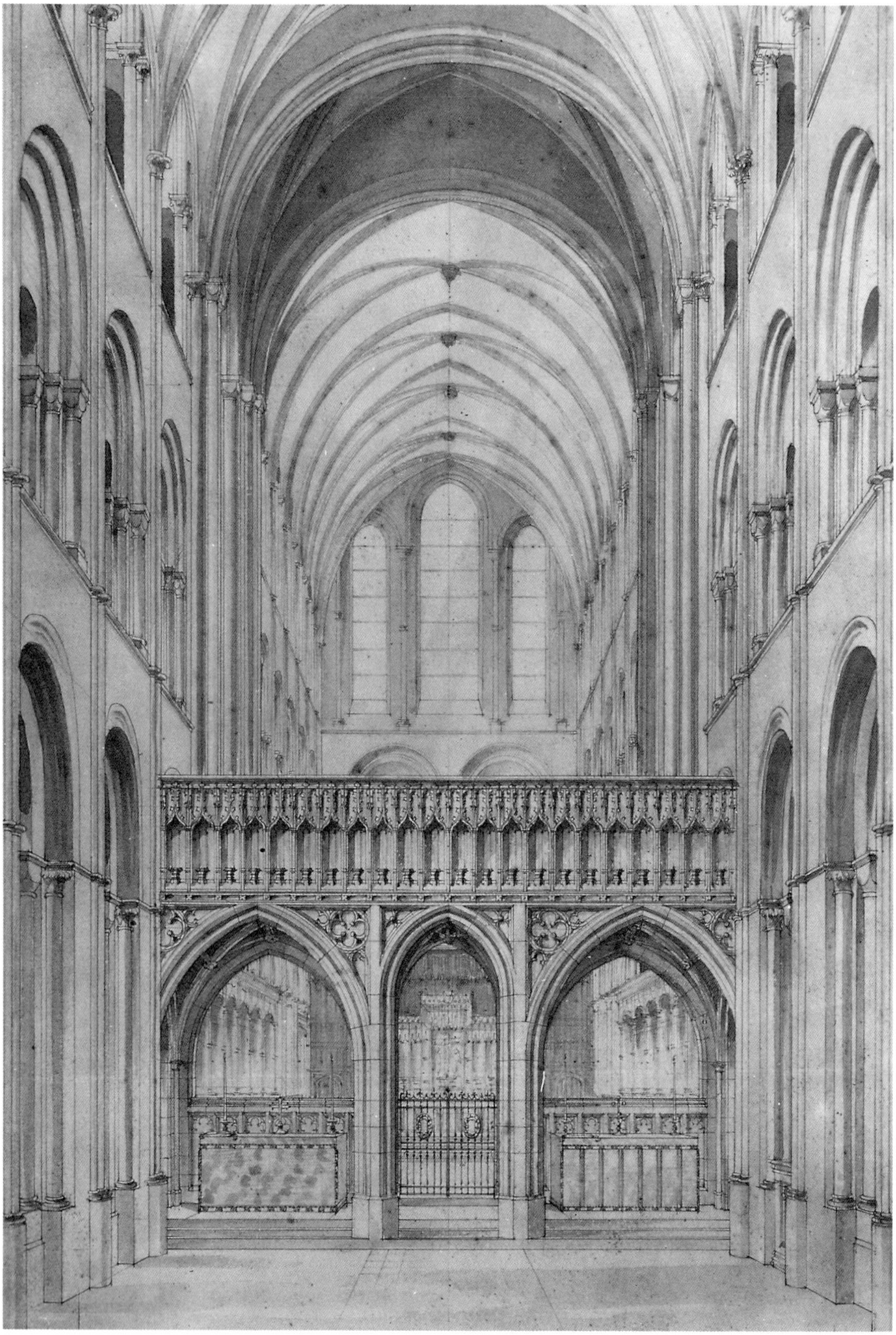

147 *Randall Blacking's plan to restore the Arundel Screen.*

was dedicated as the Bell-Arundel Screen by the Bishop of Chichester in the presence of the Archbishop of Canterbury on 4 November 1961. The memorial tablet, a bas-relief of the head of Bishop Bell, the work of Mary Gillick O.B.E., is placed at the south-east corner of the screen (fig.124).[28]

Dean Hook's memorial pulpit had been condemned even by Sir John Betjeman. Hussey's requirement was that it should be replaced by 'a pulpit hugging the pillar, with the pillar forming the back'. Geoffrey Clarke and Robert Potter together produced the design, which was implemented with the assistance of the structural engineer, Peter Taylor.[29] The free-standing structure of the pulpit is of reinforced concrete formed as a 'wish-bone' with its counter-balancing base concealed beneath the floor, the front panel being decorated with an abstract Cross-motif in bas-relief. The cladding is in aluminium, designed and cast by Geoffrey Clarke: the lining is in leather and the desk, top-rail and floor are of timber. It was completed and erected by April 1966. Robert Potter said in a letter[30] that 'It was a joy to work with Geoffrey Clarke, a "partnership" which extended throughout my time at the Cathedral. Possibly our most exciting challenge was the Nave Pulpit.'

Dean Holtby writes that Geoffrey Clarke's work runs 'like a thread throughout the Cathedral': apart from the pulpit, and the furnishings of the Mary Magdalene chapel, he also undertook other work, including a lectern, given by Lady Holland in 1972, at present moved to the retroquire. On St Richard's altar (designed by Robert Potter in 1984), is a pair of squat candlesticks, and in front of it is a pair of three-tiered votive candle-stands, all commissioned by Dean Holtby and made of cast aluminium. In 1973, Clarke was also asked to provide 12 door handles and plates for the new glass doors at the west end (a commission originally intended for Henry Moore), which he did at a cost of £1,180.[31] Two of his tripod stands are now used for flower arrangements.

By the early 1960s, the high altar and sanctuary were considered to be drab, gloomy, undistinguished and by far the least satisfactory area of the Cathedral. The 1910 reredos by Somers Clarke in painted wood, considered to be mediocre, was removed, revealing the full expanse of the wooden Sherburne screen with its seven plain bays separated by slim carved buttresses and crowned with Gothic canopies. Discussions between Robert Potter and Walter Hussey led to the search for some strong colour in this area. In the matter of selecting the most suitable artist, Hussey sought the advice of Henry Moore, who suggested John Piper.[32] There was some idea that Moore himself might have been involved in the design of the high altar, but this was not to be.

148 *The restored screen, with Robert Potter's and Geoffrey Clarke's new pulpit.*

For the high altar Hussey thought a painting was required, but Piper suggested tapestry strips, to hang between the buttresses, and to be read as a whole across the full width of the screen.

A letter from Piper to Hussey of 24 January 1966 reveals a little of the decision-making processes and explains his suggestion. Robert Potter and he had a long meeting

> to consider the High Altar and Reredos, and he [Potter] has produced a large (and excellent) photograph which is almost as good as being at Chichester. After considering all possible treatments, we have come to think again in the end of *tapestry*. I hope you won't be shocked at this, on grounds of expense or otherwise. Would you give it a thought in terms of 7 separate tapestries 36" wide and about 15' high ... I would like to invent a *figure* scheme ... We feel that finely-wrought work (such as enamels) would make too small a show in the long view, and that any material such as fibre glass would look too 'unprecious' and unsympathetic for such a position ... I see them in my mind at present as a sort of development, in weaving terms, of the kind of figures you have in my Oundle [window] sketch.[33]

Although this was Piper's first venture into tapestry, he was, of course, familiar with Graham Sutherland's *Christ in Glory* for Coventry, and there was already in Chichester another modern tapestry, the *Creation* by Jean Lurçat (1962), in the chapel of Bishop Otter College. Together with Madame Marie Cuttoli at Aubusson, Lurçat (1892-1966) had been responsible for the revival of tapestry in France from the late 1930s. Like Lurçat, Piper was interested in tapestry as an art form in its own right, not merely as a vehicle for the enlargement of paintings, and he spent much time studying renaissance examples 'to see how they managed it'.[34] In the same article, Piper admits that the commission caused many problems, while teaching him a great deal.

> ... it drove me nearly mad. You have to think out a way of working one colour into other: it's a problem each artist has to solve in his own way, and eventually I adapted the marbling technique which I use a lot in my paintings. Above all I wanted to avoid the jagged edges which you always get in Jean Lurçat's tapestries.

He says that the Chichester Tapestry was 'in some ways the most frightening commission I have received'.

In March 1964, Piper sent Hussey four sketches 'very early and immature ... like scribbles on the back of an envelope for a poem. Show any, or all, or none of them to the Friends' Council, as you think best.'[35] The Friends were enthusiastic about the scheme, and immediately contributed £200 towards initial costs, later approving the project as an objective for fund-raising.[36]

One of the original four sketches[37] was based on a single figure in each of the seven bays, but the Friends' Council, probably on Hussey's advice, tended towards the more abstract and Kandinskyesque approach of other sketches, which were based on an idea put to the artist by his old friend the Rev. Dr. Moelwyn Merchant; 'and in working out the design over the following long period, I found his suggested arrangement worked well in practice, without any alterations (see Plates XXII and XXIII).'[38]

The principal scheme, taking up the three wider central bays of the screen, and slightly raised so as not to be obscured by the altar, is *The Trinity* (the dedication of the Cathedral), represented by a bright green triangle amongst flames, overlayed by symbols for *The Father* (a white light), *The Son* (a Tau cross with a symbolic wound on each arm), and *The Holy Spirit* (a feathered flame). This central feature of the Trinity is set between the four elements of the natural world—*Earth*, *Air*, *Fire* and *Water*—all depicted as abstract pattern, and the messengers of the spiritual world, the *Four Evangelists*, symbolically shown (as described in the *Book of Revelation*) below the elements in the outer four bays. The symbols of the evangelists bear more than a passing relationship to Graham Sutherland's treatment of the same subject in the Coventry tapestry.

Following approval of the artist's final sketch, shown to the Council of the Friends in January 1965 along with some quarter-size cartoons that could be hung in position,[39] Piper started work on the full-sized cartoon, executed in collage with poster-paint background, and details picked out in gouache, occasionally mixed with ink or acrylic, on white cartridge paper.[40] These cartoons were executed full size by Piper and not, as is usual, photographically enlarged.

In the meantime, and having spoken to Norman Thurston the Coventry bursar, Piper had approached Pinton Frères at Felletin near Aubusson, who had woven the Sutherland Tapestry (about eight times as large).[41] Pinton accepted Piper's ideas as practicable, and wrote to Hussey that the designs were very beautiful and that they would be very honoured to be able to make the tapestries to embellish the Cathedral.[42]

One major problem was raised at the January meeting by the Archdeacon, Lancelot Mason, who pointed out the absence of a symbol in the central composition for God the Father:

> I find the Archdeacon's comments, at this 11th hour, unnerving; and I foresee the greatest trouble in meeting his demands. Why did he not make them in October when he saw earlier sketches, since when the idea has crystallized in three large paintings which it is very difficult to go back on? *Must I*?[43]

But after a visit in February to a friend, Victor Kenna, rector of Farringdon near Exeter, whose advice the artist had sought, Piper wrote, with a sketch

> The answer to our problem is: to have a white light up on the left. Will work on this plan as soon as I am home, first wk. in March.[44]

By the beginning of October, Pinton had prepared a sample (*l'échantillon*), showing the winged calf of St Luke on a blue ground,[45] and, following approval of this, the tapestry itself was woven between February and July 1966.

Transport was arranged through the Arts Council, customs clearance and duty-free status authorised by the Board of Trade and Mr. Dick Doman, a Chichester upholsterer, appointed to line and hang the strips, all in time for the unveiling on 20 September 1966.[46]

There was a good deal of public reaction to the tapestry, much of which is preserved in the Hussey archive[47] in the form of letters of praise for its warmth and liveliness or protest at its garishness. Hussey himself wrote that

> There were perhaps more words of disapproval of the Tapestry than of anything else done at Chichester during my twenty-two years there. I think this was largely due to its prominent position; it couldn't be ignored, but drew the eye to that part of the cathedral, as indeed it was meant to do.

The new altar fronting the tapestry was made from Purbeck stone by Haysom to the design of Robert Potter: it was installed by the Cathedral Works Organisation on 17 June 1967.

Soon after the installation of the tapestry, Piper designed for the Cathedral a set of festival vestments consisting of a chasuble, dalmatic and tunicle. These were in yellow Thai silk with appliquéd purple spiral motifs. Made by Louis Grossé in time for Christmas

1967, they were designed to complement the tapestry and were purely decorative in intent.[48]

Both the Piper and the Richards vestments were really intended for special use only, so Robert Potter designed an 'everyday' set of copes, of two different shades of colour running vertically from hood to hem, also made by Grossé, in 1969.[49]

In July 1972, the Dean and Chapter's minutes record that Mr. Richard Cox wished to donate an altar frontal for St Clement's Chapel in the south aisle in memory of his wife, Muriel. The first design he submitted was rejected but a second one was accepted in October.[50] Nothing else is said about this in the minutes, and Walter Hussey does not mention it in *Patron of Art*, but he was, by the end of that year, in correspondence with Cecil Collins (1908-89) about the frontal.[51] Cecil Collins' painting, *The Icon of Divine Light*, was completed and installed by August 1973 and dedicated at Allhallowtide, the third of November.[52]

At the top of the wooden frame is inscribed 'Behold I make all things new. Rev. XXI.5.' The iconography of the painting is complex, but the following extract from the artist's own explanation gives the basic symbolism:

> The icon represents a vision of God as the Divine Sun, the Renewer of the world, the eternal Spring Time, which Returns man's consciousness from exile to the original Beauty of his true destiny ... this Sun is the creative Heart of eternal life, it is both dynamic and expanding in Light, and simultaneously in Peace and Harmony unifying all things ... the stars are all the souls in this world, and in all the worlds, who are conscious and aware of the Prescence [*sic*] of the Divine Light, and who Reflect it in their lives, who therefore live in a continuum of eternal life ... It is painted in one single colour only, so that it radiates one basic harmony. The function of the Icon is to serve as a Support for contemplation of the mystery of Divine Light.[53]

One contemporary critic says of the painting: 'Mr Collins infuses it with a Byzantine authority and a majestic presence that pervades the Chapel with a reassuring tranquillity, inducing a mood of repose in the spectator, conducive to achieving an inner spiritual peace'.[54]

Cecil Collins was approached again early in 1977 by Hussey with plans for a painting for St Richard's Shrine in the retroquire.[55] A sketch was produced for the Chapter's approval as well as of an anonymous sponsor, but this scheme was dropped after the retirement of Dean Hussey in August of that year.

The crowning achievement of Hussey's time at Chichester and the one that properly sums up his patronage is the window *The Arts to the Glory of God* by Marc Chagall installed in the northern retroquire. Unveiled by the Duchess of Kent on 6 October 1978, it was the culmination of an idea dating back to Hussey's first approach to the artist in 1969. The choice of Chagall as the artist for the Chichester window may have been influenced by Robert Potter's involvement as the architect for a window in the small church at Tudely in Kent commissioned from Chagall by Sir Henry and Lady d'Avigdor Goldsmid in memory of their daughter.[56] John Piper wrote to Hussey, 'The Chagall window at Tudely is quite a success, I think ... and I found Chagall a great old charmer ...'[57] Hussey had also seen, with Lancelot Mason, Chagall's remarkable new series, the Jerusalem Windows, at a special exhibition at the Louvre in the early '60s and he felt that their strong colour was exactly what Chichester needed.

Hussey's first approach to Chagall met with an encouraging response, but he found the artist too busy to take on anything else. The correspondence started again in 1975, and Chagall asked Hussey how he envisaged the window. The Dean said he imagined that 'You could treat it by putting little vignettes around representing the different arts leading up the central figure to the praise of God at the top—and that's precisely what he has done!'[58]

Mme. Chagall writes to Hussey in January 1976, 'Thank you, too, for sending your suggestions for the window. I will translate them to my husband who is very much taken by Psalm 150. He is studying it, and preparing the sketches.'[59]

By April of the following year, the Dean had seen and approved the *maquette*,[60] but envisaged problems with the fund-raising. Charles Marq of the Atelier Jacques Simon in Rheims (who had made other windows to Chagall's designs) would construct the window, and was obviously pleased with the commission. 'Ce sera comme toujours avec Marc Chagall, un vitrail tout à fait nouveau, jamais vu, une vraie création,'[61] and in December 'Je suis hereux avec ce travail, car ce travail ne ressemblera à aucun autre.'[62]

After a fraught visit by Hussey to Chagall in S. Paul de Vence[63] and numerous delays, caused by the very specialist nature of the work both in manufacturing the glass, in the assembling, and in Chagall's hand-finishing, the window arrived in Chichester on 20 September 1978, more than a year after Hussey's retirement.

> The theme of this window is Psalm 150: "O praise God in his Holiness ... Let everything that hath breath praise the Lord." The triumphal quality of this chant is expressed by the dominance in the composition of the colour red (red on white, on green, on yellow), broken up by a certain number of green, blue and yellow blobs. This is the first time that Marc Chagall has conceived a subject composed entirely of small figures: it is the people in festive mood glorifying the Lord, exalting his greatness and his creation. The musicians are playing the instruments referred to in the psalm: horn, drum, flutes, strings and cymbals. A man juxtaposed with an animal at the right-hand edge of the composition holds open a little book, indicating that the word too participates in this hymn of praise. In the centre two figures hold up the seven-branched candlestick, while David, author of the psalm, crowns the whole composition playing upon his harp.'[64]

In a notice published in the *Chichester Observer* after the dedication, Canon Keith Walker (then Precentor of the Cathedral) pointed out the appropriateness of the theme of the window to the artist. 'Chagall's parents were members of the Hassidistic sect of Judaism ... Followers of Hassidism interpret God as a deity of song, dance, and gaiety. In worship and life heaven is anticipated.'[65]

This final project of Dean Hussey, though far the most expensive,[66] partly due to French Government directive, immeasurably enriched the Cathedral with what Canon Walker called 'a new means of devotion and artistic splendour'.[67]

Interviewed on BBC's *Meeting Point* in 1967,[68] Hussey, the highly gifted patron, sums up his attitude to modern art in the Church:

> I think that the products of all sorts of artists can be some of the highest work which is done by human beings, and therefore I think it makes an extraordinarily appropriate symbol of what man offers to God. I think it is tremendously important that the contemporary artist should be brought, in this as in every age, to express the truths about God in a contemporary idiom.[68]

Robert Holtby (Dean 1977-89), Hussey's immediate successor, inherited a considerable part of the restoration programme and it must have been frustrating at times that so much effort was concentrated upon replacing decaying 19th-century masonry in the central tower. But he too carried on the beautification of the Cathedral, if in a more pragmatic

149 *The Duchess of Kent unveiling the Chagall window in 1978, watched by head verger Jim Bacon.*

150 *John Skelton's font, 1983.*

and circumspect fashion. His underlying principle was that works of art in a church should not merely be for adornment; 'their purpose is to teach, to edify, to suggest a glimpse of the Beyond, to which creative work in holy places should point'.

His first commission was for a new font, sculpted in Cornish polyphant stone by John Skelton in 1982-3; certainly one of the sculptor's most successful works. The font replaced the unsatisfactory and awkward Victorian piece of 1894 and was intended to complement the colours of the Feibusch *Baptism* mural. The dark green stone, polished to reveal warm brown flecks and subtle variations in its structure, was selected by the sculptor from the quarry of Messrs. Harris on Bodmin Moor. The original block measured 180 cu. ft., and was sawn out by hand in the traditional way. The shallow bowl, set into the upper block, is of beaten copper, also echoing and reflecting the colours of the mural. With five assistants,[69] the work involved almost 1,000 man hours over a period of some two years. The *maquette* is at present fixed on a bronze bracket to the west wall of the baptistry as a candle sconce, an adaptation not favoured by the artist, but nevertheless an interesting insight into the working methods of one whose work can be seen in many sites in and around Chichester. Skelton, who has lived and worked in Sussex for many years, started his career as a pupil of his uncle, Eric Gill.

During Dean Holtby's time, the Cathedral also gained a reredos (1984), in the Chapel of St John, another Baptism, by Patrick Procktor (b.1936). It was the gift of a member of the General Chapter. A major new tapestry (1985) and altar were also commissioned, for St Richard's shrine.

Both of Dean Holtby's major commissions, the font and the tapestry, celebrate the life and work of Bishop George Bell; John Skelton's font was dedicated on the very day, 4 February 1983, of the centenary of Bell's birth, and the Anglo-German Tapestry, with its very rich symbolism of St Richard's life and work, testifies to the association between England and Germany, having been designed by a German artist, Ursula Benker-Schirmer, and woven partly at her factory in Marktredwitz (Bavaria), and partly at the West Dean tapestry studio, near Chichester. This is particularly significant because of Bell's work with German refugees and his strong links with German churches.

Dean Hussey emphasised that artistic commissions should always be of their period and, whether ancient or modern, should form an integral part of the church and its purpose. This is especially evident in Chichester:

> The Cathedral is rich in history, architecture, music, art, all speaking in their way of the manifold truth of God. At the same time it must be seen to try to use the best in contemporary

> arts—this was always the way. Never trying to live in the past, always absorbing the best of any age, and so never a museum, but something alive and of the present, tough with its roots in the past.[70]

If the present writers are allowed to express a personal hope, it is that the work of George Bell, Walter Hussey and Robert Holtby with living artists should be exploited as a very sound foundation for a continuing programme of contemporary commissions. The *Five Wounds* (1994) by Michael Clark (b.1954), the first conceptual work of art to find a permanent place in an English cathedral, is an imaginative example of this sort of cooperation, proving that the artists are still there, still inspired, and still just as eager for the collaboration of the creative patron as they were when Hans Feibusch wrote *Mural Painting* in 1946.

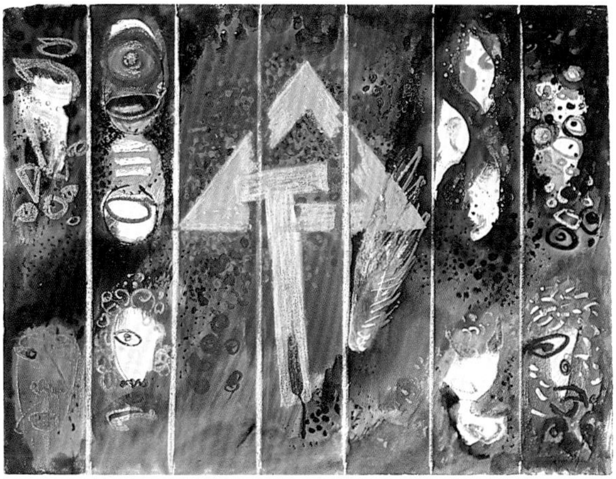

XXII *(left) Progressive sketches for the Piper Tapestry (on loan from the artist's estate): early form, collage and gouache, 366 x 553mm; preliminary sketch of the final form (gouache, ink and crayon, 582 x 778mm); and a later stage, gouache, chalk and collage, 500 x 785mm.*

XXIII *(above) The completed Tapestry in place, viewed from roof level during the recent restoration, with a unique glimpse of the Lady Chapel beyond the quire.*

XXIV *The Chagall window, depicting Psalm 150 (retroquire).*

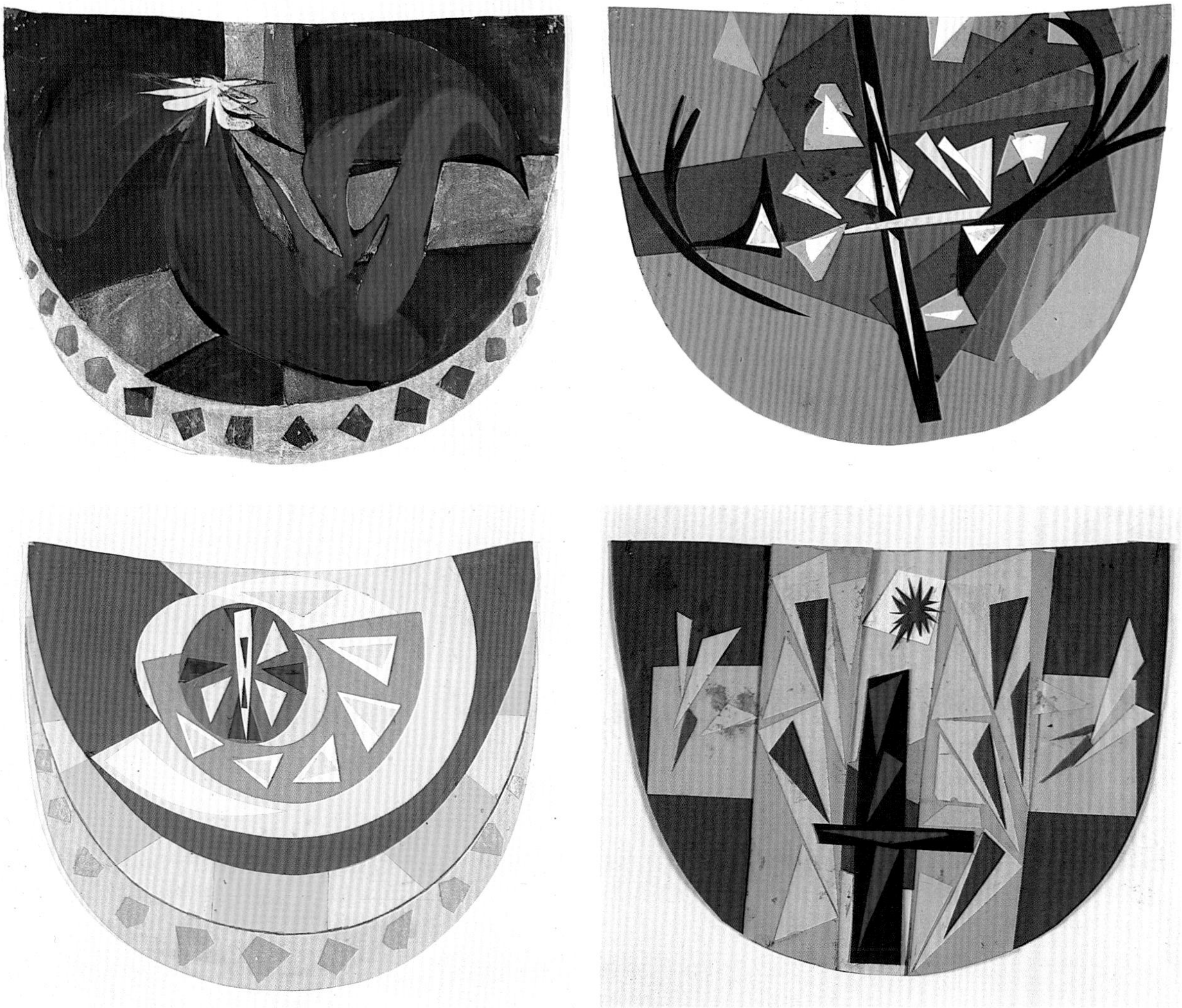

XXV *Ceri Richards's designs for cope hoods.*

XXVI *The Anglo-German St Richard tapestry.*

XXVII *The Royal Maundy at Chichester, 1986. With the Queen and the Duke are Dean Holtby, Bishop Kemp, and the Lord High Almoner (Bishop David Say of Rochester), the sub-Almoner (Canon Anthony Caesar, sub-Dean of the Chapels Royal), the Secretary and sub-Secretary of the Royal Almonry.*

XVII

The Immediate Past

Robert Holtby

The death of Dean Duncan-Jones in 1955, and the retirement (and death) of Bishop Bell in 1958, marked the opening of a new era in the life of the Cathedral. When Walter Hussey was appointed dean, Bell being a strong advocate of that choice by the Crown, he was already well-known as a patron of distinguished artists.

Hussey was a very different character from Duncan-Jones—less authoritarian, less dogmatic. Yet he was very determined, and over 22 years proved capable of achieving his ends by persuasion. Gentler than his predecessor, he was no less resolute, and presided over changes, not only in the appearance of the Cathedral, but in its liturgy, and indeed in its administration. Hussey was Dean when cathedrals experienced a revival (caused by reflection on their rôle in relation to the diocese), by liturgical, including musical, developments, and by the sharp growth in tourism, the last prompting questions about the mission of a cathedral to its many visitors.

Hussey's leadership was effective principally in two areas: the fabric, guided by Robert Potter (to whom I owe many of the details in this area), and the adornment of the building, in which he took a personal initiative.

Potter succeeded Harry Sherwood as Surveyor on 29 September 1959, when Roger Wilson was bishop. His first survey in 1961 drew urgent attention to the dangers to the fabric—cracks and settlement and the effects of atmospheric pollution. The Cathedral was therefore included in the Sussex Churches Campaign, under the leadership of Sir Kenneth Blackburne, chairman from 1963 to 1970.

The first enterprise, combining aesthetic with structural purpose, was the restoration of the Arundel Screen and pulpitum, with the now familiar three-arched openings allowing a view of the high altar. This proved of liturgical significance with the growing numbers attending the Choral Eucharist. The reordering of the sanctuary had a complementary liturgical purpose.

The work of restoration prompted Potter to propose to the Chapter the creation of a workshop and organisation to deal with masonry matters. The object, as he put it, was to provide an organisation 'not only to undertake the needs of the Cathedral, but to run on a commercial basis whereby the livelihood of the craftsmen could be ensured and not be dependent upon the success of appeals'. Thus a profitable venture was created and a whole workforce came into being in the place of one plumber and one part-time carpenter. This was a considerable contribution to Cathedral restoration. Workshops were opened on the Industrial Estate, stonemasons were trained, and the Cathedral Works Organisation

151 *The dedication of the Coronation window in the south choir aisle (1953). Left to right: Archbishop Fisher, Dean Duncan-Jones, Bishop Bell, the verger R.S. Street, the Precentor (Canon Browne-Wilkinson), the Rev. J.S. Hannon (chaplain to the Theological College), Chancellor Macmorran QC, the Treasurer (Canon Mortlock), the Cathedral Chancellor (Dr. Moorman), Archdeacon Mason, Canon Powell, Canon Lowther Clarke.*

became a Trust in 1973. The import of French stone to approximate to that of the original builders was soon a salient feature of the enterprise.

A series of operations followed: the first was the securing of the vault of the present Treasury, and with this a new roof was constructed. The ruined eastern gable was restored, and a reinforced concrete floor created, independent of the vaulting, to support a room for the Cathedral Library. That work on the north-east of the Cathedral was followed by securing the stability of the quire, rebuilding flying buttresses, restoration of the stonework of the central tower (a very lengthy undertaking), repairing the windows and walling of the Chapter House, and refacing the plinth of the Bell Tower. Within the Cathedral, underfloor heating was installed, and the paving of the floor of the retroquire was restored to its 18th-century pattern in Villhonneur stone. But what chiefly affected the appearance of the Cathedral was its main entrance at the west end. The level of the churchyard had risen almost a metre above that of the floor of the Cathedral. Ditches round it became flooded after rain, to the detriment of the building. The ground level was lowered revealing, in the west porch, the 12th-century bases of the pillars in the jambs of the original Norman doorway. The principal approach was paved and a drainage system introduced. The entrance was vastly improved by the glazing of the outer arches of the porch and inner doorway, with handles designed and made by Geoffrey Clarke.

Robert Potter was succeeded as surveyor in 1985 by Donald Buttress, who continued an extensive programme of repair, starting with the completion of the work on the lantern stage of the central tower. Two striking features have been the restoration of cloister bays, the cost of which has been borne by individuals and organisations and by *in memoriam* contributions, and the restoration of the nave ceiling, where a fragment of Lambert Barnard's painting has been revealed.

152 *Corbel-likeness of the Cathedral architect, Donald Buttress, carved by Douglas Garland, Clerk of the Works.*

Walter Hussey's artistic initiatives are described elsewhere in this volume, and he gave his own account in his book *Patron of Art*, a book largely anecdotal in character, but revealing a fine, discriminating judgement. His interest in the patronage of musical works continued at Chichester, and he was supported in his enthusiasm by John Birch, whom he had appointed organist in 1958, in succession to R.H. Hawkins, who had been in office 20 years. In 1965 Leonard Bernstein was approached, and the outcome was *The Chichester Psalms*, with 'a touch of the idiom of *West Side Story*' (for which the Dean had some liking) for the 1965 Southern Cathedrals Festival. It has since found an honoured place in concert repertoire.

Ten years later—1975—was the 900th anniversary of the Cathedral's foundation. The focal point of this, on 15 June, was a Eucharist at which the Archbishop of Canterbury presided. A small committee was established under Hugh (later Lord) Cudlipp to plan the celebrations. Sir William Walton wrote a *Magnificat* and *Nunc Dimittis*, and William Albright composed the Chichester Mass for

153 *Roman mosaic discovered during the laying of underfloor heating in the south nave aisle. John Warwick is seen here inspecting it.*

the Festival Eucharist. Hussey commissioned a book of essays on Chichester topics, elegantly produced, with a cover design by John Piper.

The Festivities of 1975 developed into an annual event, under the directorship (until 1987) of the late Richard Gregson-Williams. The 1989 programme illustrates the continuing enthusiasm for the event: it included 19 concerts in 17 days, covering a wide variety of performances. The Festival became a lively link with the local community and beyond, and revived the use of the great Church for 'secular' events.

Towards the end of Walter Hussey's time, the Worshipful Company of Goldsmiths gave generous financial assistance to equip a Treasury for the housing and display, under maximum security, of treasures and plate from the Cathedral and from churches in the diocese. The Treasury thus established occupies part of the former subdeanery church, on the east side of the north transept. The collection, apart from episcopal croziers and rings found in Cathedral sarcophagi, 'for the most part is related to the Eucharist as it was celebrated in the downland and coastal plains during the last seven hundred years'. (So the contents were described by the late Canon Geoffrey Parks, M.C., appointed in retirement to the honorary office of Sub-treasurer, to which he brought highly specialised knowledge and a fine judgement.)

When Dean Hussey retired in 1977, the furnishing of the Cathedral continued. Major projects undertaken were the reordering of the baptistery, with the John Skelton font, the reordering of the St Richard shrine area, with the Anglo-German Tapestry, the rebuilding of the great organ and the provision of a reredos for the St John Chapel, painted by Patrick Procktor. This last exemplifies the function of creative works, not merely for aesthetic delight, but for purposes of edification. Inspired by the Grünewald (Issenheim) altar at Colmar and a painting by Poussin now in Washington, it shows scenes from the life of the Baptist, preparing the way for the Saviour. The figure on the left has an extended right arm, like Mary Magdalene in the Sutherland painting. Both paintings are visible from the west of the Cathedral, the one pointing to the Cross, the other a witness to the Resurrection.

The Cathedral pipe organ had been silent since 1973. A committee under the chairmanship of (the late) Sir John Barnes, KCMG, MBE, met for the first time in 1980. The organ appeal (for £450,000) was undertaken under the umbrella of the Chichester Development Trust, a body which was to have a powerful influence on the continuing restoration of the fabric.

In spite of the valiant efforts of the Sussex Churches Campaign, and notably of the Cathedral Friends, it became clear that, given the substantial demands of restoration and maintenance, an organisation was required specifically to raise funds for those purposes. A Trust was therefore established in May 1980 for 'the restoration, improvement, development and maintenance and repair of the Cathedral Church, its furniture, ornaments and precincts'. In addition, there was provision for support for the musical foundation and for the restoration and repair of buildings owned by the Dean and Chapter. Donations reached their peak in the period 1986-9, making a total of £1,300,000 (including £300,000 raised for the special organ fund). A further £600,000 was raised between 1991 and April 1993. The first full-time secretary was Captain Blake Parker, RN, who brought to the work imagination to discern the tasks ahead and administrative gifts, combined with energy, to fulfil them.

The Trust did more than raise funds. Under successive chairmen, Leslie Weller being the first, and

154 *The Treasury, given by the Goldsmiths' Company in 1979.*

through its advisory council, representing all areas of the diocese, it stimulated a lively interest in the Cathedral and its work, and created a partnership between laity and chapter.

Another influential body in the dissemination of information, and the encouragement of support for the Cathedral, is the Company of Friends, formed in 1939, following the precedents of the Friends of Canterbury (founded under the initiative of George Bell when dean) and York. The Friends' Newsletter and their annual *Journal* have proved to be an effective means of communication concerning current Cathedral events and information on its history. Social activities have done much to encourage a corporate spirit, and the Friends therefore have been a major partner in Cathedral ministry. In 1989, 50 years after their foundation, they were able to survey their several contributions to the ongoing work of the Cathedral: support for fabric restoration, including the renovation of the west porch, help towards the adornment of the Cathedral and furnishings, the renovation of memorials and provision of assistance for the library and the choir library and for service books. There has indeed been a *crescendo* of support over the years since the Friends financed the Piper tapestry.

In the 1970s the office of Secretary was combined with that of Visitors' Officer when Mrs. Eve Shepherd was appointed to the joint office. This became a valuable amalgamation: the Secretary has worked alongside other Chapter officers, and integrated the activities of the Friends with the ministry to visitors in all its aspects—information, education, and all that makes for warmth of welcome and instruction.

One of the issues which confronted cathedrals as the country emerged from the war—along with problems of restoration and maintenance—was the growth of tourism. In March 1979, the English Tourist Board published the results of a survey, 'English Cathedrals and Tourism, Problems and Opportunities'. It was then estimated that twenty million tourists visited cathedrals annually. Chichester, one of the cathedrals surveyed, received warm commendation, and it was noted that there were more volunteer helpers there than in most cathedrals. The gift shop had been opened in 1975, at the base of the Bell Tower, and the cafeteria, designed by Robert Potter, with expert advice from Miss Barbara Frith, was opened in 1977 by Pastor Martin Niemöller, Bishop Bell's friend.

Chichester, however, does not experience the same degree of exposure to the influx of visitors as certain other cathedrals. Nevertheless, numbers have grown: the proximity of the south coast ports has been a contributory factor. The needs of visitors and pilgrims, conscious or hidden, and a 'ministry of welcome', became urgent topics for Chapter deliberation. The history and architecture of the building, the significance of its furnishings—even the meaning of the basic Christian symbols—are a closed book to increasing numbers of tourists. And there was the growing need to provide for parish groups from Sussex and beyond (some of them Roman Catholic) who came as pilgrims and for whom the reordered retroquire and the St Richard shrine area have provided appropriate surroundings for acts of worship.

Provision must be made for both the informed and the unknowing, and part of that is suitable hand-outs, aimed at showing the Cathedral primarily as a place of worship, not simply a great building, however impressive. There are the particular demands of parish groups and school parties, the planning of guided and 'stand-by' tours, the enrolling of guides fluent in languages other than English, and the training of all volunteers. The administrative tasks also include the arrangements for doorkeepers, teams of refectory and other helpers.

The establishment of an Education Centre with lending library in the Pilgrims' Room (off the Cloisters) under the direction of Sister Sarah, SSM, proved a valuable adjunct to the work. For various reasons, it was replaced after a few years by a Visitors' Centre, also manned by volunteers. The Centre was closely linked with the work of the Visitors' Officer, by then Sybil Papworth. It concentrated on the use of visual material, providing opportunities for visitors to see and touch stained glass, stone, needlecraft and tapestry. This was especially a part of school visits, as were Cathedral tours for schoolchildren and the annual Children's Day. With the coming of the National Curriculum, the Dean and Chapter appointed Estelle Morgan in 1990 to organise this work and in liaison with schools in the diocese over areas where the Cathedral could provide a resource for studies or in-service training for teachers. The search for effective communication never ceases.

Care for visitors and pilgrims involves a pastoral solicitude which has also to extend to the regular congregation, many of whom are volunteer helpers in the ministry of welcome. In the second half of the century a growing number of citizens have come to look upon the Cathedral as their 'parish church', towards whom, therefore, there is a responsibility for pastoral care. Under the provisions of the relevant measure, a Cathedral Roll was established, and a Council was elected from it. This did not diminish the statutory obligations of the Dean and Chapter, but created a very helpful consultative body—one further means of partnership with laity. The Roll and its Council initiated a Cathedral stewardship scheme, which *inter alia* has provided generous financial support for the Cathedral's work as well as stimulating interest in its ministry.

With the gradual growth of the congregation, the Sunday Choral Eucharist emerged as the principal act of worship, though the earlier said Celebration (following the Prayer Book rite) continued to be attended by a faithful number. Preaching on Sundays, therefore, became increasingly directed to the local congregation. The practice of concelebration, started in Dean Hussey's time, was a focal point in the corporate ministry of the Dean and Chapter. The relationship of the Cathedral to the rest of the diocese was a central factor in guiding Chapter policy, chiefly in regard to the liturgical rôle of the bishop, whose Cathedral it is, and the adoption by the Chapter of the diocesan calendar, with emphasis on the relationship to diocesan liturgical practice. Rite 'B' of the Alternative Service Book was adopted for the Choral Eucharist, and Rite 'A' was used on certain weekdays: it is appropriate that a Cathedral should use a variety of authorised forms. Special liturgical observances were introduced for Maundy Thursday, Good Friday and the Easter Vigil. In January 1981 Canon Christopher Luxmoore, the Precentor, was consecrated Bishop of Bermuda—the first consecration in the Cathedral since its foundation.

One feature of recent years has been the increase in the number of 'special' acts of worship, including a series of carol services. Such events have included regimental commemorations, legal services, and, uniquely, the 25th anniversary of the foundation of the University of Sussex, and the centenary of the (West) Sussex County Council. 1986 was especially memorable. Besides the S.C.F. and the Festivities, there was the Royal Maundy—a great occasion for City and County as for the Cathedral—the dedication of the rebuilt organ, and the annual conference of deans and provosts. The closure of the Theological College in 1994 marked the end of a greatly valued link over its long life. The Principal has been a residentiary canon, members of the Chapter were on its governing body, and the students took part in the Cathedral music on various occasions.

155 *The Royal Maundy at Chichester, 1986.*

For hundreds of years the Cathedral has been a nursery of church music. The traditional excellence of the choral foundation was maintained by John Birch and by his successor Alan Thurlow, who proved himself particularly sensitive to the liturgical function of music in worship and the suitability of works proffered for performance at all Cathedral events, fulfilling a dual rôle as director of the choir and general music adviser.

The recruitment of choristers has become more local. At the Prebendal School numbers have grown considerably under successive headmasters, and girls have been admitted. The Dean and Chapter agreed a change in the statutory provision for the school's governing body by adding lay members with appropriate professional experience.

The choristers are required to board. Today, with the general trend away from full boarding, as the nature of schools changes, they are therefore part of a small minority in a school largely attended by day pupils, but they share fully in its academic and musical achievements (H.R.H. Princess Alexandra opened a new music school in 1989). Already, 80 per cent of choristers obtain bursaries towards their fees. A number of free places also have been endowed by various benefactors; by 1995, indeed, these will be available for fully half the choir.

The Dean and Chapter, as Trustees of St Mary's Hospital, added to its residential accommodation by the erection of St Mary's Lodge sheltered housing in March 1987, a month after the appointment as Custos of Bishop Edward Knapp-Fisher, former Archdeacon and Sub-dean of Westminster.

The diocesan celebrations in connection with the centenary of the birth of Bishop Bell (1983) involved the Cathedral at various points. Clergy took part in an international Bell Colloquium and joined in conference in Bavaria and Berlin, the choir visiting East Berlin as part of the tour, and singing the Mass in Bamberg Cathedral also. Links with Roman Catholic and Lutheran institutions were established and, in all this, the Cathedral worked alongside parishes in the diocese. Dean Holtby attended a Kirchentag in Berlin and

156 *The opening of the Prebendal School swimming pool (the headmaster, Neville Ollerenshaw, with his wife, Bishop Wilson and Dean Hussey).*

laid a wreath on the site of the execution at Flossenburg of Dietrich Bonhoeffer whose last message was to Bell. In the Cathedral itself, the new font marked the centenary, and out of the German connection came the Benker Tapestry in the retroquire, behind the site of the St Richard shrine, where the ashes of George Bell are interred. (The commissioning is described in 'Chichester Tapestries', *Otter Memorial Paper* 7).

Cathedrals have traditionally been free from the restraint of faculty jurisdiction, but in 1984 a Commission, under the chairmanship of Eric Kemp, Bishop of Chichester, issued a report, *The Continuing Care of Churches and Cathedrals*, which, for the latter, aimed at securing *accountability*, while retaining power to *initiate*. To this end, compulsory reference to the then Cathedrals Advisory Commission was recommended, as was the establishment of a local Fabric Advisory Committee. The Chichester Chapter saw these recommendations as a formal extension of that moral accountability which undergirded their work.

The existence of statutory advisory bodies has not brought about any change in the formal constitution of the Cathedral's governing body. The Administrative Chapter still consists of the dean, precentor, chancellor, treasurer, bursalis prebendary, archdeacon of Chichester and one canon elected from the General Chapter (which meets annually to enact certain business and to hear reports). The 29 prebendaries and four Wiccamical prebendaries must be summoned for the formal election of the bishop. Members of the Administrative Chapter, save the elected prebendary, all have obligations to do 'residence', and the stipends of two of them are met by the Church Commissioners, they being engaged principally on

157 *Cardinal Hume and Bishop Kemp with Dean Treadgold at the Cathedral service during the Week of Prayer for Christian Unity, 1990.*

Cathedral duties, and fulfilling longer periods of residence than their colleagues.

The constitution of the Chapter reflects and continues in principle the historic organisation of the Cathedral body, though residence today also implies dwelling in Chichester for the whole year. Outside their statutory duties, full-time residentiary canons fulfil their ministry in the light of their own special interests and experience.

Modern developments require an efficient administrative support: the office of Communar is crucial to staff efficiency. When Canon Mason retired from the office (its last clerical holder) the statutes were changed to allow the appointment of a lay Communar. Sir John Guillum Scott, T.D., D.C.L., former Secretary-General of the Church Assembly and later of the General Synod, admirably created the pattern of work for his successors, each of whom has brought professional experience to his office, supported in finance and administration by an appropriately qualified staff.

An opportunity to reflect on the work of the Cathedral and the extent to which it was meeting its obligations occurred in 1978, when Bishop Kemp conducted a visitation. The enquiry ranged over all areas of the work: liturgy, administration, pastoral care, the relationship to the rest of the diocese. The enquiry provided the information necessary for planning the Cathedral's continuing work and the policies which should inform it. The Dean and Chapter set about fulfilling the *directions* in the Bishop's charge, and implementing its *recommendations*. It was not merely a useful undertaking, but it also exemplified the historic rôle of the Bishop in relation to the Cathedral.

In the period following the visitation what developments are significant? The Dean and Chapter retain their statutory authority. Yet in practice, through associated bodies like the Cathedral Development Trust, the Cathedral Council and the Friends' Council, and through the (statutory) Advisory Committee, along with the Cathedrals' Fabric Commission, their powers are effectively reduced. The greater involvement of these lay bodies is to be welcomed. Should all such participation become formal?

There is the constant problem of the maintenance and repair of the fabric and the necessity for its regular inspection. State aid is a help, but not a panacea. But, chiefly, there is the call to convey the Gospel to the thousands of visitors who enter the Cathedral and view its monuments and furnishings. That is a call which far exceeds the demands on the generations with which most of this volume is concerned. Medieval pilgrims to the shrine of St Richard journeyed in an age of faith: we have to explore the means of communication with those whose apprehension is dim.

But however efficient the administration or imaginative the 'presentation' of the Cathedral, its life and work must be measured by its unchanging primary purpose:

> The Chapter of the Cathedral Church of the Holy Trinity in Chichester is a body of priests surrounding the Bishop of the diocese to aid him in his work by their counsel and to maintain the regular worship of Almighty God in his Cathedral Church.

So runs the Preamble to the Cathedral statutes. It is the standard for this and every age. The heart of the worship remains the daily recitation of the Divine Office and the daily offering of the Holy Eucharist.

General Abbreviations

Bennett *et al.*	F.G. Bennett, R.H. Codrington, C. Deedes (eds.), *Statutes and Constitutions of the Cathedral Church of Chichester* (Chichester, 1904)
BL	British Library (MS)
Bodl. Lib.	Bodleian Library, Oxford (MS)
Nairn and Pevsner	I. Nairn and N. Pevsner, *The Buildings of England: Sussex* (1965)
Cal.S.P.Dom.	*Calendar of State Papers Domestic*
CCJ	*Chichester Cathedral Journal*
CDG	*Chichester Diocesan Gazette*
Chichester Papers	F.W. Steer (ed.), *Chichester Papers*, Chichester Council (1955-67)
Corlette	H.C. Corlette, *The Cathedral Church of Chichester ... with an Account of the Cathedral and See* (1905), Bell's Cathedral series
Crocker	C. Crocker, *A Visit to Chichester Cathedral* (Chichester, 1849)
Dallaway	J. Dallaway, *A History of the Western Division of the County of Sussex*, vol.1 (1815)
DNB	*Dictionary of National Biography*
Duncan-Jones	A. Duncan-Jones, *The Chichester Customary* (1948)
Fasti (1)	J.M. Horn (comp.), *Fasti Ecclesiae Anglicanae* 1300-1541 7, *Chichester Diocese* (1964)
Fasti (2)	J.M. Horn (comp.), *Fasti Ecclesiae Anglicanae* 1541-1857 2, *Chichester Diocese* (1971)
Hay	A. Hay, *The History of Chichester* (Chichester, 1804)
JEH	*Journal of Ecclesiastical History*
Kitch, *Studies*	M.J. Kitch (ed.), *Studies in Sussex Church History* (1981)
Mercurius Rusticus	B. Ryves, *Mercurius Rusticus: the Countries Complaint of the Sacrileges, Profanities and Plunderings Committed by the Schismatiques on the Cathedral Churches of the Kingdom* (1647) (2nd ed. 1685)
Morgan	R.R. Morgan, *Chichester: A Documentary History* (Chichester, 1992)
MS	Manuscript
Otter Memorial Papers	P. Foster (ed.), *Otter Memorial Papers*, WSIHE, Chichester (1990-)
Peckham, *Acts* (1)	W.D. Peckham (ed.), *The Acts of the Dean and Chapter of the Cathedral Church of Chichester, 1472-1544* (Sussex Record Society, vol.52, 1952)
Peckham, *Acts* (2)	W.D. Peckham (ed.), *The Acts ... 1545-1642* (Sussex Record Society, vol.58, 1959)
Peckham, *Chartulary*	W.D. Peckham (ed.), *The Chartulary of the High Church of Chichester* (Sussex Record Society, vol.46, 1942/3)
PCC	Prerogative Court of Canterbury
PRO	Public Record Office
SAC	*Sussex Archaeological Collections*
SCF	Southern Cathedrals Festival
SRS	Sussex Record Society
SNQ	*Sussex Notes and Queries*
Stephens, *Memorials*	W. R.W. Stephens, *Memorials of the South Saxon See and Cathedral Church of Chichester* (1876)
Swainson	C.A. Swainson, *The History and Constitution of a Cathedral of the Old Foundation* (1880)
VCH 2	W. Page (ed.), *Victoria County History of Sussex*, vol.2 (1907)

VCH 3	L.F. Salzman (ed.), *Victoria County History of Sussex*, vol.3 (1935)
Walcott	M.E.C.Walcott, *The Early Statutes of the Cathedral Church of the Holy Trinity, Chichester, with Observations on its Constitution and History*, reprinted from *Archaeologia* 45 (1877) pp.143-234.
Willis	Robert Willis, *The Architectural History of Chichester Cathedral* (1861)
WSRO	West Sussex Record Office

NOTES

I. The Bishopric of Selsey (Susan Kelly)

1. The primary sources for Wilfrid are: B. Colgrave (ed.), *The Life of Bishop Wilfrid by Eddius Stephanus* (1927) [hereafter *LW*]; and B. Colgrave and R.A.B. Mynors (eds.), Bede's *Ecclesiastical History of the English People* (1969) [hereafter *EH*]. For more detail on the South Saxon phase of his career, see H. Mayr-Harting, 'St Wilfrid in Sussex', in Kitch, pp.1-17.
2. *EH*, pp.372-3.
3. For the background, see H. von Campenhausen, 'The ascetic idea of exile in ancient and early monasticism', in his collected papers, *Tradition and Life in the Church* (1968), pp.231-51, especially pp.243-8; K. Hughes, 'The changing theory and practice of Irish pilgrimage', *JEH* 11 (1960), pp.143-51.
4. See D.P. Kirby, 'The Church in Saxon Sussex', in P. Brandon, *The South Saxons* (1978), pp.160-73 at pp.169-70.
5. *LW*, pp.82-5; *EH*, pp.374-7.
6. The foundation charter is P.H. Sawyer (ed.), *Anglo-Saxon Charters: an Annotated List and Bibliography* (Royal Historical Society Guides and Handbooks 8, 1968) [hereafter Sawyer], no.232. A new edition, with extended commentary, is forthcoming in S.E. Kelly *et al.* (ed.) *Charters of Selsey* (British Academy, 1995), no.1.
7. F.G. Aldsworth, 'The mound at Church Norton, Selsey, and the site of St Wilfrid's church', *SAC* 117 (1979) pp.103-7; F.G. Aldsworth and E.D. Garnett, 'Excavations on "The Mound" at Church Norton, Selsey, in 1911 and 1965', *SAC* 119 (1981), pp.216-21. For Pagham see J. Munby, 'Saxon Chichester and its predecessors', in J. Haslam (ed.), *Anglo-Saxon Towns in Southern England* (1984), pp.315-30 at pp.321-3.
8. For an introduction to new ideas about the pastoral role of minsters, see J. Blair, 'Minster Churches in the Landscape', in D. Hooke, *Anglo-Saxon Settlements* (1988), pp.35-58; R. Morris, *Churches in the Landscape* (1989); J. Blair and R. Sharpe (eds.), *Pastoral Care Before the Parish* (1992).
9. In 1086 Chichester was certainly a secular chapter, and it seems unlikely that there had been any radical change since the move from Selsey. Domesday Book (fol.17r) mentions that the canons of Chichester held 16 hides in common, which had never paid tax; this may represent lands which had previously been allocated to the Selsey community. Part of these 16 hides may be represented by two hides of a manor at Treyford, which are said to be in the prebend of Chichester church (fol. 23r). The existence of individual prebends after the Conquest may be indicated by the fact that parts of the episcopal manors of Aldingbourne and Amberley are said to have been held by sundry priests and clerics in 1086 (fols. 16v, 17r: note that these men are not explicitly linked to Chichester).
10. *EH*, pp.380-3, 514-17.
11. Bede's letter is translated in D. Whitelock (ed.), *English Historical Documents c.500-1042*, 2nd edn. (1979) [hereafter *EHD*], pp.799-810 (no.170). See C. Cubitt, 'Wilfrid's "usurping bishops": episcopal elections in Anglo-Saxon England, *c*.600-*c*.800', *Northern History*, 25 (1989), pp.18-38 at 21-4.
12. *EH*, pp.516-17; Sawyer no.44 (see Kelly *et al.*, *Charters of Selsey*, no.5). It has been suggested that the so-called Bossington Ring in the Ashmolean Museum belonged to Eolla of Selsey: see A. Anscombe, 'The ring of Eolla, bishop of Selsey, *circa* A.D. 720', *SNQ* 1 (1926-7), pp.136-9. But this is probably mistaken: D.A. Hinton, *A Catalogue of Anglo-Saxon Ornamental Metalwork 700-1000 in the Department of Antiquities, Ashmolean Museum* (1974), pp.9-12.

13. *EH*, pp.516-17, 558-9, 572-3.
14. All the charters from Selsey itself are edited in Kelly *et al.*, *Charters of Selsey*. For other Sussex documents, see E. Barker, 'Sussex Anglo-Saxon Charters', *SAC* 86 (1947), pp.42-101; *SAC* 87 (1948), pp.112-63; *SAC* 88 (1949), pp.51-113.
15. Sawyer no.1184 (Kelly *et al.*, *Charters of Selsey*, no.11). Another apparently eighth-century charter which survives in single-sheet form (Sawyer no.43; Kelly *et al.*, *Charters of Selsey*, no.4) is a 10th-century forgery.
16. Sawyer nos. 44-6, 48-9, 1178, 1183 (Kelly *et al.*, *Charters of Selsey*, nos.2, 5, 7, 9-10, 12-13); see also S 50, 108.
17. N. Brooks, *The Early History of the Church of Canterbury: Christ Church from 597 to 1066* (1984), pp.174-206; C. Dyer, *Lords and Peasants in a Changing Society: the Estates of the Bishopric of Worcester, 680-1540* (1980), pp.13-15.
18. Sawyer nos.158, 1435 (Kelly *et al.*, *Charters of Selsey*, nos.14, 15).
19. For the background, see P. Wormald, 'The Ninth Century', in J. Campbell (ed.), *The Anglo-Saxons* (1982), pp.132-57.
20. See M. Bell, 'Saxon Settlements and Buildings in Sussex' in P. Brandon (ed.), *The South Saxons* (1978), pp.36-53 at p.45.
21. See Sawyer no.160 and Brooks, *Church of Canterbury*, pp.34-5, 203-6.
22. See R. Radford, 'The pre-Conquest boroughs of England, 9th-11th centuries', *Proceedings of the British Academy* 64 (1980 for 1978), pp.131-53; M. Biddle and D. Hill, 'Late Saxon Planned Towns', *Antiquaries' Journal* 51 (1971), pp.70-85.
23. See D. Hill, 'The Origins of the Saxon Towns', in P. Brandon (ed.), *The South Saxons* (1978), pp.174-89 at 179-84.
24. The information comes from the Anglo-Saxon Chronicle: see Whitelock, *EHD*, p.204.
25. The Selsey episcopal lists are discussed in detail in the introduction to Kelly *et al.*, *Charters of Selsey*. See also M.A. O'Donovan, 'An interim revision of episcopal dates for the province of Canterbury, 850-950: part II', *Anglo-Saxon England*, vol.2 (1973), pp.91-113 at pp.101-3; F.B. Fryde *et al.*, *Handbook of British Chronology*, Royal Society Guides and Handbooks 2, 3rd edn. (1986), p.221.
26. Sawyer no.506 (Kelly *et al.*, *Charters of Selsey*, no.18).
27. Sawyer no.1291 (Kelly *et al.*, *Charters of Selsey*, no.20).
28. Sawyer no.230; for the background to its fabrication, see Brooks, *Church of Canterbury*, pp.240-3. The charter mentions land at North Mundham; territory there was also claimed by Selsey (see Sawyer nos.45, 1172; Kelly *et al.*, *Charters of Selsey*, no.2).
29. See Sawyer nos.714, 776, 779, 1377.
30. D. Knowles *et al.*, *The Heads of Religious Houses England and Wales 940-1216* (1972), pp.80-1.
31. Sawyer nos.845, 869.
32. Anglo-Saxon Chronicle, *sub annis* 994, 998, 1001, 1009, 1011 (Whitelock, *EHD*, pp.235, 236, 237, 242, 244).
33. F. Barlow, *The English Church 1000-1066*, 2nd edn. (1979), p.222.
34. By contrast, the Archbishop of Canterbury's holdings in Sussex alone brought in over £143 (he also held extensive lands in Kent, Middlesex and elsewhere). One survey indicates that more than twenty English monasteries and nunneries had an annual income of over £100 in 1086, with the wealthiest, Glastonbury, receiving more than £800: see D. Knowles, *The Monastic Order in England*, 2nd edn. (1963), p.702.
35. Great Domesday Book, fols.16v-17r, 18v. Bexhill was lost after the Conquest, but regained in 1166. The bishopric or bishop also had interests in small estates at Treyford and at Hazelhurst in Ticehurst (fols.19r, 23r).
36. See Barlow, *English Church*, pp.164-5.
37. Hill, 'Origins of Sussex Towns', pp.187-9 (note 23).
38. Great Domesday Book, fol.16v. See also Munby, 'Saxon Chichester', pp.327-8 (note 7).
39. N.E.S.A. Hamilton (ed.), *Willelmi Malmesbiriensis Monachi De Gestis Pontificum Anglorum Libri Quinque*, Rolls Series (1870), p.205.
40. W.D. Peckham, 'The Parishes of the City of Chichester', *SAC* 74 (1933), pp.65-97 and 69-73;

Munby, 'Saxon Chichester', pp.323-6.

41. There are two charters in the archive which seek to establish a connection between the Selsey community and Chichester in the Anglo-Saxon period, but they are both late forgeries: Sawyer nos.47, 616 (Kelly *et al.*, *Charters of Selsey*, nos.8, 19). A third document (Sawyer no.403; Kelly *et al.*, *Charters of Selsey*, no.17) concerns a grant to the bishop in 930 of land in the Selsey peninsula; a section which is clearly a later interpolation refers to dependent meadow-land 'near the city', apparently Chichester.
42. A. Clapham, *English Romanesque Architecture* (1930), pp.84-5 and pl. 31c; *VCH* 2, pl. opposite p.16; *VCH* 3, pp.105-6.
43. See the discussion of a similar Canterbury seal, and of the sketch of a Carolingian church in a Canterbury manuscript, by Brooks, *Church of Canterbury*, pp.46-9.

II. The Medieval Cathedral (Diana E. Greenway)

1. The document is found in WSRO, Ep. I/1/3, Reg. Storey fols.43v-44r; a large section of it is printed, though with some errors and omissions, by Walcott, p.175.
2. See M. Brett, *The English Church under Henry I* (Oxford, 1975), pp.162-4.
3. H. Mayr-Harting (ed.), *The Acta of the Bishops of Chichester, 1075-1207* (Canterbury and York Society, 56, [1964]) [hereafter *Acta*], no.8.
4. Deuteronomy 16: 16, 17.
5. St Richard's ordinance, calendared in Peckham, *Chartulary*, no.77, is printed in full in F.M. Powicke and C.R. Cheney (eds.), *Councils and Synods*, vol.2, *1205-1313* (Oxford, 1964) [hereafter *Councils & Synods*, vol.2], pp.416-17; the bishops' indulgences are calendared in Peckham, nos.79-85, 88-9; and Dean Geoffrey's calculation is translated in Peckham, no.70.
6. C. Deedes (ed.), *The Episcopal Register of Robert Rede ... Bishop of Chichester, 1397-1415* (2 vols., SRS, 8, 11 [1908-10]) [hereafter *Reg. R. Rede*], vol.2, pp.415-18.
7. See St Richard's mandate, calendared in Peckham, *Chartulary*, no.87, printed in full in *Councils & Synods*, vol.2, p.418.
8. The notes by Dean Geoffrey of Gloucester are useful in assessing the indulgences granted at the different feasts, Peckham, *Chartulary*, no.70. A Kalendar, giving the feasts, saints' days and commemorations observed at Chichester, which was drawn up for Bishop William Reede (1368-85), survives in Bodl. Lib. MS Ashmole 1146 fols.1v-7r. Another, of 15th-century date, is found in Bodl. Lib. MS Laud lat. 95, fols.16-20.
9. For the changing of the date of the fair, see Peckham, *Chartulary*, no.130.
10. The order of Bishop Adam Moleyns (1446-50) is printed in Swainson (an admirable collection), no.165, p.91, from 'Dean Hayley's book' (now WSRO Cap. I/12/3) p.163. For the summer readings (called *historie*) and responsories, including *Peto Domine*, see Andrew Hughes, *Medieval Manuscripts for Mass and Office: a guide to their organization and terminology* (Toronto, 1982), paragraphs 107, 835-6.
11. On this subject there is no better introduction than the brilliant book by Kathleen Edwards, *The English Secular Cathedrals in the Middle Ages*, 2nd edn. (Manchester, 1967).
12. The record known as the taxation of Pope Nicholas IV lists the estimated values of all ecclesiastical incomes in the year 1291. For the diocese of Chichester it may be conveniently consulted in translation in Peckham, *Chartulary*, no.954. A full transcript is printed in *Taxatio Ecclesiastica Angliae et Walliae auctoritate P. Nicholai IV circa A. D. 1291* (Record Commission, 1802), pp.134-42.
13. See Walcott, pp.179-80.
14. *ibid.*, pp.183-4, also p.149 n. *b*; Peckham, *Chartulary*, no.379.
15. At medieval Westminster Abbey servants outnumbered monks by more than 2:1; see B.F. Harvey, *Living and Dying in England, 1100-1540: The Monastic Experience* (Oxford, 1993), pp.164-5. An estimate on this basis would give 60 servants at Chichester.
16. The Latin text is given in *Acta*, no.101; for an English abstract, see Peckham, *Chartulary*, no.198.
17. These three statutes are printed in Walcott, pp.160-84, 184-213, 213-17.
18. The documents are printed in Swainson, no.108, pp.51-4.

19. *ibid.*, no.140, p.75.
20. The archbishop's award is printed in Swainson, no.115, pp.57-9, and the list of questions *ibid.*, no.116, pp.59-62. For comment, see Edwards, *English Secular Cathedrals*, p.131.
21. The records of the three visitations are printed in translation in *Reg. R. Rede*, vol.1, pp.99-107, 107-23, vol.2, pp.363-73.
22. *Fasti* (1), pp.48-9.
23. Walcott, pp.207-8, calendared Peckham, *Chartulary*, no.40.
24. *Fasti* (2), pp.4-5.
25. For details of his career, see A.B. Emden (ed.), *A Biographical Register of the University of Oxford to 1500* (3 vols., Oxford, 1957-9), vol.2, pp.1246-7.
26. Haseley's career is given *ibid.*, p.884. For the full documentation of the election, with English translation, see *Reg. R. Rede*, vol.2, pp.387-402.
27. See Edwards, *English Secular Cathedrals*, pp.50-3.
28. Walcott, pp.216-17.
29. *Reg. Storey* fols.3r-5v, 69r.
30. Peckham, *Acts* (1).
31. For these buildings see T. Tatton-Brown below, pp.236-7.
32. *Councils & Synods*, vol.2, p.460; also quoted in Swainson, no.70, p.33. A service-book from Chichester, dating from the first half of the 13th century, survives in Bodl. Lib. MS Laud lat. 95, fols. 23v-149: it includes a Psalter, with canticles and litany, a breviary and a hymnal.
33. *Reg. R. Rede*, vol.1, p.114; E.F. Jacob (ed.), *The Register of Henry Chichele, Archbishop of Canterbury, 1414-43*, vol.3 (Canterbury and York Society, 46, 1945), p.505.
34. For the first records of these altars, see Peckham, *Chartulary*, nos.91, 472, 542. For the flanking chapels, see T. Tatton-Brown, below p.27.
35. First recorded Peckham, *Chartulary*, nos.68, 656, 461, 212, 466, 688. The chapel of St Catherine and her fellows became known as 'of the Four Virgins'.
36. *ibid.*, no.361; cf. *Reg. R. Rede*, vol.1, p.124.
37. *ibid.*, no.903 (37).
38. Walcott, pp.168, 170-1.
39. Peckham, *Chartulary*, no.954, p.308.
40. A charter of Archbishop Richard of Canterbury, printed in C.R. Cheney and B.E.A. Jones (eds.), *English Episcopal Acta*, vol.2, *Canterbury, 1162-90* (1986), no.103, and calendared in Peckham, no.74.
41. J. Bolland, *Acta Sanctorum, Iulii*, vol.6, pp.397-426, at p.406.
42. St Richard's will is printed, with translation, in *SAC* 1 (1848), pp.164-92; for his stipulation about his place of burial and his bequest of relics, see pp.166-9. In 1248 Beatrix de Lindefeld gave to St Richard a reliquary in the shape of a cross, which was to be kept in the Cathedral, Peckham, nos.34-5.
43. Among these interesting documents, a few may be singled out for notice: Bishop Seffrid II, *Acta*, no.86; Dean William of Bracklesham, Peckham, *Chartulary* nos.663, 680, 696, 698-700; Stephen de Colemere, *ibid.*, no.538. For the 'martilogy', see nos.294, 930.
44. Fifteen are listed in 1291, Peckham, *Chartulary* no.954, pp.307-8.
45. Of the 28 vicars in 1397, 13 were also chantry chaplains, *Reg. R. Rede*, vol.1, pp.104-6.
46. For an account of St Richard's career, see C.H. Lawrence, 'St Richard of Chichester', in Kitch, *Studies*, pp.35-55, and D. Jones, *The Life of St Richard of Chichester* (SRS 79, 1993/4 [forthcoming]).
47. For St Richard's will, see above, n.42.
48. The miracles, briefly discussed by D.L. Jones, 'The cult of St Richard of Chichester in the Middle Ages', *SAC* 121 (1983), pp.79-86, are described in the early Life of St Richard, by Ralph Bocking, printed in *Acta Sanctorum, Aprilis*, vol.1, pp.282-318, at pp.302-14.
49. On the cult and the medieval shrine, see Jones, *art. cit.* On the destruction of the shrine in 1538, see also J. Fines, below, p.62.
50. See Morgan, chapter 2 and p.198.
51. For a discussion and useful map, see W.D. Peckham, 'The parishes of the city of Chichester', *SAC* 74 (1933), pp.65-97, with map facing p.65.

52. See, e.g., *Reg. R. Rede*, vol.1, p.99.
53. For an account of the hospital, see *VCH* 2, pp.100-2. For the appointment of the warden in 1301 and his oath of obedience to the Dean and Chapter, see Peckham, *Chartulary*, no.709.
54. *ibid.*, nos.443, 500.
55. *ibid.*, nos.485, 489.
56. This is a topic that would merit investigation. For some of the documentary references, see *ibid.*, subject index, s.v. Lights.
57. *ibid.*, no.724.
58. *ibid.*, no.523; *VCH* 3, pp.102-4.
59. *VCH* 3, pp.92-3.

III. The Medieval Fabric (Tim Tatton-Brown)

I am extremely grateful to John Atherton Bowen, who has discussed many aspects of the interpretation of the fabric with me, while making excellent drawings of various parts of the building; also to my wife, Veronica, for word-processing this text and that of Chapters IX and XIV and wrestling with computer problems and rewritten drafts.

Architectural terms used in Chapters III, IV, IX and XIV can be found in Nairn and Pevsner's list or (in greater detail) in Thomas Cocke, Donald Finlay, Richard Halsey and Elizabeth Williamson, *Recording a Church: An Illustrated Glossary* (Council for Brit. Archaeology, 1982).

1. Julian Munby, 'Saxon Chichester and its predecessors', in J. Haslam (ed.), *Anglo-Saxon Towns in Southern England* (1984), pp.315-30.
2. SRS 45 (1940-1), p.102, quoted in F.G. Aldsworth, '"The Mound" at Church Norton, Selsey, and the site of St Wilfrid's church,' *SAC* 117 (1979), p.104.
3. It finally fell in the late 17th century and was replaced by a tower at the west end of the parish church. See Aldsworth, *ibid.* (note 2), and F.G. Aldsworth and E.D. Garnett, 'Excavations on "The Mound" at Church Norton, Selsey, in 1911 and 1965', *SAC* 119 (1981), pp.217-21.
4. G.J. Copley (annot. and ed.), *Camden's Britannia: Surrey and Sussex* (1977), p.35; also Stephens, *Memorials*, p.31 and A.S. Duncan-Jones, *The Story of Chichester Cathedral* (revised edition 1955), p.13.
5. F. Goodwin, *Catalogue of the Bishops of England* (1601), p.334, and W.H. Godfrey and J.H. Bloe, 'Cathedral historical survey' in *VCH* 3 (1935), pp.105-6.
6. R.D.H. Gem, 'Chichester Cathedral: when was the Romanesque church begun?' in R.A. Brown (ed.), *Proceedings of the Battle Conference in 1980* (1981), pp.61-4.
7. Willis, p.5. This brilliant account is still the starting point for the fabric of the cathedral. Godfrey and Bloe's survey (*op. cit.* [note 5] pp.105-46) in the *VCH* is still the most complete account.
8. Florence of Worcester, ii p.67, quoted in full in Gem, *op. cit.* (note 6), p.62.
9. The foundations for the north-east and south-east chapels were briefly recorded in the early 1960s during underpinning work. (A. Down and M. Rule, *Chichester Excavations* I [1971], pp.127-41.)
10. Scars for this can still be seen in the transept walls. When the gallery was removed in the late 12th century, a new spiral staircase was built outside the east wall of the north transept to give access to the upper chamber. An original spiral staircase already existed in a similar position outside the south transept. See also, W.D. Peckham, 'Some notes on Chichester Cathedral', *SAC* 113 (1973), p.22.
11. This was a common practice at this time. Both the contemporary St Augustine's Abbey and the Cathedral at Canterbury only had their naves completed on the west in a second, later 11th-century phase. The evidence for the latter has only come to light very recently, during the 1993 excavations under the nave floor.
12. West of this break, the abaci flanking the windows have a carination or kink, and there is a chamfer around the edge of the window.
13. See M.R.G. Andres, 'Chichester Cathedral, the original east end: a reappraisal', *SAC* 118 (1980), pp.299-308. A tiny fragment of this blind arcading can also be seen at the north-west corner of the nave north aisle.
14. Many of the original round arches and roll-mouldings in the presbytery were badly damaged when

galleries were put in here in the 18th century. The masonry of these arches now mostly dates from the 19th-century restorations.

15. The original external corbel-table can also be seen externally at the west end of the presbytery and (close to) in the present Cathedral Library. A very similar, and probably contemporary corbel-table can be seen at the top of the west tower of Bosham church. See F.G. Aldsworth, 'Recent observations on the tower of Holy Trinity Church, Bosham', *SAC* 128 (1990), pp.55-72 and Brighton p.71 below.
16. See Holtby p.285 below and T. Tatton-Brown, 'The west portal of Chichester Cathedral', *CCJ* (1990), pp.8-11.
17. There are, however, remains of cross arches in the triforium galleries of the presbytery (but not in the nave) and Martin Andrew has suggested that there was a large barrel-vault over the presbytery; see his 'Chichester Cathedral: the problem of the Romanesque choir vault' in *Journal British Archaeol. Assocn.* 135 (1982), 11-22. I am not convinced.
18. Willis, p.x.
19. See G. Zarnecki, 'The Chichester reliefs', *Archaeol. Journal* 110 (1954), pp.106-19.
20. Walcott, p.14.
21. *Chronica Rogeri de Hoveden*, vol.2, p.333 and *Annales Monastici* (Rolls Series), vol.2, pp.245, etc.
22. Willis, pp.13-15.
23. *ibid.*, plate IV. At this time the original blind arcading in the presbytery aisle walls was removed.
24. *Rotuli Litt. Patent.* (Records Comm.), vol.1, p.65; '*ducendi marmor suum per mare a Purbic usque Cicestr' ad reparationem ecclesiae suae de Cicestr*'.
25. An early start was made by Edward Prior in his 'A table of the styles of masoncraft used from 1090 to *c*.1450', *Proceedings of the Harrow Architectural Club* (1904).
26. These were first studied by Cecil Hewett in his *English Cathedral Carpentry* (1974), pp.127-8.
27. *Annales Monastici* (Rolls Series 36) vol.3, p.32; *impetu ceciderunt ... duae turres Cicestrae.*
28. *Calendar Close Rolls* (1231-4), p.34 and Liber 'Y' fol.80v (W.S.R.O.).
29. J. Munby, 'Medieval carpentry in Chichester: 13th-century roofs of the Cathedral and Bishop's Palace' in A. Down (ed.), *Chichester Excavations* 5, pp.243-4.
30. L. Salzman, *Building in England down to 1540* (1953), p.175.
31. Historical MSS. Commission, *Report on MSS in Various Collections* 1 (1901), p.193.
32. The south porch is, however, contemporary with the sacristry (now the Canons' Vestry) to the east. The doorway behind it, into the south aisle, was rebuilt in the late 13th century.
33. Peckham, *Chartulary*, p.37.
34. See D. Greenway, p.22 above and W.H. Blaauw, 'Will of Richard la Wych,' *SAC* 1 (1848), pp.64-192, esp. 116-17.
35. Blaauw, *ibid.*, p.166, note 3.
36. See D. Greenway, p.23 above and Walcott, p.31. (This work very usefully summarises the documentary evidence for the various altars and chapels in the Cathedral.)
37. The adding of rows of chapels to nave aisles can be found in many 13th-century French cathedrals, for example Rouen, Evreux or Amiens, but it is exceptionally rare in Britain. Elgin Cathedral in Scotland is the only other example, and this was apparently more like most of the French examples in having the altar against the outer wall. At Chichester, the altar was always on the east, and the small reredos above it survives, in part, in many of the chapels, with flanking aumbries and piscinas.
38. This is not the place to give a detailed analysis of all the mouldings, etc., but the mid-13th-century bases are of a 'water-holding' type, while the later 13th-century ones have three rolls. Mid-13th-century capitals have volutes with square abaci above, while the later ones are moulded and have round abaci.
39. Walcott, pp.26 and 28. Both chapels are first documented in the 15th century.
40. The dating of these chapels is still uncertain, and the Purbeck marble crocketed capitals and water-holding bases in the arches that open into them certainly seem to be early 13th-century in style. However, the writer feels that they, and other architectural fragments, may have been stockpiled

and re-used. For a brief discussion of this, see N. Pevsner and P. Metcalf, *The Cathedrals of England: Southern England* (Harmondsworth, 1985), p.96. It has to be admitted, however, that the start of the work on all these chapels could still be in the early 13th century.

41. See O.H. Leeney, 'References to ancient Sussex Churches in *The Ecclesiologist* mainly as regards restoration and repair', *SAC* 86 (1947), p.162.
42. Part of the cusping from within these windows can still be seen inside the roof, re-used in the 15th century. Only above the smaller gable on the north side of the chapel of St Edmund does a hexafoil survive *in situ*.
43. There was much discussion about the form of the new window in the 1840s in *The Ecclesiologist*, see Leeney, *op. cit.* (note 41), 161.
44. Tatton-Brown, *op. cit.* (note 16).
45. To the ground-level of before the 1187 fire.
46. In the presbytery the earlier thinner flying buttresses can still be seen, though those on the south side were completely rebuilt in 1974.
47. To stop water penetration into the interior, there is an original 13th-century 'damp-proof' course of lead below the pipes.
48. The tops of these flying buttresses were covered in lead in the 18th century and new pipes to gutters under the chapel roofs were put in. These led to hoppers outside the walls which fed downpipes to drains. This system remains. It is also worth noting that the presbytery flying buttresses were covered in lead in 1533, according to the Communar's Accounts. Cap. I/23/1 fol.69a, 70a and 83b.
49. For a detailed study of this roof, see Munby, *op. cit.* (note 29).
50. See unpublished report, dated 16 January 1991, by Nottingham University Tree-ring Dating Laboratory (copy in the Chapter Office). Also summary by Julian Munby, 'Chichester Cathedral roofs', *CCJ* (1993), pp.7-11.
51. Peckham, *Chartulary*, p.903, no.37; also caps. 7 and 35 of Gilbert's Synodal Statutes of 1289.
52. Traces of an earlier 13th-century scheme of painted decoration survives inside on the lower (12th-century) wall faces.
53. Peckham, *ibid.*, p.903, no.38.
54. A ridge rib was also added to the reconstructed south side of the south transept vault.
55. As can be seen from Buckler's fine drawing of 1812, fig.18, reproduced from *VCH* 3. At Wells Cathedral, the north transept had earlier been used as the Chapter House.
56. C. Tracy, 'Medieval choir stalls in Chichester: a re-assessment', *SAC* 124 (1986), pp.141-55.
57. H. Tummers, 'The Medieval effigial tombs in Chichester Cathedral', *Church Monuments* 3 (1986), p.10.
58. This was put back in its original place after the crossing was rebuilt. See note 55.
59. Quoted in *VCH* 3, p.111.
60. Larger blocks of Upper Greensand were also introduced to the nearby Winchester Cathedral at about the same time. See T. Tatton-Brown, 'Building stones of Winchester Cathedral' in J. Crook (ed.), *Winchester Cathedral: Nine Hundred Years 1093-1993* (1993), p.43.
61. This chapel was built in the late 12th century, and was apparently dedicated to the 'Four Virgins'.
62. It is not known when the parochial altar moved to the north transept, but it was certainly there by the very early 16th century.
63. But the decoration of the Chichester spire is now clearly Perpendicular work, rather than in the Decorated style, used at Salisbury.
64. Sir Gilbert Scott himself described how he did this in his *Personal and Professional Recollections* (1879), p.310. Quoted in full below, p.150.
65. Walcott, p.28.
66. See below, Chap.XV.
67. See *VCH* 3, p.135.
68. E. Croft-Murray, 'Lambert Barnard; an English Renaissance painter', *Archaeol. Journal* 113 (1956), pp.108-25 and T. Brighton, pp.80-1 below.

IV. Cathedral and Reformation (John Fines)

1. Peckham, *Acts* (1).
2. W.D. Peckham, 'The Valuation of Chichester Cathedral, 1535', *SAC* 92 (1954), pp.157-77.
3. M.J. Kitch, 'The Chichester Cathedral Chapter at the time of the Reformation', *SAC* 116 (1978), pp.277-92.
4. Kitch, *op. cit.* 278.
5. Walcott, pp.143-243.
6. Legacies record only £2 8s. 10d. for the period 1500-19 and £1 17s. 11d. for the period 1520-39. There were some legacies late in Mary's reign, though no record of the shrine's restoration. *SRS* 41 (1935), pp.270-271.
7. Cap 1/51/14 transcribing Cap 1/23/1.
8. Cap 1/26/2.
9. Cap 1/51/14.
10. Cap 1/51/10.
11. W.K. Jordan, *The Chronicle and Political Papers of King Edward VI* (1966), p.41.
12. SRS 16 (1913), pp.79-81.
13. *ibid.* pp.18-19 and 74-5.
14. SRS 74 (1984/5), item 88.
15. SRS 16 (1913), pp.4-5.
16. *ibid.*, pp.17-18.
17. SRS 41 (1935), pp.284, 278, 286.
18. J. Cornwall, 'Sussex Wealth and Society in the reign of Henry VIII', *SAC* 114 (1976), p.9.
19. W.D. Peckham, 'The Parishes of the City of Chichester', *SAC* 92 (1954), pp. 74, 90.
20. References in this section are to SRS 36 (1930) except where otherwise stated.
21. The income recorded in the *Valor* is only £84 15s. 9d. (Peckham, *SAC* 92, pp.157-177.)
22. *English Chantries, the Road to Dissolution* (Harvard, 1979), pp.20-21.
23. Peckham, *Acts* (1) pp.146 and 229.
24. *ibid.*, pp.14, 15.
25. *ibid.*, p.424.
26. *Letters and Papers Foreign and Domestic of the reign of Henry VIII* ed. J.S. Brewer, J. Gairdner and R.H. Brodie, 1862-1932, p.8.1001.
27. *ibid.*, pp.10.547, 997, 1119.
28. L.F. Salzman, 'Sussex Religious at the Dissolution', *SAC* 92 (1954) pp.24-36. Dress was a matter of some significance. At the Dissolution Thomas Chapman, warden of the Friars Minor in London wrote to Cromwell, 'I remain in such apparel as you saw me in Chichester.' *Letters & Papers*, p.13.3.252.
29. *ibid.*, p.13.2.1062.
30. *ibid.* 1049, 1280.
31. SRS 36, pp.133-5.
32. For a thorough study of Chichester deprivations see T.J. McCann, 'The Clergy and the Elizabethan Settlement in the Diocese of Chichester', in Kitch, *Studies*, pp.99-124.
33. C.E. Welch, 'Three Sussex Heresy Trials', *SAC* 95 (1957), pp.59-70—one might just note that Thomas Hoth, Augustinian Canon of the New Priory of Hastings, claimed that he was brought to trial to cover 'the lewde conversacion and unthrifty lyvyn of predyaux and our master t'gether'. John Prideaux was prebendary of Ipthorne.
34. A.G. Chester, *Hugh Latimer, Apostle to the English* (New York, 1978), p.152.
35. Strype, *Annals*, 1, pp.442-3.
36. R.B. Manning, *Religion and Society in Elizabethan Sussex* (Leicester, 1969), p.44.
37. Peckham, *Acts* (1) pp.666, 688 & 730; Manning, p.43. See also Hobbs (below), chapter XI, n.9.
38. SRS 45; Peckham, *Acts* (1) pp.506 and 539.
39. Peckham, *Acts* (1) p.323.
40. Manning, 171.
41. W.D. Peckham, 'Chichester Cathedral in 1562', *SAC* 96 (1958) pp.1-8.

V. Art in the Cathedral from the Foundation to the Reformation (Trevor Brighton)

1. For an account of these with some suggested identifications see F.W. Steer and G.L. Remnant, 'Chichester Cathedral Library', *Chichester Papers* 44 (1964).
2. The hidden corbel sculptures have never been recorded and a full assessment of the imagery is not possible at present.
3. The following description is based on a report on the wall paintings in the Treasury (January 1988) by Dr. Wolfgang Gärtner, director of the Wallpaintings Workshop, Canterbury Cathedral. (Copy in the Cathedral Library.)
4. See B. Smith, A. Robinson, B. Astor, 'The Chichester Roundel', *Otter Memorial Paper* 4 (1988).
5. The fullest analysis of these sculptures is G. Zarnecki, 'The Chichester Reliefs', *Archaeological Journal* 110 (1954), pp.106-19.
6. Zarnecki (*op. cit.*, pp.107-8) discussed the dates attributed by various writers. He suggested the date *c.*1140 in his earlier work, *English Romanesque Sculpture, 1066-1140* (London, 1951), pp.24 and 39.
7. C.S.P. Cave, 'The Roof Bosses in Chichester Cathedral', *SAC* 71 (1930), p.9.
8. G. Gordon, *The Sculptures in the Retrochoir at Chichester* (Talbot Press, Saffron Walden, n.d.).
9. Nairn and Pevsner, pp.147-8.
10. F.W. Steer and G.L. Remnant, 'Misericords in Chichester Cathedral', *Chichester Papers* 22 (1961).
11. C. Tracy, 'Medieval Choir Stalls in Chichester: a reassessment', *SAC* 124 (1986) pp.141-55.
12. See M. Campbell, 'Metalwork in England c.1200-1400', *The Age of Chivalry: Art in Plantagenet England*, ed. J. Alexander and P. Binski, catalogue of The Royal Academy exhibition, 1987 (in which the V & A grill was exhibited).
13. Drawn by J. Buckler in 1825 (reproduced in *VCH* 3).
14. Preb. R.H. Codrington, 'Ancient Coats of Arms in Chichester Cathedral', *SAC* 48 (1905), p.139. The arms are (gules) 3 leopards' faces (argent).
15. For Barnard's work, see E. Croft-Murray, *Decorative Painting in England 1537-1837*, vol.I (Early Tudor) (1962) and 'Lambert Barnard: an English early Renaissance painter', *Archaeological Journal* 113 (1957); K. Coke, *The Amberley Castle Panels* (Pallant House Gallery, Chichester, 1992).
16. BL Add. MSS 5675, fol.62 and 36389, fol.131, reproduced in *VCH* 3 (see figs.18 and 36).
17. Dallaway, p14.
18. The line of Kings continues after Henry VIII down to and including George I. Croft-Murray considers that Lambert Barnard may have painted Edward VI, Mary I and perhaps Elizabeth. He considers that Lambert's son, Anthony, may have painted James I and his grandson, Lambert II, the portrait of Charles I (destroyed in the fall of the spire in 1861). The rest of the Stuarts and George I were probably the work of Tremaine.
19. Early guide books attribute the repainting to 'Tremayne' but his Christian name is given neither in these nor in the Chapter records. The Communar's Accounts for 1749 give a date: 'By ye Painter's Bill for painting ye Kings 12-12-0'. In 1735, 1743 and 1748, apprentices were bound at Chichester to *William* Tremaine (Tremain, Trimain), a master glasier (R. Garraway Rice (ed.), 'Sussex Apprentices and Masters 1710-52', *SRS* 28, 1924. If he were the restorer, it could perhaps account for the somewhat crude style of the repainting. On the other hand, in the absence of any proof of Tremayne's involvement, it is tempting to consider another surname, 'Mason the Gilder and Painter', who in the next year, 1750, was paid the unusually large sum by the Cathedral of £233 5s. (Ed).
20. E. Duffy, *Stripping the Altars: Traditional Religion in England 1400-1580* (Yale U.P., 1992), pp.494, 577.
21. H.N. Birt, *Elizabethan Religious Settlement* (1907), pp.427-30. Quoted by Duffy (*op. cit.*).
22. *Mercurius Rusticus*, p.140.

VI. The Dean and Chapter 1570-1660 (Andrew Foster)

Versions of this article have been tested on kind audiences in Chichester, at the inauguration of the Chichester Centre for Ecclesiastical Studies in 1993, and at the Institute of Historical Research in

London, and I am most grateful for advice received on those occasions. In particular, I would like to thank John Fines, Kenneth Fincham, Nicholas Tyacke and Robert Holtby for general encouragement and advice. Our editor, Mary Hobbs, has of course been a tower of strength and saved me from many errors, while my wife Liz has provided her customary constant support.

1. For full discussion of this theme see: C. Cross, 'Dens of Loitering Lubbers: Protestant protest against Cathedral foundations, 1540-1640' in D. Baker (ed.), *Studies in Church History* 9 (1972), pp.231-7; D. Marcombe, 'Cathedrals and Protestantism: The Search for a new identity, 1540-1660' in D. Marcombe (ed.), *Close Encounters* (Nottingham Univ., 1991), pp.43-61.
2. Peckham, *Acts (2)*, pp.85-7; see p.142 for 'Masters of the Church'.
3. The two individuals who had converted to Catholicism were Stephen Goffe and Richard Mileson; Bruno Ryves immediately departed to become Dean of Windsor; Thomas Lockey had resigned in 1642; William Oughtred, Aquila Cruso, Nathaniel Field and John Langhorne were those who died in 1660; for fuller discussion of restoration problems, see Robert Holtby (below); see also: Mary Hobbs, *The Sermons of Henry King (1592-1669), Bishop of Chichester* (AUP, New Jersey and Scolar Press, Aldershot, 1992), pp.25-31.
4. For developments here see: Diana Greenway (above), John Fines (above) and *Fasti* (2).
5. *Fasti* (2), p.37.
6. The five archdeacons who did not become members of the Chapter were: John Spencer, John Coldwell, John Langworth, Henry Hammond and William Cotton; James Marsh held the post of chancellor, while James Mattock served as the precentor; only eight of the 19 archdeacons who held office during this period gained a real say in the running of Cathedral affairs through service as canons residentiary.
7. *Fasti* (2), p.64.
8. WSRO: Cap I/3, Cap I/23, Cap I/26 and Cap I/27; for full details see: *Diocese of Chichester. A Catalogue of the Records of the Dean and Chapter, Vicars Choral, St Mary's Hospital, Colleges and Schools*, F.W. Steer and I. Kirby (compilers) (Chichester, 1967).
9. For comparison, see: G.R. Aylmer and R. Cant (eds.), *A History of York Minster* (1977) and S. Eward, *No Fine but a Glass of Wine. Cathedral Life at Gloucester in Stuart Times* (1985).
10. W. Camden, *Britannia*, *c.*1586, quoted in Timothy McCann (comp.), *Restricted Grandeur: Impressions of Chichester 1586-1948* (Chichester, 1974), p.1.
11. 'The Supplication of John Large of Chichester to the Burgesses of the Parliament', 1586, quoted in T. McCann, *Restricted Grandeur*, p.3.
12. This statement is based on work of some of my past students who have sampled will bequests for the period 1570-1640. A more systematic survey of diocesan wills may shed more light on this interesting feature of local bequests.
13. For full discussion of the work of Curteys and the Catholic nature of this region see R.B. Manning, *Religion and Society in Elizabethan Sussex* (Leicester University Press, 1969).
14. Lieutenant Hammond's remarks are quoted in T. McCann, *Restricted Grandeur*, pp.6-7.
15. *Cal.S.P.Dom. 1635*, p.xlii.
16. *SAC* 86 (1947), pp.185-6; *VCH* 3, p.112; T. Tatton-Brown, Chap.IX.
17. Figures based on analysis of WSRO Cap I/23/3 and 4.
18. *Mercurius Rusticus*, p.139.
19. C. Carlton, *Going to the Wars. The Experience of the British Civil Wars, 1638-1651* (Routledge, 1992); I. Gentles, *The New Model Army in England, Ireland and Scotland, 1645-1653* (Blackwell, 1992).
20. *Fasti* (2), *passim*.
21. Peckham, *Acts (2)*, pp.85-7; Manning, *Religion and Society*, pp.63-90; the point about the senior canon residentiary acting as the President of the Chapter in the absence of the Dean is important, for it confirms the status of those canons over the Cathedral dignitaries; much later the Precentor came to act as second in command, as indeed he does today.
22. Peckham, *Acts (2)*, pp.93-4.
23. Figures based on analysis of WSRO: Cap I/23/3 and 4.
24. Peckham, *Acts (2)*, pp.68, 78.
25. Peckham, *Acts (2)*, pp.69-70; this was obviously a hasty move to forestall Curteys, for Clarke and

Willoughby never took up their positions and received a dividend.

26. Peckham, *Acts (2)*, pp.83-4; Manning, *Religion and Society*, pp.74-5.
27. The bishops were in order: Richard Curteys (1570-82), Thomas Bickley (1585-96), Anthony Watson (1596-1605), Lancelot Andrewes (1605-1609), Samuel Harsnett (1609-19), George Carleton (1619-28), Richard Montagu (1628-38), Brian Duppa (1638-1641), Henry King (1641-1669).
28. I owe this observation to Dr. Mary Hobbs; for more on Henry King see her excellent *The Sermons of Henry King (1592-1669), Bishop of Chichester.*
29. Harsnett's temperament is well exposed in a letter to the Earl of Arundel of December 1617, when he remarked that 'if your lordship had but the least taste of the unsavoury government of Chichester, you would do like Almighty God, - spew both it and them out of your mouth'—as quoted by me in 'Chichester Diocese in the early 17th century', *SAC* 123 (1985), pp.187-94.
30. Peckham, *Acts (2)*, pp.190-1, 199, 206-9.
31. For material on Weelkes see P. Barrett (below); Kenneth Fincham has recently edited a valuable first edition for the Church of England Record Society on *Visitation Articles and Injunctions of the Early Stuart Church* (1994), which contains Harsnett's articles of 1616, pp.139-41.
32. WSRO: Ep.I/20/9—materials relating to Carleton's visitation.
33. *Cal.S.P.Dom., 1631-3*, p 254.
34. *Cal.S.P.Dom., 1635*, pp.xlii-xliii; John Donne and Henry King shared this concern about standards of worship as Mary Hobbs has rightly noted in *The Sermons of Henry King*, pp.36, 76.
35. A valuable study of the history of properties in Chichester is to be found in R. Morgan, *Chichester: A Documentary History*.
36. John Ecton, *Thesaurus Rerum Ecclesiasticarum* (3rd edition, 1763), pp.52-3 reveals that the value of the prebends ranged from Firles, worth a mere ten shillings per annum (hence perhaps its annexation to the post of treasurer), to the wealthy prebends of Woodhorn and Wightring worth over twenty pounds per annum, with the average prebend worth just under ten pounds per annum.
37. These figures are based on close analysis of *Fasti* (2); as this figure includes all those holding office in 1570, there is some overlap with the figures supplied by John Fines, but this is less of a problem with the period after 1660.
38. R. O'Day, *The English Clergy: The Emergence and Consolidation of a Profession 1558-1642* (Leicester University Press, 1979).
39. See Diana Greenway and John Fines (above) on this subject; D. Lepine, 'The Origins and Careers of the Canons of Exeter Cathedral 1300-1450' in C. Harper-Bill (ed.), *Religious Belief and Ecclesiastical Careers in Late Medieval England* (Boydell Press, 1991) provides useful comparative material.
40. These figures are drawn from close analysis of the relevant editions of J. and J.A. Venn (eds.), *Alumni Cantabrigiensis* (4 vols., 1922-7) and J. Foster (ed.), *Alumni Oxoniensis* (4 vols., 1891-2); Curteys attended St John's College, Cambridge and 11 of the 15 appointments made from that college came in the late 16th century; Watson, Andrewes and Harsnett all attended Pembroke Hall, Cambridge; Duppa and King went to Christ Church, Oxford and 11 of the 15 appointments from that College date from the 1630s, '40s and '50s.
41. Mary Hobbs reminds me that William Oughtred had cause to complain about his association with Chichester for he claimed that his daughter had been seduced by Bishop Henry King's son John: Mary Hobbs, *The Sermons of Henry King*, p 16; useful biographical details on many of these lawyers may be found in B. Levack, *The Civil Lawyers in England 1603-1641* (OUP, 1973).
42. The most recent biography is that by Thomas Mason, *Serving God and Mammon. William Juxon, 1582-1663* (AUP, New Jersey, 1985).
43. Peckham, *Acts (2)*, p.241.
44. Kenneth Fincham views Thorne's work rather less favourably than I do in his *Prelate as Pastor: The Episcopate of James I* (OUP, 1990), pp.141-5; I am impressed by the fact that Thorne did attend meetings more than most, but I am grateful to Kenneth Fincham for reminding me that Thorne was being recommended for promotion *c*.1606-7: PRO: SP 14/24/46.
45. Reference to Lockey raises the intriguing question as to how much the library of Chichester Cathedral was used during this period. See Mary Hobbs (below) for fuller discussion of the Library.
46. A. Foster, 'Chichester Diocese in the early 17th century', *SAC* 123 (1985), pp.187-94. Deans and

chapters were formally abolished on 30 April 1649, but effectively, they ceased to exist in 1646.

47. A. Foster, 'The function of a bishop: the career of Richard Neile, 1562-1640' in R. O'Day and F. Heal (eds.), *Continuity and Change* (Leicester University Press, 1976), pp.33-54.
48. 41 per cent of all deans from this period became bishops, but only two of Chichester's deans gained that exalted status: Curteys and Dee; Oxford and Westminster were much better billets if one sought promotion at this time.
49. Again, at Exeter for an earlier period, D. Lepine found that two-thirds of Exeter canons died in post.
50. The deans in question were: Curteys, Rushe, Culpepper, Thorne, Dee, Steward, Aglionby and Ryves. Thorne is known to have attended 135 Chapter meetings, but it is not clear that the rest attended that number between them.
51. I owe this typically sardonic observation to Robert Holtby.
52. The eight precentors of the period were: Willoughby, Beacon, Reynolds, Ball, Mattock, Murriell, Stokes and Potter. John Beacon, the civil lawyer, should perhaps also be mentioned for he was the only other precentor who served as a canon residentiary, but he held office as such for less than four years, scarcely time to exert much influence.
53. See Harry Tummers (below); note also the short piece on 'The Reverend Henry Ball DD c1553-1603' by the late Ronald Tibble in *West Sussex History* 53 (April 1994), pp.25-27.
54. Peckham, *Acts (2)*, p.189.
55. The six chancellors were: Bradbridge, Chantler, Blaxton, Roger Andrewes, Scull and Marsh; full details of Roger's life may be found in P. Welsby, *Lancelot Andrewes, 1555-1626* (SPCK, 1958).
56. Compare this analysis with that provided by Claire Cross concerning who really mattered at York Minster in Chapter V 'From the Reformation to the Restoration' in G. Aylmer and R. Cant (eds.), *A History of York Minster* (1977), pp.193-232.
57. Of these four individuals, three owed their appointment to Bishop Barlow; only Gardiner was a Curteys nominee.
58. Again Exeter offers an interesting comparison from the medieval period, with 50 per cent of all canons serving for more than ten years.
59. The crucial test of influence really relates to how many canons residentiary a bishop could appoint. In this respect Barlow and Harsnett had most impact with five appointments each, next came Curteys, Bickley and Montagu with four each, then Watson and Andrewes with two apiece, and Duppa and Carleton with only one each. Even here, however, one still has to calculate length of service and those appointed in the 1630s served for far less time than those placed earlier in the period.
60. *Fasti* (2), p.37.
61. *Alumni Cantabrigiensis* and *Alumni Oxoniensis*, *op. cit.*
62. B. Levack, *The Civil Lawyers in England 1603-1641* (OUP, 1973), pp.208-9.
63. Peckham, *Acts (2)*, p.219.
64. *Fasti* (2), p.59; Diana Greenway (above).
65. Peckham, *Acts (2)*, p.75; *Fasti* (2), p.60.
66. I owe confirmation of this point to Nicholas Tyacke, who refers to Corro in his excellent *Anti-Calvinists: The Rise of English Arminianism c.1590-1640* (OUP, 1987), p.58.
67. *Cal.S.P.Dom,1628-29*, pp.257, 260; *Fasti* (2), p.75.
68. *Cal.S.P.Dom,1631-33*, p.254.
69. *Cal.S.P.Dom.1637*, p.517.
70. PRO: PCC 11/175/123; I am grateful to Kenneth Fincham for this point.
71. WSRO: the bulk of Chichester Corporation Records dates from *c*.1688.
72. *VCH* 3, p.96; WSRO: Cap I/21/3 & Chichester City, J3.
73. *Cal.S.P.Dom, 1635-6*, pp.166, 538-9, 542; *Cal.S.P.Dom. 1636-7*, pp.215-6.
74. *Cal.S.P.Dom. 1635*, pp.xlii-xliii.
75. *ibid.*
76. For a general introduction to the problems of the Church of England between 1640 and 1660 see: J. Morrill, 'The Church in England, 1642-49' in J. Morrill (ed.), *Reactions to the English Civil War,*

1642-1649 (Macmillan, 1982), pp.89-114; C. Cross, 'The Church in England 1646-1660' in G. Aylmer (ed.), *The Interregnum: The Quest for Settlement 1646-1660* (Macmillan, 1972), pp.99-120.

77. F. Sawyer, 'Proceedings of the Committee of Plundered Ministers Relating to Sussex', *SAC* 36 (1888), pp.136-59.
78. J. Walker, *Sufferings of the Clergy* (1714); D. Lloyd, *Memoires of the Lives, Actions, Sufferings & Deaths of ... Personages that suffered ... from 1637 to 1666* (1668).
79. M. Hobbs, *Sermons of Henry King*, p.274.
80. Peckham, *Acts (2)*, pp.142, 206-9.
81. Discussions with Claire Cross, Bill Sheils, Ian Atherton and Kenneth Fincham have convinced me that an article such as this can merely scratch the surface of a desirable major research project on the rôle of cathedrals in the early modern period. When a full comparative study comes to be written, it will have to take into account a wide range of pastoral rôles performed by canons in their local communities, give greater consideration to issues of estate management, and look closely at the range of services and activities conducted within Cathedral precincts.

VII. The Restoration to 1790 (Robert Holtby)

1. J.B. Mullinger in *DNB*.
2. *Fasti* (2), p.36. This authority is followed throughout.
3. *Cal.S.P.Dom.* (May 1684-Feb. 1685) 29 June 1684, p.81.
4. eg. WSRO Cap. 1/26/10, Dr. Edes Rental, 1664; and Cap. 1/26/15, fol.47, 1667 (tenements in St Pancras).
5. WSRO Cap. 1/1/8, fol.89.
6. *ibid.*, fol.92.
7. See Watkins Shaw, *The Succession of Organists of the Chapels Royal and the Cathedrals of England and Wales from c.1538* (Oxford, 1991), pp.75-79.
8. Nairn and Pevsner, p.153.
9. Walcott, p.17.
10. *SAC* 42 (1899), pp.246-7.
11. Sometimes called Dean Healey's Memorandum.
12. WSRO Cap. 1/26/17.
13. James Elmes's biography of Wren (1813), quoted in Corlette, p.40, but see T. Tatton-Brown, p.146 below.
14. Edmund Venables in *DNB*.
15. C.E. Whiting, *Nathaniel Lord Crew ... and his Diocese* (1940), p.30.
16. Edes was a residentiary from 1662. He was not precentor until 1696.
17. Stephens, *Memorials*, p.301, from Bodl. Lib. MSS Tanner 384.
18. *ibid.*, pp.301-2.
19. *Cal.S.P.Dom.* 1683, p.70. See also Carleton to the Duke of York (*ibid.*, pp.61-2) on disloyalty of City officers.
20. *ibid.*, pp.312-13.
21. Thomas Seccombe in *DNB*.
22. Thomas Cooper in *DNB*.
23. W.D. Peckham, 'Chichester Non-Jurors', *SNQ* 9 (1942-3), pp.115-16. See also McCann, p.193 below.
24. WRSO Cap. 1/4/4/106, 3 May 1674.
25. WSRO Ep.149; Cap. 1/7/1, fol.65ff., quoted in L.P. Curtis, *Chichester Towers* (Yale, 1966), p.115.
26. WSRO Ep.149; Cap. 1/7/1, fol.195ff., 9 September 1666.
27. WSRO Cap. 1/26/17.
28. WSRO Cap. 1/1/5, fol.192. The 'sermon place' was probably, as in the 19th century, the south transept, see Yates, p.120 below.
29. WSRO Cap. 1/1/2, fol.155, 10 October 1695.
30. WSRO Cap. 1/2/7, 28 August 1742.

31. Bennett *et al.*, p.43.
32. *ibid.*, p.43.
33. *ibid.*, pp.44-5.
34. Described in Curtis, *op. cit.* (note 25).
35. J.M. Scott in *DNB.*
36. N. Sykes, *Edmund Gibson* (Oxford, 1926), pp.55-6.
37. Edward Carpenter, *Thomas Sherlock* (1936), p.25.
38. Curtis, *op. cit.*, p.15.
39. C.N.L. Brooke, J.M. Horn, N.L. Ramsay, 'A Canon's Residence in the Eighteenth Century: the case of Thomas Gooch', *JEH* 39 (no.4, October 1988), p.555. On Gooch see also John Venn, *Gonville and Caius College, Biographical History*, vol.2, Cambridge, 1901.
40. Studied in detail by Curtis, *op. cit.*, esp. pp.16-29.
41. Curtis, *op. cit.*, p.64.
42. 'The Correspondence of the Duke of Richmond and Newcastle 1724-1750', ed. Timothy J. McCann, SRS 73 (1982/3), p.41, 2 September 1740.
43. *ibid.*, p.62, 14 June 1741. See also G.H. Nadel, 'The Sussex Election of 1741', *SAC* 91, 1953.
44. Curtis, *op.cit.*, p.64, quoting William Hayley.
45. BL Add. MS 32692, fol.24, 15 August 1739.
46. BL Add. MS 32694, fol.335, 28 July 1740.
47. BL Add. MS 32688, fol.445, 3 October 1737.
48. BL Add. MS 32985, fol.263, 28 September 1767. The Newcastle correspondence has very many letters from Ball. There are also letters in WSRO Goodwood (110, 111). WSRO MP 708 is a list of sources for *Chichester Towers*.
49. Anthony Fletcher, *A County Community in Peace and War, Sussex 1600-1660* (1975), p.235.
50. WSRO c/2, fol.159.
51. WSRO Lists and Indexes, no.11, 31 December 1740.
52. Hay, pp.364-5.
53. 'The Memoirs of James Spershott', ed. F.W. Steer, *Chichester Papers* 30 (1932), p.14.
54. WSRO Cap 1/4/8/10, 12 January 1727 (OS). The accounts include regular provision for bread, e.g. Cap 1/28/270; 1718/1730.
55. Neville Ollerenshaw, *A History of the Prebendal School* (Chichester, 1983), p.12.
56. Ollerenshaw corrects some of the material in A.F. Leach, 'Chichester Prebendal School' in *VCH* 2, p.399. Christopher Fry in *Chichester 900* (Chichester 1975) says that Collins probably went to the Prebendal before going to Winchester. Some boys went on to other schools.
57. See Julian Munby, *St Mary's Hospital* (Leeds, 1981), and C.A. Swainson, 'The Hospital of St Mary in Chichester', *SAC* 24 (1872) pp.41-62.
58. See Hilda Johnstone and F.W. Steer, 'Alexander Hay, Historian of Chichester', *Chichester Papers* 20, 1961.
59. Walcott, p.203.
60. *SNQ* 14, p.58.
61. F.W. Steer, 'The Vicars' Hall, Chichester and its Undercroft', *Chichester Papers* 12 (1958) (WSRO Cap 1/1/2, fol.47).
62. W.K. Lowther Clarke, 'Chichester Cathedral in the Nineteenth Century', *Chichester Papers* 14 (1959), p.12.
63. WSRO Cap 1/1/8, fol.100. See further T. Tatton-Brown, chapter XIV below.
64. Stephens, *Memorials*, p.345.
65. *ibid.*, p.345.
66. WSRO Cap 1/28/263. *See also* I.C. Hannah, 'Houses in the Close at Chichester', *SAC* 63 (1923), pp.133-58.
67. Geoffrey Holmes and Daniel Szechi, *The Age of Oligarchy, Pre-Industrial Britain 1722-1783* (1993), p.101.
68. See John and Hilary Vickers, *Methodism in a Cathedral City* (Chichester, 1977).
69. WSRO, Cap 1/2/11.

70. The South Sea Company.
71. *loc. cit.*, p.23.
72. *ibid.*
73. *ibid.*
74. *ibid.*, p.24.
75. *ibid.*

VIII. Change and Continuity, 1790-1902 (Nigel Yates)

1. The best study of the Church of England in this period is W.O. Chadwick, *The Victorian Church*, 2 vols. (1966-70). However, it begins with the debate on Catholic Emancipation in the late 1820s. The period between 1790 and then has no comparable study. W.R. Ward, *Religion and Society in England 1790-1850* (1972), is good on the changing relationship between the Anglican establishment and dissent but does not really deal with the internal history of the Church of England. The most recent significant contribution covering the period is P. Virgin, *The Church in an Age of Negligence* (Cambridge, 1989) but it is somewhat idiosyncratic. The liturgical issues have been explored in W.N. Yates, *Buildings, Faith and Worship: The Liturgical Arrangement of Anglican Churches 1600-1900* (Oxford, 1991), which concentrates heavily on the period 1780-1840. The most recent research on cathedrals has been undertaken by P. Barrett, *Barchester: English Cathedral Life in the Nineteenth Century* (1993).
2. Chadwick, *op. cit.*, vol.1 pp.39-40.
3. C. Dewey, *The Passing of Barchester* (1991), p.151.
4. W.N. Yates, 'The Parochial Impact of the Oxford Movement in South-West Wales', *Carmarthenshire Studies*, ed. W.T. Barnes and W.N. Yates (Carmarthen, 1974), p.222.
5. WSRO Cap I/4/5/10-11.
6. Corlette, pp.42-3, 46. See also Brighton, pp.80-1 above.
7. WSRO Cap I/3/6, 21 January 1822.
8. *Chichester Observer*, 2 June 1897.
9. WSRO Cap I/24/5.
10. Barrett, *op. cit.*, p.159.
11. WSRO Cap I/3/5, 10 October 1792.
12. WSRO Cap I/3/6, 2 August 1802.
13. *First Report of Her Majesty's Commissioners appointed to inquire into the State and Condition of the Cathedral and Cathedral and Collegiate Churches in England and Wales* (1854), pp.143-54.
14. WSRO Cap I/7/1, fols.131-66.
15. Chadwick, *op. cit.*, vol.1 p.137.
16. WSRO Cap I/3/7, 10 October 1859, 20 January 1864, 20 January and 1 August 1865. See also W.K. Lowther Clarke, 'Chichester Cathedral in the Nineteenth Century', *Chichester Papers* 14, (1959), pp.5, 10.
17. Chadwick, *op. cit.*, vol.2 p.367.
18. WSRO Cap I/3/7, 20 January 1860.
19. WSRO Ep I/53/9/1, p.45
20. W.R.W. Stephens, *The South Saxon Diocese: Selsey—Chichester* (1881), pp.261-4.
21. Lowther Clarke, *op. cit.*, pp.9, 14.
22. *Post Office Directories of Sussex*, 1887 and 1890.
23. Lowther Clarke, *op. cit.*, p.12.
24. The information in this section, and other information in this chapter relating to the careers of Chapter members, is drawn from the revised edition of le Neve's *Fasti Ecclesiae Anglicanae*, Foster's *Alumni Oxoniensis*, Venn's *Alumni Cantabriensis*, Crockford's *Clerical Directory* and relevant entries in the *DNB*.
25. Lowther Clarke, *op. cit.*, pp.16. For the correspondence between Chandler and Manning see E.S. Purcell, *Life of Cardinal Manning* (1895), vol.1 p.170-9.
26. See Chadwick, *op. cit.*, pp.372-3.

27. Authoritative but somewhat hagiographical memoir by his son-in-law, W.R.W. Stephens, *Life and Letters of Walter Farquhar Hook* (1879). Very thin modern biography by C.J. Stranks, *Dean Hook* (1954). For Hook's period in Leeds see W.N. Yates, *Leeds and the Oxford Movement* (publications by the Thoresby Society, vol.55, Leeds, 1975), pp.13-18, and 'The Religious Life of Victorian Leeds', *History of Modern Leeds*, D. Fraser (ed.) (Manchester, 1980), pp.253-6.
28. *Chichester Observer*, 17 October 1888.
29. F. Pigou, *Phases of My Life* (1898), p.370.
30. WSRO EP I/53/9/1, p.92.
31. Thin memoir by J.F. Briscoe and H.F. B. Mackay, *A Tractarian at Work* (London and Oxford, 1932). For Randall's period at All Saints', Clifton, see P.G. Cobb, *The Oxford Movement in Nineteenth Century Bristol* (Bristol, 1988), pp.17-18, 22-3.
32. Chadwick, *op. cit.*, vol.2, p.52.
33. E.M. Goulburn, *John William Burgon* (1892), vol.2 p.125.
34. WSRO EP I/53/9/1, p.204.
35. Chapter Act Book 1876-96, January, May and August 1878.
36. Goulburn, *op. cit.*, pp.196-7.
37. Barrett, *op. cit.*, pp.49-51.
38. See J.F. White, *The Cambridge Movement* (Cambridge, 1962), and Yates, *Buildings, Faith and Worship*, pp.127-74.
39. Corlette, pp.43-4; Crocker, p.40.
40. T.G. Willis, *Records of Chichester* (Chichester, 1928), pp.154-5.
41. Crocker, pp.10-11, 30-6.
42. *Handbook to the Cathedrals of England, Southern Division* (1903), vol.2, p.662.
43. WSRO Cap I/4/5/13-14; Clarke, *op. cit.*, p.19.
44. Barrett, *op. cit.*, p.137.
45. WSRO Cap I/11/1. This volume, which is the chief source of much that follows, contains a very detailed account of the restoration of the Cathedral, and the building of the new church of St Peter the Great, between 1847 and 1867.
46. Lowther Clarke, *op. cit.*, p.3.
47. WSRO Cap I/3/7, 10 October 1853.
48. *Handbook*, vol.2, pp.631-2.
49. Crocker, p.39.
50. Letter from Hook to Charles Swainson, prebendary of Firle and Principal of Chichester Theological College, in June 1859, quoted in Stephens, *Hook*, vol.1, pp.393-5.
51. Corlette, pp.46-7.
52. WSRO Cap I/11/1.
53. Article in *The Builder*, 2 March 1861, quoted in Stephens, *South Saxon Diocese*, pp.267-9. This is actually a quotation from Prof. R. Willis, see his 'introductory essay', p.xviii in his *Architectural History*, though *The Builder*'s report (p.134) is also valuable.
54. Slater (1819-72) was a pupil of the former cathedral architect, R.C. Carpenter, who had died in 1855. Neither Slater nor his successor, G.M. Hills (1826-94), another of Carpenter's pupils, was really in the top rank of Victorian architects, which explains the pedestrian nature of much of the work in the cathedral after 1860.
55. WSRO EP I/53/9/1, p.148.
56. Barrett, *op. cit.*, p.238.
57. *VCH* 3, p.113.
58. WSRO Cap I/3/7, 1 August 1861; Clarke, *op. cit.*, p.13.
59. WSRO Cap I/3/7, 2 May 1865; Corlette, p.48.
60. WSRO Cap I/3/7, 12 November 1866; 21 January, 2 May, 10 October and 18 November 1867.
61. Stephens, *Hook*, vol.1, p.441; Barrett, *op. cit.*, p.238.
62. WSRO Cap 2/3/7, 20 January and 4 May 1869; Clarke, *op. cit.*, p.4; *VCH* 3, p.123. Now in St Mary's Portfield, Chichester (a redundant church and mechanical music museum).
63. *Handbook*, vol.2, pp.638, 654-5 (note 42).

64. WSRO Cap I/3/7, 1 August 1867 and 3 August 1869.
65. *VCH* 3, p.113.
66. Chapter Act Book 1876-96, August 1876, May 1877 and October 1878.
67. *Chichester Observer*, 12 September 1888.
68. Chapter Act Book 1876-96, May and November 1888, October 1889 and October 1890.
69. Willis, p.181.
70. Chapter Act Book 1876-96, August 1891, October 1892 and January 1894; Chapter Act Book 1896-1919, October 1897.
71. Chapter Act Book 1876-96, October 1881; Pigou, *op. cit.*, p.258; Barrett, *op. cit.*, p.120.
72. See W.N. Yates, *The Oxford Movement and Parish Life: St Saviour's, Leeds, 1839-1929* (York, 1975).
73. WSRO Ep I/53/9/1, p.176; Stephens, *Hook*, vol.1, p.500; for the details of the Purchas case see P.T. Marsh, *The Victorian Church in Decline* (1969), pp.125-8.
74. Goulburn, *op. cit.*, ii p.188.
75. Pigou, *op. cit.*, p.363.
76. Hook Papers, L2/14. I am grateful to the owner of these private papers, Mrs. Barnaby Green, for supplying me with a copy of this letter.
77. WSRO Cap I/3/7, 10 October 1871.
78. *ibid.*, 2 May 1873; Chapter Act Book 1876-96, January 1877.
79. WSRO Cap VI/2.
80. Chapter Act Book 1876-96, October 1877 and January 1878; Barrett, *op. cit.*, p.153.
81. WSRO EP I/53/9/1, p.205.
82. Chapter Act Book 1876-96, January, May and October 1889; January and May 1890; May 1891.
83. *ibid.* May 1892, August 1894, January 1895 and October 1896.
84. Chapter Act Book 1896-1919, October 1898, May 1900 and October 1901.
85. *ibid.*, January and May 1897.
86. *Chichester Observer*, 12 May 1897; see also Willis, *op. cit.*, pp.216-18 and Briscoe and Mackay, *op. cit.*, pp.186-7.
87. Chapter Act Book 1896-1919, May 1901.
88. Chadwick, *op. cit.*, vol.1, p.140, vol.2, pp.382-3 and *The Founding of Cuddesdon* (Oxford, 1954), pp.1-9. The first students at Lampeter were not admitted until 1827 and the college was subsequently granted the right to award both BA and BD degrees. See D.T.W. Price, *A History of St David's University College, Lampeter*, vol.1 (Cardiff, 1977).
89. J.W. Burgon, *Lives of Twelve Good Men* (1891), pp.159-60. See also W.M. Jacob, 'The Diffusion of Tractarianism: Wells Theological College, 1840-9', *Southern History* 5 (1983), pp.189-96.
90. A. Haig, *The Victorian Clergy* (1984), pp.81-6.
91. WSRO Cap I/3/7, 1 August 1872.
92. Barrett, *op. cit.*, p.283.
93. PRO HO 92/2/1-11; published in *The Religious Census of Sussex 1851*, ed. J.A. Vickers, SRS 75 (1989), pp.166-71.
94. B.I. Coleman, 'Southern England in the Census of Religious Worship, 1851', *Southern History* 5 (1983), pp.154-88 and W.N. Yates, 'The Major Kentish Towns in the Religious Census of 1851', *Archaeologia Cantiana* 100 (1983), pp.399-423.
95. Lowther Clarke, *op. cit.*, p.11.
96. WSRO, Cap I/3/7, 20 January 1872.
97. *ibid.*, 2 May 1865 and 10 October 1866.
98. *ibid.*, 20 January 1868.

IX. Destruction, Repair and Restoration (Tim Tatton-Brown)

1. Walcott, p.34.
2. *ibid.*, p.35. But see Fines, p.54 above.
3. Stephens, *Memorials*, pp.230-7.
4. E. Croft-Murray, 'Lambert Barnard : an English Renaissance Painter', *Archaeol. Journal* 113 (1956), pp.111-12.

5. Walcott, p.89 and N. Plumley and J. Lees, *The Organs and Organists of Chichester Cathedral* (1988), p.1.
6. Appendix to O.H. Leeney, 'References to Ancient Sussex churches in *The Ecclesiologist*, mainly as regards restoration and repair', *SAC* 86 (1947), pp.185-6, printing S.P. Dom., Charles I, vol.342, no.98.
7. See T. Brighton (p.84, above), A. Foster (p.88, above), and P. Barrett (p.252, below).
8. Corlette, p.64.
9. Illustrated in C. Hewett, *English Cathedral Carpentry* (1974) p.127, fig.107, though Hewett suggests a 15th-century date. He also points out the unusual use here of eaves-blades with spur-ties, and plate-hooks for the top plate.
10. Walcott, pp.20-1, and see Robert Holtby (p.103, above).
11. It was apparently copied, not very accurately, by Hollar for use in the first edition of Dugdale's *Monasticon Anglicanum* (1673) vol.3, p.115. King's engraving (fig.44), which shows the ruined north-west tower, was only published in the English abridgement of the *Monasticon* of 1722. It was, however, used by King himself in his *The Cathedrall and Conventuall Churches of England and Wales* (1672), p.74. For King's plan (fig.67), see C.E. Welch, 'An Early Plan of Chichester Cathedral,' *SNQ* 14 (Nov. 1956), pp.199-203.
12. We know of this from the paper by Dr. Ede, the precentor, quoted by Robert Holtby (above, pp.103-5).
13. *VCH* 3, p.143, notes, that in 1724 there was another proposal to rebuild the 'West Tower'. The Dean and Chapter were authorised to make contracts up to £900 for it (BL Add. MS. 39331, fol.66).
14. J. Elmes, *Memorials of the Life and Works of Sir Christopher Wren* (1823), Part 2, p.520.
15. This scaffold was fixed to the apex of the spire by some original ironwork. See T. Tatton-Brown, 'Building the tower and spire of Salisbury Cathedral,' *Antiquity* 65, no.246 (March 1991), p.92.
16. Elmes, *op. cit.*, p.521, where the pendulum weight inside the tower is described in detail (also quoted in Corlette, p.42).
17. Walcott, p.199.
18. *VCH* 3, p.114 and Willis, p.31, who saw the chapel before its restoration in 1871 (see fig.97), and said that the raised floor level 'robbed the chapel of its due altitude'.
19. See plan of the chapel in James Storer (1814) *The History and Antiquities of the Cathedral Churches of Great Britain* (4 vols., 1814-19), and Le Keux's longitudinal section through the Cathedral (*c.*1815) fig.69.
20. Essex *was* employed to take down the 'little cloister' in the Vicars' Close (p.237, below), and he then went on to Ely Cathedral to carry out major restorations for Bishop Manson, see T. Cocke, 'The Architectural History of Ely Cathedral from 1540-1840', *Medieval Art and Architecture at Ely Cathedral* (BAA Conference Transactions, 1978), pp.73-5.
21. For Grimm's drawings (reproduced in *VCH* 3), see figs.36, 72 and 97. For a description of the state of the Cathedral in 1803 see also *Gents. Mag.* Part I (1803), pp.22-5, quoted in Corlette, pp.41-2.
22. W.K. Lowther Clarke, 'Chichester Cathedral in the Nineteenth Century', *Chichester Papers* 14 (1959), p.2. Also Corlette, p.46.
23. G. Zarnecki, 'The Chichester Reliefs', *Archaeol. Journal* 110 (1954), pp.106-19.
24. V.H.A. Vallance, *Great English Church Screens* (1947), pp.57-61.
25. See T. Brighton (pp.79-80, above).
26. Lowther Clarke, *op. cit.* (note 22), p.3 and N. Yates (p.120, above) and *ibid.*, pp.128-9.
27. See N. Yates (p.129, above). For a fuller discussion and documentation of these changes see O.H. Leeney, *op. cit.* (note 6), pp.155-64.
28. *Transactions of the Archaeological Institute at Chichester, July 1853* (1856), pp.35-6; first published in1861.
29. See N. Yates, p.130, above. The blocks remained there until removed to the Bell Tower in 1881. In 1905, the Arundel Screen was re-erected inside the first floor (i.e. above the basement vault) of the Bell Tower (see J. Halliburton, below, p.159 and fig.83).
30. Quoted in Leeney, *op. cit.*, pp.168-70. For the fall of the spire, see also N. Yates (pp.130-2, above).

31. Willis, p.xviii. For some contemporary local press accounts, see *CCJ* (1961), pp.19-21.
32. Willis, pp.xviii-xix.
33. Leeney, *op. cit.*, p.141.
34. G. Gilbert Scott (ed.), *Personal and Professional Recollections* (1879), pp.39-311, quoted in Leeney, *op. cit.*, p.171. Unfortunately the moulded and carved stone taken from the rubble does not seem to survive, though a little stone was re-used and the capstone is preserved in the north transept. Record drawings made at the time of the fall can be found at the WSRO. Add. MSS., 1850-1861.
35. Scott, *ibid.*, p.309 and Leeney, pp.171-2. Also quoted in Corlette, *op. cit.* (note 8), 48. Scott also tells us that: 'The piers to some height above the floor of the church are wholly of Purbeck stone set in cement, but as this was found ruinously costly they were carried up above that level with dressings of Portland stone, but the mass of Purbeck. The superstructure was partly of Chilmark stone and partly of the rag from Purbeck.'
36. See illustration in Corlette, *op. cit.* (note 8), p.98.
37. Corlette, p.85, and N. Yates, p.134 above and *passim*.
38. Some excellent drawings (now at the Society of Antiquaries of London) were, however, made of the platform and tombs in 1852 by Sir George Scharf (figs.11 and 79).
39. Corlette, p.85.
40. There is a useful 'Report on the Repairs necessary to Chichester Cathedral' by G.M. Hills (dated 30 Sept.1892), in which the state of the western towers is discussed, as well as the proposed rebuilding. Hills disagreed with Blomfield's advice on opening up the south-west tower (Cathedral Library).
41. Leeney, pp.78-9 and T.G. Willis, *Records of Chichester* (1928). A full discussion by Godfrey and Bloe of all these chapels and their furnishings up to 1935 can be found in the *VCH*.
42. For a list of all the newly carved corbelled (portrait) heads here, see *CCJ* (1961), p.21. There is a useful summary report on the state of the fabric in early 1934 by the architect, Philip M. Johnston; also another, much longer, report nearly three years later by the new architect, W.A. Forsyth (dated 26 October 1936).

X. Deans, Chapters and Bishops (John Halliburton and Jeremy Haselock)

1. For an outline of Dean Hannah's achievements see *DNB sv.*
2. There is much about Hannah's career up to his becoming Vicar of Brighton in *John Hannah—a Clerical Study* by J.H. Overton, 1890.
3. Hannah owned quarries at West Hoathly which supplied materials to repair the Cathedral fabric, see Tatton-Brown, p.324, n.71, below.
4. See *DNB* entry *cit. supra.*
5. For a summary account of conditions in England before 1914, see A.J.P. Taylor, *English History 1914-1945* (Oxford, 1965), p.1.
6. Minutes of the Dean and Chapter of Chichester 1914, p.349.
7. See *The Times* obituary, 3 June 1931.
8. Chapter Minutes, 1915, p.364.
9. Chapter Minutes, 1918, p.417.
10. Chapter Minutes, 1904-7, esp. pp.188 and 192.
11. Chapter Minutes, 1923, p.33.
12. On George Bell, see R.C.D. Jasper, *George Bell, Bishop of Chichester* (OUP, 1967) and Kenneth Slack, *George Bell* (SCM Centrebook, London, 1971). A new biography by Frank Field MP is in preparation.
13. See Slack, *op. cit.*, pp.94, 95.
14. Jasper, *op. cit.*, p.276.
15. For an account of the life and achievement of Duncan-Jones see S.C Carpenter, *Duncan-Jones of Chichester* (London, 1956).
16. W.H. Frere, *Principles of Liturgical Reform* (Murray, 1911), p.187.
17. Carpenter, *Duncan-Jones*, p.41.

18. A.S. Duncan-Jones, *Why Change the Communion Service?* (Alcuin Club Miscellaneous Publications, Mowbray, 1934).
19. Carpenter, *op. cit.*, pp.39, 53, 54.
20. Bell's Charge delivered after his Primary Visitation was published as *Common Order in Christ's Church* (Mowbray, 1937).
21. *ibid.*, p.47.
22. *ibid.*, pp.34-6.
23. *ibid.*, p.37.
24. Duncan-Jones, p.xiii.
25. P. Dearmer, *The Parson's Handbook* (1899).
26. A.S. Duncan-Jones, S. Gaselee, E.G.P. Wyatt (eds.), *A Directory of Ceremonial* (Alcuin Club Tracts 13, Mowbray, 1921).
27. *Customary*, p.xi.
28. Quoted in Carpenter, *op. cit.*, p.68.
29. A.G. Hebert, SSM, *Liturgy and Society* (Faber, 1935).
30. A.G. Hebert (ed.), *The Parish Communion* (SPCK, 1937).
31. Donald Gray, *Earth and Altar* (Alcuin Club Collections Vol.68, 1986).
32. I am grateful to Dr. Mary Hobbs for a detailed verbatim account of this incident.
33. *A Charge at his Primary Visitation of Chichester Cathedral* by the Bishop of Chichester, 4 November 1948. Printed for Private Circulation.

XI. The Cathedral Library (Mary Hobbs)

1. Bennett *et al.*, p.3
2. *ibid.*
3. N.R. Ker, *Mediaeval Libraries of Great Britain: a list of surviving books* (Oxford, 1964). They are: Cambridge, UL, Hugo Floriacensis (*Eccles. Hist.*); Trinity Coll., St Ambrose (*Hexameron*); Emmanuel Coll., St Augustine (*Sermons*), St Jerome (*Contra Rufinum; Contra Jovinianum*), Boethius, (*De Trinitate*); Glasgow UL, Hegesippus; Lincoln Cathedral, *Liber florum*; BL, *Annales*, Isidorus; Coll. of Arms, Bede; Oxford: Bodl. Lib., gloss on Job, St Augustine (two works), *Psalter*, Avicenna; St John's Coll., Peter Lombard, Rabanus Maurus, Orosius; Paris (Sorbonne), *Kalendar*. I must thank the present custodians of these MSS for their generous help. For the characterisation of medieval manuscripts similar to those at Chichester see T. Webber, *Scribes and Scholars at Salisbury Cathedral, c.1075-c.1125* (Oxford, 1994).
4. See Fines, p.54, above.
5. Walcott, p.66.
6. Peckham, *Acts* (1), p.117.
7. *ibid.*, p.110, esp. n.3.
8. R. Garraway Rice, *Sussex Wills: Aldbourne to Chichester*, *SRS* 41 (1935), p.274.
9. Peckham, *Acts* (2), pp.65, 66. If a 'super-altar' was not a book, it may gave been one of numerous fittings sold off, as the Communar's books show, in 1550. For Way and for the sacking of the shrine, see Fines, p.66, above. See also A.T. Way, 'Blessed William Way', *Devon & Cornwall Notes and Queries* 37, 38 (1984, 1985), which suggests that the vicar choral was probably the martyr's uncle.
10. Peckham *Acts* (2), p.208, and Andrew Foster, p.95, above, to whom I owe the reference to Lockey.
11. C. Thomas-Stanford, *Sussex in the Great Civil War and the Interregnum* (1910), p.61. Other cathedrals were luckier: Winchester, for instance, quietly transferred their books to the College, and Thomas Pury (as Andrew Foster reminded me) persuaded the corporation of Gloucester to take over the Cathedral books as a public library.
12. The book appears among Bishop Henry King's books after his death, possibly retrieved for him by a friend of whose will he was executor, the Dutch London merchant Francis Tryon, whose name is on the list in the South Transept (fig.45) of those who gave money to restore the cathedral after the Civil War. For William Nicolson, see Alison McCann, p.190, below.
13. 1653 (*PCC* 136 Coke). John King's will was *PCC* 48 Duke. The whereabouts of these books

during the Interregnum is a puzzle; some may have been with King or his sons; others, taken by John Downes or William Cawley, who were granted the Bishop's properties and rents, may have been returned, perhaps by William's son John, an intruded minister in the diocese who was later regularly ordained by King. I owe the consideration that follows to Andrew Foster.

14. Hobbs, 'Henry King, John Donne and the Refounding of Chichester Cathedral Library', *The Book Collector* 33 (1984), pp.189-205.
15. Unless the 'etc' which follows 'Buck's Bible' after his name in all the donors' lists denotes a quantity of further unspecified gifts.
16. 'Reading Vogues at English Cathedral Libraries of the Eighteenth Century', *Bulletin of the New York Public Library* (1963-6).
17. Walcott, p.66. Dean Ball's letter of thanks to the Duke of Newcastle (note 25 below), in which he records the Chapter having made 'an elegant room' in a place 'hitherto neglected and almost ruinous', is indeed dated 9 April 1750, the year the Duke of Richmond was granted a vault beneath the Lady Chapel, see T. Tatton-Brown, p.146, above.
18. Botfield, *Notes on English Cathedral Libraries* (William Pickering, 1849).
19. *A Visit to Chichester Cathedral* (William Hayley Mason, Chichester, 1849), p.35.
20. Mr Leslie Holden kindly brought it to my notice.
21. There is a wonderful field for detailed research here into the contents of this 18th-century library, the reading habits of the period, and the people of Chichester at the time.
22. It is perhaps significant that, when Clarke died in 1771, the separate library section in the Communar's Accounts ends. See further Robert Holtby, 'The Restoration to 1790' above, and Alison McCann's chapter on the Archives.
23. Alison McCann, *St Andrew Oxmarket, Chichester* (WSRO, 1978).
24. Kaufman (n.16), p.651.
25. BL Add. MS 32879, f.124. I owe this reference to the kindness of Dean Holtby.
26. 'Cui debemus non tantum utilem, elegantem et sumptuosam Librorum copiam; Sed et ipsam magna ex parte Bibliothecam.'
27. I am most grateful to Mrs Elaine Bishop for providing me with references from the relevant documents for the 19th century: WRSO, Cap.I/3/7, the volume 1876-96 (recently also deposited in the WSRO), and the *Diocesan Gazette*, 1916-37.
28. Canon Lowther Clarke, quoted in a letter from Hilda Johnstone to Bishop Bell, November 1947.
29. Bishop Eric Kemp kindly deposited this file in the Library in 1989.
30. Including the Sealed Bible of 1662 which Botfield singled out for special admiration, containing the original Letter Patent of Charles II on vellum 'for lodging a corrected and authentic copy of the Common Prayer Book in this Cathedral'. He adds a note that 'the Great Seal attached to these Patents is preserved in the Chapter House': it has now apparently disappeared altogether.
31. My appeal with a list of titles in *The Book Collector* of 1984 has brought little further information about their present whereabouts. For further detail of the affair see my forthcoming article 'Books in Crisis at Barchester', *The Book Collector* (1994/5).
32. F.W. Steer, 'Chichester Cathedral Library', *Chichester Papers* 44 (1964).

XII. Archives and Antiquaries (Alison McCann)

1. WSRO Ep VI/1/4 f.52v; Cap I/1/1 f.82v.
2. WSRO Ep VI/1/4 f.55v; Cap I/1/1 f.88v.
3. WSRO Ep VI/1/6.
4. WSRO Cap I/3/0 f.160r. For the probable position of the Treasury, see Hobbs, p.173 below.
5. WSRO Cap I/17/25.
6. WSRO Cap I/1/1 f.81r.
7. WSRO Cap I/12/2 p.306.
8. WSRO Ep VI/1/6 f.227v.
9. WSRO Ep VI/1/5 f.1v. His collections are now WSRO Ep VI/1/1-5 and Bodl. Lib. MS Ashmole 1146. See WSRO Ep I/88/44 for an account of their original structure and compilation.

10. WSRO Ep I/1/2 and Ep I/1/3.
11. WSRO Cap I/3/0 f.160r.
12. WSRO Cap I/1/2 f.5v.
13. WSRO Cap I/3/0 f.141r.
14. WSRO Cap I/23/3.
15. WSRO Cap I/27/1.
16. WSRO Cap I/1/2 f.5v.
17. WSRO Cap I/1/2 ff.27v-28.
18. WSRO STC III/H ff.193v-194r.
19. WSRO *The English Historical Library* (ed.3, 1736), p.128, quoted by R. Lane Poole in Hist. MSS. Comm., *Report on MSS in Various Collections*, vol.1 (1901), pp.187-8.
20. WSRO Cap I/21/1 contains Swayne's extracts from act books and statutes; WSRO Cap I/12/2 also includes extracts from act books and cartularies.
21. WSRO Cap I/1/2 ff.24-6.
22. WSRO Cap I/4/9/29.
23. WSRO Cap I/4/6/5.
24. WSRO Cap I/12/3 f.107.
25. WSRO Cap I/4/9/40.
26. WSRO Cap I/12/3 p.238 and p.257.
27. WSRO STD III/3 f.28r Dean's Peculiar Court Diary.
28. WSRO Cap I/1/2 f.30r, 1673 Visitation Articles.
29. WSRO Cap I/1/2 f.37r.
30. WSRO Cap I/1/2 f.33v.
31. Bodl. Lib. MSS Tanner 148, 149 (WSRO MF 37). For Edes's escapades, see further R.T. Holtby, pp.105-6, above.
32. WSRO Cap I/1/2 ff.45v.,46r.
33. WSRO Cap I/1/2 f.47r.
34. WSRO Cap I/1/2 f.75r.
35. WSRO Cap I/1/2 f.77v.
36. WSRO Cap I/24/1 ff.252-3.
37. WSRO Cap I/1/5 ff.295-314.
38. Possibly WSRO Cap I/1/4.
39. WSRO Cap I/4/9/47.
40. WSRO Cap I/3/2 ff.106r, 107r. See also R.T. Holtby, p.107, above.
41. WSRO Cap I/3/2 f.107r. No record exists of Covert's reinstatement but he was attesting Chapter Acts again from July 1691 (WSRO Cap I/3/2 f.129v).
42. WSRO Cap I/3/3 f.97r.
43. WSRO Cap I/5/3 ff.131r, 133r.
44. *Report from the Select Committee appointed to enquire into the state of the Public Records of the Kingdom etc.* 1800, vol.15, p.333, Appendix (N4).
45. WSRO Cap I/7/1 pp.139, 141 (1825); pp.154, 160 (1832).
46. WSRO Cap I/3/7 p.62.
47. WSRO Cap I/3/7 p.270.
48. Historical Manuscripts Commission, *Report on Manuscripts in Various Collections*, vol.1 (1901) pp.187-204.
49. *op. cit.* p.204. The Cathedral Library now contains several copies of each.
50. WSRO Cap I/21/12.
51. Information supplied by Dr. K.M.E. Murray. See further Hobbs, p.183, above.
52. WSRO Cap I/3/11 p.387.
53. Information supplied by Leslie Holden.
54. WSRO Ep I/88/14.
55. WSRO Cap I/7/3 Answers of the Dean and Administrative Chapter No.28.
56. WSRO Ep I/88/10.

57. *A Catalogue of the Records of the Dean and Chapter, Vicars Choral, St Mary's Hospital, Colleges and Schools*, comp. Francis W. Steer and Isabel M. Kirby (WSCC, 1967).
58. A catalogue of his papers is in an advanced state of preparation.
59. See *DNB*.
60. WSRO Ep VI/1/5 f.IV. 'Qui vero instigante diabolo de libra hoc aliter ordinare praesumserit sit perpetuo anathema maranatha partemque recipiat cum Juda traditore domini in inferno inferiore, prout Cædwalla Rex Sussex ... imprecatur in carta prima fundationis eiusdem'.
61. Lambeth Palace Lib. Reg. Courtenay ff.212-213.
62. WSRO Cap I/12/2 f.37.
63. WSRO Cap I/4/9/40.
64. WSRO Cap I/12/2 f.161.
65. WSRO Cap I/12/2 ff.671-2.
66. WSRO Cap I/19/2 f.161.
67. WSRO Cap I/12/2 f.265.
68. WSRO Cap I/1/2 ff.24-6.
69. See L.P. Curtis, *Chichester Towers* (Yale Univ. Press, 1966), pp.74-9, and R.T. Holtby, p.109, above.
70. WSRO Cap I/1/5 ff.295-314.
71. WSRO Cap I/1/5.
72. WSRO Cap I/1/1.
73. WSRO Cap I/17/1.
74. Hay, pp.384 and ff.
75. WSRO Cap I/3/6 p.229.
76. WSRO Ep I/52/1-10.
77. WSRO Ep I/52/11.
78. *A few words to those who have the welfare of Chichester at heart*, WSRO MP 784. See also fig. 66.
79. Philip Barrett, *Barchester* (SPCK, 1993), pp.49-51, and see Yates, pp.125 and 128, above.
80. Dr. Augustus Jessopp, author of theological and historical works.
81. Now in the Peckham Library at WSRO.
82. WSRO Add. MS. 2547.
83. WSRO Lib. 4431.
84. Eric Gill, *Autobiography* (1940).
85. *SAC* 38 (1892) and 48 (1905).
86. WSRO MP 94 f.156.
87. *Chichester Observer*, 3 March 1937.
88. WSRO Cap I/21/12.
89. SRS 4 (1905), 8 (1908) and 11 (1910).
90. WSRO MP 94 ff.102-107. Heron-Allen's book is the source of figs.2, 3 and 4.
91. WSRO MP 93 f.106; the early charters were edited by Eric E. Barker in *SAC* 86-88 (1947-9).
92. *Chichester Observer*, 4 August 1920 and see Hobbs, pp.182-3, below.
93. *Chichester Observer*, 13 October 1920.
94. His unpublished autobiography *Both Ways from Corfu* is WSRO Add. MS. 10981.
95. Add. MS 10981.
96. W.D. Peckham Papers, WSRO Acc. 5517.
97. WSRO Correspondence file AV7.

XIII. Church Monuments (H.A. Tummers)

1. Nairn and Pevsner, p.153.
2. A full inventory of Cathedral monuments (copy in the Cathedral Library) was prepared in 1992 by Dr John Physick for the purposes of the new Cathedral Measure. An early comprehensive account was published by Godfrey (*VCH* 3, pp.105-69). The following lists are held by the Cathedral Library: W.K. Lowther Clarke (1951), Betty Legh-Pope, enlarged by Lady (Frances) Cooke (1975), Canon Geoffrey Parks (1979), Douglas Eagleton (1989, based on the former: for

sale from the Cathedral Office) and 'Ledgerstones in the Cathedral' (Anne Blakeney, 1994).

3. Unless otherwise stated, for the the medieval monuments see H. Tummers, 'The medieval effigial tombs in Chichester Cathedral', *Journal of the Church Monuments Society* 3 (1988), pp.3-41.
4. For the latest conservation treatment, executed in 1961, see *CCJ* (1961), p.4 and the Dean and Chapter Act Books 1955-1959, pp.81, 350, 352 and 1959-1963, *passim*.
5. Bennett *et al.*, p.60, and Stephens, *Memorials*, pp.191-2.
6. See my 'De vorm en plaats van de middeleeuwse grafmonumenten in de kathedraal van Chichester', in *Nader beschouwd. Een serie kunsthistorische opstellen aangeboden aan Pieter Singelenberg bij zijn afscheid van de Universiteit van Nijmegen*, Kunsthistorisch Instituut (Nijmegen, 1986), pp.1-10; see also Clarke's list (note 2 above), pp.7-9.
7. J. Bertram, 'Incised slabs in Sussex', *Transactions of the Monumental Brass Society* 3 (1988), pp.387-9.
8. Probably it was a pulpitum, made by Walter Walton in *c.*1410: J. Harvey, *English Mediaeval Architects* (2nd ed., 1984), p.314.
9. T. Tatton-Brown, 'The tomb of John Arundel', report written for the Dean and Chapter, July 1991, pp.1-3.
10. Lowther Clarke's list (note 2 above), pp.4-5.
11. Early plan by Thomas King, WSRO F PD102; Dean and Chapter Act Book K (1920-1937), p.32. The Act Books A to L, to 1944, are preserved in the WSRO; later books in the office of the Chapter Clerk, Thomas Eggar Verrall Bowles, 5 East Pallant, Chichester.
12. The design of the niche is by the otherwise unknown 'Mr. Roos'; Edward Richardson executed it and designed and executed the effigy: Crocker, p.35; O. Leeney, 'References to ancient Sussex churches in *The Ecclesiologist*', *SAC* 86 (1947), p.177.
13. For two contrasting opinions: Stephens, *Memorials*, p.388, and Nairn and Pevsner, p.160.
14. Parks's list (note 2 above), p.22 and R.T. Holtby, *Chichester Cathedral of the Holy Trinity* (Pitkin, 1981), p.5.
15. *VCH* 3, p.112.
16. John Bertram, 'A suggestion made with authority', *Friends of the Cathedral. Newsletter* (Advent 1990), and an answer by Douglas Eagleton, 'Some Comments on St Richard's brass', *idem (Lent 1991)*.
17. J.E. Butler, 'The monumental brasses of Chichester Cathedral', MS in the Cathedral Library.
18. Bodl. Lib., MSS Willis 38, 41, 46 and 50.
19. The first to say so was I. Valentine, *The Chichester Guide* (Chichester, 1810), p.34.
20. See my 'The medieval effigial tombs' (note 3 above), p.19, and also Lowther Clarke's list (note 2 above), p.6.
21. C. Welch, 'An early plan of Chichester Cathedral', *SNQ* 14 (1956), pp.199-203.
22. A recent suggestion that a female effigy at Hornsea is a still earlier example is based on a confused stylistic analysis (B.and M. Gittos, 'A survey of East Riding sepulchral monuments before 1500', *Medieval Art and Architecture in the East Riding of Yorkshire*, ed. C. Wilson, The British Archaeological Association Conference Transactions for the Year 1983 (Leeds, 1989), p.95.
23. See note 3 above.
24. See Philip Lankester, 'Notes and queries on a mediaeval tomb at Chichester', *The Church Monuments Society Newsletter* 5 (Summer 1989), pp.15-18. Also P. Foster, T. Brighton and P. Garland, 'An Arundel tomb', *Otter Memorial Paper* 9 (Chichester, 1987). The MS of the Cartulary is: BL MS Cotton Vespasian F XV, fols.106v and 107v.
25. B. Winkles, *Winkles' architectural and picturesque illustrations of the cathedral churches of England and Wales* (1838), vol.2, engraving opposite p.35.
26. For the different sites of these three monuments: Th. Abingdon, *The antiquities of the cathedral church of Worcester ... Lichfield* (1717), pp.230-4; Th. Horsfield, *The history, antiquities and topography of the County of Sussex* (Lewes, 1835), p.23; and Crocker, p.48.
27. M. Hobbs, *The Sermons of Henry King (1592-1669), Bishop of Chichester* (AUP, New Jersey, & Scolar Press, Aldershot, 1992), pp.30-1.
28. Abingdon, *op. cit.*, p.239, mentions Smalpage's memorial in the south transept, but Walcott, p.51, records it in the cloisters. For Cawley's memorial see H.R. Mosse, *The Monumental Effigies of Sussex*

1250-1650 (2nd ed., Cambridge, 1933), p.46 and W. Hussey, 'Cathedral Notes', *CCJ* (1972), p.3.

29. See W.D. Peckham, 'The epitaph of William Chillingworth', *SNQ* (1948-1949), pp.79-83.
30. The best authority for bishops and other cathedral clergy is Le Neve, *Fasti*. (Far more memorial inscriptions are to be found in Chichester Cathedral than mentioned.) See also G. Hennessy, *Clergy of the Diocese of Chichester* (Chichester 1911).
31. Mentioned by R.T. Holtby, 'Bishop William Otter', *Otter Memorial Paper* 6 (Chichester, 1989).
32. Corlette, pp.87-8, is the only author so far to note the excellency of the design of this memorial.
33. D. Meara, *Victorian Memorial Brasses* (1983), p.165, merely mentions Burgon's brass, though it would have deserved more attention than some other examples given. E. Goulburn, *John William Burgon. A Biography with Extracts from his Letters and Early Journal* (2 vols., London, 1892), has an engraving of the Dean as frontispiece, which shows how faithful a likeness this brass is (with thanks to the Rev. Colin Lawlor, who let me read his thesis on Burgon).
34. An interesting 'parchment memorial' once hung near this tomb: F.W. Steer, 'A parchment memorial in Chichester Cathedral', *SNQ* 16 (1963), pp.1-4.
35. *VCH* 3, p.145; also, for Bradbridge's mayoralty, R. Newman, 'An Unrecorded Chichester Mayoralty', *SAC* 16 (1963), p.134. Further on this and other early brasses in the Cathedral: C. Davidson-Houston, 'Sussex Monumental Brasses, 2, Chichester Cathedral', *SAC* 77 (1936), pp.130-9.
36. See F.W. Steer, 'Naval memorials in Chichester Cathedral', *The Monumental Journal* (1958), pp.329-33.
37. The earliest mention is in I. Hannah, 'Chichester Cathedral', *SAC* 63 (1922), p.237.
38. From *c.*1750 till about 1870: see W.K. Lowther Clarke, *Shilling guide to Chichester Cathedral* (2nd ed., Chichester, 1957), p.16. The Lady Chapel was restored to its original use in memory of Bishop Gilbert, whose memorial is on the south wall (Leeney, *op. cit.* [note 12], p.177).
39. The first removal is recorded in Act Book J (1896-1919), pp.58 and 64. About 1900 another tablet is added (*idem*, p.162), but when in 1938 a request is made for a new floor brass, there is a resolution to find out whether the Nicolls family has still any connection with the Cathedral: Act Book L (January 1937-June 1944), pp.119 and 121.
40. Described thus by Lieut. Hammond in 1635: 'A relation of a short survey of the Westerne Counties', edited by L.G. Wickham Legg in *Camden Miscellany*, vol.16, Part 3 (1936), p.34.
41. For these altar tombs see Dallaway, p.134 and *VCH* 2, pp.361-2. The best description is *VCH* 3, pp.45, 125, 132-3 and 145.
42. Kathleen Esdaile was the first to notice the naval monuments by Charles Harris: *English Church Monuments 1510-1840* (1946), p.100. As the names of the persons commemorated are cited wrongly and Harris's name was not incorporated in the index, this item was not taken up by later authors, such as R. Gunnis, *Dictionary of British sculptors* (2nd ed., 1968), generally an inexhaustible source for post-medieval sculptors. For the general history of naval monuments see Esdaile, pp.96-100.
43. See particularly: C. Teniswood, 'Memorials of Flaxman', *Art Journal* (1867), pp.101-4; 161-4; 201-5; 241-4; *idem* (1868), pp.1-4; 81-4; 145-8 and 241-4 (an early evaluation); M. Whinney, 'Flaxman and the eighteenth century: a commemoration', *Journal of the Warburg and Courtauld Institutes* 19 (1956), pp.269-82 and M. Whinney, *Sculpture in Britain 1530 to 1830*, The Pelican History of Art (Harmondsworth, 1964), pp.183-95 (the best art-historical analysis); R. Gunnis, 'Monuments by John Flaxman in Sussex', *SAC* 95 (1959), pp.82-8; M. Whinney and R. Gunnis, *The collection of models by John Flaxman, R.A. at the University College London* (1967) (the models, several of which are for Chichester monuments, are now on show in the Victoria and Albert Museum); D. Irvin, *English Neoclassical Art: Studies in Inspiration and Taste* (1966) (Flaxman compared with other contemporary English and European sculptors); N. Penny, *Church Monuments in Romantic Britain* (New Haven/London, 1977); and D. Bindman (ed.), *John Flaxman* (1979) (the most reliable publication for exact dates).
44. For the Murray monument see Parks's list (note 2 above), p.10.
45. Gunnis, *Dictionary of British Sculptors*, pp.199-200.
46. *ibid., passim.*
47. For the statue in Liverpool and Gibson's connection with Canova and Thorvaldsen in Rome, see *The Age of Neoclassicism*, Exhibition Catalogue Victoria and Albert Museum (1972), p.239.
48. Lowther Clarke, *op. cit.* (note 2, above), pp.7, 68. Tower was Kempe's partner, see Nairn and

Pevsner, p.160. For Wilberforce's monument, see Lowther Clarke, p.68.
49. The firm of Gaffin is the only one named in Gunnis, *Dictionary of British Sculptors*, p.160.
50. *ibid.*, p.224.
51. For Bell's memorial see the Act Books for 1955-1959 and 1959-1963, *passim* and Coke, p.330, n.28.
52. Parks's list (note 2 above), p.22.

XIV. The Buildings of the Bishop's Palace and the Close (Tim Tatton-Brown and the Right Revd Eric W. Kemp)

I am most grateful to Richard Meynell for all his help during my visits to the many buildings in his care in the Close. At the Bishop's Palace, I was greatly helped both by Bishop Kemp and Richard Andrews, the architect.

1. Walcott, p.13, records the gift of the land from the Earl of Arundel.
2. *VCH* 3, p.146.
3. Some of the documentary evidence for this is usefully summarised in Morgan, p.146.
4. Paradise was originally the name for the whole of the graveyard around the cathedral and not just the area within the cloister.
5. Chron. Rogeri de Hoveden (Rolls Series 2), p.333 and Peckham, *Chartulary*, p.903, no.29.
6. Quoted in Morgan, p.157.
7. *ibid.*, p.75.
8. M.J. Kitch, 'The Chichester Cathedral Chapter at the time of the Reformation', *SAC* 116 (1978), pp.277-92.
9. Quoted in full in Morgan, p.158.
10. *ibid.*, p.75.
11. Walcott, p.92.
12. N. Ollerenshaw, *A History of the Prebendal School* (1984).
13. Why the bishop needed such a large area is not clear. His 'park' on the west is now a public garden.
14. Note 5 above.
15. I.C. Hannah, 'Bishop's Palace, Chichester', *SAC* 52 (1909), p.9.
16. *ibid.*, p.10-11.
17. *ibid.*, p.7.
18. H. Chapman, G. Coppack and P. Drewett, 'Excavations at the Bishop's Palace, Lincoln, 1968-72', *Occasional Papers in Lincolnshire History and Archaeology* (1975), p.6 ff.
19. There was a room here called 'the pastry' in 1607. Work carried out there is said to be 'at the north end of the entry from the pastry to the churchyard', see F.W. Steer, 'Repairs to the Bishop's Palace', *CCJ* (1961), p.15.
20. South of this wall the 'pastry' referred to in 1607 (see note 19 above) must have been situated. To the east of it, is a 16th-century stair-turret.
21. J. Munby, 'The Bishop's kitchen', *Archaeol. Journal* 142 (1985), pp.14-16.
22. There were at least two, possibly three, original doorways. One has a cusped head and is shown in Munby (note 21), p.16, fig.7.
23. A 15th-century crown-post roof survives over the southern end of this range.
24. Steer, *op. cit.* (note 19), pp.17-18.
25. The crenellations further east only date from the early 19th century, and were put up after the Treasurer's House had been demolished.
26. Episcopal Rec. Liber B, fol.76 quoted in *VCH* 3, p.152. The vaults were presumably destroyed in the mid-17th century.
27. Steer, *op. cit.* (note 19), pp.17-18.
28. Quoted in Hannah, *op. cit.* (note 15), p.16.
29. F.W. Steer, 'The heraldic ceiling at the Bishop's Palace, Chichester', *Chichester Papers* 10 (1958). Bishop Kemp writes: Every alternate panel has the Tudor Rose, and the letters H [for Henry VIII] and K [for Katherine of Aragon, from whom he was even then contemplating divorce].
30. These crenellations are not proper battlements, and were clearly made for show.

31. J. Gardner (ed.), *Letters and Papers, Foreign and Domestic, of the Realm of Henry VIII* (1885), p.201, no.530, quoted in E. Croft-Murray, 'Lambert Barnard: an English Renaissance Painter', *Archaeol. Journal* 113 (1956), p.110.
32. Steer, *op. cit.* (note 19), pp.15-16.
33. Hannah, *op. cit.* (note 15), p.21. (There is, however, an interesting 1622 survey of the Palaces at Chichester and Aldingbourne in Lambeth Palace Library, MS *Arches Sentences* B2/37/4.)
34. In 1670, the palace is recorded as having 25 hearths, Morgan, p.160. Similar contemporary building work, with new casement windows, took place at the Bishop's Palace at Salisbury, *RCHM Salisbury. The Houses of the Close* (1993), p.55.
35. A plaque in the front corridor gives the date, 1727, see Hannah, *op. cit.* (note 15), p.22.
36. *ibid.*, pp.22-3.
37. I.C. Hannah, 'Houses in the Close at Chichester', *SAC* 68 (1927), p.136. See also Stephens, *Memorials*, p.287.
38. Morgan, p.163.
39. See Kitch, *op. cit.* (note 8), p.278. Perhaps there was a canon's house in this area as early as 1327, when an exchange of land with the bishop took place during the building of his new gatehouse. See Steer, *op. cit.* (note 19), pp.17-18.
40. See figure, p.8 in T. Tatton-Brown and R. Meynell, 'The houses in the Close at Chichester Cathedral', *CCJ* (1994), pp.5-20. Other re-used material can be seen in the garden wall of this house.
41. In 1649 it was described as 'a large decayed hall now divided into three parts, an old wainscotted parlour and another also wainscotted, an adjoining closet, buttery, kitchen, pantry, with a large gallery over the hall, 2 further closets, 3 chambers over the parlour and other chambers, a yard, an orchard and stable and a garden of 1 acre 2 roods'. Morgan, p.161.
42. Cap. 1/4/4/3, quoted in Morgan, p.161.
43. The original of this drawing is now in the Deanery.
44. See Hannah, *op. cit.* (note 37), pp.143-8 and Tatton-Brown and Meynell, *op. cit.* (note 40), pp.9-12.
45. The 1649 survey mentions the 'mansion house with great and little parlour, little hall, 4 chambers and 2 closets above, and 4 little chambers on the top floor; also a buttery, pantry, 2 cellars, kitchen, wash house and stable', Morgan, p.63.
46. This house was also much rebuilt after the Civil War and in the 18th century. In 1649 it was called 'a mansion house with an old high hall, 2 parlours wainscotted, a buttery, 2 cellars, kitchen, bakehouse, wash-house and 3 chambers over the parlour, a gatehouse (used as a malthouse), courtyard, 4 chambers over the kitchen and a small porter's lodge', Morgan, p.163.
47. Described in *VCH* 3, p.154 as 'chamfered lintels on shouldered corbels'. There is an original chimney-flue in between the windows.
48. Walcott, p.60. See also Hannah, *op. cit.* (note 37), pp.151-4.
49. The floor level in the hall seems to have been lowered at this time, see Hannah, *op. cit.* (note 37), pp.148-51.
50. W.D. Peckham, 'The Vicars Choral of Chichester Cathedral', *SAC* 78 (1957), p.138.
51. K. Edwards, *The English Secular Cathedrals in the Middle Ages* (1949), p.283. For the buildings of the Vicars' Close at Lincoln and Wells see S. Jones, K. Major and J. Varley, *The Survey of Ancient Houses in Lincoln vol.2: Houses to the south and west of the Minster* (1987), pp.40-64 and W. Rodwell, 'The buildings of the Vicars' Close', in L.S. Colchester (ed.), *Wells Cathedral* (1982), pp.212-26.
52. Fully recorded in Bishop Robert Rede's register. See F.W. Steer, 'The Vicars' Hall, Chichester and its undercroft', *Chichester Papers* 12 (1958), pp.3-5.
53. Steer, *op. cit.*, p.6.
54. A blocked dooway into it survives. For further details, see I.C. Hannah, 'The Vicars' Close and adjacent buildings, Chichester', *SAC* 56 (1914), p.104.
55. W.A. Pantin, 'Chantry Priests' Houses and other Medieval Lodgings', *Med. Archaeol.* 111 (1959), p.248 suggests that the houses of the Vicars' Close were a later 15th-century addition, but by this time there were only between sixteen and twenty-four vicars to be housed, see Peckham, *op. cit.* (note 50), p.139.

56. T. Tatton-Brown, 'The Vicars' Close and Canon Gate', *CCJ* (1991), pp.14-24.
57. In the roof of 3 Vicars' Close, see Tatton-Brown, *ibid.*, p.19.
58. Quoted in Hannah, *op. cit.* (note 54), p.94 who thought this only referred to the covered passage (called the 'Dark Cloister') on the south side of St Faith's Chapel. The latter was not, however, demolished until the early 19th century.
59. Peckham, *op. cit.* (note 50), 140.
60. Morgan, p.158.
61. This fair, running for eight days in October, was originally held around the Cross at the centre of the city, see Hannah, *op. cit.* (note 54), pp.97-8.
62. Hannah, *ibid.*, pp.96-7.
63. The 1396 bridge at York has gone, but the magnificent structure at Wells, beside the Chapter House, still survives.
64. Most closely paralleled by Hereford where a fine later 15th-century College of Vicars Choral still survives around a cloister on the south-east side of the Cathedral, with a long covered passage leading up to the south-east transept. Unlike Chichester, this passage was always separate from the 'bishops' cloister' on the south side of the nave, see plan in T. Tatton-Brown, 'The cloister at Chichester Cathedral', *CCJ* (1992), p.17. The vicars' houses at Hereford have similar internal timber partitions to Chichester, but the cloister here is an internal one, tucked under the front of the upper chamber.
65. Walcott, pp.91-2, who also notes that the Principal of the Vicars Choral kept the keys of the cloister gates which were locked at 9p.m. See also *VCH* 3, p.153.
66. The general form of the cloisters is similar to the almost contemporary cloisters at Winchester College. John Harvey, *Cathedrals in England and Wales* (1974), p.223 suggests that they were designed by William Wynford. William of Wykeham's arms are on the door leading from the cloisters into the presbytery.
67. Described and illustrated by Cecil Hewett, *English Cathedral and Monastic Carpentry* (1985), pp.135-6.
68. It is just possible that the Vicars had a small chapel on the north-east side of their hall above the 'Turnstyle', Hannah, *op. cit.* (note 54), p.104.
69. Quoted by Hannah, *ibid.*, p.105. The doors have long since disappeared; later in the 19th-century iron gates, were put into the south and west walks.
70. Wills confirm the stylistic date. Money was left in 1375 'to the work of the belfry', and in 1408 'towards building the belfry', in 1436 to 'the fabric of the new belfry', see *VCH* 3, p.159 and R.J. Christophers, 'The Bell Tower of Chichester Cathedral', *Chichester Papers* 48 (1965), p.7 where the legend is told that the stone was originally intended for Ryman's Castle at Apuldram.
71. The stone came from Philpots Quarry at West Hoathly, at that time owned by the Dean, J.J. Hannah. The stone facing was heavily scraped and then 'chemically treated so as faithfully to preserve the existing form and surface' (inscription on contemporary plaque inside the tower). The two western pinnacles were also completely rebuilt, while those on the eastern side were partially rebuilt.
72. These, along with the Close wall, were not removed until 1848-52.
73. Christophers, *op. cit.* (note 71), pp.8-9. See also list of bells in Appendix F. In 1873 there was a proposal, supported by Canon Swainson, to turn the bell tower into a water tower (see fig.66).

XV. The Musical History of Chichester Cathedral (Philip Barrett, Noel Osborne and Alan Thurlow)

1. Bennett *et al.*, cited in K. Edwards, *The English Secular Cathedrals in the Middle Ages* (2nd edition, Manchester, 1967), pp.263-4.
2. C. Deedes (ed.), *The Episcopal Register of Robert Rede, 1397-1415* (2 vols., SRS, 1908-10), vol.1, pp.104-6.
3. K. Edwards, pp.270, 278, 284.
4. W.D. Peckham, 'The Vicars Choral of Chichester Cathedral', *SAC* 78 (1937), p.144. Eight were choristers and four were thurifers (F. Harrison, *Music in Mediaeval Britain*, 2nd edition [1963], p.12).
5. Bennett *et al.*, p.13.

6. BL Lansdowne MS 431, described briefly in J.H. Cooper, 'A Chichester Psalter', *SAC* 43 (1900), pp.280-1. (He was not aware that the Kalendar of the MS was that of Barnwell Priory, Cambridge, though three Chichester obits have been added. Ed.)
7. MS 148.
8. Walcott, p.1; cf. also p.62.
9. Swainson, p.33.
10. *ibid.*, p.85; cf. E.F. Jacob and H.C. Johnson, *The Register of Henry Chichele 1414-43* (Canterbury and York Society, 4 vols., 1937-47), pp.287, 505; Duncan-Jones, p.84.
11. Walcott, pp.81, 83; Swainson, p.30; cf. the account for the enthronement of the proxies of Bishop Sampson in 1536 and Bishop Day in 1543 (Peckham *Acts* (1), pp.51, 68). The orders for the enthronement of a bishop and the installation of a dean are described in detail in Peckham, *Acts* (2), pp.1-3.
12. Bennett *et al.*, pp.13-14.
13. Peckham, *Acts* (1), pp.9-11. For discussions of medieval cathedral liturgies, cf. E. Bishop, 'Holy Week Rites of Sarum, Hereford and Rouen compared', *Liturgica Historica* (1918), pp.276-300; and J. Harper, *The Forms and Orders of Western Liturgy from the Tenth to the Eighteenth Century* (Oxford, 1991).
14. Swainson, pp.77-8, 80, 87; Walcott, p.39; Peckham, *Vicars Choral*, p.145.
15. Swainson, pp.98-9 (cf. p.80).
16. Bennett *et al.*, p.21; Walcott, p.28; Harrison, p.84.
17. Harrison, pp.84, 87.
18. Peckham, *Acts* (1), pp.21-3.
19. Harrison, pp.181-2. The refreshments were a glass of milk, with egg, sugar and saffron (Stephens, *Memorials*, p.192).
20. Bennett *et al.*, pp.32ff; Peckham, *Vicars Choral*, p.134.
21. Peckham, *Acts (1)*, p.50; cf. pp.126-7.
22. Harrison, p.182. For references to organs in the cathedral in the early 16th century, cf. *ibid.*, p.209 and N. Plumley and J. Lees, *The Organs and Organists of Chichester Cathedral* (Chichester, 1988), p.1.
23. Harrison, p.336. He may well have been the musician John Mason who was also a prebendary and Treasurer of Hereford Cathedral (*ibid.*, p.460; J.M. Horn, *Fasti Ecclesiae Anglicanae 1300-1541: 2—Hereford Diocese* [1962], p.48); for details of his music, cf. M. Hofman and J. Morehen, *Latin Music in British Sources c.1485-c.1610* (1987), pp.45-6.
24. Peckham, *Acts* (2), pp.71-2.
25. Thurston Dart, 'Music and Musicians at Chichester Cathedral 1545-1642', *Music and Letters*, 42-3 (1961), pp.221-6; Wyn K. Ford, 'Chichester Cathedral and Thomas Weelkes', *SAC* 100 (1961), pp.156-72; P. le Huray, 'Music in a Provincial Cathedral: Chichester from Reformation to Restoration', *Musical Times* (March 1987), vol.128, no.1729, pp.161-5. The standard authority on Weelkes is David Brown, *Thomas Weelkes: a biographical and critical study* (1969), but cf. also C.E. Welch, 'Two Cathedral Organists', *Chichester Papers* 8 (1957); W.S. Collins, 'Recent discoveries concerning the biography of Thomas Weelkes', *Music and Letters*, 62 (1981), pp.352-3; T.J. McCann, 'The Death of Thomas Weelkes 1623', *Music and Letters*, 55 (1974), pp.45-7; G.A. Philipps, 'Patronage in the Career of Thomas Weelkes', *Musical Quarterly*, 67 (Jan 1976), pp.46-57; J. Shepherd, 'Thomas Weelkes: A Biographical Caution', *Musical Quarterly*, 66 (1980), pp.505-21; K. Fincham, 'Contemporary Opinions of Thomas Weelkes', *Music and Letters*, 62 (1981), pp.352-3; *Prelate as Pastor: The Episcopate of James I* (Oxford, 1990), pp.141-4; cf.also letters by Wyn K. Ford and W.S. Collins in *Music and Letters*, 43 (1962), pp.92-5. Weelkes' collected anthems were published in *Musica Britannica*, vol.23 (ed. D. Brown, W. Collins and P. le Huray) and studied by W.S. Collins, 'The Anthems of Thomas Weelkes' (unpublished Ph.D. thesis, University of Michigan, 1960) and Peter Phillips, *English Sacred Music 1549-1649* (Oxford, 1991), pp.145-70.
26. Cf. P. le Huray, *Music and the Reformation in England*, 1549-1660 (1967), p.15; cf. T. Dart, p.221; W.S. Collins, letter in *Music and Letters*, 43 (1962), p.94 and P. le Huray, *art. cit.*, p.161. The number of vicars choral appears to have declined gradually from 10 in 1551 to four in 1570, with five being found in 1578. Four was the accepted figure from 1596 (Peckham, *Vicars Choral*, pp.139-40).

27. Peckham, *Acts (2)*, pp.18, 76-7, 86, 139, 141, 153, 183 and 220. For a summary of these difficulties, cf. D. Brown, pp.28-32. For further details cf. R.B. Manning, *Religion and Society in Elizabethan Sussex* (Leicester, 1969), pp.170-1.
28. Peckham, *Acts (2)*, pp.106-7 (10 October 1581); p.109 (2 May 1581); p.118 (2 May 1587); p.124 (1 August 1589) and p.126 (2 May 1590); p.124 (1 August 1589); cf. N. Plumley and J. Lees, 45.
29. Wyn K. Ford, *art. cit.*, 156-7, quoting Peckham, *Acts (2)*, nos.951 and 954 (Act Book A, Cap.1/3/1. f.115v and f.116v.).
30. P. le Huray, *art. cit.*, 161-3 (note 25).
31. Peckham, *Acts (2)*, p.191; cf. injunctions of Bishop Samuel Harsnett, Statute Book B (Cap. 1/1/2, p.25); pp.161-3.
32. Brown, pp.21-6.
33. Fincham, *art. cit.*, 352-3.
34. Brown, pp.33, 35.
35. Collins, *art. cit.*, 352-3.
36. *ibid.*, p.131; Brown, p.43; Collins, *art. cit.*, p.131; Welch, pp.4-5; Shepherd, p.517; Wyn K. Ford, p.168 (note 25).
37. Brown, pp.44-5; cf. McCann, *art. cit.*, pp.45-7 (note 25).
38. Philipps, *art. cit.*, pp.47, 57; Shepherd suggests rather unconvinvingly that Weelkes' life-style was not that of 'a progressively declining wastrel and drunkard' and adopts 'a more cautious approach' (p.521).
39. Cf. Wyn K. Ford, *art. cit.*, p.161 n.2; cf. Collins, *art. cit.*, p.120.
40. Peter Phillips, p.165 (note 25).
41. Cap.1/1/2 Statute Book B, p.26; cf. Collins, p.127.
42. *ibid.*, p.13 (27 September 1616); cf. Act Book of the Dean and Chapter (hereafter ABDC), same date; Peckham, *Acts (2)*, p.207.
43. ABDC, 6 May; cf. Peckham, *Acts (2)*, p.204, Collins, p.128, Shepherd p.513 and Wyn K. Ford, pp.162-3.
44. Statute Book B, p.16; cf. Bennett *et al.*, p.31. The Dean and Chapter ordered that each boy should have 'eyther a duble psalter or a Communion booke' and bring it to services (ABDC, 6 May 1616; Peckham, *Acts (2)*, p.204).
45. Statute Book B, p.17; cf. Bennett *et al.*, p.31; ABDC, 27 September 1616; Peckham, *Acts (2)*, p.207; Collins, pp.129-30.
46. Statute Book B, p.18; cf. Bennett *et al.*, p.32; cf. Peckham, *Acts (2)*, p.208, Collins, pp.129-30.
47. Statute Book B, p.25; cf. Bennett *et al.*, p.32 and Peckham, *Acts (2)*, p.208.
48. Cap.1/4/6/3. The list is printed in Welch, p.10; Brown, pp.39-40 and le Huray, *op. cit.*, p.94. It is discussed by Wyn K. Ford, pp.165-6 (note 25). Lilliat was a chorister at Christ Church, Oxford, and a vicar choral at Wells Cathedral. He was admitted as a vicar choral at Chichester in 1591 and in 1606 also became a Gentleman Extraordinary to the Chapel Royal. His son Edward became a chorister at Chichester in 1616. His common-place book, with poems, songs, phrases and other items is Bodl. Lib. MS Rawlinson Poetry 148 and has been published: E. Doughtie (ed.), *Liber Lilliati: Elizabethan Verse and Song* (Newark USA, 1985).
49. William Cox, son of Dean Francis Cox, was admitted as a chorister in 1582, became a prebendary in 1611 and a canon residentiary in 1616. He died in 1632. He is known to have influenced Weelkes and the anthem 'Deliver us, O Lord', often ascribed to Weelkes, is probably by Cox. This may be the 'Mr William Cox, his anthem', included in Lilliat's list.
50. Brown, pp.40, 169.
51. cf. ABDC, 2 August 1617, 10 October 1617, 12 October 1618, 24 March 1618-9, 25 & 26 March 1619, 13 May 1624, 13 October 1630, 20 January 1630/1, 3 May 1631, 12 May 1631, 1 August 1631; cf. Peckham, *Acts* (2), pp.212, 214, 219, 220, 241-5, 251.
52. ABDC, 12 May 1631; Peckham, *Acts* (2), p.244; Wyn K. Ford, 164.
53. Ep. I/20/10, f.35, quoted in K. Fincham, *Prelate as Pastor*, p.141.
54. Fincham, p.143.
55. Walcott, p.20, quoting Bruno Ryves, *Mercurius Rusticus*, cf. T.J. McCann, *Restricted Grandeur*, pp.8-10.

56. ABDC, 14 September 1661 (Statute Book B, 1660-1710, f.22).
57. Cf. ABDC, 31 August 1665, 2 August 1666, 11 October 1667, 19 January 1668/9, 11 October 1669.
58. ABDC, 24 March 1669/70.
59. Cap. 1/1/2 (Statute Book B), pp.115, 126.
60. ABDC, 2 May 1678; cf. Bennett *et al.*, p.37.
61. ABDC, 27 April 1680; cf. Bennett *et al.*, p.39.
62. ABDC, 23 April 1684.
63. Statute Book B, p.139.
64. *ibid.*, pp.146-7. In 1689 the number of Sherburne clerks was reduced from four to three (*ibid.*, p.166).
65. *ibid.*, p.152.
66. *ibid.*, p.155. They also complained about the vergers walking round the nave during services.
67. *ibid.*, p.156; cf. Bennett *et al.*, p.42.
68. ABDC, 23 September 1699.
69. Statute Book B, p.159.
70. ABDC, 10 October 1701; cf. 23 September 1699, 23 August and 18-19 September 1701, 22 June 1702, 28 May 1714, 2 August 1714.
71. ABDC, 2 August 1708, 5 October 1709.
72. ABDC, 20 January 1710.
73. Statute Book B, p,168.
74. ABDC, 10 December 1714, 1 May 1716, 6 May 1717.
75. ABDC, 2 November 1718, 1 August 1733, 3 January 1736, cf. Welch, 5-9; R. Tibble, 'Thomas Kelway (1695-1744), organist and composer', *West Sussex History* (1992) 49, pp.15-17.
76. Statute Book B, p.187; cf. Bennett *et al.*, p.43.
77. *ibid.*, pp.202-3; cf. Bennett *et al.*, p.46.
78. ABDC, 2 May 1743, 6 & 9 December 1746, 23 February 1746/7.
79. Cap. I/21/7 p.80; cf. Welch, pp.10-12 (note 25).
80. ABDC, 20 January 1767.
81. C. Dearnley, *English Church Music 1650-1750* (1970), p.282.
82. Communar's Accounts, *ad. loc.*
83. Cap. VI/1/1; Cap. VI/1/3; Cap. VI/1/4.
84. Chichester Cathedral Library case B/4.
85. E. Thomas, 'John Marsh and Chichester Cathedral Music', *SCF Programme 1992*, p.59. For further details of Marsh, cf. E. Thomas and R. Iden, 'John Marsh and the Seaside', *West Sussex History* 51, April 1993, pp.3-14.
86. E. Thomas, p.59.
87. Marsh's diary, March 1788, p.15 (microfilm in WSRO); Thomas, p.60.
88. Marsh's diary, April 1802, p.80.
89. Marsh's diary, August 1803, p.154.
90. Thomas, pp.60-1.
91. Marsh's diary, June 1806, p.24.
92. *ibid.*, April 1810, p.14.
93. Peckham, *Vicars Choral*, p.154; ABDC, 18 October 1790, 2 May 1798. He was also addicted to fox hunting and would slip out from his stall to go to the meet when the choir turned east for the creed.
94. For details of Atkins, cf. WSRO MP2822.
95. Quoted in T.J. McCann, *Restricted Grandeur: Impressions of Chichester 1586-1948* (Chichester, 1974), p.26.
96. W. K. Lowther Clarke, 'Chichester Cathedral in the 19th century', *Chichester Papers* 14 (1959), p.13; ABDC, 1 August 1850, 1 August 1866; cf. also P.L.S. Barrett, 'Chichester Cathedral Choir in the 19th century', *SCF Programme 1980*, pp.29-31.
97. ABDC, 2 May 1853.

98. *Gentleman's Magazine*, 88, part I (1818), p.392.
99. ABDC, 20 January 1818; 20 January 1819; 20 January 1828.
100. Bennett *et al.*, p.50.
101. ABDC, 20 January 1857.
102. M.E.C. Walcott, *Traditions and Customs of Cathedrals* (1872), p.64.
103. Bennett *et al.*, p.50; Cathedral Visitation Book, p.135.
104. ABDC, 2 May 1826.
105. Lowther Clarke, p.13 (note 96).
106. Parliamentary Papers (hereafter PP) 1854 xxv, p.933.
107. ABDC, 1 August 1854.
108. 'A Collection of Anthems used in the Cathedral Church of Chichester', arranged by T. Bennett, organist (Chichester, 1823); Communar's Accounts, 1843; Cap.VI/1/3.
109. Cf. WSRO MP 1278 (list of printed music in the muniment room of Chichester Cathedral). For the comparative picture at Winchester, where there were 122 anthems in the repertoire in 1765 and 289 in 1827, cf. A. Parker, 'The Cathedral Choir and its music, 1660-1800' in J. Crook (ed.), *Winchester Cathedral: 900 years* (Chichester, 1993), pp.308-9.
110. For details of his appointment, see P.L.S. Barrett, *Barchester: English Cathedral Life in the 19th century* (1993), p.186.
111. ABDC, 10 October 1866, 20 January 1871, 31 August 1876, 1 August 1890.
112. M. Hackett, *A Brief Account of Cathedral and Collegiate Schools* (2nd edition, 1873), p.5.
113. Barrett, *Barchester*, p.192; ABDC, 4, 22 and 25 May 1875; Barrett, *art. cit.*, p.30.
114. ABDC, 3 February 1876.
115. Draft Chapter Acts, July 1878.
116. In 1832 there had been three practices a week—see Visitation Book, p.155.
117. PP 1884-5 xxi, p.378.
118. For details of Allen's time at Chichester and especially of the different choir-training methods of Read and Allen, see C. Bailey, *Hugh Percy Allen* (Oxford, 1948), pp.9-15.
119. T.G. Willis, *Records of Chichester* (Chichester, 1928), p.217.
120. ABDC, 2 May 1902, 4 June 1904, 10 October 1904, 10 October 1913, 20 January 1914, 11 October 1915. The three cathedral choirs continued to sing together from time to time—see *CDG*, July 1934.
121. ABDC, 11 December 1915.
122. *CDG*, June 1918, May 1919.
123. ABDC, 28 February 1923, 4 February 1925. For another tribute to Read, see CDG, March 1925.
124. *CDG*, February 1931.
125. ABDC, 9 March 1931.
126. R.C.D. Jasper, *George Bell, Bishop of Chichester* (Oxford, 1937), p.83. For the programme of the 1930 festival, see *CDG*, June 1930 and *Chichester Observer*, 11 June 1930. Holst also brought a special choir to sing Vaughan Williams' *Mass in G minor* on August Bank Holiday 1931 (*CDG*, August 1931 and I. Holst, *Gustav Holst: a biography* [2nd edition, 1969], p.150). Vaughan Williams conducted the 'Holst Whitsuntide Singers' for their visit in 1938 (*CDG*, June 1938); see also G. Barnard, 'A Recollection of Gustav Holst and Chichester', *CCJ* (1984), pp.2-5. For Bell's tribute to Holst's work at Chichester, see *CDG*, June 1934. The composer's ashes are buried in the north transept. For details of his funeral, see *Chichester Observer*, 27 June 1934 and I. Holst, pp.168-9.
127. ABDC, 8 May 1936.
128. ABDC, 17 September 1937, 8 October 1937, 8 April 1938, 6 May 1938, 7 October 1938.
129. For further details of Grace and Hawkins, see Plumley and Lees, p.54.
130. ABDC, 1 December 1939.
131. ABDC, 26 July 1940. In 1948 Miss Monica Head was appointed as a second female lay vicar (ABDC, 13 and 27 February, 19 March 1948; for her resignation, see 14 June 1957). Mrs Powell (Salwey) sang as an alto until 1956 (ABDC, 1 June 1956).
132. ABDC, 28 August 1944, 5 July 1946, 4 December 1953, 21 October 1955.
133. *CDG*, November and December 1939.

134. ABDC, 5 July 1946, 1 August 1947, 19 December 1947. For further details, see *CDG*, May, June and September 1931, July 1932, September 1934, September 1938 and *The Cicestrian*, Advent 1951, no.1; Trinity 1952, no 2; Advent 1952, no.3; Trinity 1954, no.6.
135. See S.C. Carpenter, *Duncan-Jones of Chichester* (1956), pp.70-1. For the origin of this service, see *CDG*, December 1930, January 1931, January 1935, January 1936.
136. ABDC, 4 May 1956; see 22 June 1956, 11 January 1957, 25 January 1957.
137. ABDC, 8 February 1957, 10 January 1958, 7 February 1958, 21 February 1958, 7 March 1958, 25 April 1958, 23 May 1958, 27 June 1958, 17 October 1958. Birch actually began work in September 1958—see J. Birch, 'Close Encounter', *CCJ*, 1980, pp.7-9.
138. For the present-day choir, see Alan Thurlow, 'In Quires and Places ...', parts 1 and 2, *West Sussex History* (WSRO), 38 (September 1987) and 39 (January 1988).

XVI. The Cathedral and Modern Art (David Coke and Robert Potter)

1. Hans Feibusch, *Mural Painting* (1946).
2. *op. cit.*, p.92.
3. *Dean and Chapter Minutes*, 29 Sept. 1950, p.3, Item 7.
4. By the sketches provided at this meeting.
5. Plate XXI, see also *The Studio*, April (1954), p.106, Hans Feibusch, 'Mural Paintings in Churches', pp.104-9.
6. *ibid.*, p.105.
7. Reproduced in *The Studio*, April 1954, p.106.
8. Letter from George Bell to Walter Hussey, 22 July 1943, quoted in Hussey, *Patron of Art, The Revival of a Great Tradition among Modern Artists* (1985), p.30.
9. Hans Feibusch, *Mural Painting* (1946), pp.29, 91-2.
10. St Michael's Chapel was refurbished through the initiative of the Chichester branch of the Royal Naval Association as a memorial to the men and women of Sussex who lost their lives at sea during World War Two, and who have no known grave. It was dedicated as the Sailors' Chapel on 30 July 1956 in the presence of HM Queen Elizabeth II and HRH The Duke of Edinburgh.
11. Robert Potter succeeded Harry Sherwood as Surveyor of the Cathedral in 1959, and was succeeded by Donald Buttress in 1985.
12. Photographs of the Chapel as it was (in 1943), and of three of the pictures of the *Life of St. Richard* (in 1942), are held by the National Monuments Record (and see fig.146b). Three of the frescoes, on wood, are at present stored in the Canons' vestry; they were displayed until 1984 on the back of the old organ case.
13. WSRO, *Hussey Archive*, Sutherland to Hussey, 26 Aug. 1959.
14. *Patron of Art*, p.103.
15. WSRO, *Hussey Archive*, Sutherland to Hussey, 22 Oct. 1960.
16. John 20: v17: 'Jesus saith unto her, Touch me not; for I am not yet ascended to my Father: but go to my brethren and say unto them, I ascend unto my Father, and your Father: and to my God, and your God.'
17. *Studio International*, March 1965.
18. WSRO, *Hussey Archive*, Clarke to Hussey, 28 May 1962.
19. Cost in total £1,535 including £550 for the Sutherland altarpiece.
20. *Chichester Observer*, 8 Feb. 1963.
21. *Dean and Chapter Minutes*, 25 April 1958, Item 109; WSRO, *Hussey Archive*, Stone to Hussey, 6 July 1958 and 12 Feb. 1959.
22. WSRO, *Hussey Archive*, Piper to Hussey, 25 Jan. 1958.
23. *Patron of Art*, p.127.
24. Hussey interviewed by Oliver Mathews in *Antique Collector*, April 1984.
25. Letter, Hussey to Potter, 3 March 1960.
26. WSRO, *Hussey Archive*, Richards to Hussey, 11 Aug. 1962.
27. Pallant House, Chichester, a Queen Anne town house, was restored and opened as an art gallery

in May 1982, as a result of Walter Hussey's offer to leave his private fine art collection to the City on the understanding that it would be displayed at Pallant House. The permanent collection includes items related to Hussey's Cathedral commissions.

28. The circular bronze bas-relief portrait (signed 'M Gillick') is set onto a Purbeck stone slab, inscribed 'GEORGE KENNEDY ALLEN BELL, BISHOP OF CHICHESTER 1929-1958, A PASTOR POET & TRUE PATRON OF THE ARTS, CHAMPION OF THE OPPRESSED AND TIRELESS WORKER FOR CHRISTIAN UNITY. The Bell-Arundel screen removed a century ago is erected in his memory in 1961 by friends and admirers in many lands & of many faiths.' The tablet was dedicated on 2 November and the total cost was 600 guineas.
29. Peter Taylor was an Associate of the firm of Gifford and Partners who were involved with Robert Potter in the strengthening of the foundations and structure of the choir.
30. Letter, Potter to David Coke, 15 Nov. 1992.
31. *Dean and Chapter Minutes*, 20 Nov. 1973.
32. *Patron of Art*, p.121.
33. WSRO, *Hussey Archive*, Piper to Hussey, 24 Jan. 1966.
34. *Weekend Telegraph*, 23 Sept. 1966, p.37.
35. WSRO, *Hussey Archive*, Piper to Hussey, 3 March 1964.
36. The Friends had made a decision to donate their funds to projects other than the restoration of the fabric of the building itself.
37. Some of the preparatory work for the tapestry is now at Pallant House.
38. *Pitkin Guide to Chichester Cathedral* (1974), p.13.
39. WSRO, *Hussey Archive*, notes.
40. Trevor Brighton, 'The Piper Tapestry' in 'The Chichester Tapestries', *Otter Memorial Paper* 7 (1991), p.20.
41. At a cost of £17,475.
42. Trans. from the French quoted in Brighton, *op. cit.*, p.22.
43. WSRO, *Hussey Archive*, Piper to Hussey, 22 Jan. 1965.
44. WSRO, *Hussey Arch*ive, Piper to Hussey, 19 Feb. 1965.
45. Now at Pallant House.
46. The final cost of the tapestry was over £6,000—£3,269 to Pinton Frères, £2,000 artist's fee, and about £1,000 for transport, display etc.
47. WSRO.
48. WSRO, *Hussey Archive*, Piper to Hussey, 26 May 1967. *Liberty's* bill for the silk was £51 16s. 3d.; Grossé's fee was £198, and Piper's 'if any more money is available (say £50)', otherwise he was quite happy to make a gift of the design to the Cathedral 'which has been kind to me and which I love'. (WSRO, *Hussey Archive*, Piper to Hussey, 28 Dec. 1967.)
49. *Dean and Chapter Minutes*, 28 Oct. 1969; *Patron of Art*, p.128.
50. *Dean and Chapter Minutes*, 25 July, p.77, Item 232/72 and 3 Oct. 1972, p.82, Item 250/72.
51. WSRO, *Hussey Archive*, Ms. 364. J.98, Collins to Hussey, 2 Dec. 1972 and 26 Aug. 1973.
52. Although Collins had expressed a wish for it to be used as a reredos mounted on a grey velvet-covered board over the altar rather than a frontal in a letter to Hussey of 26 Aug. 1973 (WSRO, *Hussey Archive*).
53. The story of the commission is given in William Anderson, *Cecil Collins, The Quest for the Great Happiness* (London, 1988), p.106 and pl.70. Elisabeth Collins designed the kneelers for the chapel. The full version of Collins' text is in the WSRO, *Hussey Archive*.
54. James Burr, *Apollo* (Nov. 1973), pp.394-5, fig.5: *Icon of Divine Light*, by Cecil Collins, 1973. Tempera on board, 60.9 x 152.4 cm.
55. According to Keith Walker in Judith Robinson (ed.), *The Journey: A Search for the Role of Contemporary Art in Religious and Spiritual Life* (Lincoln, 1990), p.109, this was to be an *Icon of Divine Love*.
56. Letter from Lady d'Avigdor Goldsmid to David Coke, 21 Oct. 1985. Dean Hussey 'was a great help to me when I wanted to "do up" my village chapel—he sent me to Robert Potter. I visited him at Chichester and saw all his lovely things, and helped him get his Chagall window.'
57. WSRO, *Hussey Archive*, Piper to Hussey, 19 Nov. 1967.

58. Hussey interviewed by Robert Walker in *Patron of Art*, BBC2, 4 Nov. 1985.
59. WSRO, *Hussey Archive*, Chagall to Hussey, 4 Jan. 1976.
60. WSRO, *Hussey Archive*, 16 April 1977.
61. WSRO, *Hussey Archive*, 2 March 1977.
62. WSRO, *Hussey Archive*.
63. *Patron of Art*, pp.139-42.
64. Translation of a letter, 22 May 1978 from Marq to Hussey, reproduced in the service sheet for the Dedication, 6 Oct. 1978.
65. *Chichester Observer*, 'Chagall in Chichester', 3 Nov. 1978, p.13.
66. Eventually costing over £20,000, including Chagall's fee of £8,392.16; Charles Marq's fee £9,178.19; transport £229.02; metalwork £155.52; stonework £885.60; dedication service £1,506.49; photographs £96.36; and the exterior safety mesh £426.84. Funds were contributed by one of the Sainsbury family trusts; the Arts Council; Ian Askew's Trust; the Idlewild Trust; the Warbeck Fund; the Anthony Hornby Charitable Trust; Percy and Oona Cartwright; and the Dean and Chapter's Common Fund; Walter Hussey himself was a major contributor.
67. *op. cit.*
68. An extract of which is shown in BBC2's *Patron of Art*, 4 Nov.1985 (Hussey interviewed by Robert Walker).
69. Christopher Pellett and Fiona Dennis cut and polished the stones, Reuben Walters assisted in copper beating, Myrtle Skelton in fitting the bowl, and Sarah Moore assisted with the lettering, 'ONE LORD·ONE FAITH·ONE BAPTISM· '.
70. The so-called Anglo-German Tapestry, made of wool, silk and cotton, is fully described, explained and documented by Robert Holtby himself and by the designer Ursula Benker-Schirmer in 'Chichester Tapestries', pp.25-30 (note 40). The Cathedral Friends generously contributed funds for the tapestry, but the principal share of the finance came from the German churches, Catholic and Lutheran, who were fully represented at the dedication in June 1985. Particular thanks were offered to Cardinal Höffner, President of the German Catholic bishops, for his strong support. The stone altar is a companion to those in the Mary Magdalen Chapel and in the sanctuary, also by Robert Potter, made by Haysom, in 1984, and the candlesticks and votive stands by Geoffrey Clarke, described above (p.271) were made at this time.

Further reading: Michael Day, *Modern Art in English Churches* (1984); Tom Devonshire-Jones, 'Art-Theology-Church, A survey 1940-1990', *Theology* (Sept/Oct 1992), pp.360-70; Joan Morris (ed.), *Modern Sacred Art* (1938); George Pattison, 'The Achievement of Walter Hussey: A Reflection', *Images of Christ*, Exhibition Catalogue (Northampton, 1993).

SELECT BIBLIOGRAPHY

The chapter notes contain full specialist, critical guides to particular topics and people. This bibliography lists books and articles relating to the Cathedral in more than one chapter, and those mentioned in the notes of subsequent date to the classified, chronological list of books which prefaces Steer and Kirby, *Diocesan Records*, 1967.

Aldsworth, F.G., 'The mound at Church Norton, Selsey, and the site of St Wilfrid's Church', *SAC* 117 (1979)

Aldsworth, F.G. and Garnett, E.D., 'Excavations on "The Mound" at Church Norton, Selsey, in 1911 and 1965', *SAC* 119 (1981)

Andrew, Martin, 'Chichester Cathedral: the problem of the Romanesque choir vault', *Journal British Archaeol. Assocn.* 135 (1982)

Andres, M.R.G., 'Chichester Cathedral, the original east end: a reappraisal', *SAC* 118 (1980)

Barnard, G., 'A Recollection of Gustav Holst and Chichester', *CCJ* (1984)

Barrett, P.L.S., *Barchester: English Cathedral Life in the Nineteenth Century* (1993)

Barrett, P.L.S., 'Chichester Cathedral Choir in the 19th century', *SCF Programme 1980*

Bell, Bp George, *Common Order in Christ's Church* (Mowbray, 1937)

Bennett, F.G., Codrington, R.H., Deedes, C. (eds.), *Statutes and Constitutions of the Cathedral Church of Chichester* (Chichester, 1904)

Birch, J., 'Close Encounter', *CCJ* (1980)

Brighton, Trevor, 'The Piper Tapestry' in 'The Chichester Tapestries', *Otter Memorial Paper* 7 (1990)

Brooke, C.N.L., Horn, J.M., Ramsay, N.L., 'A Canon's Residence in the Eighteenth Century: the case of Thomas Gooch', *JEH* 39 (no.4, October 1988)

Butler, D.J., *The Town Plans of Chichester 1595-1898* (1972)

Butler, J.E., 'The monumental brasses of Chichester Cathedral', MS in the Cathedral Library

Cave, C.S.P., 'The Roof Bosses in Chichester Cathedral', *SAC* 71 (1930)

Christophers, R.J., 'The Bell Tower of Chichester Cathedral', *Chichester Papers* 48 (1965)

Clarke, W.K. Lowther, 'Chichester Cathedral in the Nineteenth Century', *Chichester Papers* 14 (1959)

Codrington, Preb. R.H., 'Ancient Coats of Arms in Chichester Cathedral', *SAC* 48 (1905)

Cooper, J.H., 'A Chichester Psalter', *SAC* 43 (1900)

Corlette, H.C., *The Cathedral Church of Chichester ... with an Account of the Cathedral and See* (1905), Bell's Cathedral series

Crocker, C., *A Visit to Chichester Cathedral* (Chichester, 1849)

Croft-Murray, E., 'Lambert Barnard; an English Renaissance painter', *Archaeol. Journal* 113 (1956)

Curtis, L.P., *Chichester Towers* (Yale, 1966)

Dallaway, J., *A History of the Western Division of the County of Sussex*, vol.1 (1815)

Dart, Thurston, 'Music and Musicians at Chichester Cathedral 1545-1642', *Music and Letters*, 42-3 (1961)

Davidson-Houston, C., 'Sussex Monumental Brasses, 2, Chichester Cathedral', *SAC* 77 (1936)

Deedes, C. (ed.), *The Episcopal Register of Robert Rede ... Bishop of Chichester, 1397-1415* (2 vols., SRS 8, 11 (1908-10)

Doughtie, E. (ed.), *Liber Lilliati: Elizabethan Verse and Song* (Newark USA, 1985)

Duncan-Jones, A.S., *The Story of Chichester Cathedral* (revised edition 1955)

Duncan-Jones, A.S., *The Chichester Customary* (1948)

Edwards, K., *The English Secular Cathedrals in the Middle Ages*, 2nd edn. (Manchester, 1967)

Fletcher, A., *A County Community at Peace and War, Sussex 1600-1660* (Chichester, 1975)

Ford, Wyn K., 'Chichester Cathedral and Thomas Weelkes', *SAC* 100 (1961)

Foster, A., 'Chichester Diocese in the early 17th century', *SAC* 123 (1985)

Foster, P., Brighton, T., Garland, P., 'An Arundel Tomb', *Otter Memorial Paper* 9 (1987)

Gem, R.D.H., 'Chichester Cathedral: when was the Romanesque church begun?', Brown, R.A. (ed.), *Proceedings of the Battle Conference in 1980* (1981)

Gordon, G., *The Sculptures in the Retrochoir at Chichester* (Talbot Press, Saffron Walden, n.d.)

Greenway, D.E. (Comp.), *Fasti Ecclesiae Anglicanae* 1066-1300 5, *Chichester Diocese* (forthcoming 1996)

Hannah, I.C., 'Bishop's Palace, Chichester', *SAC* 52 (1909)

Hannah, I.C., 'Chichester Cathedral', *SAC* 63 (1922)

Hannah, I.C., 'Houses in the Close at Chichester', *SAC* 63 (1923)

Hannah, I.C., 'The Vicars' Close and adjacent buildings, Chichester', *SAC* 56 (1914)

Hay, A., *The History of Chichester* (Chichester, 1804)

Hennessy, G., *Clergy of the Diocese of Chichester* (Chichester, 1911).

Hewett, C., *English Cathedral Carpentry* (Chichester, 1974)

Hobbs, M., 'Henry King, John Donne and the Refounding of Chichester Cathedral Library', *The Book Collector* 33 (1984)

Hobbs, M., *The Sermons of Henry King (1592-1669),* Bishop of Chichester (AUP, Scolar Press, Aldershot, 1992)

Horn, J.M. (comp.), *Fasti Ecclesiae Anglicanae* 1300-1541 7, *Chichester Diocese* (1964)

Horn, J.M. (comp.), *Fasti Ecclesiae Anglicanae* 1541-1857 2, *Chichester Diocese* (1971)

Hussey, W., *Patron of Art, The Revival of a Great Tradition among Modern Artists* (1985)

Johnstone, Hilda and Steer, F.W., 'Alexander Hay, Historian of Chichester', *Chichester Papers* 20, 1961

Jones, D.L., 'The cult of St Richard of Chichester in the Middle Ages', *SAC* 121 (1983)

Jones, D., *The Life of St Richard*, SRS 79 (1993/4)

Kelly, S.E. *et al.*, *Charters of Selsey* (British Academy, 1995)

Kitch, M.J., 'The Chichester Cathedral Chapter at the time of the Reformation', *SAC* 116 (1978)

Kitch, M.J. (ed.), *Studies in Sussex Church History* (1981)

Lankester, P., 'Notes and queries on a mediaeval tomb at Chichester', *Church Monuments Society Newsletter* 5 (Summer, 1989)

le Huray, P., 'Music in a Provincial Cathedral: Chichester from Reformation to Restoration', *Musical Times* (March 1987)

Leeney, O.H., 'References to ancient Sussex Churches in *The Ecclesiologist* mainly as regards restoration and repair', *SAC* 86 (1947)

Manning, R.B., *Religion and Society in Elizabethan Sussex* (Leicester U.P., 1969)
McCann, Alison, *St Andrew Oxmarket, Chichester* (WSRO, 1978).
McCann, Timothy (comp.), *Restricted Grandeur: Impressions of Chichester 1586-1948* (WSRO, 1974)
Morgan, R.R., *Chichester: A Documentary History* (Chichester, 1992)
Munby, J., 'The Bishop's kitchen', *Archaeol. Journal* 142 (1985)
Munby, J., 'Chichester Cathedral Roofs', *CCJ* (1993)
Munby, J., 'Medieval carpentry in Chichester: 13th-century roofs of the Cathedral and Bishop's Palace', Down, A. (ed.), *Chichester Excavations* 5 (Chichester, 1981)
Munby, J., 'Saxon Chichester and its predecessors', Haslam, J. (ed.), *Anglo-Saxon Towns in Southern England* (Chichester, 1984)
Munby, J., *St Mary's Hospital* (Leeds, 1981)
Nairn, I. and Pevsner, N., *The Buildings of England: Sussex* (1965)
Newman, R., 'An Unrecorded Chichester Mayorality', *SAC* 16 (1963)
Ollerenshaw, Neville, *A History of the Prebendal School* (Chichester, 1983)
Page, W. (ed.), *Victoria County History of Sussex*, vol.2 (1907)
Peckham, W.D. (ed.), *The Acts of the Dean and Chapter of the Cathedral Church of Chichester, 1472-1544* (SRS 52, 1952)
Peckham, W.D. (ed.), *The Acts of the Dean and Chapter of the Cathedral Church of Chichester, 1545-1642* (SRS 58, 1959)
Peckham, W.D. (ed.), *The Chartulary of the High Church of Chichester* (SRS 46, 1942/3)
Peckham, W.D., 'Chichester Cathedral in 1562', *SAC* 96 (1958)
Peckham, W.D., 'Chichester Non-Jurors', *SNQ* 9 (1942-3)
Peckham, W.D., 'The Parishes of the City of Chichester', *SAC* 74 (1933)
Peckham, W.D., 'Some notes on Chichester Cathedral', *SAC* 113 (1973)
Peckham, W.D., 'The Vicars Choral of Chichester Cathedral', *SAC* 78 (1937)
Plumley, N. and Lees, J., *The Organs and Organists of Chichester Cathedral* (Chichester, 1988)
Ryves, B., *Mercurius Rusticus: the Countries Complaint of the Sacrileges, Profanities and Plunderings Committed by the Schismatiques on the Cathedral Churches of the Kingdom* (1647) (2nd ed. 1685)
Salzman, L.F. (ed.), *Victoria County History of Sussex*, vol.3 (1935)
Steer, F.W., 'Chichester Cathedral Library', *Chichester Papers* 44 (1964)
Steer, F.W. and Kirby, I. (comp.), *Diocese of Chichester. A Catalogue of the Records of the Dean and Chapter, Vicars Choral, St Mary's Hospital, Colleges and Schools* (Chichester, 1967)
Steer, F.W., 'The heraldic ceiling at the Bishop's Palace, Chichester', *Chichester Papers* 10 (1958)
Steer, F.W., 'A parchment memorial in Chichester Cathedral', *SNQ* 16 (1963)
Steer, F.W. and Remnant, G.L., 'Misericords in Chichester Cathedral', *Chichester Papers* 22 (1961)
Steer, F.W., 'Naval memorials in Chichester Cathedral', *The Monumental Journal* (1958)
Steer, F.W., 'Repairs to the Bishop's Palace', *CCJ* (1961)
Steer, F.W., 'The Vicars' Hall, Chichester and its undercroft', *Chichester Papers* 12 (1958)
Stephens, W. R.W., *Memorials of the South Saxon See and Cathedral Church of Chichester* (1876)
Stephens, W. R.W., *The South Saxon Diocese: Selsey-Chichester* (1881)
Swainson, C.A., *The History and Constitution of a Cathedral of the Old Foundation* (1880)
Swainson, C.A., 'The Hospital of St Mary in Chichester', *SAC* 24 (1872)
Tatton-Brown, T., 'The cloister at Chichester Cathedral', *CCJ* (1992)

Tatton-Brown, T. and Meynell, R., 'The houses in the Close at Chichester Cathedral', *CCJ* (1994)

Tatton-Brown, T., 'The west portal of Chichester Cathedral', *CCJ* (1990)

Tatton-Brown, T., 'The Vicars' Close and Canon Gate', *CCJ* (1991)

Thomas-Stanford, C., *Sussex in the Great Civil War and the Interregnum* (1910)

Tracy, C., 'Medieval choir stalls in Chichester: a re-assessment', *SAC* 124 (1986)

Tummers, H., 'The Medieval effigial tombs in Chichester Cathedral', *Church Monuments* 3 (1986)

Vickers, John and Hilary, *Methodism in a Cathedral City* (Chichester, 1977)

Walcott, M.E.C., *The Early Statutes of the Cathedral Church of the Holy Trinity, Chichester, with Observations on its Constitution and History,* reprinted from *Archaeologia* 45 (1877), pp.143-234.

Welch, C.E., 'An Early Plan of Chichester Cathedral,' *SNQ* 14 (1956)

Welch, C.E., 'Two Cathedral Organists', *Chichester Papers* 8 (1957)

Willis, Robert, *The Architectural History of Chichester Cathedral* (1861)

Willis, T.G., *Records of Chichester* (Chichester, 1928)

Zarnecki, G., 'The Chichester reliefs', *Archaeol. Journal* 110 (1954)

APPENDIX A

CHICHESTER CATHEDRAL SENIOR CLERGY FROM 1900

For earlier lists, see:
George Hennessy, *Chichester Diocese Clergy Lists* (1900)

1. Bishops of the Diocese

[1895-1907 Ernest Roland Wilberforce DD]
1908-1919 Charles John Ridgeway, DD (d.1927)
1919-1929 Winfrid Oldfield Burrows, DD (d.1929)
1929-1958 George Kennedy Allen Bell, DD (d.1958)
1958-1974 Roger Plumpton Wilson, DD
1974- Eric Waldron Kemp, DD

2. Deans

[1892-1902 Richard William Randall, DD,]
1902-1929 John Julius Hannah, DD
1929-1955 Arthur Stuart Duncan-Jones, BD
1955-1977 John Walter Atherton Hussey, MA
1977-1989 Robert Tinsley Holtby, BD
1989- John David Treadgold, LVO, BA

3. Precentors

[1889-1918 John Henry Mee, MA]
1918-1925 Henry David Jones, MA
1925-1937 The Rt. Revd. Henry Kemble Southwell, DD, CMG
1937-1945 Edward Mortlock, MA
1945-1961 Arthur Rupert Browne-Wilkinson, MC, MA
1961-1971 Deryck Reeves Hutchinson, MA
1971-1980 Arthur Keith Walker, PhD
1981-1984 Christopher Charles Luxmoore, MA
1985- John Frear Hester, MA

4. Chancellors

[1877-1900 William Douglas Parish, S.C.L.]
1900-1914 Henry Mahoney Davey, M.A.

1914-1930	Edward Leighton Elwes, MA
1930-1946	Reginald John Campbell, DD
1946-1956	John Richard Humpidge Moorman, DD
1956-1970	Cheslyn Peter Montague Jones, MA
1970-1975	Vernon Kingsbury Lippiett, MA
1975-	Roger Tagent Greenacre, MA

5. Treasurers

[1898-1903	The Hon. George Wingfield Bourke, MA]
1904-1911	Robert Edward Sanderson, DD
1911-1918	Henry David Jones, MA
1918-1928	John Jackson Mallaby, MA
1929-1949	The Rt. Revd. Hugh Maudslay Hordern, MA
1950-1967	Charles Bernard Mortlock, MA, FSA
1970-1972	Walter William Seymour March, MA, BD
Vacant 1972-1978	
1978-1981	Richard Montague Stephens Eyre, MA
1981-	Francis John Hawkins, MA

6. Archdeacons of Chichester

[1887-1903	Francis John Mount, MA]
1903-1914	Edward Leighton Elwes, MA
1914-1920	The Rt. Revd. Herbert Edward Jones, MA
1920-1933/34	Benedict George Hoskyns, MA
1934-1945	Charles Philip Stewart Clarke, MA
1946-1973	Lancelot Mason, MA
1973-1975	Frederick George Kerr-Dineen, MA
1975-1981	Richard Montague Stephens Eyre, MA
1981-1991	Keith Hobbs, MA
1991-	John Michael Brotherton, MA

R.T. Greenacre

Appendix B

The Stained Glass

(Roman numerals on phased Cathedral plan, p.xx.)

Location and Number	Date	Artist	Donor	In Memoriam
East Window I	1905	Charles Eamer Kempe		The 6th Duke of Richmond
		The Second Adam above the first The Burning Bush and the Annunciation The Baptism of Christ *The arms of Richmond impaling Greville*		
North QuireAisle n II	1952	Christopher Webb *St John the Baptist*	War Damage Commission	
n IV	1978	Marc Chagall *Psalm 150*		
n VI	1912	Unknown *Arms of post-reformation bishops*	Dean Hannah	Archdeacon John Hannah and Dean Robert Gregory
North Transept				
n XII	1886	Clayton & Bell	Family 'and many loving friends & old shipmates'	Lt. Charles Gordon Spring RN
		Jesus stills the tempest (Matt 8: 23-27)		
North Nave Aisle n XIV	ca 1868	Clayton & Bell *King David*		George Croke Rowden, Precentor, and his daughter Grace Emily
n XV	1923	Caroline Townshend	Lady Dilke	Sir Charles Wentworth Dilke
		St Edumnd of Pontigny and St Thomas of Canterbury		
n XVI to n XIX	1949	Christopher Webb	War Damage Commission	
n XVI		*Bishop Reginald Pecock Bishop Luffa St Wilfrid*		
n XVII		*Bruno Ryves Thomas Weelkes Bishop Richard Montagu*		
n XVIII		*Charles Marriott Oliver Whitby Bishop John Lake*		
n XIX		*Nathaniel Woodard John Mason Neale George Chandler*		
n XX	1960	John Baker	J.A. Jones and J.V. Alexander	
		Jesus saves St Peter from drowning (Matt. 14: 24-32)		
West Window w I	Lancets 1847 Decorated 1848	William Wailes William Wailes	Parish of All Souls, London 'The faithful of Chichester'	George Chandler
		Lancets: Four great forerunners The Annunciation Visitation Nativity		
	Decorated windows:	*Our Lord with the Four Evangelists, his charge to St Peter, blessing the children* *Christ in glory with angel musicians*		
South Quire Aisle s II	1894	Charles Eamer Kempe	Archdeacon F.J. Mount, replacing a window in memory of Maria Chandler (now in St Peter the Great) given by Dean Chandler	
		St Joseph of Arimathea, Our Lord, St Mary Magdalene		
s IV	1847	William Wailes	Henry Manning? [The plaque naming the donor only dates from 1904]	(traditionally) Caroline Manning
		The Martyrdom and Vision of St Stephen		

Location and Number	Date	Artist	Donor	In Memoriam
s V	1953	Christopher Webb *Arms of the Boroughs of Sussex*		The Coronation of Queen Elizabeth II
s VI	1912	Unknown	The Hannah family and architect Somers Clarke	Annie Barbara Hannah
s VII	1950	Christopher Webb *St David*	'A Friend of the Cathedral'	Lt. Henry Arthur Evans, Welsh Guards
South Transept				
s VIII	1873	Clayton & Bell *Joshua*	'Brother Officers' *St Michael*	Col. Richard Atkinson, 35th Royal Sussex Rgt. *St Alban*
s IX	1873	Clayton & Bell *The Lamb of God, (Rev 7: 10)*	Canon Francis Alfred Bowles	*The Robing of Aaron, Ex 28*
s X	1877	Charles Parrish & Charles-Laurent Maréchal *Paradise Lost and Regained: OT types and NT anti-types*	John Abel Smith	Anna Smith
South Nave Aisle				
s XI	1872	Ward and Hughes *Acts of St Peter*	Mrs. Smith (widow)	Canon Henry Smith
s XII	1864	Clayton & Bell *Acts of St Peter*	Henry Roberts	Fanny Hersee
s XIII	1870	Arthur O'Connor *Acts of St John*	Edward Johnson Chapter Clerk (son)	Mary Johnson
s XIV	1862	John Hardman *Acts of St Paul*	Charles Pilkington (Canon Residentiary 1850, Chancellor 1854)	Parents
s XV	1862	Michael O'Connor *Dorcas (Acts 9: 36-42), Jesus cures the sick man at the pool of Bethesda (John 5: 2-9)*	Alexander Clark Forbes (son)	Sir John and Lady (Elizabeth) Forbes
s XVI	1871	William Miller *'Feed my Lambs'*		Canon Charles Edward Hutchinson
Lady Chapel				
LC I	1873	Clayton & Bell *The Crucifixion*	John F. France	Richard, Eliza and Harriet Owens
LC n II	1879	Clayton & Bell *Jesus and his Brethren (Matt. 12: 50)*	John F. France	William and Harriet France
LC n III	1882	Clayton & Bell *Jesus in the workshop at Nazareth*	John F. France	Daniel and Anna Barnard
LC n IV	1888	Clayton & Bell *The Flight into Egypt*	'grieving friends and colleagues'	Dean John Burgon
LC n V	1877	Clayton & Bell *The Nativity*	The Officers and staff of the Royal Sussex Militia	Colonel Gage
LC s II	1879	Clayton & Bell *The Wedding at Cana*	John F. France	Elizabeth (wife) and Beatrice (daughter)
LC s III	1880	Unknown *Mary and Joseph find the boy Jesus in the Temple*	Canon Arthur Rawson Ashwell	
LC s IV		Clayton & Bell *The Presentation of Jesus in the Temple*	Percy Ricardo (father)	Mary, Countess of March
LC s V	1879	Clayton & Bell *The Annunciation; Visitation; 'No room at the inn'*		Canon George Henry Woods, Treasurer

D. Eagleton

Appendix C

Monuments

Dates are those of death (dates in square brackets denote date of monument if known to differ).

I. Monuments to 1600, augmented from the plan in *VCH* (1935) facing p.112. (Upright numbers on the phased Cathedral plan, p.xx)

1 Coffin slab with hipped roof: Bp Ralph Luffa 1123
2-3 Coffin slabs with hipped roofs: 12th-century bishops
4-7 Flat coffin slabs: ?Bp Seffrid II 1204; Bishops Simon of Wells 1207; Ranulph Wareham 1222; Ralph Neville 1244
8 Shrine of St Richard 1254
9 Tomb recess: ?Bp Stephen de Berghsted 1287
10 Tomb recess: Bp Gilbert de St Leofard 1305
11 Tomb recess: Bp John Langton 1337
12 Table tomb with effigy: Bp Robert de Stratford 1362
13-17 Floor slabs, 4 with indents of former brasses: Bps John de Climping 1262; William Reede 1385; Robert Rede 1417; Simon Sydenham 1438; Richard Praty 1446
18-20 Floor slabs with indents of former brasses: Bps Henry Ware 1421; Adam Moleyns 1450; Reginald Pecock 1459
21 Table tomb formerly with brass: Bp John Arundel 1478
22 Tomb recess formerly with effigy: Bp John Rickingale 1429
23 Table tomb with (Rickingale's) effigy—burial place of Bp Edward Storey 1503
24 Tomb recess with effigy: Bp Robert Sherburne 1536
25 Plain table tomb: Bp George Day 1556
26 Plain table tomb: Bp William Barlow 1570
27 Tomb recess: ?Dean Milton 1424
28 Mural monument (anon.) 15th-century
29 Altar tomb niche (anon.) late 15th- or early 16th-century
30 Base of tomb: ?Dean Cloos *c.*1500
31-34 Altar tomb niches (anon.) late 15th- or early 16th-century
35 Coffin lid found in Paradise 1829
36 Wall tablet formerly with brass 15th-century
37 Wall monument (anon.) *c.*1530-40
38 Brass plaque: William Bradbridge 1546 [1592]
39 Wall monument: Percivall Smalpage 1595
40 Wall monument: Bp Thomas Bickley 1596
41 Small brass from heart burial *c.*1500 [now in Cathedral Library]

A Heart burial slab: Maude, Countess of Surrey 13th-century
B Table tomb with effigy: Lady Joan de Vere 1293
C Double table tomb with effigies: Richard Fitzalan, 2nd Earl of Arundel 1376 and Eleanor his wife 1372

II. Monuments 1600-1995 (sideways numbers on phased Cathedral plan, p.xx)

1 William Collins 1759 [Flaxman 1795]
2 Ernest Udny 1808 [Westmacott]
3 Jane Smith 1780 [Flaxman]
4 Henry Blaxton 1606; Edward Blaxton 1770
5 Lt Col. Sir Edward Wheeler 1903 ['A & N.AUX. C.S.L.']
6 Wall brass plaques: Col. Arthur Gem 1918; Lt Edward Tyacke 1918 [Culn Cawthorpe & Sons]
7 Floor brass tablets: Maj. Gen. James Young 1926; Brig. Gen. William Osborn 1951; Col. C.G.H.A. Herbert Hankey 1940; Col. Herbert Edwards 1946; Brig. Richard Birkett 1942, in
8 The chapel of the Royal Sussex Regiment
9 Archbould Udny 1828
10 Bp Charles Ridgeway 1927
11 Sarah Udny 1811 [Flaxman]
12 Francis Dear; Bridget his wife, 1802 [Flaxman]
13 Agnes Cromwell 1797 [Flaxman]
14 Muriel Cox 1970
15 Bp Richard Durnford 1896 [Bodley, Garner & Chavalliaud]
16 George Bell 1958 [Gillick 1961]
17 Archdeacon John Walker 1887
18 Wall tablets: Percy Hiscock 1900; George Hiscock 1919; H. H. Moore 1911 [Eric Gill]
19 Frederick J. Read (organist) 1925
20 John Smith 1842 [Roos & Richardson] & brass to his wife Emma 1852
21 Wall memorial: Herbert Jones, Bp of Lewes 1926
22 Brass: Dean John Burgon 1888 [Kempe]
23 Wall memorial: Charles Eamer Kempe 1907 [W. Tower]
24 Benedict Hoskyns 1935 [M. Gill]
25 Lt Col Richard Buckner 1837 & wife 1851 [Robert Brown]
26 Bp John Buckner 1824
27 Maj. Hugh Drummond 1855
28 Sarah Matthews
29 Thomas Wheeler 1769 & 2 daughters
30 Dean Walter Hook 1875 [G. G. Scott]; wall board to Henry King junior, 1668
31 Frances Waddington 1728; Bp Edward 1731. Wall tablet to Archdeacon Lancelot Mason 1990 [Garland]
32 Dean Walter Hussey 1986 [Peever]
33 Rev. George Farhill 1790 & wife
34 Floor tablets: Bp Philip Shuttleworth 1842; Bp Winfrid Burrows 1929; Dean Arthur Duncan-Jones 1955
35 Charles Lennox, 6th Duke of Richmond 1903
36 Charles Lennox, 5th Duke of Richmond 1860 [Gaffin]
37 Bp Ashhurst Gilbert 1870

38 Rev. Percival Webb 1903
39 John Farhill 1830 [William Pitts]
40 Charles Lennox, 7th Duke of Richmond 1928
41 Lord Arthur Lennox 1864
42 Mary Lennox 1843
43 Margaret Miller 1701 & family
44 Canon William Clarke 1771; Bp William Otter 1840; Archdeacon C.P.S. Clarke 1947
45 John Peckham 1782 & family
46 Sarah Peckham 1784; Rev. Henry 1795 [Harris]
47 Dean Samuel Slade 1829
48 Dean Lambrook Thomas 1672
49 Hugh Hordern, Bp of Lewes 1949
50 Wall tablets: Thomas Cook, Bp of Lewes 1928 [Hadlow & sons]; Henry Southwell, Bp of Lewes 1926 [M. Gill]; Bp William Streatfield, Bp of Lewes 1929 [Hadlow & sons]
51 Bp William Otter 1840 [Towne]
52 Bp Ernest Wilberforce 1907 [John Tweed]
53 John Cawley 1621; son William (regicide) 1666 [restored by Thomas King, 1840—from St Andrew's Oxmarket, 1980s]
54 Archdeacon Henry Ball 1603
55 Francis Goater 1734 & family
56 Prebendary Cecil Deedes 1920 (Librarian)
57 Prebendary James Fraser 1913 (Librarian)
58 John Michelbourne (centenarian) 1620
59 Rev. Richard Tireman (vicar of St Peter's) & family 1792-1810
60 Robert Sandham 1776 & family
61 Rachel Harris 1734; husband George 1741
62 Eliza Huskisson 1856 [Gibson]
63 Bp Guy Carleton 1685 & daughter 1683
64 Bp Henry King 1669; son John 1671
65 Bp Robert Grove 1696
66 Frederick J. Crowe (organist) 1921
67 Floor tablets: Gustav Holst 1934
68 Thomas Weelkes 1623 [1923]
69 Dean Thomas Hayley 1739; wife Sarah 1730
70 Henry Baker 1730; wife Penelope 1734
71 Edmund Woods & family 1833-34 [J.E. Carew]
72 John Mackie 1831 [Clark & son, Reading]
73 Lt Noel Abbey 1918; wife Florence; memorial to F.W. Steer 1978 (Librarian)
74 Maj. Gen. John Fraser 1804; wife Maria 1846 [M.W. Johnson]
75 Maj. Gen. Sir George Teesdale 1840 [M.W. Johnson]
76 Alicia Murray 1853 [Richardson]
77 Dean Thomas Ball 1770; wife Margaret 1783 [Flaxman 1785]
78 John Quantock 1820; wife Mary 1820 [Hinchcliff]
79 Edward Madden 1819 [John Bacon the younger]
80 Vice-Admiral Henry Frankland 1814 & daughter [Flaxman]
81 Charles Cullen [George Karn, Chichester]
82 Joseph Baker 1789 [Hickey]
83 William Huskisson MP 1830 [Carew]

84 Matthew Quantock 1812 [Flaxman]
85 Capt. Thomas Allen RN 1781 [Harris]
86 Vice-Admiral Sir George Murray 1819 & daughter [Kendrick]
87 Capt. James Alms RN 1791 [Harris]
88 Lt George Alms RN [Harris]
89 Admiral Swinton Holland 1922
90 Canon Thomas Hurdis 1784; wife Naomi 1781
91 William Nembhard 1829
92 Dorothy Lane 1807
93 Window inscriptions: Canon Vernon Lippiett 1980; Amey Mitchell 1985
94 Elizabeth Shore 1759; Canon Thomas Briggs 1713; John Shore 1721
95 Richard Smith 1767 [W. Tyler]
96 Canon Richard Green 1775 & wife Anna 1790
97 Canon John Frankland 1779; wife Mary 1778
98 John Shore 1773 & family
99 Rev. Thomas Baker 1831
100 George Dixon 1838 & children
101 (L to R) Ann Pilkington 1816; sister Theophania; Rev. Charles Pilkington 1828; wife Harriet 1850; George Pilkington 1842
102 William Williams 1828; sister Emma 1846
103 Richard Pope 1823; wife Mary 1828
104 Mayor Henry Mullins & family 1780-1829
105 Alderman John Harris 1730
106 William Ridge 1829 & family
107 Lieut-Col George Thomson 1898
108 William Chillingworth 1643; Oliver Whitby 1702; Canon Thomas Woodward 1696; wife Hannah 1722; Charles Wentworth Dilke 1762; wife Sarah 1825
109 Rev. Evan Griffiths 1954
110 Three large tablets: Mary Johnson & descendants 1784-1945
111 Godfrey Rokeling 1953; wife Mary c.1973
112 James Whitwood (Collector of Customs) 1701 & family
113 Richard Fuller & family 1812-1961 [Skelton 1962]
114 William Laver 1829
115 Canon C.B. Mortlock 1967
116 Edward Mortlock 1945
117 Buxton Whalley 1943 & sister
118 John Sherer 1730 & family
119 Major Anthony Greene 1814
120 Mary Dilke & family 1852-85
121 Emma Dilke [Vich]
123 Eight tablets to the Nicholls family 1829-1920 [Gaffin]
124 Midshipman George Heming 1827 & wife
125 Roundels in the cloister bays:

Margaret Fielden 1990; Terence Morrison-Scott 1991; 3 Bates sisters of Iden [1992]; Rev. Herbert Ward 1987; Sir John Guillum Scott (Communar) [1983]; Edward Hall 1986

Appendix D

Textiles

The Cathedral Banner

Designed by the Revd. Ernest Geldard, made by Miss Harvey of London, *c.*1900. St Wilfrid and St Richard in an architectural framework, embroidered in coloured silks and padded gold thread. Given by Canon Barwell, Prebendary of Fittleworth.

Altar Frontals

1. Designed by G.F. Bodley (Cathedral architect), made by Watts & Co. of London 1899. Former High Altar frontal, with 7 panels, alternating red silk (designed by Garner) and velvet; heavily embroidered in gold thread in motifs of pomegranates and fleurs-de-lys, with a lettered superfrontal fringed in red and gold. Given by Revd. J.F. Fixon in memory of Canon and Mrs. Ashwell.
2. Designed by Mrs. Harriet Wyatt, made by her 1892/3 and enlarged under the direction of her daughters by the Cathedral Guild of Embroiderers, *c.*1900. Former High Altar frontal, embroidered in coloured silks and gold thread; three heavily padded medallions based on pictures by Fra Angelico at San Marco, Florence.
3. Blue and gold fabric used at the 1937 Coronation in Westminster Abbey. Design of crowns and roses, tasselled superfrontal. Formerly on altar of St Michael's (Sailors') Chapel; given by Commander Inglefield, 1959.

Panel Backing Bishop's Throne

Design by Joan Freeman, made by Cathedral's Seffrid Guild, 1993. Cathedral arms framed in a lozenge of gold thread, surrounded by ears of corn and willow-leaves between the points of a star, in coloured silks on light green ground. Given in memory of Mr. H. Hood.

Copes

1. The Diocesan Cope:
Cream and gold metallic brocade, the morse and orphreys with motifs in gold thread; Cathedral arms in coloured silks and gold thread on hood and IHS on mitre, both the latter set with precious stones from various donors. Made in 1911 by the Sisters of St Margaret, East Grinstead; given by the [Bishop] Ridgeway Gift Fund.
2. Set of six copes desigend by Ceri Richards, made at Bromley College of Art, 1960/1. Heavy silk with appliqué decoration in gold and silver lurex representing heavenly bodies; similarly on the velvet orphreys (2 each, red, blue and yellow); the hoods, all different, are decorated in coloured appliqué.

3. Set of four copes designed by Robert Potter, made by Louis Grossé, London, 1967 in four shades of cream and gold dupion with cowl hoods. Given by the Friends of the Cathedral.
4. Yellow Chinese silk cope with cowl hood bearing appliqué cross in dark gold Lurex, designed and made by Anne Blakeney and the Seffrid Guild 1993; also matching stole. Given in memory of Dr. E.M.M. Alexander.

High Mass Set

Designed by John Piper and made by Louis Grossé, 1967: chasuble, dalmatic and tunicle with stoles in yellow Thai silk with appliqué in gold leather and purple, green & white. Given in memory of Canon Frith.

Three Chasubles

Each with ten matching stoles, in green, purple and red respectively, also ten white stoles, in heavy Kilbride silk with appliqué design in contrasting shade. Designer and date unknown (presumably early 1970s).

The St Richard of Chichester Embroideries

A set of twelve panels, designed by Yvonne Hudson and Rosalie Williams and worked by 15 'Thimbles' for the 900th anniversary of the Cathedral in 1975: panels 1-4 depict the building of the new Cathedral in Chichester, 5-12 the life of St Richard, in a mixture of stitches and appliqué.

Kneelers

Lady Chapel: designed by Robert Potter and made by members of the Sussex Branch of the Embroiderers' Guild, in the early 1970s, members of the Mothers' Union making the long kneelers for the altar-rail. Design reflects vaulting, in shades of gold in various stitches.

Chapel of St Clement: designed by Elisabeth Collins to reflect her husband Cecil's altar frontal 'Icon of Divine Light' and worked by the Cathedral Embroidery group, in petit-point in shades of gold, orange and grey. Early 1970s.

Chapel of St George: designed by Margaret Maclean and made by the Cathedral embroidery group: crests of the two battalions of the Royal Sussex Regiment.

Chapel of St. Michael: designed by Margaret Maclean and made by the Cathedral embroidery group: Royal Naval crown, worked in blue and gold, framed, on a blue ground, *c.*1980.

Chapel of St Thomas and St Edmund: designed by Philippa D'Este Eastes and worked by her and members of the West Sussex Women's Institutes to commemorate the Diamond Jubilee of the W. Sussex Federation of W.I.'s, 1980.

Cushions in Mayoral Pew: designed and made by Margaret Maclean, 1980s.
Alms Bags: designed and made by Anne Blakeney, 1986/88: 24 bags in two designs in gold thread and kid on green.

A. Blakeney

Appendix E

Plate

The only plate that survives from the medieval period is what was found in Paradise, formerly the burial-ground in the Cloisters, in or close to the tombs of bishops which were opened during excavations in the 1830s. It consists of: two chalices and patens of silver-gilt, one of lead and one of pewter (the paten a fragment only). These pieces date from the late 12th or 13th centuries. They could have been made for Cathedral use or for the bishop's personal use, or simply for burial. The pieces are of great rarity and historical interest, but are not outstanding examples of their kind. The decoration and inscription on the two silver patens is, however, of particular interest.

Whatever other medieval plate the Cathedral possessed must have been lost or destroyed at or before the time of its sacking by Parliamentarian troops after the siege of Chichester in 1642. There are written records of gifts of plate to the Cathedral after the Restoration, to subsequent sellings, and to a melting-down of later plate to be made into the set now in regular use. This dates from 1855 and consists of: two matching chalices with patens, and a pear-shaped flagon—agreeable but unexceptional Victorian pieces.

In addition to this set there are a number of miscellaneous pieces in Cathedral ownership, of varying periods from the 17th century to the present day. Some are known to be gifts or bequests, the provenance of others is obscure. They include: four silver alms-basins, of dates ranging from 1681 to 1844, very similar in appearance and each bearing a different text to encourage the alms-giver; and a number of chalices, mostly with patens, some decorated with precious (or semi-precious) stones, of dates ranging from 1632 to present times. These are attractive pieces though none is of outstanding quality or interest. Worthy of mention among 20th -century pieces are a squarish-shaped chalice with an elaborate paten, made by the silver-smith Gerald Benney (1957) and presented to Dean Duncan-Jones, and a set (chalice-paten-alms dish) made by Desmond Clem-Murphy (1953) in an attractive modern style and bearing the insignia of the Royal Sussex Regiment.

A number of the pieces referred to above are on permanent display, along with other Cathedral possessions, in the Treasury, which is housed in the Chapel of the Four Virgins off the north choir aisle, and is devoted chiefly to the display of church plate on loan from parishes in the Diocese.

References: *Couchman*, in Sussex Archaeological Collections Vol. LIII (1910) pp.224-7.
Oman, 'English Church Plate'.

R. & M. Moriarty

Appendix F

The Bells

Treble	R. Phelps	1729	5cwt.	0qtr.	
2	do.	do.	5	2	
3		1583	5	3	Give thanks to God.
4	Eldridge	1674	7	3	Wm. Eldridge me fecit.
5		1665	8	3	Deus di[vin]a omnia fecit.
6	W.P	1665	10	0	Dominus providebit.
7	I W	1587	13	3	Be meek and lo[w]ly to hear the word of God.
TENOR	Ric. Phelps	1706	21	3	Soli Deo Gloria
Hour Bell	J. Taylor	1877	60	13	Great Walter

The peal used is 'Surprise Major' and for the quarter hours, the Cambridge Chime.

Index

compiled by Ann Hudson

Note: The index is to persons, places and subjects in the main text; places outside Chichester are indexed selectively. Major additional material in the notes is also indexed. An asterisk after a page reference indicates a note giving bibliographical details.

4
3